CW00431611

Bristol City

The Early Years

1894-1915

Desert Island Football Histories

Club Histories	ISBN
Aberdeen: A Centenary History 1903-2003	1-874287-49-X
Aberdeen: Champions of Scotland 1954-55	1-874287-65-1
Aberdeen: The European Era – A Complete Record	1-874287-11-2
Bristol City: The Modern Era – A Complete Record	1-874287-28-7
Bristol City: The Early Years 1894-1915	1-874287-74-0
Cambridge United: The League Era – A Complete Record	1-874287-32-5
Cambridge United: 101 Golden Greats	1-874287-58-9
The Story of the Celtic 1888-1938	1-874287-15-5
Colchester United: Graham to Whitton – A Complete Record	1-874287-27-9
Coventry City: The Elite Era – A Complete Record	1-874287-51-1
Coventry City: An Illustrated History	1-874287-59-7
Dundee: Champions of Scotland 1961-62	1-874287-72-4
Dundee United: Champions of Scotland 1982-83	1-874287-71-6
History of the Everton Football Club 1878-1928	1-874287-14-7
Halifax Town: From Ball to Lillis – A Complete Record	1-874287-26-0
Hereford United: The League Era – A Complete Record	1-874287-18-X
Huddersfield Town: Champions of England 1923-1926	1-874287-66-X
Ipswich Town: The Modern Era – A Complete Record	1-874287-43-0
Ipswich Town: Champions of England 1961-62	1-874287-56-2
Luton Town: The Modern Era – A Complete Record	1-874287-05-8
Luton Town: An Illustrated History	1-874287-37-6
Matt Busby: A Complete Man U record 1945-1971	1-874287-53-8
Motherwell: Champions of Scotland 1931-32	1-874287-73-2
Norwich City: The Modern Era – A Complete Record	1-874287-67-8
Peterborough United: The Modern Era – A Complete Record	1-874287-33-3
Peterborough United: Who's Who?	1-874287-48-1
Plymouth Argyle: The Modern Era – A Complete Record	1-874287-54-6
Plymouth Argyle: 101 Golden Greats	1-874287-64-3
Portsmouth: From Tindall to Ball – A Complete Record	1-874287-25-2
Portsmouth: Champions of England – 1948-49 & 1949-50	1-874287-38-4
The Story of the Rangers 1873-1923	1-874287-16-3
The Romance of the Wednesday 1867-1926	1-874287-17-1
Stoke City: The Modern Era – A Complete Record	1-874287-76-7
Stoke City: 101 Golden Greats	1-874287-55-4
West Ham: From Greenwood to Redknapp	1-874287-19-8
West Ham: The Elite Era – A Complete Record	1-874287-31-7
Wimbledon: From Southern League to Premiership	1-874287-09-0
Wimbledon: From Wembley to Selhurst	1-874287-20-1
Wimbledon: The Premiership Years	1-874287-40-6
Wrexham: The European Era – A Complete Record	1-874287-52-X
World Cup Histories	
England's Quest for the World Cup – A Complete Record	1-874287-61-9
Scotland: The Quest for the World Cup – A Complete Record	1-897850-50-6
Ireland: The Quest for the World Cup – A Complete Record	1-897850-80-8
Miscellaneous	
Red Dragons in Europe – A Complete Record	1-874287-01-5
The Book of Football: A History to 1905-06	1-874287-13-9
Football's War & Peace: The Tumultuous Season of 1946-47	1-874287-70-8

BRISTOL CITY

The Early Years

— 1894-1915 —

Series Editor: Clive Leatherdale
Series Consultant: Leigh Edwards

David Woods

DESERT ISLAND BOOKS

First Published in 2004

DESERT ISLAND BOOKS LIMITED
89 Park Street, Westcliff-on-Sea, Essex SS0 7PD
United Kingdom
www.desertislandbooks.com

© 2004 David Woods

The right of David Woods to be identified as author of this work has been asserted under The Copyright Designs and Patents Act 1988

British Library Cataloguing-in-Publication Data
A catalogue record for this book is available from the British Library

ISBN 1-874287-74-0

All rights reserved. No part of this book may be reproduced or utilised in any form or by any means, electronic or mechanical, including photocopying, recording or by any information storage and retrieval system, without prior permission in writing from the Publisher

Printed in Great Britain
by Biddles, King's Lynn

~ Contents ~

~ *Author's Note* ~

The task of producing the statistical section has been much helped by contemporary records kept by Bristol City FC director Joseph Daveridge for the 1897-1906 period, and those compiled by Thomas Bowden between 1897 and 1915. Unfortunately, these records often fail to agree, and whilst one might think – given his position with the club – that Daveridge's information would be the more reliable, the fact that he often leaves gaps relating to holiday games suggests that this was not necessarily the case. Indeed, the disharmony between these two suggests their differing choice of newspaper, rather than any specialist inside knowledge.

With numbering of players' shirts not being adopted by the Football League until 1939, it is not surprising that the researcher is often confronted by conflicting views of various newspapers in regard to positions and goalscorers. Keen readers will therefore note some changes to my previous work, following further investigation of the local press both in Bristol and other centres. It will be appreciated that goal-times were not always readily available and many have been estimated in order to convey the scoring sequence.

David Woods

DEDICATION:

In memory of Bill Pinnell – (called the 'Traveller' on account of his reporting so many away games involving both Bristol City and Rovers) – who died at the age of 89 in January 1977. Starting his journalistic career on the *Bristol Times & Mirror* in 1919, Bill was Sports Editor of the *Bristol Evening Post* for almost 25 years from the first day of publication in April 1932. Following his retirement, Bill continued his 'Traveller Looks Back' column in the *Green 'Un*. It was his column and the author's visit to his Greenmore Road home in Knowle, Bristol, where Thomas Bowden's three-volume contemporary record was first seen in November 1964, which provided the inspiration for this book.

Also in fond remembrance of a bygone part of Bedminster, the Bristol Technical School of Engineering (1940-1967) and all its pupils, including my brother Tony and myself, who ever kicked a ball against the adjoining Tannery wall.

~ Acknowledgements ~

Particular thanks are due to Anton Bantock of the Malago Society. His permission to reproduce narrative from his book on Bedminster (published by Tempus Publishing as part of their Archive series in 1997) enables the reader to more fully appreciate the historical background of the very special area of Bristol in which City's roots are so deeply imbedded. I am also grateful to Tony Robinson for kindly supplying the foreword and for the assistance of the staff at libraries in Barnsley (Joan Fareham), Birmingham (Richard Abbott), Blackpool (Vivienne Greaves), Burton-upon-Trent (Gillian Johnson), Chesterfield (Ann Krawszik), Colindale, Doncaster (Helen Wallder), Exeter, Gainsborough (Lynne Claxton), Grimsby, Huddersfield, Lincoln (Magaret Hill), Middlesbrough (Jenny Parker), Newbury (Kerry Taylor), Isle of Wight (Richard Smout – County Archivist), Oxford (Sheila Weatherhead), Plymouth (Joyce Brown), Preston (Ann Dennison), Southampton, Southport (Matthew Tinker), Stockport (Carole Perry), Hanley (Lesley Chadwick), Treorchy (Alun Prescott), Trowbridge (Daphne Perkins), Weston-super-Mare (Joy Hodges), and particularly all those at the Bristol Central Library who have had to put up with my foraging for the past 25 years.

Others have helped in various ways including numerous members of the AFS, but special thanks are due to Mervyn Baker, Tony Brown, Stephen Byrne, Andrew Crabtree, Leigh Edwards, David Farmer, Mick Hunter, Mike Jay, Colin Jones, Jonathan Morgan, Lorna Parnall, Gerry Pearce, Geoff Rose, Richard Sartin, Steve Small, Roy Shoesmith, Monica Spencer, Matthew Stevens, Colin Timbrell, Jerry Wolstenholme, Andrew Woods. It is also fitting to acknowledge the help and encouragement received in the past from well-known Bristol journalists David Foot, Peter Godsiff and the late George Baker. Finally, last but not least, a big thank-you to Scott Davidson who, when he was the Bristol City Chairman, kindly let me borrow, amongst other things, Club Minute books for the 1897-1900 period.

~ *Foreword* ~

I'm often away from my Bristol home, filming in far-flung places. Yet around 2.30 British Time every Saturday afternoon, wherever I am, and whatever time the local clocks say, I start to get nervous. In my mind's eye I'm walking along the discussed railway line bridge over the River Avon. Then I am exchanging ribald pleasantries with the overweight footballers in Greville Smyth Park. A few minutes later I'm zig-zagging across the crowded road, between Wedlock's and the red-brick toilets. Then I'm heading for the turnstiles, stopping only to pick up my programme, my copy of 'One Team In Bristol' and my half-time draw ticket. It's five to three now, and I'm squeezing into my seat next to my mate Dave. Finally the Ashton roar begins, and I'm one of 10,000 Bristolians cheering our heroes onto the pitch.

And what's so great about this feeling of solidarity, whether it's in person or in my imagination, is that I'm part of a great continuum. For over a hundred years fans have felt like I feel, just as my son does, and hopefully his son will after him. We are as much part of the history of Bristol City Football Club as Billy Wedlock, John Atyeo, Brian Tinnion, and all the countless, talented young men in red we've cheered and saluted as well as moaned at and despaired of over the years.

Will we go up this season? Will we be able to hold onto our talented striker? How are we going to replace our aging play-maker? These aren't just issues for today. Followers of the Mighty Reds have been asking similar questions since 1894! Turn the pages of this book and share the passion of other generations who are as much a part of the Red Army as you and I are today.

Tony Robinson
March 2004

~ Introduction ~

Contrary to custom – and despite having represented a district not wholly incorporated into the boundary of the City & County of Bristol until 1897 – it was the youngest of the major soccer sides formed in late Victorian Bristol that had the honour of being the 'City' club. It was not until their election to the Southern League and the adoption of professionalism in 1897, that Bristol South End sought permission to change their name. Initially, the Gloucestershire FA rebuffed the request, and it took a direct appeal to the Football Association to pave the way for the 'Babe' of local football to become Bristol City.

Due to the amalgamation with Bedminster in 1900, the club's genealogical tree is complex, with two family lines. The Bedminster organisation was formed as Southville in 1887, and City started up as Bristol South End in 1894. The Southville district, which adjoins Bedminster, was a new affluent suburb at this time, whilst Bedminster itself had been for many centuries a separate town. Its origins may be Roman – its main thoroughfare, East Street/West Street, is certainly Roman – and it was already an important township when Bristol was little more than a river crossing. The mission church of St John's predates any Christian foundation in the City, and in the twelfth century St John's became the mother church of St Mary Redcliffe, reputed to have been described by Queen Elizabeth I as the 'fairest church in all England'.

The priests of St John were accorded the special status of 'prebendaries', and a place for the 'Prebend of Redcliffe with Bedminster' can be seen in the choir of Salisbury Cathedral to this day. The Royal Manor of Bedminster comprised all land south of the Avon from the Gorge up to Brislington and, according to the Domesday Book, had 25 villains, three slaves and 27 smallholders with ten ploughs, one cob, nine cattle, 22 pigs and 112 sheep. The Manor was bestowed by Norman kings on powerful magnates and finally became a fief of Robert FitzHarding in about 1130. Despite being awarded the Manor of Berkeley in 1154, the Lords of Berkeley preferred their fair Manor of Bedminster to the gloomy castle on the Severn and as such played a prominent part in the development of Bristol by fostering trade as well as founding abbeys and churches.

The power of the Berkeleys waned in the fourteenth century, and after 1416 the Manor of Bedminster passed to heiresses and their families until being finally purchased in 1605 by the Smyths of

Ashton Court, who continued as Lords of the Manor until their feudal powers fell into abeyance in the nineteenth century.

Until the seventeenth century, Bedminster was a prosperous community clustered around its parish church in a fertile valley. In the 1630s it was assessed for ship money at £47 which established its economic equality with Glastonbury (£56) and Frome (£49), but the town was sacked and burnt in 1644 by Prince Rupert prior to the second siege on Bristol and needed over a century to recover. When John Wesley preached at the Paddock in the 1760s, Bedminster was a sprawling, decayed market town, with orchards rubbing shoulders with brickworks, rope-walks and cottage industries.

However, dramatic change lay around the corner. Open-cast mining had first been recorded in the 1670s, and in 1744 Jarrit Smith – who was to become Sir Jarrit Smyth of Ashton Court – called in a mining surveyor from the East Bristol Coalfield at Kingswood. The first shafts were sunk at South Liberty Lane in 1748 and within 60 years there were eighteen coal-pits operating in the Bedminster and Ashton Vale Coalfield. Not only did the Smyths do very well from the royalties, but on the threshold of the Industrial Revolution Bedminster had coal and easy access to the City docks, not to mention the insatiable demands of its larger neighbour Bristol, which was second only to London in size at this time.

The transformation of Bedminster was rapid and traumatic. The population jumped from 3,000 in 1801 to 78,000 by 1884 as people from depressed rural Somerset flocked to the new coalfields for work. Almost overnight, Bedminster became a power-house of heavy industry, manned by a huge workforce packed into high-density terraced housing. Coal-mining and smelting generated other industries: engineering, tanneries, glue-works, paint factories, glass-works. In the late Victorian era the paper-bag manufacturers E. S. & A. Robinson, as well as the tobacco business of W. D. & H. O. Wills moved into new factories in Bedminster.

By the 1870s Bedminster had overflowed to the surrounding hills and hollows, creating its own suburbs in the Chessels, Windmill Hill, Southville, Totterdown, as well as Ashton Gate. Although brought finally within the City boundary in 1897, the construction of the New Cut of the River Avon (1804-09) had ensured that Bedminster remained geographically separate from the rest of Bristol, hence keeping its own dialect, as well as distinct sense of humour, the latter proving to be an invaluable attribute for those watching Bristol City over the years.

1

~ *Beginnings* ~

Compared with the urban areas of northern England, the Association game was a late starter in Bristol. It wasn't until 1882 that a local club, Warmley, was formed to play the 'dribbling' code. They were quickly followed that same year by St George, who started up on 21 October, and just six weeks later what would become great rivals met for the first time when St George triumphed on their own ground.

The following season saw the birth of Bristol Rovers, then known as the Black Arabs, and also the Clifton Association club, which produced Bristol's first international in Charles Wreford-Brown. Credited with coining the term 'soccer', Wreford-Brown won the first of his four England caps against Ireland in 1889, when playing for Oxford University in term-time, and his home club, Clifton, during vacations. Clifton, who played in distinctive chocolate and cardinal shirts, never embraced professionalism, which arrived in Bristol for the 1897-98 season when both City and Rovers – as well as St George and Warmley – took the plunge. With Bedminster following suit twelve months later, the situation was economically unsustainable and within a couple of years 'survival of the fittest' had reduced the numbers to the two we have today.

Had Warmley and St George acted on an amalgamation proposal, first mooted in the spring of 1897, the future might have been different. Poor form and inclement weather took Warmley to the brink, but it was crowd trouble during the course of a 1-5 home defeat by Millwall Athletic on the 7 January 1899 that brought matters to a head. With debts of £900, the club had little option but to fold when an FA Inquiry ordered the closure of its Chequers enclosure for four weeks from 30 January.

St George, who had added the Bristol prefix on joining the Birmingham & District League in 1897 – to distinguish themselves from Birmingham St Georges – soldiered on until the end of the campaign, before they too folded with debts of £340. Strangely enough, they had applied to take over Warmley's Southern League fixtures a few months earlier, but their application, alongside that of the Thames Ironworks club, had been rejected.

On the other side of the Avon, wiser heads prevailed and the amalgamation of City and Bedminster in 1900 probably prevented a similar catastrophe. It was thanks to the good sense of the Bedminster officials that petty rivalry was put aside to enable the setting-up of a combined South Bristol club that went on to accomplish great things in the following decade.

Whilst the cradle of the Association game in Bristol was to be found in the east of the City, it wasn't long before clubs sprung up south of the river. Much enthusiasm was created by the first County match played by Gloucestershire, which took place in front of a 600 crowd on the Bedminster Cricket Club ground on 7 April 1885. Pocock's first-half shot brought success against Somerset, but despite further fixtures, including a 1-10 defeat by Aston Villa at Perry Barr, it wasn't until 7 September 1886 that the official formation of the County FA took place. This led to the instigation of the County Cup, following a meeting in September 1887 attended by Clifton Association, Eastville Rovers, Globe, St Agnes, St George, St Simon's and Southville. Details were finalised at a further gathering held at the Montpelier Hotel on the 5 October.

The first final was contested on 10 March 1888 in front of a 2,000 crowd on the old St George enclosure, near the Lord Rodney Public House on Two Mile Hill. Honours ended even, with Howard Henry Francis, a Bristol-born sportsman who later played Test cricket for South Africa, scoring for Clifton, and Riddell being on the mark for Warmley. A replay took place at the same venue a week later. This time Clifton, who brought in Wreford-Brown, Russell and Colthurst (in place of Newnham, Falcon and Francis), were not to be denied and with Colthurst and Russell both grabbing a pair they triumphed 4-1 against their unchanged opponents, for whom Riddell had opened the scoring.

CLIFTON ASSOCIATION: F J Baines; W F Gorton, P F Newnham; G Innes-Pocock (capt), C Wreford-Brown, G R Lowndes; R Innes-Pocock, C Lacy-Sweet, C H Russell, A B Colthurst, H H Francis.
WARMLEY: G Godfrey; G Gay, S Peacock; J Peacock, W Noble, H Williams; T Nelmes, J Mackay, J R Riddell, P Fussell (capt), W Bowler.
REFEREE: F M Ingram (Essex). UMPIRES: Dr W G Grace (Wanderers); W J Somerton (Eastville Rovers).

Southville, formed in 1887, were one of the early pioneers of the soccer code in the Bedminster area, and they took part in the inaugural Gloucestershire Cup match on 12 November 1887 when they drew 1-1 on Durdham Down. Their opponents were the Globe club, formed by old boys of Queen Elizabeth's Hospital School at a meeting in the Coffee Tavern a few months earlier on 29 August. Whilst the actual date of Southville's formation is unknown, details as to their formation and first match are well recorded. It was at a small gathering of Southville Cricket Club members that the decision form a soccer section was taken.

The new club kicked off on 15 October 1887 on their home ground in Bedminster (now Greville Smyth) Park, when a goal by Jack McCarthy brought a 1-0 win over Criterion. Their best victory was achieved in beating Bristol East (h) 5-0 on 14 January, and they ended the season with the record: P18, W9, D6, L3, F22, A4.

Star of the side was goalkeeper Charlie Gyles, who took over from his brother Fred as Secretary the following season. Faced by tougher opposition, 1888-89 proved to be a difficult campaign, though the game at Warmley on 8 December is notable for the fact that the full Southville line-up appears in the press for the first time. C E Gyles; F W Gyles, S Bendall; S J Harris, H Morris, G Gerrish; E T Harris, R Hanover, Rev B Morris, W G Griffiths, and A Brown were the eleven players who did duty that day, but a second-half goal from Hanover wasn't enough to prevent a 1-3 defeat.

The season was hardly successful, with a record of P19, W5, D3, L11, F27, A26. However, home wins of 9-1 and 4-0 over North Rovers and Beaufort respectively, together with a fine display in a 1-2 Gloucestershire Cup defeat at Warmley, gave indication of the side's potential, but the lack of an enclosed ground held back Southville's ambitions. However, encouraged by the comments of Dr W G Grace – who had refereed their cup clash with Warmley – and with the active help of Bedminster Chairman Dr Ernest Cook, they joined forces with the 42-year-old Cricket Club. The 1889-90 season saw the adoption of the Bedminster name, and the team, in their maroon and old-gold colours, played on the cricket ground, at the junction of Greenway Bush Lane and North Street.

With the stage now set for south Bristol to produce a rival to the east Bristol giants of St George and Warmley, it wasn't long before Bedminster made their mark, though they received an initial shock. A 0-6 defeat at Clevedon on 12 October 1889 was hardly a good start, but Bedminster's excuse was that they could only muster ten players. Fortunately matters improved and the end-of-season summary of P20, W8, D1, L11, F54, A53 included wins of 10-0 and 8-0 over St Agnes (a) and St Simon's (h) respectively, as well as a satisfying 7-0 home victory over below-strength Warmley on 22 March. Progress continued apace the following campaign, when Gloucestershire Cup success established the Minster as one of the top local clubs.

After disposing of Eastville Rovers 3-2, Craigmore College were thumped 12-0 to set up a final against old rivals Warmley, which took place in front of a 2,500 crowd on neutral territory at St George on 28 March when the sides lined up as follows:

BEDMINSTER: C E Gyles; F W Gyles (capt), J W Welham; H A Marshall, S J Harris, F E Skeates; J F McCarthy, W G Griffiths, H J Batchelor, F J Harris, E T Harris.

WARMLEY: J Summerhill; G Britton, G Bowler; G Reeves (capt), P Britton, W Jefferies; G.Peacock, J Mackay, T Nelmes, A W Rickard, W Phipps.

REFEREE: C Lacy-Sweet (Glos FA). LINESMEN: G E Snailum (Wilts FA) and G Innes-Pocock (Clifton Association).

Warmley were without the services of regular captain George Peacock, who had suffered a broken collarbone against Clevedon earlier in the week, but this didn't prevent them dominating the first half. Playing against the wind, the Minster – for whom McCarthy fired against the bar in a rare attack – were fortunate to reach the interval with their goal intact, but after the break shots by Billy Griffiths and Batchelor brought a hard-earned 2-0 success. This set the seal on an outstanding season (P21, W15, D3, L3, F78, A22) which had brought high-scoring victories over Bethesda (h) 9-0, Clevedon (a) 6-1, Craigmore College (a) 6-1 and Clifton (h) 5-1.

The third season at Greenway Bush Lane saw the Minster enter the FA Cup for the first time, following in the pioneering footsteps of Clifton and Warmley, who had both tested the waters the previous campaign. Unfortunately, after a bye, and then a walkover, they were outclassed by Luton Town in the third qualifying round on 14 November, and gifted the visitors a couple of own-goals in a 1-4 defeat. Better fortune attended their efforts in the Gloucestershire Cup, however, as they again won through to the final, but this time Warmley gained their revenge in front of a 6,000 crowd paying receipts of £100 on the Kingswood Athletic Ground, a venue that was to become better known as the Chequers from the following season.

WARMLEY: J Summerhill; G Britton, G Bowler (capt); G Reeves, P Britton, H Wilshire; G Peacock, J Mackay, T Nelmes, J King, W Phipps.
BEDMINSTER: D L Courtice; G E Jones (capt), J W Welham; H A Marshall, F E Skeates, G Rich; J F McCarthy, Rev A B Macfarlane, H J Batchelor, W G Griffiths, E G Miles.
REFEREE: W H Jope (Wednesbury).

The Minster kicked off up the slope and defended the Pavilion End in front of a large gathering of spectators, many of whom bore cards urging their favourites to 'Play Up'. Macfarlane opened the scoring with a high shot after about quarter of an hour, but before another fifteen minutes had elapsed King drove in Warmley's leveller. Shortly before half-time Peacock notched up what proved to be the winner.

Conceding thirteen goals without reply at Swindon Town on 7 November prevented any chance of parity for the Minster in the goal column (F58, A65), although the results of their 26 games were evenly divided – thirteen were won and thirteen lost.

With the formation of the Football League in 1888, there was a growing trend to formalise fixtures, and 1892-93 heralded the start of the first league in the Bristol area. Acting on a recommendation by Percy Wyfold Stout, who was to win five rugger caps for England towards the close of century, the Bedminster Chairman W A Deakin and G T Bryant of St George convened a meeting, presided over by A W Francis, at the Earl Russell Hotel, Lawrence Hill, Bristol, on 30 March 1892. Representatives of Bedminster, Clifton Association, Eastville Rovers, Mangotsfield, St George and Warmley unanimously agreed to establish what became the Western League, though at this time they settled on the title of the Bristol & District League.

The competition commenced on 24 September, but Bedminster didn't play their first fixture until four weeks later, when they drew an exciting game with Wells on the Tor Firland enclosure. Warmley had the honour of being the first Champions, finishing the campaign one point ahead of runners-up Trowbridge Town, whilst Bedminster, with the Reverend Macfarlane as their captain, were in fourth place with a record of P16, W6, D5, L5, F30, A34 Pts 17. A crowd of 3,000 at Greenway Bush Lane saw goals from Macfarlane and Mayger bring victory over Warmley on 21 January, but the Minster's best win in the competition was a 5-0 success over Eastville Rovers in front of 1,000 spectators on 3 December. In the FA Cup, Bedminster had come a cropper, 1-7 at Uxbridge.

The heaviest defeat of the season was in losing 0-9 at Warmley on 19 November, but the fact that Bedminster only had nine men in the first half and ten in the second was reasonable excuse. In the County tourney, Craigmore College were overcome 5-0 before the Minster suffered a similar reverse at home to Gloucester in the semi-final. Bedminster's only loss in eight friendlies, 2-7 at Swindon Athletic early in the season, contributed to an overall record of P28, W11, D9, L8, F62, A62.

At this time, social conditions were gradually improving for the masses and with the introduction of half-day working on Saturdays many were encouraged to attend soccer games in the afternoon. This extra interest, coupled with much-improved literacy following the Public Elementary Education (Forster's) Act of 1870 – which brought about compulsory education up to the age of eleven – led to the first Special Saturday Football Edition of the *Bristol Evening News* on 14 October 1893, though it was to be another twelve years before a complete Saturday night sports paper, the *Echo Sports Final – Green Edition* – hit the Bristol streets on 11 November 1905. This became the *Sports Times* when the *Echo* was taken over by the *Bristol Evening Times* in late 1909, but wasn't printed on green paper until 24 March 1917 when it became the *Sports Times – Green 'Un. The Evening News* didn't bring out their own special sports paper (the *Sports News*, which was to become the *Sports News – Pink 'Un*) until after the Great War.

Yet again Uxbridge proved to be Bedminster's nemesis in the FA Cup by winning 6-2 at Greenway Bush Lane on 14 October, whilst in the newly instigated Amateur Cup, no luck was forthcoming either as, despite home advantage on 4 November, victory went to the Home Park side from Plymouth 3-0. Whilst a 1-10 thrashing was sustained at Warmley in the Gloucestershire Cup, form was better in the League. Victories of 7-2, 5-0 and 5-1 over Mangotsfield (h), Staple Hill (a) and Clevedon (h) respectively, had the Minster at the top of the table at various times during the campaign, but a run of four consecutive defeats, including a 1-6 hammering at St George, brought a final placing of fourth. The season closed with the League's inaugural Six-a-Side Tournament, when as a consequence of their goalkeeper, Charlie Gyles, breaking a leg, Bedminster conceded 21 'points' to Eastville Rovers at the Chequers.

The Minster were, however, more successful in a similar competition at Trowbridge that ushered in the following season. Disposing of Bradford-on-Avon 15-4 and St George 7-5, Bedminster won through to the final before losing 5-10 to Southbroom in front of a 3,500 crowd on 1 September 1894. It was a struggle in the League, though, despite beating Clevedon 8-2 on 10 November. With defeats of the magnitude of 0-9 at St George and 0-7 at Trowbridge, it was scarcely surprising that Minster finished just three off the bottom in ninth place.

Internal dissention, which had seen departures to the newly formed Bristol South End, was partially responsible for the poor form, but despite this the crowds held up well. Around 3,000 were present at Greenway Bush Lane to see Warmley beaten 2-1 on 17 November, whilst the 800 spectators at the game with Hereford Thistle on Easter Saturday got their money's worth. Disappointed they may have been at losing 1-4 to the Champions elect, but they didn't have time to brood as straight afterwards they were treated to a thrilling contest in which a select Bedminster Combination XI beat the 1st Scots Guards 4-3.

Team-raising problems saw the Minster scratch from their fixture at Warmley towards the end of the season, rather than attempt the policy Mangotsfield had tried against them seven weeks earlier. Faced with a player shortage on 9 March, the Country Boys looked to the offside rule to prevent defeat as they turned out with only two men! Hardly a good ruse, as Bedminster scored from a corner early on, whereupon their opponents conceded defeat and left the field. Wisely, perhaps, the Minster chose to forsake the FA Cup in favour of the Amateur tournament, and they put up a good fight before losing 2-3 at home to the Old Weymouthians. The visit of the lady footballers on 16 April provided an interesting diversion. Unfortunately, three of the ladies were indisposed, so a couple of gents took over between the sticks as 2,000 curious spectators at

Greenway Bush Lane saw the Blues side – despite being one lady short – beat the Reds 5-2.

The doings of the Bristol & District League, which was renamed the Western League in 1895-96, stimulated much local interest and it wasn't surprising that similar operations for the more junior clubs sprung up in its wake. The 1893-94 season heralded the start of the South Bristol & District League, the championship of which was won by Bristol South, who played at the Chessels. Strangely, this club, which had been formed around 1888, then chose to disband, though there is a suggestion in the local press, later denied, that they amalgamated with the cuckoo in the Bedminster nest – the newly formed Bristol South End.

The following campaign saw the birth of the East Bristol, as well as the North Bristol & District League. The former adopted the original title of the Western League in 1899-1900, and the latter became known as the Bristol & Suburban League in 1906-07. The South Bristol & District League fell by the wayside at the end of 1897-98, when it was known as the Bristol & District Alliance. Doubtless much of this activity had been encouraged by periodic missionary visits by famous clubs in the days before professionalism was adopted in the capital of the West.

One of the earliest such visits was by West Bromwich Albion, who delighted a 1,730 crowd on the old St George enclosure on 20 April 1892 by bringing with them the FA Cup that they had won by defeating Aston Villa 3-0 at the Oval a month earlier. The Baggies, who were three goals to the good at the interval, were not much troubled by the Gloucestershire XI that confronted them as they won at a canter, 7-0.

In the period up to 1897 there were sixteen such treks to Bristol by the likes of Aston Villa, Blackburn Rovers, Corinthians, Derby County, Nottingham Forest, Preston North End, Sunderland, Stoke, Tottenham Hotspur, Wolverhampton Wanderers, but the most momentous occasion took place on 7 April 1896 when the Western League XI beat Aston Villa 2-0 in front of a 5,380 crowd on the new St George ground at Bell Hill. The Trowbridge Town goalkeeper, William George, was the star of the show and it was no surprise when Villa signed him for £200 seventeen months later.

2

~ *New Kid on the Block* ~

Such was the local soccer scene when the Bristol Babe was born on 12 April 1894. Internal dissension within the ranks of the Bedminster club, coupled with the decision of Bristol South to disband, led to erstwhile Minster members Fred Keenan and John Durant calling a meeting to discuss the future of the Association game in south Bristol.

The eighteen enthusiasts gathered in the front parlour of Keenan's residence (Bovey Tracy House, Milford Road, Southville) included Bill Hodgkinson, one time Secretary of Eastville Rovers, notable players 'Hammer' Clements and Arthur Jones, as well as J A Stevens, Secretary of the Bristol & District League, and F W Thomas. All agreed on the need for the formation of a new club. After much discussion, chaired by Harry Locke, it was decided to name the new organisation in accordance with the proposal of Mr Stevens who, being an admirer of Preston North End, voiced the thought, 'Why not Bristol South End'?

The princely sum of £6 8s 6d was pledged before the meeting broke up, and four days later at John Durant's Rock Lodge home in Southville Road the officials were appointed. Bill Hodgkinson became Secretary, with Fred Keenan as his assistant, whilst Harry Locke shared the Treasurer's role with his brother Ted. The first Chairman was W R Nurse, while Colonel Plant became President with John Durant as his deputy. The fledgling Club was ambitious right from the outset, as it wasn't interested in filling the niche left by Bristol South. Wishing to compete with the major local clubs – Bedminster, Clifton Association, Eastville Rovers, St George and Warmley – it was resolved that application be made for admission to the Bristol & District League.

A meeting at the General Elliott public house, in East Street, on 24 April, saw a committee of fourteen elected to assist the Club officers. Colours of red shirts and navy blue knickers were chosen, and it was agreed that gentlemen would pay an annual subscription of five shillings, whilst for ladies the cost would only be half-a-crown (half of five shillings). Unfortunately, the very next day the club's ambitions met with an early rebuff as the Bristol & District League rejected their application on the basis that 'They couldn't entertain a club without any history'.

Despite another setback, on 23 May, when, at a meeting held at the Hope & Anchor, Redcliffe Hill, the club's reserves were denied admittance to the South Bristol & District League – even though Bedminster's third XI were successful – the Club responded with a resourcefulness that was to be demonstrated on many occasions in the early years.

Heartened by being granted affiliation to the Gloucestershire FA, which cleared the way for participation in various cup competitions, the club compiled a fixture list of friendlies, attracting to their St John's Lane ground – which was leased from the trustees of the Ashton Court Estate at a rent of £20 per annum – such notable sides as Swindon Town, Tottenham Hotspur, 1st Scots Guards, the London Welsh Regiment, and Preston North End. Several sub-committees were formed to co-ordinate the work necessary to prepare the site, and frenzied activity throughout the summer of 1894 had the ground ready at a cost of £109 for the opening match on 1 September.

Swindon Town, billed as Champions of the West of England, were South End's opponents on this momentous day. In gloriously hot weather, the 3,500 crowd were entertained prior to the start by the Bristol South Band, conducted by George Godfrey who was to remain in this role for the first 53 years of the Club's existence. He would take his final bow with the baton on 23 August 1947, when namesakes Southend United were the visitors.

A 2-4 defeat to Swindon ensued for the new boys, but the local morning papers (*Bristol Mercury, Western Daily Press, Bristol Times & Mirror*) were full of praise, describing the proceedings as exciting and well-contested throughout. Much credit was extended to South End for their gallant fight, as well as frequent unselfish play and clever tactics. Afterwards, the players and officials of both sides were entertained to a burlesque performance of the Water Babies at the Theatre Royal.

That week had brought a further setback to hopes of Bristol & District League membership. Swindon Wanderers had withdrawn due to financial problems, which saw them relinquish their County Ground home to neighbours Swindon Town. South End applied to take over their fixtures but the League resolved to carry on with one club less. In the event, Wanderers' circumstances soon improved, and they resumed their membership the following month.

No doubt South End felt they had proved a point when, a week later, they beat a side composed mainly of Wanderers players by a huge margin of 11-0. All in all, an auspicious start for a club that had attracted a membership of 300. The first local derby with the Minster took place on 23 March, when a 4,000 crowd at St John's Lane saw the visitors triumph 2-0, though the highlight of the season was undoubtedly when Preston North End came to town on

6 April. It was quite a coup for the Bristol Babe to induce to St John's Lane such a famous side – otherwise known as the Old Invincibles (founder members of the Football League and the first Champions in 1888-89, when they didn't lose a match as well as winning the FA Cup).

Not surprisingly, South End proved no match for their illustrious visitors. Despite the torrential rain, a 3,500 crowd saw Clements score a disputed goal, when the opposing goalkeeper was illegally charged. The referee (South End Committee man George Elmes) didn't demonstrate much impartiality as he ran back to the centre-circle in raptures exclaiming 'Goal! Goal'! Unfortunately, Preston notched up six as the homesters were well and truly put in their place.

At that time, South End were often referred to as the 'Garabaldians', on account of their red shirts, like those worn by the followers of the Italian revolutionary Garibaldi. The club was also simply known as the 'Reds' or 'Red Shirts', but as 'City' they became the 'Citizens', before their rapid rise to prominence ushered in the 'Bristol Babe'. The first mention of their present popular nickname of the 'Robins' appeared in the *Bristol Magpie* match report of the game against Bedminster on 28 December 1895, when South End were referred to as 'Cock Robin', but the term does not appear to have entered public parlance until 1926, when the song 'When The Red, Red, Robin Goes Bob, Bob, Bobbing Along' – written by Harry Woods – was the hit of the moment. Moreover, it wasn't until the late 1940s that the 'Robin' finally supplanted the 'Babe'.

Somewhat surprisingly, at a meeting of South End members on 13 April 1895, it was decided by a large majority that application for B&DL membership would not be made for 1895-96. The following communiqué was issued: 'This meeting of Bristol South End Football Club desires to add its appreciation of the good work done by the Bristol & District League and that this resolution is in no way antagonistic to that body. This Club will always be glad to work and cordially co-operate with the League for the advancement of football in the district'.

Another season of friendlies was therefore arranged, with the likes of the Seaforth Highlanders, Berwick Rangers (Worcester), and the Royal Artillery (Portsmouth) visiting St John's Lane for the first time. South End marked their FA Cup debut by beating Slough 5-1, before a solitary goal saw them dumped them out of the competition by Great Marlow.

With their reserve team (South End Athletic) gaining admittance to the South Bristol & District League, South End formed a Wednesday side that commenced its career with a 1-0 St John's

Lane success over Redland Grove College on 20 November. This midweek side won five and drew five of their sixteen games, a record that included the game against a representative side put together by Mr J A Stevens on Christmas Day, when a virtual 1st XI won 4-0 in front of a 2,000 St John's Lane crowd.

Notwithstanding South End's earlier decision, the expulsion of Cardiff from the Western League at the turn of the year – in consequence of their failure to fulfil fixtures and pay fines – prompted South End to propose taking over the fixtures of the South Wales Club. This offer was considered at a meeting at the Earl Russell Hotel, Lawrence Hill, on 15 January 1896, but the vote went against South End 9-7 and the following statement issued: 'The Western League thank the South End Club for their offer, but regret that they cannot see their way clear, owing to the question of points and other various difficulties of the case, to accept it, but the League trust that the South End Club will renew its application next season, and the South End Club is further assured that this resolution has nothing to do with any personal matter between the League and the South End Club'.

South End were unhappy by this further rejection, but good sense prevailed by the end of the campaign when they resolved to make another bid for membership. This time they were successful, being elected on the 3 June at a meeting held at the Conservative Club, Old Market Street. Strengthened by the addition of the Fielding brothers from Gloucester, South End soon justified their status, but they were brought back to earth by the eventual champions, Warmley, on 28 December. Losing 0-4 on the Tennis Court Ground in front of a record 4,464 crowd was a shock, but even worse was to follow. Defeat at St George and losing at home to Eastville Rovers and Bedminster put South End out of contention for the championship before Warmley came and completed the double near the end of the season. Despite obvious disappointment, finishing as runners-up was no mean achievement, especially as South End were four points clear of third-place Bedminster.

On losing at home against Eastville Rovers on 9 January, South End had lodged a complaint in regard to their rivals playing an ineligible man in John McLean. The Rovers had two points deducted and were fined £1, but South End, who had offered the selfsame player £1 5s to work at the Lane, failed in their dubious objective of getting the game replayed. Honours were even in derby clashes with the Minster: in the League, each won the away fixture, whilst Bedminster's success in the FA Cup was avenged by South End's victory in the Amateur competition. Following on from this, victories of 3-0 and 2-0 over Trowbridge Town and St George respectively took them through to the first round proper. Against the renowned Old Carthusians, who had beaten the Casuals 2-1 to clinch the inaugural tournament two years earlier, a couple of goals adrift at the break wasn't too bad, but by the finish South End had conceded eight more as they slumped to their worst ever defeat. Such a hammering confirmed the thoughts of the Committee that the Club had progressed as far as it could with local amateur players, giving added impetus to plans already in motion.

An Investigation Committee had been formed to explore the possibility of turning professional and gaining entry to the Southern League. The results of their labours culminated in a meeting at the Albert Hall, Bedminster, on 3 April 1897, when professionalism was adopted, following assurances from Southern League representatives that the club would be admitted to its ranks.

At the time, the name of the Club had not been settled upon, even though the Investigation Committee had quickly agreed that a new identity was necessary. They plumped for the title of 'Bristol City', but they reckoned without the opposition that a club barely three years old would provoke by such an ambitious declaration of intent. The Gloucestershire FA ruled against South End's proposal at a meeting at the Full Moon Hotel, Stokes Croft, Bristol on 27 April 1897 commenting: 'It would be detrimental to the interests of the clubs in the city and neighbourhood if any one club was allowed to take the name Bristol City.' *The Bristol Times & Mirror* was in agreement with this refusal: 'This ruling should put a stopper on any club calling itself by this name and even if they had not taken this action, surely the Bristol Rugby Club would have the right to protest'.

The Garibaldians were not easily dissuaded, however, and they continued to press for the right to adopt their preferred name, even though the rugby club complained to the Rugby Union that they considered the name to be too similar to their own. It took a visit to London by director Walter Tozer to plead the Club's case directly to the Football Association to get things moving. Approval was eventually received on 7 August, after the Gloucestershire FA had checked that the older established clubs like Eastville Rovers did not have any objections.

Unfortunately, all this uncertainty had delayed the issue of the share subscription list until September, when the public only took up 531 of the 1,400 shares on offer. Setting a precedent for events 85 years later, the directors made up the shortfall. According to the share prospectus, H C Ewens had taken over as Chairman, but within twelve months both he and his predecessor, A E Denby, had retired from the board. No doubt both were exhausted by their efforts in establishing the club at the forefront of the professional game in Southern England.

The Club's new status produced a flurry of activity at St John's Lane during the summer, with many improvements to complement the 500-seat grandstand. These included banking at both ends, as well as the provision of a canvas screen. This screen, raised by pulleys attached to a number of 30ft-high poles, served to block out the free view of spectators from what was dubbed 'scroungers' gallery' perched on Windmill Hill, as well as being profitably employed as advertising hoardings.

3

~ *Southern League Days* ~

The adoption of professionalism prompted South End to advertise for a manager, and of those who applied the name of Samuel Woodroffe Hollis stood out like a beacon. Trainer at Woolwich Arsenal, Hollis was invited to Bristol by Albert Denby on Easter Wednesday, 21 April 1897. Hollis was among the 5,000 crowd that saw Derby County beat West Bromwich Albion 2-1 in the special exhibition match at Bedminster's new Ashton Gate home. Afterwards he agreed to become manager, even though there was little money available to buy players.

On his return to London, Hollis 'tapped' a number of the Woolwich players before meeting up again with Denby a week later at the Hampshire County Cricket ground, where his Arsenal side beat Southampton St Mary's in a friendly 5-0. Mr McMinn, the Southampton secretary, not only assured the Bristol representatives of his club's support for their Southern League application, but also offered some of the Saints' surplus players. The first offer was gratefully accepted, but the second brought forth a 'No thank you,' from Hollis. If they are not good enough for you, they're not good enough for us. We want players that you want.'

Big words indeed from the manager, especially as he still hadn't been informed of the amount of money available for bargaining. Hollis insisted on knowing where he stood before he left to return to London, and was handed a cheque from the Chairman for £30 and told to do his best. Given that there was no limit as to the fee a man could receive for signing on, this was hardly a princely sum, but Hollis proved equal to the task. His smooth tongue worked overtime on the way back to London as he persuaded four of his Arsenal players – Alex 'Sandy' Caie, 'Paddy' O'Brien, 'Jock' Russell and Finlay Sinclair – of the honour of playing for the Club without even asking for a signing-on fee.

This clever bit of business gave Hollis scope to cast his sights further afield for other newcomers. With the addition of but a further £10, the services of club captain Billy Higgins were secured from Grimsby Town, together with Tom Wyllie (Bury), George Mann (Manchester City), Albert Carnelly and Harry Davy (Leicester Fosse), as well as a useful trio of Loughborough Town stalwarts – Jack Hamilton, Billy Jones and goalkeeper Hugh Monteith.

The manager had certainly done his best: in fact he achieved a minor sensation as the team he assembled for just £40 almost proved good enough to win the Southern League Championship. The season started with a home friendly against a Southampton side that had dropped the 'St Mary's' part of their name. Events on the pitch went well as City opened their professional career with a 3-1 success, but the occasion was marred by tragedy. A little girl, taken to the match by her parents, drowned in the swollen waters of the brook that ran alongside the ground. Further home friendly wins of 3-1 and 6-2 followed against Swindon Town and Lancashire League Champions Chorley, before the opening Southern League engagement on 11 September 1897.

The Wolverton & London North West Railway outfit were not expected to prove difficult opponents and this is how it appeared at half-time when City held a 6-1 advantage, but after the break the Railwaymen made a spirited fight-back before Carnelly struck to seal a 7-4 victory. A week later, Millwall Athletic, the previous campaign's runners-up, and champions of 1895-96, were expected to provide a sterner test, but City, helped by the vicissitudes of the Millwall goalie, astounded the soccer world with a 6-2 success.

It was not until New Year's Day that City suffered their first Southern League defeat, but after holding pole position for a good third of the season, they had to settle for the runners-up spot at the finish. In the Western League, however, they were not to be denied and received the ultimate accolade, from the League Secretary, J A Stevens, by being described as 'the best team ever seen in the competition'. Indeed, such was the side's prowess that Eastleigh, who had suffered 14-1 League defeat and a 10-3 Charity Cup hammering at City's hands, scratched from their home match with the 'Babes' on 2 March. In the FA Cup, the 'Citizens', as City were also popularly known, dealt a mortal blow to the Clifton Association organisation with a 9-1 success, before experiencing their first ever defeat as a professional club when losing to a Southampton side that went onto to reach the semi-finals. Fortunately, the Gloucestershire Cup hoodoo was exorcised by a 2-0 victory over Eastville Rovers. Progressing to the final, staged at the Rovers' Stapleton Road ground on 11 April, City became the sixth club to win the trophy after beating the holders Warmley 2-1 in front of a 11,186 crowd.

The season was celebrated at a special complimentary dinner at the Prince Hotel, Totterdown, on 18 April, but in what was a notable campaign for attendance records, it was surprising that an operating profit of only £66 (£18 after depreciation, etc) was declared at the AGM held at the Temperance Hall, East Street, Bedminster, on 5 July 1898. A new high was reached in Southern League circles with a crowd of 12,170 (inclusive of 300 season ticket holders) to watch City's 5-2 home victory over Southampton on 15 January, whilst a few months later the feat was repeated in the Western League, when the visit of Warmley to St John's Lane on 8 April brought forth a 10,250 crowd. A total of £3,263 was taken at the gate throughout the season, with a further £101 being earned through season ticket sales.

All in all, it had been a successful introduction to professionalism for the Bristol Babe, but it wasn't enough to satisfy the ambitions of the club directors. No doubt influenced by the fact that, of eight games against Football League clubs during the course of the season, only two were lost, City made an audacious bid for Football League membership. Entering the ballot along with the three Second Division clubs (Darwen, Lincoln City, and Loughborough) up for re-election, together with fellow non-leaguers Burslem Port Vale, Nelson and New Brighton Tower, City got short shrift at the League AGM in Manchester on 20 May. The delegates were unimpressed: City finished bottom of the poll with just one vote. Lincoln, Burslem and Loughborough were successful with 21, 18 and 16 votes respectively, whilst Darwen 15, New Brighton 13 and Nelson 3 missed out.

Darwen's disappointment was brief, however, as within half an hour it was decided to increase the size of the two divisions and they were re-admitted. Eight days later New Brighton, Glossop North End and Barnsley also gained entry to the fold in an apparently uncontested election, but quite why City and Nelson were not involved is unclear. Whatever the reason, it meant another bid for Southern League honours in 1898-99 with Bedminster numbering among City's rivals.

Bedminster, who had failed in their own attempt to gain admission to the Second Division of the Southern League in 1897-98, had remained amateur and romped away with the championship of the Amateur Section of the Western League. Racking up the goals at home by beating Fishponds 7-0, St Paul's 7-1, Mangotsfield 6-0, and Radstock 5-0, they had also accounted for Midsomer Norton 10-1 on New Year's Day. Unfortunately, in the last game of the season, Midsomer Norton gained more than ample revenge. Despite being reduced to ten men for more than half the game, they won 3-2 to deprive Bedminster of their 100 per cent record.

After winning away at Newbury 3-1, the Minster's FA Cup cause wasn't helped by the fact that they found themselves in dispute with their landlords, the Bedminster Athletic Ground Company. As a consequence, the club agreed to switch their second qualifying round match to Stapleton Road and paid the price as Eastville Rovers won 3-2.

Bedminster did better in the Amateur tourney, however, as victories against Yeovil Casuals and the Old Weymouthians brought about a place in the fourth qualifying round. Home advantage, though, was to no avail against Street, who won easily 4-1. In the Bristol Charity Cup, Mangotsfield were beaten 2-1, Clifton Association 3-1, Staple Hill 4-1 and Barton Hill 5-1 to set up a clash with Warmley, who won 4-0 to inflict what was destined to be Bedminster's last-ever defeat in the competition.

By this time, the Minster had been at Ashton Gate for almost two seasons, having vacated Greenway Bush Lane at the conclusion of the 1895-96 campaign. It was at a meeting held in the offices of the Bedminster club solicitor, W H Brown, on 12 December 1895 that the news of the new ground was released. The Bedminster Cricket & Football Club – recently formed as a Limited Company to obtain a new ground, now that Greenway Bush Lane was to be built upon – had successfully obtained an advantageous lease from Sir Greville Smyth for eleven acres of land opposite Bedminster Park.

The final season at Greenway Bush Lane had been disappointing, as yet again the side finished fourth from bottom, though the reduction in numbers meant a placing of eighth compared with ninth the previous campaign. The team never really recovered from a disastrous start that saw four successive defeats. A 1-2 loss was also forthcoming against St Paul's on the Bower Ashton ground on 7 December, though Bedminster made amends with a 3-0 home success just over a month later. They did well to obtain a point in a goalless draw at home to Gloucester on 21 December, as they had three men missing at the kick-off, and no sooner did the threesome turn up than the team lost Walters with a leg injury.

With victories over St George, Swindon Wanderers and Clifton Association prior to Christmas, the Minster fans were expecting further improvement in the New Year, but this isn't how it worked out. Following Cardiff's failure to show up on Boxing Day, the team suffered a procession of defeats that was only relieved by victories over St Paul's and Eastville Rovers. Fortunately for their long-suffering supporters, the best was kept to last as Mangotsfield were beaten 7-0 on 21 March. Finishing with a league record of P20, W6, D2, L12, F36, A42, Bedminster were probably a point better off than they had the right to expect, as the game at Gloucester – cancelled due to a smallpox epidemic – was adjudicated to stand as a goalless draw.

Ten friendlies were contested during the season, including a game against Mr J A Stevens' Bristol City XI. This attracted a record 5,000 crowd to Greenway Bush Lane, on 14 September, to see the representative side thrashed 6-2. The 85th King's Light Infantry (Portland) were beaten 4-1 in early November, and near the end of the month the Royal Artillery (Plymouth) were also summary dispatched 6-2. The best, though, was the victory over South End in front of a 3,000 crowd at Greenway Bush Lane on 28 December, though Bedminster paid the price at St John's Lane four months later. In both the FA and the Amateur Cups, the Minster fell at the first time of asking, but they won through to a meeting with Eastville Rovers in the semi-final of the Gloucestershire Cup.

Unfortunately this game, in front of a 4,000 crowd at Greenway Bush Lane on 28 March, was marred by tragedy which made Bedminster's 0-1 defeat of little consequence. Herbert Edward Smith, the Minster's clever right-winger, sustained an early head injury when challenging Frederick Lovett for the ball. Smith continued after receiving treatment, but twice had to go off for further attention before retiring from the fray early in the second half. None of those present appreciated the seriousness of his condition and on returning home he collapsed and died at his Islington Road home at 6.45 the following morning without ever regaining consciousness.

The inquest was held the following Tuesday at Bedminster Police Station. Dr Henry Cook stated that death was due to shock and compression of the brain from haemorrhage due to a ruptured artery. The City Coroner, H G Doggett, in summing up, remarked: 'Football is a game attended with a certain amount of risk, and the players went into it with that knowledge. Of course it ought to be played fairly and honestly, and in this case there was no evidence to show it was not'. A verdict of 'accidental death' was recorded.

Crowd disorder saw one of its earliest manifestations in Bristol during the season, when Barton Hill beat Bedminster's reserves by the only goal in a Second Division Western League game on 7 March 1896. The Greenway Bush Lane crowd were so incensed that the referee, Sam Peacock, feared for his safety. The former Warmley player had to be protected and escorted back across the Cut into Bristol in order to save falling into the hands of rowdy youths. Feeling it was hardly worth risking life and limb for the match fee of just five shillings, Peacock said he had no wish to officiate again, but relented after further reflection.

Bedminster's punishment for the crowd's indiscipline was determined by the Western League Management Committee at their fortnightly meeting four days later, when it was announced that the club should print and exhibit 1,000 handbills warning of ground closure should the disgraceful scenes ever be repeated.

The season concluded with the Minster engaged in the Western League Six-a-Side tournament. Facing Eastville Rovers in a semi-final at Staple Hill on 23 April, the Minster were unable to avenge the defeat they had suffered in the inaugural event two years previously. A poor League record meant that, for the second time, Bedminster had to face up to a re-election ordeal. This was to have taken place at the Conservative Club in Old Market Street on 6 May, but the meeting was adjourned for four weeks. Fortunately, Bedminster were safely restored to membership on the same day that South End were voted in.

Although Ashton Gate, then known as the Bedminster Athletic Ground, would not be ready to stage cricket until 1897, it opened for football on 12 September 1896, when Staple Hill were beaten in a friendly after the visiting inside-left, Bracey, had the honour of scoring the first goal on the ground. The official opening, however, took place two weeks later when a 3,000 crowd witnessed a 1-1 Western League draw with Warmley. The *Western Daily Press* expressed the hope that Ashton Gate would become one of the finest grounds in the West of England, but at that time work had not yet started on the proposed grandstand, whilst the dressing rooms still awaited completion. The football pitch wasn't where it is today, being confined to a small corner of the available space, where the Bristol Bowling Club now carry out their activities. The main area was reserved for cricketing pursuits, which saw its first contest seven months later when, in a two-day match starting on 30 April, Dr W G Grace's team of 'twelve' Gloucestershire men restricted V T Hill's Somerset XII to 68 for 8 in reply to their 212.

With victories over Trowbridge (h) 4-0, St George (h) 2-1, South End (a) 3-1 – as well as completing the double over Clifton 5-0 (h) and 7-1 (a) – it wasn't surprising that the Minster finished high up the table in third place, but the Champions, Warmley, proved to be their nemesis in both local cup competitions. After losing to them in the Bristol Charity Cup, the Minster performed better in the final of the Gloucestershire Cup, but still lost. A 6,705 crowd paying record receipts of £191 on the new St George ground at Bell Hill saw the Minster start well, but Berry's twelfth-minute blunder in letting in Phil Britton's long-shot unsettled them and they went down 0-2.

BEDMINSTER: W Berry; A E Talbot-Lewis, G Brooks; C Jordan, M O McAuliffe, H Morris; F J Harris, A Hargett, W Harrison, G Cottle, W Burley.
WARMLEY: W Davis; J Carter, F Reeves; G Bowler, P Britton, H Wilshire; F Webley, R Preddy, S Stone, W Rooke, G ('Nip') Britton.
REFEREE: T W H Saywell (Chatham). LINESMEN: A Farrant (St George) and J Fagan.

In the FA Cup, Freemantle were beaten 2-0 after the Minster had come out on top in the local derby clash with South End at St John's Lane, but Reading Amateurs proved much too good in the third qualifying round, winning 5-0 at Ashton Gate. Hopes of making progress in the Amateur tourney were raised by having to face South End yet again, but this time it was to be a different story as the Garibaldians extracted revenge with a 2-1 replay success.

All in all, it had been a good first season for Bedminster at their new home, which saw a glimpse of the big time on 21 April, when First Division clubs Derby County and West Bromwich Albion played each other for a purse reputed to be ten guineas.

With Bedminster's election to the First Division of the Southern League at that organisation's AGM held in London on 21 May 1898, the scene could have been set for a similar situation to that which was to overwhelm St George and Warmley in East Bristol. Fortunately, at the third AGM of the Bedminster Cricket & Football Club, held some months earlier on 7 February at the Hope & Anchor, Redcliffe Hill, A W Francis – who was to be a prime mover in the amalgamation with Bristol City – was appointed to the board along with E J Pilliers.

David Copeland, signed from Walsall Town Swifts, opened Bedminster's professional career with a goal against Southampton in a friendly nine days before the first Southern League game on 10 September. David Proudfoot's strike at Northumberland Park brought a commendable share of the spoils with Tottenham Hotspur, but it wasn't until their sixth match that both points were secured. Beating New Brompton 4-1 at Ashton Gate on 12 November set up a sequence of four straight wins, and a further run of four successive victories at the end of the campaign brought a final placing of eighth.

Local derby honours were shared. Bedminster lost 2-5 at St John's Lane in front of a 10,250 crowd on 17 December – when Albert Carnelly grabbed a pair to mark his comeback to City's ranks after his brief sojourn with Ilkeston Town. But John Leonard's goal earned revenge in the return fixture three months later. A successful season was cemented by lifting the Bristol Charity Cup. Bedminster beat Reading 3-2 in a thrilling game watched by barely 500 spectators at St John's Lane on 24 April.

Warmley, despite all their troubles, still proved too good, winning 3-2 at the Chequers on Boxing Day, just a month before their unfortunate demise, whilst in the FA Cup the White Shirts had also demonstrated their pedigree by emerging triumphant in a second replay at St John's Lane on 24 October. The best win of the season was achieved over the rump of the old Bedminster side that had disagreed over the decision to adopt professionalism. A 9-2 success over Bristol Amateurs confirmed the enormous gulf that existed.

The stars of Bedminster's first professional side included captain Robert Kelso, a Scottish international signed from Dundee, James

Whitehouse, a talented goalkeeper from the Aston Villa side which did the League and Cup double in 1896-97, and Irish international Robert Crone, who should have become the only player to be capped for his country whilst at the club. He was selected for the game against Wales on 4 March 1899, but had to decline the honour as Bedminster insisted that he turn out in the local derby played on the same day.

For City, the 1898-99 campaign, with William Panes-Kingston, having taken over as Chairman, was a case of so near, yet so far. City, who had been reinforced by the acquisition of Jim Stevenson from Bristol St George towards the end of the campaign, had the championship within their grasp before contriving to lose it in the final 45 minutes of the season on 29 April. Having not suffered a defeat in the competition until going down 1-2 at Brighton United on 11 January, City went into this last game tied at the top of the table with the defending champions, Southampton. City needed to win to be sure of the toppling their rivals, although a draw would still give them a chance of honours. According to Rule 8 of the competition, the Saints' superior goal-average would count for nothing. Instead, a deciding match on neutral territory would be necessary.

A new record St John's Lane crowd of 13,000, generating receipts of £440, saw City win the toss after the Saints, in white shirts and black shorts, had been the first to enter the field. With City holding a two-goal lead at the break, the Championship appeared to be theirs, but the Saints had other ideas as they stormed back to win by the odd goal in seven. Southampton deserved full credit for their stirring comeback, but sadly this epic contest has been marred by suspicions of match fixing.

Years later the matter still rankled and 'On-looker' in his regular column in the Saturday Sports Edition of the *Bristol Evening News* on 14 January 1911 refers to the fact that a prominent City player was accused of a grave illegality and didn't play for the club again. To lose the championship in such a way was a bitter blow to Sam Hollis, in what was his last match in charge. After announcing his intention to resign on 18 March, because of increasing interference by the directors, as well as certain conditions attached to his new £200 per annum contract, he took over from Harry Smith as secretary-manager of bitter rivals Bedminster.

Despite winning their opening four fixtures, City's performances in the United League were less notable, and they had to be satisfied with a final placing of fifth. In the FA Cup, though, they became the first local club to reach the first round proper. Meeting Sunderland – whose General Secretary and Manager Robert Campbell was to take charge of City the following season – at St John's Lane on 28 January the ground record was broken when a crowd of 16,945 saw Billy Langham open the scoring with a fine shot. Sadly, the famous visitors, who included England international Phil Bach, a future City player, at right-back, quickly retaliated to progress to the next round with a 4-2 success.

Tragedy marred this great cup run, however, as, after winning at Cowes in the third qualifying round, City were paired with Bristol St George. This clash attracted much interest and so large was the crowd on the Bell Hill ground on 19 November that many sought better vantage-points. Pat Finnerhan's great first-half strike served to win the game for the visitors, but spectator Charles Hayden lost his life when falling from a tree. The City directors sent £10 to his widow to start up a relief fund for her and her six children.

The Gloucestershire Cup was retained with a 2-1 victory over the newly named Bristol Rovers on 3 April. This set the seal on another successful season. Following a congratulatory banquet for the players and directors at the Club's Angel Hotel, Redcliffe Street, headquarters on 22 April, a Complimentary Dinner took place at the Prince Hotel, Totterdown, three weeks later.

However, success on the pitch came at a price for City, who had paid their players £3 per week basic, plus £2 win bonus and £1 for a draw. Despite innovations such as having the United Kingdom Commercial Travellers Association sponsor the Southern League fixture with Reading on 25 March, and with revenue from season tickets (priced at 15s, 12s 6d and 10s), increasing to just over £131, the financial situation gave cause for concern. A loss of £112 was posted.

This, though, did not detract from the optimism that heralded the start of the new season. Whilst Ted Locke retained the post of Financial Secretary, the engagement of Campbell, a former Scottish international, as Secretary-Manager at a salary of £270 per annum ended Hodgkinson's tenure as General Secretary.

Campbell appeared to be the ideal man to build on the foundations laid by Hollis and he recruited what appeared to be a good set of players. He persuaded former City and Bedminster goalkeeper Talbot-Lewis to return from Everton, as well as signing Clyde pair Alex Crawford and Alex McDonald, together with Alex Downie (Third Lanark) Adam Godsman (Inverness), and Fred Molyneux (Stoke). Crowds of up to 7,000 flocked to St John's Lane for the pre-season trial games and all seemed set for another bold bid for Southern League honours.

Whilst the 'Play up, Play up', song that was printed in the 1899-1900 Club Handbook captured some of the new season's optimism, it failed to inspire the team. Despite the capture of James Blessington from Derby in October, City struggled to hold a mid-table position during the campaign. Indeed, so bad was the side performing that on 1 December the directors held a crisis meeting at their headquarters in the Angel Hotel, Redcliffe, having moved from the Star Hotel, North Street, Bedminster some thirteen months earlier. At the end of the season, City were indebted to their better goal-average, which gave them ninth spot above Bristol Rovers, but they trailed three places behind Bedminster. The supporters were disillusioned by the procession of defeats, 29 in all, including twelve in the Southern League, as well as a 0-6 hammering by Bedminster in the Charity Cup.

City carried a large playing staff and ran a reserve side for the first time since 1896-97, when they had had finished fourth in the South Bristol & District League. City's poor form had a grave impact on finances. The Southern League home average was down from 5,462 to 4,125, but even so it was a surprise when, despite the staging of their first Annual Sports on 12 August 1899, a huge financial loss of almost £1,200 was revealed. However, by this time the necessary steps for the salvation of South Bristol football had already been implemented. Renewed optimism was in the air, even though Bedminster fans were entitled to feel somewhat cheated.

The Minster, with average Southern League home crowds of just 2,458 in 1898-99 and 2,757 in 1899-1900, had shown the fruits of good husbandry, with a surplus of £62 announced at their AGM held at the Bedminster Hotel on 6 February 1899. With new players arriving – of the calibre of England internationals Francis Becton from Sheffield United, Albert Flewitt (West Bromwich Albion), and goalkeeper George Toone (Notts County), not to mention Scottish cap Hugh Wilson (Sunderland), who was appointed captain, Tommy Boucher (Notts County) and Peter Chambers (Blackburn Rovers) – it is obvious that Hollis had lost but little of his smooth-talking ways.

No doubt the profit of £57 for year ending September 1899 was boosted by staging the England v Wales Home International on 20 March, though the use of Ashton Gate for this fixture engendered much local jealously. Despite Bedminster's grandstand, described as the finest in Bristol, being full, only £320 was realised from a crowd that barely reached 6,000 to witness England's 4-1 win. Whilst City supporters might have been miffed by the non-selection of St John's Lane, the main problem was caused by the Gloucestershire FA sulking over not being consulted over choice of venue. They preferred the Rovers' ground at Stapleton Road, but arrangements had been left in the hands of the ground owners.

The GFA were so aggrieved that they issued a statement: 'The Council regrets that not having received any official intimation from the Football Association respecting the International at Bedminster, and consequently the council do not see their way clear to send representatives to the committee as suggested by Mr A W Francis.' The *Bristol Evening News* of 11 March commented: 'The unpardonable sin in the local football world would seem to be to offend the Gloucestershire Football Association. Whilst it is salaamed and bowed to as omnipotent, all to the well, but directly a club or organisation – in this instance the Football Association – dares to have a mind of its own, then the GFA acts like a spoilt child.'

The City supporters amongst the crowd were no doubt disappointed that their very own George Barker, described as the 'best back in the Southern League', was not selected, despite having played a starring role for the South in their 1-3 defeat by the North in the trial match at the Crystal Palace, in front of a 5,000 crowd on 1 February.

As the 1899-1900 campaign neared its end, it was clear that South Bristol could not sustain two clubs operating within a mile of one another. Just as Warmley and St George had folded in east Bristol, there were dangers of the deadly rivalry between City and Bedminster bringing about the same fate south of the river. Fortunately, wisdom prevailed amongst the Bedminster board, particularly A W Francis and Financial Secretary W H (Billie) Burland. They resurrected moves regarding the establishment of one professional club in south Bristol, first proposed almost three years previously in the summer of 1897, when the Minster Secretary E E T Matthews entered into dialogue with City director Walter Tozer. Tozer, alone among his colleagues, was of the opinion that 'amalgamation would lead to the early establishment of a first-rate club, and enable it to steer clear of the dangers appertaining to football enterprise'.

The general feeling was that amalgamation was necessary. Most people, though, including the local press, thought that City's response during the first week of April 1900 – that 'amalgamation would only be considered on the basis that everything of theirs would be retained' – would close the matter. But Bedminster would not be deterred this time, however, and Francis organised a further meeting. Compromise won the day, and agreement was reached by the City shareholders at the Temperance Hall on 10 April. Whilst the name, colours and ground of Bristol City would be retained, the board of the new amalgamated club would comprise an equal number of City and Bedminster directors. However, due to the conditions of the lease for Bedminster's Ashton Gate ground, and to keep faith with erstwhile Minster supporters, it was decided that home matches be split between both clubs' grounds for the next three seasons.

The Minster – who had retained the Bristol Charity Cup by beating Bristol Rovers 4-1 in front of a 6,034 St John's Lane crowd on 24 March – lost form and heart following the announcement of amalgamation. Suffering three straight Southern League defeats, they bounced back with a 4-1 home success over Queen's Park Rangers in front of barely a hundred spectators on 25 April. Completing their Southern League career three days later with a goalless draw at Reading, their curtain call was a Gloucestershire Cup final against City at the end of the month. Firm favourites for this clash, played on the Rovers ground at Stapleton Road on 30 April, the Minster seized the opportunity to depart the football scene on a high with a 2-1 success, and leave no one in any doubt that they were fully deserving of their title as 'the best team in Bristol'.

So passed into history the maroon and old-gold shirts of the renowned Minster, who in 1893 had one of the largest followings in local football with a membership of some 400. The future of the Association game in the capital of the West of England was now to rest with City and Rovers, though both Bristol St George and Warmley were to reform as amateur organisations.

4

~ A New Era ~

With a board of directors comprising former Bedminster officials A W Francis, D Thomas, F V Larway, F W Mapson, Frank N Bacon, and City men William Panes-Kingston, Joseph Daveridge, Harry King, E C Tyack, and E C Hanson, the newly fused organisation looked ahead to the 1900-01 season with confidence. Francis became the first Chairman, but by the following year Panes-Kingston had regained the pre-eminence he had held with the old Bristol City Club.

Whilst much of what was City's had been retained, this did not apply to the field of play. It was mainly ex-Bedminster men who were destined to take the club into a new era. Hugh Wilson (often recalled as the most versatile and cleverest footballer ever seen in Bristol) assumed the captaincy from Jack Hamilton. Other additions included Dave McDougall (Patrick Thistle), Billy Michael (Hearts), Dave Nichol (Millwall), Jimmy Stevenson (Newcastle), as well as Phil Bach and Billy Fulton from Sunderland. All told, it was an unrecognisable City that made a strong bid for the Southern League Championship.

The Bristol Coat of Arms, woven in the Minster's maroon and old-gold colours, graced the players' shirts for the first time, though the practise was dropped in 1903-04. Except for the occasion of the 1909 FA Cup final, it did not return until 1950-51, when the Bristol Coat of Arms, with 'BCFC' scrolled in red lettering underneath, decorated City's shirts until the end of the 1960-61 campaign.

The 1900-01 season commenced with a trial match at Ashton Gate on 28 August, where a City team comprising: Toone; Bach, Davies; Jones, Wilson, Chambers; Whelan, Stevenson, Michael, Fulton, Nichol, beat local side Arlington Rovers 4-0 in front of a 4,000 crowd. City were not so convincing in Western League action, however, but as FA approval for the enlarged competition was not granted until 12 November, it is likely that the 'league' wasn't taken that seriously.

In the Southern League it was Southampton who again proved just that little bit better as, for the third time in four seasons, City had to be content with the runners-up spot. The disbanding of the Chatham club on 20 December was a blow to championship aspirations as not only did it mean the loss of the four points gained from two victories against them at the beginning of the month, but also the relinquishing of a healthy 8-1 goal return. In truth, though, City threw away the championship near the end of the season. They should have at least have drawn with Queen's Park Rangers at Kensal Rise, whilst their failure to defeat a Spurs side that included nine reserves was inexcusable.

The loss of top scorer Michael, following his injury at Portsmouth in January, was a blow, as were injuries to Whelan, Geddes and Fulton at various times throughout the campaign. Fortunately, skipper Hugh Wilson proved to be a splendid handyman by filling every position except that of goalkeeper. Billy Jones played for the South side that drew 3-3 with the North in the English International trial in front of a 6,000 crowd at the Crystal Palace on 25 February, and did well enough to become City's first international in a 3-0 win over Ireland at the Dell a few weeks later.

By now, the Gloucestershire Cup competition was much diminished in stature, with only City and Rovers remaining of the leading clubs. The void was filled by Arlington Rovers, Barry Unionists, Bedminster St Francis, Bristol East, Fishponds, St Philip's, and Staple Hill, all of whom had to contest for the right to play either City or Rovers in a semi-final. This arrangement continued until the establishment of the Gloucestershire Immediate Cup in 1907-08, whereupon the senior competition became a straight fight each year between the two senior clubs. In the interim, however, none of the lesser lights proved able to threaten the status quo, despite there being considerable talent within their ranks. Staple Hill, for example, gave Manchester United a shock by opening the scoring, in front of future Prime Minister Winston Churchill, in an FA Cup-tie at Clayton in January 1906. Consequently, all the finals from the start of the new century resolved themselves into City and Rovers affairs. After the Rovers had beaten Bristol East 3-0 at Stapleton Road in the semi-final, the new order was established on 29 April 1901 when just 2,800 fans were present at St John's Lane to witness City's easy 4-0 success.

The newly constituted City club had uprooted their administrative headquarters from the Angel Hotel to Bank Chambers, East Street, Bedminster, but despite retaining St John's Lane as their home ground, fourteen games (nine Southern League, three Western League and two friendlies) were also played at Ashton Gate. The erstwhile Bedminster home was initially used on 22 September, when a crowd in excess of 8,000 witnessed a 1-1 Southern League draw with Tottenham Hotspur, an occasion which also saw the presence of the St John's Ambulance Brigade for the first time. Given the animosity that had existed between City and Bedminster, this was a highly encouraging turnout, but this figure was soon to be exceeded again.

Four weeks later it was estimated that 15,000 were present for the game with Bristol Rovers, in which Michael make amends for having his penalty-kick saved by Richard Gray on the stroke of half-time. His 53rd-minute header settled a contest that had aroused much interest. All manner of vehicles had been used to convey spectators to the game. The Ashton Gate ground was packed and there was occasion for surprise when receipts of only £352, representing a crowd of only 13,500, were announced. This discrepancy between appearance and reality led to local reporter Harry J Slater-Stone ('Half-Back') – who would continue writing in the local press almost up to his death in September 1938 – to investigate. But he was rebuffed by the club's Secretary-Manager Bob Campbell, who refused point-blank to shed light on the discrepancy.

The interest caused by the use of Bedminster's ground waned as the campaign wore on. By the end of the season the average Southern League gathering at Ashton Gate of 6,056 was almost identical to the figure of 6,083 for St John's Lane. No thought, therefore, was given in regard to making any permanent move, even though events in the summer were to bring a premature end to the dual-ground arrangement.

Despite this reasonable support, finance was still a concern, with many players said to be paid far in excess of their worth. At that time, the status of the Southern League, founded in 1894, was almost on an equal footing with the Football League (formed 1888). But whereas the older competition sought to put a brake on players' earnings (£4 per week maximum) the Southern League was a virtual free-for-all. With a loss of almost £1,000 for 1900-01 – following on from the previous campaign's even bigger deficit – City thought they might be able to trim their expenses by making another application for Football League membership.

At a meeting held at the Temperance Hall on 10 May 1901, Bill Hodgkinson's proposal, seconded by Joseph Crompton, was accepted. Manager Robert Campbell was despatched to send a telegram, whereupon City entered the ballot alongside the three clubs up for re-election – Burton Swifts, Walsall and Stockport County – plus fellow non-leaguers Crewe Alexandra, Darwen, Doncaster Rovers and Stalybridge Rovers. This time, City's boldness, helped no doubt by Campbell's many contacts in the soccer world, came up trumps. At the Football League's AGM in Manchester a week later, City topped the poll with 23 votes, together with Burton Swifts, soon to amalgamate with Burton Wanderers and become Burton United. They were followed by Doncaster (16), Stockport (16), Stalybridge (7), Walsall (7), Crewe (5), and Darwen (0). For the third and final vacancy, a second ballot was required. It resulted in

Stockport, with 21 votes, retaining their place in preference to Doncaster, who polled 13. But Rovers' disappointment was short-lived. Just prior to the start of the season they took over the vacancy created by New Brighton Tower's late resignation.

Despite his three-year managerial contract at £260 per annum that still had a year to run, a major internal disagreement saw Campbell depart soon afterwards. Once again City turned to Hollis, who now faced a situation similar to that four years earlier. With few players retained, due to the need to cut the previous season's wage bill of £2,719 plus £137 bonuses, Hollis faced a daunting task, but this time he extracted a pledge from the directors that they would heed his advice and not interfere.

On taking the job Hollis commented: 'They've given me a free hand now – with nothing in it!' Still, it was a task he relished, and Hollis called upon the club's benefactors for financial assistance. The appeal raised £345, added to which he introduced economies that included a cut in his own salary. Scouring the country for bargains, Hollis picked up three players from the Walsall side whom City had displaced in the Football League – Joe Connor, Jack Flynn and Billy Tuft – not to mention Bertie Banks (Aston Villa), Tommy Boucher (Bristol Rovers), John Bradbury (Barnsley), Walter Cookson (Nelson), Steve Jones (Aberdare), Wally Moles (Tottenham Hotspur), James Robertson (New Brompton), Harry Clay (Kimberley St John's), Jimmy Jay (Bristol East) and Hanley lad Ernie Vickerstaffe, who somewhat surprisingly hailed from local club Eastville Athletic.

With only Richard Davies, Billy Jones, Peter Chambers, John McLean and Paddy O'Brien being retained, City entered the Football League with their cheapest side since the adoption of professionalism. One of those released was the peerless William John Wedlock, destined to become one of the best centre-halves ever to play for England. The economies worked, as a City side, costing some £800 less than that of the previous season, turned in some outstanding displays to confound the critics. Among them were many of their own fans, who had barely contributed £75 in season ticket sales compared to the previous year's figure of £132.

City commenced their Football League career at Bloomfield Road, where Blackpool took the field in their new light-blue colours. Two goals from City's old stalwart Paddy O'Brien brought success, but a rude awakening came on the Cobridge enclosure two days later. City were well beaten by Burslem Port Vale, but it was all smiles at the first home game on the following Saturday as strikes by Jones, O'Brien and Connor brought a comfortable victory over Stockport County in front of a 6,489 crowd.

The visit of Woolwich Arsenal on 26 October attracted an attendance in excess of 10,000, but many in the crowd were annoyed to find City turning out in an all-white strip as the visitors insisted on playing in their normal red and white colours. Arsenal were acting within the rules, as the older established club had the right to play in their own colours at all times, even though many visitors to Bristol, including Manchester United, chose not to exercise the option.

In mid-December, the game scheduled at Gainsborough Trinity was switched due to the Northolme enclosure being under suspension. The change of venue didn't much help Trinity, who were an hour late in arriving in Bristol, forcing a late kick-off. Consequently, with City leading, the game had to be abandoned at the end of the first half due to fading light. Taking no chances for the re-arranged fixture a month later, the visitors stayed overnight, but couldn't prevent City's thumping success.

The visit of leaders West Bromwich Albion in mid-February saw a crowd of 14,175 crammed into St John's Lane, but many left disappointed as City lost 1-2, despite seeing John Bradbury almost taking out the roof of the net with his goal.

The fans who took advantage of the seven-shilling excursion to Plumstead, where City were beaten 0-2, were not much cheered by the following week's 3-1 success over Barnsley. The local press reported that the second-half play was the worst of the season. Form slumped and five of the last six games were lost.

Failure from the penalty-spot in the 0-2 home defeat by Burton United made the fans' misery complete, though many probably took a more philosophical view. A collection for the Ibrox Disaster Fund made many realise there were worse things that could happen at a football match than losing two points. There was also the Old English Sports and Archery Tournament, to be held on the ground on 17 May, to look forward to.

Overall, the Second Division was considered to be weaker than usual, but City's performances, which saw them finish sixth, were still noteworthy. The one blot on the season was that, in losing to the Rovers in a marathon FA Cup-tie, City allowed their rivals to become the first Bristol club to claim a League scalp in the competition. Fog had saved City in the first meeting at Stapleton Road on 16 November, when they trailed by two goals, but in the re-arranged game a week later they deserved their draw. With a replay at St John's Lane, City felt confident, but the Rovers surprised them by overcoming a half-time deficit to pull off a 3-2 success.

All home fixtures were now played at St John's Lane, in accordance with the Football League stipulation that for each club all games must be staged at one venue. Interestingly, the *Bristol Magpie* had held a poll amongst its readers, which by the start of the 1901-02 campaign produced a vote of 582 to 470 in favour of retaining City's original home in preference to Ashton Gate.

During that season, a testimonial fund was established for one of the club's founders, Fred Keenan, who had lost the use of his lower limbs following an accident. The fund enabled Keenan to be presented with a cycle chair, in which he was to become a familiar sight on the touchline for a good few years.

The demise of three of Bristol's professional clubs meant that the Bristol Charity Cup wasn't contested in 1900-01. The competition for a handsome bowl donated by C H Flook – a jeweller with shops in Bristol and South Wales – had commenced as a knock-out tournament when Barton Hill and Eastville Wanderers drew 2-2 in a first-round match on 19 December 1896. Warmley, who beat South End in the inaugural final, retained the trophy by beating Reading 3-0 in 1897-98, before Bedminster took the honours in both 1898-99 and 1899-1900. The Bristol Charity Cup was revived on a league basis in 1901-02 and was eventually discontinued in 1942.

In the Gloucestershire Cup, City – who had scarcely extended themselves in defeating Bristol East – found goals hard to come by in the final. Richard Davis set the trend by firing wide from the penalty-spot in front of a 13,835 crowd at Stapleton Road. Matters did not improve in the replay three weeks later as, with the dearth of goals continuing, City had to settle for sharing the trophy with the Rovers.

Despite declaring a small profit of just under £40, it was felt that the club was at last running on the right lines. But although Football League membership had resulted in gate receipts increasing to £3,835 it was ironic that Southern League Bristol Rovers, boosted by their great FA Cup run, bettered this figure by more than £300. Interest, though, was on the up and the public responded with season ticket sales rising to £118 for 1902-03.

The general opinion of Association Football enthusiasts in Bristol at this time, as expressed by Burleigh's 1902-03 Football Annual was that: 'Professionalism had passed successfully through its critical period and that the City and Rovers clubs have come to stay. The optimist must look forward to one or the other of them to embrace a policy that shall, within a few seasons, have them regularly meeting, as members of the First Division, the best in the country, even though they may fall short for many seasons to come in the struggle for the English Cup'.

City fans were hopeful of promotion at the start of a season that ushered in the pitch markings (except for the addition of the penalty arc in 1937) which we are familiar with today. Hitherto, with the introduction of the penalty-kick at the instigation of J Reed, the Honorary Secretary of the Irish FA in 1891, the penalty area had extended right across the pitch twelve yards from the goal-line, whilst two six-yard arcs marked the goal-area.

A first-day defeat at the hands of Bristol Rovers dented the optimism somewhat, but spirits were cheered when Chesterfield were beaten in the League opener. With a side including Irish international Andrew Gara from Nottingham Forest, Micky Good (Preston North End), George Lewis (Notts County), Dickie Wombwell (Derby County), Alf Dean and Walter 'Swappy' Leigh from Grimsby Town, City were even more impressive than they had been in the previous season. Winning their first five League games, and only conceding one goal, City bestrode the table prior to their visit to the Manor Ground, on 4 October.

All good things come to an end, but the defeat at Plumstead was unfortunate in that the errant hand of Lewis gave away the penalty that allowed Fergus Hunt to fire in Woolwich Arsenal's late winner. This was trainer Robert Crone's last game for City, as the former Bedminster player, appointed in the 1901 close season, took up a similar post with Brentford. Victory over Doncaster Rovers had City back on top of the table, but despite an unbeaten run of seven games, too many draws dropped them down to third place by the time of their visit to Burslem Port Vale in early December. A frozen pitch did little to help the Babes' cause, though the real reason for their defeat was said to be their timorous attitude. Decline continued with failure at Gainsborough Trinity, before a couple of home fixtures gave hope of stopping the rot.

Barnsley, the Christmas Day visitors, insisted on playing in their regular colours, so the City turned out in their change blue and chocolate strip. City fell behind in the first minute when, from Dickie Bourne's centre, Davies had the misfortune to send the ball into his own net. It did not appear that City would be any luckier playing in the new strip than they had been in their all-white outfit. Matters improved, however, and the final whistle saw the points shared at the end of an exciting 3-3 draw.

Two days later City hit top form against Burton United, winning 3-1 as well as having four goals disallowed. New Year's Day saw a trip to Blackpool, where Dean's magnificent shot secured victory. Subsequent form was patchy: soft goals from Leigh and Good brought an unexpected success against Manchester United on the Bank Street enclosure on 17 January, whilst Jay struck four times as City ran up a 7-1 home success against Stockport County a week later. Blackpool, despite being outplayed, turned the tables at the end of the month, but the bad luck evened itself out on 7 March. City, who should have been three goals behind early on against Leicester Fosse, eventually won 6-1. A much better run-in this term made sure that City's final placing was a creditable fourth.

The Club's prowess was reflected in their FA Cup performances, with Middlesbrough becoming City's first ever top-flight scalp. In the intermediate round, a crowd of 8,666 at St John's Lane on 13 December saw goals from Leigh, Boucher and Wombwell earn a 3-1 victory over the high-flying Teesside club.

Even though he didn't play in that game, City's Bertie Banks, a great showman and personality, went out to celebrate during the evening. He resolved to trade on his reputation as the 'Penalty King' and gain free admission at the evening's variety entertainment at the People's Palace in Baldwin Street. Much to his chagrin he wasn't initially recognised, but eventually got in on the promise that he would grab a hat-trick in the next round.

As good as his word, Banks did indeed do the necessary as City caused a sensation by winning 5-0 at First Division strugglers Bolton Wanderers in the first round proper. The run couldn't last, of course, but it was unfortunate that a fine chance of making progress was then squandered by losing at Southern League Spurs in the next round.

Whilst FA Cup success helped generate record gate receipts of £4,756, which yielded a profit of £360, the Gloucestershire Cup brought disappointment at the end of a marathon contest that needed three games to decide the matter. Heavy snowfall after the interval added to the entertainment during a goalless draw at Stapleton Road, which was refereed by the FA Cup final referee, Jack Adams. The replay on 20 April at St John's Lane saw one of the most thrilling and keenest battles for the county trophy yet seen. Fred Corbett, shortly to join City, gave the Rovers their first-half lead, and it wasn't until just before the finish that Banks found the net for the equaliser. There was still time, though, for Dean to grab what would have been City's winner three minutes later, but the referee stilled the celebrations by disallowing the effort. The Reds, though, were not unduly concerned: the re-match again dealt them home advantage and they had every confidence of eventual success. The Rovers, however, had other ideas and a week later they chalked up a 4-2 victory.

Trainer J Pavey had been awarded a benefit match against the Bristol & District League XI at the conclusion of South End's first season, and manager Sam Hollis was the fortunate recipient against Burslem Port Vale two years later. However, it wasn't until 14 April 1903 that Billy Jones became the first City player to be so honoured.

A 7,000 crowd turned out to see a 1-1 draw with Third Lanark and Jones received £102 as his share of the proceeds. In the period up to the Great War, Peter Chambers, Billy Tuft, Harry Clay, Bill Demmery, Sammy Gilligan, Billy Wedlock, Andy Burton, Archie Annan, Arthur Spear and Reuben Marr were also to have benefits.

Reinforced by Alf Gilson (Brentford), Jim Hosie (Stockport), Fred Corbett (Bristol Rovers), Jack Morris (Notts County), Albert Fisher (Aston Villa) and ex-Bedminster player Andrew Hargett, there was every expectation of a real promotion challenge in 1903-04. Unfortunately, a disastrous start, with just one win in the first five games, had City down in twelfth spot by early October. Thereafter matters greatly improved with high-scoring wins of 6-0, 5-0 and 4-0 against Burnley, Grimsby and Blackpool respectively before the turn of the year. The three successive draws that started the New Year set things back a little, but only five defeats in the second half of the season saw City once again end the campaign in fourth place.

With Bristol Rovers' Stapleton Road pitch waterlogged, Southern League football made a brief return to St John's Lane on 17 October. A crowd numbering some 8,000 turned up to see a Billy Beats goal in the second half bring the Rovers a 1-0 victory over Tottenham Hotspur. Although Bristol Rugby club were to play two trial games on the ground at the start of the following season, further opportunity of ground-sharing at the Lane didn't arise, as City had decamped to Bedminster's old home at Ashton Gate.

It was City's pairing with Sheffield United in the FA Cup that highlighted the need to develop St John's Lane or move to a more suitable venue. This clash had all Bristol agog with excitement. Not only were the Blades renowned Cup fighters, winners in 1899 and 1902, as well being losing finalists in 1901, but they also held top place in Division One. So great was the interest that City decided to increase the seating accommodation. A temporary covered stand to accommodate 500 people was erected at the Lane end, whilst 1,000 ring seats were provided within the railings, a double row behind both goals, and a single row along each side. Whilst incentive was scarcely necessary, those purchasing tickets by the Friday before the game paid sixpence less.

With rain falling heavily at midday, there were many who – acquainted with the peculiarities of St John's Lane – doubted whether the match would be played. The referee, however, Thomas Kirkham, had no qualms when he inspected the pitch half an hour later. A record 17,909 crowd paying receipts of £754 saw City lose a thrilling game 1-3, after Dean had been robbed of a goal just after the interval when Billy Foulke scooped his shot out from behind the goal-line.

Unable to obtain a ten-year extension to their short lease at the Lane, the City directors felt unable to justify any outlay on permanent improvements. In consequence, meetings were held with the Bedminster Athletic Ground Company, with whom agreement was reached for the football club to take over the lease at Ashton Gate on 1 May 1904. City took over the whole arena, comprising an area of six acres and 1.5 roods, and moved the football pitch to the centre of the site. Laid out with a ten-yard border, fenced in by 3ft 9in iron railings, a pitch measuring 120 x 80 yards was certainly much more spacious than City had been used to at St John's Lane. It also allowed Bedminster Cricket Club to continue playing at this venue until their move to the Clanage in 1912.

A collection for the new ground raised nearly £3, when City brought the curtain down on League action at St John's Lane with a 2-1 success over Burslem Port Vale on 23 April. A week later the band played 'Auld Lang Syne' as 1,500 fans bid their farewells to the ground after the first team beat the reserves 3-2. The reserves, who had only started up again after a three-year break, had enjoyed an exceptional season. A prolific attack, which brought victories such as a 14-1 success over Trowbridge Town on 28 November and 8-1 v Staple Hill on 18 March, ensured that the championship of both the Second Division of the Western League and the Bristol Charity League were easily secured.

So ended life at the Lane, though City were still to use the ground for their successful Wednesday League side between 1908 and 1912, as well as holding the club's Annual Sports there on 10 September 1904. On being taken over by Messrs E. S. & A. Robinson, the venue was eventually renamed the Robinson Sports Ground. The company's works side played Somerset Senior League football there until the 1990s. The ground was sold and developed for housing in late 2003.

When City played at the Lane, facilities included provision for the playing of lawn tennis and bowls, and running parallel with the south-west side of the ground there was a rifle range. The overall record of first-team games played by South End/City at the venue reads P274, W187, D31, L56, F784, A391 – such details not including the 2-3 home defeat by Street on 9 March 1895. That game was played on the ground of the Waverley Club, behind the Talbot Public House in the Bristol district of Knowle.

Little more than an enclosed field in its early days, St John's Lane was gradually developed and by the 1897-98 season a grandstand to seat 500 had been erected on the south-west side of the ground. At that time there was some banking behind the goals, and during the following season the pitch was enclosed with white painted wooden railings. The summer of 1899 saw the banking at both ends enhanced, glass windbreaks fitted to the sides of the stand, installation of hot baths in the dressing rooms, and the erection of a flag pole in the corner of the stand, upon which a silk flag in the club's colours (a gift of Chairman W P Kingston) could be flown.

The news of City's impending move from their spiritual home was released on 5 March 1904, when a sketch appeared the local press showing how the new ground would eventually look. Showing all four sides under cover – a futuristic concept which only came to fruition 90 years later – it proved even in 1904 to be somewhat over-ambitious.

With the club spending in excess of £2,000 on the new Ashton Gate, the football action commenced on 27 August 1904 with the Probables beating the Possibles 9-0 in front of a 5,000 crowd. The *Western Daily Press* reported the new venue as having two grandstands, each of which seated 1,200. Admission to Number One stand on the south-west side of the ground was one shilling, whilst for Number Two on the opposite side it was threepence cheaper. The south-east end of the ground – destined to be variously known by generations of City fans as the East End/ Covered End/ Winterstoke Road End – provided shelter for 8,000 spectators before it was demolished in December 1917, having suffered gale damage the previous year. No doubt affected by some of the costs incurred in the move, the club's finances took a dip for the worse. A loss of £416 was disclosed at the AGM held at the Temperance Hall on 21 June 1904, this despite the final campaign at the Lane producing record season ticket sales of £200.

The pressure was now really on manager Sam Hollis. With a fine new ground at Ashton Gate, City were ready for First Division soccer. Unfortunately, success was elusive, despite the capture of prolific scorer Sammy Gilligan from Celtic, Freddie Fenton (West Brom) and Harry Thickett (Sheffield United). For the third successive season, a final placing of fourth was to be City's fate. This disappointment was exacerbated by the fact that across the river Bristol Rovers performed extremely well. With an experienced and settled side comprising Arthur Cartlidge; Hugh Dunn and Dick Pudan; Tommy Tait, Ben Appleby, Gavin Jarvie; Billy 'Darkie' Clark, Jack Lewis, Billy Beats, Andrew Smith, and Albert Dunkley, the Rovers were deservedly crowned as Southern League Champions, an accomplishment that brought them a place in the renowned *Book of Football*, a twelve-part publication that was produced during the early part of the following season (and subsequently published in book form by Desert Island Books).

The official opening of Ashton Gate was somewhat spoiled by Bolton Wanderers winning an exciting game 4-3 on 3 September. (City have subsequently had the last laugh, as the famous Trotters have won but twice more in 23 visits.) A 1-4 defeat at Manchester United followed, but a 2-0 home success over Glossop sparked a run of five successive wins. Despite losing 0-1 at Barnsley on 22 October, only four more points were dropped before the chance of revenge over top-of-the-table Bolton offered itself on New Year's Eve. Following Sammy Gilligan's opener, the fans who travelled to Burnden Park in two special trains were on good terms with themselves, but by the finish they had to concede that Bolton deserved their 3-1 victory. A stirring 1-1 draw seven days later ended injury-hit Manchester United's fourteen-match winning run and set up City's good spell of form.

Blackpool's acceptance of a £200 offer to switch venues allowed the Reds to edge home in the FA Cup. This set up an away trip to Woolwich Arsenal, after Chesterfield and Bradford City had been beaten in the League. Robbed of a second-half penalty at Plumstead, City had to be content with a goalless draw, but in the replay at Ashton Gate, Dean's hot-shot brought a deserved victory for the green-shirted homesters. A record 19,371 crowd at the home second-round game with Preston North End on 18 February had only Harry Clay's penalty save to cheer in a 0-0 draw. In the replay, City were the better side, but couldn't prevent Dickie Bourne's winner right on the final whistle.

A spell of four League games without a win, sparked by a 1-2 defeat at Leicester, was interrupted by the club being honoured with the staging of the International trial game. On 13 February a 7,500 crowd turned up at Ashton Gate to see the North beat a South side containing City's Chambers and Jones, as well as Arthur Cartlidge (of Bristol Rovers) 3-1. The *Western Daily Press* summed up the game: 'A fascinating contest for those who love the pure science of the sport in preference to the rush and flurry so often associated with League matches. It was a fine game, which absorbed every moment of an hour and a half of splendid and very brilliant football'.

With Wombwell having been transferred to Manchester United, Arthur Capes' early opener against Blackpool at Ashton Gate on 18 March was timely. It set up a 2-0 success that got matters back on track and things looked rosy when the following two matches were won without conceding any goals. Unfortunately, a dropped point at home to Gainsborough Trinity was the prelude to three successive defeats. Despite the capture of ex-England international 'Cocky' Bennett from Sheffield United, the losing run was only halted by beating Lincoln City 2-0 at the end of the season. Four days earlier, on 21 April, the Heart of Midlothian club had raised City's hackles by failing to honour an engagement at Ashton Gate. After lodging a £75 claim against the Edinburgh club, City were awarded the sum of £40 following a meeting by the Scottish FA at the Carlton Rooms, Glasgow on 5 September 1905.

Despite finishing in fourth place for the third consecutive campaign, inconsistent form left City well short of claiming a promotion prize. Whilst, on the pitch, the season was not as successful as hoped, financially the move to Ashton Gate proved justified with an increase in gate receipts from £4,020 to £5,199.

Given this largesse, it was perhaps something of a surprise that the recorded profit was just £71. Sam Hollis decided enough was enough at the end of the season, and he departed to spend more time on his hotel business. This was fortuitous for ex-England full-back Harry Thickett, who had lost his place in the City team. He was among many applicants for the vacant position and, on being given a glowing reference by his old club Sheffield United, he was chosen to replace Hollis. The board appeared to have no doubts about the ability of the new man, stating: 'We are confidently of the opinion that the Club has selected a manager of ripe experience in the practical knowledge of the game and players generally, and under whose supervision of the team should go far towards securing promotion to the First Division'.

One of Thickett's first tasks was to follow up on Vice-Chairman Frank Bacon's attempts to woo his ex-Arlington Rovers playing colleague Billy Wedlock back into the City fold. Wedlock who, between his shifts as a stonemason, had been turning out for Aberdare since leaving City four years earlier, was attracting many scouts to South Wales, who even offered bribes to the Aberdare trainer Bob Jones. Thickett, though, got his man and secured probably the most important signing in the Club's history. Never slow to take advice, he then acted on the information of ex-United colleague Peter Boyle, and signed Andy Burton, a brilliant dribbler and ball-player, for just £75 from Motherwell.

Public expectations, already high, were raised considerably by other newcomers such as Archie Annan (Sheffield United), Frank Hilton (Doncaster St John's), and Billy Maxwell (Millwall). Also safely secured as a professional was promising local lad Joe Cottle, who had made two appearances in friendlies towards the end of the previous season. Well-known referee Bob Lethaby, who later became Chairman of the Gloucestershire FA, had recommended Cottle to the club, but the player failed to show for a trial with the reserves because his pal, Tommy Radford, a fellow member of Bristol &

District League side Dolphins FC, wasn't included. Rather than run the risk of losing Cottle's services, City not only picked his pal for the game, but signed him on as well.

With the First Division being expanded by two clubs, City sought to gain easy admission to the realm of the elite on 29 May 1905. At the League AGM, the Bristol Babe took part in a special ballot but they were doomed to disappointment. Bury and Notts County retained their status by topping the poll, whilst Manchester United, City, and West Bromwich trailed behind with thirteen, nine and three votes respectively.

Despite general dismay, it wasn't expected that elevation would be long delayed. Strangely, the optimists reigned supreme for a while in south Bristol. Not even a 1-2 defeat for the Reds by the Greens in the pre-season trial match on 23 August could dampen expectations, though the pessimists were back in force when the season's opener was lost 1-5 at Manchester United. However, very few of those not present on the Bank Street enclosure fully appreciated the extent to which City were handicapped by being deprived of the invaluable services of Peter Chambers. Otherwise, the defeat would not have been magnified into the disaster it was portrayed.

The new manager's confidence in the side he had assembled with much care was unshaken, and the line he took was abundantly justified by subsequent events. More than three months elapsed before another point was lost, and meanwhile fourteen successive league victories were racked up, equalling Manchester United's record set the previous season. Unfortunately, Morgan's late headed leveller for Leeds City on 9 December prevented City from setting a new benchmark, but the record still remains to this day, having only subsequently been matched by Preston North End in 1950-51, whilst Arsenal, in the Premiership, also put together a run of fourteen straight successes straddling the 2001-02 and 2002-03 campaigns.

Once City's fine sequence was broken, the pessimists anticipated trouble, but the team remained unbeaten in the League until the visit of Leicester Fosse on 17 February. Perhaps the players were over-confident, following the great reception they had received from the fans gathered at Temple Meads Station on their return from winning at the Hawthorns a week earlier. The Albion fans were not best pleased that their side had *five* goals disallowed in a contest that was viewed as the most crucial of the season for both clubs. The *Bristol Daily Mercury*, commenting on the game, paraphrased Lord Macaulay's 'Lays Of Ancient Rome':

> 'Even the ranks of Bromwich / Could scarce forbear to cheer'

Fosse's fine away record should have acted as a warning, as City, frustrated by a solid defence, slumped to a 1-2 defeat. This marked the end of a difficult period: two weeks earlier Bristol Rovers had triumphed 3-0 in a friendly at Ashton Gate, this not long after City had tumbled out of the FA Cup against Southern League Brentford. With hindsight, the 1-2 loss at Griffin Park, on the day that the red tide of Liberalism swept the Tories out of power, probably helped City to romp away with the championship, but at the time the humiliation was keenly felt. Lincoln City would have been the visitors to Ashton Gate in the next round, so a comparatively easy task of making headway in the competition was missed.

Recovering from this blip, City won 3-0 on the Circle ground at Hull on 24 February to kick-start an end-of-season unbeaten run that would see only two points dropped in twelve games. In the first, a gale and snowstorm at Barnsley acted as a leveller, though the draw at Burnley was fair enough.

Runners-up Manchester United could not keep pace, and City pulled away to take the championship with a new points record of 66. West Bromwich Albion and newcomers Chelsea offered the only threat to the top two, but by the end of the season – when goals by Sammy Gilligan and Andy Burton secured victory over the Pensioners at Ashton Gate – both were a considerable way adrift.

Promotion was celebrated with a banquet at the Royal Hotel, when the Lord Mayor, Alderman A J Smith and the High Sheriff, H L Riseley, were in attendance. The menu was fit for a king, and there were 21 speeches interposed with the piano playing of Percy Smith, as well as performances of various artistes including the Apollo Glee Party and J M Dingle giving a rendition of the Club song 'Play up! Play up! Bristol City'.

5

~ The Promised Land ~

With matchday seats priced at two shillings and ground admission sixpence, season tickets costing £1 5s represented good value. Not surprisingly, sales reached a new record in excess of £464 as interest quickened for City's top-flight debut. A crowd reported as being in the region of 21,000 was attracted to Ashton Gate for the opener against promotion partners Manchester United. To mark the occasion, City reintroduced an elaborate match programme after a lapse of a number of years. On the pitch, City experienced a rude awakening to the demands of the higher division; Walter Bennett's fifth-minute penalty could not prevent a 1-2 defeat. On a blisteringly hot day, United, with their keeper wearing a white floppy hat, quickly levelled with a Charlie Roberts header and took the points with a well-placed shot by future City player John Picken.

Matters improved slightly with a 2-2 draw in the next game at Birmingham, before the Bristol Babe exploded into life with a 3-0 victory at Stoke. Thereafter, apart from a three-match losing spell in early October, the wins came on a regular basis. Indeed, so consistent were the City that they emerged as strong contenders for the championship. Unfortunately, the opportunity was squandered following a 2-1 Good Friday success at Bolton. The team hit the buffers in losing 0-3 against the leaders Newcastle, and came completely off the rails with two home defeats against Bolton and Aston Villa. A 4-2 away success at Anfield ended the rot, and three more victories left runners-up City to reflect on the fact that failure at St James' Park had cost them the crown.

Ashton Gate Halt, a railway station built to cater for the greater crowds, was opened on the occasion of Blackburn's visit on 15 September 1906. Despite Burton and Maxwell having goals disallowed for offside, City won 2-0 against opponents reduced to ten men when Albert Houlker had to depart with a bad injury ten minutes into the second half.

The visit of Woolwich Arsenal a month later brought a welcome change from previous meetings, as City played in their normal colours. The Gunners turned out in similar kit to that which Manchester United wore in the season's opener, white shirts with red trimmings. The Arsenal supporters, many of whom sported red top-hats, caused some alarm by letting off fireworks each time their side scored in a 3-1 success, and again a minute before the finish when their keeper Jimmy Ashcroft saved Bennett's spot-kick.

After six weeks without a win, City got back on track in the next home game against Bury. New signing George Smith from Gainsborough Trinity created a favourable impression in a 2-0 success, though most of the afternoon's amusement was provided by an errant dog that invaded the pitch shortly before the interval.

With Arsenal having backed down, City fans could have been forgiven for thinking that the kit-changing problem was a thing of the past. No doubt, therefore, they were surprised on 10 November to find their favourites turning out at Ashton Gate in Prussian blue, when Middlesbrough proved unwilling to change. In this game, City were not discouraged by Maxwell having a goal disallowed on twenty minutes, and almost immediately afterwards Hanlin found the net from distance. Gilligan doubled the advantage shortly before the interval, and in the second half Smith's fine acute-angled volley ensured City had the last laugh.

The Club faced criticism in the *Bristol Evening News* match report of the Sheffield United game on Christmas Eve. The question was posed as to why City didn't do as other clubs, and send someone round the pitch with a board advising spectators of team changes. Obviously the lack of this service caused some problems in regard to identification – even at a time when numbers were not worn on shirts – but there was no doubt that it was Gilligan who saved a valuable home point in the dying seconds of a 3-3 thriller. The kit problem reared its head again against Stoke in early January, with City turning out in blue, whilst Stoke played in claret.

Following that game, City decamped to Clevedon for a week to prepare for their FA Cup clash with Second Division Leeds City, who completed their arrangements in nearby Portishead. City were scarcely troubled as they commenced on the Cup trail with a 4-1 success, but being second out of the hat against Woolwich Arsenal, the next round at Plumstead was to be a different story. Over 3,000 fans took advantage of the special excursion organised by the Great Western Railway, but they were doomed to disappointment. Despite having most of the play on the Manor Ground, City's chance of Cup glory vanished for yet another season as they lost 1-2. The only consolation was the comment in the *Bristol Evening News* that: 'The better side lost.'

Out of the Cup, the City could now concentrate their energies on the League, and concentrate they did. After beating Everton at Ashton Gate, they returned to the Manor Ground on 16 February, where Hilton's late drive allowed the tables to be turned with a 2-1 victory. A 2-0 win over a superior Manchester City side at Ashton Gate in early March was remarkable as the Babes were without the services of the injured Hilton for more than half of a game. But with

Wedlock absent on international duty, City's three-month immunity from League defeat came to an end a week later. Jim Thackeray's first-half strike proved insurmountable in wretched weather at Ayresome Park.

At Goodison Park on 16 February 1907, Billy Wedlock followed in the footsteps of Billy Jones by turning out for England. Playing at centre-half in a 1-0 win, he went on to make a total of 26 appearances (25 consecutively) for his country up to 1914. He owed his opportunity to the fact that England's regular centre-half, Colin Veitch, was injured playing for Newcastle on the day City lost a thriller against Aston Villa 2-3. On returning from Villa Park, Wedlock was informed that he was required for the England trial at Owlerton on Monday. Unfortunately, he was only able to travel up on the morning of the game and, with the train running late, barely quarter of an hour remained before the scheduled kick-off time of 2.15pm. He was met at Sheffield station by Fred Milnes (the Pilgrims' captain) and J A H Catton, one of the great football journalists of the day, who wrote under the name of 'Tityrus'. Wedlock had changed on the train and, after being conveyed to the ground by motor car for the delayed 2.20pm start, he gave an impressive display for the Professionals, who beat the Amateurs 4-2 in front of an 8,000 crowd.

Later on, 'Tityrus' paid a glowing tribute to Wedlock, who stood just 5ft 4in and scaled 10st 7lbs, stating: 'He is one of the World's wonders in getting the ball – whether in the air or on the turf. Here, there, and everywhere, intervening and doing his work with a contempt for fatigue, he dominated many a game.' Football League referee, the Reverend J W Marsh, vicar of Nelson in Lancashire, remarked that Wedlock was: 'One of the finest gentleman I have ever met on the football field.' Known throughout football as 'Fatty', Wedlock's amazing powers of recovery also had him known as 'the India-Rubber man' because he could bounce so quickly into attack or defence. Local journalist Harry Slater-Stone found him scrupulously fair, modest to the point of shyness, and recalled that he only once had a penalty given against him. He wrote: 'It would be infinitely easier to stage Hamlet without the Prince of Denmark than to imagine Bristol City without Wedlock.'

Defeating the Rovers in front of a 12,629 Stapleton Road crowd to retain the Gloucestershire Cup on April Fools Day was City's only reward of a memorable 1906-07 season. But this didn't mean there wasn't anything else to celebrate. By finishing as championship runners-up they became the first ever Southern Club to finish in the top two, not to mention setting a new record for a debut club on gaining promotion to the top flight. It was not until after the

Great War that Arsenal improved on City's Southern eminence, and it was to take until 1960-61 before Ipswich Town's championship success beat the record, which had by then been equalled by Charlton Athletic in 1936-37. City's rise to almost the pinnacle of the game in little more than thirteen years, since their formation as Bristol South End in 1894, was certainly deserving of a party. Accordingly, another banquet was held, this time at the Grand Hotel in Broad Street, on 27 May 1907. Not surprisingly, a club record profit of £2,879 was announced for the year.

Everything, therefore, looked rosy for the new campaign, with City looking to go one better in the League or, alternatively, accomplishing the long-held desire of many supporters by winning what was commonly referred to as the English Cup. City flew out of the traps. Despite Archie Annan and Andy Burton being on the injured list, City followed a 3-2 home success with a famous 4-0 away win over Woolwich Arsenal. Unfortunately, Sheffield's other team, the Wednesday, proved too strong in the next game, and with only one more point accumulated up to early October, City found themselves sliding into trouble.

Referee Millward helped stop the rot as Manchester City were beaten 2-1, thanks to the official disallowing centre-forward Irvine Thornley's strike. The following week Preston's Deepdale enclosure fully lived up to its reputation as a graveyard for City hopes. A 1-1 home draw with Bury did little to lift the fans' spirits, but enthusiasm returned for the away game with Aston Villa, which saw a mass exodus from Bristol. A strong constitution was needed as City fought back from a 1-3 deficit to draw 4-4 in a real thriller. A useful point earned, but the fact that City could, and should, have won was of little consolation to those who made the trip. (It was to be almost 61 years before City's first ever win over the famous Villains would be secured.) Three straight wins followed, before City made only their second visit to Stamford Bridge. On a ground where to this day the Bristol Babe still seek success, struggling Chelsea, strengthened by new acquisitions, proved irresistible.

Forest were easily accounted for in Harry Clay's Benefit and, despite in and out form, matters looked bright until early February, when Preston completed the double with a 3-1 victory at Ashton Gate. Ten matches without a win saw City plummet from sixth place into the relegation zone. It looked decidedly bleak when the Trotters came to town on 18 April, but fortunately Sammy Gilligan proved up to the task as he twice struck gold. City concluded the season with three wins and a draw, which lifted them up to tenth spot, a placing that gave a totally false impression of the season's events. Bolton and Birmingham proved to be the unfortunate fall-guys in what had been a well-matched division. Only 22 points separated the top and bottom, whist Bolton would have scrambled to safety at City's expense had they had won at Ashton Gate just a week earlier.

Despite the accustomed Gloucestershire Cup success, with the Rovers being beaten 2-0 on 29 April, City's record in the major cup competition this term was embarrassing. Drawn at home against Second Division strugglers Grimsby Town, the Reds were hot favourites to make progress, but the Mariners' goalkeeper produced a magnificent performance to earn his side a replay. City weren't unduly perturbed, as they were confident of success at Cleethorpes, but they found that Pat Hilton's strike was not enough to carry them through.

Frank Hilton became the very first City player to be honoured by the Football League. He played and scored for their representative XI in a 6-3 win over the Irish League at Roker Park on 12 October 1907. Wedlock was similarly honoured four months later at Villa Park, when he obtained the first of his three inter-league caps in a 2-0 success over the Scottish League. Sandwiched between these events, Ashton Gate was again the venue for an international, though this time for the English Rugby Union, shortly before their move to their new Twickenham home. Despite the fog on 18 January 1908 rendering much of the pitch invisible, a crowd estimated at 29,000 – though official sources gave 21,000 – ensured the venture was a financial success, even though England lost 18-38 to Wales after trailing 8-15 at the interval.

Another profit was declared, but it had dropped considerably to a little over £573, even though season ticket sales had only fallen marginally. City had, however, splashed out on full-back Bob Young from Dundee Violet the previous summer, and this 21-year-old was to remain for thirteen season. That City got their man, despite fierce competition from Spurs, Middlesbrough and Sunderland, was entirely due to Young's friendship with Sammy Gilligan. The two would lodge together for three years until Gilligan was sold to Liverpool amid a storm of criticism from the City fans who idolised him.

Given their somewhat fortunate escape from relegation the previous term, City supporters could have been forgiven for any misgivings they might have harboured for 1908-09. Little did they know it, but they were in for one of the most exciting seasons in the club's history. Matters didn't auger well early on, as it took until the fifth game before the first victory was achieved. The side was playing well, though, and eventually the rub of the green turned in their favour as strikes from Gilligan and Frank Hilton proved enough to beat Woolwich Arsenal at Ashton Gate on 19 September. Progress was maintained throughout the autumn, and a 2-0 success at Roker Park on 12 December was notable for the fact that the previous week Sunderland had won the North-East derby at Newcastle 9-1. A 1-0 Christmas Day success in front of a record 36,000 crowd at Valley Parade left City well placed in fifth spot. The following day, though, at Ashton Gate, the 23,000 spectators were disappointed as the lowly Bantams extracted full revenge. A 2-5 defeat at Everton and a 1-1 home draw with Leicester Fosse that followed was hardly the form to encourage much optimism in the run-up to City's FA Cup opener against Southern League side Southampton.

When Saints' goalkeeper Herbert Lock saved Andy Burton's spot-kick shortly before the close, City fans must have given up all hope. Faced with a replay at the Dell, the team now faced a daunting prospect on a ground where they had never won. Fortunately, the Babe came good with a 2-0 success to set up a meeting with First Division Bury. Yet again, success wouldn't come at the first time of asking, as a 2-0 lead was squandered, though Gilligan's effort was enough to secure victory in the Gigg Lane replay and leave City to face the surprise conquers of Liverpool in the third round. Only one attempt was necessary to negotiate the challenge of Southern League Norwich in front of a record 24,009 Ashton Gate crowd, which carried City through to a quarter-final clash with Glossop. It might have been different if the Canaries' left-winger Tommy Allsopp hadn't fired his spot-kick against the base of an upright shortly after Burton had opened the scoring.

By this time, all Bristol was in the grip of Cup fever. With City facing the Derbyshire minnows – Glossop had dropped the North End part of their title in 1899 when they had their solitary season among the ranks of the elite – it was confidently expected that a semi-final place was all but assured. Unfortunately, with blizzards sweeping the country on match-day, conditions on the North Road enclosure were less than ideal and City were glad to escape with a goalless draw. The weather for the Ashton Gate replay was much improved, but this time City encountered such firm resistance from Glossop's defence that it wasn't until just six minutes from the close that Gilligan was able to break the hearts of the injury-stricken visitors.

City's luck held in the draw for the semi-final, as they found themselves paired with Second Division Derby, but they were to be the recipients of even greater fortune during the match. With barely seconds remaining, the 33,878 Stamford Bridge crowd must have thought that City were out. They trailed to a goal by Davis shortly after the break, but with the referee ready to blow for time, the County right-back Jack Nicholas gave City a lifeline by handling Bob Hardy's last-gasp effort. With time extended to allow the penalty-kick to be taken, Willis Rippon kept his nerve and sent a pile-driver into the net to the keeper's left. Rippon kept up the good work in the St Andrew's replay, but this time City had no real difficulty in progressing through to the final.

When Cup final opponents Manchester United came to town on league business on Easter Monday, a 20,000 crowd paid record League receipts of £780. Unfortunately City, who had beaten United on the Bank Street ground at Clayton on Good Friday, were held to a goalless draw, but that didn't dampen the ardour of the fans, who descended on London in their thousands for the final after threats of a soccer strike by the embryonic Players Union had been averted.

The Great Western Railway ran dozens of special trains, but the players travelled up on the day before the game and stayed overnight at the Queen's Hotel, Norwood. City, however, had problems with injuries. Both Reuben Marr and Fred Staniforth had to visit well-known London specialist Mr H A Barker, whilst Rippon required surgery on the knee he had injured in the Easter Tuesday clash with Blackburn Rovers. Fortunately, Staniforth safely came through tests at the club's Cup headquarters at Portishead, but City had to make do without the others. Given these problems, it was not surprising that Manchester United were favourites in what was also their first final. United had been fortunate when a snowstorm brought abandonment of their quarter-final at Burnley, when they were a goal down with eighteen minutes left, but they had injury problems of their own, taking a calculated gamble in playing 'Sandy' Turnbull.

The great day dawned at the Crystal Palace on 24 April, where a 71,401 crowd – the largest ever to watch a City game, before or since – gathered within the shadow of Joseph Paxton's magnificent glass structure, moved here from the site of the 1851 Great Exhibition in Hyde Park. Previously called Penge Place, this location on Sydenham Hill was a perfect setting for Paxton's brilliant creation, after which it was named. The nation would be deprived of a great treasure by the fire that consumed it in November 1936, just days after Bristol Rovers had beaten the Corinthians 2-0 in an FA Cup-tie at the same venue. The grounds had been officially opened in 1854, though the spectacular fountains did not arrive until two years later.

When the fountains fell into disuse, their huge basins were utilised for other things. The southern basin was turned into a football arena in 1894, with stands built by John Aird & Sons. All

FA Cup finals from 1895 to 1914 were staged here, whereupon the ground was requisitioned by the Royal Navy. Never again would the Crystal Palace reverberate to the special carnival atmosphere engendered by a day out at this unique venue. Later, it would resonate to the roar of speedway before eventually becoming the site of the athletics stadium. The National Sports Centre was officially opened in July 1964. The northern 'basin' was mainly utilised as a cycle track and skating rink, but it was also used for soccer when the arena was renovated following the end of hostilities in 1918. It was not until 1982 that football finally ceased to feature at the Palace.

In 1909, no doubt many spectators would also have been intrigued by the life-sized dinosaur exhibits in the vast 200-acre Victorian playground, whilst others would have enjoyed the switchback railway that was a feature of the site. Unfortunately, in the windy and cloudy conditions, the contest was to prove disappointing. City turned out in royal blue shirts with a white shield on their left breast bearing the Bristol Coat of Arms, whilst United wore white shirts with a thin red 'V' running from their shoulders to their midriff, with the red rose of Lancashire on their left breast, a special gift of keen supporter George Robey, the Music Hall comedian.

A rough game was won by United with a goal from 'Sandy' Turnbull midway through the first half. Gilligan missed City's best chance, when the United keeper pulled off a remarkable save, but had Rippon played it might have been a different story. Newspaper opinion of the time described the game as being of a generally uninteresting nature, with neither side playing well. There was much foul play and the referee was criticised for apparently being unable to differentiate between fair shoulder charges and illegal tackling. The most interesting topic appeared to be the opportunity afforded of judging the merits of the two great centre-halves on view. The consensus was that Wedlock had fairly established his right to be called the best in the land. From start to finish he was always on the ball, accurate with his passing and, despite his lack of inches, was able to beat opponents with ease when heading.

The Bristol Babe's only consolation was to finish five places above United in the League, even though only a point separated the sides. Moving images of the final were shown in both the Empire and the Palace Theatres the week following the event, and after beating Manchester City 1-0 at Ashton Gate on 28 April the players of both sides attended the second house at the Empire. This film resurfaced 25 years later, purchased for ninepence from a London junk shop. It was shown at the Town Hall cinema, Bedminster, in February 1935, when City were involved in another lengthy cup run. At the outbreak of World War II it was put into the care of Bristol City Council, but was among a number of items that were 'lost' when the City Museum was hit during the Blitz.

City's Cup form highlighted the brilliant play of local lad Joe Cottle, who was rewarded by being called up for England. He turned out, with Wedlock, in a 4-0 win over Ireland on the Bradford Park Avenue enclosure on 13 February – the first time that City had supplied two players in an international. Sadly, despite his more than competent performance, Cottle was not selected for England again, and a broken leg at Preston two years later virtually ended his career, though he did manage a short spell with Bristol Rovers.

City's fine season was mirrored by their reserves retaining the Western League Second Division Championship. Weymouth were beaten 8-1 at Ashton Gate on 31 October, whilst away from home their best result was beating Barry District 4-0 on 20 March. Home crowds for the reserves averaged 2,000, but twice this figure turned out on 12 September when, thanks to Channon's goal, Aberdare were dismissed 1-0. The attraction, however, wasn't the football: it was another of Professor Stephen's balloon ascents and parachute jumps. This was the second of three seasons when Professor Stephens thrilled the local crowds with his ballooning exploits.

Further success for City's second string came when securing the Bristol Charity League – a 7-0 hammering of Kingswood Rovers on 26 April cementing their success. Only a 0-2 defeat at Bristol Rovers on 3 April served to spoil a procession of victories in the competition. The season was also notable for City starting up a Wednesday League side again. In their South End days they had fielded a Wednesday side in 1895-96 and 1896-97, but with the formation of the Bristol Wednesday League in 1907 a more organised structure presented itself. City would continue with a Wednesday side for four seasons, completing the double on every occasion, but they resigned shortly prior to the start of the 1912-13 season when the Gloucestershire FA barred them from participation in the Wednesday Cup competition. It wasn't until the 1920s – they were champions in 1928-29 – that they again fielded a side, and this was followed by another brief revival that saw the Second Division Championship won in 1949-50.

Of City's first-team stars, Wedlock was delighted to add to his England appearances in the close season by playing all three games on the FA tour of Austro-Hungary. Despite City's purchase of John Cowell from Rotherham Town to replace injury-prone Rippon, and the cost of extending the main stand towards the Covered End, a record profit of £3,134 was declared. The shareholders received 2s in the £1 dividend, the last ever paid by the Club.

6

~ *Decline and Fall* ~

The fans didn't realise it, but City had reached the high-point of their existence and were heading for a fall. What can appear to modern eyes as a regular yo-yo pattern of the club's existence, would probably have been different had regular First Division status been cemented at this time. Unfortunately, it didn't happen and City's opportunity to be one of the top clubs was not only lost, but made worse over the intervening years by a lack of any real desire to regain lost ground.

The signs were ominous as the 1909-10 season started with City failing to win any of their opening four games. A 4-1 victory over Middlesbrough stopped the rot and matters picked up until the usual defeat was suffered at Preston. After beating a Notts side whose physical tactics had provoked the Ashton Gate crowd into unruly action the previous term, three successive defeats had City tumbling. Victories over Bolton and Everton were all they could muster up to the end of the year, and a 0-4 loss at Sunderland on New Year's Day hardly augured well for the second half of the season.

Following a 2-0 home League win over Bradford City, hopes of better things arose with FA Cup success over Liverpool. But another poor spell coincided with being dumped out of the Cup by Second Division West Bromwich Albion on 9 February, and the decline continued with a 2-3 loss at newly promoted Spurs before the team perked up. Three successive League victories without conceding a goal had City confident of beating Villa, in a match that saw Sammy Gilligan take his benefit, on 19 March. In the event, the Villa hoodoo still exerted itself, even though City kept their goal intact in a 0-0 draw. Next up was a Good Friday trip to Manchester United's new home at Old Trafford, where the Babe came to grief. Losing 1-2 in what was only the fourth League played on the ground, it got worst before it got better. A 0-4 hammering followed at Bramall Lane, but on Easter Monday a 2-1 victory brought revenge over the Red Devils at Ashton Gate.

Despite being in fourteenth place with six matches left, City's top-flight status was still under threat. It took a 1-0 success over Chelsea and a last-day blitz of Nottingham Forest – when Cowell scored all of the goals in a 4-0 win, to ensure survival. Ironically, he never scored for City again, and after playing the opening five games of the following term was sold to Sunderland.

An FA Cup exit at the Hawthorns was probably a welcome relief to the players, as their involvement in the County tourney turned into a long drawn out affair. Already faced with having to play two finals – their exploits the previous season had brought about postponement of the annual local spat – the delayed contest turned into a marathon. Two replays proved necessary before City won 2-1 on 26 January. By the time the up-to-date contest came round on 6 April, the fans had had enough. Only 1,175 made the trek to Ashton Gate to witness City's 2-0 success.

Failure to make progress in the FA Cup, coupled with a drop in season ticket sales, contributed to City declaring their first loss (£78) in six years. The summer of 1910 saw City's captain Wedlock playing in South Africa as a member of the FA touring side. Such was his popularity in the Southern Hemisphere that a further £86 was collected towards his Benefit Fund. By the end of the following season this total had swelled to £451. Happy as he was with this sum, Wedlock would probably have swapped it for City's salvation. Unfortunately, it wasn't to be, even though the 1910-11 campaign kicked off with a 1-0 win at Newcastle. Lack of goals was the main problem as – apart from a point at Preston, of all places – defeat followed defeat.

Some amusement came at Notts County's new Meadow Lane home in early October, where the referee had to bring the players back out onto the field after blowing for time too early. He had failed to allow for the time lost when the flight overhead of famous aviator de Lesseps had brought play to a halt. That defeat, which dumped City at the bottom of the table, ended manager Harry Thickett's reign. Director Francis (Frank) Noot Bacon assumed temporary control and, following a settling in period, halted the rot with a 2-0 home success over Bury on 22 October. Recovery continued with a 4-0 win at Sheffield United, but a 3-4 Christmas Eve defeat at Goodison Park had City back at the bottom of the pile. By New Year's Eve matters had improved with City up to fourteenth place after taking five points from three games.

Two New Year League defeats was a blow, but it was FA Cup humiliation that would inflict most damage to morale. Drawn against Birmingham League minnows Crewe Alexandra in the first round at Ashton Gate on 14 January, no one anticipated one of the greatest pre-Great War Cup shocks, which saw City lose 0-3. In the aftermath, Bacon requested to be relieved of his duties, though he remained in control of the reserves until the appointment of ex-City player Jack Hamilton on 16 September 1911.

The directors turned to Sam Hollis yet again, and he took over for the third time on 19 January. A 3-2 home win over Middlesbrough was a good start, but only one victory in the following twelve games left the Bristol Babe in dire straights with just three matches remaining.

A 5-1 victory over Nottingham Forest wasn't enough to lift City off the bottom, but an unexpected 2-1 success against Manchester City at Hyde Road brought genuine hope of survival. A win over Everton at Ashton Gate in the final game of the season was all that was required. Somewhat strangely, this important game only attracted 8,000 spectators, though the missing hordes probably could sense that an Ashton Gate let-down was in the offering. They weren't wrong, as an out of sorts City meekly succumbed to a 0-1 defeat and thereby lost their place at soccer's top table.

With a sizeable outlay expended on the vain fight against relegation, it was no surprise that City posted a record loss of £3,842. Heads rolled and Chairman William Panes-Kingston – who had also resigned from the board along with Harry King – was replaced at the helm by former Bedminster man Ernest G Murdock.

Ironically, demotion coincided with better opposition for the reserves, who had to be content with Western League fare during much of City's First Division days. Elected to the South Eastern League for 1910-11, they faced the second strings of the likes of Chelsea, Tottenham Hotspur, and Woolwich Arsenal. A good first season saw City finish in third place, followed by placings of fourteenth, ninth, and sixth, before goal average cost them the 1914-15 championship to Fulham reserves.

Few expected the Bristol Babe to prosper in the Second Division, but their fight against having to apply for re-election was a shock. They started well enough with a 1-0 win over Fulham in front of an encouragingly large 12,000 Ashton Gate crowd, but were soon struggling. With the loss of many of their First Division side, City recruited six players from Scotland – Ferguson Anderson, 'Jock' Nicholson, Tommy Brand, Tommy Cairns, 'Jock' Butler and Johnny Forbes. Of these, Nicholson was to become a stalwart of City's team, whilst eighteen-year-old Cairns emerged as one of the best players of his day. Unfortunately, this was not to be with Bristol City. After playing eleven games and scoring just once, he became homesick and returned to his native heath. Two years later he was signed by Glasgow Rangers and went on to play a number of times for his country.

Throughout the season, City were never higher than tenth, and with only six victories up to the turn of the year matters were cause for concern. A 4-1 victory over Leeds City on 27 January was the best of the campaign, but barely two months later a 0-3 defeat at top-of-the-table Burnley left City struggling in seventeenth spot.

Thankfully, with seven matches left, matters picked up and safety was assured by securing eleven points out of the fourteen available. Such improved form offered hope for the future, though the 5,000 spectators who witnessed the goalless draw with Hull that concluded the season would probably have thought differently. One hopes they got some enjoyment from watching the Olympic Marathon trial that started with the runners completing one lap of the Ashton Gate ground shortly before kick-off.

Consolation of sorts came with Gloucestershire Cup victory over the Rovers at Ashton Gate, but in the FA Cup City were unable to overcome Southern League Northampton Town or their manager Herbert Chapman (later to find fame as boss of Huddersfield and Arsenal). Further success over the Rovers was more poignant, as it occurred in consequence of the sinking of the *Titanic* on her maiden voyage. Special Disaster Fund matches were held throughout the country, and at Ashton Gate on 4 May 1912 a paltry crowd of 1,500 saw City overcome a 0-1 deficit to win 3-1. The £47 receipts from this game were added to the £7 collected at half-time in the game against Hull a week previously.

Compared with the previous pessimism, promotion was a confident expectation among supporters for 1912-13. Interest was high from the start, and a record 6,000 crowd attended the Public Trial on 24 August to see the Reds beat the Blues 3-0. Optimism intensified during an opening sequence of seven unbeaten games, but form deteriorated following a 1-3 defeat in muddy conditions at bottom of the table Glossop, where Wedlock scored one of his rare goals. Despite 'Ginger' Owers firing City's early winner against Clapton Orient, a barren spell then endured until 21 December. Beating Bury 1-0 set up a sequence of three victories before City came a cropper at Bradford Park Avenue on New Year's Day. A sparkling 7-2 home win over Stockport on 18 January relieved the gloom, but, missing the inspiration of Wedlock, a long-term casualty following his Christmas Day injury against Fulham, the 1-5 loss at Preston that followed brought the dark clouds down again.

Lincoln's visit on 8 March produced an outcry from a larger than normal crowd who were attracted to the game by the expectation of Wedlock making his long-awaited return. City provoked the situation by their failure to announce that the great man had failed a fitness test. It was to be another two weeks before he made his comeback, following defeats of 1-4 at Nottingham Forest and 1-7 at Barnsley, but even his presence couldn't prevent Birmingham's 3-0 Ashton Gate triumph.

Next up was a visit to Huddersfield, where nothing could prevent Town extending their unbeaten run into double figures. The penultimate game, a 0-3 defeat by Grimsby Town on 19 April, was the last with Hollis at the helm. Four days later former England international George Hedley replaced him.

A humiliating 1-5 home loss to Bury brought the curtain down on what ultimately proved to be another disappointing season, in which City surrendered their Gloucestershire Cup crown to the Rovers for the first time in seven years. In the FA Cup they fared no better, though it wasn't surprising that First Division Liverpool proved too strong at Anfield on 15 January.

Wedlock's injury brought his long sequence of 25 consecutive England appearances to an end. Unfit for selection against Ireland in Belfast, he was chosen for the Home International arranged for Ashton Gate on 17 March. He received every fitness remedy known at the time, but was fighting a losing battle. Much to the disappointment of the home fans, he had to cry off at the eleventh hour. Perhaps his absence kept the crowd down to 9,000, though the poor weather obviously had an effect as England beat Wales 4-3 in an exciting game.

Form improved in 1913-14 with an eighth-place finish, but the sensation of the season concerned newly acquired amateur centre-forward Tommy Howarth. Signed following a trial game over Christmas, City 'arranged' his discharge from the Army and subsequent employment, but the Football Association stepped in. Howarth was suspended for twelve months from April 1914, whilst City were fined £50 for their involvement in a practice that the FA were determined to stamp out. At the same meeting they also dealt with Manchester United, who had been fielding a soldier under an assumed name.

City's campaign had started with a 4-1 home success over Glossop, and the Babe's were top of the embryonic table with the 5-0 victory over Stockport which followed. A thriller at Park Avenue toppled City off their perch, but the last-gasp victory obtained by Jimmy Smith's disputed penalty was to prove vital for the Bradford club. Come the end of the season they grabbed the second promotion spot on goal average from Arsenal, who had received approval for their change of name (dropping 'Woolwich') the day before City's visit to their new Highbury home.

Following City's early goal spree, which had them as the country's top scorers, the team's shooting prowess declined. At Fulham on 20 December, Fred Chapple, who had cost a big fee on account of his 39 goals in 56 games for Brentford, pulled a goal back from the penalty-spot, but City still trailed when the referee blew for time ten minutes early. The errant official brought the teams back out, only for the Cottagers to score again and finish 3-1 winners.

It wasn't until Christmas Day that City found the net on more than one occasion, but after leading 2-0 at Homerton, the Reds were shocked by Clapton's second-half comeback. Howarth's debut did little to change matters in a 0-4 defeat at Meadow Lane on 17 January, but he did open his account during a 2-0 success at Wolves three weeks later. Goalscoring remained a problem throughout the rest of the campaign, though a 4-1 victory was gained at Lincoln's expense on a waterlogged Ashton Gate pitch on 14 March.

The signing of centre-forward James Morton from Barnsley was rushed through in time for him to make his debut in the home game against Leeds City on 10 April. Morton didn't score, but he notched the winner against Grimsby in the following game, when the attention of many in the 12,250 Ashton Gate crowd was diverted by the antics of world-famous aviator Hucks, high in the sky above the Cabot Tower. This constituted City's last win of the season: a 2-2 draw at Birmingham was the best that could be managed in the remaining three games. Progress in the FA Cup was also short-lived: following a 2-2 draw against Queen's Park Rangers at Park Royal, the Southern Leaguers came to Ashton Gate and grabbed an extra-time win. Habits returned to normal in the Gloucestershire Cup, however, with City beating the Rovers 2-0 on 14 April. Wedlock's long international career came to a close at Cardiff on 16 March 1914 when he bowed out in style by scoring in a 2-0 win over Wales.

The 1914-15 season was a strange affair. The outbreak of the Great War and the decision of the football authorities to continue as normal gave the campaign an unreal feel. Many in the country were off the opinion that football should have shut down, though opposition was assuaged by recruitment campaigns at many games. There was also bad feeling in regard to the many fit young professional footballers who had declined their country's call to arms, though the morale-boosting effects of football matches were eventually appreciated.

These sentiments were illustrated by the attitude of much of the Bristol press, where by late-November match reports had disappeared from all but the Saturday night sports papers. With minds on other things, City's season ticket sales dropped to just £79, the lowest figure since the adoption of professionalism. Only 3,000 attended the season's opener at Ashton Gate, when new signing Cliff Brooksbank from Exeter helped defeat Blackpool. Early form, including a 4-0 home victory over Preston, had City looking likely promotion candidates, but by Christmas they were slipping into mid-table. A 7-0 Boxing Day success over Grimsby improved the goal-average, though doubtless the fans were frustrated by City's failure to add to their half-time advantage. Despite losing 1-4 at Preston in mid-February, City still had outside hopes of making a promotion challenge, but a 1-2 loss at Glossop followed by a 0-1 home defeat to Wolves put them out of contention. Apart from away successes at Fulham and Leicester Fosse, form slumped, though City played their part in a thrilling 3-5 defeat at Huddersfield that was captured on the silver screen. A 2-1 home win over Lincoln, followed by a 1-1 draw at Birmingham, brought the season to a close with City having to settle for a disappointing position of thirteenth. Jerry Wolstenholme,

In the FA Cup, Cardiff's sturdy defence proved a formidable barrier in the first half on 9 January. Fortunately, Edwin Burton, who had been signed from Shildon Athletic twenty months earlier, broke the deadlock after the interval and City beat their Southern League opponents 2-0. Through to the second round for the first time in five years, the Bristol Babe faced a difficult task at Everton, where they had their moments, but were unable to prevent the First Division club winning 4-0 in front of a 24,500 Goodison Park crowd on 30 January.

In view of the War, the Gloucestershire FA decided not to proceed with their competition for the County trophy, and it was to be five years before this contest was revived. All were saddened by the death of GFA Secretary Bill Hodgkinson during the season. He had done much to establish Bristol City as a first-class club. He died at the Bristol General Hospital on 10 March and was buried in Arno's Vale Cemetery.

Whilst an inferior goal-average to that of Fulham cost City's second-string the championship of the South Eastern League, mutterings by various London clubs threatened future participation. Matters came to head during the last week of the season, with two London clubs threatening to resign because of the travelling costs involved unless City and Plymouth were ejected.

~ *Postscript* ~

With the Great War bringing to an end what many would say was the only successful era in Bristol City's history, the question arises as who were the best players during this very special time. A contemporary view was provided by some of those who were closely connected with the Club. W R Nurse (South End's first President), Sam Hollis (thrice Manager), Tom Locke (Programme Editor during First Division days), John Valentine (City's one-time Poet Laureate), and William Panes-Kingston (Chairman 1897-1911) gave their thoughts on the matter in response to an article by 'Half-Back' (H J Slater-Stone) in his 'Stray Leaves' column in the *Bristol Sports Post* during July 1932.

'Half-back' proposed the following names as constituting City's best eleven players since the advent of professionalism – Hugh Monteith; Archie Annan, Joe Cottle; Reuben Marr, Billy Wedlock, Hugh Wilson; Walter Bennett, Billy Maxwell, Alex Caie, Andy Burton (or 'Paddy' O'Brien), Dickie Wombwell (or 'Jock' Russell).

Panes-Kingston was basically in agreement, except for selecting Sammy Gilligan (or Willis Rippon) for the centre-forward berth, whilst both Nurse and Hollis plumped for a forward line-up comprising Bennett, Maxwell, Gilligan, O'Brien and Joshua Harris. Valentine, however, differed with 'Half-Back' by choosing Phil Bach at right-back, Alex Carnelly (right-wing), Burton (centre-forward), O'Brien (inside-left) and Russell (outside-left), whilst Locke came up with this eleven: Monteith; Bach, Laurie Banfield; Wilson, Wedlock, Pat Hanlin; Maxwell, Bennett, Gilligan, Burton, Harris.

They helped City to defeat Blackpool in 1905 Cup-tie

TWO elderly men were looking back more than half-a-century today—to the time when they were among the 11 heroes of Ashton Gate who beat Blackpool in the F.A. Cup competition (writes JOHN BARBER).

It happened during season 1904-05, four years before Bristol City reached the F.A. Cup Final.

'Did not deserve it'

'About the best'

VETERANS OF THE 1905 CUP-TIE.—Billy Jones (left) and Harry Clay, who played for Bristol City when they beat Blackpool in 1905 as they are today.

This article appeared in the *Bristol Evening Post's Green 'Un* on 24 January 1959 – the day City drew 1-1 with Blackpool in an FA Cup-tie

Balance sheet in respect of City's first season as a professional club

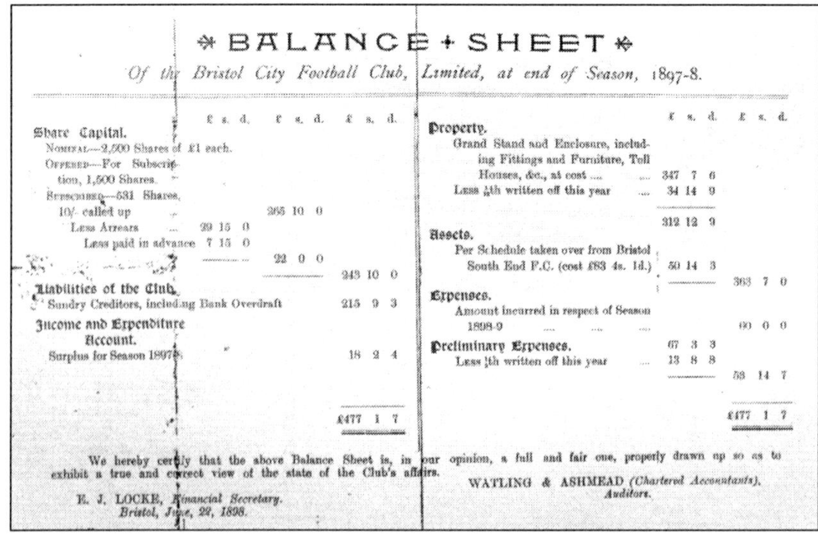

BALANCE SHEET

Of the Bristol City Football Club, Limited, at end of Season, 1897-8.

	£ s. d.	£ s. d.	£ s. d.
Share Capital.			
Nominal—2,500 Shares of £1 each.			
Offered—For Subscription, 1,500 Shares.			
Subscribed—531 Shares, 10/- called up		265 10 0	
Less Arrears	29 15 0		
Less paid in advance	7 15 0		
		22 0 0	
			243 10 0
Liabilities of the Club.			
Sundry Creditors, including Bank Overdraft			215 9 3
Income and Expenditure Account.			
Surplus for Season 1897-8			18 2 4
			£477 1 7

	£ s. d.	£ s. d.
Property.		
Grand Stand and Enclosure, including Fittings and Furniture, Toll Houses, &c., at cost	347 7 6	
Less [illegible]th written off this year	34 14 9	
	312 12 9	
Assets.		
Per Schedule taken over from Bristol South End F.C. (cost £83 4s. 1d.)	50 14 3	
		363 7 0
Expenses.		
Amount incurred in respect of Season 1898-9		60 0 0
Preliminary Expenses.	67 3 3	
Less [illegible]th written off this year	13 8 8	
		53 14 7
		£477 1 7

We hereby certify that the above Balance Sheet is, in our opinion, a full and fair one, properly drawn up so as to exhibit a true and correct view of the state of the Club's affairs.

E. J. LOCKE, *Financial Secretary.*
Bristol, June, 22, 1898.

WATLING & ASHMEAD *(Chartered Accountants),*
Auditors.

City lost this game against Chelsea at Stamford Bridge 1-4 on 23 November 1907

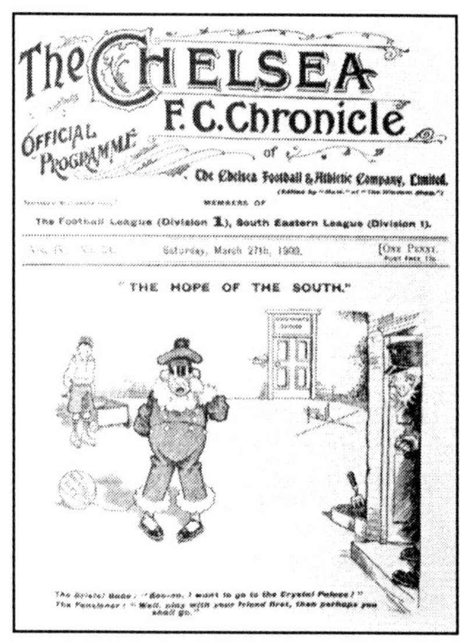

City drew with Derby in this FA Cup semi-final at Stamford Bridge on 27 March 1909

Above: City are about to play Manchester United in their first FA Cup final

Right: Billy Wedlock's first England cap in 1907

Bristol City *v.* Leicester Fosse, 1905/06. The Fossils proved to be anything but sacrificial victims as they shocked City at Ashton Gate by winning 2-1 in front of 8,000 fans on 17 February 1906. This was published in *The Bristol Magpie* on 15 February 1906.

THE FOOTBALL WORLD BY "ON-LOOKER"

WEDLOCK'S PROSPECTS

'On-Looker's' articles, along with 'Shots for Goal', were regular features in the Saturday night sports edition of the *Bristol Evening News*. This one appeared on 7 January 1911

St John's Lane ground, 1898/99. This sketch appeared in *The Bristol Magpie* of 20 April 1899. Note the canvas screens at the end of the ground.

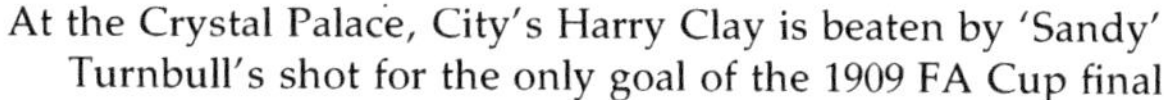

At the Crystal Palace, City's Harry Clay is beaten by 'Sandy' Turnbull's shot for the only goal of the 1909 FA Cup final

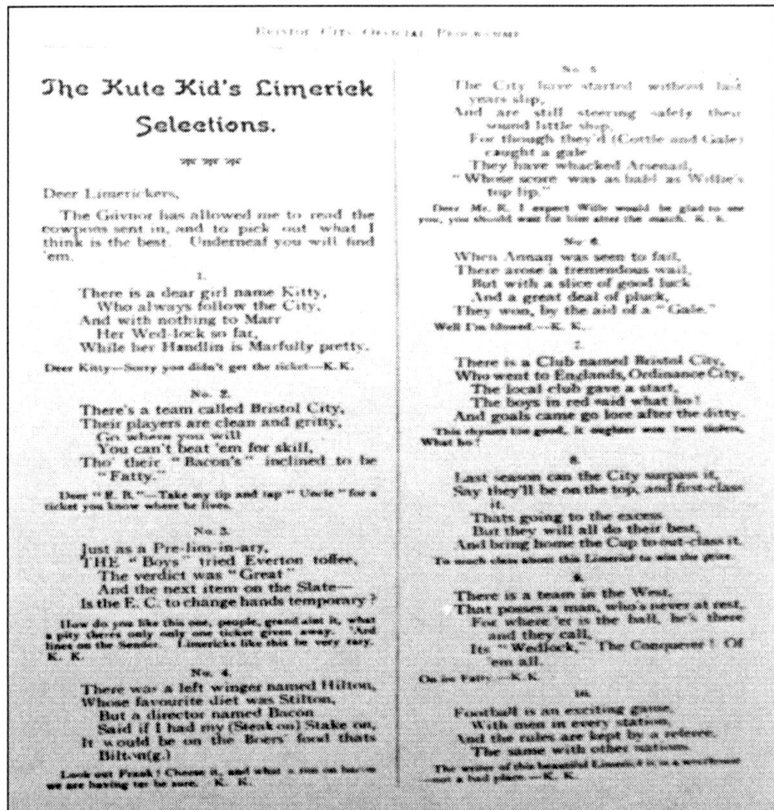

The Kute Kid's Limerick Selections.

Deer Limerickers,

The Givnor has allowed me to read the cowpons sent in, and to pick out what I think is the best. Underneat you will find 'em.

1.

There is a dear girl name Kitty,
Who always follow the City,
And with nothing to Marr
Her Wed-lock so far,
While her Handlin is Marfully pretty.

Deer Kitty—Sorry you didn't get the ticket—K. K.

No. 2.

There's a team called Bristol City,
Their players are clean and gritty,
Go where you will
You can't beat 'em for skill,
Tho' their "Bacon's" inclined to be "Fatty."

Deer "E. B."—Take my tip and tap "Uncle" for a ticket you know where he lives.

No. 3.

Just as a Pre-lim-in-ary,
THE "Boys" tried Everton toffee,
The verdict was "Great"
And the next item on the Slate—
Is the F. C. to change hands temporary?

How do you like this one, people, grand aint it, what a pity there's only only one ticket given away. 'And lines on the Sender. Limericks like this be very easy. K. K.

No. 4.

There was a left winger named Hilton,
Whose favourite diet was Stilton,
But a director named Bacon
Said if I had my (Steak on) Stake on,
It would be on the Boers' food thats Bilton(g.)

Look out Frank! Cheese it, and what a [illegible] we are having [illegible]. K. K.

No. 5.

The City have started without last years slip,
And are still steering safely their sound little ship,
For though they'd (Cottle and Gale) caught a gale
They have whacked Arsenal,
"Whose score was as bald as Willie's top lip."

Deer Mr. K. I expect Willie would be glad to see you, you should wait for him after the match. K. K.

No. 6.

When Annan was seen to fail,
There arose a tremendous wail,
But with a slice of good luck
And a great deal of pluck,
They won, by the aid of a "Gale."

Well I'm blowed.—K. K.

7.

There is a Club named Bristol City,
Who went to Englands Ordinance City,
The local club gave a start,
The boys in red said what ho!
And goals came go lore after the ditty.

This rhymes too good, it oughter won two tickets. What ho!

8.

Last season can the City surpass it,
Say they'll be on the top, and first-class it.
Thats going to the excess
But they will all do their best,
And bring home the Cup to out-class it.

To much class about this Limerick to win the prize.

9.

There is a team in the West,
That posses a man, who's never at rest,
For where 'er is the ball, he's there and they call,
Its "Wedlock," The Conquerer! Of 'em all.

On ire Fatty.—K. K.

10.

Football is an exciting game,
With men in every station,
And the rules are kept by a referee,
The same with other nations.

The writer of this beautiful Limerick is in a [illegible]—not a bad place.—K. K.

The Kute Kid's programme feature of 21 September 1907, against Newcastle

The *Bristol Magpie*, 20 January 1898, after City had thrashed Southampton 5-2

THE RETREAT FROM MOSCOW, OR THE DEFEAT OF THE SOUTHAMPTON CHAMPIONS.

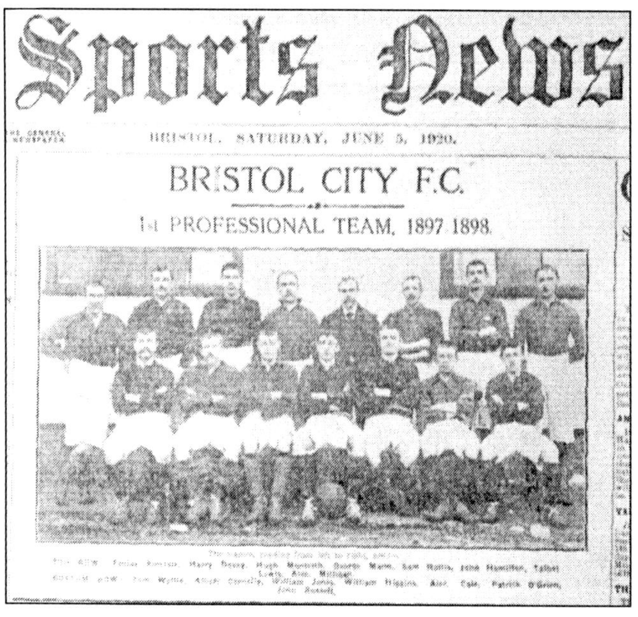

Sports News

BRISTOL, SATURDAY, JUNE 5, 1920.

BRISTOL CITY F.C.

1st PROFESSIONAL TEAM, 1897-1898.

Cigarette cards clockwise: The Bristol 'Babe', Archie Annan, Billy Wedlock, Billy Tuft

Below: *Green 'Un*, 4 August 1962

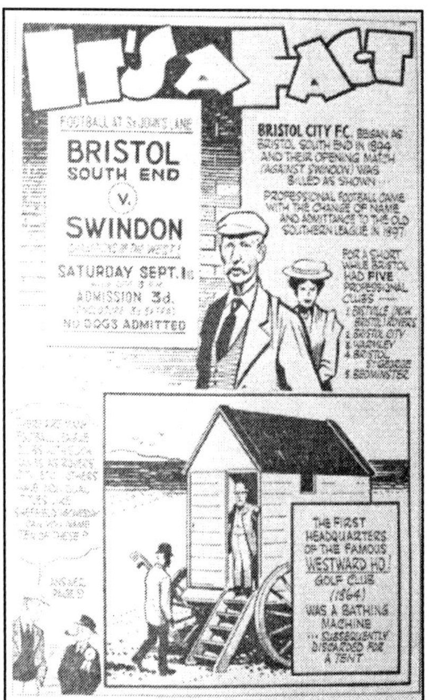

Above: Souvenir card, produced by Messrs WH Smith for the 1909 FA Cup final

Bristol South End's team and officials on 1 September 1894 before the club's first game
Below: Manchester United (in white), win 2-1 at Ashton Gate, 1 September 1906

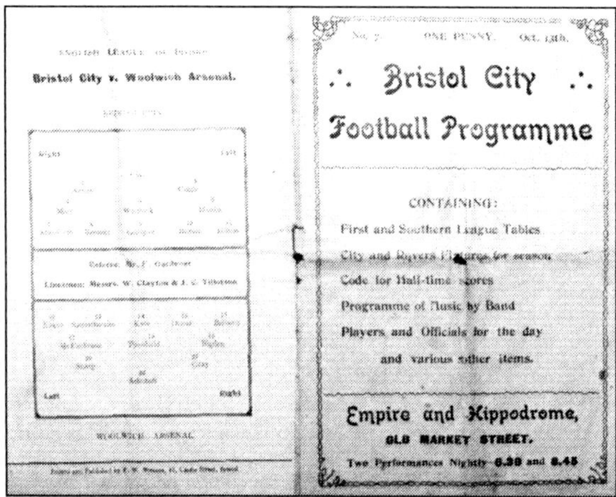

Bristol City v. Woolwich Arsenal.

WOOLWICH ARSENAL

ONE PENNY. Oct. 13th.

∴ Bristol City ∴

Football Programme

CONTAINING:

First and Southern League Tables

Code for Half-time scores

Programme of Music by Band

Players and Officials for the day

and various other items.

Empire and Hippodrome,

OLD MARKET STREET.

Above: 22,000 packed into Ashton Gate to see Woolwich Arsenal on 13 October 1906

A sketch from the *Bristol Observer*, after a friendly with Notts Co on 12 February 1898
Below: Advertisement from the *Bristol Evening News* on 1 September 1909

Bedminster 1898-99 Back: Mountford (trainer), Whitehouse, Crone, Smith (manager); Middle: Cox, Lamont, Massie, Kelso (capt), McDonald, Stewart, Livesley; Front: McVean, Bell, Leonard, Copeland, Gray

Disc to accompany film of the 1909 FA Cup final

Bristol City 1902-03

GUIDE TO SEASONAL SUMMARIES

Col 1: Match number (for league fixtures); Round (for cup-ties).
e.g. 2:1 means 'Second round; first leg.'
e.g. 4R means 'Fourth round replay.'

Col 2: Date of the fixture and whether Home (H), Away (A), or Neutral (N).

Col 3: Opposition.

Col 4: Attendances. Home gates appear in roman; Away gates in *italics*.
Figures in **bold** indicate the largest and smallest gates, at home and away.
Average home and away attendances appear after the final league match.

Col 5: Respective league positions of Bristol City and their opponents after the match.
Bristol City's position appears on the top line in roman.
Their opponents' position appears on the second line in *italics*.
For cup-ties, the division and position of opponents is provided.
e.g. *2:12* means the opposition are twelfth in Division 2.

Col 6: The top line shows the result: W(in), D(raw), or L(ose).
The second line shows Bristol City's cumulative points total.

Col 7: The match score, Bristol City's given first.
Scores in **bold** indicate Bristol City's biggest league win and heaviest defeat.

Col 8: The half-time score, Bristol City's given first.

Col 9: The top lines shows Bristol City's scorers and times of goals in roman.
The second line shows opponents' scorers and times of goals in *italics*.
A 'p' after the time of a goal denotes a penalty; 'og' an own-goal.
The third line gives the name of the match referee.

Team line-ups: Bristol City line-ups appear on the top line, irrespective of whether they are home or away. Opposition teams appear on the second line in *italics*.
Players of either side who are sent off are marked !
Bristol City players making their league debuts are displayed in **bold**.

N.B. For clarity, all information appearing in *italics* relates to opposing teams.

BEDMINSTER (Southern League Division 1) Manager: Harry Smith SEASON 1898-99

No	Date		Att	Pos	Pt	F-A	H-T	Scorers, Times, and Referees	1	2	3	4	5	6	7	8	9	10	11
1	A	TOTTENHAM			D	1-1	0-1	Proudfoot 82	Whitehouse	Stewart	**Crone**	Lamont	Proudfoot	McDonald	McVean	Bell	Leonard	Copeland	Gray
	10/9		*5,500*		1			*Cameron 13*	*Cullen*	*Melia*	*Cain*	*Jones*	*McNaught*	*Stormont*	*Smith*	*McKay*	*Joyce*	*Cameron*	*Bradshaw*
								Ref: F King	The Minster won the toss at Northumberland Park and chose to play with the slight wind in their favour, but fell behind to Cameron's early opener. In the second half Cameron had a fine shot kept out by the crossbar shortly before the ball was scrimmaged through for an equaliser.										
2	H	BRIGHTON UTD			L	1-2	0-1	Stewart 50p	**Cox**	Stewart	Crone	Lamont	Proudfoot	McDonald	McVean	Leonard	Bell	Copeland	Gray
	14/9		**1,000**		1			*McArthur 35, Longair 70*	*Bullimer*	*Hendry*	*Caldwell*	*McWhirter*	*Longair*	*Low*	*Davidson*	*McLeod*	*McArthur*	*Willocks*	*Malloch*
								Ref: C Moss	Cox was handicapped by a first-half injury to his leg, which brought about his departure from the fray after Longair headed in the visitors' winner. With Crone taking over between the sticks, the Minster played up for all they were worth but were unable to obtain an equaliser.										
3	A	READING		12	L	**0-4**	0-0		Whitehouse	Kelso	Crone	Stewart	Lamont	McDonald	Leonard	McVean	Bell	Gray	Copeland
	8/10		*4,000*	*7*	1			*Millar 55, 65, Boyne 75, Bamford 85*	*Neale*	*Henderson*	*O'Brien*	*Ballantyre*	*Holt*	*Eccleston*	*Sharp A*	*Goldie*	*Millar*	*Bamford*	*Boyne*
									There wasn't anything to choose between the two sides after a well-contested first half but, following the break, the Biscuitmen put on a brilliant exhibition. They were constantly attacking and reaped their reward with strikes from Boyne and Bamford adding to Millar's double.										
4	A	NEW BROMPTON		12	L	2-5	1-3	McVean 30, Callender 60	Whitehouse	Kelso	Brooks	Stewart	Lamont	Crone	Whittle	McVean	Copeland	Bell	**Callender**
	22/10		*3,000*	*1*	1			*Frettingham 20, 35, Campbell 40,*	*Bunyan*	*King*	*Watson*	*Innes*	*Atherton*	*Hutcheson*	*Grieve*	*Macdonald*	*Frettingham*	*Lennox*	*Campbell*
								[Watson 70p, 80p]	There has been nothing about Bedminster's play this season to arouse expectation that they would hold their own against the league leaders and so this result was practically a foregone conclusion. The windy weather didn't help, but at least with two goals the Minster made a fight of it.										
5	A	SHEPPEY UTD		12	D	2-2	1-1	Leonard 44, Kelso 75	Whitehouse	Kelso	Crone	Lamont	Proudfoot	McDonald	Leonard	McVean	Copeland	Stewart	Gray
	5/11		***1,000***	*14*	2			*Rule 7, Trainer 50*	*Leitch*	*Penney*	*Macfarlane*	*Lissenden*	*Abbott*	*Walker*	*Harrison*	*Trainer*	*Rule*	*Collins*	*Peters*
									A rough game in good weather on the Botany Ground at Sheerness, where the Minster were helped by the fact that Sheppey lost the services of the injured Lissenden for a quarter of an hour. Rule netted the opener from Harrison's centre, but Crone's free-kick set up Leonard's equaliser.										
6	H	NEW BROMPTON		12	W	**4-1**	4-0	McVean 10, Copeland 25,	Whitehouse	Kelso	Crone	Lamont	Proudfoot	McDonald	Leonard	McVean	Stewart	Copeland	Gray
	12/11		3,000	*1*	4			*Frettingham 85* [Stewart 30, 45]	*Bunyan*	*King*	*Watson*	*Hutcheson*	*Atherton*	*Graham*	*Grieve*	*Macdonald*	*Frettingham*	*Lennox*	*Campbell*
								Ref: H Platt	The Minster placed their strongest XI in the field, but Brompton were without Innes and Gallacher. Just after McVean had fired Bedminster in front the visitors were awarded a penalty, which Watson placed outside. Stewart's overhead kick right on the interval brought up goal No 4.										
7	A	CHATHAM		9	W	1-0	0-0	McVean 75	Whitehouse	Kelso	Crone	Lamont	Proudfoot	McDonald	Leonard	McVean	Stewart	Copeland	Gray
	19/11		*5,000*	*8*	6				*Frail*	*Harper*	*Dunn*	*Smith*	*Chapman*	*Perrins*	*Lawrence*	*McNeill*	*Brearley*	*Clements*	*Johnson*
									Bedminster, who travelled up on the Friday, took the field at Chatham fully refreshed. The fine weather drew a large crowd to witness a very vigorous game, but it wasn't until the second-half was well advanced that McVean fired in a loose ball to bring the Minster their due reward.										
8	H	SHEPPEY UTD		8	W	3-1	2-0	Gray 5, Stewart 10, Leonard 75	Whitehouse	Brooks	Crone	Lamont	Proudfoot	McDonald	Leonard	McVean	Stewart	Copeland	Gray
	26/11		**1,000**	*14*	8			*Trainer 47*	*Leitch*	*Macfarlane*	*Penney*	*Jenner*	*Abbott*	*Lissenden*	*Harrison*	*Collins*	*Rule*	*Trainer*	*Peters*
								Ref: J Le Grand	A small crowd in the stormy weather saw the Minster dominate this game, but only put away a small percentage of their many chances. When Stewart's shot rebounded off a post, Leonard put across for Gray to shoot in the early opener. Trainer's header was Sheppey's sole response.										
9	A	BRIGHTON UTD		6	W	2-0	1-0	Leonard 40, Stewart 75	Whitehouse	Brooks	Crone	Lamont	Proudfoot	McDonald	Leonard	McVean	Stewart	Copeland	Gray
	30/11		*1,560*	*11*	10				*Bullimer*	*Caldwell*	*Hendry*	*Longair*	*Low*	*McWhirter*	*Malloch*	*Willocks*	*McArthur*	*McLeod*	*Davidson*
									After much give and take play, Leonard's fine shot gave Bedminster a slender advantage at the break. The second half opened with the Minster pressing, but Brighton soon became aggressive and Whitehouse had to be at his best. A run down the flank led to Stewart clinching victory.										
10	A	GRAVESEND		7	D	1-1	1-1	Bull 15og	Whitehouse	Brooks	Crone	Lamont	Proudfoot	Bell	Leonard	McVean	Stewart	Copeland	Gray
	3/12		*1,500*	*8*	11			*Hulme 25*	*Wilkinson*	*Barbour*	*Struthers*	*Bull*	*Regan*	*Davies*	*Garfield*	*Yates*	*Mobley*	*Hulme*	*Ross*
									No sooner had play commenced than it was halted due to an injury to Bell, but this didn't trouble Bedminster, who took the lead when Bull put Gray's centre into his own net. Hulme soon equalised and by the end of play the Minster had cause to be thankful for much keen defending.										
11	A	BRISTOL CITY		8	L	2-5	1-1	Leonard 44, McVean 70	Whitehouse	Kelso	Crone	Lamont	Proudfoot	Bell	Leonard	McVean	Stewart	Copeland	Gray
	17/12		***10,250***	*4*	11			*Finnerhan 18, 65, Kelso 50og,*	*Monteith*	*Barker*	*Davy*	*Jones*	*McLean*	*Hamilton*	*Langham*	*Finnerhan*	*Caie*	*Carnelly*	*Russell*
								Ref: T Saywell *[Carnelly 60, 85]*	In the heavy, drifting, rain, Finnerhan rolled in City's opener, but shortly before the break Leonard sent in a great shot that gave Monteith no chance of saving. City went back in front when Kelso, in attempting to clear from Carnelly, had the bad luck to head the ball into his own net.										

No		Opponent			FT	HT	Scorers											
12	A	WARMLEY*	8	L	2-3	1-2	Gray 20, Copeland 70	Whitehouse	Kelso	Crone	Lamont	Proudfoot	McDonald	Leonard	McVean	Stewart	Copeland	Gray
26/12		*4,000*	*13*	11			*Bishop 44, 86, Preddy 45*	*Douglas*	*McDermid*	*Warburton*	*Manson*	*Britton P*	*Woods*	*Preddy*	*Browett*	*Henderson*	*Reid*	*Bishop*
							Ref: G Landragin	Losing the toss and starting against a cross-wind, the Minster's first effort went wide, but at last Stewart set up Gray to put the ball into the net. A shot against the post allowed Bishop to gallop up and knock in Warmley's leveller. Copeland rushed through for Bedminster after the break.										
13	A	SOUTHAMPTON	8	L	0-1	0-1		Whitehouse	Kelso	Crone	Lamont	Proudfoot	McDonald	Leonard	McVean	Stewart	Copeland	Gray
31/12		*2,000*	*1*	11			*Wood 5*	*Robinson*	*Meehan*	*Haynes*	*Meston*	*Chadwick*	*Durber*	*Smith*	*Stevens*	*Hartley*	*Wood*	*Seeley*
								Bad weather quite spoilt the attendance at this game, which went ahead despite protests over the state of the pitch. In a fairly even contest, a less than full-strength Saints' side were slightly fortunate to beat the Minster by the narrowest of margins, thanks to an early strike by Wood.										
14	H	CHATHAM	9	D	0-0	0-0		Whitehouse	Kelso	Crone	Lamont	Proudfoot	McDonald	Leonard	McVean	Stewart	Copeland	Gray
7/1		3,000	*10*	12				*Frail*	*Harper*	*Humphreys*	*Smith*	*Chapman*	*Perrins*	*Johnson*	*Lawrence*	*Brearley*	*Clements*	*Dickenson*
							Ref: Sgt Barrow	Frail's fine display between the sticks kept Bedminster at bay after the break and thereby prevented them from recording the double over the Kent side. In the first half though, the visitors' speedy forwards caused the Minster rearguard problems so a share of the spoils was a fair result.										
15	A	SWINDON	10	L	3-4	3-0	Stewart 5, McVean 7, Gray 35	Cox	Kelso	Brooks	Lamont	Proudfoot	McDonald	Leonard	McVean	Stewart	Copeland	Gray
14/1		*3,000*	*5*	12			*Richardson W 50, Kelso 73og,*	*Menham*	*Shutt*	*Richardson G*	*Henderson*	*Logan*	*Smith*	*Sharples*	*Coupar*	*Richardson W*	*Little*	*Kirton*
							Ref: E McDonald *[Richardson G 80, Coupar 85]*	The Minster took full advantage in the first half when the home side had the strong sun in their eyes, but what a change after the break when Swindon made a number of positional changes. A stirring fight-back was rewarded when, despite offside appeals, Coupar scored the winner.										
16	H	GRAVESEND	9	W	**4-1**	3-1	McVean 25, Gray 35, Copeland 36,	Whitehouse	Kelso	Crone	Lamont	Proudfoot	McDonald	Leonard	McVean	Stewart	Copeland	Gray
21/1		**1,000**	*8*	14			*Hulme 7* [Leonard 80]	*Wilkinson*	*Barbour*	*Struthers*	*Bull*	*Regan*	*Davies*	*Garfield*	*Hulme*	*Mobley*	*Parkinson*	*Ross*
							Ref: H Platt	Considering the weather, the pitch was in fair condition, though there were small pools of water in evidence. The Minster looked a beaten side for the first 25 minutes. Hume shot in the opener, but McVean hooked in the equaliser before Gray's grounder put Bedminster into the lead.										
17	H	MILLWALL ATH	9	L	1-4	0-2	Leonard 75 *[Geddes 85]*	Whitehouse	Kelso	Crone	Lamont	Proudfoot	McDonald	Leonard	McVean	Stewart	Copeland	Gray
4/2		2,000	2	14			*Hill 30, Cavey 43, Turnbull 80,*	*Sunderland*	*Burgess*	*Davis*	*Crawford*	*Stewart*	*Millar*	*Tannahill*	*Calvey*	*Hill*	*Turnbull*	*Geddes*
							Ref: G Muir	It can hardly be said that the final return of four goals to one in favour of the Dockers represented the run of the game, as the Minster had more of the play. The visitors' were, however, more clinical in front of goal, in this snowbound game, following on from Hill's side-footed opener.										
18	H	BRISTOL CITY	9	W	1-0	0-0	Leonard 70	Whitehouse	Kelso	Crone	Lamont	Proudfoot	Stewart	Leonard	Massie	McVean	Copeland	Gray
4/3		**7,000**	*4*	16				*Monteith*	*Barker*	*Stewart*	*Jones*	*McLean*	*Hamilton*	*Langham*	*Finnerhan*	*Caie*	*Carnelly*	*Russell*
							Ref: J Albert	McVean hooked the ball back for Leonard to fire home the goal that settled this fast and exciting local derby. Robert Crone therefore at least had the pleasure of performing on the winning side after the Bedminster directors had decided that they couldn't spare him to play for Ireland.										
19	A	MILLWALL ATH	9	L	0-3	0-1		Whitehouse	Kelso	Crone	Lamont	Proudfoot	McDonald	Leonard	Massie	McVean	Copeland	Gray
11/3		*3,000*	*2*	16			*Crawford 30, Stewart 70, Tannahill 75*	*Sunderland*	*Burgess*	*Davis*	*Crawford*	*Stewart*	*Millar*	*Tannahill*	*Calvey*	*Gettins*	*Turnbull*	*Geddes*
								At East Ferry Road, the Minster won a corner at the outset, but thereafter it was Millwall who controlled most of the first-half play. Fortunately the Dockers' shooting was erratic, but eventually Crawford scored for them. The visitors improved after the break, but didn't have any luck.										
20	H	ROYAL ARTILLERY	10	L	0-1	0-0		Whitehouse	Kelso	Crone	Lamont	Proudfoot	Stewart	Leonard	Massie	McVean	Copeland	Gray
31/3		2,000	*13*	16			*Jardine 85*	*Reilly*	*Turner*	*Phillips*	*Coutts*	*Hill*	*Patterson*	*McGibbin*	*Hanna*	*Phinn*	*Brazier*	*Jardine*
							Ref: V Daines	Reilly, the visiting custodian, had to be on his best form as Bedminster dominated this game. His opposite number was fortunate however soon after the break when McGibbon netted only to be given offside. Jardine put away a rebound off of a post to snatch an unlikely Artillery victory.										
21	H	SWINDON	10	L	0-1	0-0		Whitehouse	Kelso	Crone	Lamont	Stewart	McDonald	Leonard	Massie	McVean	Copeland	Bell
1/4		1,500	*8*	16			*Richardson W 85*	*Menham*	*Shutt*	*Mills*	*Richardson G*	*Logan*	*Henderson*	*Sharples*	*Anthony*	*Richardson W*	*Coupar*	*Little*
							Ref: J Tillotson	The fairly large gathering of spectators were kept waiting at the start as it wasn't until a quarter of an hour after the advertised time that Swindon kicked-off from the Lower End. They witnessed Richardson's swift low-shot, which brought about another unlucky home defeat.										
22	H	SOUTHAMPTON	10	W	2-1	0-0	Copeland 80, Leonard 85	Whitehouse	Kelso	Crone	Lamont	Stewart	McDonald	McVean	Massie	Leonard	Copeland	Gray
4/4		3,000	*1*	18			*Haynes 65*	*Robinson*	*Meehan*	*Durber*	*McLean*	*Chadwick*	*Robertson*	*Yates*	*Stevens*	*Hartley*	*Wood*	*Haynes*
							Ref: J Platt	The Saints were under so much pressure that, after Haynes had fired them in front in a breakaway, they played one of their forwards in defence. Fortunately their ploy didn't work as Robinson carried Copeland's drive over the line, then Leonard fired in the close-range winner.										
23	A	ROYAL ARTILLERY	9	W	2-0	0-0	Copeland 85, Gray 89	Whitehouse	Kelso	Crone	Lamont	Stewart	McDonald	McVean	Massie	Leonard	Copeland	Gray
8/4		*2,000*	*13*	20				*Field*	*Leach*	*Clarke*	*Whitehouse*	*Sutherland*	*Smith*	*Hanna*	*Harrison*	*Phinn*	*McBirnie*	*Woods*
								A good crowd turned up for this game despite the Soldiers having to field their reserve side after losing an appeal against suspension. The Artillery proved no match for Bedminster, but it wasn't until near the finish that the Minster scored the goals to secure a deserved victory.										

BEDMINSTER (Southern League Division 1) Manager: Harry Smith SEASON 1898-99

No	Date	Att	Pos	Pt	F-A	H-T	Scorers, Times, and Referees	1	2	3	4	5	6	7	8	9	10	11
24	H TOTTENHAM		9	W	1-0	0-0	Gray 85	Whitehouse	Kelso	Crone	Lamont	Stewart	McDonald	McVean	Massie	Leonard	Copeland	Gray
	15/4	3,000	*8*	22				*Cullen*	*Erentz*	*Melia*	*Downie*	*McNaught*	*Leach*	*Smith*	*Atherton*	*Joyce*	*Cameron*	*Bradshaw*
							Ref: F King	Windy weather prevailed at Ashton Gate, where a late goal from Gray, following a rush, brought victory for the Minster. A deserved success, though they were perhaps fortunate that no one else touched a Spurs free-kick that went straight into the net just prior to the half-time interval.										
25	H READING		8	W	2-1	2-0	Copeland 35, Gray 40	Whitehouse	Kelso	Crone	Lamont	Proudfoot	Stewart	Leonard	Massie	McVean	Copeland	Gray
	29/4	2,000	*5*	24			*Sharp 75*	*Whittaker*	*Henderson*	*O'Brien*	*Foster*	*Ballantyne*	*White*	*Bamford*	*Johnson*	*Davies*	*Sharp A*	*Plant*
	Home	Away						This was a much easier win than the scoreline suggests. Up until the last 20 minutess the Biscuitmen, who had lost the services of Plant shortly before half-time, offered little. After the break Leonard failed from the spot before Sharp ran through to beat Whitehouse with a capital shot.										
	Ave 2,458	3,524																

* *Warmley disbanded late Jan - record expunged.*

WESTERN LEAGUE DIVISION 1

No	Date	Att	Pos	Pt	F-A	H-T	Scorers, Times, and Referees	1	2	3	4	5	6	7	8	9	10	11
1	A TROWBRIDGE*			W	**4-1**	2-0	Copeland 25, Livesey 35, 60, 85	Whitehouse	Kelso	Brooks	**Lamont**	Proudfoot	McDonald	McVean	**Massie**	**Livesey**	Copeland	Leonard
	7/9	***200***		2			*Richards 89*	*West*	*Stevens*	*Smith*	*Haslam*	*Rose*	*Hyman H*	*Belcher*	*O'Brien*	*Richards*	*Love*	*Hyman W*
							Ref: T Saywell	Whitehouse, who had as much to do as his opposite number, was fortunate that O'Brien had a shot ruled offside before Copeland gave the Minster the lead when he caught West off his line. Towards the close the gathering gloom made it almost impossible to follow the ball.										
2	H SOUTHAMPTON			W	2-1	2-1	Copeland 35, Massie 40	Whitehouse	Kelso	Crone	Stewart	Proudfoot	Lamont	Leonard	Massie	**Whittle**	Bell	Copeland
	17/9	2,500		4			*Unknown 10*	*Joyce*	*Durber*	*Thomas*	*McLean*	*Dewar*	*Petrie*	*Cust*	*Stevens*	*Buchanan*	*Cavendish*	*Mackenzie*
							Ref: Sgt Barrow	After rushing the ball into the net for an early lead, the Saints wasted a spot-kick midway through the first half. Whitehouse saved the first attempt, whilst the second effort was blasted against the crossbar. Copeland levelled with a grand shot, before Massie poked in the winner.										
3	H BRSTL ST GEORGE		4	L	1-4	0-2	Copeland 55	Whitehouse	Kelso	Crone	Lamont	Proudfoot	McDonald	Leonard	McVean	Livesey	Bell	Copeland
	10/10	1,500	*2*	4			*Stevenson 5,85, Barr 30, Boyd 80*	*Carter*	*Halley*	*Cole*	*Underwood*	*Beak*	*Scotchbrook*	*Allen*	*Barr*	*Stevenson*	*Boyd*	*Henderson*
							Ref: T Saywell	Stevenson, who put the green-shirted visitors in front with a beauty, was unlucky right on the interval with a shot that cannoned off the bar. After the break Copeland registered with a fierce drive, but by the finish Stevenson's touch-in completed a much-deserved St George victory.										
4	H TROWBRIDGE*		4	W	3-1	1-0	Copeland 35, Massie 46, 75	Whitehouse	Kelso	Crone	Lamont	Proudfoot	McDonald	McVean	Bell	Massie	Copeland	**North**
	26/10	**1,000**	*7*	6			*Hyman W 80*	*West*	*Haslam*	*Robson*	*Hyman H*	*Rose*	*Smith*	*Hyman W*	*Richards*	*O'Brien*	*Terry*	*Sheldon*
							Ref: A Farrant	Despite the score, Trowbridge were by no means outclassed by the Minster, who started from the Road End. The keeper erred with Copeland's soft effort that gave the homesters' the lead, then after the break his failure to hold Proudfoot's long-shot allowed Massie to tap in the rebound.										
5	H BRSTL EASTVILLE R		2	W	1-0	0-0	Gray 47	Whitehouse	Kelso	Crone	Lamont	Proudfoot	McDonald	Leonard	McVean	Stewart	Copeland	Gray
	24/12	**6,000**	*3*	6				*Julian*	*Bunch*	*Griffiths*	*Farnall*	*Burton*	*Kinsey*	*Brown*	*Jones*	*McCairns*	*Fisher*	*Paul*
							Ref: A Millward	A large crowd witnessed a capital game at Ashton Gate where, after the Rovers had monopolised play for the opening quarter of an hour, the Minister gave their opponents a hot time. Gray settled the contest when, from Crone's free-kick shortly after the interval, he rushed the ball in.										
6	A BRSTL EASTVILLE R		4	D	2-2	2-0	Copeland 5, McVean 35	Whitehouse	Kelso	Crone	Lamont	Proudfoot	McDonald	Leonard	McVean	Stewart	Copeland	Gray
	28/1	***3,500***	*3*	7			*Fisher 55, Unknown 84*	*Cook*	*Bunch*	*Griffiths*	*Farnall*	*Burton*	*Kinsey*	*Brown*	*Jones*	*McCairns*	*Fisher*	*Paul*
								The Minster had decidedly the better of the play up to half-time, with Copeland netting the opener with a fine drive and McVean's tight shot doubling the advantage. In the second half, though, a misunderstanding between Crone and Whitehouse enabled Fisher to reduce the arrears.										
7	A BRSTL ST GEORGE		4	L	2-3	1-1	Halley 25og, Stewart 65p	Whitehouse	Kelso	Crone	Lamont	Proudfoot	McDonald	Leonard	Bell	Stewart	Copeland	Gray
	11/2	*3,000*	*2*	7			*Henderson 35, Stevenson 75, 85p*	*Macfarlane*	*Halley*	*Mackay*	*Underwood*	*McCreadie*	*Beak*	*Allan*	*Barr*	*Stevenson*	*Henderson*	*Scotchbrook*
							Ref: J Knight	On the Bell Hill pitch, which in places resembled a bog, St George were a man short early on, with Halley going off injured. He soon returned, however, only to put Stewart's tame shot into his own net. McDonald's foul on Allan allowed Stevenson to settle the game with a penalty-kick.										
8	A SOUTHAMPTON		4	L	**0-3**	0-1		Whitehouse	Kelso	Crone	Lamont	Proudfoot	McDonald	Leonard	McVean	Stewart	Copeland	Gray
	22/2	*1,000*	*5*	7			*Buchanan 35, 60, Smith 75*	*Joyce*	*Durber*	*Thomas*	*McLean*	*Dewar*	*Petrie*	*Smith*	*Stevens*	*Buchanan*	*Cavendish*	*Mackenzie*
								With the Minster commencing play against the wind and sun, the Saints had the better of the early exchanges until Gray finished off a fine run with a shot that Joyce did well to clear. Buchanan opened the scoring from a pass from Smith, before heading in a second following the break.										

9	H	SWINDON		5	D	0-0	0-0		Whitehouse	Brooks	Crone	Lamont	McDonald	Stewart	Leonard	Massie	McVean	Copeland	Gray
	6/3		**1,000**	*1*	8				*Menham*	*Shutt*	*Mills*	*Smith*	*Logan*	*Henderson*	*Kirton*	*Coupar*	*Little*	*Sharples*	*Anthony*
								Ref: A Millward	As goalless draws go, this was a good game. The nearest either side came to scoring was in the opening half when, first Swindon appealed that Whitehouse had carried Logan's shot over the line, then a little later Coupar fired against the bar. After the break neither keeper was troubled.										
10	A	SWINDON		5	L	1-3	0-0	McVean 50	Cox	Brooks	Crone	Stewart	Proudfoot	McDonald	Bell	McVean	Massie	Copeland	Gray
	22/4		*3,000*	*1*	8			*Sharples 60, 87, Little 89*	*Menham*	*Shutt*	*Richardson G*	*Henderson*	*Logan*	*Smith*	*Sharples*	*Coupar*	*Richardson W*	*Little*	*Kirton*
		Home	Away					Ref: J Tillotson	Needing a win to clinch the title, Swindon, with only the injured Mills missing, put their strongest side in the field. Shocked when McVean and Massie combined well for the former to fire the Minster in front, Swindon improved by switching Coupar and Kirton and drove on to victory.										
	Ave	2,400	2,140																

** Trowbridge Town disbanded end of Oct - record expunged.*

FRIENDLIES

1	H	SOUTHAMPTON		L	1-2	1-1	Copeland 35	**Whitehouse**	**Kelso**	**Brooks**	**Stewart**	**Proudfoot**	**McDonald**	**McVean**	**Bell**	**Leonard**	**Copeland**	**Gray**
	1/9		1,000				*Nicol 15, Hartley 50*	*Robinson*	*Nicol*	*Durber*	*Weston*	*Chadwick*	*Robertson*	*Smith*	*Wood*	*Hartley*	*Keay*	*Mackenzie*
							Ref: W Pollett	Despite the fine weather, Bedminster's first professional game attracted only a moderate crowd. Nicol opened the scoring with a long shot, but Copeland levelled before the break. Hartley's winner into the right-hand corner caught Whitehouse stranded on the opposite side of his net.										
2	H	WARMLEY		W	2-0	1-0	Leonard 15, Unknown 88	Whitehouse	Kelso	Brooks	Stewart	Proudfoot	McDonald	McVean	Bell	Leonard	Copeland	Gray
	3/9		2,000					*Walker*	*McDermid*	*Warburton*	*Woods*	*McManus*	*McHardy*	*Hamilton*	*Manson*	*Reid*	*Andrews*	*Bishop*
							Ref: N Whittaker	The continuing fine weather helped draw a fair sized crowd to see the Minster secure a deserved win over the famed visitors. A scrimmage a few paces from goal ended with the opener being secured; then, shortly before the call of time, Warmley's rearguard was breached yet again.										
3	H	BLACKPOOL		D	1-1	1-1	Callender 31	Whitehouse	Kelso	Crone	Stewart	Proudfoot	McDonald	Whittle	Massie	Copeland	Callender	North
	29/10		600				*Stirzaker 30*	*Fletcher*	*Parr*	*Scott*	*Howson E*	*Stirzaker*	*Howson W*	*Cartmell*	*Banks*	*Williams*	*Atley*	*Leadbetter*
							Ref: J Matthews	Bedminster started from the Park End and the early play took place around the Blackpool citadel. However the visitors took the lead when Stirzaker put the leather away after Whitehouse had saved from Banks and Howson. Fortunately, Callender straight away notched a hot one.										
4	A	SWINDON		L	0-2	0-2		Whitehouse	Brooks	Crone	Lamont	Proudfoot	Bell	Leonard	McVean	Massie	Copeland	Whittle
	10/12		*1,000*				*Sharples 30, Anthony 40*	*Menham*	*Shutt*	*Mills*	*Richardson G*	*Munro*	*Henderson*	*Sharples*	*Coupar*	*Logan*	*Little*	*Anthony*
							Ref: S Major	With a stiff wind at their backs, Swindon had much the better of matters in the first half. Sharples opened the scoring on the half-hour mark; then Whitehouse spoilt an otherwise faultless display when he misjudged Anthony's high-shot, which doubled the Railwayman's advantage.										
5	H	SWINDON		W	3-0	2-0	Copeland 5, 30, 75	Whitehouse	Brooks	Crone	Lamont	Proudfoot	McDonald	Leonard	Bell	Stewart	Copeland	Gray
	27/12		2,000					*Menham*	*Munro*	*Mills*	*Richardson G*	*Logan*	*Smith*	*Anthony*	*Coupar*	*Richardson W*	*Little*	*Kirton*
							Ref: T Hanson/Sgt Barrow	With no referee at the start, this game was played as a friendly with Mr Hanson taking over in the middle. Bedminster pressed from the start and opened the scoring just before the missing official turned up. Copeland brought up his hat-trick with a shot that quite baffled Menham.										
6	A	RYDE		D	2-2	2-1	McVean 5, 40	Whitehouse	Kelso	Crone	Lamont	Proudfoot	McDonald	Leonard	McVean	Stewart	Copeland	Gray
	2/1		*500*				*Jones 20, 82*	*Hammett*	*Walker FM*	*Ponting*	*King*	*Halliday*	*Flux W*	*Jones*	*Christie*	*Woodhouse*	*Maidment E*	*Mellanby*
			(£20+)					Colonel Smith, the president of the Ryde club, paid Bedminster's travel expenses and was rewarded by a good turnout despite the unfavourable wet weather. The Minster did most of the pressing, but had to settle for a draw after twice being pegged back by the resilient seasiders.										
7	H	BRISTOL AMTRS		W	9-2	5-2	Bell 5, Leonard 10, 65, Lamont 20,	Cox	Kelso	Crone	Lamont	Proudfoot	Stewart	Leonard	Massie	McVean	Bell	Whittle
	25/2		500				*Langford 1, Callender 30*	*Thomas E*	*Slade E*	*Cowcill L*	*Mayo L*	*McAuliffe MO*	*Littleton B*	*Taylor C*	*Stolz W*	*Langford E*	*Callender W*	*North A E*
							Ref: T Hanson [Unk'n 31,46,85,McVean44,Massie70]	Despite Langford giving them the lead directly after the kick-off, the Amateurs (the rump of the old Bedminster organisation) were easily disposed of by their professional brethren. Leonard's smart shot from the extreme right had the goal-hungry Minster in seventh heaven.										
8	H	GLOSSOP NTH END		W	4-2	0-0	Copeland 50, 80, 81, Massie 60	Cox	Kelso	Crone	Lamont	Proudfoot	McDonald	Leonard	Massie	Bell	Copeland	Gray
	18/3		1,000				*Colville 55, Lumsden 75*	*Etchells*	*Rothwell*	*Orr*	*Clifford*	*Colville*	*Collier*	*Gallacher*	*Vaughan*	*Connachan*	*McCosh*	*Lumsden*
							Ref: W Pollett	Copeland, who opened the scoring with an easy shot, made amends for blasting his 65th-minute penalty against the crossbar by netting two late goals to bring up his hat-trick. Timely strikes indeed for the Minster as, shortly before, Lumsden had headed in the Football Leaguers' leveller.										

FA Cup/Glos Cup/Charity Cup				F-A	H-T	Scorers, Times, and Referees	1	2	3	4	5	6	7	8	9	10	11
P A NEWBURY		-	W	3-0	1-0	Whittle 30, Bell 60, Lamont 75	Whitehouse	Kelso	Crone	Stewart	Proudfoot	Lamont	Leonard	Massie	Whittle	Bell	Copeland
24/9	*600*						*Ingram*	*Marty*	*Justins*	*Pope*	*Booker*	*Freebody*	*George*	*Willis*	*Francis*	*Marshall*	*Dolton*
						Ref: T Saywell	The home side kicked off and soon had a shot from a free-kick, but failed to score. The Minster then responded and twice had efforts ruled out for offside. George made a fine run and shot for the homesters, but generally Bedminster were not troubled as they coasted to an easy victory.										
1Q H RYDE		-	W	3-1	2-0	McVean 25, Bell 28, Gray 65	Whitehouse	Kelso	Crone	Stewart	Lamont	McDonald	Leonard	McVean	Copeland	Bell	Gray
1/10	1,000					*Woodhouse 85*	*Hammett*	*Walker FM*	*Ponting*	*King*	*Halliday*	*Pook*	*Jones*	*Christie*	*Woodhouse*	*Maidment E*	*Judge*
						Ref: N Whittaker	Bell's tricky play lead to McVean's opener; then shortly after he got in on the act himself with a shot that gave Hammett no chance. After the break Gray was unfortunate to have his header disallowed for offside, before registering with a long dropping shot, which the keeper fisted in.										
2Q A WARMLEY		12	D	1-1	0-1	Stewart 50p	Whitehouse	Kelso	Brooks	Stewart	Lamont	Crone	Whittle	McVean	Massie	Bell	Copeland
15/10	*1,500*	*13*				*Manson 35*	*Douglas*	*Warburton*	*Walker*	*Woods*	*McDermid*	*Britton*	*Manson*	*Andrews*	*Henderson*	*Reid*	*Bishop*
						Ref: T Saywell	A tie of very moderate character on the Chequers ground, where the passing left much to be desired. Bedminster were fortunate early on when Bishop slipped with the goal at his mercy. Walker's handling offence within the twelve-yard line allowed the Minster to level from the spot.										
R H WARMLEY		12	D	2-2	2-0	McVean 10, Copeland 25	Whitehouse	Kelso	Crone	McDonald	Lamont	Stewart	Whittle	McVean	Copeland	Bell	**Clements**
19/10	500	*13*				*Andrews 55, Henderson 80*	*Douglas*	*McDermid*	*Warburton*	*Woods*	*McManus*	*Britton*	*Manson*	*Andrews*	*Henderson*	*Hamilton*	*Bishop*
						Ref: T Saywell	Despite the continuous rain of the past few days the turf was in fine condition for this replay. Although being without the injured Clements for most of the game, Bedminster were much the better side. McVean's shot, which gave the Minster the lead, went in off of Warburton's head.										
2R N WARMLEY		12	L	1-2	1-1	McVean 30	Whitehouse	Kelso	Brooks	Stewart	Lamont	Crone	Whittle	McVean	Livesey	Bell	Copeland
24/10	*1,000*	*13*				*Andrews 44, Hamilton 88*	*Douglas*	*McDermid*	*Warburton*	*Woods*	*McManus*	*Britton*	*Hamilton*	*Manson*	*Henderson*	*Andrews*	*Bishop*
						Ref: T Saywell *(at 'St John's Lane')*	Warmley pressed from the start, but the Minster took the lead when McVean's shot from just beyond the halfway line found the corner of the net. Hamilton's fine centre allowed Andrews to equalise, then in the second half the Warmley outside-right fired the winner past Whitehouse.										
1 H BRSTL ST GEORGE		9	W	3-2	1-0	Copeland 44, McVean 65, 70	Whitehouse	Kelso	Crone	Lamont	Proudfoot	Stewart	Leonard	Massie	McVean	Copeland	Gray
GC 27/2	2,000	*BL:5*				*Stevenson 75, Boyd 80*	*Carter*	*Halley*	*Cole*	*Underwood*	*McGreadie*	*McKay*	*Allan*	*Barr*	*Stevenson*	*Boyd*	*Scotchbrook*
						Ref: T Helme	Copeland opened the scoring shortly before the interval, when the injured McKay was off the field receiving treatment. After the break McVean doubled the Minsters' advantage by shooting in when Carter was on the ground. Boyd ended the scoring from a bully around goal.										
SF A BRISTOL ROV		10	L	0-1	0-1		Whitehouse	Crone	Kelso	Stewart	Proudfoot	Lamont	Leonard	Massie	McVean	Copeland	Gray
GC 25/3	*3,500*	*BL:4*				*Jones 10*	*Cook*	*Bunch*	*Griffiths*	*Farnall*	*Burton*	*Kinsey*	*Brown*	*Jones*	*McCairns*	*Fisher*	*Paul*
						Ref: A Millward	Despite the rain a good crowd were present to see this game, decided early on when Jones fired in from a fine pass by McCairns. It was rough luck on Bedminster, who felt that Massie was denied a goal in the second half. Upon consulting with his linesman, the referee ruled offside.										
SF H SWINDON		9	W	2-0	1-0	McVean 15, Copeland 75	Whitehouse	Brooks	Crone	Lamont	Stewart	McDonald	McVean	Massie	Leonard	Copeland	Gray
CC 17/4	500	*7*					*Menham*	*Shutt*	*Mills*	*Henderson*	*Logan*	*Richardson G*	*Sharples*	*Anthony*	*Little*	*Coupar*	*Kirton*
						Ref: Sgt Barrow	The small gathering at Ashton Gate saw Whitehouse twice tested in the first five minutes, before McVean opened the scoring with a stiff shot high into the net. After the break, Swindon pressed and gave the Minster an anxious time before Copeland put on number two with a low shot.										
F N READING		8	W	3-2	0-1	Gray 75, 89, McDonald 80	Whitehouse	Kelso	Crone	Lamont	Stewart	McDonald	McVean	Massie	Leonard	Copeland	Gray
CC 24/4	*500*	*5*				*Sharp 30, Plant 60*	*Whittaker*	*Henderson*	*O'Brien*	*Foster*	*Ballantyne*	*Hosie*	*Bamford*	*Goldie*	*Davies*	*Sharp A*	*Plant*
						Ref: J Tillotson *(at 'St John's Lane')*	Bedminster had looked out of it when Plant raced away to put Reading 2-0 up just after Stewart's spot-kick had been repelled by an upright. Fortunately, Gray revived the Minster when he shot in a rebound, and then headed the winner after McDonald's send-up had levelled matters.										

	SOUTHERN LEAGUE	Home						Away					
		P	W	D	L	F	A	W	D	L	F	A	Pts
1	Southampton	24	9	2	1	34	9	6	3	3	20	15	35
2	Bristol City	24	11	0	1	39	16	4	3	5	16	17	33
3	Millwall Ath	24	7	2	3	34	17	5	4	3	25	18	30
4	Chatham	24	6	4	2	19	8	4	4	4	13	15	28
5	Reading	24	9	2	1	24	4	0	6	6	7	20	26
6	New Brompt'	24	7	3	2	24	9	3	2	7	14	21	25
7	Tottenham H	24	8	2	2	24	11	2	2	8	16	25	24
8	BEDMINSTER	24	7	1	4	19	13	3	3	6	16	26	24
9	Swindon T	24	7	4	1	33	21	2	1	9	10	28	23
10	Brighton Utd	24	6	2	4	23	13	3	0	9	14	35	20
11	Gravesend U	24	6	3	3	31	20	1	2	9	11	32	19
12	Sheppey Utd	24	5	2	5	16	18	0	1	11	7	35	13
13	Royal Artillery	24	3	4	5	11	16	1	0	11	6	44	12
		312	91	31	34	331	175	34	31	91	175	331	312
	Warmley*	17	2	0	6	13	23	0	2	7	12	35	6

	WESTERN LEAGUE	P	W	D	L	F	A	W	D	L	F	A	Pts
1	Swindon T	8	3	0	1	9	5	2	1	1	7	5	11
2	Brs St George	8	2	1	1	10	8	2	0	2	8	7	9
3	Southampton	8	4	0	0	15	3	0	0	4	3	12	8
4	Bristol Rov	8	1	1	2	8	8	1	1	2	6	11	6
5	BEDMINSTER	8	2	1	1	4	5	0	1	3	5	11	6
		40	12	3	5	46	29	5	3	12	29	46	40
	Warmley*	5	2	0	2	8	10	0	0	1	0	5	4
	Trowbridge*	5	0	0	2	1	6	0	0	3	3	12	0

* *Disbanded*

Odds & ends

Double wins: SL: (0). WL: (1) Trowbridge Town.
Double losses: SL: (2) Swindon, Millwall. WL: (1) Bristol St George.

Won from behind: SL: (2) Gravesend United (h), Southampton (h). WL: (1) Southampton (h). BCC: (1) Reading (n). Fr (1) Bristol Amateurs (h).
Lost from in front: SL: (2) Warmley (a), Swindon Town (a). WL: (1) Bristol St George (h). FAC: (1) Warmley (n).

High spots: The 1-0 win over Bristol City at 'Ashton Gate' on 4 March. The stirring fight-back against Reading at 'St John's Lane' that secured the Bristol Charity Cup on 24 April.

Low spots: Losing to Warmley in the FA Cup replay at 'St John's Lane'. A 2-5 loss against Bristol City at 'St John's Lane' on 17 December. Succumbing to Bristol Rovers in the semi-final of the Gloucestershire Cup.

Player of the Year: Robert Crone.
Ever-presents: League: (1) David Copeland.
Hat-tricks: (2) B. Livesey, David Copeland.
Leading scorer: Overall: David Copeland (21). League: Copeland (11).

AGM (Bedminster Hotel, East Street, Bedminster, 6 February 1899): Profit (year-ending 31 December 1898) £61.17s.10d.

	Appearances			Goals			
	Lge	Cup	Fr	Lge	Cup	Fr	Tot
Bell, J	**12**	5	6		2	1	**3**
Brooks, G	**8**	3	4				
Callender, W	**1**		1	**1**		1	**2**
Clements, 'Hammer'		1					
Copeland, David	**35**	9	7	**11**	3	7	**21**
Cox, W	**3**		2				
Crone, Robert	**33**	9	6				
Gray, Robert	**29**	5	5	**8**	3		**11**
Kelso, Robert	**28**	8	6	**1**			**1**
Lamont, James	**34**	9	5		1	1	**2**
Leonard, John	**32**	6	7	**8**		3	**11**
Livesey, B	**2**	1		**3**			**3**
McDonald, W	**28**	4	6		1		**1**
McVean, Malcolm	**33**	8	5	**8**	6	3	**17**
Massie, W	**13**	6	4	**3**		2	**5**
North, A	**1**		1				
Proudfoot, David	**28**	3	8	**1**			**1**
Stewart, Alexander	**31**	9	6	**7**	1		**8**
Whitehouse, Jimmy	**32**	9	6				
Whittle	**2**	4	3		1		**1**
Opponents og				**2**			**2**
Unknown scorers						4	**4**
20 players used	**385**	**99**	**88**	**53**	**18**	**22**	**93**

Note: Games against disbanded clubs included.

No	Date		Att	Pos	Pt	F-A	H-T	Scorers, Times, and Referees	1	2	3	4	5	6	7	8	9	10	11
1	A	SHEPPEY UTD			W	2-0	1-0	Flewitt 30, Wilson 88	Toone	Crone	Davies RH	Draycott	**Davies WH**	Chambers	Whelan	Flewitt	Boucher	Wilson	Geddes
	2/9		*2,000*		2				*McClelland*	*Osborne*	*Penney*	*Macfarlane*	*Blair*	*Lissenden Jr*	*Harrison*	*Hall*	*Lester*	*Spence*	*Bamford*
								Ref: S Carr	The Minster started their League campaign with a slightly fortunate success on the Botany Ground at Sheerness. The Islanders had most of the play, but were let down by some poor finishing. Bedminster took the lead when Flewitt's free-kick was deflected into the net off of Osborne.										
2	H	BRIGHTON UTD*			W	3-1	1-1	Saxton 3, Boucher 85, Geddes 86	Toone	Crone	Davies RH	Wilson	Davies WH	Chambers	Whelan	Flewitt	Boucher	Saxton	Geddes
	9/9		3,000		4			*Malloch 20*	*Howes*	*Ashby*	*Mills*	*Low*	*McAvoy*	*Parry*	*Oakden*	*Mercer*	*McArthur*	*Willocks*	*Malloch*
								Ref: C Landragin	The play started briskly and Saxton netted a beauty that gave United's custodian little chance. For a long time the Minster looked like being frustrated, but in the closing stages a hot-shot at close quarters from Boucher and a Geddes scrambled-in effort brought a hard-earned victory.										
3	A	BRISTOL ROV		3	W	3-0	1-0	Flewitt 40, 75, Boucher 85	Toone	Davies RH	Crone	Wilson	Davies WH	Draycott	Whelan	Flewitt	Boucher	Geddes	Saxton
	23/9		*7,207*	*9*	6				*Stone*	*Ritchie*	*Griffiths*	*Lamont*	*Lee*	*Robertson*	*Leonard*	*Jones*	*Fisher*	*Lewis*	*Paul*
								Ref: Capt Simpson	In front of a large crowd, which the *Bristol Mercury* recorded as 7,207 paying for admission, the Minster pulled off an easy win at Stapleton Road. Flewitt fired in the opener; then, after the interval, made victory certain by racing through for another, before Boucher shot in the third.										
4	A	THAMES IRNWKS		6	L	0-1	0-1		Toone	Davies RH	Crone	Draycott	Wilson	Chambers	Whelan	Becton	Flewitt	Saxton	Geddes
	7/10		*5,000*	*7*	6			*Joyce 30p*	*Moore*	*Dunn*	*King*	*Dove*	*McManus*	*McEachrane*	*Hird*	*McKay*	*Joyce*	*Carnelly*	*Bradshaw*
									A good first half at Canning Town where, despite the home side starting in excellent style, the Minster more than held their own until Crone brought down Bradshaw close to the twelve-yard line. Joyce scored from the hotly disputed penalty and thus consigned Bedminster to defeat.										
5	H	TOTTENHAM		5	W	2-1	1-1	Boucher 35, Flewitt 75	Toone	Crone	Davies RH	Draycott	Wilson	Chambers	Whelan	Flewitt	Boucher	Becton	Geddes
	14/10		**6,250**	*1*	8			*Copeland 25*	*Clawley*	*Erentz*	*Tait*	*Jones*	*Morris*	*Stormont*	*Smith*	*Pratt*	*Copeland*	*Cameron*	*Kirwan*
									A truly great game at Ashton Gate, where the Minster were slightly fortunate to garner the points from this encounter, though this is not to say they didn't display the ability to match the high-class of their opponents. Ex-Bedminster player Copeland fired in the opener from close range.										
6	A	NEW BROMPTON		6	-	0-1	0-1		Toone	Crone	Davies RH	Draycott	Wilson	Chambers	Whelan	Flewitt	Boucher	Becton	Saxton
	21/10		*2,500*	*11*	8			*Frettingham 30*	*Carter*	*Lockie*	*Glover*	*Innes*	*Atherton*	*Hutchinson*	*Nobbs*	*Macdonald*	*Frettingham*	*Pangbourn*	*Seeley*
								Ref: F King (*Abandoned due to fog 50 mins*)	The sun was shining bright when Becton had his second-minute effort disallowed for offside but the mist came down suddenly after the break. With no improvement after a lengthy wait, the game was abandoned with Brompton leading thanks to Frettingham's dispatch of Nobbs' centre.										
7	A	SWINDON		8	L	1-2	1-1	Wilson 43	Toone	Crone	Davies RH	Draycott	Davies WH	Chambers	Whelan	Flewitt	Boucher	Wilson	Geddes
	4/11		*3,000*	*3*	8			*Henderson 44p, Sharples 51*	*Menham*	*Shutt*	*Wilson J*	*Richardson*	*Logan*	*Henderson*	*Sharples*	*Coupar*	*Turner*	*Smith W*	*Wilson T*
								Ref: F King	The boisterous wind caused Menham to misjudge a shot from Geddes, and Wilson was able to slip the ball into the back of the net, but almost immediately Henderson levelled with a penalty for the Railwaymen. After the break, Menham redeemed himself by saving Wilson's spot-kick.										
8	H	BRISTOL CITY		8	D	1-1	1-0	Monteith 40og	Toone	Crone	Davies RH	Draycott	Wilson	Chambers	Whelan	Flewitt	Boucher	Becton	Geddes
	11/11		5,500 (£160)	*7*	9			*Davies 80og*	*Monteith*	*McDonald*	*Robson*	*McLean*	*Britton*	*Hamilton*	*Langham*	*Blessington*	*Caie*	*Jones*	*Crawford*
								Ref: A Barker	City included Blessington, their signing from Derby, in this exciting game. Toone was in brilliant form between the sticks and he was unlucky to be beaten when Davies put the ball into his own goal. Poetic justice perhaps as Monteith had helped a Geddes curling corner into his net.										
9	H	SOUTHAMPTON		8	L	0-2	0-2		Toone	Crone	Davies RH	Draycott	Wilson	Chambers	Whelan	Flewitt	Boucher	Becton	Saxton
	25/11		4,000	*1*	9			*Milward 30, Farrell 43*	*Robinson*	*Meston*	*Durber*	*Greenlees*	*Chadwick*	*Englefield*	*Turner*	*Yates*	*Farrell*	*Wood*	*Milward*
								Ref: J Stark	An exciting opening 20 minutes, with both sides attacking in turn, but no goals until later when Milward shot in for the Saints. Not long after the referee had halted play to admonish someone in the enclosure for uncomplimentary expressions, Wilson's slip let in Farrell to net a beauty.										
10	A	MILLWALL ATH		8	W	2-1	1-1	Wilson 12, Becton 75	Toone	**Barker**	Davies RH	Draycott	Wilson	Chambers	Whelan	Flewitt	Boucher	Becton	Saxton
	2/12		*5,000*	*6*	11			*Smith 32*	*Cox*	*Burgess*	*Davis*	*Smith*	*Goldie*	*Millar*	*Bevan*	*Brearley*	*Robertson*	*Banks*	*Nichol*
								Ref: C Landragin	A fortunate win for the Minster as their opponents, who were the better side, suffered wretched luck in being denied by the woodwork on no fewer than six occasions. Wilson's grand-shot put Bedminster in front, but Smith's similar effort restored parity before the half-time interval.										
11	A	CHATHAM		8	L	0-3	0-1		Toone	Barker	Davies RH	Davies WH	Wilson	Crone	Whelan	Draycott	Boucher	Saxton	Geddes
	16/12		***1,500***	*14*	11			*Dickenson 30, Kaye 70, Collins 80*	*Bennett*	*Harper*	*Tranter*	*Collins*	*Chapman*	*Perrins*	*Kaye*	*Burton*	*Johnson*	*Clements*	*Dickenson*
								Ref: T Sweetman	The Minster, who lost the services of Boucher with a dislocated right thumb ten mins before the interval, were easily beaten on the Maidstone Road enclosure. Chatham, without their fast winger May, opened the scoring when Dickenson's shot was allowed despite an appeal for offside.										

No	Venue	Opponent / Date / Att	Pos	Res / Pts	F-A	H-T	Scorers, Times, Referees	1	2	3	4	5	6	7	8	9	10	11
12	A	NEW BROMPTON	9	L	**0-5**	0-4	*[Swan 35, 40, Gray 65]*	Toone	Barker	Davies RH	Draycott	Davies WH	Crone	Whelan	Becton	Wilson	Saxton	Geddes
	18/12	***1,500***	*8*	11			*Macdonald 15, Frettingham 25,*	*Carter*	*Robertson*	*Glover*	*Innes*	*Atherton*	*Graham*	*Gray T*	*Macdonald*	*Frettingham*	*Pangbourne*	*Swan*
								This game took place in dismal weather before a very moderate attendance. New Brompton put the same XI in the field as were vanquished by Bristol City on the weekend. Macdonald's cross-shot opened the scoring, but Frettingham looked decidedly offside when he got the second.										
13	H	READING	8	W	1-0	0-0	Saxton 47	Toone	Barker	Davies RH	Draycott	Wilson	Chambers	Whelan	Becton	Flewitt	Saxton	Geddes
	23/12	2,000	*7*	13				*Whittaker*	*Henderson*	*Sharp*	*Watts*	*Holt*	*Hosie*	*Barlow*	*Goldie*	*Ross*	*Davies*	*Kelly*
							Ref: J Stark	Although Bedminster brought their bad run to an end with this success, they cannot be congratulated upon making a good show. In fact there was little to be commended apart from the display of Whelan, whose centre laid on the only goal for Saxton to find the net from close range.										
14	A	PORTSMOUTH	8	L	0-2	0-1		Toone	Barker	Davies RH	Draycott	Wilson	Chambers	Whelan	Becton	Flewitt	Saxton	Geddes
	26/12	***11,000***	*4*	13			*Cunliffe 43, Smith 55*	*Reilly*	*Turner E*	*Struthers*	*Blyth*	*Stringfellow*	*Cleghorn*	*Marshall*	*Cunliffe*	*Clark*	*Smith*	*Barnes*
							Ref: F Crabtree	The entry of the Bedminster side onto the field at the start had the crowd singing *For Old Time's Sake*. They deserved more from this game, but didn't get the best of luck. Smith used his hand to net Pompey's second, this shortly before Chambers went off with a broken collar-bone.										
15	A	BRIGHTON UTD*	8	W	**4-1**	1-1	Flewitt 43, 70, Davies R 67, Geddes 80	Toone	Crone	Barker	Wilson	Davies WH	Bramley	Whelan	Davies RH	Flewitt	Geddes	Saxton
	6/1	*2,000*	*16*	15			*Malloch 44*	*Howes*	*Farrell*	*Mills*	*Parry*	*McAvoy*	*Low*	*Baker*	*Mercer*	*Hill*	*Davidson*	*Malloch*
							Ref: A Roston-Bourke	Despite losing the services of the injured Saxton after the break, this turned out to be an easy win for the Minster. Flewitt put on the opener, but Malloch equalised with a brilliant header. Whelan's fine run set up Davies to score after the break, then a scrimmage brought up number three.										
16	H	BRISTOL ROV	10	L	2-5	1-2	Whelan 15, Ritchie 65og *[Brown 82]*	Toone	Barker	Davies RH	Bramley	Draycott	Wilson	Whelan	Stolz	Saxton	Flewitt	Geddes
	20/1	4,000	*9*	15			*Paul 24, Jones 37, 75, Lewis 80,*	*Gray*	*Ritchie*	*Griffiths*	*Lamont*	*Brown G*	*Robertson*	*Brown R*	*Lewis*	*Jones*	*McInnes*	*Paul*
							Ref: F Crabtree	An exciting game on a heavy pitch, yet the football was not of a high class. Bedminster started with plenty of confidence and took the lead when Whelan headed in off a post, but Paul soon levelled matters. Jones fired in another and Rovers were on their way to a deserved success.										
17	H	PORTSMOUTH	11	W	2-0	1-0	Boucher 40, Davies R 75	Toone	Barker	Crone	Draycott	Davies WH	Wilson	Whelan	Flewitt	Boucher	Davies RH	Geddes
	3/2	500	*3*	17				*Reilly*	*Wilkie*	*Struthers*	*Blyth*	*Stringfellow*	*Hunter*	*Barnes*	*Cunliffe*	*Brown A*	*Smith*	*Clark*
							Ref: F Crabtree	Whilst Bedminster deserved every praise for coming out on top in this fixture, Pompey, who were without Cleghorn, Turner and Marshall, also had Brown rendered *hors de combat* long before the close. Following the break, Richard Davies shot in the Minster's second to clinch victory.										
18	H	THAMES IRNWKS	6	W	3-1	1-1	Davies W 35, Geddes 65, Flewitt 80	Toone	Barker	Crone	Draycott	Davies WH	Wilson	Whelan	Flewitt	Boucher	Davies RH	Geddes
	10/2	2,000	*13*	19			*Carnelly 30*	*Moore*	*King*	*Dunn*	*Craig*	*Stewart*	*McEachrane*	*Allan*	*McKay*	*Joyce*	*Carnelly*	*Taylor*
							Ref: V Daines	Carnelly was unlucky not to have been awarded a second goal directly after William Davies had scored Bedminster's equaliser with a quick shot. Barker, in trying to clear, just touched the ball, and Carnelly who ran past him and put the sphere into the net was strangely given offside.										
19	H	SHEPPEY UTD	4	W	4-2	2-1	Wilson 3, Saxton 20, Whelan 46,	Toone	Barker	Crone	Draycott	Davies WH	Ayre	Whelan	Wilson	Boucher	Saxton	Geddes
	12/2	1,000	*16*	21			*Chapman 35, Hall 55* [Boucher 47]	*Cotton*	*Macfarlane*	*Penney*	*Lissenden Jr*	*Blair*	*Jenner*	*Hall*	*Chapman*	*Spence*	*Buchanan*	*Horrocks*
							Ref: H Platt	The small crowd at Ashton Gate saw Sheppey start from the Road End, but the Minster took an early lead when Wilson beat Cotton all the way with a great shot. Saxton then netted from close in to doubled the advantage, before Chapman responded for the visitors with an oblique drive.										
20	A	TOTTENHAM	4	L	2-5	1-4	Flewitt 13, 80	Toone	Barker	Davies RH	Draycott	DaviesWH	Wilson	Whelan	Flewitt	Boucher	Saxton	Geddes
	17/2	*7,000*	*1*	21			*Pratt 3, 30, 40, Kirwan 25, 75*	*Haddow*	*Melia*	*Tait*	*Morris*	*McNaught*	*Stormont*	*Smith*	*Rule*	*Pratt*	*Copeland*	*Kirwan*
								In spite of the mud and the rain, this was an interesting game at Northumberland Park, where much fine football was displayed. A pass by Geddes allowed Flewitt to equalise Pratt's early opener. Spurs turned up the pressure after this and Pratt's screw-shot put them 3-1 in front.										
21	H	NEW BROMPTON	4	W	3-1	3-1	Wilson 8, Geddes 25, Whelan 43	Toone	Barker	Davies RH	Draycott	Davies WH	Chambers	Whelan	Flewitt	Boucher	Wilson	Geddes
	24/2	1,000	*8*	23			*Swan 35*	*Carter*	*Robertson*	*Glover*	*Innes*	*Atherton*	*Graham*	*Gray T*	*Pangbourne*	*Frettingham*	*Swan*	*Seeley*
								Yet again, dreadful weather coinciding with Bedminster home games had an adverse effect on the attendance. Those that did attend, however, saw a capital game in which Brompton, though outplayed, never gave up. Whelan's rocket-shot was reminiscent of Carnelly in his best vein.										
22	A	GRAVESEND	5	L	2-3	1-2	Geddes 36, Wilson 75	Toone	Barker	Davies RH	Draycott	Davies WH	Chambers	Whelan	Flewitt	Boucher	Wilson	Geddes
	3/3	*2,000*	*8*	23			*Bright 35, Pugh 43, Regan 65p*	*Ashcroft*	*Regan*	*Bagnall*	*Richards*	*Bull*	*Ford*	*Bright*	*Parkinson*	*Henderson*	*Pugh*	*Otty*
								Played on the Overcliffe ground, where in the fine weather the Shrimpers enjoyed the rare luxury of a good gate. Bright, playing instead of the injured Grieves, fired in the opener, but, despite responding immediately, the Minster were unable to prevent United from completing a double.										
23	H	SWINDON	4	W	2-1	1-0	Saxton 7, Boucher 82	Toone	Barker	Davies RH	Draycott	Davies WH	Ayre	Whelan	Saxton	Boucher	Wilson	Geddes
	10/3	3,000	*6*	25			*Sharples 70*	*Menham*	*Shutt*	*Smith A*	*Richardson*	*Logan*	*Henderson*	*Sharples*	*Coupar*	*Green*	*Smith W*	*Wilson*
							Ref: A Cooper	Saxton's shot gave the Minster their opener then, early in the second half, they should have doubled their advantage when Shutt handled the ball. Unfortunately Menham saved Wilson's spot-kick and Whelan's follow-up. Boucher's late winner curled into the net off the foot of a post.										

BEDMINSTER (Southern League Division 1) Manager: Sam Hollis SEASON 1899-1900

No	Date	Att	Pos	Pt	F-A	H-T	Scorers, Times, and Referees	1	2	3	4	5	6	7	8	9	10	11
24	A BRISTOL CITY		4	W	2-0	2-0	Geddes 30, Saxton 40	Toone	Barker	Davies RH	Draycott	Davies WH	Chambers	Whelan	Saxton	Boucher	Wilson	Geddes
	17/3	*5,000*	*8*	27				*Monteith*	*McDonald*	*Robson*	*Downie*	*McLean*	*Hamilton*	*Langham*	*Goldie*	*Jones*	*Pollock*	*Potter*
							Ref: G Muir	In spite of the snow, which fell so heavily during the afternoon, there was a capital crowd at Ashton Gate for this local derby. A well-deserved success for the much quicker Minster side, despite City appealing for offside when Saxton put away Boucher's neat pass for goal number two.										
25	A SOUTHAMPTON		7	L	2-3	0-3	Davies R 80, Wilson 85	Toone	Barker	Davies RH	Ayre	Davies WH	Chambers	Saxton	Flewitt	Boucher	Wilson	Geddes
	31/3	*4,000*	*3*	23			*McLeod 2, Milward 30, 43p*	*Robinson*	*Meehan*	*Durber*	*Meston*	*French*	*Greenlees*	*Turner*	*McLeod*	*Farrell*	*Wood*	*Milward*
							Ref: F King	During the opening half Bedminster showed much of the listlessness that had so characterised their play when they were freely dropping points in the closing weeks of the previous season. However, they rallied in a most admirable manner and deserved the consolation of two late goals.										
26	H MILLWALL ATH		6	W	2-0	1-0	Boucher 40, Wilson 60	Toone	Barker	Davies RH	Draycott	Davies WH	Chambers	Whelan	Wilson	Boucher	Saxton	Geddes
	7/4	4,000	*7*	25				*Cox*	*Burgess*	*Allan*	*Robertson*	*Goldie*	*Millar*	*Dryburgh*	*Brearley*	*Caie*	*Nichol*	*Banks*
							Ref: G Landragin	Despite the counter-attraction of Southampton's visit to play the Rovers, there was a good gathering at Ashton Gate, where a capital game was witnessed. A slip by Smith left Boucher free to shoot in the opener then, after the break, a melee lead to Wilson being able to rush the ball in.										
27	A QP RANGERS		7	L	1-2	1-1	Geddes 30	Toone	Barker	Davies RH	Draycott	Davies WH	Chambers	Whelan	Flewitt	Boucher	Wilson	Geddes
	14/4	*3,000*	*9*	25			*Bedingfield 44, Turnbull 60*	*Clutterbuck*	*Knowles*	*McConnell*	*Keech*	*Misslewhite*	*Skinner*	*Crawford*	*White*	*Bedingfield*	*Turnbull*	*Hannah*
								After having an early goal disallowed for offside, the Rangers fell behind when Geddes fired in for Bedminster. On recent form the Minster were expected to win this game, but Bedingfield equalised just before the break and then Turnbull notched the homesters' second-half winner.										
28	H GRAVESEND		6	L	1-2	0-0	Geddes 60	Toone	Barker	Crone	Draycott	Davies WH	Chambers	Whelan	Davies RH	Saxton	Wilson	Geddes
	17/4	3,000	*11*	25			*Henderson 75, 80*	*Ashcroft*	*Regan*	*Bagnall*	*Richards*	*Bull*	*Ford*	*Grieve*	*Bright*	*Henderson*	*Pugh*	*Otty*
							Ref: B Lockyer	Saxton was unlucky early on with a shot that ran along the crossbar. After the break the visitors continued to defend against the Minster's rather impotent attack before Geddes registered from close range. Barker then struck the bar, before Henderson twice shot in for Gravesend.										
29	H CHATHAM		7	L	0-1	0-0		Toone	Barker	Davies RH	Draycott	Davies WH	Chambers	Whelan	Flewitt	Boucher	Saxton	Geddes
	21/4	2,000	*13*	25			*Kaye 50*	*Bennett*	*Humphreys*	*Tranter*	*Perrins*	*Chapman*	*Burton*	*Dickenson*	*Clements*	*Kaye*	*Appleby*	*Johnson*
								Despite losing the services of Saxton after 15 minutes, the Minster were on top throughout. Toone only had three shots to deal with, whilst his opposite number was tested by quite a multitude. The referee disregarded his offside signalling linesman when Kaye slipped in the only goal.										
30	H QP RANGERS		6	W	**4-1**	2-0	Geddes 2, Whelan 35, Boucher 70, [Davies R 80]	Toone	Barker	Crone	Draycott	Davies WH	Chambers	Whelan	Stolz	Boucher	Davies RH	Geddes
	25/4	**100**	*9*	27			*Bedingfield 85*	*Clutterbuck*	*Knowles*	*McConnell*	*Keech*	*Tennant*	*Skinner*	*Crawford*	*Evans*	*Bedingfield*	*Turnbull*	*Hannah*
								The recent announcement of amalgamation with Bristol City was part of the reason for such a low turnout. Despite the number of goals scored, this was a very tame affair. A fast drive by Geddes brought the opener; then Whelan doubled the Minster's advantage by firing in a hard-shot.										
31	A READING		6	D	0-0	0-0		Toone	Barker	Davies RH	Draycott	Davies WH	Chambers	Whelan	Stolz	Boucher	Flewitt	Geddes
	28/4	*2,000*	*4*	28				*Hosie*	*Henderson*	*Watts*	*Boyd*	*Holt*	*Nelson*	*Evans*	*Barlow*	*Ross*	*Davies*	*Barnes*
	Home Away Ave 2,757 3,982						Ref: J Stark	Delightfully fine weather, that was more comfortable for the spectators than the players, prevailed at Elm Park where the Minster brought the curtain down on their League career with a point from a capital game. Whelan was unlucky with a header that hit a post just prior to the break.										

* *Brighton United disbanded 29/3 – record expunged.*

WESTERN LEAGUE DIVISION 1

No	Date	Att	Pos	Pt	F-A	H-T	Scorers, Times, and Referees	1	2	3	4	5	6	7	8	9	10	11
1	H BRISTOL ROV			D	1-1	1-1	Boucher 35	Toone	Crone	Davies RH	Draycott	Davies WH	Wilson	**Banyon**	Flewitt	Boucher	Becton	Saxton
	30/9	2,250		1			*Jones 25*	*Stone*	*Ritchie*	*Griffiths*	*Lamont*	*Lee*	*Kinsey*	*Brown G*	*Jones*	*Leonard*	*Lewis*	*Paul*
							Ref: E Jarvis	In unfavourable weather, the Rovers made their customary brilliant opening and Jones put them in front with a splendidly judged shot. The Minster soon levelled when Boucher put away a centre from Banyon, but despite all their efforts, however, they were unable to score again.										
2	H SWINDON			L	1-2	0-0	Becton 75	Toone	Crone	**Ayre**	Draycott	Davies WH	Chambers	Whelan	Flewitt	Boucher	Becton	Geddes
	15/11	**1,000**		1			*Logan 85, Smith W 88*	*Menham*	*Shutt*	*Wilson J*	*Richardson*	*Henderson*	*Smith A*	*Sharples*	*Coupar*	*Logan*	*Smith W*	*Wilson T*
								At 11.10am Swindon, facing the wind, kicked-off from the Upper End. The early exchanges favoured the visitors, but there was no score until after the break, when Becton found the net after Menham had twice cleared. Undeterred, Swindon notched up a late double to take the points.										

No	Ven	Opponent	Att	Pos		Res	H-T	Scorers, Times, Referees	1	2	3	4	5	6	7	8	9	10	11
3	A	BRISTOL CITY		4	L	**1-8**	1-3	Geddes 40	**Clapp**	Ayre	Crone	Bramley	Davies WH	Baynon	**Stolz**	Whelan	Becton	Geddes	Saxton
	6/12		*2,000*	*3*	1			*Russell 25, 75, 77, 85, Jones 26, 44,*	*Watts*	*McDonald*	*Robson*	*Downie*	*McLean*	*Britton*	*Langham*	*Blessington*	*Jones*	*Russell*	*Crawford*
								Ref: A Barker *[Crawford 60, Blessington 70]*	The Minster paid the price for fielding only a moderate team, due to their forthcoming English Cup game with Cowes. Russell's low shot, the first of a remarkable four-goal haul, was followed by a fierce drive by Jones, before a Geddes grounder brought Bedminster's sole response.										
4	A	SWINDON		4	W	1-0	0-0	Wilson 50	Toone	Barker	Ayre	Bramley	Draycott	Wilson	Whelan	Davies WH	Saxton	Flewitt	Geddes
	17/1		***1,000***	*3*	3				*Menham*	*Shutt*	*Wilson J*	*Richardson*	*Logan*	*Smith A*	*Sharples*	*Henderson*	*Smith W*	*Turner*	*Wilson T*
								Ref: G Peacock	In dull weather at the County Ground, it was the excellent display of Bedminster's defence, in which Barker starred, that paved the way for success. Flewitt had a goal disallowed for offside shortly before Wilson, with an absolutely splendid shot, registered the game's only score.										
5	H	BRISTOL CITY		3	W	**4-1**	2-1	Whelan 1, Flewitt 30, Boucher 85,	Toone	Barker	Davies RH	Draycott	Davies WH	Chambers	Whelan	Flewitt	Boucher	Wilson	Geddes
	7/3		**4,000**	*4*	5			*Langham 40* [Downie 86og]	*Monteith*	*McDonald*	*Robson*	*Downie*	*McLean*	*Hamilton*	*Langham*	*Blessington*	*Jones*	*O'Brien*	*Crawford*
								Ref: A Farrant	A sensational opening to what proved to be a keen tussle. Robson's poor clearance allowed Wilson to put the ball across for Whelan to net with a lovely shot in off the post. Flewitt looked decidedly offside when he doubled the advantage, before Langham headed home for City.										
6	A	BRISTOL ROV		1	W	2-0	2-0	Davies R 35, Lee 37og	Toone	Barker	Crone	Draycott	Davies WH	Chambers	Whelan	Davies RH	Saxton	Wilson	Geddes
	16/4		***6,000***	2	7				*Gray*	*Lee*	*Griffiths*	*Lamont*	*Robertson*	*Brown G*	*Brown R*	*Lewis*	*Horsey*	*Fisher*	*Paul*
		Home Away						Ref: A Barker	A good crowd in the threatening weather at Stapleton Road, saw the Minster take the lead shortly after Paul had seen his shot ripple along the bar. From a well-placed corner, Davies found the net via the crossbar; then a few minutes later Geddes headed in off of the unfortunate Lee.										
	Ave	2,417 3,000																	

FRIENDLIES

No	Ven	Opponent	Att	Res	H-T	Scorers, Times, Referees	1	2	3	4	5	6	7	8	9	10	11
1	A	SWINDON		W 2-0	0-0	Whelan 55, 75	**Toone**	Crone	**Davies RH**	**Draycott**	**Wilson**	**Chambers**	**Whelan**	**Flewitt**	**Boucher**	**Becton**	**Geddes**
	1/9		*3,000*				*Menham*	*Shutt*	*Wilson J*	*Richardson*	*Henderson*	*Smith A*	*Sharples*	*Chapman*	*Smith W*	*Logan*	*Wilson T*
						Ref: V Daines	Becton was injured in this season opener, which meant he missed the following day's Southern League fixture at Sheerness. Whelan secured victory with his double; then, shortly before the fading light brought play to an early 80th-minute conclusion, Sharples was denied by a post.										
2	H	LLANDUDNO		W 7-0	1-0	Saxton 35, 70, 75, Boucher 50, 55,	Toone	Crone	Davies RH	Draycott	Davies WH	Chambers	Whelan	Flewitt	Boucher	Wilson	Saxton
	16/9		2,000			[Wilson 60, 65]	*Robinson WJ*	*Brookes SJ*	*Jones FW*	*Parry J*	*Knight A*	*Jones C*	*Webb F*	*Jones S*	*Bartley T*	*Lowrie F*	*Welch RC*
						Ref: W Pollett	The Swifts, who brought down a strong team, started well before Saxton steered in the opener for Bedminster. After the break, Boucher registered with a low drive, then doubled his tally with a header. Wilson got in on the act with a cross-shot, before firing in the fifth goal.										
3	H	STOCKPORT		W 3-2	0-2	Draycott 70, Saxton 75, Becton 80	Toone	Crone	Davies RH	Draycott	Wilson	Ayre	Stolz	Becton	Flewitt	Saxton	Geddes
	30/12		1,000			*Chesworth 10, Foster 12*	*Moores*	*Wainwright*	*Harding*	*Harvey*	*Yates*	*Hall*	*Foster*	*Parker*	*Worth*	*Chesworth*	*Betteley*
						Ref: F Matthews	Bedminster, with Chambers and Boucher on the sick list, could only put out a weak side to oppose a Stockport XI that came with an excellent reputation. Fortunately County, who opened the scoring with a low-drive, tired in the final 20 mins and the Minster were able to snatch victory.										
4	A	WLCH ARSENAL		L 0-3	0-1		Toone	Barker	Davies RH	Draycott	Davies WH	Wilson	Whelan	Flewitt	Boucher	Saxton	Geddes
	27/1		*2,000*			*Logan 40, 60, Gaudie 75*	*Orr*	*McNichol*	*Jackson*	*Murphy*	*Dick*	*Anderson*	*Lloyd*	*Logan P*	*Gaudie*	*McCowie*	*Tennant*
							For the opening 20 mins the Minster kept their opponents on the defensive, but found Orr in inspired form between the sticks. Shortly before the break the Gunners made a determined attack and Logan registered the opening goal. Arsenal were much the better side in the second half.										

FA Cup/Glos Cup/Charity Cup			F-A	H-T	Scorers, Times, and Referees	1	2	3	4	5	6	7	8	9	10	11
3Q A WEYMOUTH	6	W	6-0	4-0	Flewitt 20, Boucher 25, 55,	Toone	Crone	Davies RH	Draycott	**Bramley**	Chambers	Whelan	Flewitt	Boucher	Wilson	Geddes
28/10 *2,000*					[Wilson 35, 40, 65]	*Williams*	*Burke*	*Brown*	*McGinn*	*Newport*	*Taylor*	*Sargeant*	*Steadman*	*Patterson*	*Dennis*	*Zealey*
					Ref: N Whittaker	Weymouth, in twice turning down monetary inducement to switch the venue, gave the reason as 'whilst they held out no hope of victory, they desired a visit from one of the finest teams in the South'. Alas for Weymouth fans, it did indeed prove to be an easy win for the visitors.										
4Q H BRISTOL EAST	8	W	4-1	3-1	Wilson 10p, 15, Becton 30, Geddes 89	Toone	Crone	Davies RH	Draycott	Davies WH	Chambers	Whelan	Becton	Flewitt	Wilson	Geddes
18/11 400 *WL:1*					*Godwin 35*	*Demmery*	*Carter*	*Miles*	*Rooke W*	*Cooke*	*McKay*	*Godwin*	*Rooke J*	*Alderwick*	*Bridge*	*Jay*
(£10.2.0)					Ref: A Farrant	The Minster had no need to over-exert themselves in this victory over the side formed to take over the mantle of the late-lamented Warmley club. Even after Wilson netted with a fine shot, and Becton put on the third, the East never gave up and deserved Godwin's consolation effort.										
5Q H PORTSMOUTH	8	L	1-2	1-1	Becton 18	Toone	Barker	Davies RH	Draycott	Wilson	Chambers	Whelan	Flewitt	Boucher	Becton	Saxton
9/12 6,000 *4*					*Hunter 25, Smith 50*	*Reilly*	*Turner*	*Wilkie*	*Blyth*	*Stringfellow*	*Hunter*	*Marshall*	*Cunlife*	*Brown*	*Smith*	*Clark*
					Ref: J Strawson	Pompey, who trained at Berkeley, were cheered on by 500 of their fans, who took over a large part of the grandstand. After falling behind to Becton's fine shot, they levelled when Hunter's effort found the net off one of the home players, before Smith popped up with a fine winner.										
SF H STAPLE HILL	5	W	2-0	2-0	Saxton 35, 40	Toone	Barker	Davies RH	Ayre	Davies WH	Chambers	Whelan	Saxton	Boucher	Wilson	Geddes
GC 28/3 500 *WL:2*						*Bailey J*	*Grundy W*	*Harding*	*Nicholls H*	*Nicholls F*	*Fussell W*	*Rogers A*	*Stone F*	*Hendy G*	*Fry*	*Fussell B*
					Ref: A Farrant	Staple Hill had ground advantage when the cup draw was made, but Bedminster induced them to go to Ashton Gate. The Hillians, who arrived over half an hour late, were somewhat over-physical in their approach, but the Minster won through with a close-range shot and a tap in.										
F N BRISTOL CITY	6	W	3-1	2-0	Boucher 25, Geddes 27, 85	Toone	Barker	Davies RH	Draycott	Davies WH	Chambers	Whelan	Flewitt	Boucher	Wilson	Geddes
GC 30/4 *1,975* *9*					*Russell 86*	*Lewis*	*McDonald*	*Robson*	*Downie*	*McLean*	*Hamilton*	*Potter*	*Blessington*	*Jones*	*O'Brien*	*Russell*
(£61.9.3)					Ref: T Armitt *(at 'Stapleton Road')*	Hugh Wilson, the Bedminster skipper, was deservedly presented with the Cup by the Gloucestershire FA President (JA Tayler). A fitting finale for the Minster prior to their amalgamation with the City. McDonald's back-pass set-up Boucher to race onto the leather and slot in the opener.										
SF H BRISTOL CITY	9	D	1-1	1-1	Flewitt 25	Toone	Barker	Crone	Draycott	Davies WH	Wilson	Whelan	Davies RH	Boucher	Flewitt	Geddes
CC 13/1 4,200 *6*					*Barker 18og*	*Monteith*	*McDonald*	*Robson*	*Downie*	*McLean*	*Hamilton*	*Langham*	*Blessington*	*Jones*	*Caie*	*Russell*
					Ref: F Crabtree	Wilson won the toss at Ashton Gate and chose to play from the Lower End. Bedminster's defence was resolute, apart from when star player Barker back-heeled McLean's shot into his own net. The Minster drew level in this capital game when Flewitt headed in from Whelan's centre.										
R A BRISTOL CITY	4	W	6-0	3-0	Flewitt 4, 50, Geddes 20,	Toone	Barker	Davies RH	Draycott	Davies WH	Chambers	Whelan	Flewitt	Boucher	Wilson	Geddes
CC 21/2 *2,000* *10*					[Wilson 35p, 55, Boucher 75]	*Lewis*	*Robson*	*Pollock*	*Downie*	*McLean*	*Hamilton*	*Langham*	*Blessington*	*Jones*	*O'Brien*	*Potter*
					Ref: F Crabtree	Pollock's injury, sustained when Geddes scored Bedminster's second, disrupted City. Off the field for most of the rest of the first half, he was a limping passenger thereafter. McLean's handling offence gave away a penalty, which had to be re-taken after Lewis had saved the first effort.										
F N BRISTOL ROV	5	W	4-1	1-1	Saxton 4, Boucher 65, Wilson 80,	Toone	Barker	Davies RH	Draycott	Davies WH	Chambers	Whelan	Saxton	Boucher	Wilson	Geddes
CC 24/3 *6,034* *9*					*Lewis 35* [Geddes 85]	*Gray*	*Ritchie*	*Griffiths*	*Lamont*	*Robertson*	*Lee*	*Brown*	*Lewis*	*Jones*	*Fisher*	*Paul*
(£172.11.7)					Ref: T Armitt *(at 'St John's Lane')*	The final of the Charity Cup proved a complete success with this game being as good as the attendance. After twice firing over the crossbar, Saxton had more luck with his third attempt, which opened the scoring. Geddes headed in the last goal to put the icing on the Minster's cake.										

	SOUTHERN LEAGUE	P	Home W	D	L	F	A	Away W	D	L	F	A	Pts
1	Tottenham H	28	13	1	0	43	9	7	3	4	24	17	**44**
2	Portsmouth	28	14	0	0	39	5	6	1	7	20	24	**41**
3	Southampton	28	11	0	3	52	14	6	1	7	18	19	**35**
4	Reading	28	10	2	2	25	6	5	0	9	16	22	**32**
5	Swindon T	28	12	1	1	30	11	3	1	10	20	31	**32**
6	BEDMINSTER	28	9	1	4	27	18	4	1	9	17	27	**28**
7	Millwall Ath	28	9	0	5	25	17	3	3	8	11	20	**27**
8	QP Rangers	28	8	2	4	29	20	4	0	10	21	38	**26**
9	Bristol City	28	9	0	5	33	23	0	7	7	11	24	**25**
10	Bristol Rov	28	9	2	3	31	16	2	1	11	15	39	**25**
11	New Brompt'	28	7	3	4	27	16	2	3	9	13	32	**24**
12	Gravesend U	28	7	4	3	28	25	3	0	11	10	33	**24**
13	Chatham	28	9	1	4	26	16	1	2	11	12	42	**23**
14	Thames Iron	28	6	4	4	19	13	2	1	11	10	33	**21**
15	Sheppey Utd	28	1	5	8	9	24	2	2	10	15	42	**13**
		420	134	26	50	443	233	50	26	134	233	443	420
	Brighton U*	22	1	2	8	8	22	2	1	8	14	34	**9**
	Cowes*	13	2	0	5	9	26	1	1	4	8	17	**7**
*	*Disbanded*												

	WESTERN LEAGUE	P	Home W	D	L	F	A	Away W	D	L	F	A	Pts
1	Bristol Rov	6	2	0	1	4	3	1	1	1	4	3	**7**
2	BEDMINSTER	6	1	1	1	6	4	2	0	1	4	8	**7**
3	Swindon T	6	2	0	1	3	1	1	0	2	4	6	**6**
4	Bristol City	6	2	0	1	11	5	0	0	3	1	7	**4**
		24	7	1	4	24	13	4	1	7	13	24	24

Odds & ends

Double wins: (3) Sheppey United, Brighton United, Millwall Athletic.
Double losses: (3) Southampton, Chatham, Gravesend United.

Won from behind: (2) Tottenham Hotspur (h), Thames Ironworks (h).
Lost from in front: SL: (4) Swindon Town (a), Bristol Rovers (h), Queens Park Rangers (a), Gravesend United (h). WL: (1) Swindon Town (h).

High spots: Finishing the season as the top Bristol club.
Beating Bristol Rovers at 'Stapleton Road' on 23 September.
Beating Bristol City 6-0 in the semi-final of the Bristol Charity Cup.
Cleaning up in the local cup competitions, thrashing Bristol Rovers 4-1 at 'St John's Lane' to retain the Bristol Charity Cup, thrashing Bristol City at 'Stapleton Road' to win Gloucestershire Cup.

Low spots: Being beaten 5-2 at 'Ashton Gate' by Bristol Rovers.
Succumbing 1-8 against Bristol City in the Western League game at 'St John's Lane' on 6 December.
Amalgamation with Bristol City at the end of the season.

Player of the Year: Hugh Wilson.
Ever-presents: SL: (1) George Toone.
Hat-tricks: (3) Hugh Wilson (2); Arthur Saxton.
Leading scorer: Overall: Hugh Wilson (19). League: Tommy Boucher & Alf Geddes (10).

AGM (Bedminster Hotel, East Street, Bedminster, 5 February 1900):
Profit (year-ending 31 December 1899) £57.1s.2d.

	Appearances Lge	Cup	Fr	Goals Lge	Cup	Fr	Tot
Ayre	**6**	1	1				
Barker, George	**25**	6	1				
Baynon	**2**						
Bramley, Charles	**4**	1					
Becton, Francis	**13**	2	2	**3**	2	1	**6**
Boucher, Tommy	**27**	7	3	**10**	5	2	**17**
Chambers, Peter	**24**	7	2				
Clapp, A	**1**						
Crone, Robert	**21**	3	3				
Davies, Richard	**33**	8	4	**5**			**5**
Davies, William	**28**	6	2	**1**		1	**2**
Draycott, William	**33**	7	4				
Flewitt, Albert	**27**	6	4	**9**	4		**13**
Geddes, Alf	**33**	7	3	**10**	5		**15**
Saxton, Arthur	**23**	3	3	**5**	3	4	**12**
Stolz, Bill	**4**		1				
Toone, George	**36**	8	4				
Whelan, Micky	**35**	8	3	**5**		2	**7**
Wilson, Hugh	**32**	8	4	**9**	8	2	**19**
Opponents og				**4**			**4**
19 players used	**407**	**88**	**44**	**61**	**27**	**12**	**100**

Note: Games against disbanded clubs, and abandoned, included.

No	Date		Att	Pos	Pt	F-A	H-T	Scorers, Times, and Referees	1	2	3	4	5	6	7	8	9	10	11
1	H	SWINDON TOWN			L	2-4	2-2	Clements 2, Fry 35 *[Selwood 90]*	**Trestrail A**	**WelhamJW**	**Taylor A**	**Davis FS**	**Jones A**	**Jones GE**	**Walters R**	**Fry G**	**Lewis W**	**Clements H**	**Mayger FE**
	1/9		3,500					*Walman 30, Jones 40, Mills 70,*	*Williams C*	*Allen T*	*Richards'n W*	*Webb H*	*Dibsdale A*	*Spackm'n HJ*	*Ricks H*	*Jones RL*	*Walman H*	*Selwood F*	*Mills P*
									The Champions of the West are given a hard time by the fledgling South End before running out clear winners after the break. The homesters' rushed the ball through for an early lead when a shot by Lewis hit a post. Fry put them in front again after Walman had brought Town level.										
2	H	SWINDON WDRS*			W	**11-0**	2-0	Lewis 5,60,70,71, Fry 44,62,78,80,	**Jackson W**	**Thomas E**	**Hunt RP**	Jones GE	Jones A	Davis FS	Walters R	Fry G	Lewis W	Clements H	Mayger FE
	8/9		1,500					[Walters50,Mayger75,Clements 85]	*Cardno J*	*Howard FW*	*Hockey W*	*Major ST*	*Mantell W*	*Selwood C*	*Smith JH*	*Jerrom H*	*Howard FH*	*Beddows J*	*Sessions J*
								Ref: J Bloor	This game, against a side composed of the late Swindon Wanderers players, turned into a stroll for South End. With his side nine goals behind, Howard took over between the sticks when Cardno had to retire with a thigh strain. A melee from a George Jones corner brought the last score.										
3	A	ST GEORGE			L	0-2	0-2		Jackson WA	Thomas E	Hunt RP	Jones GE	Jones A	Davis FS	Walters R	Fry G	Lewis W	Mayger FE	Clements H
	15/9		*800*					*Gerrish 25, Harris G 30*	*Thompson W*	*Davis S*	*Garland T*	*Winstone F*	*Bennett W*	*Baugh A*	*Harris G*	*Harris W*	*Gerrish DS*	*Britton W*	*Lane R*
								Ref: A Greenough	St George won the toss and kicked-off from the Pavillion End at 3.48pm. A hot shot from Gerrish opened the scoring and not long after Harris notched a second. Play became rough after the break and South End had cause to be thankful for the brilliant form of keeper Warren Jackson.										
4	H	EASTVILLE ROV			W	2-1	2-0	Mayger 25, Clements 40	Jackson WA	Taylor A	Jones GE	Davis FS	Jones A	**Cridland CH**	**Quinlan J**	**Pilman S**	Lewis W	Clements H	Mayger FE
	22/9		1,500					*Horsey 70*	*Stone W*	*Llewellyn C*	*Lovett FA*	*Hodgson CC*	*John LE*	*Furze E*	*McBain H*	*Rogers W*	*Horsey B*	*Hockin GE*	*Laurie A*
									Due to the Lifeboat Parade, this game didn't kick-off until 4.40pm. Ernest Carpenter, the lessee of the Theatre Royal, set the ball in motion, and the Rovers, who had won the toss, started well. South End, however, soon awoke and put on two goals so as to be in control by half-time.										
5	H	MANGOTSFIELD			W	4-1	2-1	Quinlan 25, Clements 35, 60,	Jackson WA	**Webber**	Jones GE	Davis FS	Jones A	Cridland CH	Quinlan J	Walters R	Lewis W	Clements H	Mayger FE
	29/9		1,500					*Coles 4* [Lewis 50]	*Bennett D*	*Webb M*	*Spearing WY*	*Nolan WH*	*Brain M*	*Bateman J*	*Preddy R*	*Coles S*	*Brain G*	*Stiddard G*	*Palmer T*
								Ref: F Yates	The visitors had the best of the early exchanges and Coles, on receiving the ball from Bateman, evaded G Jones before firing into the net. For South End, Clements hit the crossbar before Quinlan shot in a leveller. Good work by Mayger and Clements set up Lewis early after the break.										
6	A	SWINDON ATH			W	2-1	0-0	Clements 80, Quinlan 82	Jackson WA	Jones GE	Thomas E	Cridland CH	Jones A	Davis FS	Walters R	Quinlan J	Mayger FE	Clements H	Lewis W
	6/10		300					*Hollister 55*	*Wells J*	*Vowles B*	*Hamlin C*	*Biggs F*	*McCleave P*	*Fulton F*	*Passmore J*	*Price WB*	*Webb W*	*Westlake FS*	*Hollister W*
									This meeting with Swindon Town's second team, took place in miserable weather and in front of a poor attendance. South End won the toss and Athletic kicked-off against the wind 30 minutes late and a man short for a time. South End twice registered with shots in the second half.										
7	H	WELLS			W	4-0	1-0	Mayger 28, Clements 70, 72,	Jackson WA	Thomas E	Jones GE	Davis FS	Jones A	Cridland CH	Walters R	**Cooke**	Lewis W	Clements H	Mayger FE
	13/10		1,300					[Walters 75]	*Sheldon E*	*Ellicott C*	*Wesley*	*Gibbons*	*Luffman F*	*Fry S*	*Tulk W*	*Ellicott EA*	*Colman H*	*Sadler*	*Annandale*
								Ref: E Nettle	A much-changed home side, but the visitors, playing a substitute, were about their usual strength. Wells kicked off, and after some even play, Sheldon saved a fine shot from Walters. More pressure from South End saw Lewis graze the crossbar, before Mayger fired in the opening goal.										
8	H	CARDIFF**			W	2-0	2-0	Lewis 20, Walters 40	Jackson WA	Jones GE	Thomas E	Cridland CH	Jones A	Davis FS	Mayger FE	Clements H	Lewis W	**Adams**	Walters R
	20/10		1,500						*Becker WH*	*Farthing F*	*Scott*	*Thackeray H*	*Moon*	*Finn*	*Beasley EO*	*McNaughton*	*Cochrane*	*Luther E*	*Dale A*
								Ref: J Bloor	South End were on the offensive right from the start, but it wasn't until some 20 minutes had elapsed that good play down the left by Mayger and Clements laid on the chance for Lewis to fire in the opener. Walters then doubled South End's advantage before the break with a fine shot.										
9	A	STREET			D	2-2	1-1	Lewis 25, Hollister 55	Jackson WA	Thomas E	Jones GE	**Tutton**	Jones A	**Luffman F**	**Tooth**	**Cleak A**	Lewis W	Clements H	**Hollister W**
	27/10		*250*					*Hooper 43, Ball 87*	*Reynolds G*	*Ware H*	*Marsh F*	*Underwood H*	*Fienne I*	*Stacey F*	*Day A*	*Hooper A*	*Miles*	*Ball J*	*Badman G*
								Ref: T Hooper	The Redshirts played five reserves in this give-and-take contest at Street. In fairly good weather, Lewis gave South End the lead with a fine shot, but Hooper equalised just before half-time. Hollister rushed through after the break, but a defensive slip allowed Ball to restore parity.										
10	H	CALNE			W	3-0	2-0	Lewis 2, Clements 10, Cleak 70	Jackson WA	Jones GE	Thomas E	Cridland CH	**Whitnell**	Davis FS	Mayger FE	Clements H	Cleak A	Lewis W	Walters R
	3/11		1,200						*Pointing*	*Clark W*	*Chivers*	*Broomham*	*Cleverley*	*Nock*	*Ricks H*	*Price*	*Garaway*	*Joles*	*Young*
								Ref: A Jones	The visitors, who started with ten men, were no match for a South End side who took an early lead. Clements then doubled the advantage before the missing player turned up. Despite doing better for a while after the break, Calne were unable able to breach South End's rearguard.										

11 A **BURNHAM** 17/11 — Att: *250* — W 1-0 (HT 0-0)
Luffman 85
Ref: F Baker

Jackson WA	Jones GE	**Day S**	Cridland CH	Jones A	Davis FS	**Godsell H**	Fry G	Lewis W	Clements H	Luffman F
Puddy J	*Clatworthy*	*King F*	*Stone F*	*Bradford R*	*Leaker A*	*Ash C*	*Gard H*	*Stokes C*	*Tucker WH*	*Blake*

Burnham, who had to rely on reserve men, held their own until Blake had to leave on becoming indisposed some ten minutes before the close. Luffman then registered with a shot to take the homesters' unbeaten tag. A deserved South End success as they had had three goals disallowed.

12 H **GLOS COUNTY XI** 1/12 — Att: 1,000 — W 2-0 (HT 1-0)
Jones A 25, Clements 60
Ref: E Nettle

Jackson WA	Jones GE	Taylor A	Davis FS	Jones A	Cridland CH	Fry G	Walters R	Lewis W	Clements H	Mayger FE
Bennett R	*Nolan WH*	*Dickenson*	*Millard F*	*Palmer T*	*Brain M*	*Preddy R*	*Cranfield B*	*Rogers W*	*King J*	*Davis G*

After Arthur Jones put South End in front with a fast, low shot, their bad luck with disallowed goals continued in this game. They were not discouraged, however, when Fry had his second-half shot struck-off for offside, and Clements registered shortly after to make sure of victory.

13 H **SWINDON ATH** 8/12 — Att: 700 — W 1-0 (HT 1-0)
Walters 30
Ref: G Gay

Bellamy AJ	Day S	Jones GE	Luffman F	**Lillington T**	Hunt RP	Fry G	Clements H	Adams	Walters R	**Cranfield B**
Leighfield	*Goodman*	*Gray*	*Bailey*	*Orpwood*	*Nash*	*Roweir*	*Prior*	*Hamlin*	*Ricks H*	*Jerrom H*

South End spurned most of their chances in this close, hard-fought, affair, in which both sides pressed in turn. At the finish they had to be satisfied with a Walters shot that brought them victory. The Swindon forwards failed to utilise the openings made for them by their halves.

14 H **CLIFTON ASSOC** 15/12 — Att: 1,200 — W 2-4 (HT 2-3)
Clements 15, Mayger 25
Taylor 12, Jones 30og, Unk'n 35,75

Southall	Jones GE	**Bolt N**	Day S	Webber	Cridland CH	Jackson WA	Walters R	Clements H	Mayger FE	Cranfield B
Bailey J	*Woodco'k HC*	*Heyward H*	*Thomas DJ*	*Ormiston JP*	*Pratt R*	*Bidwell*	*Francis HH*	*Taylor C*	*Britton LF*	*Symes A*

Though not strongly represented, Clifton won this St John's Lane encounter. Taylor put them in front early on, but South End fought back to take the lead before Jones headed into his own-net. South End's shooting was poor in the second half, when the play was often extremely fast.

15 H **TROWBRIDGE** 22/12 — Att: 1,000 — L 0-1 (HT 0-0)
Everett 50
Ref: E Nettle

Jackson WA	**Hockey**	Jones GE	Webber	Davis FS	Cridland CH	Fry G	Walters R	Lewis W	Clements H	Mayger FE
Thorne R	*Smith EC*	*Jeynes J*	*Billett J*	*Readings AF*	*Spackm'n HJ*	*Grist H*	*Quinlan JW*	*Booker WE*	*Everett F*	*Hyman W*

Despite losing the services of Smith early on with a twisted ankle, Trowbridge managed to win a contest that the Garabaldian's had dominated throughout. Everett made South End pay for their failure to put away first-half chances by netting with a soft shot not long after the interval.

16 H **GLOUCESTER** 26/12 — Att: 1,200 — D 3-3 (HT 1-2)
Clements 21, Mayger 46, Lewis 75
Fielding F 20, Stout P 35, [Sherwood 50]
Ref: S Peacock

Jackson WA	Taylor A	**Binding J**	Davis FS	Trestrail A	Cridland CH	Jones A	**Williams H**	Lewis W	Clements H	Mayger FE
Speck G	*Cragg AC*	*Vaughan*	*Sessions Wilf*	*Sessions Wal*	*Stout FM*	*Robbins AT*	*Sherw'od HG*	*Stout PW*	*Fielding AF*	*Fielding FB*

South End's side included Clevedon players Taylor and Trestrail for this attractive holiday game. Two goals in a minute, with a Williams centre enabling Clements to equalise Frank Fielding's opener, excited the spectators and the thrills kept coming in this ding-dong struggle.

17 H **ST GEORGE** 27/12 — Att: 2,500 — D 2-2 (HT 2-1)
Clements 30, Mayger 43
Harris G 25, Baugh 75
Ref: A Jones

Jackson WA	Jones GE	Taylor A	Davis FS	Trestrail A	**Gray R**	**Ricks HJ**	**Stout PW**	Lewis W	Clements H	Mayger FE
Phipps TB	*Saunders*	*Davis F*	*Baugh A*	*Bryant F*	*Beak S*	*Harris G*	*Harris W*	*Whippie A*	*Garland T*	*Winstone F*

The Dragons in their green shirts and the Garabaldian's in red, managed to put on a fine game at St John's Lane, despite both being short of some prominent players. Winstone's magnificent throw-ins led to the visitors drawing first blood. Baugh looked offside with his late leveller.

18 H **WARMLEY** 29/12 — Att: 900 — W 4-0 (HT 2-0)
Clements 5, Binding 25, 75, [Stout 50]
Ref: S Thomas

Jackson WA	Jones GE	Taylor A	Cridland CH	Trestrail A	Gray R	Ricks HJ	Lewis W	Binding J	Stout PW	Clements H
Bennett R	*Fry J*	*Reeves F*	*Fry P*	*Whitchurch*	*King J*	*Bowler G*	*Britton Nip*	*Hendy R*	*Mackay J*	

In this game of which, due to a late start, only 80 minutes was played, South End made short shift of a Warmley side playing in blue and white, who were only able to put ten men in the field. Clever play between Ricks, Clements and Binding allowed the latter to secure the second goal.

19 A **CARDIFF**** 5/1 — Att: *500* — L 1-3 (HT 0-2)
Lewis 75
Coyne 5, Beasley 6, Brown 60
Ref: W Thomas

Jackson WA	Jones GE	Gray R	Luffman F	Jones A	Cridland CH	Ricks HJ	Walters R	Lewis W	Clements H	Cranfield B
Becker WH	*Johnson J*	*Winter RE*	*Thackeray H*	*Farthing F*	*Callow W*	*Beasley EO*	*Coyne C*	*Luther E*	*Godley F*	*Brown G*

Cardiff kicked-off and within five minutes had secured the lead from a scrimmage, then straight from the re-start Beasley added another. After the break Brown got through for the visitors again, before Lewis brought South End some consolation by netting a particularly fine effort.

20 A **CLEVEDON** 26/1 — Att: ***100*** — L 1-3 (HT 0-2)
Unknown 75
Grey J 2, Beavan 40, Unknown 60

Jackson WA	Hunt RP	Jones GE	Jones A	Davis FS	Clements H	Lewis W	Fry G	**Chambers**	Cranfield B	
Blackm're JA	*Taylor A*	*Pethick AH*	*Kirkpatrick F*	*Horsey E*	*Grey H*	*Beavan J*	*Weaver R*	*Blackmore C*	*Grey J*	*Taylor H*

At Dial Hill, South End were only able to field ten men. Clevedon notched an early opener, but it was nearly half-time before much else of note happened. The homester's third goal came from a scramble, before South End, who had a goal disallowed for offside, got in on the act.

21 A **WELLS** 23/2 — Att: *200* — W 3-2 (HT 2-2)
Luffman 25, Binding 40, Fry 70
Unknown 15, 30

Jackson WA	Jones GE	Taylor A	Cridland CH	Jones A	Davis FS	Luffman F	Clements H	Binding J	Lewis W	Fry G
Laver	*Gibbons*	*Fry S*	*Tulk W*	*Wesley*	*Barnes*	*Tasy*	*Salisbury C*	*Ellicott EA*	*Sadler*	*Annadale*

Both sides appeared out of sorts in this game, which commenced at 4pm. After Clements had been prominent in South End's early attacks, the home side attacked determinedly and scored after Jackson had twice saved. Luffman soon levelled with a brilliant shot after beating the back.

No	Date		Att	Pos	Pt	F-A	H-T	Scorers, Times, and Referees	1	2	3	4	5	6	7	8	9	10	11	12 sub used
22	H	EASTVILLE ROV			L	2-5	0-3	Lewis 55, 56 *[Brown 44]*	Jackson WA	Jones GE	Gray R	Davis FS	Jones A	Cridland CH	Luffman F	Fry G	Lewis W	Clements H	Mayger FE	
	2/3		650					*Horsey 2, 50, 85, Thompson 25,*	*Stone W*	*McBain H*	*Thomps'n ML*	*Hodgson CC*	*John LE*	*Hockin GE*	*Laurie A*	*Brown G*	*Horsey R*	*Rogers W*	*Thomps'nWT*	
								Ref: G Gay	The Rovers, playing in green and yellow, soon showed that they meant business as barely had the game begun than Horsey scored. A fusillade											
									followed from the Reds, but with no success, before Thompson evaded G Jones to run in another. Lewis completed his brace with a beauty.											
23	H	STREET			L	2-3	2-2	Clements 30, 32	Jackson WA	Gray R	**Elmes H**	Davis FS	Jones A	Cridland CH	Luffman F	**Martell SS**	Lewis W	Clements H	Mayger FE	
	9/3		**500**					*Unknown 20, Stacey 35, Hooper 47*	*Potter W*	*Wallace AW*	*Marsh F*	*Underwood H*	*Marsh A*	*Pearce A*	*Stacey F*	*Hooper A*	*Day A*	*Ball J*	*Badman G*	
								Ref: G Gay	South End were almost completely camped in their opponents' half at the outset of this game played on the ground of the Waverley club, in											
								(on the Waverley ground)	Knowle. A foul in front of goal, however, allowed Street to register from a bully before Clements did the necessary from Luffman's centre.											
24	A	CALNE			D	2-2	1-0	Lewis 44, Jones A 51	Jackson WA	Taylor A	Jones GE	Cridland CH	Jones A	Davis FS	Luffman F	Hollister W	Lewis W	Ricks HJ		
	16/3		*250*					*Chivers 50, Withers 75*	*Garaway*	*Clark W*	*Chivers*	*Stevens*	*Dibsdale*	*Cleverley*	*Young*	*Joles*	*Currie ES*	*Jerrom H*	*Withers*	
								Ref: E Gunning	South End, who journeyed to Calne without Clements and Mayger - playing for the Glos County side at Wells - were also missing Gray, which											
									meant they were only able to put ten men in the field for this game. Lewis fired in the opener after Garaway had palmed away his first effort.											
25	A	BEDMINSTER			W	2-0	2-0	Clements 20, Luffman 35	Jackson WA	Jones GE	Hunt RP	Davis FS	Jones A	Gray R	Ricks HJ	Lewis W	Clements H	Mayger FE	Luffman F	
	23/3		***4,000***						*Gyles FW*	*Hemmens GH*	*Wallace JW*	*Hunt TA*	*Milne SJ*	*Britton T*	*McCarthy JF*	*Phillips JD*	*Smith HE*	*Popham G*	*Giles G*	
									In this the first meeting of the two South Bristol rivals, which took place at Greenway Bush Lane, South End kicked off with the wind in their											
									favour. Clements opened the scoring with a smart effort, then Luffman headed in the second before having another disallowed for offside.											
26	H	STAPLE HILL			W	2-1	0-1	Clements 50, Gray 75	Jackson WA	Jones GE	**Fulton R**	Davis FS	Jones A	**Millard F**	Ricks HJ	Lewis W	Clements H	Gray R	Mayger FE	
	30/3		1,000					*Punter 30*	*Hudson S*	*Grundy W*	*Britton A*	*Nicholas H*	*Peacock A*	*Davis C*	*Millard H*	*Rogers A*	*Punter CR*	*Drury E*	*Bracey E*	
									Staple Hill, third in the Bristol & District League, provided a stern test for South End in this game. Punter put the visitors in front shortly after											
									Millard gave away a free-kick for handling. Clements levelled after the break from a Davis pass, before Gray notched a well-deserved winner.											
27	H	PRESTON			L	1-6	1-3	Clements 35 *[Drum'nd 30, Grier 80]*	Jackson WA	Jones GE	Fulton R	Millard F	Jones A	Gray R	Ricks HJ	Lewis W	Clements H	Davis FS	Mayger FE	
	6/4		3,500					*Henderson 4, 60, 75, Smith 15,*	*Trainer*	*Dunn*	*Holmes*	*Sharpe*	*Saunders*	*Grier*	*Henderson*	*Barr*	*Smith*	*Drummond*	*Blythe*	
			(£49.12.7)					Ref: G Elmes	Proud Preston had no trouble in winning this game, despite Hammer Clements scoring a disputed goal. The referee, South End Committee											
									member George Elmes, did little to conceal his excitement when awarding the goal, running back to the centre-circle exclaiming 'Goal! Goal!'											
28	H	SB&DL XI			D	2-2	1-2	Davis 44, Clements 75	Jackson WA	Taylor A	Hunt RP	Millard F	Jones A	Luffman F	Wiliams H	Lewis W	Clements H	Davis FS	Cranfield B	
	10/4		**500**					*Young 20, 30*	*Nash AW*	*Isherw'd WH*	*Brimble WJ*	*Slade E*	*Fishlock*	*Nash E*	*Monks*	*Thayer C*	*Young W*	*Mcfarlane M*	*Osborne G*	
								Ref: W Somerton	South End are given a scare by the local league side and it takes a second-half Clements effort to save their faces. In the opening period the											
									representative side took full advantage of having both the wind and the sun at their backs as Young twice registered to put them 2-0 ahead.											
29	H	HRFRD THISTLE			L	1-4	1-2	Clements 5 *[Williams 85]*	Jackson WA	Fulton R	Taylor A	Millard F	Jones A	**Vowles VH**	Ricks HJ	Lewis W	Clements H	Mayger FE	Davis FS	**Dickenson T**
	12/4		**4,000**					*Sharp J 25,75p, Phillips 40,*	*Clutterbuck*	*Clayton N*	*Bassett A*	*Edwards A*	*Sharp B*	*Williams J*	*Hamer B*	*Phillips W*	*Sharp J*	*Dutton F*	*Williams G*	
								Ref: S Peacock	Jackson, in fisting out an early shot, dislocated his thumb and had to retire from the fray with the score 1-0 in favour of his side. With the											
									arrangement being suitable to Hereford Thistle, Dickenson, the Waverley keeper, took over and was soon beaten by Sharp's long, fierce, drive.											
30	H	LONDON WELSH			L	1-3	0-0	Ricks 77	Bellamy AJ	Fulton R	Vowles VH	Millard F	Jones A	Cridland CH	Ricks HJ	Lewis W	Davis FS	Clements H	Mayger FE	
	13/4		1,800					*Jones C 50, Owen 65, Rea 75*	*Thomas T*	*Davies WR*	*Evans TP*	*Jones C*	*Hughes ET*	*Jones RL*	*Roberts W*	*Owen ML*	*Hughes MR*	*Jones R*	*Rea JC*	
								Ref: G Gay	Bellamy let C Jones' shot slip through his fingers to give the visitors the lead just after the break. Millard conceded the corner from which											
									Owen's drive doubled the advantage; then Rea added another before Ricks shot in to make the keeper pay for fumbling his first effort.											
31	H	SCOTS GUARDS			L	0-1	0-1		Bellamy AJ	Jones GE	Taylor A	Millard F	Jones A	Cridland CH	Ricks HJ	Lewis W	Clements H	Davis FS	Mayger FE	
	15/4		2,500					*Barker 35*	*Fairclough*	*Dawson*	*Milligan*	*Gash*	*Calder*	*Cresswell*	*Crabbe*	*Kirk*	*Ganson*	*Patterson*	*Barker*	
								Ref: W Somerton	The 1st Scots Guards, with future Bristol City player Milligan in their ranks, won this closely contested game when a bully close to goal in the											
									opening half resulted in Barker netting the only goal. Milligan was a thorn in South End's side, constantly thwarting the many home attacks.											

No	Venue / Date	Opponent	Att	Res	FT	HT	Scorers / Ref	1	2	3	4	5	6	7	8	9	10	11
32	H	TOTTENHAM H		L	**0-7**	0-1	*[Pryor 75, 77, 82, McEllany 85]*	Bellamy AJ	Jones GE	Taylor A	Davis FS	**Calder**	**Cresswell**	Ricks HJ	Lewis W	Clements H	**Crabbe**	Mayger FE
	16/4		2,000				*Payne 25, 70, Hunter 65,*	*Ambler*	*Burrows*	*Jull*	*Shepperd*	*Stirling*	*Julian*	*Pryor*	*Clements*	*Hunter*	*McEllany*	*Payne*
							Ref: S Peacock	Even though South End borrowed Privates Calder, Cresswell and Crabbe from yesterday's opponents the 1st Scots Guards, they were no match for Spurs. A screw shot from Payne brought the opener midway through the first half, before Hunter's shot after the break heralded a goal riot.										
33	H	CARDIFF**		L	0-3	0-3		Bellamy AJ	Elmes H	Fulton R	Millard F	Jones A	Davis FS	Ricks HJ	Lewis W	Clements H	Hollister W	Mayger FE
	20/4		2,000				*Brown 10, Coyne 30, Godley 40*	*Wilding G*	*Johnson J*	*Rowness J*	*Becker WH*	*Farthing F*	*Davies DJ*	*Dale A*	*Coyne C*	*Luther E*	*Godley F*	*Brown G*
							Ref: S Peacock	A capital game was witnessed by a large gathering of spectators at St John's Lane. Despite South End pressing from the start, Cardiff took an early lead when Brown beat Bellamy with a grand shot. Coyne put the visitor's two goals up with a shot that the goalkeeper should have saved.										
34	H	EASTVILLE ROV		L	2-3	0-3	Davis 55, Clements 70	Dickenson T	Taylor A	Fulton R	Millard F	Jones A	Cridland CH	Ricks HJ	Lewis W	Clements H	Davis FS	Mayger FE
	27/4		1,500				*Thompson W 5, Horsey15,*	*Stone W*	*Thomps'n ML*	*Lovett FA*	*McBain H*	*John LE*	*Hockin GE*	*Laurie A*	*Brown G*	*Horsey R*	*Thomps'nWT*	*Osborne R*
							Ref: G Gay *[Osborne 30]*	Missed opportunities and bad luck cost South End in this encounter. Against the run of play, the visitors thrice scored before the interval. Facing an uphill task in the second half, South End kept the Rovers under siege, but could only net with a Davis shot and a Clements header.										
35	H	B&DL XI		W	4-1	1-0	Lewis 40, Mayger 65, 75, Cleak 80	**Mercer**	Jones GE	Taylor A	Millard F	Jones A	Hunt RP	Davis FS	Lewis W	Cleak A	Cranfield B	Mayger FE
	29/4		800				*Gallier 85*	*Gyles FW*	*Thomps'n ML*	*Pook J*	*Popham G*	*Welham JW*	*Ross JS*	*Bracey E*	*Osborne R*	*Gallier H*	*Brown G*	*Rogers W*
		Home	Away				Ref: G Elmes	Special permission was obtained from the FA, through EH Nettle, for the playing of this benefit for J Pavey, the South End trainer. Mayger headed in from Millard's throw-in to double South End's advantage before again adding to the register from a Davis centre shortly afterwards.										
	Ave	1,587	739				*(Benefit for SE trainer J Pavey)*											

** The Swindon Wanderers Club, who withdrew from the Bristol & District League due to financial problems that saw them give up their County Ground home to Swindon Town, were thought to have folded at the time of this match. Fortunately their circumstances improved so as to allow them to take up League membership from October 1894.*

*** This Cardiff Club has no connection with Cardiff City who were formed as Riverside in 1899.*

FA Amat Cup/Glos Cup		F-A	H-T	Scorers, Times, and Referees	1	2	3	4	5	6	7	8	9	10	11
2 H HRFRD THISTLE	L	2-4	1-2	Lewis 35, Clements 46	Jackson WA	Jones GE	Thomas E	Cridland CH	Jones A	Davis FS	Mayger FE	Clements H	Cleak A	Lewis W	Fry G
10/11 800 *4*				*Sharp J 39, 40, 75, 76*	*Wigley F*	*Clayton N*	*Bassett A*	*Williams W*	*Edwards A*	*Williams J*	*Hamer B*	*Read W*	*Sharp J*	*Sharp B*	*Dutton F*
				Ref: J Bloor	This game, played in heavy rain, will be remembered as an unusually fast and spirited encounter from start to finish. Mayger centred for Lewis to put on the opener, but J Sharp soon levelled when finishing his fine run with a shot past Jackson, and within a minute registered once more.										
1 A MANGOTSFIELD	L	0-2	0-0		Jackson WA	Jones GE	Gray R	Cridland CH	Jones A	Davis FS	Mayger FE	Clements H	Lewis W	Walters R	Fry G
GC 19/1 *500 10*				*Palmer 50, Unknown 80*	*Nicholls WH*	*Nolan WH*	*Gardiner F*	*Harding W*	*Brain M*	*Bateman J*	*Preddy R*	*Palmer T*	*Coles S*	*Bryant G*	*Davis G*
				Ref: J Bloor	Both sides pressed in turn throughout the first half, without any success as the defences held sway. After the break the South End captain, Arthur Jones, drove the ball well up the left-wing, but Preddy got it back quickly and Palmer got through the backs to fire in the opening goal.										

	Home						Away				
	P	W	D	L	F	A	W	D	L	F	A
Friendlies	35	11	3	12	59	55	4	2	3	14	15
Cups	2	0	0	1	2	4	0	0	1	0	2
	37	11	3	13	61	59	4	2	4	14	17

Odds & ends

Double wins: (2) Swindon Athletic, Wells.
Double losses: (1) Eastville Rovers.

Won from behind: Friendlies (4) Mangotsfield (h), Gloucester (h), Wells (a), Staple Hill (h).
Lost from in front: Friendlies (1) Hereford Thistle (h), Cup (1) Hereford Thistle (h).

High spots: An exciting opening to South End's career despite losing to Swindon Town on 1 September.
Beating Swindon Wanderers 11-0 on 8 September.
Winning the first ever match against Eastville Rovers 2-1 on 22 September.
The thrilling 3-3 Boxing Day draw with Gloucester.
Beating Bedminster at 'Greenway Bush Lane' on 23 March.
Scoring against Preston North End on 6 April.

Low spots: Succumbing to Eastville Rovers on 2 March and 27 April.
Being beaten at home by Street on 9 March.
Conceding seven goals versus Tottenham Hotspur on 16 April.
Losing to Cardiff 0-3 at 'St John's Lane' on 20 April.
Being sent packing out of the Amateur Cup by Hereford Thistle on 10 November.
Losing 0-2 at Mangotsfield in the Gloucestershire Cup on 19 January.

Player of the Year: Hamlet Horatio ('Hammer') Clements.
Ever-presents: (0).
Hat-tricks: (2) W. Lewis, G. Fry.
Leading scorer: 'Hammer' Clements (23).

AGM (Ford Memorial Hall, Mill Lane, Bedminster, 29 May 1895):
Profit £62.4s.4d. Gate Receipts £400.9s.4d.

Players (Cont'd): Bolt, N; Calder, Private; Chambers; Cooke; Crabbe, Private; Cresswell, Private; Godsell, H; Hockey; Lillington, T; Martell, SS; Mercer; Pilman, S; Southall; Tooth; Tutton; Welham, JW; Whitnell (all 1 appearance).

	Appearances			Goals		
	Fr	*Sub*	Cup	Fr	Cup	Tot
Adams	**2**					
Bellamy, AJ	**5**					
Binding, J	**3**			**3**		**3**
Cleak, A	**3**		1	**2**		**2**
Clements, 'Hammer'	**33**		2	**22**	1	**23**
Cranfield, B	**6**					
Cridland CH	**20**		2			
Davis, FS	**30**		2	**2**		**2**
Day, S	**3**					
Dickenson, T	**1**	*1*				
Elmes, H	**2**					
Fry, G	**10**		2	**6**		**6**
Fulton, R	**6**					
Gray, R	**8**		1	**1**		**1**
Hollister, W	**3**			**1**		**1**
Hunt, RP	**7**					
Jackson, Warren	**27**		2			
Jones, Arthur	**28**		2	**2**		**2**
Jones, George	**28**		2			
Lewis, W	**33**		2	**14**	1	**15**
Luffman, F	**10**			**3**		**3**
Mayger, Frank	**26**		2	**8**		**8**
Millard, Fred	**9**					
Quinlan, J	**3**			**2**		**2**
Ricks, HJ	**13**			**1**		**1**
Stout, Percy	**2**			**1**		**1**
Taylor, A	**14**					
Thomas, E	**7**		1			
Trestrail, AEY	**4**					
Vowles, VH	**2**					
Walters, R	**13**		1	**4**		**4**
Webber	**3**					
Williams H	**2**					
Players (Cont'd)	**17**					
Players short	**2**					
Unknown scorer				**1**		**1**
50 players used	**385**	*1*	22	**73**	2	**75**

BRISTOL SOUTH END (Friendlies) — Trainer: J Pavey — SEASON 1895-96

No	Date		Att	Pos	Pt	F-A	H-T	Scorers, Times, and Referees	1	2	3	4	5	6	7	8	9	10	11
1	H	ST PAUL'S			W	3-1	1-0	Grindley 30, 70, Towle 60	Jackson WA	Taylor A	**Skelding R**	Millard F	Jones A	**Ross JS**	Davis FS	Lewis W	Grindley WH	**Towle**	Mayger FE
	4/9		800					*Unknown 50*	*Berry W*	*Hone AH*	*Ellis S*	*Marsh P*	*Cranfield W*	*Moth'sd'le W*	*Rider C*	*Elmes F*	*Ford G*	*Pook J*	*Belcher C*
								Ref: F Gyles	South End took the lead when Grindley registered from Mayger's corner. Hands in front of goal allowed the Bower Ashton club St Paul's to level shortly after the break, but Mayger's through ball set up Towle to put the homesters' back in front before Grindley tied matters up.										
2	H	SWINDON WDRS			W	4-1	2-0	Grindley 20, 35, 55, 75	Jackson WA	Taylor A	Skelding R	Millard F	Jones A	Ross JS	Davis FS	Lewis W	Grindley WH	**Mcfarlane A**	Mager FE
	7/9		**500**					*Howard 85*	*Vipond*	*Taylor*	*Hockey JW*	*Elkins*	*Jarman TA*	*Selwood C*	*Peder*	*Walman H*	*Shaw*	*Jerrom H*	*Howard FH*
								Ref: D Jepson	Although Wanderers put a strong side in the field at St John's Lane, South End had more dash and deservedly won this encounter. Grindley, who scored twice in the first half and twice in the second, was South End's star. Howard notched the visitors' sole response close on time.										
3	A	WARMLEY			L	**0-4**	0-4		Jackson WA	Taylor A	Skelding R	Millard F	Jones A	Ross JS	Lewis W	Towle	Clements H	Mcfarlane A	Mayger FE
	14/9		*1,500*					*Rooke 15, 30, Carter 20, 40*	*Demmery W*	*Nelmes T*	*Yeoman G*	*Bryant F*	*Wilshire H*	*Wilmott L*	*Webley F*	*Stone S*	*Carter J*	*Rooke W*	*Britton Nip*
								Ref: A Farrant	The visitors had plenty of the play but were unable to match Warmley's finishing prowess. Shortly after Towle had a shot disallowed for offside, Rooke fired in the opener. Mayger then blasted narrowly wide before Carter concluded a Warmley rush by netting number two.										
4	H	HEREFORD TOWN			D	4-4	1-2	Lewis 10, 72, Clements 60, 70	Jackson WA	Taylor A	Skelding R	Millard F	Jones A	Gray R	Ricks HJ	Lewis W	Clements H	Mcfarlane A	Mayger FE
	21/9		2,000					*Edwards 25, Thomas 40, 85,*	*Sund'rl'nd HS*	*Preece J*	*Cole J*	*Reynolds C*	*Edwards AR*	*Owens A*	*Lowes E*	*Botchett C*	*Thomas AJ*	*Davis G*	*Dutton F*
								Ref: D Jepson *[Davis 88]*	An exciting tussle, which saw South End put up a brilliant display against the team who defeated St George 7-1 a fortnight ago. After keeping their opponents waiting for 20 minutess past the kick-off time, South End took an early lead, when Lewis, from a corner, put the ball through.										
5	H	MANGOTSFIELD			W	**5-0**	1-0	Macfarlane 40, 65, 70, Lewis 50, [Clements 88]	Jackson WA	Taylor A	Skelding R	Gray R	Jones A	Millard F	Mayger FE	Mcfarlane A	Clements H	Lewis W	Ross JS
	28/9		1,500						*Bennett R*	*Nelmes E*	*Webb M*	*Preddy G*	*Cross J*	*Harding W*	*Preddy R*	*Hollister A*	*Coles S*	*Britton W*	*Bateman J*
									In this game, which kicked off an hour late at 4.30pm due to the late arrival of the Villagers, South End certainly had their shooting boots on as, besides the goals that counted, they also had seven efforts disallowed for offside. The Mangotsfield keeper received an ovation at the end.										
6	H	EASTVILLE ROV			D	1-1	0-1	Davis 65	Jackson WA	Skelding R	**Skeates FE**	Millard F	Hamlin C	Gray R	Davis FS	Lewis W	Clements H	Mcfarlane A	Mayger FE
	19/10		2,000					*Gallier 40*	*John LE*	*Horsey R*	*Lovett FA*	*McBain H*	*Ross JS*	*Hockin GE*	*Butler*	*Laurie A*	*Gallier H*	*Thomps'nWT*	*Rogers W*
									South End dominated the early play, but Rovers took the lead from their first corner. After the break the Southerners' were fortunate when Ross put in a drive which struck the bar and went behind. From the goal-kick, Mayger raced away and set up Davis to level with a smart shot.										
7	H	CLIFTON ASSOC			W	6-4	1-0	Macfarlane 35, 85, Clements 55,	Jackson WA	Skelding R	Hunt RP	Millard F	Jones A	Gray R	Davis FS	Lewis W	Clements H	Mcfarlane A	Mayger FE
	26/10		1,200					*Symes 50, 65, Britton 66, 83*	*Bailey J*	*Woodc'ck HC*	*Heyward H*	*Thomas DJ*	*Pratt R*	*Sharp GA*	*Taylor C*	*Symes A*	*Webb*	*Lewis*	*Britton LF*
								Ref: V Daines [Lewis 57, Millard 75, Mayger 80]	Clifton were dangerous at the start before South End woke up with Clements having his fine effort saved by Bailey prior to taking the lead. The second half was characterised by end-to-end play, but after Britton's pretty shot brought the visitors level at 3-3, South End raced away.										
8	H	ROYAL ARTILLERY			D	0-0	0-0		Jackson WA	Skelding R	Taylor A	Millard	Jones A	Binding J	Davis FS	Lewis W	Clements H	Mcfarlane A	Mayger FE
	9/11		2,000						*Reilly*	*Kinman*	*Phillips*	*Harper*	*Hogg*	*Patterson*	*Maggs*	*Maxwell*	*Williams*	*Jardine*	*McDonald*
								Ref: D Jepson	A good crowd were in attendance at St John's Lane for this visit of the Army Cup holders side, based in Portsmouth. Binding proved a very able deputy for Gray, but South End were unable to find the net in this great ding-dong struggle in which the play raged from end to end.										
9	H	FREEMANTLE			L	0-1	0-0		Jackson WA	Binding J	Taylor A	Millard F	Jones A	Skeates FE	Davis FS	Lewis W	Clements H	Mcfarlane A	Mayger FE
	23/11		2,000					*Goodwin 60*	*Domeny*	*Long*	*McKay*	*Ridges G*	*Ellaby*	*Fowett*	*Sims*	*Nineham*	*Goodwin*	*Englefield*	*Ridges H*
								Ref: W Thomas	Another large crowd at the Lane to see South End do battle with the Freemantle club from Southampton. Jackson had to be at his best to keep the impressive visitors at bay before the break, but he was powerless when Goodwin ran through and fired in Freemantle's deserved winner.										
10	H	SWINDON WDRS			W	2-0	1-0	Clements 1, Lewis 70	Jackson WA	Skeates FE	Taylor A	Gray R	Jones A	Millard F	Clements H	Mcfarlane A	Mayger FE	Lewis W	Binding J
	30/11		1,200						*Vipond*	*Lane R*	*Webb W*	*Selwood C*	*Jarman TA*	*Howard FW*	*Westlake FS*	*Howard FH*	*Walman H*	*Ricks H*	*Spackm'n HJ*
									The Wanderers were completely outclassed, but at the finish South End only had two goals to show for all their dominance. Clements did the needful from a Binding centre; then after the interval Lewis was able to turn the ball in when the keeper could only parry Macfarlane's shot.										

No	Venue	Opponent / Att	Res	Score	HT	Scorers / Referee	1	2	3	4	5	6	7	8	9	10	11
11	H	SEAFRTH HLNDRS	W	4-3	2-1	Binding 2, Welham 25, 52, 88	Jackson WA	Skelding R	Taylor A	Gray R	Welham JW	Millard F	Mayger FE	Mcfarlane A	Clements H	Lewis W	Binding J
7/12		1,200				*Banks 15, Osborne 50, Unknown 60*	*Harris*	*Cotterell*	*Low*	*Ferguson*	*Grey*	*MacIntosh*	*Hamilton*	*Osborne*	*Banks*	*Fairburn*	*Bull*
						Ref: J Bloor	Binding's swift low shot, which put South End into an early lead, set the scene for a cracking contest with the Army Cup runners-up side based in Aldershot. Welham clinched victory by following up to put the ball away when the keeper saved, but couldn't hold, his late penalty kick.										
12	H	WELLS	W	5-2	1-2	Macfarlane 7,Lewis 74, 80,Gray 75,	Jackson WA	Skelding R	Skeates FE	Millard F	Jones A	Gray R	Binding J	Lewis W	Clements H	Mcfarlane A	Mayger FE
14/12		750				*Sheldon 5, 35* [Clements 88]	*Richardson*	*Ellicott C*	*Fry S*	*Gibbons*	*Hopkins*	*Barnes*	*Parfitt*	*Ross*	*Sheldon E*	*Tulk W*	*Sadler*
						Ref: J Beanland	In heavy drizzle, South End pressed from the start, but Wells took the lead with Sheldon's terrific long-shot from midfield. Despite levelling, South End looked likely losers when Sheldon's cross-drive put the visitors back in front, but an amazing finale turned the game on its head.										
13	H	ST PAUL'S	W	**5-0**	3-0	Clements 5, 25, Mayger 35, 65, [Macfarlane 75]	Jackson WA	Skelding R	Taylor A	Millard F	Jones A	Gray R	Binding J	Lewis W	Clements H	Mcfarlane A	Mayger FE
21/12		1,000					*Berry W*	*Hone AH*	*Ellis S*	*Marsh P*	*Cranfield W*	*Moth'sd'le W*	*Rider C*	*Elmes F*	*Ford G*	*Pook J*	*Belcher C*
						Ref: J Beanland	Clements headed through South End's early opener and, despite the temporary loss of Mayger following a kick in the face, the centre-forward soon added another before a post deprived him of a hat-trick. Macfarlane's stinging shot from close in brought the scoring to a conclusion.										
14	H	GLOUCESTER	W	4-1	4-1	Millard 2, Jones 25, Grindley 28,	Jackson WA	Taylor A	Skelding R	Millard F	Jones A	Gray R	Binding J	Lewis W	Grindley WH	Clements H	Mcfarlane A
26/12		**500**				*James 3* [Binding 40]	*Speck G*	*Frith AP*	*Morris FM*	*Spence A*	*Mackay AD*	*Scott HH*	*James E*	*Clutterbuck G*	*Pearce*	*Fielding FB*	*Fielding AF*
							In cold and damp conditions on a snow-covered pitch, South End kicked off from the Rifle Range end and soon took the lead when Millard's long shot found the net. James then fired in an equaliser within a minute, but two goals in a three-minute spell put South End firmly in charge.										
15	A	ST GEORGE	D	2-2	1-2	Davis 44, Clements 75	Jackson WA	Skelding R	Taylor A	Millard F	Jones A	**Cranfield W**	Binding J	Lewis W	Clements H	Mcfarlane A	Davis FS
27/12		700				*Luther 20, Rooke 35*	*Brislington W*	*Garland T*	*Nolan WH*	*Bryant F*	*Winstone F*	*Beak S*	*Harris W*	*Harris G*	*Coyne C*	*Rooke W*	*Luther E*
							At Bell Hill a strong South End side were faced by the green shirts of St George, who included Bryant (Warmley) and Rooke (Staple Hill) in their ranks. South End were in deep trouble when, after falling behind to Luther's fine shot, Rooke doubled their deficit with a clipper.										
16	A	BEDMINSTER	L	1-2	0-0	Grindley 50	Jackson WA	Skelding R	Taylor A	Millard F	Jones A	Gray R	Binding J	Lewis W	Grindley WH	Clements H	Mcfarlane A
28/12		***3,000***				*Rhodes 60, Harris 75*	*Gyles FW*	*Hemmens GH*	*Burke D*	*Daniells TC*	*Milne SJ*	*Baugh A*	*Smith HE*	*Harris ET*	*Rhodes E*	*Drury W*	*Nicholls W*
						Ref: F Howard	Despite the dreadful weather, a large crowd attended this game on the Greenway Bush Lane enclosure, where Grindley put South End into a well-deserved lead. Taking advantage when Hemmens failed to control Macfarlane's long-distance shot, he got to the ball before keeper Gyles.										
17	A	EASTVILLE ROV	L	0-3	0-1		Jackson WA	Skelding R	Taylor A	Millard F	Trestrail A	Gray R	Binding J	Mcfarlane A	Clements H	**Leslie H**	**Belcher C**
4/1		*2,000*				*Brown 45, Thompson 50, Gallier 75*	*John LE*	*Horsey R*	*Lovett FA*	*McBain H*	*Ross JS*	*Hockin GE*	*Thomps'nWT*	*Osborne R*	*Gallier H*	*Brown G*	*Bubb L*
						Ref: J Riddell	The Rovers had most of the first-half play and deservedly went in front when Brown registered with a pretty shot right on the half-time whistle. They maintained their dominance after the break and Thompson banged home their second before centring neatly for Gallier to tie things up.										
18	H	BERWICK RNGRS	D	3-3	2-0	Macfarlane 30, 35, Millard 75	Jackson WA	Skelding R	Taylor A	Millard F	Jones A	Gray R	Binding J	Lewis W	Clements H	**Mackay J**	Mcfarlane A
11/1		1,700				*Green 53, Unknown 55, 65*	*Banwell*	*Bevan*	*Croft*	*Griffiths*	*Nott*	*Harris*	*Green*	*Purslow*	*Barrett*	*Roberts*	*Clegg*
							A thrilling game with Birmingham League side Berwick Rangers (Worcester) as South End fall behind after holding a two-goal lead. Despite Macfarlane twice firing in before the break, it takes Millard to save the day. He sends in a well-placed corner that curls in under the crossbar.										
19	H	STAPLE HILL	W	1-0	0-0	Macfarlane 55	Jackson WA	Jones A	Taylor A	Gray R	**Ormiston JP**	Millard F	Mcfarlane A	Davis FS	Clements H	Mackay J	Lewis W
18/1		1,500					*Hudson S*	*Grundy W*	*Nicholls H*	*Stiddard G*	*Rooke W*	*Davis C*	*Millard H*	*Rogers A*	*Punter CR*	*Phipps W*	*Bracey E*
						Ref: G Gay	This match, played in aid of the Gloucestershire FA, was a one-sided affair. South End pressed for the majority of the time, but were only able to break through on one occasion when Macfarlane put the ball away. Jackson kept out some sporadic Hillians attacks towards the finish.										
20	H	SWINDON T RES	D	2-2	1-0	Clements 30, Elmes 80	Jackson WA	Skelding R	Taylor A	Millard F	Jones A	Gray R	Binding J	**Elmes F**	Cleak A	Clements H	Hollister W
1/2		2,000				*Calderwood 55, 57*	*Leighfield*	*Webb H*	*Vowles B*	*Fulton R*	*Elkins*	*Taylor*	*Bailey*	*Haggard*	*Calderwood*	*Jones RL*	*Potter*
						Ref: G Gay	With Town's League fixture being postponed due to Millwall's FA Cup involvement, South End found themselves opposed by a strong side. Despite Jackson letting in Calderwood's tame shot, South End fought back for a well-deserved draw, thanks to Elmes netting from a bully.										
21	H	SE WEDNESDAY	W	6-3	1-2	Hollister 10, Unk'n 50, 60, 75, 85,	Jackson WA	Taylor A	Skelding R	Gray R	Jones A	Millard F	Hollister W	Adams	Binding J	Lewis W	
15/2		**500**				*Davidson 15, Preddy 35, Dean 55* [Binding 70]	*Bennett R*	*Bellamy AJ*	*Leslie H*	*Dean G*	*Ormiston JP*	*Taylor WHW*	*Davidson*	*Hollister*	*Preddy R*	*Blackmore*	
							A thriller versus South End's Wednesday side, with both only able to put ten men in the field. Hollister knocked in the opener, but Davidson equalised with a good shot before the foot of Preddy put Wednesday in front. After Binding put on the fourth goal it became one-way traffic.										

BRISTOL SOUTH END (Friendlies) Trainer: J Pavey SEASON 1895-96

No	Date		Att	Pos	Pt	F-A	H-T	Scorers, Times, and Referees	1	2	3	4	5	6	7	8	9	10	11
22	H 22/2	READING AMTRS	1,500		W	5-3	1-2	Binding 25, 60, Millard 65,	Jackson WA	Skelding R	Taylor A	Cridland CH	Welham JW	Jones A	Adams	Clements H	Binding J	Lewis W	Millard F
								Green 35, Hawkins 36, 70	*Boulderstone*	*Baker PT*	*Morrell W*	*Vassell A*	*Dean F*	*Salmon J*	*Hurrin R*	*Hawkins A*	*Green W*	*Goadby H*	*McKean H*
								Ref: G Gay [Lewis 55, 72]	In the delightful weather, a large concourse of spectators were present to see Reading Amateurs. Binding's fast shot opened the scoring, but the visitors levelled when Green got the leather past Jackson in fine style, and immediately took the lead when Hawkins put on their second.										
23	H 29/2	TROWBRIDGE	1,500		W	4-1	3-1	Osborne 25, Lewis 27, 40, Elmes 70	Jackson WA	Taylor A	Skelding R	Gray R	Welham JW	Millard F	Adams	**Osborne R**	Clements H	Elmes F	Lewis W
								Terry 10	*George W*	*Jeynes J*	*Smith EC*	*Billett J*	*Thompson*	*Spackm'n HJ*	*Everett F*	*Terry*	*Belcher C*	*Clegg*	*Williams*
									Terry got the visitors off to a good start with a shot well out of Jackson's reach, but South End came storming back to deservedly win this encounter. Osborne levelled with a swift shot, and then two efforts from Lewis and a shot from Elmes put the home side firmly in control.										
24	A 7/3	MIDSOMER NRTN	***250***		W	1-0	?-0	Unknown	Midsomer Norton were missing three of their best players, in this close game, played in miserably wet conditions. There aren't any details in the local press in regard to line-ups, but as end-of-season comment mentions the fact that Jackson was ever-present this campaign, it has been assumed that he played in both of the games played by South End on this day, which the Bristol papers clearly record as having taken place.										
								Ref: H Mears											
25	H 7/3	CLIFTON ASSOC	650		W	3-1	1-1	Lewis 30, Elmes 65, Binding 80	Jackson WA	Taylor A	**Taylor WH**	Gray R	Welham JW	Dickenson	Adams	**Holland**	Binding J	Lewis W	Elmes F
								Cook 35	*Bailey J*	*Woodc'ck HC*	*Heyward H*	*Mayo L*	*Thomas DJ*	*Hurn*	*Taylor C*	*Cook*	*Bidwell*	*Francis HH*	*Britton LF*
								Ref: G Elmes	In the rain, and with the wind in their favour, South End assumed the offensive right from the start. Apart from two early offside strikes, they only had a Lewis shot, equalised shortly after by Cook, to show for it at the break. Fortunately, Elmes put away a rebound in the second half.										
26	H 14/3	SMALL HEATH RES	2,000		L	0-3	0-1		Jackson WA	Welham JW	Skelding R	Millard F	Jones A	Gray R	Lewis W	Elmes F	Binding J	Clements H	Adams
								Abbott 40, 60, Unknown 62	*Roach*	*Forrester*	*Pratt*	*Ollis*	*Fountain*	*Devey*	*Landells*	*Jones*	*Izon*	*Abbott*	*Deeley*
								Ref: J Bloor	Faced by a Small Heath side that included first-team players in Roach, Ollis, Devey, Jones and Izon, South End put on a creditable display against their illustrious opponents. Abbott opened the scoring with a great shot; then soon after the break he raced through to fire in another.										
27	A 21/3	ST PAUL'S	*500*		W	3-0	0-0	Clayton 60, 80, Welham 75	Jackson WA	Jones A	Taylor A	Millard F	Welham JW	Clements H	**Clayton**	Lewis W	Elmes F	Binding J	**Curtis**
									Berry W	*Hone AH*	*Ellis S*	*Marsh P*	*GreenwayGD*	*Yendol*	*Rider C*	*Ford G*	*Cranfield B*	*Belcher C*	*Williams*
								Ref: Mr Saunders	A fair sprinkling of spectators on the Bower Ashton ground where Clayton opened the scoring with a brilliant shot almost from the touchline. Welham then doubled South End's advantage by finding the net with a lofty shot, before Clayton notched his second with a swift drive.										
28	A 28/3	TROWBRIDGE	*750*		D	0-0	0-0		Jackson WA	Skelding R	Taylor A	Millard F	Jones A	Gray R	Clayton	Elmes F	Clements H	Lewis W	Adams
									George W	*Smith EC*	*Jeynes J*	*Billett J*	*Thompson*	*Hathaway*	*Belcher C*	*Terry*	*Currie ES*	*Edwards*	*Clegg*
								Ref: W Hurn	The high wind spoilt this game, though there were some interesting moments. Clements demonstrated some smart form and was frequently dangerous, whilst Elmes missed an easy chance of scoring. Aided by the wind after the break, the visitors should have clinched victory.										
29	H 3/4	SCOTS GUARDS	**3,000**		L	0-3	0-1		Jackson WA	Skelding R	Welham JW	Gray R	Jones A	Cranfield W	Curtis	Adams	Clements H	Lewis W	Binding J
								Rough 30, 70, Thompson 75	*Pennington*	*Kelly*	*Milligan*	*Cresswell*	*Gash*	*Harrison*	*Kirk*	*Kilkenny*	*Rough*	*Ganson*	*Thompson*
								Ref: G Gay	In delightful weather the game started fast, with both citadels undergoing narrow escapes before Pt Rough headed through the opener. Weight often told against South End and, after the break, Rough put the visitors further in front before Thompson applied the final touch for the third.										
30	H 4/4	WARMLEY	2,000		W	3-2	2-1	Clements 15, Elmes 17, Adams 75	Jackson WA	Skelding R	Welham JW	Gray R	**Milne SJ**	Millard F	Elmes F	Lewis W	Binding J	Clements H	Adams
								Wootton 10, 65	*Davis W*	*Yeoman G*	*Trotman J*	*Batt W*	*Bartlett D*	*Dix V*	*King H*	*Brain W*	*Yeoman T*	*Brain G*	*Wootton T*
									Warmley, who wished to keep their side fresh for the Glos Cup final on Easter Monday, upset the South End Committee by not including any first-team men in their side. Wootton headed the visitors into an early lead, but Clements, with a close in shot, soon brought South End level.										
31	H 7/4	BEDMINSTER	2,500		W	2-1	2-1	Clements 30, McCarthy 44og	Jackson WA	Skelding R	Taylor A	Jones A	Welham JW	Millard F	Mayger FE	Adams	Clements H	Elmes F	Binding J
								Burland 15	*Gyles FW*	*Hemmens GH*	*McCarthy JF*	*Thayer C*	*Ross JS*	*McAuliffeMO*	*Slade H*	*Harris ET*	*Thomas HJ*	*Burland FW*	*Marsh D*
								Ref: V Daines	The visitors included Ross of Eastville Rovers, as Milne was playing for the Western League XI against Aston Villa. Burland shot in out of Jackson's reach to put Bedminster in front, but Clements levelled before an Adams header was headed into his own net by McCarthy.										

No	H/A	Date	Opponent	Att	Res	Score	HT	Scorers	1	2	3	4	5	6	7	8	9	10	11
32	H	8/4	HRFRD THISTLE	800	L	1-2	0-0	Adams 50	Jackson WA	Skelding R	Jones A	Millard F	Cranfield W	Gray R	Binding J	Elmes F	Clements H	Lewis W	Adams
								Cooper 65, Harper 80	*Taylor*	*Jones*	*Belcher*	*Williams W*	*Crump*	*Oakes P*	*Oakes T*	*Edwards A*	*Cooper*	*Harper*	*Wilson*
								Ref: D Jepson	Both sides were under-represented, the visitors without the two Sharps, whilst South End were missing Taylor and Mayger. The Thistle were on the offensive from the start, but they could find no way through before the interval. After the change of ends, Adams shot in for South End.										
33	H	11/4	ST GEORGE	1,200	L	0-3	0-2		Jackson WA	Taylor A	Jones A	Millard F	Ormiston JP	Gray R	Binding J	Elmes F	Clements H	Adams	Mayger FE
								Harris G 9, 15, Harris W 70	*Phipps TB*	*Nolan WH*	*Garland T*	*Bryant F*	*Beak S*	*Luther E*	*Harris W*	*Coyne C*	*Harris G*	*Lane R*	*Winstone F*
								Ref: F Gyles	South End were handicapped in the second half when Ormiston, who had injured his ankle early in the game, had to retire just before St George put on their third goal. South End improved, however, and were only prevented from obtaining a goal by Phipps' remarkable save.										
34	H	18/4	EASTVILLE ROV	1,000	W	1-0	0-0	Adams 75	Jackson WA	Skelding R	Leslie H	Gray R	**McAuliffe M**	Millard F	Cranfield B	Elmes F	Cleak A	Adams	Mayger FE
									Stone W	*Lovett FA*	*Horsey R*	*Hockin GE*	*Ross JS*	*McBain H*	*Leese C*	*Brown G*	*Gallier H*	*Osborne R*	*Thomps'nWT*
								Ref: J Bloor	The Rovers, who kicked off in favourable weather, fielded the side that recently lost against Warmley in the Gloucestershire Cup final. Both sides had their chances in the first half, but were unable to make them count. After the interval Adams registered close in from Mayger's pass.										
35	H	25/4	MIDSOMER NRTN	750	L	1-2	0-1	Ford 55	Jackson WA	Skelding R	Leslie H	Millard F	Jones A	McAuliffeMO	Mayger FE	Adams	Clements H	**Ford G**	Cranfield B
								Matthews F 35, Unknown 60	*Parfitt S*	*Shearn H*	*Naish W*	*Gay G*	*Box A*	*Shearn J*	*Barter T*	*Matthews S*	*Matthews F*	*Woods H*	*Smith A*
			Home / Away Ave 1,400 / 1,243						After keeping the visitors penned in their own half of the field, South End are shaken when a breakaway results in Jackson being beaten by a neat shot. Ford equalised after the break from a well-directed pass from Clements, but in another breakaway Midsomer Norton got the winner.										
	H	30/4	SOUTH END ATH					*(Benefit for SE Trainer J Pavey)*	Unable to find any result of this match, which was scheduled as a second benefit game for South End's trainer J Pavey. The Bristol South End first team were due to play their successful reserve side, who had secured the Championship of the South Bristol & District League.										
	A	4/3	CLEVEDON		L	0-4	0-?		The result of this game is as originally recorded in the *Bristol Evening News*, but later comments, allied to summary of the Club's seasonal record, suggest that this wasn't a Bristol SE match or even a fixture of their Wednesday side. Possibly it was a Weston South End game.										

FA Cup/FA Amat Cup/Glos Cup		F-A	H-T	Scorers, Times, and Referees	1	2	3	4	5	6	7	8	9	10	11
P H SLOUGH	W	5-1	4-1	Grindley 13, Clements 15, 35, 70,	Jackson WA	Taylor A	Skelding R	Millard F	Jones A	Gray R	Lewis W	Clements H	**Grindley W**	Mcfarlane A	Mayger FE
5/10 800				*Abrahams 44* [Mayger 30]	*Finch W*	*Fisher CD*	*Fidler H*	*Rideout A*	*Stacey W*	*Kimber H*	*Leach JA*	*Poole C*	*Abrahams C*	*Brades W*	*SummersbyA*
				Ref: F Crossley	Slough kicked off in showery conditions, but it wasn't long, though, before South End took up the offensive. A clever pass set up Grindley to open the scoring; then almost immediately Clements got away to double the advantage before Mayger's overhead kick made it three.										
1 H GREAT MARLOW	L	0-1	0-1		Jackson WA	Taylor A	Skelding R	Millard F	Jones A	Gray R	Lewis W	Clements H	**Hamlin C**	Mcfarlane A	Davis FS
12/10 1,800				*Corby 25*	*Wheeler E*	*Handsomb'dy*	*Morton G*	*Lovell JH*	*Shaw E*	*Meaker JG*	*Davis W*	*Sedgwick M*	*Nicholls FO*	*Shaw CA*	*Corby H*
				Ref: F Crossley	Punctual to time, Great Marlow kicked off towards the Lane End. South End's erratic shooting allowed Corby's well-judged shot to bring the visitors a somewhat fortunate success over opponents reduced to nine men following a 20th-minute collision between Jones and Taylor.										
2 A OLD WEYMTHIANS	L	1-3	1-2	Mayger 25	Jackson WA	Skelding R	Taylor A	Millard F	Jones A	Gray R	Mayger FE	Mcfarlane A	Clements H	Lewis W	Davis FS
AC 2/11 *1,000*				*Unknown 20, Long 35, 47*	*Farrer CR*	*Pope WH*	*Budge LG*	*Mast'm'n HW*	*Mayo*	*Ellis*	*Thomas*	*Long*	*Hopkins*	*Barnes LC*	*Whitcomb C*
				Ref: P McLaughlin	On the Westham ground, South End faced opponents composed largely of present boys of the College, some of whom recently played for the Dorset County side. After South End levelled from a free-kick, Long twice registered with fine shots to bring the Old Weymouthians victory.										
P A EASTVILLE ROV	L	0-4	0-0		Jackson WA	Taylor A	Jones A	Gray R	Millard F	Ormiston JP	Mercer	Mackay J	Clements H	Mcfarlane A	Davis FS
GC 25/1 *2,000 WL:3*				*Osborne 55,80, Brown 57, Leese 70*	*John LE*	*Horsey R*	*Lovett FA*	*McBain H*	*Thomps'n ML*	*Hockin GE*	*Hodgkins G*	*Osborne R*	*Gallier H*	*Brown G*	*Leese C*
				Ref: S Major	Although hardly entertaining hope of victory, a weakened South End side were not prepared for this size of defeat. Holding their opponents at the break, South End were optimistic, but they fell apart after Osborne registered with a fine shot. Almost immediately Brown fired in another.										

	P	W	D	L	F	A	W	D	L	F	A
		Home					Away				
Friendlies	35	17	5	6	75	47	2	2	3	7	11
Cups	4	1	0	1	5	2	0	0	2	1	7
	39	18	5	7	80	49	2	2	5	8	18
SE Wed	16	5	5	5	35	29	0	0	1	0	3

Odds & ends

Double wins: (3) St Paul's, Swindon Wanderers, Clifton Association.
Double losses: (0).

Won from behind: Friendlies (4) Wells (h), Trowbridge Town (h), Warmley (h), Bedminster (h).
Lost from in front: Friendlies (2) Bedminster (a), Hereford Thistle (h).

High spots: An exciting home 4-4 draw with Hereford Town on 21 September.
Thrashing Mangotsfield 5-0 at 'St John's Lane' on 28 September.
Defeating Clifton Association 6-4 on 26 October.
A keen 3-3 tussle with Worcester side Berwick Rangers on 11 January.
Beating Reading Amateurs 5-3 on 22 February.
A 2-1 success over Bedminster on 7 April.
Defeating Eastville Rovers 1-0 on 18 April.
A thrilling FA Cup debut that saw Slough beaten 5-1 on 5 October.

Low spots: Being beaten 1-2 by Bedminster at 'Greenway Bush Lane' on 28 December.
Losing 0-3 at home to St George on 11 April.
Ending the season with a 1-2 defeat by Midsomer Norton.
Going out of the FA Cup 0-1 to Great Marlow.
Losing 0-4 against Eastville Rovers in the Gloucestershire Cup on 25 January.

Player of the Year: Warren Arnold Jackson.
Ever-presents: (1) Warren Jackson.
Hat-tricks: (4) W.H. Grindley, A.B. Macfarlane, J.W. Welham, 'Hammer' Clements.
Leading scorer: 'Hammer' Clements (15).

AGM (Ford Memorial Hall, Mill Lane, Bedminster, 12 May 1896):
No financial information has been found.

Players (Cont'd): Belcher, C; Cridland, CH; Dickenson; Holland; Hunt, RP; Milne, 'Scottie'; Ricks, HJ; Taylor, WHW; Trestrail, AEY (all 1 appearance).

	Appearances Fr	Appearances Cup	Goals Fr	Goals Cup	Tot
Adams	**13**		**3**		**3**
Binding, J	**22**		**6**		**6**
Clayton	**2**		**2**		**2**
Cleak, A	**2**				
Clements, 'Hammer'	**29**	4	**12**	3	**15**
Cranfield, B	**3**				
Cranfield, W	**2**				
Curtis	**2**				
Davis, FS	**8**	3	**2**		**2**
Elmes, F	**11**		**4**		**4**
Ford, G	**1**		**1**		**1**
Gray, R	**24**	4	**1**		**1**
Grindley, WH	**4**	1	**8**	1	**9**
Hamlin, C	**1**	1			
Hollister, W	**2**		**1**		**1**
Jackson, Warren	**35**	4			
Jones, Arthur	**27**	4	**1**		**1**
Leslie, H	**3**				
Lewis, W	**28**	3	**12**		**12**
McAuliffe, MO	**2**				
Macfarlane, AB	**18**	4	**10**		**10**
Mackay, J	**2**	1			
Mayger, Frank	**17**	2	**3**	2	**5**
Mercer		1			
Millard, Fred	**32**	4	**4**		**4**
Osborne, R	**1**		**1**		**1**
Ormiston, JP	**2**	1			
Ross, JS	**4**				
Skeates, FE	**4**				
Skelding, Robert	**28**	3			
Taylor, A	**25**	4			
Towle	**2**		**1**		**1**
Welham, JW	**9**		**4**		**4**
Players (Cont'd)	**9**				
Players short	**1**				
Unknown players	**10**				
Unknown scorers			**5**		**5**
Opponent og			**1**		**1**
52 players used	**385**	**44**	**82**	**6**	**88**

No	Date		Att	Pos	Pt	F-A	H-T	Scorers, Times, and Referees	1	2	3	4	5	6	7	8	9	10	11
1	H	STAPLE HILL			W	3-1	1-0	Fielding 30, Clements 70, Porter 85	Speck G	Skelding R	Sinden	Clements H	Ross JS	Gray R	Quinlan J	Sharp J	Porter H	**Fielding FB**	Smith W
	19/9		1,500		2			*Punter 75*	*Hudson S*	*Grundy W*	*Britton A*	*Nicholls H*	*Brain M*	*Bracey E*	*Ford*	*Rogers A*	*Punter CR*	*Drury E*	*Miles C*
								Ref: A Farrant	In splendid weather, South End commenced their league career in front of a good crowd at St John's Lane. Ex-Gloucester man Frank Fielding had the honour of scoring the first goal when he registered with a hot-shot. The Hillians played a good game, but were clearly outpaced.										
2	A	EASTVILLE ROV			W	2-0	1-0	Porter 25, Ross 70	Speck G	Skelding R	Sinden	Clements H	Ross JS	Gray R	Quinlan J	Porter H	Cleak A	Fielding FB	Smith W
	26/9		*3,000*		4				*Stone W*	*Jones*	*Marriott*	*McBain H*	*Nolan WH*	*Shenton G*	*Leese C*	*Brown G*	*Gallier H*	*Osborne R*	*Thomps'nWT*
								Ref: A Farrant	In dull but dry weather on the Ridgeway ground, Cleak kicked-off for South End. Even play ensued until, from Smith's splendidly placed centre, Fielding passed to Porter, who shot the opener into the net. After the break a splendid free-kick by Ross brought South End's second.										
3	H	TROWBRIDGE		1	W	3-0	1-0	Quinlan 30, Fielding F 60, [Fielding A 65]	Speck G	Skelding R	Sinden	Binding J	Ross JS	Gray R	Quinlan J	Clements H	Cleak A	Fielding FB	Fielding AF
	24/10		**800**	*8*	6				*George W*	*Slugg F*	*Terry*	*Hathaway*	*Thompson*	*Everett G*	*Belcher C*	*Silcocks*	*Hayes*	*Everett F*	*Jerrom H*
								Ref: F Yates	The stormy weather kept the gate down for this game, which brought the two best keepers in the Western League into opposition. Trowbridge lost Thompson's services just after Quinlan fired in the opener, and he was little more than a passenger when he returned for the second half.										
4	H	ST GEORGE		2	W	2-1	0-1	Smith 65, Quinlan 80	Speck G	Robson E	Sinden	Clements H	Ross JS	**Hockin GE**	Thomps'nWT	Quinlan J	Fielding FB	Fielding AF	Smith W
	28/11		2,500	*3*	8			*Harris W 45*	*Jackson WA*	*Parsons W*	*Jay J*	*Harris G*	*Luther E*	*Beak S*	*Harris W*	*Coyne C*	*Weston*	*Dutton FW*	*Britton W*
								Ref: A Stacey	Despite the absence of Porter, who was sick, South End maintained their 100 per cent league record in a fast and exciting game. The visitors though were a shade the better side, and deserved the lead given them by a Harris shot. Smith scrambled the ball home to equalise matters.										
5	A	BEDMINSTER		2	W	1-0	0-0	Smith 70	Speck G	Robson E	Frith AP	Millard F	Clements H	Hockin GE	Thomps'nWT	Quinlan J	Sinden	Fielding AF	Smith W
	26/12		*3,000*	*3*	10				*Berry W*	*Brooks G*	*Baugh A*	*Bennett*	*McAuliffeMO*	*Pearson GA*	*Harris ET*	*Hargett A*	*Currie ES*	*Cottle G*	*Burley W*
								Ref: G Gay	Despite the heavy pitch, South End secured a well-deserved victory before a large Ashton Gate crowd. Sinden should have scored early on, and it wasn't until after the interval that the only goal was obtained. Robson sent in a free-kick which Smith headed neatly into the Minsters' net.										
6	A	WARMLEY		2	L	**0-4**	0-1	*[Britton N 85]*	Speck G	Robson E	Frith AP	Clements H	Ross JS	Sinden	Thomps'nWT	Quinlan J	Porter H	Fielding AF	Fielding FB
	28/12		***4,464***	*1*	10			*King 10, Preddy 60, Rooke 75,*	*Demmery W*	*Carter J*	*Reeves F*	*Bowler G*	*Britton P*	*Wilshire H*	*Webley F*	*Preddy R*	*King J*	*Rooke W*	*Britton Nip*
								Ref: A Farrant	A record crowd on the Tennis Court ground where Warmley demolished the young pretenders. The defending league champions kicked off up the hill and it wasn't long before King rushed through the opening goal. Right on half-time, Frank Fielding had a header disallowed for offside.										
7	H	ST PAUL'S		2	W	3-2	1-1	Ross 10, Cleak 50, Lewis 75	Speck G	Robson E	Sinden	Clements H	Ross JS	Gray R	Thomps'nWT	Lewis W	Cleak A	Fielding FB	Smith W
	2/1		1,500	*7*	12			*North 13, Slade 60*	*Field A*	*Hone AH*	*Sage AA*	*Ormiston JP*	*Cranfield W*	*Littleton*	*Rider C*	*Elmes F*	*Slade H*	*Stolz W*	*North AE*
								Ref: J Bloor	Despite only starting with eight players, South End took the lead when Ross registered with a lofty shot. The visitors soon levelled from the foot of North but, from a scrimmage after the break, South End went in front again before a fine dribble by Elmes resulted in Slade equalising.										
8	H	EASTVILLE ROV		3	L	1-3	0-3	Fielding A 80	Speck G	Robson E	Frith AP	Clements H	Ross JS	Hockin GE	Thomps'nWT	Lewis W	Fielding AF	Fielding FB	Smith W
	9/1		1,000	*4*	12			*Gallier 2, 25, O'Grady 10*	*Stone W*	*Horsey R*	*Marriott*	*McBain H*	*Nolan WH*	*Furze E*	*McLean J*	*Osborne R*	*Gallier H*	*O'Grady*	*Turner*
								Ref: F Matthews	The wretched weather meant a smaller than expected crowd who saw the visitors secure an early corner. This proved fruitless however, but not long after Gallier registered with a good shot. Despite much attacking South End's only reward was a late neat-shot from Arthur Fielding.										
9	A	ST PAUL'S		2	W	**4-1**	3-1	Quinlan 15, Smith 25, 35, [Fielding 55]	Speck G	**Breaker**	Frith AP	Clements H	Ross JS	Hockin GE	**Andrews**	Quinlan J	Porter H	Fielding AF	Smith W
	23/1		***500***	*7*	14			*North 35*	*Field A*	*Hone AH*	*Sage AA*	*Ormiston JP*	*Cranfield W*	*Littleton*	*Ewens*	*Elmes F*	*Slade H*	*Stolz W*	*North AE*
								Ref: J Beanland	A fair number of spectators at Bower Ashton see South End win the toss and elect to kick uphill with the wind in the first half. A corner-kick lead to Quinlan netting the opener; then Smith doubled the advantage with a good cross-shot, before North fired in St Paul's sole response.										
10	A	ST GEORGE		3	L	1-2	1-2	Fielding 40	Speck G	Robson E	Frith AP	Clements H	Jones A	Hockin GE	Quinlan J	Thomps'nWT	Sinden	Fielding FB	Smith W
	6/2		*1,500*	*2*	14			*Luther 1, Harris 25*	*Jackson WA*	*Marsh H*	*Jay J*	*Oakes*	*Parsons W*	*Beak S*	*Harris W*	*Coyne C*	*Callender W*	*Dutton FW*	*Luther E*
								Ref: G Gay	St George got off to a cracking start with Harris sending in a high shot that Speck could only save at the expense of a corner. The kick was grandly placed by Beak for Luther to fire in a fine opener. A Harris drive then doubled the advantage, before Fielding shot in for South End.										

11	A	CLIFTON ASSOC	2	W	3-1	2-1	Smith 25, 55, Fielding 35	Speck G	Robson E	Sinden	Clements H	**Edwards A**	Hockin GE	Thomps'nWT	Lewis W	Quinlan J	Fielding AF	Smith W
	20/2	*1,000*	9	16			*Graham 40*	*Bailey J*	*Miles*	*Heyward H*	*Pratt R*	*Thomas DJ*	*Mayo L*	*Thomas AW*	*Parr*	*Graham*	*Bidwell*	*McCarthy JF*
							Ref: A Farrant	On the Chequers' ground at Kingswood, bottom of the table Clifton opened the game facing the sun and immediately secured an unproductive corner. After Smith had put South End ahead, Fielding doubled their advantage when he did the necessary from Robson's well-placed corner.										
12	A	TROWBRIDGE	2	W	2-1	2-1	Porter 20, Fielding 30	Speck G	Robson E	Taylor A	Sinden	Edwards AR	Hockin GE	Thomps'nWT	Porter H	Clements H	Fielding FB	Smith W
	6/3	*1,500*	*6*	18			*Terry 40*	*George W*	*Slugg F*	*Fulton*	*Billett J*	*Everett G*	*Spackm'n HJ*	*Belcher C*	*Terry*	*Currie ES*	*Hayes*	*Beards*
							Ref: A Farrant	South End were able to field their strongest team at Trowbridge, where a big crowd was present. Smith's fine pass set up Porter to fire in the opener, then shortly after Sinden gave Fielding the chance to shoot in the second. Trowbridge rushed through their reply during a scrimmage.										
13	A	STAPLE HILL	2	W	1-0	1-0	Brown 31	Speck G	Robson E	Taylor A	Clements H	Edwards AR	Hockin GE	Thomps'nWT	Quinlan J	Porter H	Brown J	Smith W
	27/3	*600*	*8*	20				*Hudson S*	*Grundy W*	*Smith H*	*Nicholls H*	*Brain M*	*Bracey E*	*Rowlands J*	*Rogers A*	*Brain W*	*Drury E*	*Punter CR*
								South End made their first half advantage of the high wind count when, after spurning many chances, Brown fired in what was to prove to be the winner. The wind upset all South End's attempts of combination after the break during which time Robson and Taylor had a difficult task.										
14	H	CLIFTON ASSOC	2	W	1-0	1-0	Fielding 35	Speck G	Robson E	Sinden	Clements H	Edwards AR	Hockin GE	Thomps'nWT	Porter H	Brown J	Fielding FB	Smith W
	3/4	2,000	*9*	22				*Gidding*	*Heyward H*	*Brennan*	*Clay*	*Thomas DJ*	*Pratt R*	*Taylor A*	*Taylor C*	*Parr*	*McCarthy JF*	*Thomas AW*
							Ref: N Whittaker	Given the cold conditions a fair crowd witnessed a hapless display as South End's forwards were out of sorts against a much under-strength Clifton side. Frank Fielding found the net with a pretty side-kick to inflict on unlucky Clifton their ninth single-goal defeat of the campaign.										
15	H	BEDMINSTER	2	L	1-3	1-1	Quinlan 2	Speck G	Frith AP	Sinden	Clements H	Edwards AR	Hockin GE	Thomps'nWT	Quinlan J	Porter H	Brown J	Smith W
	16/4	**3,500**	*3*	22			*Harrison 30, Pearson 75, Burley 80*	*Berry W*	*Brooks G*	*Lewis AE*	*Jordan C*	*McAuliffeMO*	*Pearson GA*	*Harris ET*	*Hargett A*	*Harrison W*	*Cottle G*	*Burley W*
							Ref: P McLaughlin	In stormy conditions, South End kicked-off towards the Country end. Straight away Thompson had an effort disallowed for offside, but Quinlan soon fired in the opener. A swift shot brought the Minster level, and they took the points after South End spurned many chances.										
16	H	WARMLEY	2	L	0-3	0-0		Speck G	Sinden	Frith AP	Clements H	Edwards AR	Hockin GE	Thomps'nWT	Quinlan J	Ross JS	Brown J	Smith W
	24/4	2,500	*1*	22			*Wilshire 55, Stone 60, Rooke 80*	*Demmery W*	*Carter J*	*Reeves F*	*Bowler G*	*Britton P*	*Wilshire H*	*Stone S*	*Preedy R*	*Hyman W*	*Rooke W*	*Britton Nip*
	Home	Away					Ref: N Whittaker	The Champions Warmley always had the measure of South End, who only forced Demmery to make three saves in the first half when their opponents were facing the sun. Wilshire's long shot opened the scoring, then a high one from Stone beat Speck, before Rooke tied things up.										
Ave	1,913	1,946																

FRIENDLIES

Trainer: J Pavey

SEASON 1896-97

No	Date	Att	Pos	Pt	F-A	H-T	Scorers, Times, and Referees	1	2	3	4	5	6	7	8	9	10	11
1	H BEDMINSTER 5/9	3,000		W	1-0	0-0	Porter 65	**Speck G**	Skelding R	**Sinden**	Gray R	Ross JS	Quinlan J	**Painter**	**Sharp J**	**Porter H**	Clements H	**Smith W**
							Ref: G Gay	*Gyles FW*	*McCarthy JF*	*Hemmens GH*	*Baugh A*	*Milne SJ*	*McAuliffeMO*	*Burley W*	*Pearson GA*	*Cottle G*	*Elmes F*	*Harris ET*
							The South End team, with six men new to the Club, including the impressive Sinden who hails from London way, had more dash and staying power than their local rivals. The only goal was scored when Ross passed to Porter, who slipped the ball past the bemused Minsters' keeper.											
2	A ST PAUL'S 12/9	*500*		L	1-2	0-2	Unknown 75	Speck G	Skelding R	**Frith AP**	Clements H	Ross JS	Sinden	Quinlan J	Sharp J	Porter H	Mayger FE	Smith W
							Rider 5, Elmes 30	*Field A*	*Hone AH*	*Sage AA*	*Woodman*	*Cranfield W*	*Littleton*	*Rider C*	*Elmes F*	*Young W*	*Slade H*	*Yendol*
							South End kicked off at Bower Ashton, but it was St Paul's who created the early pressure. Assisted by the wind, Rider fired in the Saints' early opener. The visitors started the second half with vigour and kept the home defence busy, but Hone and Sage proved equal to the task.											
3	H HORFIELD GRSN 3/10	1,000		W	3-1	2-1	Fielding F 5, 47, Fielding A 10	Speck G	Skelding R	Sinden	Clements H	Ross JS	Gray R	Quinlan J	Binding J	**Fielding FB**	**Fielding AF**	Smith W
							Ward 35	*Eaton*	*Jones*	*Keath*	*Stanley*	*Mann*	*Higgins*	*Horton*	*McKeown*	*Ward W*	*Vasey*	*Prince*
							Horfield Garrison were no match for South End, who notched up two early goals. Frank Fielding fired in the early opener, and his brother Arthur headed in the second a little later. After Ward kicked a fine goal for the visitors, Frank Fielding's fine run and shot tied matters up.											
4	H GRENADIER GRDS 31/10	1,500		D	1-1	1-1	Fielding A 10	Speck G	**Robson E**	Sinden	Clements H	Ross JS	Binding J	Quinlan J	**Th'ps'n WT**	Smith W	Fielding FB	Fielding AF
							Moor 40	*Murdon*	*McGuire*	*Powell*	*Siddall*	*Shicknell*	*Selwyn*	*Godfrey*	*Burke*	*Hooton R*	*Mathers*	*Moor*
							Ref: D Jepson											
							With Bedminster engaged in the FA Cup, South End's game with them in the amateur tourney was postponed. The 2nd Grenadier Guards (Windsor) thus filled in to give South End a game that started with Ross having a goal disallowed when he netted direct from a free-kick.											
5	A STAPLE HILL 5/12	*250*		W	2-1	1-1	Quinlan 30, Porter 85	Speck G	Robson E	Sinden	Clements H	Ross JS	Hockin GE	Thomps'nWT	Quinlan J	Porter H	Fielding AF	Smith W
							Drury 5	*Hudson S*	*Britton A*	*Grundy W*	*Bracey E*	*McBain H*	*Nicholls H*	*Humphries A*	*Drury E*	*Brain W*	*Punter CR*	*Miles C*
							Ref: J Bloor											
							Only a small gathering of spectators at Staple Park for this clash that the Hillians were a trifle unlucky to lose. Both sides had their chances after the break, but it wasn't until near the finish that Somerset cricketer Robson ran through to set up Porter with South End's late winner.											
6	H KING'S OWN 19/12	1,000		W	4-0	2-0	Thompson 31, 50, Fielding A 32, [Fielding F 80]	Speck G	Robson E	Frith AP	Fulton R	Ross JS	Hockin GE	Thomps'nWT	Quinlan J	Sinden	Fielding AF	Fielding FB
								Faugell	*Ford W*	*Crook*	*Edwards*	*Wilkins*	*Humphries*	*Sharples*	*Jones*	*Worsley*	*Greatbanks*	*Ford C*
							A fast and interesting game that saw South End deprive the King's Own Lancaster Regiment team from Devonport, who impressed with their passing, of their unbeaten record. Thompson opened the scoring by putting away the rebound when Arthur Fielding's shot hit the crossbar.											

No	Venue/Date	Opponent/Att	Res	Score	HT	Scorers	1	2	3	4	5	6	7	8	9	10	11
7	A	BEDMINSTER	W	3-1	0-0	Davis 60, 80, Smith 70	Speck G	Sinden	Frith AP	Clements H	Ross JS	Hockin GE	**Davis A**	Lewis W	Porter H	**Young W**	Smith W
	16/1	*2,500*				*McAuliffe 89*	*Berry W*	*Brooks G*	*Hemmens GH*	*Thomas FH*	*McAuliffeMO*	*Parsons*	*Harris FJ*	*Hargett A*	*Weston*	*Brown WSA*	*Burley W*
						Ref: W Somerton	South End kicked off as the snow was falling, but reached the interval without scoring after a keenly contested first half. Leading thanks to shots by Davis and Smith, Ross sent his spot-kick high over the crossbar. McAuliffe's fierce grounder brought the Minster their sole reward.										
8	H	STAPLE HILL	W	3-1	1-1	Thompson 20, Smith 70, Niblett 85	Speck G	**Barrett**	Sinden	Millard F	**Th'mps'n AT**	Hockin GE	Thomps'nWT	Lewis W	**Niblett F**	Smith W	
	13/2	1,000				*Drury 30*	*Osborne*	*Grundy W*	*Trubody*	*Rowland*	*Hooper W*	*Brain M*	*Rogers A*	*Millard H*	*Brain W*	*Drury E*	*Bracey E*
						Ref: F Matthews	Thompson's fine shot put South End, who were only able to place ten men in the field, into the lead, but Drury netted from close quarters to bring Staple Hill level. Midway through the second half the homesters woke up and Lewis got clear to set up Smith to fire them back in front.										
9	H	SCOTS GUARDS	W	4-3	1-3	Brown 30, Quinlan 60, 85,	Speck G	Robson E	Taylor A	Clements H	Edwards AR	Hockin GE	Thomps'nWT	Quinlan J	Sinden	**Brown J**	Smith W
	13/3	2,500				*Rough 10, 25, Unknown 40*	*Pennington*	*Dawson*	*Kelly*	*Cresswell*	*Campbell*	*O'Neill*	*Currie*	*Kirk*	*Rough*	*Ganson*	*Innes*
						[Edwards 89]	South End started well, but the Guards soon retaliated and Private Rough put them in front with a shot that struck the upright before finding the net. South End, who opened their account with a good goal from Thompson's centre, were indebted to a tricky shot for their late winner.										
10	H	GLOS REGIMENT	D	3-3	3-1	Fielding 10, Quinlan 20, Unknown 35	Speck G	Davis FS	Sinden	Clements H	Ross JS	Hockin GE	Thomps'nWT	Quinlan J	**Davis A**	Fielding FB	Smith W
	10/4	1,500				*Heath 40, Pitney 55, Unknown 70*	*Hathway*	*Burke*	*Livingstone*	*Heath*	*Beard*	*Amos*	*Wethered*	*Russell*	*Hill*	*Johnson*	*Pitney*
						Ref: G Peacock	Fielding opened South End's account when netting from Smith's fine centre. Quinlan soon doubled the advantage with a shot that struck the crossbar and dropped into the net. Private Heath brought the Regimental side back into the game with a grand drive that Speck couldn't stop.										
11	H	VAMPIRES	L	0-2	0-1		Speck G	Sinden	Frith FP	Millard F	Clements H	Hockin GE	Quinlan J	Fielding AF	Brown J	Fielding FB	Smith W
	17/4	1,000				*Cane 40, McLachlan 75*	*Waller*	*Handsomb'dy*	*Marshall*	*Masterman*	*Bentley*	*Spierpoint*	*Fry*	*Wilkins*	*Cane*	*McLachlan*	*Hay*
						Ref: P McLaughlin	The stormy weather kept the crowd down at St John's Lane, where the Vampires started well. Cane shot over when well placed, but made amends not long after when he netted with a splendid ground-shot. After the break, McLachlan returned to good effect when Speck cleared.										
12	H	BARKING WDVILLE	W	1-0	1-0	Porter 25	Speck G	Breaker	Sinden	Clements H	Ross JS	Hockin GE	Thomps'nWT	Quinlan J	Porter H	Brown J	Smith W
	19/4	2,000					*McCappin*	*Chalk*	*Hirst*	*Chalk*	*Breens*	*Grant*	*Campbell*	*Randall*	*Inglis*	*Langford*	*Deane*
							A large crowd at St John's Lane for this holiday morning game against Barking Woodville, who won the Essex County Cup in 1894 and 1896, as well as securing the West Ham Charity Cup in 1894 and 1895. Porter's hot-shot settled the contest; he neatly converted Thompson's centre.										

FAC/Amt Cup/Glos Cup/Ch Cup		F-A	H-T	Scorers, Times, and Referees	1	2	3	4	5	6	7	8	9	10	11
Q1 H BEDMINSTER 2	L	2-4	2-3	Fielding A 30, Smith 32	Speck G	Skelding R	Sinden	Clements H	Ross JS	Gray R	Quinlan J	Porter H	Fielding FB	Fielding AF	Smith W
10/10 4,500 *5*				*Currie 5, 75, Cottle 15,*	*Lewis AE*	*Brooks G*	*Hemmens GH*	*Baugh A*	*McAuliffeMO*	*Pearson GA*	*McCarthy JF*	*Harris ET*	*Currie ES*	*Cottle G*	*Burley W*
				Ref: M Plomer *[McCarthy 25]*	The Minster, strengthened by the inclusion of Currie from Corsham, who fired in their early opener, thoroughly deserved this victory. Three goals in the opening 25 minutes almost killed off South End, but two quick strikes kept the game alive until Currie shot in Bedminster's fourth.										
Q2 A BEDMINSTER 2	D	3-3	3-2	Stout 21, Fielding F 30, Ross 45	Speck G	Robson E	Frith AP	Clements H	Ross JS	Sinden	Thomps'nWT	Porter H	Stout PW	Fielding AF	Fielding FB
AC 7/11 *2,500* *5*				*Burley 9, Currie 20, McAuliffe 57*	*Berry W*	*Fudge*	*Hemmens GH*	*Baugh A*	*McAuliffeMO*	*Pearson GA*	*Harris FJ*	*Bennett*	*Currie ES*	*Cottle G*	*Burley W*
				Ref: A Farrant	On Bedminster's new Ashton Gate ground, South End were soon in trouble when Burley registered with a capital shot. Things got bleaker when Currie slid in number two, but Stout and Frank Fielding fired through to even matters before Ross put them ahead with a high shot.										
R H BEDMINSTER 2	W	2-1	1-0	Smith 30, Thompson 50	Speck G	Robson E	Sinden	Clements H	Ross JS	Hockin GE	Thomps'nWT	Quinlan J	Porter H	Fielding FB	Smith W
AC 14/11 1,500 *5*				*Unknown 70*	*Berry W*	*Fudge*	*Hemmens GH*	*Baugh A*	*McAuliffeMO*	*Pearson GA*	*Harris FJ*	*Bennett*	*Currie ES*	*Cottle G*	*Harris ET*
				Ref: F Goff	With the return of last week's rain – though this time a perfect deluge, accompanied by a tempest – both sides did well to put on an entertaining game. A bully around goal saw Smith notch the opener, then after the break Thompson shot in the second, before the Minster forced in a reply.										
Q3 H TROWBRIDGE 2	W	3-0	1-0	Thompson 15, 70, Quinlan 75	Speck G	Robson E	Sinden	Clements H	Ross JS	Hockin GE	Thomps'nWT	Quinlan J	Porter H	Fielding AF	Fielding FB
AC 21/11 800 *7*					*George W*	*Slugg F*	*Lane*	*Hathaway*	*Everett G*	*Spackm'n HJ*	*Belcher C*	*Terry*	*Sheldon*	*Adams F*	*Jerrom H*
				Ref: N Whittaker	An enthusiastic crowd saw Thompson put South End in front when George could only partially fist away Arthur Fielding's effort. Despite exerting much pressure thereafter, the Town were still trailing at the break. It took Thompson's headed effort to quell the dangerous visitors.										
QF A ST GEORGE 2	W	2-0	2-0	Fielding F 30, Fielding A 31	Speck G	Frith AP	Robson E	Clements H	Ross JS	Hockin GE	Millard F	Quinlan J	Sinden	Fielding AF	Fielding FB
AC 12/12 *2,000* *4*					*Jackson WA*	*Parsons*	*Jay J*	*Harris G*	*Luther E*	*Beak S*	*Harris W*	*Coyne C*	*Weston*	*Dutton FW*	*Britton W*
				Ref: A Stacey	Despite the match being played as a friendly, due to the poor condition of the pitch, the fact that it was played to a conclusion made it a cup-tie according to rule 12 of the competition. Frank Fielding opened the scoring with an easy shot, before his brother netted almost from the re-start.										
1 H OLD CARTHSIANS 2	L	0-10	0-2	*[Tringham 15, 52, 65, Buzzard 63]*	Speck G	Robson E	Frith AP	Clements H	Ross JS	Hockin GE	Thomps'nWT	Quinlan J	Porter H	Fielding AF	Fielding FB
AC 30/1 1,700 -				*Smith 10,50,57,80,85,Cl'mts 55og,*	*Wilkinson B*	*Bray EH*	*Timmis WW*	*Bliss EC*	*Brown C*	*Darvell S*	*Jameson EM*	*Tringham E*	*Smith GO*	*Buzzard EF*	*Hewitt CD*
				Ref: P McLaughlin	The Old Carthusians were not put off by the terribly muddy conditions as they thoroughly outclassed South End. After Smith put them in front with a hot shot early on, six goals in a quarter of an hour spell following the break has the fans marvelling at the skill of the famous visitors.										
2 A FISHPONDS 2	L	1-3	1-3	Davis 30og	Speck G	Millard F	Sinden	Clements H	Ross JS	Hockin GE	Thomps'nWT	**Tucker W**	Quinlan J	Fielding AF	Fielding FB
GC 27/2 *600* *2:5*				*Nash F 3, Roberts 20, Mitchell 35*	*Nash AW*	*Brimble WJ*	*Strange*	*Davis*	*Osborne*	*Bees*	*Monks*	*Mitchell*	*Nash E*	*Roberts A*	*Isles B*
				Ref: A Farrant	South End's Glos Cup hoodoo continued at Fishponds, where an early corner-kick was so well placed that Speck was unable to clear. Matters got worse when Roberts notched another goal for the underdogs, whilst South End's only response was when Davis fired into his own net.										
1 H EASTVILLE WDRS 2	W	4-1	1-1	Brown 5, Th'pson 75, Quinlan 85, 90	Speck G	Taylor A	Sinden	Ross JS	Edwards AR	Hockin GE	Thomps'nWT	Quinlan J	Clements H	Brown J	Smith W
CC 20/3 2,000 *2:2* (£21.17.7)				*Horseman 40*	*Rodway*	*Llewellyn C*	*Harding*	*Hodgkins E*	*Higgs*	*Smith*	*Ogborne*	*Hodgkins G*	*Horseman*	*Brain*	*Moss*
				Ref: F Gyles	This 1st Round Bristol Charity Cup clash opened in South End quarters where the Wanderers secured a fruitless corner. Then the home side attacked and Clements made a splendid opening, which Brown turned to account. The visitors levelled by charging Speck into his own net.										
SF H ST PAUL'S 2	W	2-1	1-0	Brown 20, Thompson 70	Speck G	Frith AP	Sinden	Clements H	Ross JS	Hockin GE	Thomps'nWT	Quinlan J	Brown J	Tucker W	Smith W
CC 20/4 1,500 *7* (£24)				*Cranfield 75*	*Lloyd*	*Hone AH*	*Ewens*	*Ormiston JP*	*Cranfield W*	*Littleton*	*Rider C*	*Elmes F*	*Slade H*	*Stolz W*	*North AE*
				Ref: P McLaughlin	In delightful weather, the visitors lost the toss and had the sun in their eyes at the start. From Thompson's fine centre, Brown put in South End's opener. St Paul's spurned their chances before Cranfield shot in for them, but by then South End had added to their score from a rush.										
F N WARMLEY 2	L	1-2	0-1	Porter 75	Speck G	Clements H	Sinden	Millard F	Ross JS	Hockin GE	Thomps'nWT	Quinlan J	Porter H	Brown J	Smith W
CC 30/4 *1,800* *1* (£25+)				*Stone 40, Hyman 77*	*Davis W*	*Carter J*	*Reeves J*	*Bowler G*	*Britton P*	*Wilshire H*	*Stone S*	*Preedy R*	*Hyman W*	*Rooke W*	*Britton Nip*
				Ref: W Somerton *(at 'Stapleton Road')*.	The final of the Bristol Charity Cup was played, before a fair sized crowd, on the Rovers new Stapleton Road ground. Warmley raced away from the start and quickly obtained two unproductive corners. After the break, Smith's centre was rushed through for South End's equaliser.										

WESTERN LEAGUE	P	W	D	L	Home F	Home A	W	D	L	Away F	Away A	Pts
1 Warmley	16	7	1	0	23	3	6	1	1	19	6	28
2 SOUTH END	16	5	0	3	14	13	6	0	2	14	9	22
3 Bedminster	16	4	1	3	14	6	4	1	3	18	10	18
4 St George	16	5	1	2	17	10	3	0	5	10	13	17
5 Eastville Rov*	16	2	1	5	9	11	5	1	2	16	12	14
6 Trowbridge T	16	4	1	3	13	9	1	2	5	8	21	13
7 St Paul's	16	2	2	4	11	14	1	3	4	18	17	11
8 Staple Hill	16	2	0	6	12	22	3	0	5	6	17	10
9 Clifton Assoc	16	2	1	5	14	26	2	0	6	5	22	9
* *Two points. deducted*	144	33	8	31	127	114	31	8	33	114	127	142
Friendlies	12	6	2	1	20	11	2	0	1	6	4	
Cups	10	4	0	2	13	17	1	1	2	7	8	
	38	15	2	6	47	41	9	1	5	27	21	
SE Wed	6	4	0	2	19	12	0	0	0	0	0	

Odds & ends

Double wins: (4) Staple Hill, Trowbridge Town, St Paul's, Clifton Association.
Double losses: (1) Warmley.

Won from behind: (1) St George (h).
Lost from in front: (1) Bedminster (h).

High spots: The winning start to South End's Western League career by beating Staple Hill 3-1.
Beating Eastville Rovers on 26 September.
Winning 1-0 against Bedminster at 'Ashton Gate' on Boxing Day.
Beating Bedminster in the Amateur Cup.
Reaching the 1st Round Proper of the Amateur Cup.

Low spots: Losing 0-4 at Warmley on 28 December.
Succumbing 1-3 at home to Bedminster on 16 April.
Losing 0-3 at home to Warmley on 24 April.
Going down to a record home defeat versus the Old Carthusian's in the Amateur Cup.
Failing to break the Club's Gloucestershire Cup duck by losing at Fishponds on 27 February.
Warmley's success in the Final of the Bristol Charity Cup on 30 April.

Player of the Year: 'Hammer' Clements.
Ever-presents: (2) George Speck, 'Hammer' Clements.
Hat-tricks: (0)
Leading scorer: Overall: Frank Fielding and J. Quinlan (11). League: W. Smith (6).

Players (Cont'd): League: Andrews; Jones, Arthur. Friendlies: Barrett; Davis, FS; Fulton; Painter; Thompson, A; Young, W (all 1 appearance).

	Appearances Lge	LC	FAC	Goals Lge	LC	FAC	Tot
Binding, J	**1**		2				
Breaker	**1**		1				
Brown, J	**4**	3	3	**1**	2	1	**4**
Cleak, A	**3**			**1**			**1**
Clements, 'Hammer'	**16**	10	10	**1**			**1**
Davis, A			2			2	**2**
Edwards, AR	**6**	1	1			1	**1**
Fielding, Arthur	**7**	6	5	**4**	2	3	**9**
Fielding, Frank	**10**	7	6	**5**	2	4	**11**
Frith, AP	**7**	4	3				
Gray, R	**4**	1	3				
Hockin, GE	**11**	8	8				
Lewis, W	**3**		2	**1**			**1**
Millard, Fred	**1**	3	2				
Niblett, F			1			1	**1**
Porter, H	**8**	6	5	**3**	1	3	**7**
Quinlan, J	**12**	9	10	**4**	3	4	**11**
Robson, E	**10**	5	4				
Ross, JS	**9**	10	9	**2**	1		**3**
Sharp, J	**1**		2				
Sinden	**13**	9	12				
Skelding, Robert	**3**	1	3				
Smith, W	**14**	5	11	**6**	2	2	**10**
Speck, George	**16**	10	12				
Stout, Percy		1			1		**1**
Taylor, A	**2**	1	1				
Thompson, WT	**12**	8	7		5	3	**8**
Tucker, W		2					
Players (Cont'd)	**2**		6				
Players short			1				
Opponents og					1		**1**
Unknown scorers						2	**2**
36 players used	**176**	**110**	**126**	**28**	**20**	**26**	**74**

No	Date		Att	Pos	Pt	F-A	H-T	Scorers, Times, and Referees	1	2	3	4	5	6	7	8	9	10	11
1	H	WOLVERTON			W	7-4	6-1	Russell 4, Caie15,32,40,Higgins 20,	Monteith	Davy	Sinclair	Mann	Higgins	Hamilton	Wyllie	Carnelly	Caie	O'Brien P	Russell
	11/9		4,000		2			*Worsley 30,55,Radford 65,Poole 70*	*Waller*	*Moss*	*Worker*	*Mack*	*Edwards*	*Dormer*	*Wesley*	*Radford*	*Worsley*	*Poole*	*Frost*
								Ref: J Beanland [Carnelly 23,80]	Despite having the sun in their eyes at the start, City's shooting was not impaired. Russell beat Waller with a fine shot to open their account, and not long after Caie netted with a beauty. Carnelly fired in the final goal of the game to end Wolverton's spirited second-half comeback.										
2	A	MILLWALL ATH			W	6-2	2-1	Caie 5, O'Brien 30, 75, 80, 85,	Monteith	Davy	Sinclair	Mann	Higgins	Hamilton	Wyllie	Carnelly	Caie	O'Brien P	Russell
	18/9		*6,000*		4			*Davies 40, Almond 65* [Carnelly 55]	*Traynor C*	*Graham*	*Robson*	*King*	*Almond*	*Curley*	*Davies J*	*Calvey*	*Traynor A*	*Davis W*	*Geddes*
								Ref: A Cecil-Knight	Caie shot in City's early opener; then O'Brien fired past Traynor to double the advantage despite Higgins being off the field receiving treatment. Davis got Millwall back into the game with a cross-shot, but there was to be no stopping City as they pulled off a brilliant success.										
3	A	GRAVESEND		4	D	2-2	2-1	Higgins 35, 40	Monteith	Davy	Caie	Mann	Higgins	Hamilton	Wyllie	Carnelly	**Jones**	O'Brien P	Russell
	2/10		*3,000*	*7*	5			*Reynolds 10, Mobley 80*	*Bagnall*	*Buist*	*Cole*	*Innes*	*Bull*	*Turner E*	*Reynolds*	*McDonald*	*Mobley*	*Andrews*	*Johnson*
								Ref: H Walker	City didn't wake up until after Reynolds had put the homesters in front. Higgins, who twice earlier had been denied by the crossbar, equalised with a fine shot after Wyllie had a goal disallowed for offside. City protested to no avail that Mobley had fisted in Gravesend's late point saver.										
4	A	NEW BROMPTON		3	W	2-1	0-1	Davy 70, Higgins 89	Monteith	Davy	Lewis	Clements	Higgins	Hamilton	Wyllie	Mann	Caie	O'Brien P	Russell
	9/10		*5,000*	*5*	7			*Ford 5*	*Jones*	*King*	*Watson*	*Gentle*	*Meager*	*Graham*	*Hutcheson*	*Frettingham*	*Ford*	*Skea*	*Gallacher*
								Ref: E McDonald	A new record crowd at New Brompton saw City captain 'Sandy' Higgins obtain a deserved late winner to settle this keen and exciting struggle. Davy equalised Ford's early opener with a splendid shot, but was injured in the process and was but a passenger for the rest of the game.										
5	H	NORTHFLEET		2	W	3-2	2-1	Mann 22, Carnelly 35, 75	Monteith	Davy	**Milligan**	Mann	Higgins	Hamilton	Wyllie	Carnelly	Caie	O'Brien P	Russell
	23/10		4,500	*12*	9			*Moody 27, Nicholl 50*	*Clare*	*Weaver*	*Bagnall*	*Wright*	*Bundock*	*Bailey*	*Cook*	*Wolfe*	*Nicholl*	*Moody*	*Campbell*
								Ref: H Platt	A fast and extremely even game is witnessed by the crowd, which included the Lord Mayor, Ald RH Symes, who kicked off the second half. Mann opened the scoring with a beauty that grazed the underside of the crossbar after a free-kick for hands, but Moody levelled from close in.										
6	A	CHATHAM		3	D	0-0	0-0		Monteith	Davy	Milligan	Mann	Higgins	Hamilton	Wyllie	Carnelly	Caie	O'Brien P	Russell
	6/11		*5,000*	*2*	10				*Robertson*	*McKie*	*Humphreys*	*Smith*	*Hughes*	*Russell*	*Lawrence*	*Leatherbar'w*	*Vail*	*Atkinson*	*Dickenson*
								Ref: G Landragin	City were at full-strength for this top of the table clash in the Medway town, where they had all the early play but were unable to beat the opposition keeper. Chatham then woke up and a very even, exciting, contest took place without either side being able to break the deadlock.										
7	A	TOTTENHAM		3	D	2-2	2-1	Jones 5, O'Brien 35	Monteith	Davy	Milligan	Mann	Higgins	Hamilton	Wyllie	Carnelly	Jones	O'Brien P	Russell
	13/11		*8,250*	*5*	11			*Black 25, Burrows 75*	*Cullen*	*Burrows*	*Knowles*	*Hall*	*Jones*	*Crump*	*Tannahill*	*Meade*	*Joyce*	*Stormont*	*Black*
								Ref: G Muir	Higgins won the toss and City, with the wind in their favour, started strongly at Northumberland Park. Wyllie tested Cullen with a hot shot before Jones found the net with a beauty. Black then levelled with a fierce drive, before an offside looking O'Brien shot City ahead once more.										
8	H	TOTTENHAM		3	W	3-1	0-0	Caie 65, O'Brien 75, Mann 80	Monteith	Davy	Milligan	Mann	Higgins	Hamilton	Wyllie	Carnelly	Caie	O'Brien P	Russell
	27/11		4,000	*5*	13			*Joyce 70*	*Ambler*	*Burrows*	*Knowles*	*Hall*	*Jones*	*Crump*	*Tannahill*	*Davidson*	*Joyce*	*Stormont*	*Black*
								Ref: T Saywell	The miserable weather resulted in a crowd smaller than expected for this keenly awaited clash. Despite playing against a strong wind in the first half, City controlled most of the play. Caie hit the crossbar, but he put City ahead after the break when Ambler was caught out of his goal.										
9	H	SHEPPEY UTD		1	W	**7-0**	2-0	Russell 25, Caie 40, 65, 75,	Monteith	Davy	Milligan	Mann	Higgins	Hamilton	Wyllie	Carnelly	Caie	O'Brien P	Russell
	4/12		4,000	*7*	15			[Wyllie 60, Mann 70, Carnelly 85]	*Leitch*	*Penney*	*Hendry*	*Lissenden*	*Abbott*	*Walker*	*Cottrell*	*Collins*	*Trainer*	*Rule*	*Peters*
								Ref: E McDonald	Russell put City in front with a high-shot through the keeper's outstretched arms. Caie registered with a tame shot; then after the break Higgins fired wide from the spot before Wyllie grabbed City's third. By the time Carnelly got in on the act United were a contradiction of their name.										
10	A	SWINDON		2	D	2-2	1-0	Russell 40, Caie 80	Monteith	Davy	Milligan	Mann	Higgins	Hamilton	Wyllie	Carnelly	Caie	O'Brien P	Russell
	18/12		*4,000*	*11*	16			*Bell 60, Morris 89*	*Cook*	*Shutt*	*Mellars*	*Boggie*	*Munro*	*Almond*	*Richards'n*	*W Cox*	*Bell*	*Morris*	*Wilson*
								Ref: B Lockyer	On the balance of play it would not have been surprising if City had lost, but were it not for Swindon's last-gasp equaliser they would have won. Wyllie burst through to set up Russell's opener then, after Bell met a splendid centre to bring Swindon level, Caie netted with a grounder.										

No	Ven	Opponent / Att	Pos	Res / Pts	F-A	H-T	Scorers, Times, and Referees	1	2	3	4	5	6	7	8	9	10	11
11	A	SOUTHAMPTON	3	L	**0-4**	0-2		Monteith	Davy	Sinclair	Caie	Higgins	Mann	Wyllie	Jones	Carnelly	O'Brien P	Russell
1/1		***8,000***	*1*	16			*Keay 30,70, Chadwick 35, Petrie 80*	*Clawley*	*Nicol*	*Haynes*	*Meston*	*Chadwick*	*Petrie*	*Yates*	*Buchanan*	*Farrell*	*Keay*	*Turner*
							Ref: Capt Simpson	The dull weather didn't deter a record Southern League crowd at the Dell, the majority of whom were delighted with this win over one of the Saint's biggest Championship rivals. City pressed strongly without success for the first half-hour, and were unlucky to lose by such a margin.										
12	A	READING	2	D	2-2	0-2	Jones 60, Wyllie 65	Monteith	Davy	Milligan	Mann	Higgins	Hamilton	Wyllie	Jones	Caie	O'Brien P	Russell
8/1		***8,000***	*3*	17			*Hadley 20, Johnson 45*	*Bullimer*	*Henderson*	*O'Brien*	*Sharp*	*Watts*	*Eccleston*	*Crawford*	*Barr*	*McWhinnie*	*Johnson*	*Hadley*
							Ref: T Saywell	Ninety-nine times out of a hundred Monteith would have saved Johnston's shot, but this was the hundredth and this time the ball went between his legs right on the half-time whistle. City fought back after the interval and would have won, but for Caie being thwarted by one of the posts.										
13	H	SOUTHAMPTON	1	W	5-2	1-1	Caie 17, 60, 85, Carnelly 50,	Monteith	Davy	Milligan	Mann	Higgins	Hamilton	Wyllie	Carnelly	Caie	O'Brien P	Russell
15/1		**12,170**	*2*	19			*Farrell 15, Yates 65p* [Russell 75]	*Clawley*	*Nicol*	*Haynes*	*Meston*	*Chadwick*	*Petrie*	*Yates*	*Buchanan*	*Farrell*	*Keay*	*Turner*
		(£377.2.8)					Ref: Capt Simpson	Turner looked offside when he got through before passing for Farrell to put the Saints in front. Yates' initial penalty was saved, but the referee ordered it to be retaken. Turner was injured and retired shortly after the spot-kick. Russell and O'Brien's clever play set up Caie's final goal.										
14	H	CHATHAM	1	W	6-1	3-1	Caie 20, 75, Carnelly 21, 40, 65, 85	Monteith	Sinclair	Milligan	Mann	Higgins	Hamilton	Wyllie	Carnelly	Caie	O'Brien P	Russell
22/1		4,500	*4*	21			*Mortimer 15*	*Jones*	*Robertson*	*McKie*	*Smith*	*Hughes*	*Russell*	*Vail*	*Leatherbar'w*	*Lawrence*	*Mortimer*	*Dickenson*
							Ref: V Daines	Mortimer put the visitors in front with a hot shot, which went in off the crossbar, but City responded with two goals in a minute. Caie put away Russell's centre, then Carnelly shot into the corner of the net. Only Carnelly is able to take advantage of the injured Jones in the closing stages.										
15	A	WOLVERTON	1	W	3-0	1-0	Carnelly 25, Russell 47, Mann 70	Monteith	Davy	Milligan	Mann	Higgins	Hamilton	Wyllie	Carnelly	Caie	Jones	Russell
5/2		*3,000*	*11*	23				*Waller*	*Wain*	*Ufton*	*Dormer*	*Edwards*	*Wesley*	*Espley*	*Poole*	*Worsley*	*Radford*	*Frost*
							Ref: A Cecil-Knight	In front of an above-average attendance, Carnelly opened the scoring with a soft shot; then almost straight after the break Russell put on a second. Poor shooting subsequently restricted them to just one more score, when Mann notched a beauty following a bully around the goal.										
16	H	SWINDON	1	W	4-1	2-1	Caie 25, Carnelly 35, Hamilton 70,	Monteith	Davy	Milligan	Mann	Higgins	Hamilton	Wyllie	Carnelly	Caie	O'Brien P	Russell
19/2		4,600	*6*	25			*Morris 30* [Higgins 85]	*Cook*	*Shutt*	*Mellars*	*Boggie*	*Munro*	*Almond*	*Anthony*	*Richardson*	*Bell*	*Morris*	*Murray*
							Ref: B Lockyer	Fine weather greeted the large contingent of Swindon supporters, who came by special excursion. Caie drove in City's fine opener, but a tame shot by Morris brought an equaliser. A rush around goal saw Carnelly fire City back in front, then after the break Hamilton netted a beauty.										
17	A	NORTHFLEET	1	W	4-1	1-1	O'Brien 40, Mann 60, 70, 80	Monteith	Jones	Milligan	Mann	Higgins	Hamilton	Lewis	Carnelly	Caie	O'Brien P	Russell
5/3		*1,000*	*11*	27			*Nicholl 4*	*Clare*	*Pittaway*	*Bagnall*	*Wright*	*Craig*	*Johnson*	*Bundock*	*Grieve*	*Nicholl*	*Moody*	*Campbell*
							Ref: E McDonald	In the fine weather City, trailing to the Cementers' early goal, were helped by an injury to Pittaway that brought his absence from the game just before half-time. Mann notched a well-earned second-half hat-trick to keep City on course for the Championship with a handsome away win.										
18	H	READING	1	W	3-2	1-0	Caie 30, 80, Carnelly 47	Monteith	**Gibson**	Milligan	Davy	Higgins	Hamilton	Mann	Carnelly	Caie	O'Brien P	Russell
12/3		6,250	*3*	29			*Barr 60, Hadley 70*	*Bullimer*	*Henderson*	*Sharp J*	*Foster*	*Watts*	*Eccleston*	*Crawford*	*Barr*	*Cockshutt*	*Johnson*	*Hadley*
							Ref: T Saywell	The large crowd enjoyed excellent weather for this thrilling game. Caie shot in the first-half opener; then straight after the break Carnelly registered with a stinging shot into the roof of the net. Monteith pulled off a great double save but was unable to keep out Hadley's follow-up.										
19	H	MILLWALL ATH	1	D	1-1	1-0	Caie 15	Monteith	Davy	Milligan	Jones	Higgins	Hamilton	Mann	Carnelly	Caie	Russell	O'Brien
19/3		2,100	*10*	30			*Calvey 75*	*Allan*	*Robson*	*Davis W*	*Millar*	*Morrison*	*King*	*Whelan*	*Calvey*	*Turner*	*Davies J*	*Geddes*
							Ref: F Crabtree	The rain, which fell throughout the game, restricted the attendance at St John's Lane. Caie fired in a hard left-footer to put City into the lead, but, after Jones had to retire with an injury, Calvey headed in Millwall's equaliser. As the visitors pressed, Calvey missed the winning chance.										
20	A	SHEPPEY UTD	2	L	0-2	0-1		Monteith	Gibson	Lewis	Sinclair	Davy	Hamilton	Milligan	Mann	Caie	Russell	Carnelly
9/4		***1,000***	*8*	30			*Trainer 35, Peters 80*	*Osborne*	*Penney*	*Hendry*	*Lissenden*	*Abbott*	*Walker*	*Trainer*	*Collins*	*Rule*	*Murray*	*Peters*
							Ref: Mr Avery	A high wind made things difficult at Sheerness, where City never looked likely to notch up a double. Trainer shot in the homesters' opener from a pass by Peters. After the break, a brilliant run by Russell almost brought City a goal, before Peters tied up Sheppey's deserved success.										
21	H	NEW BROMPTON	2	D	1-1	1-1	Carnelly 40	Monteith	Davy	Milligan	Jones	Hamilton	Sinclair	Mann	Carnelly	Caie	Higgins	Russell
16/4		4,000	*5*	31			*Frettingham 3*	*Gentle*	*King*	*Watson*	*Janes*	*Meager*	*Graham*	*Gladwell*	*Hutcheson*	*Frettingham*	*Ford*	*Gallacher*
							Ref: J Beanland	A disappointing game for a large crowd at St John's Lane, which saw City gain a rather fortunate share of the spoils after Frettingham had put the visitors into an early lead. Carnelly equalised near the break, although much earlier Russell had sent his corner-kick directly into the net.										

SOUTHERN LEAGUE DIVISION 1

No	Date	Opponent	Att	Pos	Pt	F-A	H-T	Scorers, Times, and Referees	1	2	3	4	5	6	7	8	9	10	11
22	H	GRAVESEND		2	W	4-0	0-0	Higgins 60, Carnelly 70, Caie 75,	Monteith	Davy	Gibson	Jones	Hamilton	Sinclair	Higgins	Mann	Caie	Carnelly	Russell
	20/4		**2,000**	*7*	33			[Russell 88]	*Bagnall*	*Buist*	*Macfarlane*	*Innes*	*Bull*	*Slater*	*Janes*	*McDonald*	*Mobley*	*Turner*	*Johnson*
	Home Ave 4,738		Away 4,750					Ref: A Partridge	Gravesend put up a fine display but were undone by an injury to Janes that brought his retirement from the fray when they were only trailing to a Higgins shot. Carnelly fired in from a rebound; then Caie rushed in a third from a corner, before Russell's header completed City's success.										

WESTERN LEAGUE PROFESSIONAL SECTION

No	Date	Opponent	Att	Pos	Pt	F-A	H-T	Scorers, Times, and Referees	1	2	3	4	5	6	7	8	9	10	11
1	H	SWINDON			D	3-3	3-2	Wyllie 2, 35, Caie 40	Monteith	Davy	Lewis	Mann	Higgins	Hamilton	Wyllie	Carnelly	Caie	Jones	Russell
	6/10		1,500		1			*Bell 15, Morris 36, 80*	*Cook*	*Shutt*	*Munro*	*Clark*	*Boggie*	*Almond*	*Richards'n W*	*Cox*	*Morris*	*Bell*	*Wilson*
								Ref: A Farrant	Wyllie netted from Russell's centre early on, but Bell levelled with a close in shot. Play then became very exciting with Carnelly having a goal disallowed just prior to Wyllie registering from a melee. Morris equalised within a minute then Jones had to retire from the fray with a cut leg.										
2	H	EASTVILLE ROV			W	4-0	1-0	Caie 40, Carnelly 50, 80, Wyllie 70	Monteith	Davy	Lewis	Mann	Higgins	Hamilton	Wyllie	Carnelly	Caie	O'Brien P	Russell
	13/10		3,000		3				*Roach*	*Bunch*	*Griffiths*	*Farnall*	*Turley*	*Kinsey*	*Field*	*Cotterell*	*Jones*	*Gallier*	*McLean*
								Ref: J Lewis	It took City a long time to break through as it wasn't until nearly half-time that Caie turned a brilliant centre to account. The Rovers missed their chances, and after the break City quickly made them pay. Russell set up Carnelly to net a beauty; then Wyllie registered with a hot shot.										
3	A	BRISTOL ST G'RGE		2	W	2-0	0-0	Caie 50, Russell 55	Monteith	Davy	Sinclair	**Milligan**	Higgins	Hamilton	Wyllie	Mann	Caie	O'Brien P	Russell
	27/10		*3,000*	*5*	5				*Cox*	*McKay*	*Pennington*	*Harris G*	*Brownlie*	*Forrester*	*Britton*	*Christie*	*Finlayson*	*Edge*	*Lee*
								Ref: G Gay	The homesters, now called Bristol St George, made a better fight than was expected, though their best work was carried out when Davy was temporarily absent with a leg injury. Caie put City ahead from Wyllie's centre; then, not long after, Russell added the second with a fine shot.										
4	H	READING		2	W	4-2	1-1	Caie 35, Hosie 55og, Wyllie 70,	Monteith	Davy	Milligan	Mann	Higgins	Hamilton	Wyllie	Carnelly	Caie	O'Brien P	Russell
	20/11		4,500	*1*	7			*Barr 20, Cockshutt 72* [Hamilton 80]	*Bullimer*	*O'Brien*	*Hosie*	*Sharp J*	*Watts*	*Eccleston*	*Crawford*	*Barr*	*Cockshutt*	*Dewey*	*Johnson*
								Ref: V Daines	Reading stretched City all the way in this thrilling encounter. Barr headed them in front, but Caie put away Wyllie's pass to bring City level before the interval. A foul lead to the homesters taking the lead not long after the change of ends when Mann's kick was deflected in by Hosie.										
5	A	READING		2	L	1-2	1-0	Wyllie 25	Monteith	Davy	Milligan	Mann	Higgins	Hamilton	Wyllie	Carnelly	Caie	O'Brien P	Russell
	11/12		*4,000*	*1*	7			*McWhinnie 70, Barr 85*	*Bullimer*	*O'Brien*	*Hosie*	*Sharp J*	*Watts*	*Eccleston*	*Crawford*	*Dewey*	*Barr*	*Johnson*	*McWhinnie*
								Ref: V Daines	A ding-dong struggle at Elm Park was watched by a large crowd, despite the local biscuit factory working overtime. Wyllie netted the opener following Hosie's error, but after the break Reading fought back. McWhinnie shot in a disputed leveller, before Barr fired in the late winner.										
6	A	WARMLEY		2	W	5-2	3-0	Russell 5, Jones 20, O'Brien 21,	Monteith	Davy	Milligan	Caie	Hamilton	Mann	Wyllie	Jones	Carnelly	O'Brien P	Russell
	27/12		***7,250***	*4*	9			*Greenwood 75, Bishop 77*	*Meates*	*Reeves*	*Buist*	*Matthews*	*Britton*	*McWhirter*	*Greenwood*	*Browett*	*Preddy*	*Woods*	*Bishop*
			(£156)					Ref: T Saywell [Wyllie 65, Hamilton 88]	In a frantic opening Russell registered with a beauty, whilst Greenwood had his effort disallowed for offside. Warmley were weakened by the loss of Matthews with a knee injury shortly after O'Brien had added City's third, but they put up a spirited display throughout the second half.										
7	H	BRISTOL ST G'RGE		1	W	3-0	1-0	Caie 10, O'Brien 70, 80	Monteith	Davy	Higgins	Carnelly	Hamilton	Mann	Wyllie	Jones	Caie	O'Brien P	Russell
	5/1		**600**	*6*	9				*Cox*	*Harris*	*McKay*	*Beak*	*Brownlie*	*Forrester*	*Christie*	*Finlayson*	*Davies*	*Lee*	*Edge*
								Ref: T Saywell	The consequence of the miserable wet weather was a poor crowd that saw Caie's fine shot put City into an early lead, but nothing further accrued up to the interval. The St George custodian was in superb form, but even he could do nothing about O'Brien's second-half double.										
8	H	EASTLEIGH		1	W	**14-1**	8-1	H'tn 2, Wy 7, 40, Caie 15, H'gns 18, 78,	Monteith	Milligan	Lewis	Mann	Higgins	Hamilton	Wyllie	Carnelly	Caie	Jones	Russell
	26/1		1,000	*5*	11			*McDonald 17* [Carnelly 19, 85],	*Shearman*	*Brocklehurst*	*Dexter*	*Lawless*	*Bastock*	*Brockleh'st J*	*Williams*	*Sharpe*	*Cook*	*Donnelly*	*McDonald*
								Ref: G Gay [Jones 30, 31, 47, 80], [Brocklehurst 60og, Russell 75]	It didn't take City long to get in scoring mood as Hamilton's pot-shot put them in front after two minutes. The goals flowed regularly as City achieved their record competitive match success. Eastleigh packed their goal after the break, but Mann's shot found the net off of Brocklehurst.										

No	Venue	Opponents / Date	Attendance			FT	HT	Scorers / Referee	1	2	3	4	5	6	7	8	9	10	11
9	A	EASTLEIGH							City were awarded the points, whilst their opponents were fined for scratching from this fixture on 2 March.										
10	A	EASTVILLE ROV		1	W	3-2	1-1	O'Brien 25, Russell 65, Wyllie 80	Monteith	Sinclair	Milligan	Jones	Gibson	Hamilton	Wyllie	Carnelly	Caie	O'Brien P	Russell
		16/3	*4,000*	*7*	15			*Smellie 3, Jones 89*	*Stone*	*Bunch*	*Griffiths*	*Farnall*	*Turley*	*Kinsey*	*McLean*	*Jones*	*Smellie*	*Sawyer*	*Cotterell*
								Ref: T Saywell	City started from the Viaduct End, but the Rovers took the lead when Smillie fired in the opener after just three minutes. City then mounted a series of ferocious attacks and eventually O'Brien headed them level. With the breeze in their favour after the break, City took firm control.										
11	A	TROWBRIDGE		1	W	5-1	5-0	O'Brien 20, 40, Caie 21, Mann 25,	Monteith	Davy	Gibson	Sinclair	Higgins	Hamilton	Jones	Mann	Caie	O'Brien P	Russell
		6/4	***2,000***	*8*	17			*Hyman W 55* [Jones 30]	*Nash*	*Thompson*	*Smith*	*Billett*	*Ellis*	*Hyman H*	*Belcher*	*Stock*	*Terry*	*Hyman W*	*Britton*
								Ref: A Farrant	The sun in their eyes was not the only disadvantage Trowbridge had at the start, as they also commenced a man short. City attacked relentlessly from the outset and, from Russell's sixth corner, O'Brien headed in the opener and immediately after Caie put away another Russell flag-kick.										
12	H	WARMLEY		1	W	3-2	3-0	Higgins 5, Carnelly 24, Wyllie 25	Monteith	Davy	Gibson	Jones	Higgins	Hamilton	Wyllie	Carnelly	Caie	O'Brien P	Russell
		8/4	**10,250**	*5*	19			*Parkinson 47, Preddy 80*	*Matthews*	*McDermid*	*Walker*	*McWhirter*	*Britton*	*Woods*	*Greenwood*	*Manson*	*Parkinson*	*Preddy*	*Bishop*
			(£264.18.0)					Ref: B Lockyer	Warmley kicked-off at 3.30pm from the Gas Works End, but from a goalmouth scramble City took the lead. Higgins then crossed for Carnelly to head in number two and a minute later Wyllie ran through for the third. Parkinson's goal from McWhirter's cross revived Warmley's spirits.										
13	A	SWINDON		1	L	**0-1**	0-0		Monteith	Lewis	Gibson	Jones	Davy	Hamilton	Milligan	Mann	Caie	Higgins	Russell
		13/4	***2,000***	*2*	19			*Richardson W 85*	*Cook*	*Shutt*	*Mellars*	*Richards'n G*	*Munro*	*Almond*	*Cox*	*Bell*	*Richards'n W*	*Morris*	*Wilson*
								Ref: N Whittaker	Swindon were much better side and fully merited their win, even if it was but by a solitary goal. Both sides had their chances, but it looked like the deadlock would not be broken until Richardson put away Cox's corner. The referee endured a harsh reception from the crowd at the finish.										
14	H	TROWBRIDGE		1	W	4-0	1-0	Mann 25, Carnelly 65, 70,	Monteith	Davy	Milligan	Jones	Hamilton	Sinclair	Higgins	Mann	Caie	Carnelly	Russell
		18/4	2,000	*8*	21			[Milligan 85]	*Sheldon*	*Smith*	*Fulton*	*Billett*	*Booker*	*Rooke*	*Belcher*	*Stock*	*Hyman W*	*Bolt*	*Britton*
		Home / Ave 3,264	Away / 3,708					Ref: A Farrant	Play commenced at 5.30pm with Trowbridge kicking off from the Lower End and facing the sun. Mann, after earlier heading over a good chance, put City in front midway through the first half. After the break Carnelly fired in City's second, and then added another not long after.										

No	Date	Opponent	Att	Pos	Pt	F-A	H-T	Scorers, Times, and Referees	1	2	3	4	5	6	7	8	9	10	11	12 sub used
1	H	SOUTHAMPTON			W	3-1	3-0	Caie 25, Higgins 30, Carnelly 40	**Monteith**	**Davy**	**Sinclair**	**Mann**	**Higgins**	**Hamilton**	**Wyllie**	**Carnelly**	**Caie**	**O'Brien P**	**Russell**	
	1/9		600					*Farrell 80*	*Clawley*	*Meston*	*Haynes*	*Chadwick*	*Littlehales*	*Petrie*	*Yates*	*Nicol*	*Farrell*	*Keay*	*Turner*	
								Ref: V Daines	The terrible wet weather kept the crowd down on a day a young girl drowned in the brook by the St John's Lane ground. City won the toss and chose to start with the high wind in their favour. After the break, despite Farrell shooting in for the Saints, City still had the better of the game.											
2	H	SWINDON			W	3-1	1-1	O'Brien 30, 75, Carnelly 55	Monteith	Davy	Sinclair	Mann	Higgins	Hamilton	Wyllie	Carnelly	Caie	O'Brien P	Russell	
	4/9		4,000					*Richardson 35*	*Cook*	*Shutt*	*Mellars*	*Clark*	*Munro*	*Almond*	*McElheney*	*Bell*	*Morris*	*Richards'n W*	*Wilson*	
								Ref: N Whittaker	Just three years on from their inaugural match, City face the Railwaymen on equal terms. O'Brien fired in from Russell's pass to put City in front, but the visitors, who had three goals disallowed for offside during the proceedings, drew level when Richardson's shot found the net.											
3	H	CHORLEY			W	6-2	3-2	Caie 5, 10, Mann 15, Wyllie 50, 70,	Monteith	**Lewis**	Sinclair	Mann	Higgins	Hamilton	Wyllie	Carnelly	Caie	O'Brien P	Russell	
	6/9		2,000					*Lewis 11og, Ashton 30* [Russell 75]	*Pinnell*	*Ostich*	*Thornboro*	*Riley*	*McKennie*	*Parker*	*Kirby*	*Lyden*	*Fletcher*	*Jones*	*Ashton*	
								Ref: G Gay	The City were soon off the mark against the Lancs League Champions as Caie twice registered early on. A shot just out of Pinnell's reach was followed by a dropping volley. Chorley responded with a corner which found the net off Lewis, before Mann fired in the 'goal of the season'.											
4	H	BURTON SWIFTS			D	2-2	1-0	Wyllie 35, Carnelly 55	Monteith	Davy	Lewis	Clements	Sinclair	Hamilton	Wyllie	Carnelly	Caie	O'Brien P	Russell	
	20/9		1,500					*Leigh 75, Shaw 80*	*Gray*	*Cunningham*	*Ashby*	*Lowe*	*Wylee*	*Jackson*	*Waterson*	*Yardley*	*Leigh*	*Shaw*	*Sat'thwaite*	
								Ref: G Gay	A trip on Russell brought City an early spot-kick, but Gray saved Carnelly's effort. Wyllie netted the opener with a beauty, shortly after City had lost the services of the injured Sinclair for the rest of the game. Leigh opened the Football League side's account with a clinking shot.											
5	H	SCOTS GUARDS			W	7-0	7-0	Caie 1, Call'der 2, Carnelly 15, 30, 35,	Monteith	Davy	Lewis	Clements	Mann	Hamilton	Wyllie	Carnelly	Caie	**Callender**	Russell	
	29/9		100					[Wyllie 20, Hamilton 40]	*Pennington*	*Milligan*	*Rough*	*Cresswell*	*Ward*	*McNeill*	*Kirk*	*Mills*	*Crabbe*	*Marl*	*Innes*	
								Ref: A Farrant	In the pouring rain, City made good use of kicking towards the well-drained Lane End. After the break, though, they were brought up short by the waterlogged conditions in the opposite goalmouth. A bully around goal saw Caie net the opener, and Hamilton's fine shot produced No 7.											
6	H	WOOL ARSENAL			W	4-2	2-1	Russell 25, Carnelly 35, O'Brien 65,	Monteith	Davy	Milligan	Mann	Higgins	Hamilton	Wyllie	Carnelly	Caie	O'Brien P	Russell	
	15/11		3,000					*Crawford 20, Hannah 75* [Wyllie 70]	*Ord*	*McAuley*	*Anderson*	*Crawford*	*Farrell*	*Davis*	*Brock*	*Haywood*	*McGeoch*	*Hannah*	*Monteith*	
								Ref: A Farrant	Shots from Russell and Carnelly put City in front after falling behind when Crawford's flag-kick went into goal off Monteith. After the break, strikes from O'Brien and Wyllie allowed City to triumph in what was reported in the *T&M* as the 'finest display of football seen this season'.											
7	H	LUTON			W	3-2	2-1	Caie 6, Carnelly 15, Wyllie 55	Monteith	Davy	Milligan	Sinclair	Higgins	Hamilton	Wyllie	Carnelly	Caie	Jones	Mann	
	20/12		1,000					*Donaldson 5, McInnes 56*	*Williams*	*McEwen*	*McCartney*	*Davies*	*Stewart*	*Docherty*	*Gallacher*	*Coupar*	*Donaldson*	*Little*	*McInnes*	
								Ref: A Farrant	Despite the fine weather, the early start mitigated against a large gate. Luton started the better and it was no surprise when Donaldson netted with a great shot. Fortunately Caie soon fired in the equaliser, before goals from Carnelly and Wyllie took City to the hundred for the season.											
8	H	MIDDLETON			W	5-1	4-0	Caie 25, 32, Wyllie 30, O'Brien 44	Lewis	Sinclair	Milligan	Davy	Higgins	Hamilton	Wyllie	Carnelly	Caie	O'Brien P	Russell	
	25/12		4,500 (£105)					*Astley 75* [Higgins 55]	*Booth*	*Mather*	*Holt*	*Wood*	*Collier*	*Cranfield*	*Mayer*	*Lee*	*Astley*	*Wood*	*Fielding*	
								Ref: S Peacock	With Cranfield taking the place of one of the visitors, who was injured during the train journey down, and with a trialist in goal, it was hardly surprising that Middleton lost this game. In fine weather Carnelly's shot went in off Caie to give City the lead before Wyllie hit in the second.											
9	H	LOUGHBOROUGH			W	6-1	2-0	Mann 25, O'Brien 40, 65, 80,	Monteith	Caie	Milligan	Mann	Higgins	Hamilton	Wyllie	Jones	Carnelly	O'Brien P	Russell	
	29/1		2,000					*Pym 46* [Mumford 60og, Higgins 75]	*Mumford*	*Hardy*	*White*	*Smith*	*Hodgkin*	*Roulston*	*Walker*	*Turner*	*Pegg*	*Pym*	*Pike*	
								Ref: S Peacock	The dull and cold weather meant that the crowd wasn't as large as for the two previous Saturday games against Southampton and Chatham. Mann put City in front with a shot from near the halfway line; then O'Brien headed in the second before Pym dribbled through after the break.											
10	H	BEDMINSTER			W	9-2	5-0	Caie 10, 20, Carnelly 15, 55, 65, 85,	Monteith	Davy	Milligan	Mann	Higgins	Hamilton	Wyllie	Carnelly	Caie	O'Brien P	Russell	
	9/2		1,000					*Hargett 70, 80* [Wyllie 30],	*Berry W*	*Brooks G*	*Heyward H*	*Clements H*	*McAuliffeM**	*Mayo L*	*Gretton*	*Hargett A*	*Trestrail A*	*Callender W*	*Brown WSA Bidwell*	
								Ref: A Farrant [O'Brien 40, 71]	A decisive City victory in this meeting of the best professional and amateur talent. Caie screwed in the opener, which Carnelly followed with an easy one from O'Brien's pass. Hargett took advantage of City's complacency near the finish by twice steering the ball in for the Minster.											

No	Venue	Opponent / Date	Att	Res	FT	HT	Scorers, Times, Referees	1	2	3	4	5	6	7	8	9	10	11
11	H	NOTTS CO		D	2-2	1-1	Carnelly 20, Mann 75	Monteith	Caie	Milligan	Mann	Higgins	Hamilton	Wyllie	Jones	Carnelly	O'Brien P	Russell
		12/2	4,000				*Boucher 35, Fraser 60*	*Toone*	*Prescott*	*Lewis*	*Brailsford*	*Calderhead*	*Stewart*	*Langham*	*Carter*	*Boucher*	*Halliday*	*Fraser*
							Ref: V Daines	Despite the disagreeable weather the fans were satisfied after seeing yet another fine exhibition of football. Russell's well-placed corner										
								allowed City to rush the opener into the net, but then Langham got through and passed back for Boucher to crash in County's leveller.										
12	A	WLCH ARSENAL		L	1-3	1-1	Higgins 15	Monteith	Gibson	Milligan	Sinclair	Davy	Hamilton	Mann	Carnelly	Caie	Higgins	Russell
		21/3	*3,250*				*McGeoch 7, White 60, Hunt 75*	*Ord*	*McAuley*	*McConnell*	*Anderson*	*Clark*	*Davis*	*Haywood*	*McGeoch*	*Hunt*	*Hannah*	*White*
								Despite falling behind early on, when McGeoch registered, City settled down to produce a good combination display on the Manor Ground.										
							(Fred Davis Benefit)	Higgins brought them level with a splendid shot but, after the interval, White's clever shot and a beauty by Hunt brought Arsenal victory.										
13	A	LUTON		L	1-5	0-4	Mann 75 *[Coupar 60]*	Lewis	Davy	Sinclair	Jones	Hamilton	Gibson	Mann	**O'Brien J**	Caie	Carnelly	**Smith**
		28/3	*1,000*				*Little 10, Durrant 20, Gallacher 35, 40,*	*Williams*	*McCartney*	*McEwen*	*Davies*	*Stewart*	*Docherty*	*Gallacher*	*Coupar*	*Little*	*McInnes*	*Durrant*
								Luton were early in evidence and Little easily obtained their opener when Sinclair missed his kick. Durrant then doubled the advantage with a										
							(McEwen & Gallacher Benefit)	slanting drive. Before half-time, Gallacher scored twice, notching his first with City claiming offside, and following this with a firm header.										
14	H	DARWEN		W	5-1	2-0	O'Brien P 35, 50, 75, Mann 40,	Monteith	Gibson	Lewis	Jones	Davy	Hamilton	Mann	O'Brien J	Caie	O'Brien P	Russell
		2/4	3,000				*Kenyon 60* [Caie 88]	*Kingsley*	*Leach*	*Haworth*	*Moore*	*Tyrer*	*Dyson*	*Sugden*	*Kenyon*	*Salisbury*	*Bleasdale*	*Barnes*
							Ref: N Whittaker	Even with a weakened line-up, City had no trouble in disposing of a Darwen side which fielded their full League XI. With his hat-trick, Paddy										
								O'Brien was the star of the show. Sandwiched between his two headers, he grabbed his second when firing the ball in off the goalkeeper.										
15	H	CORINTHIANS		L	1-3	0-1	Carnelly 89	Monteith	Lewis	Gibson	Jones	Mann	Sinclair	Milligan	Carnelly	Caie	Higgins	Russell
		12/4	5,000				*Cotterill 40, Smith 70, Topham 80*	*Moon WR*	*Bray EH*	*Oakley WJ*	*Beasley HO*	*Wr-BrownOE*	*Middleditch B*	*Topham R*	*Cotterill GH*	*Smith GO*	*Alexander C*	*Hewitt CD*
							Ref: N Whittaker	City were robbed by the half-time whistle, which blew just as the ball was about to cross the line for an equaliser. Overall however they can										
								have no complaints, despite Caie hitting the post, as the better side won. Cotterill opened the scoring with a shot into the corner of City's net.										
16	H	WEST BROM		D	1-1	1-0	Mann 30p	Monteith	Gibson	Milligan	Jones	Hamilton	Sinclair	Higgins	Mann	Caie	Carnelly	Russell
		23/4	4,000				*Garfield 75*	*Reader*	*Cave*	*Williams*	*Perry*	*Jones*	*Banks*	*Bassett*	*Flewitt*	*Richards*	*Connor*	*Garfield*
							Ref: S Hollis	As a whole, this game was rather disappointing, neither side showing up particularly well. Even so it picked up after the opening 20 mins when										
								the visitors were unwilling to exert themselves. Garfield raced down the field and beat Monteith with a cross-shot to bring the Throstles level.										
17	H	BURSLEM PT VALE		W	2-0	1-0	Mann 20, Higgins 70	Monteith	Davy	Milligan	Jones	Higgins	Hamilton	Caie	Carnelly	Mann	O'Brien P	Russell
		30/4	1,500					*George*	*Clare*	*Spilsbury*	*Boullemier*	*Beech*	*Macdonald*	*Evans R*	*Evans J*	*Simpson*	*Peake*	*Heames*
							Ref: N Whittaker	Despite the stormy weather, a far-sized crowd turned out to see the Staffs Cup winners, who had beaten Sheffield United in the English Cup.										
							(Sam Hollis Benefit)	Injuries to Hamilton and Mann lead to their departure near the end when Milligan, who went in goal, stopped a shot on the stroke of time.										

FA Cup/Glos Cup/Charity Cup			F-A	H-T	Scorers, Times, and Referees	1	2	3	4	5	6	7	8	9	10	11
Q1 H CLIFTON ASSOC		W	9-1	5-1	W'llie2,10,25,55,C'nlly11,40,75,85,	Monteith	Davy	Sinclair	Mann	Higgins	Hamilton	Wyllie	Carnelly	Caie	O'Brien P	Russell
25/9 1,000					*McCarthy 5* [O'Brien 56]	*Bailey J*	*Heyward H*	*Gerrish DS*	*Mayo L*	*Thomas DJ*	*Pratt R*	*Taylor C*	*McCarthy J*	*Trestrail A*	*Parr W*	*Brown WSA*
					Ref: G Gay	Wyllie opened the scoring in the second minute, but McCarthy levelled for Clifton before his side were eventually overwhelmed. City lost the services of Sinclair who had to retire from the match with a twisted knee when the score was 3-1, but nothing could stop Clifton's annihilation.										
Q2 A TROWBRIDGE	3	W	5-2	3-2	Caie 16, Higgins 30,70,75, C'nlly 41	Monteith	Davy	Lewis	Mann	Higgins	Hamilton	Wyllie	Carnelly	Caie	O'Brien P	Russell
16/10 *2,000 WL:8*					*Everett 15, Jones 40*	*George*	*Fulton*	*Smith*	*Hathaway*	*Everett G*	*Hyman H*	*Hallam*	*Jones*	*Daniel*	*Rooke*	*Hyman W*
					Ref: A Farrant *(on the 'High School' ground)*	City were reported to have taken 1,000 fans to the Wiltshire town for this cup clash. George, the Trowbridge keeper, who blundered for City's fourth goal, was transferred to Aston Villa for a £200 fee immediately after the game. Higgins concluded the scoring with a clever shot.										
Q3 A SOUTHAMPTON	2	L	0-2	0-1		Monteith	Caie	Sinclair	Mann	Davy	Hamilton	Wyllie	Callender	Carnelly	O'Brien P	Russell
30/10 *10,000 3*					*Buchanan 1, Turner 60*	*Clawley*	*Nicol*	*Haynes*	*Meston*	*Chadwick*	*Petrie*	*Turner*	*Farrell*	*Buchanan*	*Naughton*	*Yates*
					Ref: S Carr	*The Sportsman* records that Buchanan opened the scoring after just ten seconds of this game, which saw a record crowd at the Dell according to the *Times & Mirror*. Callender skied the best chance for a City side that, in rarely being able to get going, failed to do themselves justice.										
2 H EASTVILLE ROV	1	W	2-0	2-0	Jones 15, Russell 40	Monteith	Davy	Milligan	Mann	Higgins	Hamilton	Jones	Carnelly	Caie	O'Brien P	Russell
GC 26/2 6,401 *BL:5*						*Stone*	*Bunch*	*Griffiths*	*Farnall*	*Turley*	*Kinsey*	*McLean*	*Cotterell*	*Horsey*	*Sawyer*	*Draycott*
(£170.5.8)					Ref: J Tillotson	With both St George and Warmley playing out of town, a large crowd assembled in fine weather at St John's Lane. Higgins won the toss and the Rovers started play from the Lower End. City controlled most of the action and Russell shot in the second goal to make sure of the points.										
SF N BRISTOL ST G'RGE	1	D	1-1	1-0	Carnelly 12	Monteith	Davy	Milligan	Jones	Hamilton	Sinclair	Higgins	Carnelly	Caie	O'Brien P	Russell
GC 26/3 *3,500 BL:8*					*Lee 80*	*Cox*	*Pennington*	*McKay*	*Brownlie*	*Harris G*	*Forrester*	*Lee*	*Christie*	*Finlayson*	*Davies*	*Hyde*
(£68)					Ref: J Brodie *(at the 'Chequers').*	The cold weather and a fierce wind resulted in a gathering way under what was anticipated for this clash. With the wind advantage in the first half, City took the lead when Carnelly got his head to a free-kick. Monteith's fumble of Hyde's shot allowed Lee to bundle in the late leveller.										
R N BRISTOL ST G'RGE	1	W	2-0	1-0	Mann 10p, Caie 75	Monteith	Davy	Milligan	Jones	Hamilton	Sinclair	Mann	Carnelly	Caie	O'Brien P	Russell
GC 31/3 *2,000 BL:8*						*Cox*	*Pennington*	*McKay*	*Harris G*	*Brownlie*	*Beak*	*Harris W*	*Christie*	*Davies*	*Coyne*	*Lee*
(£40)					Ref: J Tillotson *(at 'Ashton Gate').*	City, who are let down by some poor shooting, are fortunate that their opponents showed little in the way of good combination. Thankfully, Mann's early penalty put them in front; then, despite being denied by some brilliant saves in the second half, Russell eventually set up Caie.										
F N WARMLEY	2	W	2-1	2-0	Caie 15, Higgins 44	Monteith	Davy	Milligan	Jones	Hamilton	Sinclair	Mann	Higgins	Caie	Carnelly	Russell
GC 11/4 *11,186 2:2*					*Bishop 80*	*Matthews*	*Carter*	*Buist*	*McWhirter*	*Britton*	*Woods*	*Greenwood*	*Manson*	*Parkinson*	*Preddy*	*Bishop*
(£348.6.3)					Ref: J Tillotson *(at 'Stapleton Road').*	Although the rain fell heavily both before and throughout, a capital crowd witnessed this clash. Warmley won the toss and commenced with the wind behind them, but City took the lead when Caie's shot went through Buist's legs. The linesmen were Messrs A Stacey and F Millard.										
1 H EASTLEIGH	1	W	10-3	4-1	C'lly10,70,Wy11,25,65,Caie30,85,	Monteith	Davy	Milligan	Mann	Higgins	Hamilton	Wyllie	Carnelly	Caie	O'Brien P	Russell
CC 15/12 800 *WL:5*					*Cook 40, 75, Lawless 60*	*Shearman*	*Moorhouse*	*Dexter*	*Lawless*	*Bastock*	*Brockleh'st J*	*Sharpe*	*Cook*	*Woodhouse*	*Adams*	*McDonald*
					Ref: G Gay [Russell 55, O'Brien 62,80]	Despite the scoreline, Eastleigh played quite well at times in this game. Carnelly gave Shearman no chance with a great drive that put City in front, after which Wyllie's shot and a header had Eastleigh facing an uphill task. Cook fired in to give them some hope after Davy's mistake.										
2 H WARMLEY	1	L	0-1	0-1		Monteith	Davy	Caie	Mann	Higgins	Hamilton	Wyllie	Carnelly	Jones	O'Brien P	Russell
CC 21/2 2,000 *2:2*					*Bishop 25*	*Matthews*	*McDermid*	*Walker*	*McWhirter*	*Britton*	*Woods*	*Greenwood*	*Manson*	*Parkinson*	*Preddy*	*Bishop*
						City lost Wyllie with a knee injury midway through the first half. However, by the time Bishop headed in from Greenwood's pass, he had temporarily returned. As City piled on the pressure near the end, Walker pulled down Carnelly, but Matthews saved Mann's spot-kick.										

SOUTHERN LEAGUE	P	W	D	L	Home F	A	W	D	L	Away F	A	Pts
1 Southampton	22	10	0	1	34	7	8	1	2	19	11	37
2 BRISTOL C	22	9	2	0	44	15	4	5	2	23	18	33
3 Tottenham H	22	9	2	0	36	6	3	2	6	16	25	28
4 Chatham	22	7	4	0	37	14	5	0	6	13	20	28
5 Reading	22	7	3	1	26	11	1	4	6	13	20	23
6 New Brompt'	22	6	1	4	18	13	3	3	5	19	24	22
7 Sheppey Utd	22	9	1	1	30	9	1	0	10	10	40	21
8 Gravesend U	22	4	5	2	15	12	3	1	7	13	27	20
9 Millwall Ath	22	5	1	5	33	20	3	1	7	15	25	18
10 Swindon T	22	5	1	5	24	20	2	1	8	12	28	16
11 Northfleet	22	4	1	6	19	22	0	2	9	10	38	11
12 Wolverton	22	3	0	8	17	25	0	1	10	11	57	7
	264	78	21	33	333	174	33	21	78	174	333	264

WESTERN LEAGUE	P	W	D	L	Home F	A	W	D	L	Away F	A	Pts
1 BRISTOL C	14	6	1	0	35	8	5	0	2	16	8	23
2 Swindon T	14	7	0	0	25	2	2	1	4	7	13	19
3 Reading	14	5	1	1	15	8	2	1	4	14	17	16
4 St George	14	3	2	2	14	15	3	1	3	11	12	15
5 Eastville Rov	14	3	0	4	26	11	3	2	2	12	14	14
6 Warmley	14	4	2	1	24	10	1	1	5	12	17	13
7 Eastleigh	14	3	1	3	13	7	0	1	6	9	48	8
8 Trowbridge T	14	2	0	5	11	24	0	0	7	4	34	4
	112	33	7	16	163	85	16	7	33	85	163	112

Odds & ends

Double wins: (6) Wolverton, Northfleet, Eastville Rovers, Bristol St George, Warmley, Trowbridge Town.
Double losses: (0).

Won from behind: League (4) New Brompton (a), Southampton (h), Chatham (h), Northfleet (a). Friendlies: (2) Woolwich Arsenal (a), Luton Town (h). Cups: (1) Trowbridge (a).
Lost from in front: League (1) Reading (a).

High spots: City's record competitive victory, beating Eastleigh 14-1.
Beating Clifton Association 9-1 in the FA Cup on 25 September.
City's first ever Gloucestershire Cup victory on 26 February.
Winning the Gloucestershire Cup on 11 April by beating Warmley 2-1.

Low spots: The death of a young girl in the brook by the 'St John's Lane' ground as City opened their professional career on 1 September.
City's first defeat as a professional club at Southampton in the FA Cup.

Player of the Year: 'Sandy' Caie.
Ever-presents: League (2) Hugh Monteith, 'Jock' Russell.
Hat-tricks: (15) 'Sandy' Caie (3), 'Paddy' O'Brien (3), Albert Carnelly (4), George Mann, Billy Jones, Tom Wyllie (2), Billy Higgins.
Leading scorer: Overall: Albert Carnelly (45). League: 'Sandy' Caie (26).
AGM (Temperance Hall, East Street, Bedminster, 5 July 1898):
Profit £18.2s.4d. Season Ticket Sales £101.2s.6d.

	Appearances Lge	Cup	Fr	Goals Lge	Cup	Fr	Tot
Caie, 'Sandy'	**34**	9	17	**26**	5	10	**41**
Callender, W		1	1			1	**1**
Carnelly, Albert	**30**	9	16	**23**	8	14	**45**
Clements, 'Hammer'	**1**		2				
Davy, Harry	**31**	9	12	**1**			**1**
Gibson, Will	**7**		5				
Hamilton, Jack	**34**	9	16	**4**		1	**5**
Higgins, Billy	**32**	7	13	**9**	4	5	**18**
Jones, Billy	**18**	5	8	**8**	1		**9**
Mann, George	**33**	8	15	**9**	1	7	**17**
Milligan, Alex	**24**	5	10	**1**			**1**
Monteith, Hugh	**35**	9	15				
O'Brien, J			2				
O'Brien, 'Paddy'	**27**	8	11	**13**	3	12	**28**
Russell, 'Jock'	**35**	9	15	**10**	2	2	**14**
Sinclair, Finlay	**11**	5	10				
Smith, W			1				
Talbot-Lewis, Albert	**7**	1	7				
Wyllie, Tom	**26**	5	11	**12**	7	8	**27**
Opponents og				**2**		1	**3**
Unplayed	**11**						
19 players used	**396**	**99**	**187**	**118**	**31**	**61**	**210**

No	Date		Att	Pos	Pt	F-A	H-T	Scorers, Times, and Referees	1	2	3	4	5	6	7	8	9	10	11
1	A	MILLWALL ATH			D	1-1	0-1	Caie 75	Monteith	Barker	Davy	Jones	Hamilton	Stewart	Langham	Finnerhan	Caie	O'Brien	Russell
	17/9		*10,000*		1			*Turnbull 30*	*Allan*	*Burgess*	*Gow*	*Morrison*	*Stewart*	*Millar*	*Crawford*	*Turner*	*Hogan*	*Turnbull*	*Geddes*
								Ref: T Saywell	With the sun and wind at their backs, Millwall deservedly took the lead when Turnbull finished off a pretty piece of play between himself and Geddes. Despite the extremely hot weather, City came back strongly and were full value for the point earned when Finnerhan set up Caie.										
2	H	WARMLEY*		9	W	4-2	1-0	Finnerhan 43, Russell 60, Caie 70,	Monteith	Barker	Davy	Jones	McLean	Hamilton	Langham	Finnerhan	Caie	O'Brien	Russell
	8/10		8,000	*14*	3			*Henderson 75, Bishop 80*	*Douglas*	*McDermid*	*Warburton*	*Woods*	*McHardy*	*Britton P*	*Manson*	*Andrews*	*Henderson*	*Reid*	*Bishop*
								Ref: A Cecil-Knight [McDermid 85og]	The visitors had the best chances early on, but it was City who took the lead when Finnerhan's shot hit the inside of the post before crossing the line. Offside ruled out O'Brien's effort early in the second half, but it wasn't long before Russell netted and McLean struck the crossbar.										
3	H	CHATHAM		8	W	2-1	2-1	Finnerhan 10, Mann 15	Monteith	Barker	Davy	Stewart	McLean	Hamilton	Langham	Finnerhan	Caie	Mann	Murphy
	22/10		4,000	*9*	5			*Johnson 40*	*Frail*	*Harper*	*Dunn*	*Smith*	*Chapman*	*Slater*	*Brearley*	*Lawrence*	*Johnson*	*Clements*	*Dickenson*
								Ref: E Fox	City, who dropped O'Brien and Russell, won the toss and played with the wind in the first half. Finnerhan registered with a high one; then Mann added a second when meeting Caie's cross. Chatham responded with a shot that went through the legs of Barker and Monteith's hands.										
4	H	SWINDON		7	W	4-2	3-1	Russell 15, Caie 26, 40, Langham 70	Monteith	Barker	Davy	Jones	Mann	Hamilton	Potter	Langham	Caie	O'Brien	Russell
	5/11		4,000	*9*	7			*Morris 25, 80*	*Boulton*	*Shutt*	*Mills*	*Henderson*	*Munro*	*Smith*	*Sharples*	*Coupar*	*Little*	*Morris*	*Kirton*
								Ref: A Cooper	Despite injuries depriving City of the services of McLean and Finnerhan, a capital game was witnessed against the full-strength visitors. Morris notched a deserved second goal near the finish; then a minute later sent in a shot that required Monteith to bring off a fine save.										
5	A	READING		6	W	1-0	0-0	Finnerhan 70	Monteith	Barker	Davy	Jones	McLean	Hamilton	Langham	Finnerhan	Caie	Murphy	Russell
	26/11		*4,000*	*10*	9				*Whittaker*	*Henderson*	*O'Brien*	*Ballantyne*	*Holt*	*Eccleston*	*Davies*	*Goldie*	*Millar*	*Johnson*	*Plant*
									Both sides were strongly represented, City's only prominent absentee being the injured O'Brien. The play was pretty even in the first half, but following the break it needed skilful defending to stem Reading's almost constant attacking and bring about City's somewhat fortunate victory.										
6	H	TOTTENHAM		5	W	2-1	1-1	Langham 38, Russell 86	Monteith	Barker	Milligan	Jones	McLean	Hamilton	Langham	Finnerhan	Caie	Murphy	Russell
	3/12		7,000	*6*	11			*Joyce 35*	*Cullen*	*Erentz*	*Cain*	*Jones*	*McNaught*	*Stormont*	*Smith*	*McKay*	*Joyce*	*Cameron*	*Bradshaw*
								Ref: C Crisp	City, weakened by the fact that Davy was called home following the death of his father, still took the points. In front of two England selectors, Timms and Sherrington, Russell settled this terrific contest when his centre found the net as Cullen came out and completely missed the ball.										
7	H	BEDMINSTER		4	W	5-2	1-1	Finnerhan 18, 65, Kelso 50og,	Monteith	Barker	Davy	Jones	McLean	Hamilton	Langham	Finnerhan	Caie	Carnelly	Russell
	17/12		10,250	*8*	13			*Leonard 44, McVean 70*	*Whitehouse*	*Kelso*	*Crone*	*Lamont*	*Proudfoot*	*Bell*	*Leonard*	*McVean*	*Stewart*	*Copeland*	*Gray*
								Ref: T Saywell [Carnelly 60, 85]	In the heavy, drifting rain, Finnerhan rolled in City's opener, but shortly before the break Leonard sent in a great shot that gave Monteith no chance of saving. City went back in front when Kelso, in attempting to clear from Carnelly, had the bad luck to head the ball into his own net.										
8	A	GRAVESEND		4	D	2-2	1-1	Bull 35og, Russell 70	Monteith	Barker	Davy	Jones	McLean	Hamilton	Langham	Finnerhan	Caie	Carnelly	Russell
	24/12		*1,500*	*6*	14			*Ross 30, 89*	*Wilkinson*	*Struthers*	*Bagnall*	*Davies*	*Bull*	*Buist*	*Garfield*	*Hulme*	*Mobley*	*Barbour*	*Ross*
								Ref: H Platt	City are robbed at Gravesend where, following an even first half, they dominated after the interval when they had two goals disallowed. A stirring contest ends with them pegged back by Ross heading in a late leveller to preserve Gravesend's long unbeaten run on their own ground.										
9	A	NEW BROMPTON		4	W	1-0	1-0	Russell 35	Monteith	Barker	Stewart	Jones	McLean	Hamilton	Langham	Finnerhan	Caie	Carnelly	Russell
	7/1		*3,000*	2	16				*Bunyan*	*Graham*	*King*	*Watson*	*Innes*	*Atherton*	*Grieve*	*Macdonald*	*Frettingham*	*Lennox*	*Gallacher*
								Ref: G Landragin	City were fortunate as, before Russell headed in what proved to be the only goal of the game, Watson hit the crossbar with his spot-kick after a foul on Frettingham. A keenly contested game, the result of which allowed City to confound their many critics by returning with both points.										
10	A	BRIGHTON UTD		4	L	1-2	0-2	Langham 70	Monteith	Barker	Stewart	Jones	McLean	Hamilton	Langham	Finnerhan	Caie	Carnelly	Russell
	11/1		***800***	*11*	16			*Malloch 20, McArthur 30*	*Bullimer*	*Hendry*	*Caldwell*	*Farrell*	*McAvoy*	*Longair*	*McWhirter*	*Carter*	*McArthur*	*Willocks*	*Malloch*
									City's return to the County Ground at Hove proves no more successful than their previous visit. Despite the muddy and slippery conditions, a keen and entertaining game ensued that ended with United hanging on and thereby depriving City of their unbeaten Southern League record.										

No	Date	Venue	Opponent	Att	Div	Pos	Pts	Res	F-A	H-T	Scorers, Times, Referees	1	2	3	4	5	6	7	8	9	10	11
11		H	MILLWALL ATH		4			W	2-1	1-0	Carnelly 40, Langham 50	Monteith	Barker	Davy	Jones	McLean	Stewart	Langham	Finnerhan	Caie	Carnelly	Russell
	14/1			5,000		*3*	18				*Geddes 70*	*Sunderland*	*Burgess*	*Davis W*	*Crawford*	*Stewart*	*Millar*	*Tannahill*	*Calvey*	*Hill*	*Turnbull*	*Geddes*
											Ref: J Tillotson	Millwall had the best of it early on, but it was City who took the lead when Carnelly netted from Finnerhan's pass. After the break, Langham doubled the advantage when he got up high to put away Stewart's free-kick. Geddes fired in for Millwall, after which City had many escapes.										
12		A	CHATHAM		4			L	0-2	0-1		Monteith	Barker	Stewart	Jones	Mann	Hamilton	Langham	Finnerhan	Caie	Carnelly	Russell
	21/1			*3,000*		*7*	18				*Dickenson 40, Johnson 75*	*Frail*	*Harper*	*Humphreys*	*Smith*	*Chapman*	*Slater*	*Brearley*	*Harper*	*Johnson*	*Clements*	*Dickenson*
												City put up a stirring display in a hard game at Chatham, where they were without the services of Mann for all but the first five minutes. A high wind quite spoiled accurate play, and Langham fired over from a good chance early on. Johnson's swift shot made Chatham's win certain.										
13		H	SHEPPEY UTD		4			W	4-1	3-0	Finnerhan 5, Carnelly 30, Potter 40,	Monteith	Davy	Stewart	Jones	McLean	Hamilton	Langham	Potter	Finnerhan	Carnelly	Russell
	1/2			1,500		*13*	18				*Trainer 80* [Langham 65]	*Leitch*	*Penny*	*Macfarlane*	*Lissenden*	*Abbott*	*Jenner*	*Harrison*	*Collins*	*Rule*	*Trainer*	*Peters*
											Ref: E Conquer	City, without Barker playing for the South v the North at the Crystal Palace, were not troubled by the Sheerness side seeking their first out win of the season. Finnerhan put away Carnelly's pass to give City an early lead. Penny's bad mistake allowed Carnelly to double the advantage.										
14		A	SWINDON		4			D	2-2	1-1	Langham 25, 75	Monteith	Barker	Stewart	Jones	McLean	Hamilton	Potter	Carnelly	Finnerhan	Langham	Russell
	4/2			*3,000*		*8*	19				*Kirton 28, Henderson 70*	*Menham*	*Shutt*	*Mills*	*Henderson*	*Logan*	*Smith*	*Sharples*	*Coupar*	*Richardson W*	*Little*	*Kirton*
											Ref: F Beardsley	Not long after the second half commenced in a snowstorm, City lost the services of Monteith with a thigh muscle strain and Potter took over between the sticks. Henderson's long shot gave Swindon the lead, but Langham escaped the attention of Mills to run through and equalise.										
15		H	GRAVESEND		2			W	5-2	3-2	Carnelly 10, Finnerhan 35, Langham 40,	Davy	Caie	Stewart	Jones	McLean	Hamilton	Langham	Finnerhan	Potter	Carnelly	Russell
	11/2			4,000		*11*	21				*Hulme 20, Ross 45*	*Wilkinson*	*Buist*	*Struthers*	*Bull*	*Regan*	*Davies*	*Parkinson*	*Manson*	*Mobley*	*Hulme*	*Ross*
											Ref: E Conquer [Potter 46, Russell 85]	Both sides exchanged headed goals before Finnerhan found the net with a shot after some clever individual work. Straight after the interval Potter's drive found the net off the post. Twenty minutes from the end, the injured Davy left the field and Potter took over between the sticks.										
16		A	TOTTENHAM		2			L	2-3	0-1	Caie 80p, Finnerhan 85	Potter	Barker	Stewart	Jones	McLean	Hamilton	Langham	Finnerhan	Caie	Carnelly	Russell
	18/2			***8,000***		*8*	21				*Hartley 2, Bradshaw 65, McKay 75*	*Cullen*	*Melia*	*Cain*	*Jones*	*McNaught*	*Stormont*	*Smith*	*McKay*	*Hartley*	*Cameron*	*Bradshaw*
												Bradshaw's well-placed corner brought Spurs their early goal, but City were unlucky shortly after when Russell had his effort ruled offside. Carnelly suffered the same fate with the goal at his mercy just after the break. Finnerhan scored from a rush but City couldn't find an equaliser.										
17		A	BEDMINSTER		4			L	0-1	0-0		Monteith	Barker	Stewart	Jones	McLean	Hamilton	Langham	Finnerhan	Caie	Carnelly	Russell
	4/3			*7,000*		*9*	21				*Leonard 70*	*Whitehouse*	*Kelso*	*Crone*	*Lamont*	*Proudfoot*	*Stewart*	*Leonard*	*Massie*	*McVean*	*Copeland*	*Gray*
											Ref: J Albert	McVean hooked the ball back for Leonard to fire home the goal that settled this fast and exciting local derby. Robert Crone, therefore, at least had the pleasure of performing on the winning side after the Bedminster directors had decided that they couldn't spare him to play for Ireland.										
18		A	SOUTHAMPTON		4			L	**1-4**	0-1	Langham 80	Monteith	Barker	Stewart	Jones	McLean	Hamilton	Langham	Finnerhan	Murphy	Carnelly	Russell
	11/3			*6,000*		*1*	21				*Hartley 35, 75, 85, Nicol 55*	*Robinson*	*Meehan*	*Durber*	*Meston*	*Haynes*	*Robertson*	*Nicol*	*McLean*	*Hartley*	*Wood*	*Seeley*
											Ref: J Tillotson	Whilst the Saints deserved their success, the scoreline somewhat flattered them. There didn't deserve to be more than one goal between the sides as Robinson had almost as much to do as Monteith. City's sole consolation was obtained near the end when Langham fired the ball in.										
19		A	ROYAL ARTILLERY		4			W	3-0	0-0	Carnelly 55, Finnerhan 70, Murphy 85	Monteith	Barker	Stewart	Jones	McLean	Hamilton	Langham	Finnerhan	Murphy	Carnelly	Russell
	18/3			*6,000*		*12*	23					*Reilly*	*Turner*	*Phillips*	*Coutts*	*Hill*	*Patterson*	*Coleman*	*Walsh*	*Hanna*	*Phinn*	*Jardine*
											Ref: G Muir	A good two points for City by beating the Gunners on the United Services Recreation Ground, Portsmouth. After Carnelly fired in the opener, there was only one team in it and Murphy's fierce grounder wrapped up an impressive success. Langham was the star of City's front rank.										
20		H	READING		3			W	1-0	0-0	O'Brien 75	Monteith	Barker	Stewart	Jones	McLean	Hamilton	Potter	Finnerhan	**Stevenson**	O'Brien	Russell
	25/3			4,000		*4*	25					*Whittaker*	*Henderson*	*O'Brien*	*Eccleston*	*Holt*	*Hosie*	*Davies*	*Goldie*	*Millar*	*Sharp A*	*Plant*
											Ref: J Jamieson	In this game, which was sponsored by the United Kingdom Commercial Travellers Association, City did well to overcome the loss of the injured Barker early in the second half. Stevenson (ex-St George) moved back to take his place. O'Brien notched the winner from a free-kick.										
21		H	BRIGHTON UTD		3			W	3-1	1-1	McLean 35, O'Brien 55, Stevenson 80	Monteith	Caie	Stewart	Jones	McLean	Hamilton	Langham	Finnerhan	Stevenson	O'Brien	Russell
	8/4			3,000		*10*	27				*Willocks 20*	*Spicer*	*Carter*	*Hendry*	*Low*	*McAvoy*	*Longair*	*McWhirter*	*Davidson*	*McArthur*	*Malloch*	*Willocks*
											Ref: V Daines	Despite Finnerhan firing a first-half spot-kick against the crossbar and heading the rebound over, it was easy for City after the break when Monteith was hardly called into action. A difficult afternoon for Finnerhan, though, as he had another pen saved by Spicer in the second half.										

SOUTHERN LEAGUE DIVISION 1

No	Date		Att	Pos	Pt	F-A	H-T	Scorers, Times, and Referees	1	2	3	4	5	6	7	8	9	10	11
22	H	ROYAL ARTILLERY		2	W	**6-1**	4-1	Stevenson 8, 25, 40, 85,	Monteith	Davy	Stewart	Caie	Britton	Hamilton	Langham	Carnelly	Stevenson	O'Brien	Russell
	12/4		**1,000**	*13*	29			*Harrison 35* [Carnelly 30, 75]	*Field*	*Leach*	*Clarke*	*Whitehouse*	*Sutherland*	*Smith*	*Hanna*	*Harrison*	*Phinn*	*McBirnie*	*Woods*
								Ref: H Platt	The fact that visitors were only able to field what was virtually a reserve XI following last week's FA Inquiry, produced only a limited crowd at St John's Lane. Apart from the opening few minutes, and a shot from Harrison that brought the RA their goal, City were on top throughout.										
23	A	SHEPPEY UTD		1	W	2-0	1-0	Hamilton 20, Langham 49	Monteith	Barker	Stewart	Jones	McLean	Hamilton	Langham	Finnerhan	Stevenson	O'Brien	Russell
	15/4		*1,000*	*12*					*Leitch*	*Penney*	*Macfarlane*	*Lissenden*	*Abbott*	*Jenner*	*Harrison*	*Collins*	*Edwards*	*Trainer*	*Peters*
								Ref: Mr Aylott	The home defence made matters difficult for City, for whom Hamilton opened the scoring with a capital shot. After the break, Langham's goal was allowed despite it appearing that the ball had gone out of play. Shortly after matters evened out when City were deprived of a fair goal.										
24	H	NEW BROMPTON		1	W	2-0	1-0	Carnelly 15, O'Brien 75	Monteith	Davy	Stewart	Jones	McLean	Hamilton	Langham	Carnelly	Stevenson	O'Brien	Russell
	22/4		6,250	*6*					*Bunyan*	*King*	*Robertson J*	*Innes*	*Atherton*	*Graham*	*Cooper*	*Macdonald*	*Frettingham*	*Gallacher*	*Campbell*
								Ref: A Barker	Carnelly headed City in front in the first half; then after the break, Bunyan's misjudgement of O'Brien's cross, which hit the upright before rebounding into the net, made victory certain. New Brompton didn't have much to offer, but City's wayward finishing let them off the hook.										
25	H	SOUTHAMPTON		2	L	3-4	2-0	Langham 4, O'Brien 31, Caie 87	Monteith	Davy	Stewart	Jones	McLean	Hamilton	Langham	Finnerhan	Caie	O'Brien	Russell
	29/4		13,000	*1*				*Chadwick 51, Wood 56,82, McLean 62*	*Robinson*	*Meehan*	*Durber*	*Meston*	*Chadwick*	*Haynes*	*Yates*	*McLeod*	*McLean*	*Wood*	*Robertson*
		Home	Away					Ref: Capt Simpson	Langham and O'Brien fired in to have the Championship within City's grasp at the break, but a thrilling comeback ensured a third consecutive title for the Saints. After Chadwick's long-shot gave the visitors hope, Monteith misjudged Wood's dropping effort to leave all to play for.										
	Ave	5,462	4,442					(£440)											

* *Warmley disbanded late January – record expunged.*

UNITED LEAGUE

No	Date		Att	Pos	Pt	F-A	H-T	Scorers, Times, and Referees	1	2	3	4	5	6	7	8	9	10	11
1	H	KETTERING			W	3-0	0-0	Finnerhan 50, Langham 70, Mann 85	Monteith	**Barker**	Milligan	Jones	Hamilton	**Stewart**	**Langham**	**Finnerhan**	Mann	O'Brien	Russell
	10/9		4,000		2				*Baldry*	*Raynor*	*Draper*	*Pell*	*Heskin*	*Dainty*	*McCarlie*	*Woodward*	*Beaver*	*Miller*	*Dixon*
								Ref: J Tillotson	After losing the toss and kicking off facing the sun, City's form didn't match the lovely weather. After the break they woke up slightly and Finnerhan netted with a high shot not long after the change of ends. Langham then hooked in another, before Mann headed in City's third.										
2	H	BRIGHTON UTD			W	4-0	2-0	O'Brien 12, Caie 35, 50, Finnerhan 55	Monteith	Barker	Davy	Jones	**McLean**	Stewart	**Potter**	Finnerhan	Caie	O'Brien	**Murphy**
	21/9		2,000		4				*Bullimer*	*Caldwell*	*Hendry*	*Longair*	*McWhirter*	*Low*	*Malloch*	*Willocks*	*McArthur*	*McLeod*	*Davidson*
								Ref: J Le Grand	McArthur kicked off on time for the visitors, and the early play took place in City quarters. Bullimer's stumble in trying to save from O'Brien allowed City to go in front but, undismayed, United came again. Monteith had to deal with a trio of shots before City doubled their advantage.										
3	A	READING		1	W	2-1	0-0	Caie 65, Potter 80	Monteith	Barker	Davy	Stewart	McLean	Hamilton	Langham	Potter	Caie	O'Brien	Russell
	28/9		*1,500*	*5*	6			*Sharp A 85*	*Neale*	*Sharp J*	*O'Brien*	*Foster*	*Dickinson*	*Ballantyne*	*Sharp A*	*Goldie*	*Millar*	*Davies*	*Plant*
								Ref: J Tillotson	City were at full strength for this game at Elm Park, but Reading fielded four reserves. Despite being hard pressed early on, City took the lead with a splendid drive. For Reading, Sharp's shot was ruled a goal, even though Monteith caught the ball when it dropped down from the bar.										
4	H	WELLINGBOROUGH		1	W	2-1	2-1	Caie 1, Russell 25	Monteith	Davy	Milligan	Stewart	McLean	Hamilton	Murphy	Potter	Caie	O'Brien	Russell
	1/10		4,000	*5*	8			*Hall 30*	*Shawley*	*Bennett*	*Robson*	*Morrell*	*Martin*	*Davis*	*Hall*	*Williams*	*Scriven*	*Raby*	*Hyde*
								Ref: W Cockain	Potter passed to Caie, who found the back of the net with a low shot at the start. When Russell headed in another it looked like being a rout, but Hall soon replied by rushing in Hyde's cross. O'Brien, just before the break, and Hyde, near the finish, both had offside efforts disallowed.										
5	H	TOTTENHAM		2	L	0-1	0-1		Monteith	Barker	Davy	Jones	McLean	Hamilton	Potter	Finnerhan	Caie	O'Brien	Russell
	15/10		**8,000**	*1*	8			*Cameron 10*	*Cullen*	*Erentz*	*Cain*	*Jones*	*McNaught*	*Stormont*	*Smith*	*McKay*	*Joyce*	*Cameron*	*Bradshaw*
								Ref: F Beardsley	City played a plucky and determined game, but did not have the best of luck. Monteith brought off a brilliant save from Smith's fierce shot, but Cameron ran in to tuck the ball away. After the break Spurs were lucky when the referee failed to spot that Cullen carried a shot into his net.										

6	A	BRIGHTON UTD	2	L	1-2	0-1	McLean 55	Monteith	Barker	Milligan	Stewart	McLean	Hamilton	Langham	Finnerhan	Caie	O'Brien	Russell
	26/10	*2,000*	*5*	8			*McWhirter 25, McLeod 75*	*Bullimer*	*Caldwell*	*Hendry*	*Longair*	*Farrell*	*Low*	*Halman*	*Willocks*	*McArthur*	*McLeod*	*McWhirter*
							Ref: F Walford	The visit of City brought forth a good attendance in the delightful weather. Faced by full-strength opponents, City fell to defeat in this grandly contested game. Brighton won the toss and had the assistance of the wind in the first half. City's goal was forced in off one of the home backs.										
7	H	WLCH ARSENAL	5	L	1-2	1-1	Langham 20	Monteith	Barker	Milligan	Jones	McLean	Stewart	Potter	Langham	Caie	O'Brien	Murphy
	9/11	2,250	*1*	8			*Dailly 35, Hunt 50*	*Ord*	*McAvoy*	*McConnell*	*Haywood*	*Anderson*	*Dick*	*Brock*	*White*	*Hunt*	*Hannah*	*Dailly*
							Ref: J Tillotson	Despite Langham firing City in front, the *Bristol Times & Mirror* commented that they had 'seldom played a poorer game'. Whilst the Woolwich men passed well, after Dailly's fine shot levelled matters, only Monteith, Barker, McLean and Murphy were on form for City.										
8	A	TOTTENHAM	5	L	1-2	1-2	Finnerhan 44	Mann	Barker	Milligan	Stewart	McLean	Hamilton	Langham	Finnerhan	Caie	O'Brien	Russell
	12/11	***8,000***	*1*	8			*McKay 4, Cameron 14*	*Cullen*	*Erentz*	*Cain*	*Jones*	*McNaught*	*Stormont*	*Smith*	*McKay*	*Joyce*	*Cameron*	*Bradshaw*
								The England Selection Committee witnessed this fast and exciting game. Without Monteith who strained his knee against the Corinthians, City fell behind to McKay's early effort. The Citizens only goal came as a result a breakaway, whilst Caie's rough tactics almost had him sent off.										
9	H	LUTON	4	W	**6-0**	0-0	Russell 48, 85, Finnerhan 70, [Mann 75, Murphy 76, Caie 88]	Monteith	Davy	Milligan	Jones	Mann	Stewart	Potter	Finnerhan	Caie	Murphy	Russell
	30/11	1,000	*10*	10				*Perkins*	*Dow*	*Moore*	*Ford*	*Williams*	*Crump*	*Durrant*	*Kemplay*	*McInnes*	*Hewitt*	*Ekins*
							Ref: F Walford	City, after a lifeless and ragged first-half display, were reinvigorated following the break. Russell gave Perkins no chance with his shot for the opener. Murphy then had an effort disallowed for offside, but nothing could stop rampant City, who had notched up a half-dozen by the close.										
10	A	WLCH ARSENAL	4	W	3-1	2-1	Finnerhan 5, Murphy 7, Caie 75	Monteith	Barker	Milligan	Jones	McLean	Stewart	Potter	Finnerhan	Caie	Murphy	Russell
	12/12	*700*	*1*	12			*McGeoch 30*	*Hamilton*	*McAvoy*	*McConnell*	*Moir*	*Dick*	*Gilmour*	*McGeoch*	*Haywood*	*Hunt*	*Murphy*	*Dailly*
							Ref: G West	Playing against a strong wind before the break at Plumstead, City showed much better form than a Gunners side short of five regulars. Despite exerting much pressure towards the close, Arsenal were unable to add to McGeoch's cross that found the net without the aid of Dailly's head.										
11	A	SOUTHAMPTON	5	L	**0-6**	0-4	*Hartley 2, 10, 45, Chadwick 35, [Smith 60, Wood 85]*	Monteith	Barker	Stewart	Mann	McLean	Hamilton	Langham	Finnerhan	Caie	O'Brien	Russell
	4/1	*3,000*	*7*	12				*Robinson*	*Meehan*	*Haynes*	*Meston*	*Chadwick*	*Durber*	*Smith*	*Stevens*	*Hartley*	*Wood*	*Seeley*
							Ref: J Jamieson	City, short of Davy, Milligan, Carnelly and Jones, suffered a heavy defeat that in no way represented the play. For the Saints, who were also less than full strength, everything came off, whilst Robinson kept out all that the City had to offer. Hartley dribbled through for the opener.										
12	A	WELLINGBOROUGH	6	L	0-3	0-3		Monteith	Stewart	Davy	Mann	McLean	Caie	Potter	Finnerhan	Carnelly	O'Brien	Murphy
	16/1	***500***	*7*	12			*Hyde 2, Morrell 32, Drage 44*	*Shawley*	*Bennett*	*Robson*	*Morrell*	*Martin*	*Davis*	*Hall*	*Williams*	*Drage*	*Raby*	*Hyde*
								City found both their opponents and the strong wind too difficult to handle in the first half, Monteith on one occasion conceding a corner when his goal-kick blew back over the line. Hyde got the homesters off to a good start when he netted with a beauty before City had time to settle.										
13	H	RUSHDEN	6	W	3-0	0-0	O'Brien 46, Jones 70, Caie 85	Davy	Caie	Stewart	Jones	McLean	Hamilton	Potter	Finnerhan	Carnelly	O'Brien	Russell
	8/2	1,000	*11*	14				*Daw*	*Clarke*	*Hendry*	*Sale*	*Bailey*	*Suggett*	*Webb C*	*Dunkley F*	*Hingerty*	*Pendered*	*Mellor*
							Ref: J Tillotson	City started the game from the Lane End, but despite exerting much pressure were unable to register before the break. Finnerhan's swift pass set up O'Brien to net the opener; then Jones doubled City's advantage before Caie's long shot tied matters up shortly before the final whistle.										
14	H	MILLWALL ATH	6	L	2-3	1-3	Russell 20, Gard 75	Potter	Barker	Caie	Jones	McLean	Stewart	Langham	**Gard**	Carnelly	O'Brien	Russell
	22/2	2,000	*2*	14			*Calvey 23, 25, 35*	*Sunderland*	*Burgess*	*Davis W*	*Morrison*	*Stewart*	*Millar*	*Crawford*	*Calvey*	*Hill*	*Turnbull*	*Geddes*
							Ref: Sgt Barrow	Russell opened the scoring with a grounder, which the keeper should have saved. Millwall soon equalised when Calvey put in a shot which gave Potter no chance, and then repeated the feat not long after to give his side the lead. After Gard scored from close in, City had hard luck.										
15	A	LUTON	4	W	3-1	1-0	Gard 30, Potter 65, Murphy 85	Monteith	Barker	Caie	Stewart	McLean	Hamilton	Langham	Gard	Murphy	O'Brien	Potter
	27/2	***500***	*11*	16			*McInnes 75*	*Perkins*	*Dow*	*Moore*	*Ford*	*Williams*	*Crump*	*Durrant*	*Brock*	*McInnes*	*Boutwood*	*Ekins*
								Neither side was fully represented, Luton being especially weak forward. With the brilliant sun at their backs, City took the lead when Perkins spilled Langham's shot against Murphy. Unlucky with a shot that hit a post before the break, McInnes eventually registered with a cross-drive.										
16	H	READING	4	W	5-1	3-0	Carnelly 30, Potter 35, 37, 80, [Murphy 60]	Monteith	Barker	Stewart	Jones	Caie	Hamilton	Potter	Carnelly	Murphy	O'Brien	Russell
	8/3	**700**	*7*	18			*Turner 75*	*Whittaker*	*Henderson*	*O'Brien*	*Hosie*	*Holt*	*Foster*	*Turner*	*Goldie*	*Sharp A*	*Davies*	*Johnson*
							Ref: J Jamieson	City were unlucky when Russell netted direct from his corner-kick, the goal being disallowed as no one else had touched the ball. Fortunately, a shot by Carnelly counted not long after. Potter and Murphy starred for City, the *T&M* commenting that 'they have never played better'.										

UNITED LEAGUE

No	Date		Att	Pos	Pt	F-A	H-T	Scorers, Times, and Referees	1	2	3	4	5	6	7	8	9	10	11
17	A	MILLWALL ATH		4	L	1-4	0-1	Carnelly 60	Monteith	Caie	Stewart	**Britton**	McLean	Hamilton	Potter	Carnelly	Murphy	O'Brien	Russell
	16/3		*3,000*	*1*	18			*Gettins 20, Calvey 75, 85, 89*	*Sunderland*	*Burgess*	*Davis W*	*Crawford*	*Stewart*	*Millar*	*Tannahill*	*Calvey*	*Gettins*	*Turnbull*	*Geddes*
								Ref: J Stark	Millwall demonstrated the finishing power as City found themselves constantly thwarted by Sunderland's display between the sticks. Stewart's mistake allowed Gettins to slot in the opener, but Carnelly headed City level after the break when Russell's fine shot rebounded off of the bar.										
18	A	KETTERING		6	W	3-0	3-0	Stevenson 25, 30, 40	Monteith	Barker	Stewart	Jones	Caie	Hamilton	Langham	Finnerhan	Stevenson	Potter	Murphy
	1/4		*1,000*	*8*	20				*Baldry*	*Wallis*	*Draper*	*Raynor*	*Farren*	*Dainty*	*Woodward*	*Heskin*	*Panter*	*Beaver*	*Clarke*
								Ref: S Carr	In fine weather, City were indebted to their keeper for making many fine sides that kept out a Kettering side missing the services of Pell and Winterhalder. Play was rough, fouls being frequent, but Stevenson banged through the opening goal after Baldry had kept out his initial shot.										
19	H	SOUTHAMPTON		4	W	2-1	2-0	Caie 5, 15	Monteith	Barker	Davy	Jones	Britton	Hamilton	Potter	Carnelly	Caie	O'Brien	Murphy
	19/4		3,000	*2*	22			*Buchanan 70*	*Robinson*	*Meehan*	*Haynes*	*Meston*	*Dewar*	*McLean*	*Cust*	*Stevens*	*Buchanan*	*Keay*	*Seeley*
									Splendid weather attended this game, but despite City's victory they will need to play a great deal better if they are to repeat this feat in the Southern League shortly. Caie opened the scoring with a cool lob, and then doubled City's advantage with a brilliant shot from Murphy's pass.										
20	A	RUSHDEN		5	L	1-2	0-0	Carnelly 53	Monteith	Davy	Stewart	Potter	Caie	Hamilton	Langham	Carnelly	Stevenson	Murphy	Russell
	24/4		***500***	*10*	22			*Pendered 50, 85*	*Dow*	*Clarke*	*Hendry*	*Sale*	*Bailey*	*Suggett*	*Webb C*	*Dunkley F*	*Hingerty*	*Pendered*	*Mellor*
		Home	Away						A poor attendance in the threatening weather witnessed City's almost complete first-half control. Dow stood firm between the sticks however, and after the break it was Rushden who took charge. Pendered headed in their deserved winner after Carnelly had levelled the No 9's opener.										
	Ave	2,795	2,070																

FRIENDLIES

No	Date		Att	Pos	Pt	F-A	H-T	Scorers, Times, and Referees	1	2	3	4	5	6	7	8	9	10	11
1	A	EASTVILLE ROV			L	0-1	0-0		Monteith	**Barker**	Milligan	**Stewart**	**McLean**	Hamilton	**Langham**	**Finnerhan**	Caie	**Murphy**	Russell
	1/9		*3,500*					*Fisher 75*	*Cook*	*Bunch*	*Griffiths*	*Farnall*	*Turley*	*Kinsey*	*Brown*	*Jones*	*McCairns*	*Fisher*	*Paul*
								Ref: G Gay	In the sunshine, Kinsey won the toss for the Rovers who defended the Gas Works End in the first half, during which neither goal was breached. City did most of the attacking without success after the break, and Fisher, shortly after sending over the crossbar for Rovers, beat Monteith.										
2	A	WEST NORWOOD			W	4-3	0-1	O'Brien 50, Mann 70, 85, Jones 75	Monteith	Barker	Milligan	Stewart	Jones	Hamilton	Langham	Finnerhan	Mann	O'Brien	Russell
	3/9		*1,500*					*Landels 44, Critchley 55, Fitchie 60*	*Bullock*	*Humphries*	*Stevens*	*Adams*	*Critchley*	*Landels*	*Turner*	*Fitchie*	*Folkes*	*Britton*	*Hasland*
								Ref: J Clarke	A good-sized crowd at High View Park where City, the much heavier and robust side, came out on top in a seven-goal thriller. Norwood started from the Entrance End and took a first-half lead when Landels rushed up from half-back. City did well to recover after the interval.										
3	H	NEW BRIGHTON			W	4-0	0-0	Hamilton 55, Mann 56, O'Brien 70, [Potter 85]	Monteith	Barker	Milligan	Jones	Hamilton	Stewart	**Potter**	Finnerhan	Mann	O'Brien	Murphy
	7/9		1,000						*Haddow*	*Stephenson*	*Arridge*	*McCartney*	*Mellon*	*Allison*	*Cunliffe*	*Hargreaves*	*Hammond*	*Hill*	*Becton*
								Ref: A Farrant	Despite the heat a fast and exciting game was played out with New Brighton Tower. O'Brien had a first-half header disallowed, and it wasn't until after the break that Hamilton fired in the opener from a free-kick. The play, which became rough, was concluded in gathering darkness.										
4	H	BRSTL ST GEORGE			W	2-1	2-0	Murphy 15, Caie 20	Monteith	Barker	Milligan	Mann	Hamilton	Stewart	Langham	Murphy	Caie	O'Brien	Russell
	24/9		5,000					*Barr 55*	*McKay*	*Halley*	*Cole*	*Underwood*	*McCreadie*	*Beak*	*Allen*	*Barr*	*Stevenson*	*Boyd*	*Scotchbrook*
								Ref: E McDonald	No fault could be found with the gate, but the play hardly came up to expectations after local MP (W Howell Davies) kicked-off on the Saint's behalf. Murphy headed in the opener; then Caie tricked Halley before notching City's second. Boyd's pass set up Barr to score for the visitors.										
5	A	RYDE			W	3-1	2-1	Potter 25, O'Brien 40, 55	Monteith	Davy	Milligan	Jones	McLean	Stewart	Langham	Potter	Caie	O'Brien	Russell
	31/10		*500*					*Jones 10*	*Reilly*	*Scott CW*	*Walker FM*	*King*	*Halliday*	*Ponting*	*Jones*	*Christie*	*Woodhouse*	*Maidment E*	*Yelf F*
								Ref: F Barber	The homesters played Reilly, the Royal Artillery custodian, who saved brilliantly from Caie early on. Ryde then got down and Jones netted after Monteith had saved. Potter brought City level with a shot that gave Reilly no chance. Langham then registered but was given offside.										

No	Venue	Opponent / Att	Res	FT	HT	Scorers / Referee	1	2	3	4	5	6	7	8	9	10	11
6	A	CORINTHIANS	D	1-1	1-0	O'Brien 30	Monteith	Barker	Milligan	Stewart	Mann	Hamilton	Langham	Finnerhan	Caie	O'Brien	Murphy
10/11		*1,500*				*Wilson 70*	*Campbell W*	*Coode AT*	*Oakley WJ*	*Vickers H*	*Middleditch B*	*Beasley HO*	*Hewitt CD*	*Blaker RNR*	*Smith GO*	*Wilson GP*	*Powell EO*
		(Abandoned 75 mins due to fog)				Ref: Capt Simpson *(at 'Queen's Club')*	For the first time this season, the Corinthians took the field at the Queens Club, West Kensington. Unfortunately, with the old international GF Wilson failing to turn up, they played the first half-hour with ten men until EO Powell, the old Hampshire cricketer, was pressed into service.										
7	A	NOTTS CO	W	4-2	2-0	Carnelly 22, Murphy 35,	Monteith	Barker	Milligan	Jones	Mann	Stewart	Langham	Finnerhan	Murphy	Carnelly	Russell
26/12		*6,000*				*Logan 46, Hannigan 88*	*Limer*	*Lewis*	*Montgomery*	*Bull*	*Watts*	*Sanderson*	*Hannigan*	*Dean*	*Logan*	*Boucher*	*Hadley*
						Ref: W Cockain [Finnerhan 70, Russell 75]	Despite losing the services of Carnelly soon after he scored a pretty goal, City pulled off a great win at Trent Bridge. Murphy had a goal struck off before Hannigan rushed through the final goal for a Notts side at less than full-strength, due to their impending League game with L'pool.										
8	A	BRSTL ST GEORGE	L	1-9	1-4	Caie 15 *[Henderson 30, Beak 65],*	**Giddings**	Barker	Milligan	Stewart	Davy	Hamilton	Potter	Caie	Murphy	Jones	Russell
27/12		*3,500*				*Stevenson 2,25, Boyd 10,46,55,90,*	*Macfarlane*	*Halley*	*McKay*	*Underwood*	*Beak*	*Scotchbrook*	*Allen*	*Barr*	*Stevenson*	*Boyd*	*Henderson*
						Ref: T Saywell *[Caie 75og]*	After City won the toss and elected to start with the wind, the Mayor of Bristol (Herbert Ashman) set the ball rolling for St George. With the ex-Clifton amateur Giddings in goal, City had a difficult and humiliating time at Bell Hill after Stevenson's easy shot had opened the scoring.										
9	H	BRSTL ESTVILLE R	L	2-3	1-0	Murphy 2, O'Brien 75	Mann	Barker	Davy	Jones	McLean	Hamilton	Langham	Finnerhan	Murphy	O'Brien	Russell
31/12		5,000				*Brown 65, McCairns 80, Fisher 81*	*Julian*	*Horsey*	*Griffiths*	*Farnall*	*Burton*	*Kinsey*	*Brown*	*Jones*	*McCairns*	*Fisher*	*Paul*
						Ref: E McDonald	The blame for this defeat must not be placed upon the shoulders of Mann, deputising for Monteith (away on holiday), despite his having stopped to appeal for offside when Brown ran through to fire the Rovers equaliser. He saved many fine shots from the more vigorous visitors.										
10	H	BURNLEY	W	2-1	2-1	Carnelly 5, McLean 25	Monteith	Caie	Stewart	Jones	McLean	Hamilton	Langham	Potter	Carnelly	O'Brien	Russell
25/2		5,000				*Morrison 3*	*Hillman*	*Reynolds*	*Place Snr*	*Barron*	*Taylor*	*Livingstone*	*Morrison*	*Ross*	*Toman*	*Bowes*	*Place Jnr*
						Ref: V Daines	In delightful weather Ross was making his final appearance for the visitors, having agreed to a transfer to Manchester City yesterday. Morrison opened the scoring soon after the start with a cross-shot that went into the net off an upright. Carnelly brought City level with a close in shot.										
11	H	STOCKTON	W	3-0	1-0	O'Brien 3, 55, Potter 85	Monteith	Caie	Stewart	Jones	Britton	Hamilton	Potter	Carnelly	Stevenson	O'Brien	Russell
31/3		5,000					*Fall*	*Shaw W*	*Wilson*	*Brannan*	*Baker*	*Monteith*	*Halfpenny J*	*Chatt R*	*Byron*	*Fairbairn*	*Lakey*
						Ref: G Gay	An easy win for City over the current Amateur Cup holders, who placed a full-strength side in the field. City, who found places in their team for Phil Britton (ex-Warmley) and Stevenson (ex-St George), started from the Lower End and within three mins O'Brien netted during a melee.										
12	H	CORINTHIANS	W	4-3	1-3	O'Brien 3, Stevenson 41,	Monteith	Caie	Stewart	Jones	Britton	Hamilton	Finnerhan	Carnelly	Stevenson	O'Brien	Russell
4/4		4,000				*Moon LJ 7, 27, Taylor 25*	*Moon WR*	*Oakley WJ*	*Bray EH*	*Vickers H*	*Wr-BrownOE*	*Hornby RP*	*Taylor SS*	*Snell H*	*Smith GO*	*Corbett BA*	*Moon LJ*
						Ref: T Helme [Russell 45, 65]	Due to the unfavourable weather, which fortunately didn't affect the crowd, it was agreed before kick-off to play only 40 minutes each way. O'Brien's low drive opened the scoring, but Moon levelled with a clever shot, before Taylor headed in a corner to put the visitors in front.										

FA Cup/Glos Cup	F-A	H-T	Scorers, Times, and Referees	1	2	3	4	5	6	7	8	9	10	11
3Q A COWES 8 W	5-0	2-0	Russell 6, Caie 29, 83, O'Brien 60,	Monteith	Barker	Davy	Jones	McLean	Hamilton	Langham	Finnerhan	Caie	O'Brien	Russell
29/10 *1,500 2:1*			[Langham 70]	*Bennett*	*Ward A*	*McKie*	*Docherty*	*Haxton*	*Thomson*	*Moore*	*Finlayson*	*Skea*	*Leatherbar'w*	*Spellacy*
			Ref: T Saywell	After Russell opened the scoring by shooting into an open net, Cowes could do nothing against City's superior combination in the first half. After the interval they livened up considerable, but following Ward's leg fracture early in the half it was City who were able notch the goals.										
4Q A BRSTL ST GEORGE 7 W	1-0	1-0	Finnerhan 14	Monteith	Barker	Davy	Jones	McLean	Hamilton	Langham	Finnerhan	Caie	O'Brien	Russell
19/11 *11,228 BL:5*				*Macfarlane*	*Halley*	*Cole*	*Underwood*	*McCreadie*	*Scotchbrook*	*Allen*	*Barr*	*Stevenson*	*Boyd*	*Henderson*
(£347.5.6)			Ref: A Cooper	City deserved their slender win, though St George enjoyed the majority share of the play. Early on, Finnerhan ran through to fire in what proved to be the only goal of what was, in many ways, a great game in ideal dry conditions. Monteith was frequently called into action.										
5Q H READING 5 W	3-2	2-1	Caie 6p, 17, Langham 77	Monteith	Barker	Milligan	Jones	McLean	Hamilton	Langham	Finnerhan	Caie	Murphy	Russell
10/12 6,000 *9*			*Millar 43, Sharp A 55*	*Whittaker*	*Henderson*	*O'Brien*	*Sharp J*	*Holt*	*Eccleston*	*Davies*	*Goldie*	*Millar*	*Sharp A*	*Plant*
			Ref: J Adams	At the start, City seemed to have profited from their training in the bracing air at Clevedon, as they threatened to run Reading off their feet. However, the visitors fought back well and, after equalising, it was City who were the ones all at sea until Langham scored from a free-kick.										
1 H SUNDERLAND 4 L	2-4	2-3	Langham 24, Finnerhan 37,	Monteith	Davy	Stewart	Jones	McLean	Hamilton	Langham	Finnerhan	Caie	O'Brien	Russell
28/1 16,945 *1:10*			*Leslie 34, Crawford 35, Fulton 40,*	*Doig*	*Bach*	*McNeill*	*Ferguson*	*McAlister*	*Raisbeck*	*Crawford*	*Leslie*	*Fulton*	*Wilson*	*McLatchie*
(£524.1.6)			Ref: T Helme *[Wilson 85]*	Sunderland turned out in white shirts, so City played in their normal colours. Langham put City ahead with a grand shot, but Leslie fired in the Roker men's equaliser. By the finish, City, the first local club to reach this stage of the cup, may have been beaten, but they were not disgraced.										
2 H BRISTOL AMTRS 2 W	7-3	1-2	Langham 35, O'Brien 50, 70, 73, 80,	Potter	Barker	Stewart	Jones	McLean	Hamilton	Langham	Carnelly	Caie	O'Brien	Russell
GC 20/2 1,000 *WL:4*			*Langford 10, 45, North 60*	*Thomas E*	*Cowell L*	*Felloes CE*	*Mayo L*	*McAuliffe M*	*Trestrail AE*	*Slade E*	*Stolz W*	*Callender W*	*Langford E*	*North AE*
			Ref: A Farrant [Caie 55, Carnelly 85]	City, who had been giving a bye in the first round, were surprised by their Western League Division Two opponents in the opening 45 minutes. Langford headed the Amateurs in front early on; then right on the break he was on hand to walk the ball in when Potter spilled North's shot.										
SF H FISHPONDS 4 W	8-1	3-0	Jones 5, Murphy 25, Russell 35, 55,	Monteith	Caie	Stewart	Jones	McLean	Hamilton	Potter	Carnelly	Murphy	O'Brien	Russell
GC 22/3 1,500 *WL:1*			*Mitchell 88*	*Bennett R*	*Sutton A*	*Brimble WJ*	*Hulin J*	*Nolan WH*	*Nash E*	*Roberts A*	*Mitchell J*	*Webster G*	*Preddy R*	*Iles B*
			Ref: A Farrant [Carnelly 50, 70, O'Brien 75, 80]	This comprehensive success over Fishponds, brought City revenge for their shock defeat in the same competition two years earlier. They were never extended by the Western League Division Two leaders. Most of City's attacking was done from the left, where Russell did capital work.										
F N BRISTOL ROV 3 W	2-1	0-0	Langham 50, Murphy 70	Monteith	Barker	Stewart	Jones	McLean	Hamilton	Langham	Finnerhan	Murphy	O'Brien	Russell
GC 3/4 *11,433 BL:4*			*Brown 80*	*Cook*	*Bunch*	*Griffiths*	*Farnall*	*Burton*	*Kinsey*	*Brown*	*Jones*	*McCairns*	*Smellie*	*Paul*
(£356.1.9)			Ref: T Helme *(at 'St George')*	With the wind behind them, the Rovers lost their chance by not shooting more frequently in the first half. When City had nature's assistance after the break they were not long in scoring. Langham registered with a shot that went just under the bar. Jones headed in Rovers' consolation.										

SOUTHERN LEAGUE	P	Home W	D	L	F	A	Away W	D	L	F	A	Pts
1 Southampton	24	9	2	1	34	9	6	3	3	20	15	35
2 BRISTOL C	24	11	0	1	39	16	4	3	5	16	17	33
3 Millwall Ath	24	7	2	3	34	17	5	4	3	25	18	30
4 Chatham	24	6	4	2	19	8	4	4	4	13	15	28
5 Reading	24	9	2	1	24	4	0	6	6	7	20	26
6 New Brompt'	24	7	3	2	24	9	3	2	7	14	21	25
7 Tottenham H	24	8	2	2	24	11	2	2	8	16	25	24
8 Bedminster	24	7	1	4	19	13	3	3	6	16	26	24
9 Swindon T	24	7	4	1	33	21	2	1	9	10	28	23
10 Brighton Utd	24	6	2	4	23	13	3	0	9	14	35	20
11 Gravesend U	24	6	3	3	31	20	1	2	9	11	32	19
12 Sheppey Utd	24	5	2	5	16	18	0	1	11	7	35	13
13 RoyalArtillery	24	3	4	5	11	16	1	0	11	6	44	12
	312	91	31	34	331	175	34	31	91	175	331	312
- Warmley *Disbanded*	17	2	0	6	13	23	0	2	7	12	35	6

UNITED LEAGUE	P	Home W	D	L	F	A	Away W	D	L	F	A	Pts
1 Millwall Ath	20	8	2	0	26	8	6	1	3	16	11	31
2 Southampton	20	10	0	0	40	5	2	1	7	13	28	25
3 Tottenham H	20	7	1	2	24	10	4	1	5	12	15	24
4 Wlch Arsenal	20	8	0	2	24	13	2	4	4	16	18	24
5 BRISTOL C	20	7	0	3	28	9	4	0	6	15	22	22
6 Reading	20	7	2	1	26	4	1	3	6	10	21	21
7 Brighton Utd	20	8	1	1	28	11	2	0	8	13	31	21
8 Wellingboro'	20	6	0	4	22	14	1	1	8	11	26	15
9 Kettering*	20	6	1	3	14	8	2	0	8	7	25	15
10 Rushden	20	4	1	5	19	23	2	0	8	7	22	13
11 Luton Town	20	2	3	5	17	22	0	0	10	7	49	7
	220	73	11	26	268	127	26	11	73	127	268	218

* *2 points deducted*

Odds & ends

Double wins: SL: (3) Reading, New Brompton, Sheppey United, Royal Artillery. UL: (3) Kettering, Reading, Luton Town.
Double losses: SL: (1) Southampton. UL: (2) Tottenham, Millwall Ath.

Won from behind: SL: (2) Tottenham Hotspur (h), Brighton United (h)
Lost from in front: SL: (1) South'ton (h). UL: (2) Arsenal (h), Millwall (h).

High spots: Commencing the United League campaign with four wins.
City's six goal second-half salvo versus Luton on 30 November.
Becoming the first Bristol club to reach the 1st round of the FA Cup.
Opening the scoring against Sunderland in the FA Cup in front of a new record 'St John's Lane' crowd of 16,945 on 28 January.
Beating Bristol Rovers 2-1 in the Final of the Gloucestershire Cup.

Low Spots: Losing 0-1 against Bedminster at 'Ashton Gate' on 4 March.
Southampton's amazing second-half fight-back on 29 April that cost City the Southern League Championship.
The four straight United League losses that followed City's fine start.

Player of the Year: George Barker.
Ever-presents: (0).
Hat-tricks: (4) Jim Stevenson (2), Arthur Potter, 'Paddy' O'Brien.
Leading scorer: Overall: 'Sandy' Caie (22). League: 'Sandy' Caie (15).

Supporters Match (at 'St John's Lane')
15 April Totterdown End 4(2) Bedminster End 3(2)

AGM (Temperance Hall, East Street, Bedminster, 11 July 1899):
Loss £112.10s.3d. Season Ticket Sales £131.11s.2d.

	Appearances Lge	Cup	Fr	Goals Lge	Cup	Fr	Tot
Baker, George	**33**	5	8				
Britton, Phil	**3**		2				
Carnelly, Albert	**22**	2	4	**11**	3	2	**16**
Caie, 'Sandy'	**37**	6	8	**15**	5	2	**22**
Davy, Harry	**22**	3	3				
Finnerhan, Pat	**33**	5	7	**14**	2	1	**17**
Gard, Alfred	**2**			**1**			**1**
Giddings			1				
Hamilton, Jack	**38**	7	10	**1**		1	**2**
Jones, Billy	**34**	7	9	**1**	1	1	**3**
Langham, Billy	**34**	6	8	**13**	5		**18**
McLean, John	**35**	7	4	**2**		1	**3**
Mann, George	**8**		6	**3**		3	**6**
Milligan, Alex	**8**	1	8				
Monteith, Hugh	**40**	6	10				
Murphy, John	**17**	3	7	**5**	2	3	**10**
O'Brien, 'Paddy'	**25**	6	9	**6**	7	9	**22**
Potter, Arthur	**22**	2	5	**7**		3	**10**
Russell, 'Jock'	**38**	7	10	**10**	3	3	**16**
Stevenson, Jim	**7**		2	**8**		1	**9**
Stewart, Billy	**37**	4	11				
21 players used	**495**	**77**	**132**	**97**	**28**	**30**	**155**

Note: Game against Warmley included.

No	Date	Att	Pos	Pt	F-A	H-T	Scorers, Times, and Referees	1	2	3	4	5	6	7	8	9	10	11
1	H SWINDON			W	3-2	3-1	Caie 10, 35, Downie 30	Monteith	Milligan	Stewart	Jones	McLean	Hamilton	Langham	**Molyneux**	Caie	**Downie**	**Crawford**
	2/9	6,750		2			*Sharples 40, Wilson 75*	*Menham*	*Shutt*	*Wilson J*	*Richardson*	*G Henderson*	*Smith A*	*Sharples*	*Chapman*	*Smith W*	*Crawford*	*Wilson T*
							Ref: H Walker	After Hamilton won the toss in fine weather and chose to defend the Rifle Range End, Caie got the campaign off to a good start by finding the net with a fine cross-shot. Menham's fumble then allowed Downie to double the advantage, before Caie's hot-shot put City firmly in control.										
2	A COWES*			W	5-1	2-0	Crawford 18, 80, Caie 44,	Monteith	Stewart	Milligan	McLean	Godsman	Hamilton	Langham	Crawford	Caie	O'Brien	Russell
	16/9	*1,500*		4			*Walker 65* [O'Brien 55, 70]	*Steveley*	*Ward*	*Tait*	*Nash*	*Docherty*	*Joliffe*	*Baker*	*Finlayson*	*Walker*	*Brock*	*Moore*
							Ref: W Grant	Whilst a heavy thunderstorm kept the attendance down, it didn't deter City who raced to an easy win against last season's Division Two Champions. The Isle of Wight side were outclassed from start to finish, though Walker was able to kick in a consolation goal for them.										
3	H SOUTHAMPTON		7	L	1-3	0-2	Caie 70p	Monteith	McDonald	Stewart	Jones	McLean	Hamilton	Langham	Crawford	Caie	O'Brien	Russell
	23/9	6,000	*5*	4			*Farrell 20, Milward 35p, 85*	*Robinson*	*Meehan*	*Durber*	*Meston*	*Chadwick*	*Petrie*	*Yates*	*McLeod*	*Farrell*	*Wood*	*Milward*
							Ref: A Barker	Against the current Champions, an out-of-sorts City were not helped by the fierce wind that they faced in the first half. Farrell opened the scoring in fine style, before Langham gave Milward his penalty. Crawford had a goal disallowed for City shortly before Caie's spot-kick.										
4	A MILLWALL ATH		9	L	1-3	0-2	Langham 53	Monteith	McDonald	McLean	Jones	Godsman	Hamilton	Langham	Molyneux	Caie	O'Brien	Russell
	30/9	*5,000*	*7*	4			*Banks 1, 25, 75*	*West*	*Burgess*	*Beattie*	*Smith*	*Millar*	*Goldie*	*Dryburgh*	*Brearley*	*Robertson*	*Banks*	*Nichol*
							Ref: T Sweetman	Heavy rain just prior to the start left the pitch a quagmire and Millwall, winning the toss, had the advantage of the wind. Straight away, a free-kick for hands allowed Banks to score. City had a fair share of this keen encounter, but could only net once, whilst Banks claimed a hat-trick										
5	H QP RANGERS		9	W	5-3	3-1	Russell 1, Caie 13, 30,	Monteith	McLean	Godsman	Jones	Britton	Hamilton	Langham	Potter	Caie	O'Brien	Russell
	7/10	7,500	*10*	6			*Bed'gfield 40, Evans 65, Haywood 68*	*Clutterbuck*	*Knowles*	*McConnell*	*Crawford*	*Hitch*	*Keech*	*Jordan*	*Haywood*	*Tennant*	*Bedingfield*	*Evans*
							Ref: G Muir [Langham 70, 80]	City recovered their poise in the final 20 minutes of this thrilling contest, when they had as much of the play as they had enjoyed at the outset. Straight from the kick-off Russell netted from a Jones centre, and Caie soon doubled the advantage by shooting in from Potter's astute pass.										
6	A CHATHAM		8	D	2-2	2-2	Langham 4, Caie 38	Watts	McLean	Godsman	Jones	Britton	Hamilton	Langham	Potter	Caie	**Thompson**	Crawford
	14/10	*4,000*	*13*	7			*Lawrence 3, Appleby 35*	*Fraill*	*Tranter*	*Humphreys*	*Burton*	*Chapman*	*Perrins*	*May*	*Lawrence*	*Kaye*	*Appleby*	*Johnson*
							Ref: J Jamieson	In beautiful weather, both sides were let down by some poor shooting in this fast and exciting contest. A sensational opening saw Lawrence put Chatham in front from Johnson's centre, but Crawford almost immediately raced away to set up Langham, who notched City's equaliser.										
7	H READING		8	L	1-2	1-0	Jones 25	Monteith	McLean	Godsman	Downie	Britton	Hamilton	Langham	Jones	Caie	Thompson	Crawford
	21/10	5,000	*5*	7			*Evans 65, Barlow 75*	*Whittaker*	*Henderson*	*O'Brien*	*Sharp J*	*Holt*	*Hosie*	*Evans*	*Barlow*	*Ross*	*Davies J*	*Kelly*
							Ref: J Tillotson	The Bristol public had seen few poorer games than this, with both sides unable to play up to the necessary standard. Caie set up Jones to fire City in front, but after the break Evans shot in a leveller before McLean's mix-up with Monteith allowed Barlow to slot in the visitors' winner.										
8	A SHEPPEY UTD		7	D	0-0	0-0		Monteith	Caie	Godsman	Jones	McLean	Hamilton	Langham	Potter	Molyneux	Crawford	Russell
	28/10	*1,200*	*16*	8				*Cotton*	*Osborne*	*Penney*	*Lissenden Jr*	*Blair*	*Jenner*	*Hall*	*Buchanan*	*Harrison*	*Macfarlane*	*Lester*
							Ref: F Beardsley	The fair-sized crowd which greeted City at Sheerness were disappointed by the football which was as dull as the weather. The home side had decidedly the best of a game that became rough towards the finish, and were unlucky not to score during a prolonged first-half scrimmage.										
9	H BRIGHTON UTD*		5	W	3-2	2-1	Caie 5, 75, Potter 20	Monteith	Robson	McDonald	McLean	Britton	Hamilton	Langham	Potter	Caie	Jones	Crawford
	4/11	**2,000**	*17*	10			*Hill 35, 90*	*Spicer*	*Ashby*	*Mills*	*Parry*	*McAvoy*	*Low*	*Mercer*	*Hill*	*Sharp*	*Malloch*	*Willocks*
							Ref: F Crabtree	Caie's clinking shot got City off to a good start and then a rush on goal allowed Potter to double the advantage before Hill pulled one back for the visitors. After the break, Caie registered with a low shot, but right on the call of time Hill was able to pull another one back for Brighton.										
10	A BEDMINSTER		7	D	1-1	0-1	Davies 80og	Monteith	McDonald	Robson	McLean	Britton	Hamilton	Langham	**Blessingt'n**	Caie	Jones	Crawford
	11/11	*5,500* (£160)	*8*	11			*Monteith 40og*	*Toone*	*Crone*	*Davies RH*	*Draycott*	*Wilson*	*Chambers*	*Whelan*	*Flewitt*	*Boucher*	*Becton*	*Geddes*
							Ref: A Barker	City included Blessington, their signing from Derby in this exciting game. Toone was in brilliant form between the sticks and he was unlucky to be beaten when Davies put the ball into his own-goal. Poetic justice perhaps, as Monteith had helped a Geddes curling corner into his net.										

No	Venue	Opponent / Att			F-A	H-T	Scorers, Times, Referees	1	2	3	4	5	6	7	8	9	10	11
11	H	COWES*	3	W	**5-0**	3-0	Caie 5, Blessington 43, 70, 88, [Langham 44]	Monteith	McDonald	Godsman	Downie	McLean	Hamilton	Langham	Blessington	Caie	Jones	Crawford
18/11		**2,000**	16	13				*Paley*	*Tait*	*Ward*	*Joliffe*	*Nash*	*Parrott*	*Moore*	*Frewin*	*Finlayson*	*Brock*	*Baker*
		(£55)					Ref: A Partridge	Despite dominating this game following Caie's early opener, the closest City came to another goal, before Blessington opened his account with a header shortly before the interval, was Crawford's shot that hit the crossbar. Blessington notched his second with a low-drive after the break.										
12	A	PORTSMOUTH	7	L	0-2	0-1		Monteith	McDonald	McLean	Downie	Godsman	Hamilton	Langham	Blessington	Caie	Jones	Crawford
25/11		*6,000*	*3*	13			*Brown 43, 70*	*Reilly*	*Turner E*	*Wilkie*	*Hunter*	*Stringfellow*	*Blyth*	*Marshall*	*Cunliffe*	*Brown A*	*Smith*	*Clarke*
		(£185.2.9)					Ref: T Sweetman	City, who did most of the attacking but were let down by poor finishing, were made to pay when they conceded a strange goal just before the break. Monteith's clearance-kick struck Brown on the back and rebounded into the net. McDonald's bad blunder gave Brown his second goal.										
13	H	THAMES IRNWKS	5	W	2-0	1-0	Blessington 5, Caie 70	Monteith	McDonald	Robson	Downie	McLean	Hamilton	Langham	Blessington	Caie	Jones	Crawford
2/12		4,500	*11*	15				*Sunderland*	*King*	*Craig*	*Bigden*	*McManus*	*McEachrane*	*Corbett*	*McKay*	*Carnelly*	*Walker*	*Joyce*
							Ref: E Fox	Caie started play from the Lane end and City immediately took up the offensive. Blessington notched the opener when he beat Sunderland with a fierce shot. In the second half Caie doubled City's advantage with a hot one. At this game a collection for the War Fund produced £9.3s.3½d.										
14	A	TOTTENHAM	3	D	2-2	0-1	Jones 70, Russell 75	Monteith	McDonald	Robson	Downie	McLean	Hamilton	Langham	Blessington	Jones	Russell	Crawford
9/12		*5,000*	*2*	16			*Copeland 10, Kirwan 87*	*Haddow*	*Melia*	*Tait*	*Jones*	*Morris*	*Stormont*	*Smith*	*Cameron*	*Pratt*	*Copeland*	*Kirwan*
							Ref: A Roston-Bourke	Spurs kicked off and nearly scored, before Crawford and Langham shot wide for City. It wasn't long, though, before the Spurs went in front, when ex-Minster man Copeland netted with a grounder. In the second half Jones levelled during a scrimmage after a fine shot by Russell.										
15	H	NEW BROMPTON	3	W	2-1	1-0	Jones 40, Crawford 46	Monteith	McDonald	Robson	Downie	McLean	Hamilton	Langham	Blessington	Jones	Russell	Crawford
16/12		3,500	*10*	18			*Frettingham 89*	*Carter*	*Robertson*	*Glover*	*Innes*	*Atherton*	*Graham*	*Gray T*	*Macdonald*	*Frettingham*	*Pangbourne*	*Swan*
							Ref: G Muir	Faced by the side that had put Woolwich Arsenal out of the English Cup after four draws, City's victory was by no means certain. Jones netted the opener with a fine shot just before the interval and then, from Langham's cross, Crawford doubled their advantage straight after the break.										
16	A	GRAVESEND	3	D	2-2	2-2	Langham 8, Blessington 40	Monteith	McDonald	Robson	Downie	McLean	Hamilton	Langham	Blessington	Jones	Russell	Crawford
23/12		*2,000*	*11*	15			*Henderson 22, Regan 35p*	*Ashcroft*	*Regan*	*Bagnall*	*Richards*	*Farrell*	*Bull*	*Grieve*	*Bright*	*Henderson*	*Pugh*	*Otty*
							Ref: F Crabtree	Langham fired into an open goal to put City into an early lead, but Gravesend levelled when, from a well-placed corner by Richards, the ball went into the net following a melee. After Bagnall allowed Blessington to notch City's second, Pugh had a goal disallowed right on half-time.										
17	H	BRISTOL ROV	3	W	1-0	0-0	Britton 85	Monteith	McDonald	Robson	Downie	Britton	Hamilton	Langham	Blessington	Jones	Caie	Crawford
26/12		**7,250**	*11*	17				*Gray*	*Lee*	*Griffiths*	*Lamont*	*Brown G*	*Robertson*	*Brown R*	*Lewis*	*Jones*	*Fisher*	*Paul*
							Ref: N Whittaker	Jones kicked off for the Rovers from the Lane End and Brown came nicely away before he was stopped from getting in his centre. Thereafter the visitors' defence was kept active, but City were unable to find the net until just before the close, when Britton registered with a fine effort.										
18	A	SWINDON	4	L	1-2	0-2	Jones 80	Monteith	McDonald	Robson	Downie	McLean	Hamilton	Langham	Blessington	Jones	Caie	Crawford
30/12		*2,500*	*6*	17			*Coupar 30, Sharples 44*	*Menham*	*Shutt*	*Wilson J*	*Richards'n W*	*Logan*	*Henderson*	*Sharples*	*Anthony*	*Smith W*	*Coupar*	*Smithson*
							Ref: J Stark	Midway through the first half the referee made Swindon change their jerseys as their dark red was too like City's scarlet. Upon resuming, Swindon kept up the pressure and Coupar put them in front when a shot from the right rebounded off a post. City's goal was a real stinger.										
19	H	MILLWALL ATH	10	L	0-2	0-2		Monteith	Robson	Pollock	Downie	Hamilton	McLean	Langham	Blessington	Jones	Caie	Crawford
3/2		**2,000**	*4*	17			*Robertson 15, Banks 25*	*Cox*	*Burgess*	*Allan*	*Smith*	*Goldie*	*Millar*	*Dryburgh*	*Brearley*	*Robertson*	*Banks*	*Nichol*
							Ref: G Landragin	On a snow-covered pitch, in front of a moderate crowd, City were vigorous at the start, but it was the visitors who went in front. Robertson netted with a soft shot; then shortly afterwards Banks placed Millwall two up. After the break City were unable to score despite much pressure.										
20	H	CHATHAM	10	W	4-1	3-1	Jones 6, Langham 20, O'Brien 22 [Blessington 70]	Monteith	Robson	Pollock	Downie	McLean	Hamilton	Langham	Blessington	Jones	O'Brien	Potter
17/2		**2,000**	*14*	19			*Appleby 40*	*Bennett*	*Tranter*	*Humphreys*	*Burton*	*Chapman*	*Perrins*	*Johnson*	*Appleby*	*Kaye*	*Clements*	*Dickenson*
							Ref: A Cooper	A low shot by Jones put City ahead early on; then Langham fired a beauty past Bennett to double the advantage. The third came almost straight after, following a scramble around goal, before Appleby's low-shot found the net for Chatham. Blessington wedged through after the interval.										
21	A	READING	12	L	0-3	0-1		Monteith	McDonald	Robson	Downie	McLean	Hamilton	Langham	Blessington	Jones	O'Brien	Russell
24/2		*3,000*	*5*	19			*Ross 1, 70, 85*	*Whittaker*	*Henderson*	*O'Brien*	*Sharp J*	*Holt*	*Hosie*	*Evans*	*Barlow*	*Ross*	*Davies J*	*Kelly*
							Ref: F Crabtree	The homesters pressed immediately from the start and Ross netted from a corner. City's stubborn defence kept Reading from adding to their score before half-time, but after the break they had no answer. Ross beat Monteith with a beauty before claiming his hat-trick near the finish.										

No	Date		Att	Pos	Pt	F-A	H-T	Scorers, Times, and Referees	1	2	3	4	5	6	7	8	9	10	11
22	H	SHEPPEY UTD		10	W	5-1	2-0	Jones 10, 50, 70, 72, Potter 35	Monteith	McDonald	Robson	Downie	McLean	Hamilton	Langham	Blessington	Jones	O'Brien	Potter
	3/3		2,500	*15*	21			*Spence 80*	*Cotton*	*Macfarlane*	*Penney*	*Weeks*	*Blair*	*Lissenden Jr*	*Hall*	*Warren*	*Spence*	*Buchanan*	*Lissenden Sr*
								Ref: J Hindle	The fine weather resulted in a good crowd at St John's Lane, but they were disappointed by the fact that the visitors only had five of their regular team on duty. Jones was the star performer, scoring the opener with an oblique shot early on. He ended the game with a four-goal haul.										
23	A	QP RANGERS		8	D	1-1	0-1	O'Brien 75	Monteith	McDonald	Robson	Downie	McLean	Hamilton	Langham	Blessington	Jones	O'Brien	Crawford
	5/3		*1,000*	*9*	22			*White 25*	*Clutterbuck*	*Knowles*	*McConnell*	*Crawford*	*Hitch*	*Keech*	*Smith*	*White*	*Bedingfield*	*Cowie*	*Hannah*
									A poor crowd at Kensal Rise, where McDonald's mis-kick allowed White to put Rangers in front. City struggled to come to terms with the large playing area in the first half, but following their equaliser they did most of the attacking without being able to quite end the stalemate.										
24	A	BRIGHTON UTD*		7	D	1-1	0-0	Jones 50	Monteith	McDonald	Robson	Downie	McLean	Hamilton	Langham	Potter	Jones	Pollock	Crawford
	10/3		*1,500*	*16*	23			*Hill 60*	*Spicer*	*Farrell*	*Mills*	*Parry*	*McAvoy*	*Low*	*Oakden*	*Davidson*	*Hill*	*McArthur*	*Hadden*
								Ref: E Jarvis	A good company of spectators attended this well-contested game played in fine weather. City had the better of things in the first half without being able to score. Jones got through soon after the break, but City proved unable to maintain their advantage, and United quickly levelled.										
25	H	BEDMINSTER		8	L	0-2	0-2		Monteith	McDonald	Robson	Downie	McLean	Hamilton	Langham	**Goldie**	Jones	Pollock	Potter
	17/3		5,000	*4*	23			*Geddes 30, Saxton 40*	*Toone*	*Barker*	*Davies WH*	*Draycott*	*Davies RH*	*Chambers*	*Whelan*	*Saxton*	*Boucher*	*Wilson*	*Geddes*
								Ref: G Muir	In spite of the snow, which fell so heavily during the afternoon, there was a capital crowd at Ashton Gate for this local derby. A well-deserved success for the much quicker Minster side, despite City appealing for offside when Saxton put away Boucher's neat pass for goal number two.										
26	H	PORTSMOUTH		10	L	**3-6**	1-4	Jones 16, 75, Blessington 63	Lewis	Robson	Pollock	Downie	Britton	Hamilton	Langham	Blessington	Jones	Goldie	Crawford
	31/3		4,000	*2*	20			*Clark 7, 22, Robson 27og,*	*Reilly*	*Turner E*	*Wilkie*	*Blyth*	*Stringfellow*	*Cleghorn*	*Marshall*	*Cunliffe*	*Brown A*	*Smith*	*Clark*
								Ref: F Crabtree *[Cunliffe 31, 46, Smith 55]*	Despite the beautiful weather, there wasn't a particularly large crowd present for this game. After City made the early running, Clark put the visitors in front in rather tame fashion. The referee, who incurred the wrath of the fans, was protected by the police and players at the finish.										
27	A	THAMES IRNWKS		8	D	0-0	0-0		Monteith	McDonald	Robson	Downie	McLean	Hamilton	Potter	Blessington	Jones	Goldie	Pollock
	7/4		*5,000*	*15*	21				*Moore*	*Dunn*	*Craig*	*Dove*	*Stewart*	*McEachrane*	*Allan*	*McKay*	*Joyce*	*Carnelly*	*Taylor*
								Ref: A Partridge	A fair attendance at Canning Town where, at the finish, City were still left seeking their first away success of the campaign. A point from a poor game was however a fortunate return for City, who had cause to be thankful that Carnelly and Joyce exhibited much wayward shooting.										
28	A	BRISTOL ROV		8	L	0-1	0-1		Monteith	McDonald	Robson	Downie	McLean	Hamilton	Langham	Blessington	Jones	O'Brien	Crawford
	13/4		***10,000***	*11*	21			*Fisher 30*	*Gray*	*Ritchie*	*Griffiths*	*Lamont*	*Robertson*	*Brown G*	*Brown R*	*Lewis*	*Fisher*	*McInnes*	*Paul*
								Ref: H Smith	Beautiful weather for the large crowd at Stapleton Road, who witnessed an exciting game despite a strong wind. Gray did well to save a fine header by O'Brien, before Rovers took the lead when Fisher netted following good work by McInnes. Rovers were hanging on at the finish.										
29	H	TOTTENHAM		8	W	3-0	1-0	O'Brien 5 , Langham 75, Jones 80	Monteith	McDonald	Robson	Downie	McLean	Hamilton	Langham	Blessington	Jones	O'Brien	Crawford
	14/4		4,000	*1*	23				*Haddow*	*Melia*	*Tait*	*Morris*	*McNaught*	*Stormont*	*Smith*	*Cameron*	*Pratt*	*Copeland*	*Kirwan*
								Ref: G Muir	Both sides were at full strength for this game in which all the luck, for once, was with City. Langham showed that he had not lost all his once-brilliant form when beating Stormont and dashing up the wing before centring from almost the corner flag for O'Brien to notch the opener.										
30	A	NEW BROMPTON		11	L	0-1	0-0		Monteith	McDonald	Robson	Downie	McLean	Hamilton	Potter	Blessington	Jones	Goldie	Crawford
	21/4		*1,200*	*9*	23			*Swan 80*	*Carter*	*Robertson*	*Glover*	*Innes*	*Hutcheson*	*Graham*	*Gladwell*	*Gray T*	*Frettingham*	*Swan*	*Seeley*
									Although the weather was of the most delightful character, there were only about 1,200 spectators present. Play was fast and interesting in the opening half, and both goals had narrow escapes. It wasn't until near the dying stages that Swan's grand shot was able to settle the contest.										
31	A	SOUTHAMPTON		12	L	1-4	0-2	Jones 50 *[McLeod 75]*	Monteith	McDonald	Robson	Pollock	McLean	Stewart	Langham	Blessington	Jones	Goldie	Crawford
	23/4		***200***	*4*	23			*Wood 35, Milward 40, 65,*	*Robinson*	*Meehan*	*Durber*	*Meston*	*Chadwick*	*Greenlees*	*Yates*	*McLeod*	*Farrell*	*Wood*	*Milward*
								Ref: J Jamieson	A Saints side that included all put two (Turner and Petrie) of last Saturday's XI that lost 0-4 against Bury in the FA Cup final, were too strong for City in this meeting at the Dell. Jones headed in from Langham's centre just after the break, but Milward soon registered with a clean kick.										

No	H/A	Opponent / Date	Att	Pos	Res / Pts	FT	HT	Scorers	1	2	3	4	5	6	7	8	9	10	11
32	H	GRAVESEND		9	W	3-0	1-0	Jones 12, 80, O'Brien 70	Monteith	McDonald	Robson	Downie	McLean	Hamilton	Blessington	Goldie	Jones	O'Brien	Crawford
		28/4	**2,000**	*12*	25				*Ashcroft*	*Regan*	*Bagnall*	*Richards*	*Bull*	*Ford*	*Grieve*	*Bright*	*Henderson*	*Pugh*	*Otty*
		Home Ave 4,125	Away 3,413					Ref: S Major	Gravesend were unfortunate with the loss of the injured Regan just before half-time but City, with Goldie turning in a particularly fine display, deserved their success. A capital grounder by Jones opened the scoring; then in the second half O'Brien shot in to double City's advantage.										

* *Opponents disbanded – Cowes 20 December & Brighton United 29 March – records expunged.*

SOUTHERN DISTRICT COMBINATION

No	H/A	Opponent / Date	Att	Pos	Res / Pts	FT	HT	Scorers	1	2	3	4	5	6	7	8	9	10	11
1	A	READING			W	4-2	2-1	Caie 40, 55, 75, Crawford 41	Monteith	Milligan	Stewart	McLean	**Godsman**	Hamilton	Langham	Crawford	Caie	O'Brien	Russell
		13/9	*1,500*		2			*Davies J 30, 88*	*Whittaker*	*Henderson*	*O'Brien*	*Boyd*	*Holt*	*Hosie*	*Evans*	*Goldie*	*Davies R*	*Davies J*	*Ross*
								Ref: F Walford	The ref incurs City's displeasure when, after consultation with his linesman, he allowed Reading's opener, despite having blown before Davies had run on and shot home. Caie, who charged the keeper for City's third, rushed through another after Whittaker had pushed out his spot-kick.										
2	H	CHATHAM		2	W	**5-1**	2-0	O'Brien18,86,Downie25,Russell 60, [Langham 88]	Monteith	McLean	Godsman	Jones	Britton	Hamilton	Langham	Downie	Caie	O'Brien	Russell
		4/10	1,000	*8*	4			*Lawrence 50*	*Bennett*	*Tranter*	*Humphreys*	*Burton*	*Chapman*	*Perrins*	*May*	*Lawrence*	*Johnson*	*Dickenson*	*Appleby*
								Ref: J Hindle	Miserable weather attended this game at St John's Lane where, in front of a small crowd, the visitors offered little apart from Lawrence's goal following a fine run by Johnson. They were, however, handicapped by the loss of Perrins with a cut head midway through the second period.										
3	A	WLCH ARSENAL		5	L	0-3	0-0		Monteith	Caie	Godsman	Jones	McLean	Hamilton	Langham	Potter	Molyneux	Crawford	Russell
		30/10	*1,200*	*6*	4			*Hartley 47, Lloyd 80, 89*	*Hamilton*	*Graham*	*McAvoy*	*Anderson*	*Sanders*	*Dunsbee*	*Lloyd*	*Hartley*	*Gaudie*	*Groves*	*Duff*
								Ref: A Partridge	The Arsenal, who put a virtual reserve side in the field, had slightly the better of things before the break. Gaudie and Groves nearly scored for them, but it wasn't until the second half that the breakthrough came. Groves headed through following a corner not long after the re-start.										
4	H	TOTTENHAM		5	D	3-3	2-2	Jones 30, Langham 40, 75	Monteith	McDonald	Godsman	McLean	Downie	Hamilton	Langham	Blessington	Caie	Jones	Crawford
		15/11	3,000	*3*	5			*Kirwan 20, Smith 44, Copeland 70*	*Haddow*	*Melia*	*Tait*	*Jones*	*Morris*	*Stormont*	*Smith*	*Cameron*	*Pratt*	*Copeland*	*Kirwan*
								Ref: A Cooper	City's Queen's Day fixture was well patronised, as it was an ideal morning for football. A fine display of passing down the whole length of the pitch ended with Kirwan netting a beauty to put Spurs in front. Jones volleyed in a leveller, before Langham ran through to shoot City in front.										
5	A	SOUTHAMPTON		6	L	**1-5**	0-2	Langham 75 *[Farrell 60, 70]*	Monteith	McDonald	Godsman	Downie	McLean	Hamilton	Blessington	Langham	Caie	Jones	Crawford
		22/11	*2,000*	*5*	5			*Wood 30, 35, Milward 50,*	*Robinson*	*Meston*	*Durber*	*Greenless*	*Chadwick*	*Englefield*	*Turner*	*McLeod*	*Farrell*	*Wood*	*Milward*
								Ref: F Crabtree	After kicking-off, City tested Robinson before Wood gave Monteith no chance at all with his shot, which put the Saints in front. City, despite conceding another goal soon after, were not discouraged and they continued to press. Langham's goal was scant reward for their endeavours.										
6	H	PORTSMOUTH		6	L	1-3	0-1	Crawford 85	Monteith	McDonald	Stewart	Downie	McLean	Hamilton	Potter	Langham	Caie	Jones	Crawford
		29/11	1,000	*2*	5			*Marshall 15, Cunliffe 70, 75*	*Reilly*	*Turner E*	*Wilkie*	*Blyth*	*Stringfellow*	*Hunter*	*Marshall*	*Cunliffe*	*Brown A*	*Smith*	*Clark*
								Ref: T Saywell	City had their chances but a mixture of bad luck and poor shooting cost them in this exciting game. Stewart's poor defensive header allowed Marshall to beat Monteith with a lovely shot. After the break, Cunliffe headed in off of a post five minutes prior to firing in Pompey's third.										
7	H	MILLWALL ATH		6	L	1-3	0-2	Caie 80p	Monteith	Robson	Caie	Downie	Godsman	Hamilton	Potter	Blessington	Jones	O'Brien	Russell
		25/12	**6,000**	*1*	5			*Nichol 30,Brearley40,Robertson 75*	*Clare*	*Burgess*	*Davis W*	*Smith*	*Goldie*	*Millar*	*Dryburgh*	*Brearley*	*Robertson*	*Ferne*	*Nichol*
								Ref: H Smith	For the visitors, Banks was an absentee from the advertised side, whilst City's team underwent a wholesale re-arrangement. Fernie's smart pass set up Nichol to net the opener. Then, not long afterwards, Brearley's grand shot doubled Millwall's advantage. City improved after the break.										
8	H	WLCH ARSENAL		7	L	1-3	0-1	Russell 70	Monteith	Robson	**Pollock**	Britton	McLean	Hamilton	Potter	Blessington	Jones	Stewart	Russell
		10/1	2,000	*6*	5			*Tennant 40, Logan 46, McCowie 85*	*Ord*	*McNicol*	*Anderson*	*Murphy*	*Dick*	*Dunsbie*	*Lloyd*	*Logan*	*Gaudie*	*McCowie*	*Tennant*
								Ref: T Saywell	After a bad foul on McCowie inside the area, Monteith palmed out Tennant's consequential spot-kick, but was powerless to do anything about his follow-up. Straight after the interval, City's keeper thwarted McCowie with a good save, but Logan raced up to tap the ball over the line.										
9	A	CHATHAM		8	L	0-3	0-0		Monteith	McDonald	Robson	Downie	McLean	Godsman	Stewart	Blessington	Caie	O'Brien	Russell
		17/1	***500***	*7*	5			*Kaye 75, 80, Clements 85*	*Bennett*	*Tranter*	*Humphreys*	*Burton*	*Chapman*	*Perrins*	*Appleby*	*Kaye*	*Johnson*	*Clements*	*Dickenson*
									Despite being without the services of Harper and May, and playing against a strong wind, Chatham made the early running. For City, Caie was denied by a post, but after the break Chatham made full use of having wind advantage and went in front when Kaye put away Johnson's centre.										

SOUTHERN DISTRICT COMBINATION

No	Date		Att	Pos	Pt	F-A	H-T	Scorers, Times, and Referees	1	2	3	4	5	6	7	8	9	10	11	12 sub used
10	H	SOUTHAMPTON		7	W	4-1	1-0	Langham 30, O'Brien 46, 75,	Monteith	McDonald	Robson	Downie	McLean	Hamilton	Langham	Blessington	Jones	O'Brien	Potter	
	28/2		2,000	*4*	7			*Cavendish 60* [Jones 65]	*Robinson*	*Meehan*	*Haynes*	*Meston*	*French*	*Greenless*	*Yates*	*McLeod*	*Cavendish*	*Keay*	*Englefield*	
								Ref: J Tillotson	With all the rain that had fallen, the pitch was not really fit for football. In front of a meagre gate, Meehan's mistake allowed Langham to notch the opener with a shot that went in off of Robinson. A spectator at the game, John Stevens of Upper Knowle, died after falling off a wall.											
11	A	TOTTENHAM		8	L	0-2	0-1		Lewis	McDonald	Robson	Stewart	Britton	Hamilton	Potter	Downie	Jones	Leslie	Crawford	
	12/3		*3,000*	*1*	7			*Kirwan 25, Cameron 70*	*Haddow*	*Melia*	*Tait*	*Morris*	*McNaught*	*Jones*	*Hyde*	*Raby*	*Cameron*	*Stormont*	*Kirwan*	
									With Phil Britton having not arrived by the start, City were a man short throughout the first half. Trailing to Kirwaun's opener, Britton came on after the break but, despite a fine display by Talbot Lewis, City were unable to prevent Cameron from doubling the homesters' advantage.											
12	H	READING		6	W	3-1	3-1	Jones 20, 40, Pollock 30	Monteith	McDonald	Robson	Downie	McLean	Stewart	Langham	Goldie	Jones	Osborne	Pollock	
	21/3		1,000	*7*	9			*Davies 2*	*Hosie*	*Henderson*	*O'Brien*	*Boyd*	*Watts*	*Sharp*	*Evans*	*Davies*	*Ross*	*Kelly*	*Barnes*	
								Ref: F Beardsley	After Davies had fired in Reading's early opener, a particularly fine shot by Jones brought City level. A slick pass from Jones set up Pollock to put City ahead, then the outside-left's fine centre brought the Reds a third goal. Offside deprived Kelly of a goal shortly before the finish.											
13	A	QP RANGERS		6	D	0-0	0-0		Monteith	McDonald	Stewart	Downie	Britton	Hamilton	Potter	Goldie	Jones	O'Brien	Pollock	
	26/3		***500***	*9*	10				*Clutterbuck*	*Knowles*	*McConnell*	*Crawford*	*Hitch*	*Keech*	*Hannah*	*Haywood*	*White*	*Turnbull*	*Cowie*	
									The small crowd in the fine, but cold, weather at Kensal Rise witnessed an even first half, during which Clutterbuck brought off good saves from Stewart and Jones. After the break, City did most of the pressing without being able to score and had therefore to be satisfied with a point.											
14	A	PORTSMOUTH		6	D	0-0	0-0		Lewis	McDonald	Pollock	Downie	McLean	Stewart	Potter	Osborne	Jones	Leslie	Russell	
	28/3		*1,000*	*3*	11				*Reilly*	*Turner E*	*Wilkie*	*Blyth*	*Stringfellow*	*Cleghorn*	*Marshall*	*Clark*	*Brown A*	*Smith*	*Barnes*	
								Ref: J Jamieson	Considering they were missing seven regulars, whilst Pompey, except for Cunliffe, were at full strength, City did well to draw this engagement at Fratton Park. City were occupied on the defensive throughout most of this poor game, which wasn't helped by the antics of a high wind.											
15	H	QP RANGERS		6	W	2-1	2-0	O'Brien 25, Potter 30	Lewis	McDonald	Stewart	Britton	McLean	Hamilton	Potter	Blessington	Goldie	O'Brien	Pollock	
	4/4		**500**	*9*	13			*Evans 70*	*Clutterbuck*	*Knowles*	*McConnell*	*Crawford*	*Misslewhite*	*Skinner*	*Cowie*	*White*	*Evans*	*Turnbull*	*Hannah*	
								Ref: A Farrant	In front of a limited attendance, City had the benefit of the strong wind in the first half. O'Brien cleverly headed in the opener, then shortly afterwards Potter got in a fierce low shot that Clutterbuck fumbled into the net. Evans livened up a dull game by scoring from Cowle's cross.											
16	A	MILLWALL ATH		6	L	0-1	0-1		Monteith	McDonald	Robson	McClean	Stewart	Hamilton	Langham	Blessington	Jones	Pollock	Crawford	
	16/4		*4,000*	*1*	13			*Caie 25*	*Cox*	*Burgess*	*Allan*	*Smith*	*Goldie*	*Millar*	*Dryburgh*	*Brearley*	*Caie*	*Banks*	*Nichol*	
	Ave	Home 2,063	Away 1,713						In bright weather, Millwall had rather the better of things before the break and deservedly went in front when ex-City favourite Sandy Caie registered for them. In the second half the Lions kept up the offensive, but were unable to add to their score in what was but a moderate game.											

WESTERN LEAGUE DIVISION 1

No	Date		Att	Pos	Pt	F-A	H-T	Scorers, Times, and Referees	1	2	3	4	5	6	7	8	9	10	11
1	A	SWINDON			L	0-1	0-1		**Watts**	**McDonald**	Lewis	Downie	Godsman	Britton	Potter	**Leslie**	Molyneux	**Marks**	**Osborne**
	20/9		***1,000***					*Wilson 30*	*Menham*	*Shutt*	*Sharples*	*Richardson*	*G Henderson*	*Smith A*	*Anthony*	*Coupar*	*Logan*	*Smith W*	*Wilson T*
								Ref: J Tillotson	City, represented by practically their reserve team, more than held their own early on when the wind was in their favour. Prior to Wilson heading Swindon in front, Osborne had a goal struck off for offside. Watts was on form to prevent any further scoring after the break.										
2	A	BRISTOL ROV			L	0-2	0-0		Watts	**Robson**	Godsman	Jones	Britton	Hamilton	Crawford	Potter	Caie	Downie	Russell
	1/11		*2,000*					*Kinsey 75p, 85p*	*Gray*	*Ritchie*	*Griffiths*	*Lamont*	*Robertson*	*Kinsey*	*Brown R*	*Lewis*	*Jones*	*Fisher*	*McInnes*
								Ref: J Tillotson	A good crowd at Stapleton Road witnessed an exciting game with both sides attacking in turn. Kinsey's first penalty had to be taken twice, even though he netted on both occasions. The second spot-kick followed Britton's handling offence, and it was quickly turned to account.										

No	Venue	Opponent / Date	Att			FT	HT	Scorers / Ref												
3	H	BEDMINSTER		3	W	8-1	3-1	Russell 25,75,77,85, Jones 26,44,	Watts	McDonald	Robson	Downie	McLean	Britton	Langham	Blessington	Jones	Russell	Crawford	
		6/12	**2,000**	*4*	2			*Geddes 40*	*Clapp*	*Ayre*	*Crone*	*Bramley*	*Davies WH*	*Baynon*	*Stolz*	*Whelan*	*Becton*	*Geddes*	*Saxton*	
								Ref: A Barker [Crawford 60, Blessington70]	The Minster paid the price for fielding only a moderate team due to their forthcoming English cup game with Cowes. Russell's low shot, the first of a remarkable four-goal haul, was followed by a fierce drive by Jones, before a Geddes grounder brought Bedminster's sole response.											
4	H	SWINDON		1	W	3-1	2-0	Potter 7, 15, Jones 70	Monteith	Caie	Robson	Downie	McLean	Hamilton	Potter	Blessington	Jones	Russell	Crawford	
		13/12	**1,000**	*2*	4			*Logan 50*	*Rutts*	*Shutt*	*Fulton*	*Richardson G*	*Henderson*	*Smith A*	*Sharples*	*Coupar*	*Logan*	*Smith W*	*Wilson T*	
								Ref: J Le Grande	Scottish Junior international Rutts, who was given a trial by Swindon in this game, had a hot time between the sticks. Potter raced through and beat him early on; then, in trying to clear a corner, he was judged to have carried the ball over the line. A grand shot beat him for City's third.											
5	A	BEDMINSTER		4	L	1-4	1-2	Langham 40 *[Downie 86og]*	Monteith	McDonald	Robson	Downie	McLean	Hamilton	Langham	Blessington	Jones	O'Brien	Crawford	
		7/3	***4,000***	*3*	4			*Whelan 1, Flewitt 30, Boucher 85,*	*Toone*	*Barker*	*Davies RH*	*Draycott*	*Davies WH*	*Chambers*	*Whelan*	*Flewitt*	*Boucher*	*Wilson*	*Geddes*	
								Ref: A Farrant	A sensational opening to what proved to be a keen tussle. Robson's poor clearance allowed Wilson to put the ball across for Whelan to net with a lovely shot in off the post. Flewitt looked decidedly offside when he doubled the advantage, before Langham headed in for City.											
6	H	BRISTOL ROV		4	L	0-3	0-2		Lewis	McDonald	Robson	Downie	McLean	Hamilton	Langham	Blessington	Jones	O'Brien	Crawford	
		25/4	2,000	*1*	4			*Lewis 20, Jones 35, 75*	*Gray*	*Ritchie*	*Griffiths*	*Lamont*	*Robertson*	*Lee*	*Harris*	*Lewis*	*Jones*	*McInnes*	*Paul*	
		Home / Ave 1,667	Away / 2,333					Ref: A Green	Despite the Rovers needing to win to clinch the Championship, only a moderate crowd were present for this game. Crawford had a goal disallowed for offside, before Lewis shot in the opener from close range. Just prior to the break the offside rule again cost City a score.											

FRIENDLIES

No	Venue	Opponent / Date	Att			FT	HT	Scorers / Ref												
1	H	BRISTOL ROV			L	0-2	0-1		Monteith	McDonald	Milligan	Jones	McLean	Hamilton	Langham	Downie	Caie	Crawford	Russell	
		6/9	2,000					*Jones 30, Lewis 50*	*Gray*	*Lee*	*Griffiths*	*Lamont*	*Brown G*	*Kinsey*	*Leonard*	*Jones*	*Vail*	*Lewis*	*Paul*	
								Ref: A Farrant	City did most of the early pressing and Crawford netted but was ruled offside. After a bit the Rovers pressed and when Kinsey hit the crossbar from a free-kick, Jones latched onto the rebound to put them into the lead with a grand goal. Paul's clever run set up Lewis after the break.											
2	H	DEVON COUNTY XI			W	3-1	1-0	Langham 35, 60, 72	Watts	McDonald	Milligan	McLean	Godsman	Hamilton	Langham	Osborne	Molyneux	O'Brien	Russell	
		9/9	3,000					*Northey 70*	*Meyers*	*Fawcett*	*Conry**	*Shute*	*Holman*	*Derry*	*Pascho*	*Northey*	*Rose*	*Freebairn*	*Hannaford*	*Vosper*
								Ref: W Pollett	Molyneux had his effort disallowed just after the start, but Langham eventually put City in front when Meyers could only partially stop his shot, which trickled in. Northey fired in for the visitors, but almost immediately Russell's centre allowed Langham to claim his hat-trick.											
3	A	RYDE			W	1-0	1-0	Crawford 35	Monteith	McDonald	Godsman	Downie	McLean	Hamilton	Blessington	Langham	Caie	Jones	Crawford	
		23/11	*800* (£12)						*Hammett*	*Walker FM*	*Gould*	*King*	*Flux W*	*Hanna*	*Yelf F*	*Christie*	*Maidment E*	*Hamilton*	*Hounsell*	
								Ref: Sgt D Bowden	Crawford's goal brought an easy success for City on their trip across the Solent, which provided them a welcome break between important engagements on the South Coast. Unfortunately this light work-out didn't help them as their game at Portsmouth a few days later was lost.											
4	H	KAFFIRS			W	6-5	3-1	Jones 2,50, Potter 20, Broffit 40og,	Monteith	McDonald	Lewis	Downie	Godsman	Hamilton	Potter	Blessington	Jones	O'Brien P	O'Brien J	
		1/1	3,000					*Abel 35, Unk 55og, 65og, 70og, 85*	*Adolph*	*Broffitt*	*Daniells*	*Apollis*	*Davids*	*Brown*	*Kortie*	*Abel*	*Twayi*	*Solomons*	*Stevens*	
								Ref: G Silman [O'Brien P 60, Godsman75]	City spent most of the second half either trying to set up a goal for Monteith, who had swapped places with Blessington, or supplying aid to the Kaffirs cause by putting into their own net. The crowd enjoyed the antics of the visitors, who maintained their losing four-month tour record.											
5	H	BRISTOL ROV			W	2-0	0-0	Potter 47, Jones 50	Monteith	McDonald	Robson	Britton	McLean	Hamilton	Potter	Blessington	Jones	Caie	Russell	
		6/1	1,500						*Gray*	*Ritchie*	*Griffiths*	*Lamont*	*Robertson*	*Lee*	*Brown R*	*Lewis*	*Jones*	*McInnes*	*Paul*	
								Ref: A Farrant	Despite the wet weather, there was a fair crowd at the Lane for this clash. Both sides pressed in turn at the start, but it wasn't until just after the interval that the first goal was obtained. Potter fired in Gray's poor clearance, before a long shot from Jones saw City double their advantage.											
6	A	CORINTHIANS			L	0-3	0-2		Monteith	McDonald	Stewart	Downie	McLean	Hamilton	Potter	Goldie	Jones	Pollock	Russell	
		24/3	*1,000*					*Taylor 10, Blaker 20, Gosling 70*	*Moon WR*	*Wylde CH*	*Oakley WJ*	*Beasley HO*	*Barrett HR*	*Wilson GP*	*Corbett BO*	*Taylor SS*	*Blaker RNR*	*Gosling TS*	*Burnup CJ*	
								(at 'Queens Club')	Despite the Cup semi-final taking place at the Crystal Palace, the Corinthians kept this appointment with City at the Queen's Club. In a 40-minute each-way game, Taylor and Blaker shot in for the Corinthians before half-time, and Gosling netted from Burnup's pass after the break.											
7	H	CORINTHIANS			W	2-1	1-0	Goldie 15, Crawford 65	Monteith	McDonald	Robson	Downie	McLean	Hamilton	Langham	Goldie	Jones	O'Brien	Crawford	
		17/4	1,750					*Smith 75*	*Wilkinson G*	*Wylde CH*	*Timmins WA*	*Vickers H*	*Young F*	*Beasley HO*	*Corbett BO*	*Taylor SS*	*Smith GO*	*Ryder CR*	*Burnup CJ*	
								Ref: N Whittaker	The alteration made to kick-off time for the first match of the Corinthians West Country tour had a prejudicial effect of the attendance, which did not reach 2,000. Smart work by Crawford set up Goldie for City's opener; then following the break a capital shot doubled their advantage.											

FA Cup/Glos Cup/Charity Cup					F-A	H-T	Scorers, Times, and Referees	1	2	3	4	5	6	7	8	9	10	11
1	H	STALYBRIDGE R	6	W	2-1	2-1	Jones 6, Blessington 21	Monteith	McDonald	McLean	Downie	Britton	Hamilton	Langham	Blessington	Jones	Caie	Crawford
	27/1	4,996 *LL:2*					*Carney 35*	*Wharton*	*Smith*	*Walton*	*Brown*	*Green*	*Johnson*	*Ogden*	*Carney*	*Brooks*	*Joyce*	*Bamber*
		(£131)					Ref: G Muir	The contingent of 400 fans supporting Lancashire League Stalybridge's cause at St John's Lane were disappointed by City's whirlwind start which produced terrific early goals for Jones and Blessington. Despite Carney replying for the visitors, the game petered out after the interval.										
2	A	ASTON VILLA	11	L	1-5	1-3	Jones 41	Monteith	McDonald	Pollock	McLean	Britton	Hamilton	Langham	Blessington	Jones	Downie	Potter
	10/2	*16,000 1:2*					*Garraty 2, Devey 20, 25, 48, 60*	*George*	*Spencer*	*Evans*	*Bowman*	*Cowan*	*Crabtree*	*Athersmith*	*Devey*	*Garraty*	*Wheldon*	*Smith*
		(£533)						City, who made the Colonade Hotel their headquarters prior to this game, lost the toss at a windy and snowy Villa Park. Monteith's fumble of Smith's shot allowed Garraty to score early on; then Devey doubled Villa's lead, despite City's protests that the leather had gone out of play.										
SF	A	BRISTOL ROV	10	D	1-1	1-0	O'Brien 30	Lewis	McDonald	Robson	Downie	McLean	Hamilton	Potter	Blessington	Jones	O'Brien	Crawford
GC	2/4	*3,000 11*					*Jones 49*	*Gray*	*Ritchie*	*Griffiths*	*Lamont*	*Robertson*	*Brown G*	*Brown R*	*Lewis*	*Jones*	*McInnes*	*Paul*
							Ref: A Farrant	City had the better of the early exchanges, but it wasn't until midway through the first half that a dainty tap from O'Brien put them in front. After the break, the Rovers soon levelled thanks to Jones' splendid drive. City pressed much thereafter without being able to get the winner.										
R	H	BRISTOL ROV	8	W	2-1	2-1	O'Brien 2, Blessington 10	Monteith	McDonald	Robson	Downie	McLean	Hamilton	Potter	Blessington	Jones	O'Brien	Crawford
GC	9/4	2,000 *12*					*Paul 20*	*Gray*	*Ritchie*	*Griffiths*	*Lamont*	*Robertson*	*Brown G*	*Brown R*	*Lewis*	*Jones*	*McInnes*	*Paul*
							Ref: A Green	O'Brien's and Blessington's high shots put City into an early 2-0 lead, but the Rovers responded with Paul's oblique grounder. Unlucky not to have been awarded a spot-kick, the Rovers had further misfortune just before the half-time interval when McInnes had a great shot disallowed.										
F	N	BEDMINSTER	9	L	1-3	0-2	Russell 86	Lewis	McDonald	Robson	Downie	McLean	Hamilton	Potter	Blessington	Jones	O'Brien	Russell
GC	30/4	*1,975 6*					*Boucher 25, Geddes 27, 85*	*Toone*	*Barker*	*Davies RH*	*Draycott*	*Davies WH*	*Chambers*	*Whelan*	*Flewitt*	*Boucher*	*Wilson*	*Geddes*
		(£61.9.3)					Ref: T Armitt (*at 'Stapleton Road'*)	Hugh Wilson, the Minster captain, was deservedly presented with the County Cup by JA Tayler the Glos FA President. A fitting finale for the Bedminster club prior to their amalgamation with the City. McDonald's back-pass set up Boucher to race onto the ball and slot in the opener.										
SF	A	BEDMINSTER	6	D	1-1	1-1	Barker 18og	Monteith	McDonald	Robson	Downie	McLean	Hamilton	Langham	Blessington	Jones	Caie	Russell
CC	13/1	*4,200 9*					*Flewitt 25*	*Toone*	*Barker*	*Crone*	*Draycott*	*Davies WH*	*Wilson*	*Whelan*	*Davies RH*	*Boucher*	*Flewitt*	*Geddes*
		(£110)					Ref: F Crabtree	At Ashton Gate, Wilson won the toss and chose to play from the Lower End. Bedminster's defence was resolute, apart from when star man Barker back-heeled McLean's shot into his own net. From Whelan's centre, Flewitt headed home the Minster's equaliser in this capital game.										
R	H	BEDMINSTER	10	L	0-6	0-3	*[Wilson 35p, 55, Boucher 75]*	Lewis	Robson	Pollock	Downie	McLean	Hamilton	Langham	Blessington	Jones	O'Brien	Potter
CC	21/2	2,000 *4*					*Flewitt 4, 50, Geddes 20,*	*Toone*	*Barker*	*Davies RH*	*Draycott*	*Davies WH*	*Chambers*	*Whelan*	*Flewitt*	*Boucher*	*Wilson*	*Geddes*
							Ref: F Crabtree	Pollock's injury, sustained when Geddes scored Bedminster's second, disrupted City. Off the field for most of the rest of the first half, he was a limping passenger thereafter. McLean's handling offence gave away a penalty, which had to be re-taken after Lewis had saved the first effort.										

	SOUTHERN LEAGUE	P	W	D	L	Home F	Home A	W	D	L	Away F	Away A	Pts
1	Tottenham H	28	13	1	0	43	9	7	3	4	24	17	44
2	Portsmouth	28	14	0	0	39	5	6	1	7	20	24	41
3	Southampton	28	11	0	3	52	14	6	1	7	18	19	35
4	Reading	28	10	2	2	25	6	5	0	9	16	22	32
5	Swindon T	28	12	1	1	30	11	3	1	10	20	31	32
6	Bedminster	28	9	1	4	27	18	4	1	9	17	27	28
7	Millwall Ath	28	9	0	5	25	17	3	3	8	11	20	27
8	QP Rangers	28	8	2	4	29	20	4	0	10	21	38	26
9	BRISTOL C	28	9	0	5	33	23	0	7	7	11	24	25
10	Bristol Rov	28	9	2	3	31	16	2	1	11	15	39	25
11	New Brompt'	28	7	3	4	27	16	2	3	9	13	32	24
12	Gravesend U	28	7	4	3	28	25	3	0	11	10	33	24
13	Chatham	28	9	1	4	26	16	1	2	11	12	42	23
14	Thames Iron	28	6	4	4	19	13	2	1	11	10	33	21
15	Sheppey Utd	28	1	5	8	9	24	2	2	10	15	42	13
		420	134	26	50	443	233	50	26	134	233	443	420
	Disbanded												
-	Brighton Utd	22	1	2	8	8	22	2	1	8	14	34	9
-	Cowes	13	2	0	5	9	26	1	1	4	8	17	7

	SOUTHERN DISTRICT COMB.	P	W	D	L	Home F	Home A	W	D	L	Away F	Away A	Pts
1	Millwall Ath	16	7	1	0	16	0	5	1	2	14	10	26
2	Tottenham H	16	7	0	1	26	7	3	3	2	15	11	23
3	Portsmouth	16	5	2	1	20	8	3	0	5	8	10	18
4	Wlch Arsenal	16	5	1	2	16	6	3	0	5	11	16	17
5	Southampton	16	5	1	2	17	10	1	1	6	7	19	14
6	BRISTOL C	16	4	1	3	20	16	1	2	5	5	16	13
7	Reading	16	4	2	2	12	11	0	2	6	4	17	12
8	Chatham	16	4	1	3	8	6	1	1	6	4	31	12
9	QP Rangers	16	4	1	3	14	9	0	0	8	5	19	9
		144	45	10	17	149	73	17	10	45	73	149	144

	WESTERN LEAGUE	P	W	D	L	Home F	Home A	W	D	L	Away F	Away A	Pts
1	Bristol Rov	6	2	0	1	4	3	1	1	1	4	3	7
2	Bedminster	6	1	1	1	6	4	2	0	1	4	8	7
3	Swindon T	6	2	0	1	3	1	1	0	2	4	6	6
4	BRISTOL C	6	2	0	1	11	5	0	0	3	1	7	4
		24	7	1	4	24	13	4	1	7	13	24	24

Odds & ends

Double wins: SL: (1) Cowes. SDC: (1) Reading.
Double losses: SL: (3) Southampton, Millwall, Reading, Portsmouth.
SDC: (2) Woolwich Arsenal, Millwall.
Won from behind: SDC: (2) Reading (a), Reading (h).
Lost from in front: SL: (1) Reading (h).

High spots: Beating Bristol Rov in the Southern League on Boxing Day.
The 8-1 annihilation of Bedminster in the Western League
City's good display in the FA Cup at 'Villa Park', despite losing 1-5.

Low spots: The 1-3 home Southern League defeat by Southampton.
Losing 3-6 at Portsmouth in a Southern League fixture on 31 March.
The 1-4 Southern League defeat at Southampton on 23 April.
Succumbing to Bedminster 1-4 in the Western League on 7 March.
Bedminster's Gloucestershire Cup Final success after having beaten City 6-0 in the Bristol Charity Cup

Player of the Year: Billy Jones.
Ever-presents: (0).
Hat-tricks: (5) James Blessington, Billy Jones, 'Sandy' Caie, 'Jock' Russell, Billy Langham.
Leading scorer: Overall: Billy Jones (28). League: Billy Jones (23).

AGM (Temperance Hall, East Street, Bedminster, 10 July 1900):
Loss £1,163.16s.11d.

	Appearances Lge	Cup	Fr	Goals Lge	Cup	Fr	Tot
Blessington, James	**33**	7	3	**8**	2		**10**
Britton, Phil	**15**	2	1	**1**			**1**
Caie, 'Sandy'	**26**	2	3	**15**			**15**
Crawford, Alex	**37**	3	3	**6**		2	**8**
Downie, Alex	**40**	7	5	**2**			**2**
Godsman, Adam	**17**		3			1	**1**
Goldie, Edward	**9**		2			1	**1**
Hamilton, Jack	**48**	7	7				
Jones, Billy	**49**	7	6	**23**	2	3	**28**
Langham, Billy	**41**	4	4	**14**		3	**17**
Leslie, H	**3**						
McDonald, Alex	**38**	6	7				
McLean, John	**47**	7	6				
Marks	**1**						
Milligan, Alex	**3**		2				
Molyneux, Fred	**5**		1				
Monteith, Hugh	**45**	4	6				
O'Brien, J			1				
O'Brien, 'Paddy'	**20**	4	3	**11**	2	1	**14**
Osborne, R	**3**		1				
Pollock, Robert	**13**	2	1	**1**			**1**
Potter, Arthur	**22**	5	3	**5**		2	**7**
Robson, David	**34**	5	2				
Russell, 'Jock'	**19**	2	4	**8**	1		**9**
Stewart, Billy	**14**		1				
Talbot-Lewis, Albert	**6**	3	1				
Thompson, W	**2**						
Watts, Joseph	**4**		1				
Opponent og				**1**	1	1	**3**
28 players used	**594**	**77**	**77**	**95**	**8**	**14**	**117**

Note: Games against disbanded clubs included.

No	Date	Att	Pos	Pt	F-A	H-T	Scorers, Times, and Referees	1	2	3	4	5	6	7	8	9	10	11
1 A	SWINDON			W	1-0	0-0	Whelan 82	**Toone**	**Bach**	**Davies**	Jones	**Wilson**	**Chambers**	**Whelan**	**Stevenson**	**Michael**	**Fulton**	**Nichol**
	1/9	*3,250*		2				*Menham*	*Ritchie*	*Stephenson*	*Richardson*	*Logan*	*McEleny*	*Brown*	*Gardner*	*Smith*	*Downie*	*Kirton*
							Ref: B Lockyer	Wilson won the toss and elected to play with the sun at his back in this the first game of the fused Bedminster & City clubs. Whilst the match-winning goal was a decided piece of good fortune - Menham's slip allowing Michael to pass for Whelan to fire in - it was a deserved success.										
2 H	WATFORD		1	W	6-1	3-0	Michael 2p, 5, 30, 65p, 80,	Toone	Bach	Davies	Jones	Wilson	Chambers	**McDougall**	Stevenson	Michael	Fulton	Nichol
	8/9	7,500	*10*	4			*Farnall 47* [Fulton 70]	*Hammett*	*Cother*	*Nidd*	*Farnall*	*Good*	*Wood*	*Varley*	*Wilcox*	*Price*	*Colclough*	*Ferne*
							Ref: V Daines	Despite losing the toss and starting against the sun, City soon went ahead when a handling offence allowed Michael to register from the spot. Watford were outclassed, but had the satisfaction of being the first side to score against City this campaign when Farnall shot past Toone.										
3 A	LUTON		6	L	0-2	0-0		Toone	Bach	Davies	Jones	Wilson	Chambers	Nichol	Stevenson	Michael	Fulton	McDougall
	15/9	*3,000*	*10*	4			*Burbage 60, 85*	*Smart*	*Lindsay*	*McCurdy*	*Clifford*	*Holdstock*	*Williams*	*Brown*	*Blessington*	*Burbage*	*Tierney*	*Saxton*
								A large crowd, much larger in fact than the home club were in the habit of attracting when they were members of the Second Division of the Football League, witnessed this game. They saw City beaten by Luton's determination and dash, especially Burbage's Corinthian-like rushes.										
4 H	TOTTENHAM		6	D	1-1	0-0	Michael 60p	Toone	Bach	Davies	Jones	Wilson	Chambers	Whelan	Stevenson	Michael	Fulton	Nichol
	22/9	8,250	*8*	5			*Stormont 75*	*Clawley*	*Melia*	*Hughes*	*Erentz*	*McNaught*	*Jones J*	*Smith*	*Cameron*	*Brown*	*Stormont*	*Kirwan*
		(£245)					Ref: G Muir *(at 'Ashton Gate')*	Despite the home defence being given a torrid time by the dashing Spurs forwards, City still had the chances to have won this game played at Ashton Gate. A bad tackle on Michael allowed the City centre-forward to put his side in front, but Stormont's cross-shot brought Spurs level.										
5 A	WEST HAM		3	W	2-1	1-0	Fulton 40, Michael 80	Toone	Bach	Davies	Jones	McLean	Chambers	Whelan	Wilson	Michael	Fulton	Nichol
	29/9	*6,000*	*4*	7			*Kaye 55*	*Monteith*	*Tranter*	*Craig*	*Allan*	*Dove*	*McEachrane*	*Hunt*	*Corbett*	*Reid*	*Kaye*	*Fenton*
								Play was very rarely out of West Ham territory during the first half and City got the goal their play deserved shortly before the break when Fulton found the ball at his feet. After Kaye equalised, the City had two goals disallowed before Michael got a late winner from a free-kick.										
6 H	PORTSMOUTH		2	W	3-2	3-1	Fulton 7, Wilson 15, Michael 40	Toone	Bach	Davies	Jones	McLean	Chambers	Whelan	Wilson	Michael	Fulton	Nichol
	6/10	9,000	*1*	9			*Marshall 10, 65*	*Reilly*	*Turner*	*Wilkie*	*Blyth*	*Stringfellow*	*Cleghorn*	*Marshall*	*Bedingfield*	*Joyce*	*Smith*	*Clark*
		(£236)					Ref: A Green	After the newly elected local Member of Parliament, Walter Long, kicked off, the City took up the offensive and soon went into the lead when Fulton headed home. Marshall, who later fired in a fine goal, got Pompey's equaliser with a grounder, but Wilson put City in front once again.										
7 A	NEW BROMPTON		4	D	1-1	1-0	Wilson 30	Toone	Bach	Davies	Jones	McLean	Chambers	Whelan	Wilson	Michael	Fulton	Nichol
	13/10	*3,000*	*16*	10			*Innes 55p*	*Ambler*	*Hulmes*	*Robertson*	*Innes*	*Atherton*	*Graham*	*Frettingham*	*Macdonald*	*Haywood*	*Lissenden*	*Seeley*
								Despite an appeal for offside, Wilson's low drive put City in front in this game that saw them on top throughout. Unfortunately they were let down by poor finishing, and paid the price when Bach's handling offence allowed New Brompton to grab an equaliser from the penalty-spot.										
8 H	BRISTOL ROV		2	W	1-0	0-0	Michael 53	Toone	Bach	Davies	Jones	McLean	Chambers	Whelan	Wilson	Michael	Fulton	Nichol
	20/10	**13,500**	*3*	12				*Gray*	*Kifford*	*Griffiths A*	*Draycott*	*Robertson*	*Neilson*	*Clark*	*Jones*	*Boucher*	*Griffiths H*	*Paul*
		(£352)					Ref: N Whittaker *(at 'Ashton Gate')*	Such was the interest, all manner of vehicles were pressed into service for conveying the fans to this game, while many wended their way by means of the new Cumberland Road footbridge. A grand game is settled in City's favour by Michael heading in a rebound from Gray's save.										
9 A	READING		2	W	1-0	0-0	Jones 80	Toone	Bach	Davies	Jones	McLean	Chambers	Whelan	Stevenson	Michael	Fulton	Wilson
	27/10	*3,000*	*8*	14				*Cotton*	*Henderson*	*Clinch*	*Watts*	*Mainman*	*Bull*	*Evans*	*Barlow*	*Logan*	*Spence*	*Pegg*
							Ref: G Muir	A lightning low shot that sped into the far corner of the net settled this poor encounter in City's favour. The worst culprits, in a contest that was absolutely littered with fouls, were able to grab a rather fortunate win thanks to Toone's penalty save not long after the change of ends.										
10 H	KETTERING		1	W	6-0	3-0	Michael 16, 60, Wilson 35,	Toone	Bach	Robson	Jones	McLean	Chambers	Whelan	Stevenson	Michael	Fulton	Wilson
	7/11	2,000	*10*	16			[Stev'son 40, Whelan 46, Fulton 75]	*Baldry*	*Clarke*	*Draper*	*Roulston*	*Panter*	*Farren*	*Webb*	*Becton*	*Lawrence*	*Coleman*	*Towell*
							Ref: V Daines *(at 'Ashton Gate')*	Despite the windy conditions, there was a fair crowd present when Michael kicked off. Fulton got in the first shot, which was quickly followed by another from Whelan to set the scene for an afternoon of almost constant City attacking. Fulton ran through on his own for the sixth goal.										

No	H/A	Opponent / Date	Att	Pos	Pts	Res	H-T	Scorers, Times, Referees	1	2	3	4	5	6	7	8	9	10	11
11	A	GRAVESEND		1	W	3-1	2-1	Michael 12, 30, McLean 75	Toone	Bach	Davies	Jones	McLean	Chambers	Whelan	Stevenson	Michael	Fulton	Wilson
		10/11	*1,000*	*16*	18			*Madden 40*	*Hamilton*	*Warburton*	*Lockie*	*McAvoy*	*Blair*	*Bigden*	*Jury*	*Pugh*	*Parkinson*	*Madden*	*Penney*
									Faced by a Gravesend XI containing three reserves, City obtained their first ever win on the Kentish ground. A mistake by the home defence allowed Michael to nip in and score City's opener, then get the benefit of the referee's decision when Hamilton tipped the ball against a post.										
12	H	MILLWALL		1	W	**7-1**	4-1	St'son15,17, McLean 25,Wilson 40,	Toone	Bach	Davies	Wilson	McLean	Chambers	Whelan	Stevenson	Fulton	O'Brien	**Geddes**
		17/11	5,000	*5*	20			*Sharples 35*[O'Brien 70,75,Wh'n 80]	*Joyce*	*Shutt*	*Davidson*	*Regan*	*Henderson*	*Banks*	*Dryburgh*	*Sharples*	*Bevan*	*Jones*	*Wilson*
								Ref: G Muir *(at 'Ashton Gate')*	After winning the twice-taken toss, the coin not falling flat initially, City commenced with the strong wind at their backs and proceeded to give what the *Times & Mirror* recorded as 'unquestionable their finest performance' A clever pass by Geddes saw Stevenson notching the opener.										
13	A	SOUTHAMPTON		1	L	1-2	1-1	McLean 30	Toone	Bach	Davies	Wilson	McLean	Chambers	Whelan	Stevenson	Fulton	O'Brien	Geddes
		24/11	*8,000* (£170)	*2*	20			*Lee 4, Chadwick E 75*	*Moger*	*Sharp*	*Molyneux*	*Meston*	*Chadwick A*	*Lee*	*Turner*	*Yates*	*Wood*	*Chadwick E*	*Milward*
								Ref: P Harrower	A twenty-yarder, which brought the Saints their hard-earned, but deserved success in this top of the table clash, made sure that City's long series of defeats continued at the Dell. McLean's lovely shot had earlier levelled the scores after Lee's soft-opener had given So'ton the lead.										
14	H	CHATHAM*		1	W	4-0	3-0	Macey 15og, Michael 25,	Toone	Bach	Robson	Jones	McLean	Davies	Wilson	Stevenson	Michael	Fulton	Geddes
		1/12	4,000	*16*	22			[Stevenson 44, Fulton 75]	*Macey*	*Burton*	*Humphreys*	*Woods*	*Chapman*	*Perrins*	*Bell*	*Whelan*	*Johnson*	*Clements*	*Dickenson*
								Ref: S Major	A scrappy opening, but City took the lead when the referee, after consultation with his linesman, realised that Wilson's corner was touched into the goal by the Chatham keeper. A poor game with little in the way of good football, City didn't exert themselves against weak opposition.										
15	A	CHATHAM*		1	W	4-1	2-1	McLean 35, Geddes 40, 65, 80	Toone	Bach	Davies	Jones	McLean	Chambers	Whelan	Wilson	Michael	Fulton	Geddes
		8/12	*1,500*	*16*	24			*Neyland 43*	*Macey*	*Burton*	*Humphreys*	*Chisholm*	*Chapman*	*Perrin*	*Johnson*	*Whelan*	*Neyland*	*Clements*	*Dickenson*
									Only a moderate crowd at Chatham, where the home side had the advantage of the high wind at the start. McLean's pretty shot, that gave City the lead, set up a hectic time before the interval. After the break Geddes registered with a hook-shot, before scoring again to notch his hat-trick.										
16	H	SWINDON		1	W	2-0	1-0	Fulton 6, Wilson 75	Toone	Bach	Davies	Jones	McLean	Chambers	Whelan	Wilson	Michael	Fulton	Geddes
		15/12	5,000	*15*	26				*Menham*	*Ritchie*	*Stephenson*	*Richardson*	*Downie*	*McEleny*	*Brown*	*Davies*	*Kirton*	*Smith*	*Gardner*
								Ref: G Muir *(at 'Ashton Gate')*	The Railwaymen appealed for offside to no avail as the referee allowed City's early opener after consulting with both his linesmen. During the second half, shortly after the referee, George Muir, halted the game for a while to admonish a spectator, Wilson registered with a capital shot.										
17	A	WATFORD		2	-	0-0	0-0		Toone	Bach	Davies	Jones	McLean	Chambers	Whelan	Wilson	Michael	Fulton	Geddes
		22/12	*2,000*	*15*	22				*Hammett*	*Cother*	*Nidd*	*Sharp*	*Good*	*Colclough*	*Varley*	*Wilcox*	*Price*	*Allan*	*Parkinson*
								Ref: B Lockyer *(Abandoned due to fog 75 mins)*	A heavy mist hung over the ground but, despite the soft turf, play was fast and interesting before the break when City had slightly the better of play. In the second half both McLean and Whelan spurned good chances before the worsening fog brought play to a premature end on 75 mins.										
18	H	LUTON		2	W	1-0	0-0	Stevenson 56	Toone	Bach	Davies	Jones	McLean	Chambers	Whelan	Stevenson	Michael	Wilson	Geddes
		29/12	5,000	*11*	24				*Ord*	*Clifford*	*McCurdy*	*Williams*	*Farr*	*Garratt*	*Brown*	*Hawkes*	*Barker*	*Saxton*	*Durrant*
								Ref: V Daines	Luton displayed all manner of pluck, despite losing the services of Saxton (ex-Bedminster) at half-time due to a dislocated left elbow suffered in an early collision with Bach. The Luton keeper displayed inspired form to frustrate the City, but he was unable to stop Stevenson's effort.										
19	H	WEST HAM		1	W	1-0	0-0	Michael 75	Toone	Robson	Davies	Jones	McLean	Chambers	Wilson	Stevenson	Michael	Fulton	McDougall
		12/1	4,000	*9*	26				*Monteith*	*King*	*Pudan*	*Allen*	*Kelly*	*McEachrane*	*Hunt*	*Grassam*	*Reid*	*Ratcliffe*	*Kaye*
								Ref: G Muir *(at 'Ashton Gate')*	The good-sized crowd at Ashton Gate witnessed a fast, though not a scientific, game played in the fine weather. The enigmatic Michael was again poor for most of the time before bursting past both backs and firing in a wonderful winner past ex-City goalkeeper Hugh Monteith.										
20	A	PORTSMOUTH		2	L	**0-4**	0-2	*[Smith 80p]*	Toone	Bach	Davies	Jones	McLean	Chambers	Wilson	Stevenson	Michael	Fulton	McDougall
		19/1	*7,500*	*4*	26			*Clark 20, Bedingfield 27, Joyce 52,*	*Reilly*	*Turner*	*Wilkie*	*Blyth*	*Hunter*	*Cleghorn*	*Marshall*	*Joyce*	*Bedingfield*	*Smith*	*Clark*
								Ref: P Harrower	Despite the heavy nature of the turf, the pace was fast right from the start of this game. City were on the defensive early on and Pompey took the lead when Toone could only fist Clark's shot against the inside of the upright. Bedingfield soon doubled City's deficit with a good shot.										
21	H	QP RANGERS		2	W	2-0	1-0	Fulton 6, Lennox 55og	Toone	Bach	Davies	Jones	McLean	Chambers	Wilson	Stevenson	Fulton	O'Brien	Geddes
		9/2	5,000	*8*	28				*Clutterbuck*	*Newlands*	*McConnell*	*Lennox*	*Hitch*	*Skinner*	*Gray*	*Christie*	*Ronaldson*	*Humphreys*	*Foxall*
								Ref: P Harrower *(at 'Ashton Gate')*	Even though City's defence had to be vigilant in dealing with the threat of the visitors' fast and clever inside trio, their forwards squandered numerous chances. Fulton notched the opener from Wilson's well-placed corner. Lennox put into his own net whilst trying to stop O'Brien.										

No	Date		Att	Pos	Pt	F-A	H-T	Scorers, Times, and Referees	1	2	3	4	5	6	7	8	9	10	11
22	H	READING		2	W	1-0	0-0	Geddes 80	Toone	Bach	Davies	Jones	McLean	Chambers	Wilson	Stevenson	Fulton	O'Brien	Geddes
	16/2		7,000	*9*	30				*Cotton*	*Sharp J*	*Clinch*	*Bull*	*Mainman*	*Watts*	*Evans*	*Pangbourn*	*Logan*	*Sharp A*	*Spence*
								Ref: A Green	The play opened in splendid weather and Fulton starting the ball rolling from the Lower End. Some sharp exchanges ensued, but whilst Pangbourne had a goal disallowed in the second half, the score-sheet remained blank until Geddes registered for City with a capital effort.										
23	H	NEW BROMPTON		1	W	2-0	2-0	Wilson 12, Stevenson 25	Toone	Bach	Davies	Jones	McLean	Chambers	McDougall	Stevenson	Fulton	Wilson	Geddes
	27/2		**1,500**	*9*	32				*Crane*	*Robertson*	*Humphrey*	*Innes*	*Atherton*	*Neame*	*Macdonald*	*Haywood*	*Frettingham*	*Neyland*	*Seeley*
								Ref: J Tillotson *(at 'Ashton Gate')*	An easy home success, despite Geddes being carried off shortly after Wilson opened the scoring with a fine close-range shot. The City defence easily dealt with the spasmodic visiting attacks, especially after Stevenson had doubled their advantage with a splendidly placed low drive.										
24	H	GRAVESEND		1	W	6-0	3-0	Wilson 10, 30, 60, McLean 40, 75, [O'Brien 65]	Toone	Bach	Davies	Jones	McLean	Chambers	Whelan	Stevenson	Wilson	O'Brien	McDougall
	2/3		4,000	*14*	34				*Hamilton*	*Tyler*	*Lockie*	*McAvoy*	*Blair*	*Bigden*	*Jury*	*Pugh*	*Parkinson*	*Tapp*	*Penney*
								Ref: S Major	Despite doctor's orders, Whelan made a welcome return for this game. On a rain-sodden pitch that turned into a quagmire, he showed much of his old skill until retiring from the fray shortly before the lucky final goal. Hamilton's clearance hit McLean and rebounded into the net.										
25	A	MILLWALL		2	L	**0-4**	0-2	*[Gettins 51, 85]*	Toone	Bach	Davies	McLean	Wedlock	Chambers	Whelan	Stevenson	Wilson	O'Brien	McDougall
	9/3		*5,000*	*4*	27			*Frost 10, Henderson 30,*	*Griffiths*	*Shutt*	*Davidson*	*Caie*	*Henderson*	*Millar*	*Dryburgh*	*Frost*	*Bevan*	*Gettins*	*Wilson*
									Jones was absent on international duty for England, and injury continued to deprive City of the services of Michael, Fulton and Geddes. It was therefore little wonder that Millwall avenged their recent Ashton Gate humiliation, despite City having much more of the play before the break.										
26	H	SOUTHAMPTON		2	D	1-1	1-0	Whelan 30	Toone	Bach	Davies	Jones	McLean	Chambers	Whelan	Stevenson	Fulton	O'Brien	Wilson
	16/3		10,250	*1*	35			*Sharp 83*	*Robinson*	*Fry*	*Molyneux*	*Meston*	*Killean*	*Sharp*	*Yates*	*Wood*	*Toman*	*Chadwick E*	*Milward*
								Ref: A Millward *(at 'Ashton Gate')*	Sharp's high-dropping 20-yarder, not long before the finish of this fast, exciting and splendidly contested game, deprived City of victory. It was cruel luck on the Reds, who deserved more after holding the advantage for some 53 minutes following Whelan's header past Robinson.										
27	A	QP RANGERS		2	L	0-2	0-2		Toone	Bach	Davies	Jones	**Nicholls**	Chambers	Whelan	Stevenson	Fulton	Wilson	McDougall
	23/3		*5,000*	*7*	35			*Ronaldson 10, 30*	*Clutterbuck*	*Newlands*	*McConnell*	*Bellingham*	*Hitch*	*Skinner*	*Gray*	*Downing*	*Ronaldson*	*Humphreys*	*Foxall*
									City had quite enough of the play to have won this game comfortably, but weakness in front of the sticks allowed Rangers to continue their tendency of lowering the colours of the Championship-chasing clubs. Ronaldson twice broke away to deposit the ball in the back of City's net.										
28	A	TOTTENHAM		3	L	0-1	0-0		Toone	Bach	Davies	Jones	McLean	Chambers	McDougall	Stevenson	Wilson	O'Brien	Geddes
	6/4		*4,000*	*6*	35			*Jones 65*	*Clawley*	*Melia*	*Hughes*	*Anson*	*McNaught*	*Stormont*	*Jones J*	*Burton*	*Woodward*	*Moffat*	*Hyde*
									Due to their hard game at Southampton on Good Friday and their forthcoming FA Cup semi-final, Spurs put a virtual reserve side in the field for this clash. They got away with their gamble as City squandered many chances and were made to pay when Jones scored following a rush.										
29	A	BRISTOL ROV		3	D	1-1	0-1	McDougall 55	Toone	Wilson	Davies	Jones	McLean	Chambers	McDougall	**Bartlett**	Stevenson	O'Brien	Geddes
	8/4		***10,000***	*6*	36			*Williams 30*	*Gray*	*Kifford*	*Griffiths A*	*Davies*	*Robertson*	*Neilson*	*Clark*	*Jones*	*Boucher*	*Griffiths H*	*Williams*
			(£341)					Ref: N Whittaker	Heavy rain was falling when the large gathering at Stapleton Road, who were not put off by the stormy weather, saw City kick off against the wind. After McDougall, who later fired in City's equaliser, had a header disallowed, Williams put Rovers in front with a low rasping shot.										
30	A	WATFORD		2	W	3-1	2-1	McDougall 30, Stevenson 40, [Bartlett 60]	Toone	Bach	Davies	Jones	McLean	Wilson	McDougall	O'Brien	Stevenson	Bartlett	Geddes
	17/4		*2,000*	*14*	38			*Parkinson 15*	*Hammett*	*Cother*	*Nidd*	*Farnall*	*Good*	*Sharp*	*Varley*	*Wilcox*	*Price*	*Allan*	*Parkinson*
								Ref: A Partridge	Matters didn't look promising for City early on when, after Toone made a wonderful save from Wilcox, Parkinson hooked the ball into the net. However McDougall levelled with a fine cross-shot and by the break City held the lead thanks to Stevenson sending the leather past Hammett.										
31	A	KETTERING		2	D	1-1	1-0	Fulton 44	Toone	Bach	Davies	Jones	McLean	Chambers	McDougall	Stevenson	Wilson	Fulton	Geddes
	22/4		*2,000*	*11*	39			*Winterhalder 55*	*Baldry*	*Bosworth*	*Draper*	*Roulston*	*Panter*	*Pollock*	*Webb*	*Becton*	*Winterhalder*	*Coleman*	*Hartley*
	Home		Away						In fine weather the early play ruled slightly in favour of Kettering, who had a goal by Webb struck off for offside. City, though, were similarly unlucky with Wilson's early strike being disallowed, but just before the interval Fulton was alert to finish off a magnificent McDougall shot.										
	Ave 6,067		4,141																

* *Chatham disbanded 20 December – record expunged.*

WESTERN LEAGUE DIVISION 1

No	Venue	Opponent / Att.	Pos	Res	Pts	Score	HT	Scorers	1	2	3	4	5	6	7	8	9	10	11
1	H	SOUTHAMPTON		W		4-1	2-0	Fulton 3, 70, O'Brien 25, [Stevenson 52]	Toone	Bach	Davies	Wilson	McLean	Chambers	Whelan	Stevenson	Fulton	O'Brien	McDougall
	14/11	5,000			2			*Chadwick E 70*	*Wildig*	*Meston*	*Molyneux*	*French*	*Chadwick A*	*Lee*	*Turner*	*Yates*	*Wood*	*Chadwick E*	*Milward*
								Ref: A Farrant	The goodly number of spectators at St John's Lane for the delayed start of the Western League season witnessed a game of the most attractive character. Yates fired against the bar right at the start, but City took the lead when Fulton shot home from close quarters following good play.										
2	A	TOTTENHAM		L		1-4	0-1	Fulton 82	Toone	Bach	Robson	Wilson	McLean	Davies	Whelan	Stevenson	Fulton	O'Brien	Geddes
	26/11	*4,000*			2			*Morris 35, Kirwan 60, Jones 61, 85*	*Clawley*	*Erentz*	*Tait*	*Hughes*	*McNaught*	*Stormont*	*Jones A*	*Morris*	*Brown*	*Cameron*	*Kirwan*
								Ref: A Millward	Fine weather prevailed at Gilpin Park where Morris headed in Spurs' opener during a well-contested first half. Not long after the interval Kirwan shot in to double the homesters' advantage. Near the finish, Fulton responded for City before Jones set the seal on a Spurs victory.										
3	H	READING	5	L		0-1	0-0		Toone	Bach	Robson	Jones	McLean	Chambers	Whelan	Stevenson	Michael	O'Brien	McDougall
	25/12	5,000	*3*		2			*Logan 85*	*Cotton*	*Henderson*	*Clinch*	*Bull*	*Holt*	*Watts*	*Evans*	*Logan*	*Pegg*	*Sharp A*	*Barnes*
								Ref: A Farrant (*at 'Ashton Gate'*)	Logan settled a poor game when he latched onto a Watts shot which rebounded off the crossbar. City failed to capitalise before the break when they had the strong wind in their favour, though McLean was unlucky when his first-half free-kick found the net without touching anyone else.										
4	A	BRISTOL ROV	5	D		1-1	0-0	McLean 65	Toone	Bach	Davies	Jones	McLean	Chambers	Whelan	Stevenson	Michael	Wilson	Geddes
	26/12	***12,000***	*9*		3			*Boucher 55*	*Gray*	*Kifford*	*Griffiths A*	*Davies*	*Robertson*	*Neilson*	*Clark*	*Jones*	*Boucher*	*Griffiths H*	*Williams*
								Ref: Q/M Sgt Barrow	The *Times & Mirror* reported that this match was 'a credit to Bristol football and should go a long way towards cementing the good feeling that now exists between the two clubs'. Tommy Boucher shot Rovers in front through a sea of legs, but McLean soon headed in City's leveller.										
5	H	PORTSMOUTH	5	D		2-2	0-2	Jones 48, Wilson 70p	Toone	Robson	Davies	Wilson	McLean	Chambers	Whelan	Stevenson	Jones	O'Brien	McDougall
	26/1	2,000	*3*		4			*Marshall 14, Bedingfield 45*	*Reilly*	*Turner*	*Wilkie*	*Blyth*	*Hunter*	*Cleghorn*	*Marshall*	*Lewis*	*Bedingfield*	*Smith*	*Clark*
								Ref: A Farrant	Following the death of Queen Victoria, both sides wore black crepe armbands in her memory. Marshall soon registered with a shot through Toone's legs. Not long after the break, Jones fired in from a narrow angle before Turner's foul brought Wilson his match-saving spot-kick.										
6	A	PORTSMOUTH	7	D		0-3	0-0		Toone	Bach	Davies	Jones	McLean	Chambers	Wilson	Stevenson	Fulton	O'Brien	Geddes
	13/2	*2,000*	*3*		5			*Lewis 50, Marshall 70, [Bedingfield 85]*	*Reilly*	*Turner*	*Wilkie*	*Blyth*	*Stringfellow*	*Cleghorn*	*Marshall*	*Lewis*	*Bedingfield*	*Smith*	*Clark*
								Ref: G Harston	At a bitterly cold Fratton Park, the teams changed straight round at half-time. Strange refereeing decisions did little to help the game, but Lewis gave Pompey the lead on intercepting a Chambers pass. Bedingfield put away a rebound off Bach to complete Pompey's deserved success.										
7	A	QP RANGERS	5	W		2-0	1-0	Fulton 25, 70	Toone	Wilson	Davies	McLean	**Wedlock**	Chambers	McDougall	Stevenson	Fulton	O'Brien	Geddes
	18/2	*1,300*	*7*		7				*Clutterbuck*	*Newlands*	*McConnell*	*Lennox*	*Hitch*	*Skinner*	*Gray*	*Christie*	*Ronaldson*	*Humphreys*	*Foxall*
									McConnell won the toss for Queen's Park Rangers, and City were hotly assailed during the early play, before responding with efforts from Fulton and O'Brien that were frustrated. Fulton put City in front with a simple shot; then after the break he was able to double the advantage.										
8	H	TOTTENHAM	5	W		4-1	1-0	Wilson 5, 51, 90, Fulton 70	Toone	Bach	Davies	Jones	McLean	Chambers	Whelan	Stevenson	Wilson	Fulton	McDougall
	27/3	**1,000**	*2*		9			*Jones 50*	*Haddow*	*Melia*	*Anson*	*Moles*	*McNaught*	*Buckingham*	*Hawley*	*Finch*	*Jones A*	*Stormont*	*Hyde*
								Ref: A Farrant	Snow was falling when Wilson ran through to open the scoring for the Citizens soon after the start and set up an easy success over a Spurs reserve side in consequence of their FA Cup replay with Reading. Wilson notched his hat-trick when he kicked through City's final goal.										
9	H	SWINDON	4	W		4-0	3-0	McDougall 25, Fulton 30, Whelan 35, [O'Brien 80]	Toone	Wilson	Davies	Jones	McLean	Chambers	Whelan	Stevenson	Fulton	O'Brien	McDougall
	30/3	2,500	*8*		11				*Menham*	*Ritchie*	*Stephenson*	*Richardson*	*Downie*	*McEleny*	*Anthony*	*Davies*	*Logan*	*Smith*	*Kirton*
								Ref: G Silman	Despite the high wind, the spectators at St John's Lane witnessed an entertaining game. McDougall, who had a brilliant game, opened the scoring with a fine shot that went in over Menham's head. Whelan obtained a rather soft goal, but O'Brien's effort was particularly fine.										
10	A	SOUTHAMPTON	5	L		1-2	0-2	Fulton 65	Toone	Wilson	Davies	Jones	McLean	Chambers	Whelan	Stevenson	Fulton	O'Brien	McDougall
	1/4	*1,000*	*4*		11			*Meston 30, Wilson 35og*	*Robinson*	*Sharp*	*Triggs*	*Meston*	*Killean*	*Blackburn*	*Yates*	*Wood*	*Toman*	*Small*	*Harrison*
								Ref: G Muir	City, who had a good proportion of the early play, went behind when Meston's long shot evaded Toone's fingertips. Wilson diverted Toman's effort into his own goal before pulling one back after the break. Unfortunately Fulton was injured on back-heeling the ball in and had to go off.										

No	Date	Att	Pos	Pt	F-A	H-T	Scorers, Times, and Referees	1	2	3	4	5	6	7	8	9	10	11
11	H BRISTOL ROV		4	W	3-0	3-0	Stevenson 10, Jones 35, O'Brien 40	Toone	Bach	Davies	Jones	McLean	Chambers	Wheelan	Stevenson	Wilson	O'Brien	Geddes
	5/4	**8,000**	*9*	13				*Frankham*	*Kifford*	*Bolton*	*Draycott*	*Neilson*	*Lee*	*Clark*	*Jones*	*Boucher*	*Paul*	*Williams*
		(£200)					Ref: Q/M Sgt Barrow *(at 'Ashton Gate')*	The Rovers gave a trial to Frankham (who has only let in nine goals for Oldland in the B&DL this season) and he was soon beaten when Stevenson deceived him with an easy shot. Jones then registered from long distance, before O'Brien put away one of Whelan's fine centres.										
12	H QP RANGERS		4	D	2-2	1-2	McDougall 20, O'Brien 55	Toone	Wilson	Davies	Jones	McLean	Chambers	McDougall	**Harding**	Stevenson	O'Brien	Geddes
	9/4	2,000	*6*	14			*Hitch 30, Downing 40*	*Clutterbuck*	*Lennox*	*McConnell*	*Bellingham*	*Hitch*	*Skinner*	*Gray*	*Newbigging*	*Downing*	*Ronaldson*	*Foxall*
							Ref: P Harrower	A violent storm broke over the proceedings at kick-off when City commenced with only ten men. O'Brien's long-shot lead to a corner before Harding joined the fray. McDougall opened the scoring with a capital goal following Michael's poor header, but Hitch equalised from distance.										
13	A READING		4	D	2-2	1-1	Jones 5, Fulton 80	Toone	Wilson	**Marsh**	Jones	McLean	Chambers	McDougall	Stevenson	Fulton	O'Brien	Geddes
	13/4	*200*	*7*	15			*Evans 30, Spence 60*	*Cotton*	*Henderson*	*Clinch*	*Bull*	*Holt*	*Watts*	*Evans*	*Sharp A*	*Logan*	*Spence*	*Barnes*
							Ref: S Major	Jones opened the scoring for City when his free-kick hit the post and went in, but the Biscuitmen levelled thanks to a fine cross-shot from Evans. Spence put the homesters in front after the interval with a clever shot, before Fulton ran through to obtain City's deserved point-saver.										
14	H MILLWALL		5	L	0-1	0-1		Toone	Bach	Marsh	Jones	McLean	Wilson	McDougall	Bartlett	Stevenson	O'Brien	Geddes
	20/4	3,000	*3*	15			*Bevan 30*	*Griffiths*	*Shutt*	*Davidson*	*Caie*	*Henderson*	*Regan*	*Dryburgh*	*Sharples*	*Bevan*	*Carnelly*	*Jones*
							Ref: A Cooper *(at 'Ashton Gate')*	It was almost too hot for football at Ashton Gate, yet the play went all the way. No one shirked their task, and in consequence the fans got their money's worth. The Dockers played the better football, though, and deservedly won thanks to Bevan heading in from Dryburgh's corner.										
15	A SWINDON		5	W	1-0	1-0	Fulton 15	Toone	Bach	Wilson	Jones	McLean	Chambers	McDougall	O'Brien	Stevenson	Fulton	Geddes
	24/4	*2,000*	*9*	17				*Menham*	*Logan*	*Stephenson*	*Richardson*	*Downie*	*McEleny*	*Brown*	*Selby*	*Pettican*	*Smith*	*Kirton*
							Ref: S Major	In delightful weather, City had much the better of the opening exchanges and it was no surprise when Fulton put away McDougall's centre. After changing straight round at half-time, Toone had a hot time in the City goal, but he proved equal to all that Swindon were able to offer.										
16	A MILLWALL		5	L	0-4	0-3		Toone	Bach	Wilson	Jones	McLean	Chambers	McDougall	Stevenson	Fulton	O'Brien	Geddes
	27/4	*5,000*	*2*	17			*Jones 7, 44, Gettins 12, Bevan 75*	*Griffiths*	*Davis W*	*Davidson*	*Caie*	*Henderson*	*Regan*	*Dryburgh*	*Frost*	*Bevan*	*Gettins*	*Jones*
	Home Ave 3,563	Away 3,438					Ref: G Muir	Fine weather at East Ferry Road, where a corner lead to Jones putting away the Dockers' opener. Not long after, the winger passed for Gettins to double the advantage. Notching a third on half-time, Jones laid on the pass for Bevan to tie up a comprehensive victory for the home side.										

FRIENDLIES

No	Date	Att	Pos	Pt	F-A	H-T	Scorers, Times, and Referees	1	2	3	4	5	6	7	8	9	10	11
1	H BRISTOL ROV			W	3-0	1-0	Nichol 3, Michael 46, Whelan 90	Toone	Bach	Davies	Jones	Wilson	Chambers	Whelan	Stevenson	Michael	Fulton	Nichol
	5/9	3,000						*Gray*	*Kifford*	*Griffiths A*	*Draycott*	*Robertson*	*Neilson*	*Clark*	*Williams*	*Boucher*	*Griffiths H*	*Paul*
							Ref: A Farrant	The fact that the referee had little use to make of his whistle does not imply that the play was tame. Far from it, in fact, as this was a rousing contest. Nichol opened the scoring with a fine daisy-cutter early on; then, shortly following the interval, Michael put a neat shot past Gray.										
2	H QP RANGERS			D	0-0	0-0		Toone	Bach	Robson	Jones	McLean	Wilson	McDougall	Stevenson	Michael	Fulton	Nichol
	26/9	500						*Clutterbuck*	*Bellingham*	*Newlands*	*Skinner*	*Hitch*	*Keech*	*Gray*	*Downing*	*Goldie*	*Humphreys*	*Foxhall*
							Ref: A Farrant *(at 'Ashton Gate')*	Only a small crowd at Ashton Gate for what was originally scheduled as a Western League game, but was played as a friendly as the FA didn't sanction this extension of the competition until mid-November. If Foxhall hadn't been lamed early on, it was likely Rangers would have won.										
3	A QP RANGERS			W	2-1	1-0	O'Brien 25, Stevenson 70	Toone	Bach	Robson	Jones	McLean	Chambers	Whelan	Stevenson	Fulton	O'Brien	McDougall
	24/10	*1,000*					*Lennox 80*	*Clutterbuck*	*Newlands*	*McConnell*	*Lennox*	*Hitch*	*Skinner*	*Gray*	*Downing*	*Ronaldson*	*Humphreys*	*Foxall*
								Despite the fine weather there was only a small crowd at Kensal Rise for this game which was originally arranged as a Western League fixture. O'Brien's goal was the only difference between the two sides during an even first half. After the break, Stevenson placed City further in front.										
4	H SOUTHAMPTON			D	0-0	0-0		Toone	Robson	Davies	Jones	McLean	Chambers	Wilson	Stevenson	Michael	Fulton	McDougall
	31/10	1,000						*Robinson*	*Blackman*	*Molyneux*	*Paddington*	*Finch H*	*Lee*	*Ball*	*Joyce*	*Cavendish*	*Small*	*Moore*
							Ref: S Major	Yet another of the originally scheduled Western League fixtures, this clash, according to the *Times & Mirror* turned into an 'exhibition of gallery tricks rather any real exertion in regards to winning'. City had much the better of the first half, but were unable to beat Robinson.										

No	H/A	Opponent / Date / Att	Res	F-A	H-T	Scorers, Times, Referees	1	2	3	4	5	6	7	8	9	10	11
5	H	SMALL HEATH	W	2-0	2-0	Fulton 20, Geddes 40	Toone	Robson	Davies	Jones	McLean	Chambers	Whelan	Stevenson	Fulton	Wilson	Geddes
	3/11	5,000					*Robinson*	*Archer*	*Pratt*	*Warren*	*Wigmore*	*Leake*	*Bennett*	*Main*	*Aston*	*Higginson*	*Wharton*
						Ref: A Farrant	A most enjoyable game at St John's Lane, with City putting on a first-class exhibition of football against the Football League visitors. Shortly after Fulton tucked away Whelan's centre to put City in front, Small Heath were handicapped by the loss of Pratt with a dislocated shoulder.										
6	H	LEICESTER FOSSE	W	1-0	1-0	Davies 25p	Toone	Bach	Davies	McLean	Wedlock	Chambers	McDougall	Stevenson	Fulton	O'Brien	Geddes
	23/2	3,000					*Daw*	*Cochrane*	*Swift*	*Berry*	*Hamilton*	*Robinson*	*Langham*	*Henderson*	*Hammond*	*Kyle*	*Allsopp*
						Ref: S Allen *(at 'Ashton Gate')*	Fulton started play from the Road End and, at once, the City right-wing got nicely down and forced an unproductive corner. City continued on the offensive and the Fossils' defence had a hot time before bowing to the inevitable. Davies, with a fierce low shot, registered from the spot.										
7	A	ABERDARE	W	4-0	2-0	Davies A 30og, Stevenson 35, [O'Brien 70, McDougall 90]	Toone	Bach	Davies	Jones	McLean	Chambers	Brooks	Stevenson	Wilson	O'Brien	McDougall
	4/3	*1,000*					*Stone*	*Jones*	*Davies A*	*Davies G*	*Jones B*	*Shenton*	*Leonard J*	*Wollacott*	*Jones S*	*Parker S*	*Williams H*
							The dull weather at Aberdare didn't deter a goodly gathering of spectators who assembled to see a representative South Wales side do battle with City. The homesters' had the best of things early on, but City soon took up the offensive. Davies put McDougall's cross into his own net.										

FA Cup/Glos Cup					F-A	H-T	Scorers, Times, and Referees	1	2	3	4	5	6	7	8	9	10	11
PR	A	READING	2	D	1-1	1-1	Fulton 15	Toone	Bach	Davies	Jones	McLean	Chambers	Whelan	Stevenson	Fulton	Wilson	Geddes
	5/1	*7,750*	*6*				*Pegg 16*	*Cotton*	*Henderson*	*Clinch*	*Bull*	*Holt*	*Watts*	*Evans*	*Logan*	*Pegg*	*Sharp A !*	*Barnes*
		(£219)					Ref: F King	Sharp's kick on Bach's knee, following the City right-back's foul on Barnes, brought dismissal for the Reading man on the half-hour mark. Bad blood has long existed in contests with the Biscuitmen, but never before has it lead to such a rough encounter as in this unsavoury affair.										
R	H	READING	2	D	0-0	0-0	(a.e.t).	Toone	Bach	Davies	Jones	McLean	Chambers	Whelan	Wilson	Michael	Fulton	Geddes
	9/1	3,000	*6*					*Cotton*	*Henderson*	*Sharp J*	*Bull*	*Mainman*	*Watts*	*Evans*	*Logan*	*Pegg*	*Sharp A*	*Barnes*
		(£78)					Ref: F King *(Bad light ended play 110 mins)*	Despite the severe frost, the contrast between this and Saturday's clash, which one leading member of the FA described as 'the worst cup-tie he had ever seen', couldn't have been more marked. Both sides deserved credit for their endeavours to play football in deplorable conditions.										
R2	N	READING	2	L	1-2	1-2	Michael 35	Toone	Bach	Davies	Jones	McLean	Chambers	Whelan	Wilson	Michael	Fulton	McDougall
	14/1	*5,000*	*6*				*Pegg 30, Evans 44*	*Cotton*	*Henderson*	*Sharp J*	*Bull*	*Mainman*	*Watts*	*Evans*	*Logan*	*Pegg*	*Spence*	*Barnes*
		(£112)					Ref: F King *(at the 'County Ground')*	City, who took 700 fans on a special excursion to Swindon, were out of luck in this cup-tie on neutral territory at the County Ground. They had practically all the play before the break, but found themselves trailing. Pegg sent the ball into an empty net after Toone had saved from Spence.										
F	H	BRISTOL ROV	2	W	4-0	2-0	Wilson 10, Fulton 30, 55,	Toone	Bach	Davies	Jones	McLean	Chambers	McDougall	O'Brien	Wilson	Fulton	Geddes
GC	29/4	2,800	*7*				[McDougall 70]	*Gray*	*Kifford*	*Griffiths A*	*Draycott*	*Robertson*	*Lee*	*Clark*	*Jones*	*Boucher*	*Griffiths H*	*Paul*
		(£84.5.4)					Ref: Q/M Sgt Barrow	The game opened tamely, with the ball going constantly out of play, but City soon took the lead. Gray brought off a fine double save from O'Brien and Fulton, but could do nothing about Wilson's follow up shot. McDougall's low drive after the break tied up an easy City win.										

	SOUTHERN LEAGUE	P	W	D	L	F	A	W	D	L	F	A	Pts
			Home					Away					
1	Southampton	28	13	1	0	44	12	5	4	5	14	14	41
2	BRISTOL C	28	12	2	0	40	6	5	3	6	14	21	39
3	Portsmouth	28	12	2	0	33	6	5	2	7	23	26	38
4	Millwall	28	11	1	2	36	10	6	1	7	19	22	36
5	Tottenham H	28	12	1	1	35	8	4	3	7	20	25	36
6	West Ham U	28	10	2	2	28	10	4	3	7	12	18	33
7	Bristol Rov	28	11	3	0	32	8	3	1	10	14	27	32
8	QP Rangers	28	9	1	4	28	17	2	3	9	15	31	26
9	Reading	28	7	2	5	16	10	1	6	7	8	15	24
10	Luton Town	28	9	1	4	32	20	2	1	11	11	29	24
11	Kettering	28	7	4	3	21	12	0	5	9	12	34	23
12	New Brompt'	28	6	4	4	20	16	1	1	12	14	35	19
13	Gravesend U	28	5	5	4	23	27	1	2	11	9	58	19
14	Watford	28	6	3	5	17	16	0	1	13	7	36	16
15	Swindon T	28	3	6	5	15	18	0	2	12	4	29	14
		420	133	38	39	420	196	39	38	133	196	420	420
	Chatham	10	1	1	1	4	5	0	1	6	2	27	4
	Disbanded												

	WESTERN LEAGUE	P	W	D	L	F	A	W	D	L	F	A	Pts
			Home					Away					
1	Portsmouth	16	7	1	0	16	4	4	1	3	20	19	24
2	Millwall	16	6	1	1	22	3	3	4	1	11	11	23
3	Tottenham H	16	6	2	0	31	7	2	3	3	6	12	21
4	QP Rangers	16	5	1	2	22	9	2	3	3	17	16	18
5	BRISTOL C	16	4	2	2	19	8	2	2	4	8	16	16
6	Reading	16	1	5	2	14	19	4	0	4	9	12	15
7	Southampton	16	5	1	2	17	8	0	1	7	5	21	12
8	Bristol Rov	16	3	1	4	16	13	1	0	7	2	29	9
9	Swindon T	16	2	1	5	7	9	0	1	7	2	28	6
		144	39	15	18	164	80	18	15	39	80	164	144

Odds & ends

Double wins: SL: (5) Swindon Town, West Ham United, Reading, Gravesend United, Chatham. WL: (1) Swindon Town.
Double losses: SL: (0). WL: (1) Millwall.

Won from behind: SL: (1) Watford (a).
Lost from in front: (0).

High spots: Demolishing Watford 6-1 on 8 September.
Winning the Gloucestershire Cup on 29 April.
Securing election to the Football League.
Billy Jones becoming the first City player to be capped when playing for England in a 3-0 win versus Ireland at the 'Dell' on 9 March.

Low spots: Losing out on the Championship to Southampton for the third time in four years.
Succumbing to Reading in the FA Cup on 14 January.

Player of the Year: Billy Jones.
Ever-presents: (1) George Toone.
Hat-tricks: (4) Hugh Wilson (2), Bill Michael, Alf Geddes.
Leading scorer: Overall: William Fulton (22). League: William Fulton (18).

Pre-Season Trial Match (at 'Ashton Gate'):
28 Aug Bristol City 4(0) Arlington Rovers 0
4,000 Stevenson (3), Unknown

AGM (Temperance Hall, East Street, Bedminster, 26 June 1901):
Loss £974.5s.11d. Season Ticket Sales £132.16s.10d.

	Appearances			Goals			
	Lge	**Cup**	**Fr**	**Lge**	**Cup**	**Fr**	**Tot**
Bach, Phil	**39**	4	5				
Bartlett, E	**3**			**1**			**1**
Brooks			1				
Chambers, Peter	**43**	4	6				
Davies, Richard	**41**	4	5			1	**1**
Fulton, William	**35**	4	6	**18**	3	1	**22**
Geddes, Alf	**24**	3	2	**4**		1	**5**
Harding	**1**						
Jones, Billy	**41**	4	6	**4**			**4**
McDougall, D	**24**	2	5	**4**	1	1	**6**
McLean, John	**42**	4	6	**7**			**7**
Marsh, R	**2**						
Michael, Billy	**20**	2	3	**15**	1	1	**17**
Nichol, Dave	**8**		2			1	**1**
Nicholls	**1**						
O'Brien, Paddy	**24**	1	3	**7**		2	**9**
Robson, David	**6**		4				
Stevenson, Jimmy	**40**	1	7	**9**		2	**11**
Toone, George	**47**	4	7				
Wedlock, Billy	**2**		1				
Whelan, Micky	**28**	3	3	**5**		1	**6**
Wilson, Hugh	**46**	4	5	**13**	1		**14**
Opponents og				**2**		1	**3**
22 players used	**517**	**44**	**77**	**89**	**6**	**12**	**107**

Note: Games against Watford (abandoned) and Chatham included.

LEAGUE DIVISION 2 — Manager: Sam Hollis — SEASON 1901-02

No	Date	Att	Pos	Pt	F-A	H-T	Scorers, Times, and Referees	1	2	3	4	5	6	7	8	9	10	11
1	A BLACKPOOL			W	2-0	1-0	O'Brien 25, 75	Moles	**Tuft**	Davies	Jones W	McLean	Chambers	Bradbury	Connor	Boucher	O'Brien	Flynn
	7/9	*3,000*		2				*Stirzaker*	*Scott*	*Burder*	*Threlfall*	*Brookes*	*Birchall*	*Hardman*	*Anderson*	*Birket*	*Foster*	*Evans*
								City commenced their League career as Blackpool celebrated their Bloomfield Road return. Turning out in their new light blue colours, the Pool kicked off against a slight breeze and struck a post before O'Brien headed City in front shortly after having a goal disallowed for offside.										
2	A BURSLEM PT VALE			L	0-3	0-1		Moles	Tuft	Davies	Jones W	McLean	Chambers	Bradbury	Connor	Boucher	O'Brien	Flynn
	9/9	*5,000*		2			*Capes 25, Simpson 62, 72*	*Chadwick*	*Mullineux*	*Davies*	*Boullimier*	*Beech*	*Wainwright*	*Eardley*	*Price*	*Capes*	*Simpson D*	*Heames*
								Both sides were unchanged from their weekend games. The early exchanges were even, but after Capes put Vale in front, City resorted to more physical tactics. Several of the homesters received injuries, but Simpson's second-half double ensured that they achieved a deserved success.										
3	H STOCKPORT		4	W	3-0	2-0	Jones S 35, O'Brien 40, Connor 63	Moles	Tuft	Davies	Jones W	McLean	Chambers	Bradbury	Connor	**Jones S**	O'Brien	Flynn
	14/9	6,489	*18*	4				*Wharton*	*Bunce*	*Arridge*	*Smith*	*Jeffreys*	*Perrins*	*Barker*	*Eaton*	*Patterson*	*Chesworth*	*Betteley*
		(£165)					Ref: F Beardsley	City lost the toss and defended the Country End goal at the start. Debutant Steve Jones (Aberdare) got his City career off to a good start by heading in from Flynn's corner to put his side into the lead. Two further headers from Flynn and Connor brought City a comfortable success.										
4	A NEWTON HEATH		9	L	0-1	0-0		Moles	**Robertson**	Tuft	Jones W	McLean	Chambers	Bradbury	Connor	Jones S	Davies	Flynn
	21/9	*5,000*	*10*	4			*Griffiths 85*	*Whitehouse*	*Stafford*	*Erentz*	*Morgan*	*Griffiths*	*Banks*	*Schofield*	*Williams*	*Preston*	*Lappin*	*Fisher*
								City played very well on their first visit to the Clayton enclosure, where the unfavourable weather kept the attendance down. From McLean's pass, Bradbury had hard luck in not scoring, but after the break City fell away somewhat, and were undone near the end when Griffiths netted.										
5	H GLOSSOP		5	W	2-0	1-0	Burgess 30og, Connor 86	Moles	Robertson	Tuft	Jones W	McLean	Chambers	Bradbury	Connor	Boucher	Davies	Flynn
	28/9	7,000	*6*	6				*Birchenough*	*Burgess*	*Durber*	*Norgrove*	*McCartney*	*Hall*	*Goddard*	*Crump*	*Rae*	*Parker*	*Dougal*
							Ref: J Adams	Delightful weather was enjoyed by the patrons at the Lane, but the players doubtless found the heat uncomfortable. Making a big attempt to regain top-flight status, Glossop travelled on the Friday, but City proved too good for them. Burgess deflected in Connor's shot for the opener.										
6	A DONCASTER		10	L	0-3	0-1		Moles	Robertson	Tuft	Jones W	McLean	Chambers	Bradbury	Connor	Boucher	Davies	Flynn
	5/10	*1,500*	*8*	6			*Langham 35, Bailey 75, Murphy 85*	*Eggett*	*Simpson*	*Langton*	*Longden*	*Jones*	*Wright*	*Langham*	*Murphy*	*Price*	*Goodson*	*Bailey*
							Ref: A Coulson	A strong cross-wind wasn't conducive to good football, but City settled down to give a fine display against erratic Rovers. Against the run of play, Langham opened the scoring from Bailey's centre; then after City squandered early chances in the second half they conceded two more.										
7	H LINCOLN		8	D	1-1	1-1	O'Brien 35	Robertson	Tuft	Davies	Jones W	McLean	Chambers	Bradbury	Connor	Boucher	O'Brien	Flynn
	12/10	7,983	*3*	7			*Smith 6*	*Webb*	*McMillan*	*Gibson*	*Fraser*	*Crawford*	*Blow*	*Dixon*	*Proudfoot*	*O'Donnell D*	*Smith*	*McInnes*
		(£203)					Ref: J Jamieson	A splendid crowd at St John's Lane, where the Imps, playing in cherry and red stripes, deservedly retained their record as the only unbeaten team in Division II. Smith turned Lincoln's early dominance to good account with a grand goal, but O'Brien headed home City's equaliser.										
8	A WEST BROM		9	D	2-2	1-1	Boucher 2, Connor 75	Robertson	Tuft	Davies	Jones W	McLean	Chambers	Bradbury	Connor	Jones S	Boucher	Flynn
	19/10	*7,829*	*1*	8			*Lee 30, McLean 60*	*Webb*	*Kifford*	*Adams*	*Nurse*	*Stevenson*	*Hadley*	*McLean*	*Simmons*	*Lee*	*Worton*	*Smith A*
							Ref: S Black	After Bradbury headed in City's early opener, Lee equalised with a soft shot. Connor had a fine goal controversially disallowed for offside; then after the break McLean tapped the ball past Robertson, before a pass from Steve Jones allowed Connor to fire in City's point-saver.										
9	H WLCH ARSENAL		11	L	**0-3**	0-1		Robertson	Tuft	Davies	Jones W	McLean	Chambers	Bradbury	Connor	Jones S	Boucher	Flynn
	26/10	10,500	*4*	8			*Briercliffe 30, 80, Place 65*	*Ashcroft*	*McNichol*	*Cross*	*Coles*	*Anderson J*	*Place*	*Briercliffe*	*Edgar*	*Main*	*Owens*	*Foxall*
		(£267)					Ref: J Tillotson	City, playing in an all-white strip as the visitors turned out in their normal red, monopolised the early play before Arsenal scored. Briercliffe sent in a hot shot, which Robertson got a hand to but couldn't prevent from entering the net. Place's back-heel doubled Arsenal's advantage.										
10	H LEICESTER FOSSE		8	W	2-1	1-0	O'Brien 35, Davies 85p	Robertson	Tuft	Davies	Jones W	McLean	Chambers	Bradbury	Connor	Boucher	O'Brien	Jay
	9/11	6,000	*9*	10			*Brown 70*	*Daw*	*Mills*	*Swift*	*Robinson*	*Dainty*	*Roulston*	*Webb*	*Richards*	*Brown*	*King*	*Allsopp*
							Ref: J Tillotson	City, who had looked like winning this game easily, were shocked when Brown netted the Fossils' equaliser from Webb's centre. After having dominated the play, City then fell away somewhat, but Davies secured the points, despite being ordered to take his successful spot-kick again.										
11	A PRESTON		11	D	0-0	0-0		Robertson	Tuft	Davies	Jones W	McLean	Chambers	Bradbury	Connor	Boucher	**Banks**	Jay
	30/11	*1,000*	*4*	11				*McBride*	*McMahon*	*Orrell*	*Howell*	*Good*	*Tickle*	*Rogers*	*Wilcox*	*Gara*	*Pratt*	*Jack*
								Play mainly favoured the home team at Deepdale, but City had their moments. Boucher showed some good play, but dallied too long when a chance presented itself. Robertson was in fine form between the sticks, but was fortunate after the break with a Pratt shot that hit the upright.										

No	Venue	Opponent	Pos	Res	FT	HT	Scorers	1	2	3	4	5	6	7	8	9	10	11
12	H	CHESTERFIELD	8	W	**5-2**	2-1	Connor 16, 80, Banks 40, 70,	**Clay**	Tuft	Davies	Jones W	McLean	Chambers	Bradbury	Connor	Jones S	Banks	Jay
	7/12	4,000	*16*	13			*Munday 15, Bowring 60*	*Maybury*	*Banner*	*Thorpe*	*Haig*	*O'Rouke*	*Thacker*	*Tomlinson*	*England*	*Bowring*	*Munday*	*Earl*
							Ref: J Jamieson [Chambers 50]	Despite the wet conditions, City didn't allow themselves to be put off when Bowring's low shot gave the visitors an early advantage. Almost immediately, Connor levelled with a fine effort, then Banks fired City in front. A stinging shot by Steve Jones completed a deserved success.										
13	H	GAINSBOROUGH	8	·	2-1	2-1	Cookson 2, Connor 7	Clay	Tuft	Davies	Jones W	McLean	Chambers	Bradbury	Connor	Cookson	Banks	Jay
	14/12	4,000	*18*	13			*Gettins 40*	*Bullivant*	*Pycock*	*Hempshall*	*Johnson*	*Thornley*	*Hall*	*Broadgate*	*Gettins*	*Reid*	*Raby*	*Fenton*
							Ref: J Morton *(Abandoned poor light 45 mins)*	There must have been a jinx on this game, which was switched because the Gainsborough ground was under suspension. After the visitors arrived an hour late, Cookson gave City the lead when a Banks effort rebounded off the crossbar. Connor put on the second with a fine shot.										
14	H	MIDDLESBROUGH	6	W	1-0	1-0	Banks 40	Clay	Tuft	Davies	Jones W	McLean	Chambers	Bradbury	Connor	Cookson	Banks	Flynn
	21/12	6,000	*3*	15				*Frail*	*Blackett*	*Ramsay*	*Smith*	*Jones*	*Davidson*	*Crawford*	*Brearley*	*Robertson*	*Turner*	*Cassidy*
							Ref: C Fallowfield	City dominated the early play, but the visitors were unfortunate when, after the crossbar kept out Turner's shot, Robertson was similarly frustrated. A capital shot from Banks, decided what was described in the *WDP* as 'the best game seen on the ground thus far this season'.										
15	A	BARNSLEY	6	D	2-2	0-1	Davies 60, Connor 88	Clay	Tuft	Davies	Jones W	McLean	Chambers	Flynn	Connor	Boucher	Banks	Jay
	25/12	*3,000*	*11*	16			*McCairns 30, 61*	*Seymour*	*Stevenson*	*Welch*	*Bennett*	*Carroll*	*Oxspring*	*Carlin*	*Lees*	*McCairns*	*Travers*	*Dartnell*
								For Barnsley, including new signing Bert Dartnell (Man City), McCairns slipped in the opener in what was, despite the sodden conditions, a remarkably good game. Banks rushed through a late equaliser for a City team that included Jay in place of Bradbury, who had missed the train.										
16	A	BURTON UTD	7	D	2-2	0-2	Livingstone 55og, Connor 75	Clay	Tuft	Davies	Jones W	McLean	Jay	Bradbury	Connor	Boucher	Banks	Flynn
	28/12	*2,000*	*13*	17			*Martin 10, Lewis 35*	*Garlick*	*Ashby*	*Kirkland*	*Waterson*	*Mann*	*Livingstone*	*Burton*	*Lewis*	*Joyce*	*Arkesden*	*Martin*
							Ref: J Tillotson	With ex-Rovers keeper Gray still out with injured ribs, Garlick continued for a Burton side that had created a surprise by winning at Woolwich in their previous game. Connor shot in City's equaliser after Livingstone had revived their hopes when turning in a hot-shot from the No 8.										
17	H	BLACKPOOL	7	W	3-0	0-0	Boucher 48, 89, Connor 55	Clay	Tuft	Davies	Jones W	McLean	Jay	Cookson	Connor	Boucher	Banks	Flynn
	4/1	**2,000**	*15*	19				*Dorrington*	*Boulton*	*Scott*	*Anderson*	*Stirzaker*	*Birchall*	*Anderton*	*Birket*	*Parkinson*	*Allan*	*Foster*
							Ref: J Jamieson	Despite both linesmen, WH Nicholls and TB Summers, asserting that a free-kick went into the goal off Connor, the referee thought otherwise and disallowed the effort. Nothing daunted, the City struck not long after when skilful play by Banks set up Boucher to find the back of the net.										
18	A	STOCKPORT	6	D	1-1	1-0	Banks 35	Clay	Tuft	Davies	Jones W	McLean	Jay	Bradbury	Connor	Boucher	Banks	Flynn
	11/1	*1,000*	*16*	20			*Swan 70*	*Butler*	*Smith*	*Arridge*	*Pickford*	*Jeffreys*	*Perrins*	*Davies*	*Madden*	*Swan*	*Chesworth*	*Betteley*
								Not long after failing from the penalty-spot, Banks made amends by registering with a splendid shot. After the break, Swan beat Clay with an exceptionally teasing shot from not more than three yards, but City still controlled most of the play without being able to find a match winner.										
19	H	NEWTON HEATH	6	W	4-0	3-0	Flynn 4, Boucher 20, 40, Banks 49	Clay	Tuft	Davies	Jones W	McLean	Jay	Bradbury	Connor	Boucher	Banks	Flynn
	18/1	7,500 (£200)	*10*	22				*Whitehouse*	*Stafford*	*Erentz*	*Morgan*	*Higgins*	*Cartwright*	*Schofield*	*Smith*	*Richards*	*Preston*	*Lappin*
							Ref: J Tillotson	Cash crisis club Newton Heath are no match for City, despite the presence of former St John's Lane player Billy Higgins and the old Minster custodian Jimmy Whitehouse. City scored four, but it would have been more except for Whitehouse's brilliant form after the change of ends.										
20	H	GAINSBOROUGH	4	W	4-0	2-0	Jay 25, McLean 40, Bradbury 50, [Boucher 75]	Clay	Tuft	Davies	Jones W	McLean	Chambers	Cookson	Bradbury	Boucher	Flynn	Jay
	25/1	4,000	*17*	24				*Bullivant*	*Pycock*	*Hempshall*	*Johnson*	*Thornley*	*Hall*	*Gettins*	*Reid*	*Jenkinson*	*Raby*	*Fenton*
							Ref: S Carr	No lateness problems for Trinity on this occasion, as they travelled on Friday and stayed locally. With a blackboard keeping the fans up to date with progress in the cup-ties at Tottenham and Middlesbrough, Jay ran in the opener, before McLean's low shot doubled City's advantage.										
21	H	DONCASTER	4	W	3-0	2-0	Boucher 25, Cookson 44, Banks 75	Robertson	Tuft	Davies	Jones W	McLean	Chambers	Cookson	Bradbury	Boucher	Banks	Flynn
	1/2	5,000	*15*	26				*Eggett*	*Simpson*	*Langton*	*Longden*	*Marsh*	*Wright*	*Langham*	*Murphy*	*Price*	*Jones*	*Bailey*
							Ref: F Heath	City started affairs from the Lower End and, after dominating the play, took the lead midway through the first half when Boucher put away Bradbury's good pass. Coookson's fierce shot doubled matters just before the break; then Banks made the game safe from the No 8's pass.										
22	H	WEST BROM	5	L	1-2	0-1	Bradbury 50	Clay	Tuft	Davies	Jones W	McLean	Chambers	Bradbury	Connor	Boucher	Banks	Flynn
	15/2	**14,175** (£331)	*1*	26			*Worton 30, Simmons 48*	*Webb*	*Kifford*	*Adams*	*Nurse*	*Stevenson*	*Hadley*	*McLean*	*Simmons*	*Lee*	*Worton*	*Dorsett*
							Ref: F Beardsley	Some amusement for the fans at the start as the referee chose to inspect all the boots of all the players. Flynn was unlucky with a disallowed effort, before Worton fired the visitors into the lead against the run of play. Bradbury almost took out the roof off the net with his goal.										
23	A	WLCH ARSENAL	5	L	0-2	0-2		Clay	Tuft	Davies	Jones W	McLean	Chambers	Cookson	Connor	Boucher	Banks	Flynn
	22/2	*9,000*	*4*	26			*Gooing 30, 40*	*Ashcroft*	*McNichol*	*Jackson*	*Coles*	*Dick*	*Anderson J*	*Briercliffe*	*Main*	*Gooing*	*Fichie*	*Edgar*
							Ref: J Bailey	Whilst their 200 or so fans left by an early train from Temple Meads, City paid the price of delaying their departure until 9.30am. Despite not arriving at Plumstead station until 15 minutes before the 3.15pm kick-off time, they did most of the attacking prior to Gooing's headed opener.										

LEAGUE DIVISION 2 Manager: Sam Hollis SEASON 1901-02

No	Date		Att	Pos	Pt	F-A	H-T	Scorers, Times, and Referees	1	2	3	4	5	6	7	8	9	10	11	12 sub used
24	H	BARNSLEY		5	W	3-1	3-1	Connor 2, Bradbury 40, Cookson 42	Clay	Tuft	Davies	Jones W	McLean	Jay	Bradbury	Connor	Cookson	O'Brien	Flynn	
	1/3		4,000	15	28			Gordon 30	Seymour	Stevenson	Welch	Carroll	Lees	Oxspring	Carlin	McCairns	Gordon	Dartnell	Mawson	
								Ref: F Beardsley	City, playing in white, took an early lead when Connor netted a fine goal from Flynn's headed pass – this shortly before Cookson had his shot disallowed for offside. Thereafter, the game deteriorated so much that the local press reported that 'the second half was the worst this season'.											
25	A	GLOSSOP		5	W	2-1	0-1	O'Brien 65, Cookson 80	Clay	Tuft	Davies	Jones W	McLean	Jay	Bradbury	Connor	Cookson	O'Brien	Flynn	
	4/3		2,500	9	30			Parker 30	Birchenough	Rothwell	Durber	Norgrove	McCartney	Patterson	Badenoch	Crump	Rae	Parker	Wallace	
									Clay was on his mettle in saving from Wallace early on, but he was fortunate when McCartney was just off target. Birchenough saved grandly for Glossop, before Parker scored a lovely goal for them. After the interval City's fine fight back was crowned by Cookson securing the points.											
26	A	LEICESTER FOSSE		5	W	1-0	1-0	Jones 30	Clay	Tuft	Davies	Jones W	McLean	Chambers	Bradbury	Connor	Cookson	O'Brien	Flynn	
	8/3		4,000	12	32				Daw	Mills	Roulston	Berry	Dainty	Robinson	Webb	Richards	King	Stevenson	Allsopp	
								Ref: J Tillotson	Play was fairly even for the opening half-hour when Jones fired in. Thereafter the City forwards tailed off somewhat and they had cause to be indebted to their defence for maintaining the advantage and taking a full haul of points. Wade, who hesitated, missed the Fossils' best chance.											
27	H	PRESTON		5	W	2-0	1-0	Boucher 35, Cookson 65	Clay	Tuft	Davies	Jones W	McLean	Chambers	Bradbury	Boucher	Cookson	Banks	Flynn	
	15/3		8,000	4	34				Griffiths	McMahon	Orrell	Beaver	Good	Elliott	Rogers	Wilcox	Pegg	Gara	Spence	
								Ref: R Horrocks	A case of pupil turned master, as Proud Preston were easily beaten despite staying at the George & Railway Hotel on Friday night. Clay didn't have a shot to deal with until shortly before the interval, by which time City led thanks to Boucher's fine shot that went in just under the bar.											
28	A	BURNLEY		4	W	1-0	1-0	Cookson 25	Clay	Tuft	Davies	Jones W	McLean	Chambers	Bradbury	Boucher	Cookson	Banks	Flynn	
	22/3		1,000	7	36				Brown	Ross	Lockart	Barron	Taylor	Dixon	Brunton	Watkins	Hogan	Davidson	Birchall	
								Ref: R Roberts	Play was largely in favour of City in the first half, and it was no more than they deserved when Cookson scored. Whilst Burnley improved after the break, they seldom looked capable of winning. The referee provoked the ire of the crowd, and needed police protection at the finish.											
29	H	BURSLEM PT VALE		5	W	4-0	3-0	Banks 5, 23, Cookson 40, [Bradbury 70]	Clay	Tuft	Davies	Jones W	McLean	Chambers	Bradbury	Boucher	Cookson	Banks	Flynn	
	29/3		5,000	11	38				Cotton	Mullineux	Davies	Croxton	Boullimier	Lander	Simpson T	Simpson D	Capes	Price	Heames	
								Ref: S Black	City turned on the style as they clocked up their sixth consecutive League victory, with a margin that equalled their best this season. In truth, however, it should have been more, as they totally dominated this encounter after Banks headed in the early opener from a Davies free-kick.											
30	A	GAINSBOROUGH		5	L	0-2	0-1		Clay	Tuft	Davies	Jones W	McLean	Chambers	Bradbury	Boucher	Cookson	Banks	Flynn	
	2/4		2,000	18	38			Reid 25, 70	Bagshaw	Pycock	Walker	Hall	Jenkinson	Harrison	Barnard	Ashton	Reid	Wilson	Saul	
									Despite having to put out a side half composed of reserves, Trinity opened wonderfully well. Midway through the first half, Clay failed to hold Saul's shot and Reid dashed up to deposit the loose ball into the net. After the break, Reid registered again by putting away Barnard's centre.											
31	A	CHESTERFIELD		5	L	0-1	0-1		Clay	Tuft	Davies	Jones W	McLean	Chambers	Cookson	Connor	Boucher	Banks	Flynn	
	5/4		800	14	38			Brown 20	Silcock	Banner	Thorpe	Haig	O'Rouke	McCracken	England	Howcroft	Bowring	Munday	Earl	
			(£20)					Ref: J Howcroft	The wind and rain served to keep the gate down for this game at Saltergate; then in the second half a blinding snowstorm made things worse for the players. Brown, the former Leicester Fosse man, won the game for the more aggressive Chesterfield side with a clever shot on the turn.											
32	H	BURNLEY		5	W	1-0	0-0	Banks 70	Clay	Tuft	Davies	Jones W	McLean	Chambers	Bradbury	Boucher	Cookson	Banks	Flynn	
	12/4		4,000	10	40				Brown	Ross	Lockhart	Barron	Taylor	Ridsdale	Morrison	Brunton	Hogan	Davidson	Birchall	
								Ref: F Heath	Had City met with average luck in front of goal they would have won by a much more pronounced margin. After having a good deal of the play before the break, they totally dominated the second half, but all they had to show for it was when Banks headed in from Flynn's centre.											
33	A	MIDDLESBROUGH		5	L	0-2	0-0		Clay	Tuft	Robertson	Jones W	McLean	Chambers	Bradbury	Boucher	Cookson	Banks	Flynn	
	19/4		12,000	2	40			Wardrope 46, 52	Williamson	Blackett	Ramsay	Smith	Jones	Davidson	Crawford	Brearley	Robertson	Wardrope	Tennant	
									A grandly contested opening half, during which Williamson, Middlesbrough's locally born lad, impressed on his trial between the sticks. He helped keep City at bay, but on crossing over the play degenerated after Wardrope put the game out of City's reach with his two early goals.											
34	A	LINCOLN		5	L	0-1	0-1		Clay	Tuft	Robertson	Jones W	McLean	Chambers	Bradbury	Boucher	Cookson	Banks	Flynn	
	21/4		3,000	6	40			Hartley 40	Webb	McMillan	Bentley	Fraser	Crawford	Cowley	O'Donnell D	Proudfoot	Hartley	Smith	McInnes	
									Despite being without left-back Gibson and left-half Bloor, the Imps took the points. After Bradbury fired into the side netting and Cookson was twice within an ace of scoring, Hartley registered from a scrimmage to raise Lincoln's hopes of overtaking City by the end of the season.											

No	Venue	Opponent	Att	Pos	Res	F-A	H-T	Scorers, Times, and Referees	1	2	3	4	5	6	7	8	9	10	11	12
35	H	BURTON UTD		6	L	0-2	0-1		Clay	Tuft	Robertson	Jones W	McLean	Chambers	Bradbury	Connor	Vickerstaffe	Banks	Flynn	
26/4			4,000	*10*	40			*Arkesden 20, 50*	*Gray*	*Ashby*	*Kirkland*	*Waterson*	*Mann*	*Livingstone*	*Burton*	*Lewis*	*Yardley*	*Arkesden*	*Martin*	
	Home	Away						Ref: C Fallowfield	City's poor end of season run is attributed to the fact that not many of their players have been offered new terms. Against the run of play Arkesden's low shot gave Burton the lead; then he doubled the advantage after the break, before his custodian, Gray, saved a penalty-kick.											
Ave	6,092	3,743																		

FRIENDLIES

No	Venue	Opponent	Att	Res	F-A	H-T	Scorers, Times, and Referees	1	2	3	4	5	6	7	8	9	10	11	12
1	A	BRISTOL ROV		W	1-0	1-0	Boucher 35	**Moles**	Robertson	**Tuft**	Jones W	McLean	Chambers	**Bradbury**	**Connor**	**Boucher**	O'Brien	**Flynn**	
2/9			*4,000*					*Cartlidge*	*Dunn*	*Griffiths*	*Farnall*	*Robertson*	*Neilson*	*Lyons*	*Jones*	*McIntyre*	*Pierce*	*Becton*	
							Ref: A Farrant	A fast, though somewhat scrambling game was witnessed in the season's curtain opener at Stapleton Road. Offside ruled out efforts by first McIntyre and then Connor, before Boucher registered from Fynn's return. City's smaller forwards were much quicker than their opponents.											
2	H	BRIDGWATER		W	11-1	6-0	Connor 5,8,20,45,60,JonesS15,68,	Moles	**Crone**	Davies	Robertson	McLean	Chambers	**Cookson**	Connor	Jones S	**Jay**	Flynn	
16/9			100				*Davis 36* [Cookson 25, 34],	*Major AO*	*Major H*	*Gilbert*	*Cridland*	*Speed*	*Brown*	*Taylor*	*Headford*	*Davis*	*Major WP*	*Clarke*	
		(Only 35 mins each way played)					Ref: T Wyllie [Robertson 50, Chambers 65]	Moles was wearing a mackintosh as City kicked off under deluge of rain. In a game reduced to 35 minutes each way due to the conditions, Robertson headed in City's eighth, then Connor's lightning shot brought the ninth, before a drive from Chambers brought up double figures.											
3	H	BRISTOL ROV		W	3-1	1-1	McLean 20, Connor 50, Banks 75	Clay	Robertson	Tuft	Jones W	McLean	Davies	Cookson	Connor	Boucher	Banks	Flynn	
26/12			7,000				*Lamb 43*	*Cartlidge*	*Dunn*	*Neilson*	*Farnall*	*Davies*	*Lyons*	*Muir*	*Wilcox*	*Lamb*	*Becton*	*Geddes*	
							Ref: A Farrant	Despite the approach to the ground being in a terribly muddy state, the season's fifth meeting of these local rivals attracted a good Boxing Day crowd at the Lane. McLean's drive gave City an early advantage, but Lamb's header, from Farnall's free-kick, had Rovers level by the break.											
4	A	DEVON COUNTY XI		W	6-1	2-0	Flynn 7, Boucher 30, 75, 80,	Clay	Robertson	Davies	Jones W	McLean	Chambers	Bradbury	Connor	Boucher	Banks	Flynn	
5/2			*3,000*				*Andrews 60* [Day 50og, Banks 89]	*Day*	*Cocker*	*Wyatt*	*Hawkins*	*Thompson*	*Baker*	*Hay*	*Roberts*	*Matters*	*Northey*	*Andrews*	
							Ref: E Bennett *(at Devonport)*	At the Rectory Field, City did not have to exert themselves in this easy success, though the Devon side cut up rough after the break. Flynn opened the scoring from Connor's good pass. Andrews got Devon's sole response following Hay's fine work. Thrice City fired against the bar.											
5	A	CORNWALL CO XI		W	5-0	1-0	Banks 20, 85, Flynn 55, Jones 65,	Clay	Robertson	Davies	Jones W	McLean	Chambers	Bradbury	Connor	Boucher	Banks	Flynn	
6/2			*1,000*				[Boucher 75]	*Nicholls*	*Morrell*	*Horwood*	*Moyes*	*Lovell*	*Hawke*	*Romer*	*Bennett*	*Meredith*	*Wilton*	*Jenkins*	
							Ref: G Adson *(at Truro)*	Cornwall offered more resistance than did Devon the previous day, but they were still no match for City. Steve Jones sparkled for City, firing in many fine shots besides the fast grounder he registered with. It wasn't until midway through the second half that Clay had a shot to save.											
6	A	ABERDARE		W	2-0	1-0	Banks 37, Vickerstaffe 65	Clay	Tuft	Robertson	Jones W	McLean	Chambers	Bradbury	O'Brien	**Vickerstaffe**	Banks	Flynn	
17/3			*1,500*					*Seeward*	*Golding*	*Davis A*	*Parker*	*Wedlock*	*Shenton*	*Smith RW*	*Davis G*	*Osborne*	*Williams H*	*Wollacott*	
								For this game, played in beautiful weather, City's opponents contained no fewer than six Bristolians, in Golding, Wedlock, Shenton, Smith, Osborne and Wollacott. Robbed of a goal early on, when his effort appeared to be a good foot over the line, Banks headed in City's opener.											
7	H	CLAPTON		W	2-0	0-0	Vickerstaffe 55, Flynn 85	Clay	Robertson	Tuft	Crone	Chambers	Jay	Bradbury	Connor	Vickerstaffe	O'Brien	Flynn	
28/3			3,000					*Earle E*	*Parsons AW*	*Cook HJ*	*Regan CD*	*Bell*	*Mitchell GF*	*Folks WT*	*Moule C*	*Evans R*	*Smith CH*	*Mieczn'skiWL*	
							Ref: A Farrant	Thanks to Vickerstaffe and Flynn firing in, this was an easy win for City against the London Charity Cup holders. Smith had an early second-half goal disallowed for the visitors, for whom left-winger Miecznikowski, despite being guilty of some poor finishing, played a starring role.											
8	H	ASTON VILLA		L	0-1	0-1		Clay	Tuft	Davies*	Jones W	McLean	Chambers	Bradbury	Boucher	Cookson	Banks	Flynn	Robertson
16/4			4,000				*Garraty 30*	*George*	*Noon*	*Crabtree*	*Perry*	*Wood*	*Wilkes*	*Clarke*	*Garraty*	*Johnson*	*Bache*	*Templeton*	
			(£100+)				Ref: A Farrant	The Villa had the polish, but City supplied the dash in this excellent contest. Garraty headed in the only goal of the game as City appealed in vain for offside. Banks, though, squandered the chance of a draw when, following a foul on Flynn near the finish, he fired wide from the spot.											

FA Cup/Glos Cup	F-A	H-T	Scorers, Times, and Referees	1	2	3	4	5	6	7	8	9	10	11
3Q H BRISTOL EAST 10 W	5-1	2-1	Jones S 20, 28, Cookson 53, 88,	Robertson	Tuft	Davies	Jones W	Mclean	Chambers	Bradbury	Cookson	Jones S	Boucher	Flynn
2/11 2,000 *WL:1*			*Rooke J 40* [Jones W 75p]	*Demmery*	*Carter*	*Williams*	*Rooke W*	*Cook*	*McKay*	*Britton*	*Mitchell*	*Rooke J*	*Osborne*	*Crates*
			Ref: D Campbell	City were rarely extended by the plucky Western League Div Two leaders at St John's Lane. A hot-shot from Steve Jones opened the scoring, then, following a tussle around Demmery, he notched another. Shortly before half-time, Rooke registered for Bristol East from close-range.										
4Q A BRISTOL ROV 8 -	0-2	0-2		Robertson	Tuft	Davies	Jones W	McLean	Chambers	Bradbury	Connor	Boucher	O'Brien	Flynn
16/11 *8,900 SL:15* (£290)			*Jones 5, Wilcox 32*	*Cartlidge*	*Dunn*	*Griffiths*	*Farnall*	*Neilson*	*Lyon*	*Muir*	*Wilcox*	*Jones*	*Becton*	*Geddes*
			Ref: F King *(Abandoned due to fog 80 mins)*	The referee did his best to beat the fog as, after stopping the game on the hour mark, he brought the teams back out after a ten-minute delay. Unfortunately, he was unable to give Rovers their due as he was forced to bring the proceedings to a halt with ten mins remaining to be played.										
4Q A BRISTOL ROV 10 D	1-1	1-1	Bradbury 7	Robertson	Tuft	Davies	Jones S	McLean	Chambers	Bradbury	Cookson	Jones W	Connor	Jay
23/11 *9,900 SL:15* (£283)			*Jones 40* *(aet)*	*Cartlidge*	*Dunn*	*Griffiths*	*Farnall*	*Neilson*	*Lyon*	*Muir*	*Wilcox*	*Jones*	*Becton*	*Geddes*
			Ref: F King *(Bad light ended play 116 mins)*	An FA directive meant that this game continued into extra-time in an effort to produce an outcome, but fading light brought the proceedings to a halt with four minutes still remaining to be played. City performed much better this time and Bradbury fired them into a deserved early lead.										
R H BRISTOL ROV 10 L	2-3	1-0	Connor 36, Cookson 89	Robertson	Tuft	Davies	Jones S	McLean	Chambers	Bradbury	Cookson	Jones W	Connor	Jay
27/11 4,624 *SL:15* (£143)			*Lamb 55, Becton 60, Jones 84*	*Cartlidge*	*Dunn*	*Griffiths*	*Farnall*	*Neilson*	*Lyon*	*Muir*	*Wilcox*	*Jones*	*Lamb*	*Becton*
			Ref: P Harrower	It is tempting to think that the fates decreed this Rovers win, as the fog robbed them of a deserved success in the first meeting. After Connor deservedly headed City into the lead, Lamb restored Rovers fortunes with a headed equaliser. Losing 1-2 City were denied a clear penalty.										
SF H BRISTOL EAST 5 W	2-1	1-0	Banks 40, Connor 50	Clay	Tuft	Davies	Jones W	McLean	Chambers	Bradbury	Connor	Boucher	Banks	Jay
GC 10/3 1,000 *WL:1*			*Crates 85*	*Demmery*	*Carter*	*McKay*	*Rooke W*	*Cook*	*Naish*	*Bowell*	*Williams*	*Godwin*	*Rooke J*	*Crates*
			Ref: G Gay	The East, conquerors of Barry in the previous round, were at full-strength. Banks starred for a City side that didn't extend itself, obtaining the first goal with a clever shot and setting up Connor to double the advantage, as well as later having a red-hot pile-driver disallowed for offside.										
F A BRISTOL ROV 5 D	0-0	0-0		Clay	Tuft	Davies	Jones W	McLean	Chambers	Bradbury	Boucher	Cookson	Banks	Flynn
GC 31/3 *13,835 SL:11* (£416.14.9)				*Cartlidge*	*Dunn*	*Griffiths*	*Davies*	*Neilson*	*Lyon*	*Muir*	*Jones*	*Corbett*	*Wilcox*	*Becton*
			Ref: J Adams	The wind that blew straight down the pitch behind City in the first half didn't deter a record crowd that assembled in the sunshine at Stapleton Road. Despite the lack of goals – Davies sending a 23rd-minute penalty wide after Lyons had handled the ball – a good game was witnessed.										
R H BRISTOL ROV 5 D	0-0	0-0		Clay	Robertson	Tuft	Jones W	McLean	Chambers	Bradbury	Connor	Boucher	Banks	Flynn
GC 23/4 4,223 *SL:9* (£118.13.0)				*Cartlidge*	*Dunn*	*Griffiths*	*Davies*	*Neilson*	*Lyon*	*Muir*	*Jones*	*Corbett*	*Wilcox*	*Becton*
			Ref: J Adams	Despite home advantage, the City fans were not optimistic of victory as their weakened side was again opposed by a Rovers line-up that hadn't tasted defeat this season. City opened on the offensive however, and early in the second half the Rovers keeper did well to save Jones' shot.										

		Home					Away					
	P	W	D	L	F	A	W	D	L	F	A	Pts
1 West Brom	34	14	2	1	52	13	11	3	3	30	16	55
2 Middlesbro'	34	15	1	1	58	7	8	4	5	32	17	51
3 Preston NE	34	12	3	2	50	11	6	3	8	21	21	42
4 Wlch Arsenal	34	13	2	2	35	9	5	4	8	15	17	42
5 Lincoln City	34	11	6	0	26	4	3	7	7	19	31	41
6 BRISTOL C	34	13	1	3	39	12	4	5	8	13	23	40
7 Doncaster R	34	12	3	2	39	12	1	5	11	10	46	34
8 Glossop	34	7	6	4	22	15	3	6	8	14	25	32
9 Burnley	34	9	6	2	30	8	1	4	12	11	37	30
10 Burton Utd	34	8	6	3	32	23	3	2	12	14	31	30
11 Barnsley	34	9	3	5	36	33	3	3	11	15	30	30
12 Burslem Pt V	34	7	7	3	26	17	3	2	12	17	42	29
13 Blackpool	34	9	3	5	27	21	2	4	11	13	35	29
14 Leicester Fos'	34	11	2	4	26	14	1	3	13	12	42	29
15 Newton H'th	34	10	2	5	27	12	1	4	12	11	41	28
16 Chesterfield	34	10	3	4	35	18	1	3	13	12	50	28
17 Stockport Co	34	8	3	6	25	20	0	4	13	11	52	23
18 Gainsboro' T	34	4	9	4	26	25	0	2	15	4	55	19
	612	182	68	56	611	274	56	68	182	274	611	612

Odds & ends

Double wins: (4) Blackpool, Glossop, Leicester Fosse, Burnley
Double losses: (1) Woolwich Arsenal.

Won from behind: Chesterfied (h), Glossop (a).
Lost from in front: (0).

High spots: Beating crisis club Newton Heath 4-0 on 18 January.
Defeating Preston North End 2-0 on 15 March.
Turning on the style with a 4-0 success at home to Burslem Port Vale on 29 March to chalk up a sixth consecutive League win.

Low spots: Woolwich Arsenal's 3-0 success at 'St John's Lane'.
Failing to chalk up seven wins on the spin when an under-strength Gainsborough Trinity side won 2-0 on 2 April.
Losing to Bristol Rovers in the FA Cup to allow their rivals to become the first local side to secure a League scalp in the Competition.

Player of the Year: John McLean.
Ever-presents: Billy Jones, John McLean, Billy Tuft.
Hat-tricks: (2) Joe Connor, Bertie Banks.
Leading scorer: Overall: Joe Connor (18). League: Joe Connor (10).

AGM (Temperance Hall, East Street, Bedminster, 17 June 1902):
Profit £39.14s.9d. Season Ticket Sales £75.3s.9d.

	Appearances				Goals			
	Lge	**Cup**	**Fr**	***Sub***	**Lge**	**Cup**	**Fr**	**Tot**
Banks, Bertie	**21**	3	5		**9**	1	5	**15**
Boucher, Tommy	**26**	5	5		**8**		5	**13**
Bradbury, John	**31**	7	6		**4**	1		**5**
Chambers, Peter	**29**	7	7		**1**		1	**2**
Clay, Harry	**23**	3	6					
Connor, Joe	**26**	5	6		**10**	2	6	**18**
Cookson, Walter	**17**	4	3		**7**	3	2	**12**
Crone, Robert			2					
Davies, Richard	**32**	6	5		**2**			**2**
Flynn, Jack	**31**	4	8		**1**		3	**4**
Jay, Jimmy	**12**	3	1		**1**			**1**
Jones, Steve	**5**	3	1		**1**	2	2	**5**
Jones, Billy	**35**	7	6		**1**	1	1	**3**
McLean, John	**35**	7	7		**1**		1	**2**
Moles, Walter	**6**		2					
O'Brien, 'Paddy'	**8**	1	3		**6**			**6**
Robertson, James	**12**	5	7	*1*			1	**1**
Tuft, Billy	**35**	7	5					
Vickerstaffe, Ernie	**1**		2				2	**2**
Opponents og					**2**		1	**3**
19 players used	**385**	**77**	**88**	*1*	**54**	**10**	**30**	**94**

Note: Abandoned games included.

No	Date		Att	Pos	Pt	F-A	H-T	Scorers, Times, and Referees	1	2	3	4	5	6	7	8	9	10	11
1	H	CHESTERFIELD			W	2-1	2-0	Dean 18, Wombwell 29	Clay	Tuft	Lewis	Jones	Good	Chambers	Dean	Wombwell	Leigh	Banks	Barnes
	6/9		5,000		2			*Unwin 85*	*Clutterbuck*	*Thorpe*	*Leiper*	*Haig*	*O'Rourke*	*Thacker*	*Tomlinson*	*Newton*	*Unwin*	*Munday*	*Steele*
			(£150)					Ref: A Cooknell	Well served by Clutterbuck and ex-Derby man Leiper, Chesterfield's energy and enterprise surprisingly only brought them one goal. A beauty that gave Clay no chance, but by then City held a two-goal advantage thanks to Dean's grand oblique shot, and a close-in effort by Wombwell.										
2	A	GLOSSOP			W	2-0	0-0	Wombwell 52, Dean 80	Clay	Tuft	Lewis	Jones	Good	Chambers	Dean	Wombwell	Leigh	Boucher	Banks
	13/9		*1,000*		4				*Clark*	*Burgess*	*Norgrove*	*Pell*	*McCartney*	*Coates*	*Carr*	*Badenoch*	*Thornley I*	*Goodall*	*Roberts*
								Ref: J Bailey	Glossop included their coach, the famous Johnny Goodall, in their line-up, but even he was unable to prevent City notching up a deserved success after weathering early pressure. Dean's thirty-yarder tied up an impressive win not long after Boucher had had his effort disallowed.										
3	H	MANCHESTER U		1	W	3-1	2-0	Good 20, Dean 30, 80p	Clay	Tuft	Lewis	Jones	Good	Chambers	Dean	Wombwell	Leigh	Boucher	Banks
	20/9		8,000	*11*	6			*Hurst 50*	*Whitehouse*	*Stafford*	*Read*	*Cartwright*	*Griffiths*	*Morgan*	*Schofield*	*Pegg*	*Peddie*	*Williams*	*Hurst*
								Ref: J Stark	Against a Manchester United side that played in green and white, City turned in a display that fully warranted their rising to the top of the table. Good's excellent long-distance drive gave City the lead; then Dean, with a lightening shot, doubled their advantage before the break.										
4	A	STOCKPORT		1	W	1-0	1-0	Dean 5	Clay	Tuft	Lewis	Jones	Good	Chambers	Dean	Wombwell	Leigh	Boucher	Banks
	27/9		*4,000*	*17*	8				*Butler*	*Freeborough*	*Arridge*	*Evenson*	*Dixon*	*Rathbone*	*McLachlan*	*Tomkinson*	*Stansfield*	*Raby*	*Dowdall*
								Ref: G Allwood	City had the benefit of staying in Manchester prior to the match, but there was really very little between the teams in this game. The referee was clearly at fault in disallowing Wombwell's goal, but by then Dean, with a low-shot, had already obtained what proved to be the winner.										
5	H	WLCH ARSENAL		1	W	1-0	0-0	Leigh 57	Clay	Tuft	Lewis	Jones	Good	Chambers	Dean	Wombwell	Leigh	Boucher	Barnes
	4/10		12,024	*6*	10				*Ashcroft*	*McNichol*	*Jackson*	*Coles*	*Dick*	*McEachrane*	*Briercliffe*	*Connor*	*Gooing*	*Coleman*	*Lawrence*
			(£321)					Ref: F Heath	The general fear at half-time was that Arsenal's luck would prevail as City, arrayed in blue and maroon striped jerseys, had dominated the play without success. Fortunately Leigh was able to dispel all superstition by heading in Ashcroft's poor clearance for City to achieve a notable win.										
6	A	WLCH ARSENAL		2	L	1-2	0-1	Wombwell 60	Clay	Tuft	Lewis	Jones	Good	Chambers	Dean	Wombwell	Leigh	Boucher	Barnes
	11/10		*12,000*	*5*	10			*Gooing 35, Hunt 88p*	*Ashcroft*	*McNichol*	*Jackson*	*Coles*	*Anderson J*	*McEachrane*	*Briercliffe*	*Hunt*	*Gooing*	*Coleman*	*Lawrence*
								Ref: F Heath	All good things come to an end, but it was difficult for the City fans to accept this defeat. They couldn't, however, dispute the award of the late match-winning penalty as Lewis clearly handled the ball. Gooing headed in the opener, but Wombwell equalised when firing into an open net.										
7	H	DONCASTER		1	W	4-2	3-0	Wombwell 15, Dean 30p, Jones 40,	Clay	Tuft	Lewis	Jones	Good	Chambers	Dean	Wombwell	Leigh	Boucher	Barnes
	18/10		7,000	*17*	12			*Langham 65, 75* [Good 70]	*Eggett*	*Simpson*	*Langton*	*Murphy*	*Marsh*	*Wright*	*Langham*	*Aston*	*Price*	*Ratcliffe*	*Goodson*
								Ref: A Cooknell	Langham (ex-City) notched a brace for the visitors, following his clinking-shot with an effort from near the corner flag that quite beat Clay. It wasn't enough for victory though as City, for whom Good had earlier brought up No 4 with a long-distance shot, were much the better side.										
8	A	LINCOLN		1	D	1-1	0-0	Leigh 55	Clay	Tuft	Lewis	Jones	Good	Chambers	Dean	Boucher	Leigh	Banks	Wombwell
	25/10		*4,000*	*3*	13			*Hartley 86p*	*Webb*	*McMillan*	*Gibson*	*Fraser*	*Crawford*	*Blow*	*Proudfoot*	*Hartley*	*O'Donnell D*	*Smith*	*McInnes*
								Ref: H Ward	City's magnificent defence kept the Imps out for most of this game, until Lewis fouled McInnes when he was clean through on goal just before the close. Thus City paid in this top of the table clash for attempting to hold grimly onto the lead, given them when Leigh darted up to score.										
9	H	SMALL HEATH		1	D	1-1	1-0	Boucher 12	Clay	Tuft	Lewis	Jones	Good	Chambers	Dean	Boucher	Leigh	Banks	Wombwell
	1/11		12,000	*5*	14			*McRoberts 83*	*Robinson*	*Goldie*	*Wassell*	*Beer*	*Wigmore*	*Dougherty*	*Athersmith*	*Leonard*	*McRoberts*	*McMillan*	*Field*
			(£309)					Ref: J Jamieson	Despite the fact that City's inside-men scarcely appeared equal to the task of breaking down a sterling defence, the *Birmingham Sports Argus* commented that 'the homesters were a fine team in all departments'. Leigh sent yards wide of the goal when he had only had to tap the ball in.										
10	A	LEICESTER FOSSE		2	D	2-2	0-1	Leigh 55, Boucher 75	Clay	Tuft	Lewis	Jones	Good	Chambers	Dean	Boucher	Leigh	**Gara**	Wombwell
	8/11		*5,000*	*13*	15			*Belton 40, Mills 80p*	*Ling*	*Mills*	*Robinson*	*Pollock*	*Collins*	*Roulston*	*Hadley*	*Lewis*	*Brown*	*Belton*	*Simpson*
								Ref: A Cooknell	City were a trifle fortunate to gain a point in this contest, which was full of excitement and interest right from the start. Ling should have saved Leigh's shot, whilst Mills wasted a late spot-kick to win the game after having been successful with an earlier award that had levelled matters.										

No / Date	Venue	Opponent / Att	Pos	Res / Pts	F-A	H-T	Scorers, Times, and Referees	1	2	3	4	5	6	7	8	9	10	11
11	H	MANCHESTER C	1	W	3-2	2-1	Wombwell 22, 25, Good 48	Clay	Tuft	Lewis	Jones	Good	Chambers	Dean	Leigh	Gara	Banks	Wombwell
15/11		13,000	*4*	17			*Turnbull 44, Drummond 80*	*Hillman*	*Davidson*	*Orr*	*Frost*	*Hynds*	*McOustra*	*Meredith*	*Turnbull*	*Gillespie*	*Drummond*	*Threlfall*
		(£326.13.6)					Ref: S Carr	It is a long time since two teams were more evenly matched than in this entertaining encounter, but Good kicked in the third goal to secure the points for City. Wombwell fired the opener high into the net from a difficult angle, before quickly doubling City's advantage with a low shot.										
12	A	BURNLEY	3	D	0-0	0-0		Clay	Tuft	Lewis	Jones	Good	Chambers	Dean	Leigh	Gara	Boucher	Wombwell
22/11		*1,250*	*10*	18				*Towler*	*Ross*	*Lockhart*	*Barron*	*Taylor*	*Dixon*	*Morrison*	*McInnes*	*Crawford*	*Driver*	*Lee*
		(£30)					Ref: F Broughton	A typical City display after their heroics of last week. Their attack lacked sting at Turf Moor after having made all the running during the first half-hour. Just before the finish Burnley were gifted a rather dubious penalty but, fortunately for City, Barron fired his shot against Clay's legs.										
13	H	PRESTON	3	W	2-1	0-1	Dean 63, Boucher 70	Clay	Tuft	Lewis	Jones	Good	Chambers	Dean	Leigh	Boucher	Gara	Wombwell
29/11		5,000	*8*	20			*Smith 6*	*McBride*	*McMahon*	*Orrell*	*Howell*	*Hunter*	*Tod*	*Walton*	*Smith P*	*Wilcox*	*Pratt*	*Shorrock*
							Ref: A Millward	Buoyed by gifts, following a tour of the Wills Factory, the North Enders, who had stayed overnight at the Swan Hotel, got another gift early on at the Lane. Clay's fumble left Smith with an easy tap-in, and it wasn't until midway through the second half that Dean fired in an equaliser.										
14	A	BURSLEM PT VALE	4	L	0-2	0-0		Clay	Tuft	Lewis	Jones	Good	Chambers	Dean	Leigh	Gara	Boucher	Wombwell
6/12		*2,000*	*9*	20			*Eardley 81, Loverseed 86*	*Cotton*	*Mullineux*	*Hartshorne*	*Rowley*	*Holdcroft*	*Perkins*	*Eardley*	*Simpson D*	*Loverseed*	*Capes*	*Heames*
							Ref: A Cooknell	City, who were much more concerned over the frozen Cobridge pitch than were the Burslem men, paid the price of their timorous attitude. With the ground underfoot getting harder and harder as the game progressed, Clay was eventually beaten by Eardley nine minutes from time.										
15	A	GAINSBOROUGH	4	L	1-2	1-0	Boucher 40	Clay	Tuft	Lewis	Jones	Davies	Chambers	Dean	Leigh	Gara	Boucher	Wombwell
20/12		*3,000*	*15*	20			*Gettins 50, Dixon 60*	*Bagshaw*	*Thompson*	*Davies*	*Saul*	*Jenkinson*	*Hall*	*Dixon*	*Gettins*	*Greensell*	*Jacklin*	*McQueen*
							Ref: R Horrocks	Defeat seemed to be about the last thing likely to overtake City at the break when they led, thanks to Boucher's goal. Unfortunately, their play deteriorated in the second half, and Gettins headed the homesters level. Dixon brought Trinity only their seventh point at home this season.										
16	H	BARNSLEY	3	D	3-3	2-3	Boucher 20, Wombwell 25, Banks 55	Clay	Tuft	Davies	Jones	Good	Chambers	Dean	Boucher	Gara	Banks	Wombwell
25/12		6,000	*17*	21			*Davies 1og, Green 35, Cornan 40*	*Greaves*	*West*	*Welch*	*Hay*	*Lees*	*Oxspring*	*Hellewell Alec*	*Green*	*Hellewell Alb*	*Cornan*	*Bourne*
		(£192)					Ref: F Heath	On a windy Christmas day morning City, who turned out in their alternative blue and chocolate coloured strip, found themselves immediately under pressure after losing the toss. Davies, in attempting to clear Bourne's centre, sent the ball against the goal-post and into his own net.										
17	H	BURTON UNITED	3	W	3-1	2-0	Banks 1, 85, Gara 30	Clay	Tuft	Lewis	Jones	Good	Jay	Dean	Boucher	Gara	Banks	Wombwell
27/12		7,000	*12*	23			*Joyce 80*	*Waterson*	*Ashby*	*Aston*	*Livingstone*	*Mann*	*Digweed*	*Sheffield*	*Twigg*	*Joyce*	*Arkesden*	*King*
							Ref: A Cooknell	The eventual record hardly does justice to the amount of attacking City, playing in their change colours, did in this game. Banks was back to his very brilliant best and produced a great shot for his second goal. Seven times City netted, but infringements, alas, ruled out four of them.										
18	A	BLACKPOOL	3	W	1-0	1-0	Dean 14	Clay	Tuft	Lewis	Jones	Good	Chambers	Dean	Leigh	Gara	Boucher	Wombwell
1/1		*4,000*	*11*	25				*Dorrington*	*Birkett*	*Scott*	*Threlfall*	*Anderson*	*Wolstenholme*	*Anderton*	*Cookson*	*Parkinson*	*Heywood*	*Evans*
							Ref: T Helme	After a somewhat quiet opening, apart from a nasty collision between Good and George Anderson, City took the lead when Dean registered with a magnificent low shot. City's fine defence kept a weakened Blackpool side, without Wright, Birchall and Hardman, at bay thereafter.										
19	A	CHESTERFIELD	4	L	0-3	0-1		Clay	Tuft	Davies	Jones	Jay	Chambers	Dean	Leigh	Good	Gara	Wombwell
3/1		*5,000*	*7*	25			*Taylor 13, Milward 52, Banner 60*	*Clutterbuck*	*Thorpe*	*Leiper*	*Haig*	*Banner*	*Thacker*	*Tomlinson*	*Newton*	*Taylor*	*Milward*	*Steele*
							Ref: A Cooknell	Despite being without their captain, Munday, Chesterfield proved much too good for City in quagmire conditions at Saltergate. Taylor raced clear to net a splendid opener; then after the break Milward scored when Clay failed to hold the ball. Banner's long shot clinched a fine win.										
20	H	GLOSSOP	4	D	1-1	0-1	Lewis 65p	Clay	Davies	Lewis	Jones	Good	Chambers	Wombwell	Leigh	Gara	Banks	Barnes
10/1		6,000	*11*	26			*Davies 30og*	*Clark*	*Burgess*	*Norgrove*	*Pell*	*Boden*	*Coates*	*Badenoch*	*Thornley I*	*Hunt*	*Murphy*	*Jack*
							Ref: J Bailey	In fine weather at St John's Lane, City are surprised by the clever play of the visitors, who took the lead when Davies turned Badenoch's centre into his own goal. Pell's handball enabled Lewis to level from the spot, but later a foul on Barnes inside the area went unpunished.										
21	A	MANCHESTER U	4	W	2-1	1-0	Leigh 15, Good 75	Clay	Tuft	Lewis	Jones	Jay	Chambers	Davies	Leigh	Good	Banks	Wombwell
17/1		*12,000*	*6*	28			*Preston 85*	*Birchenough*	*Rothwell*	*Read*	*Morgan*	*Downie*	*Cartwright*	*Morrison*	*Richards*	*Preston*	*Peddie*	*Hurst*
							Ref: H Ward	An unexpected success at Clayton, where only Small Heath had previously won this season. Two soft goals put City in charge, the second seeing Good presented with an open net when the keeper came racing out and missed the ball. Sweet success after last week's poor showing.										

No	Date		Opponent	Att	Pos	Pt	F-A	H-T	Scorers, Times, and Referees	1	2	3	4	5	6	7	8	9	10	11
22		H	STOCKPORT		4	W	7-1	3-0	Banks 13, 70, Jay 30, 75, 85,	Clay	Tuft	Lewis	Jones	Good	Chambers	Barnes	Leigh	Jay	Banks	Wombwell
	24/1			3,000	*18*	30			*Hosie 60* [Jones 45, Barnes 80]	*Butler*	*Arridge*	*Freeborough*	*Jeffreys*	*Hosie*	*Sharpley*	*Brittleton*	*Chorlton*	*Evenson*	*Raby*	*Stansfield*
									Ref: G Allwood	City's goal-feast certainly made up for the miserable weather that accompanied this one-sided contest. County, for whom Hosie's drive produced their only reward, rarely had a look in. Banks, with a long-range shot, put away City's third a minute after having a goal disallowed.										
23		H	BLACKPOOL		4	L	0-1	0-0		Clay	Tuft	Lamberton	Jones	Good	Chambers	Dean	Leigh	Jay	Banks	Wombwell
	31/1			4,600	*12*	30			*Cookson 70*	*Hull*	*Birkett*	*Scott*	*Wolstenholme*	*Stirzaker*	*Birchall*	*Anderton*	*Cookson*	*Parkinson*	*Heywood*	*Hardman*
									Ref: A Barker	After having 75% of the play, City are undone when Lamberton's slip allowed Cookson to nip in for the winner. City are made to pay for the fact that the referee didn't spot that Hull carried the ball over the line, shortly before missing Stirzaker's handling offence in the penalty area.										
24		A	DONCASTER		4	D	0-0	0-0		Clay	Tuft	Lewis	Jones	Good	Chambers	Wombwell	Banks	Gara	Boucher	Barnes
	14/2			*2,500*	*15*	31				*Eggett*	*Simpson*	*Langton*	*Price*	*Aston*	*Wright*	*Langham*	*Gordon*	*Drake*	*Foxall*	*Woodland*
									Ref: J Plastow	Even though City had the initial advantage of the hurricane wind, Doncaster managed an equal share of the first-half play. Despite having lost Aston with a sprained knee, the Rovers dominated the second period, except for a Wombwell effort that was cleared from behind the goal-line.										
25		A	SMALL HEATH		4	L	0-2	0-2		Clay	Tuft	Lewis	Jones	Good	Chambers	Dean	Boucher	Gara	Banks	Wombwell
	28/2			*12,000*	*2*	31			*Windridge 30, 40*	*Robinson*	*Goldie*	*Wassell*	*Beer*	*Hartwell*	*Howard*	*Athersmith*	*Leonard*	*McRoberts*	*Windridge*	*Wharton*
									Ref: T Campbell	The 200-300 Bristolians who made the trip to Birmingham were disappointed by this defeat, as they saw their favourites play well. Windridge fired in the Heathens' opener from close quarters; then doubled the advantage when, from a melee in front of goal, he got the final touch.										
26		H	LEICESTER FOSSE		4	W	6-1	3-1	Barnes 20, Leigh 30, 89, Gara 40, 80,	Clay	Tuft	Lewis	Jones	Good	Chambers	Barnes	Leigh	Gara	Banks	Wombwell
	7/3			5,000	*14*	33			*Robinson 10* [Banks 70]	*Ling*	*Whitehead*	*Atterbury*	*Pollock*	*Robinson*	*Roulston*	*Hadley*	*Lewis*	*Brown*	*Belton*	*Simpson*
									Ref: J Brodie	The Fossils started off at a rare pace and could have been three goals to the good before Robinson registered with a cross-shot from the right. City obtained a rather fortunate equaliser when a Barnes corner was deemed to have touched Ling, the visiting keeper, on its way into the net.										
27		A	MANCHESTER C		4	D	2-2	0-1	Wombwell 70, 80	Clay	Tuft	Lewis	Jones	Good	Chambers	Barnes	Leigh	Gara	Boucher	Wombwell
	14/3			*25,000*	*1*	34			*Meredith 13, Threlfall 48*	*Hillman*	*McMahon*	*Holmes*	*Bevan*	*Hynds*	*McOustra*	*Meredith*	*Bannister*	*Gillespie*	*Turnbull*	*Threlfall*
									Ref: S Carr	A grand show by City at Hyde Road, where they become the first visitors to take a point this season. Wombwell's lightening oblique drive, shortly after Bevan's retirement from the fray, did the trick. The Welsh Wizard, Billy Meredith, put away a rebound for the Light Blues opener.										
28		H	BURNLEY		4	W	3-0	1-0	Good 30, Gara 70, 80	Clay	Tuft	Lewis	Jay	Good	Chambers	Barnes	Leigh	Gara	Boucher	Wombwell
	21/3			5,000	*17*	36				*Towler*	*Ross*	*Lockhart*	*Barron*	*Taylor*	*Dixon*	*Lee*	*Crawford*	*Hogan*	*Driver*	*McInnes*
									Ref: J Adams	In the absence of Jones, who caught a nasty chill in Thurday's game at Weston, Boucher was captain and won the toss. Good beat Hillman all ends up to give City the lead; then after the break Gara doubled the advantage with a great shot, before finishing off a bully for the third.										
29		A	PRESTON		4	L	0-1	0-0		Clay	Tuft	Lewis	Jones	Good	Chambers	Barnes	Leigh	Gara	Boucher	Wombwell
	28/3			*3,000*	*7*	36			*Wilcox 48p*	*McBride*	*Orrell*	*Derbyshire*	*Howell*	*Hunter*	*Tod*	*Walton*	*Wilcox*	*Pratt*	*Beaver*	*Pearson*
									Ref: A Millward	Despite their much superior play, City found themselves thwarted by Preston's defence at Deepdale. As it was, they even had to concede both points through the impulse of an exceptionally heated moment, when Lewis, made captain for the day, gave away the match-winning penalty.										
30		H	LINCOLN		4	L	0-2	0-0		Clay	Tuft	Lewis	Jones	Good	Jay	Dean	Leigh	Gara	Banks	Wombwell
	30/3			5,000	*8*	36			*Price 47, Smith 65*	*Webb*	*Proudfoot*	*Pallister*	*Fraser*	*Simpson W*	*Blow*	*O'Donnell D*	*Hartley*	*Price*	*Simpson C*	*Smith*
									Ref: J Tillotson	Despite being almost constantly on the attack before the break, City failed to take full advantage of the gale-force wind. No such problem, though, for the Imps in the second half as Price made an early breakthrough before Clay let a shot from Smith slip out of his hands into the net.										
31		H	BURSLEM PT VALE		4	W	3-0	2-0	Dean 5p, 75, Wombwell 30	Clay	Tuft	Lewis	Jones	Leigh	Chambers	Barnes	Boucher	Dean	Banks	Wombwell
	4/4			2,000	*9*	38				*Cotton*	*Mullineux*	*Rowley*	*Croxton*	*Simpson T*	*Perkins*	*Eardley*	*Price*	*Loverseed*	*Capes*	*Heames*
									Ref: J Stark	Wombwell was involved with all the goals in this success over impoverished Vale, who have transferred Hartshorne and Holdcroft. A foul by Croxton on the outside left brought the penalty; then Wombwell netted from a great pass from Barnes, before laying on the chance for Dean.										

No		Opponent			FT	HT	Scorers											
32	A	BARNSLEY	4	L	0-2	0-1		Clay	Tuft	Lewis	Jones	Good	Jay	Dean	Leigh	Boucher	Banks	Wombwell
	11/4	*4,000*	*9*	38			*Lewis 40og, Lees 75p*	*Greaves*	*West*	*Welch*	*Bennett*	*Lees*	*Oxspring*	*Hellewell Alec*	*Green*	*Hellewell Alb*	*Cornon*	*Mawson*
							Ref: F Heath	Dean's foul gave Barnsley a spot-kick directly following the break, but Lees had his effort saved after having put away his initial attempt. He made amends later, however, as, following Tuft's offence, he made no mistake with another penalty. Lewis headed the opener into his own net.										
33	H	GAINSBOROUGH	4	W	1-0	1-0	Banks 25	Clay	Lamberton	Tuft	Jones	Good	Jay	Barnes	Leigh	Boucher	Banks	Wombwell
	18/4	4,000	*15*	40				*Bagshaw*	*Thompson*	*Hempshall*	*Pycock*	*Jenkinson*	*Hall*	*Gettins*	*McQueen*	*Dixon*	*Jacklin*	*Saul*
							Ref: C Fallowfield	Despite much brilliant approach play, City failed in front of goal, apart from a Barnes effort that managed to find the back of the net midway through the first half. The visitors didn't offer a lot, except shortly before the break when Clay had to be at his very best to twice deny them.										
34	A	BURTON UNITED	4	W	3-0	1-0	Wombwell 2, Banks 68, Boucher 89	Clay	Tuft	Lewis	Lamberton	Good	Jay	Dean	Leigh	Boucher	Banks	Wombwell
	25/4	*2,000*	*13*	42				*Gray*	*Ashby*	*Aston*	*Dimmock*	*Livingstone*	*Digweed*	*Sheffield*	*Gilchrist*	*Waterson*	*Twigg*	*King*
		Home Away					Ref: A Cooknell	At Peel Croft, Wombwell gave City an early lead when he dribbled through before firing in an oblique effort from three yards. After the break Banks neatly headed in City's second before Boucher set the seal on a comprehensive success to round off another excellent League campaign.										
		Ave 6,448 5,985																

FRIENDLIES

No		Opponent		FT	HT	Scorers											
1	H	BRISTOL ROV	L	2-4	1-2	Dean 1, 80p	Clay	Tuft	Lewis	Jones	Good	Chambers	Dean	Wombwell	Boucher	Banks	Barnes
	1/9	6,250				*Wilcox 11, Corbett 45, 65, Howie 75*	*Cartlidge*	*Pudan*	*Griffiths*	*Young*	*McLean*	*Lyon*	*Muir*	*Howie*	*Corbett*	*Wilcox*	*Marriott*
		(£161)				Ref: A Green	The play was a lot more favourable to the City than the score suggests. Dean's hot-grounder gave them an early lead, but Wilcox soon levelled with a breast-high shot. City were unlucky just after the break as Wombwell had an effort disallowed, then Banks failed with his penalty-kick.										
2	A	ABERAMAN	L	2-3	1-1	Boucher 35, Leigh 60	Demmery	Davies	Lewis	Jones	Good	Jay	Dean	Boucher	Leigh	Banks	Wombwell
	20/10	*1,000*				*Rooke J 1, 75, Hulen 89*	*Eggiston*	*Jones H*	*Bolton*	*Jones B*	*Britton*	*Rooke W*	*Hulen*	*Rooke J*	*Grinnell*	*Jones S*	*Davis*
						Ref: Q/M Sgt Quinton	Despite the counter-attraction of the visit of Doncaster Rovers to Aberdare, this game attracted a good gate. Jack Rooke rushed up and scored right at the start, but Boucher's close-range shot levelled for City before the break. Hulen drove in Aberaman's winner just before the finish.										
3	A	BRISTOL ROV	L	1-2	0-2	Banks 52	Clay	Tuft	Lewis	Davies	Jay	Chambers	Wombwell	Boucher	Gara	Banks	Barnes
	26/12	*10,000*				*Wilcox 8, 20*	*Cartlidge*	*Dunn*	*Griffiths*	*Young*	*McLean*	*Lyon*	*McColl*	*Corbett*	*Graham*	*Wilcox*	*Rowlands*
		(£298)				Ref: G Muir	Wilcox gave the Rovers an early lead when he had no difficulty in netting after Clay spilled a long shot from Dunn. He soon doubled the advantage with a hook-shot before City got in on the act after the break when Banks seized on Cartlidge's poor clearance of a shot by Barnes.										
4	A	SOMERSET XI	W	10-0	4-0	Gara 20, Leigh 22, 25, 50, 85, [W'well 40,80, Lewis 60,65, Jones 70]	Clay	Tuft	Lewis	Jones	Good	Chambers	Barnes	Leigh	Gara	Boucher	Wombwell
	19/3	*500*					*Hawkins*	*Prescott*	*Gale*	*George*	*Doran*	*Tremlett*	*Gale*	*Passmore*	*Limner*	*Bloxsome*	*Saunders*
						Ref: S Hollis (*at Weston-super-Mare*)	City had a field day on the Recreation Ground at Weston-super-Mare, against a side comprising of Old Boys of Walliscote Road and Christchurch Schools. Leigh's hot drive brought up his fourth goal of the game, as well as taking the score-line into double figures.										
5	A	SOUTHPORT	L	0-1	0-0		Clay	Tuft	Lewis	Jones	Good	Jay	Barnes	Leigh	Dean	Banks	Wombwell
	10/4	*5,000*				*Shadbolt 80*	*Garvey*	*Spink*	*Nightingale*	*Sinclair*	*Bell*	*Chorlton F*	*Chorlton J*	*Shadbolt*	*Hulligan*	*Cooper*	*Kelly*
		(£71)				Ref: F Johnson	In ideal weather, a keen game was played against Southport Central, the Lancashire League Champions. It wasn't until near the finish that the deadlock was broken, when Hulligan set up Shadbolt to score. Garvey then saved well from Leigh, before City were forced to accept defeat.										
6	H	THIRD LANARK	D	1-1	0-0	Leigh 75	Clay	Lamberton	Tuft	Jones	Good	Jay	Barnes	Leigh	Boucher	Banks	Wombwell
	14/4	7,000				*Wardrope 60*	*Raeside*	*Barr*	*Milligan*	*Cross*	*Sloan*	*Nicol*	*Johnstone*	*Graham*	*Wardrope*	*Wilson*	*Hunter*
		(£204.13.0)				Ref: A Farrant (*Billy Jones Benefit*)	After losing 0-1 at Bolton, then Millwall, before stopping the rot 0-0 at Swindon, the famous 'Thirds' ended their short English Tour at the Lane for Billy Jones' Benefit. Wardrope's shot gave Clay no chance, but Leigh equalised when Raeside pushed out Boucher's fierce effort.										
7	H	WLCH ARSENAL	L	1-2	0-0	Boucher 60	Clay	Lamberton	Lewis	Jones	Good	Jay	Barnes	Leigh	Boucher	Banks	Wombwell
	22/4	500				*Coles 40, Shanks 70*	*Ashcroft*	*McNicol*	*Jackson*	*Coles*	*Dick*	*McEachrane*	*Hunt*	*Coleman*	*Keenan*	*Shanks*	*Linward*
						Ref: A Farrant (*35 mins each way played*)	The play in this 35 minutes each-way game, which was the prelude to Arsenal's short Welsh Tour, was distinctly tame. Coles put the visitors into the lead with a high shot, but Boucher levelled with a long drive, before a last-minute Shanks effort went into the net off Lamberton.										
8	H	THE WEDNESDAY	D	2-2	1-2	Lewis 25p, Wombwell 50	Demmery	Tuft	Lewis	Lamberton	Good	Jay	Barnes	Leigh	Boucher	Banks	Wombwell
	27/4	2,000				*Spiksley 15, Chapman 33*	*Lyall*	*Layton*	*Langley*	*Ferrier*	*Crawshaw*	*Thackeray*	*Simpson*	*Chapman*	*Wilson*	*Malloch*	*Spiksley*
						Ref: A Farrant (*35 mins each way played*)	On a wet evening, Spiksley headed the League Champions in front. Layton's handball allowed Lewis to level from the spot, but Chapman netted a clever goal to put the visitors back in front in this short-time game. Wombwell's clipping-shot brought City a well-deserved draw.										

FA Cup/Glos Cup					F-A	H-T	Scorers, Times, and Referees	1	2	3	4	5	6	7	8	9	10	11
PR	H	MIDDLESBROUGH	4	W	3-1	2-1	Leigh 20, Boucher 35, Wombwell 82	Clay	Tuft	Lewis	Jones	Davies	Chambers	Dean	Leigh	Gara	Boucher	Wombwell
13/12		8,666 *1:14*					*Robertson 25*	*Macfarlane*	*Hogg*	*Ramsay*	*Smith*	*Jones*	*Davidson*	*Robertson J*	*Watson*	*Thompson*	*Cassidy*	*Carrick*
		(£268.0.3)					Ref: J Adams	St John's Lane has been the scene of many battles royal since the season began, but none could surpass this epic struggle. City, who lost the toss and started from the Lane End, took the lead when Leigh scored from Wombwell's centre, but Robertson's oblique shot levelled matters.										
1	A	BOLTON	4	W	5-0	3-0	Dean 10, Banks 30, 40, 75, [Wombwell 85]	Clay	Tuft	Lewis	Jones	Good	Chambers	Dean	Boucher	Gara	Banks	Wombwell
7/2		*7,750 1:18*						*Thompson*	*Halliday*	*Struthers*	*Freebairn*	*Greenhaigh*	*Boyd*	*Hanson*	*White*	*Marsh*	*McKay*	*Taylor*
		(£240.5.3)					Ref: A Barker	The 400 City fans who travelled North were amply rewarded for their journey by seeing their favourites end Bolton's three-match winning run. In miserable wet conditions at Burnden Park, the score somewhat flattered City, who had a fair measure of luck with all three first-half goals.										
2	A	TOTTENHAM	4	L	0-1	0-1		Clay	Tuft	Lewis	Jones	Good	Chambers	Dean	Leigh	Gara	Banks	Wombwell
21/2		*18,750 SL:5*					*Woodward 31*	*Clawley*	*Watson*	*Tait*	*Morris*	*Hughes*	*Jones*	*Dryburgh*	*Cameron*	*Woodward*	*Copeland*	*Kirwan*
		(£1,386)					Ref: P Harrower	Against the run of play, Banks thought he had fired in an early opener but was given offside. City were then unlucky when the referee failed to spot Tait's use of his arm in clearing off the goal-line shortly before Vivian Woodward put the Spurs in front with a beautifully judged shot.										
F	A	BRISTOL ROV	4	D	0-0	0-0		Clay	Tuft	Lewis	Jones	Good	Jay	Dean	Leigh	Boucher	Banks	Wombwell
GC 13/4		*11,790 SL:4*						*Cartlidge*	*Dunn*	*Pudan*	*Young*	*McLean*	*Lyon*	*Muir*	*Howie*	*Corbett*	*Graham*	*Marriott*
		(£355.3.6)					Ref: J Adams	Under the control of this season's FA Cup final referee, Jack Adams, the teams, who have been invited on a Cambpells steamer trip to Ilfracombe on Wednesday, played out an exciting goal-less draw. Jay fired against an upright; then after the interval snow fell heavily.										
R	H	BRISTOL ROV	4	D	1-1	0-1	Banks 80	Clay	Tuft	Lewis	Jones	Good	Jay	Dean	Leigh	Boucher	Banks	Wombwell
GC 20/4		4,044 *SL:5*					*Corbett 35*	*Cartlidge*	*Dunn*	*Pudan*	*Young*	*McLean*	*Lyon*	*Muir*	*Howie*	*Corbett*	*Graham*	*Marriott*
		(£113.12.6)					Ref: P Harrower	This was one of the keenest and most exciting of tussles for the County trophy. In delightful weather, Corbett fired in the opener when Good was off the pitch having treatment to his ankle. Banks levelled for City from a melee and three minutes later Dean had an effort disallowed.										
R2	H	BRISTOL ROV	4	L	2-4	1-3	Banks 30, 60	Clay	Tuft	Lewis	Jones	Good	Jay	Dean	Leigh	Boucher	Banks	Wombwell
GC 29/4		4,985 *SL:5*					*Corbett 14, 44, Marriott 25, Dunn 80p*	*Cartlidge*	*Dunn*	*Pudan*	*Davies*	*Young*	*Lyon*	*Muir*	*Howie*	*Corbett*	*Graham*	*Marriott*
		(£140.1.8)					Ref: J Adams	City had just as much of the play as their opponents, but were not so lethal in front of goal. From Muir's centre, Corbett beautifully put the ball into the net to give Rovers the lead. Banks headed in City's response after Marriott, standing close in, had doubled the Rovers advantage.										

		P	W	D	L	F	A	W	D	L	F	A	Pts
			Home					Away					
1	Manchester C	34	15	1	1	64	15	10	3	4	31	14	54
2	Small Heath	34	17	0	0	57	11	7	3	7	17	25	51
3	Wlch Arsenal	34	14	2	1	46	9	6	6	5	20	21	48
4	BRISTOL C	34	12	3	2	43	18	5	5	7	16	20	42
5	Manchester U	34	9	4	4	32	15	6	4	7	21	23	38
6	Chesterfield	34	11	4	2	43	10	3	5	9	24	30	37
7	Preston NE	34	10	5	2	39	12	3	5	9	17	28	36
8	Barnsley	34	9	4	4	32	13	4	4	9	23	38	34
9	Burslem Pt V	34	11	5	1	36	16	2	3	12	21	46	34
10	Lincoln City	34	8	3	6	30	22	4	3	10	16	31	30
11	Glossop	34	9	1	7	26	19	2	6	9	17	38	29
12	Gainsboro' T	34	9	4	4	28	14	2	3	12	13	45	29
13	Burton Utd	34	9	4	4	26	20	2	3	12	13	39	29
14	Blackpool	34	7	5	5	32	24	2	5	10	12	35	28
15	Leicester Fos'	34	5	5	7	20	23	5	3	9	21	42	28
16	Doncaster R	34	8	5	4	27	17	1	2	14	8	55	25
17	Stockport Co	34	6	4	7	26	24	1	2	14	12	50	20
18	Burnley	34	6	7	4	25	25	0	1	16	5	52	20
		612	175	66	65	632	307	65	66	175	307	632	612

Odds & ends

Double wins: (3) Manchester United, Stockport County, Burton United.
Double losses: (0).

Won from behind: (2) Preston (h), Leicester Fosse (h).
Lost from in front: Gainsborough (a).

High spots: Starting the season with six straight League wins.
Beating Leicester Fosse 6-1 in a bizarre match at 'St John's Lane'

Low spots: Failing to maintain an early position at the head of division.
Succumbing 2-4 against Bristol Rovers in the Gloucestershire Cup.

Player of the Year: Dickie Wombwell.
Ever-presents: (2) Harry Clay, Dickie Wombwell.
Hat-tricks: (2) Jimmy Jay, Bertie Banks.
Leading scorer: Overall: Dickie Wombwell (16). League: Wombwell (11).

AGM (Temperance Hall, East Street, Bedminster, 10 June 1903):
Profit £360.10s.10d. Season Ticket Sales £117.19s.4d.

	Appearances			Goals			
	Lge	**Cup**	**Fr**	**Lge**	**Cup**	**Fr**	**Tot**
Banks, Bertie	**21**	5	7	**8**	6	1	**15**
Barnes, Charles	**13**		7	**2**			**2**
Boucher, Tommy	**25**	5	7	**6**	1	2	**9**
Chambers, Peter	**29**	3	3				
Clay, Harry	**34**	6	6				
Davies, Richard	**5**	1	2				
Dean, Alf	**25**	6	3	**10**	1	2	**13**
Demmery, Bill			2				
Gara, Andrew	**18**	3	2	**5**		1	**6**
Good, Michael	**32**	5	7	**5**			**5**
Jay, Jimmy	**10**	3	6	**3**			**3**
Jones, Billy	**32**	6	6	**2**		1	**3**
Lamberton, Jim	**3**		3				
Leigh, Walter	**30**	5	6	**6**	1	6	**13**
Lewis, George	**30**	6	7	**1**		3	**4**
Tuft, Billy	**33**	6	6				
Wombwell, Dickie	**34**	6	8	**11**	2	3	**16**
17 players used	**374**	**66**	**88**	**59**	**11**	**19**	**89**

No	Date	Att	Pos	Pt	F-A	H-T	Scorers, Times, and Referees	1	2	3	4	5	6	7	8	9	10	11
1	A MANCHESTER U			D	2-2	0-0	Fisher 49, Chambers 70	Clay	Gilson	Tuft	Jones	Hosie	Chambers	Dean	Fisher	Corbett	Morris	Wombwell
	5/9	*40,000*		1			*Griffiths 60, 80*	*Sutcliffe*	*Bonthron*	*Read*	*Downie*	*Griffiths*	*Robertson A*	*McCartney*	*Gaudie*	*Robertson T*	*Arkesden*	*Robertson S*
							Ref: A Green	In ideal conditions, the large crowd witnessed an even first half. After the break City often rang rings around United, but at the finish they had to be satisfied with a point. Fisher shot high to the keeper's right to give City the lead, but the persistence of Griffiths soon levelled matters.										
2	H GLOSSOP			W	5-0	2-0	Corbett 30, Hosie 38, Fisher 65, [Jones 70, Morris 80]	Clay	Bach	Tuft	Jones	Hosie	Chambers	Dean	Fisher	Corbett	Morris	Wombwell
	12/9	10,000 (£250)		3				*Clark*	*Hancock*	*Norgrove*	*Pell*	*Boden*	*Galley*	*Bainbridge*	*Thornley*	*Jones*	*Murphy*	*Barnes*
							Ref: G Capes	After the Clifton Wood Industrial School Band had provided the music, City had to work hard to prise open Glossop's strong defence. Corbett opened the scoring by putting away Wombwell's corner. Bainbridge then had an effort disallowed before Clarke misjudged Hosie's weak shot.										
3	A BRADFORD CITY		10	L	0-1	0-0		Clay	Tuft	**Hargett**	Jones	Hosie	Chambers	Dean	Fisher	Corbett	Morris	Wombwell
	19/9	*12,000*	*9*	3			*McMillan 49*	*Seymour*	*Wilson*	*Carter*	*Robinson*	*O'Rourke*	*Millar*	*Guy*	*Forrest*	*Farnall*	*McMillan*	*Graham*
							Ref: D Hammond	City certainly didn't show the form that was expected against the League newcomers. They still should have won however but, as it was, the defeat could have been worse than McMillan's fine winner, as the inside-left shot wide from the penalty spot not long before the final whistle.										
4	H WLCH ARSENAL		11	L	0-4	0-2		Clay	Hargett	Tuft	Jones	Hosie	Chambers	Dean	Fisher	Corbett	Morris	Wombwell
	26/9	14,000 (£408.9.10)	*1*	3			*Gooing 3, 70, Coleman 5, Lindward 75*	*Ashcroft*	*Thorpe*	*Jackson*	*Dick*	*Sands*	*McEachrane*	*Briercliffe*	*Coleman*	*Gooing*	*Shanks*	*Linward*
							Ref: F Kirkham	City, who often have luck on their side when playing Reading, now regularly experience the other side of the coin when facing Arsenal. Right from the start, the hoodoo struck as the visiting keeper rather luckily kept out Wombwell's effort, before Gooing headed in a fortunate opener.										
5	A BARNSLEY		12	L	0-2	0-1		Clay	Gilson	Tuft	Jones	Hosie	Chambers	Dean	Fisher	Corbett	Morris	Wombwell
	3/10	*4,000*	*3*	3			*Lees 17p, Lake 85*	*Hewitson*	*West*	*Edwards*	*Bennett*	*Lees*	*Oxspring*	*Hellewell Alec*	*Green*	*Gullen*	*Cornan*	*Lake*
							Ref: W Gilgryst	City were certainly not two goals inferior to Barnsley, and were decidedly unlucky when the referee ignored their claims for a goal when Hewitson carried the ball over the line in the second half. Gilson's handling offence brought Barnsley their opener from the penalty-spot.										
6	H LINCOLN		10	W	3-1	2-1	Dean 7, Wombwell 44, Barnes 85	Clay	Tuft	Gilson	Jones	Hosie	Chambers	Dean	Fisher	Corbett	Wombwell	Barnes
	10/10	7,000	*9*	5			*O'Donnell 5*	*Webb*	*Groves*	*McMillan*	*Fraser*	*Simpson W*	*Blow*	*Hindson*	*Watson*	*Higgins*	*O'Donnell D*	*Parker*
							Ref: T Kyle	City stopped the rot of three successive defeats with this win over a side, previously unbeaten this season, against whom they hadn't tasted success before, either home or away. It didn't look likely when O'Donnell smartly shot in the opener, but Dean was able to fire in a leveller.										
7	A STOCKPORT		10	D	1-1	0-0	Wombwell 85	Clay	Gilson	Tuft	Jones	Hargett	Chambers	Dean	Fisher	Corbett	Barnes	Wombwell
	17/10	*5,000*	*17*	6			*Wallwork 64*	*Butler*	*Allan*	*Ray*	*Rooke*	*Freeborough*	*Codling*	*Wallwork*	*Price*	*Pass*	*Brown*	*Scotson*
							Ref: W Chadwick	Stockport, with ex-Bristol East player W Rooke in their ranks, proved stubborn opponents in this game. At the close, City were grateful for Wombwell's low, close-range, shot for their point saver, but given all the chances that had come their way, they should have won with ease.										
8	H CHESTERFIELD		8	W	3-2	1-1	Wombwell 25, Dean 70, Morris 75	Clay	Gilson	Tuft	Jones	Hargett	Chambers	Dean	Morris	Corbett	Barnes	Wombwell
	24/10	5,000	*14*	8			*Ball 40, Munday 85*	*Hardy*	*Simpson*	*Wragg*	*Haig*	*Shuflebotham*	*Thacker*	*Arnold*	*Newton*	*Hutton*	*Munday*	*Ball*
							Ref: S Carr	During the opening ten minutes, the visitors rarely got over the halfway line; then Newton wasted a chance. Wombwell fired in the opening goal, but Ball equalised with a shot that gave Clay no chance. After the break, Corbett hit a post, whilst offside ruled out a shot by Wombwell.										
9	A BOLTON		8	D	1-1	0-1	Morris 75	Clay	Gilson	Tuft	Jones	Hosie	Chambers	Dean	Morris	Corbett	Wombwell	Barnes
	31/10	*9,000*	*3*	9			*White 4*	*Davies*	*Struthers*	*Ostick*	*Boyd*	*Greenhaigh*	*Taylor*	*Gardner*	*Wright*	*Marsh*	*White*	*Stokes*
							Ref: A Green	Against a Bolton side completely reorganised since City's outstanding FA Cup success last season, it wasn't expected that the Westerners would experience anything other than defeat this campaign. Completely on top after the break, Morris secured City's much-deserved point.										
10	H BURNLEY		6	W	6-0	4-0	Dean 10p, 30, 46, Wombwell 14, [Morris 35, Corbett 65]	Clay	Gilson	Tuft	Jones	Hosie	Chambers	Dean	Morris	Corbett	Wombwell	Barnes
	7/11	6,000	*8*	11				*Towler*	*Ross*	*Dixon*	*Barron*	*Walders*	*Taylor*	*Crawford*	*Hogan*	*Jenkinson*	*Jackson*	*Williams*
							Ref: G Simmons	In delightful weather City hit form against opponents who had only conceded seven goals in nine League games this season. Dixon's foul on Morris allowed Dean to give City the lead from the penalty-spot. Corbett's header brought to an end his long run of bad luck in front of goal.										

No	Venue	Opponent / Date	Att	Pos	Pts	Res	HT	Scorers / Ref	1	2	3	4	5	6	7	8	9	10	11
11	A	PRESTON		6	L	0-3	0-1		Clay	Gilson	Tuft	Jones	Hosie	Chambers	Dean	Morris	Corbett	Wombwell	Barnes
		14/11	*9,000*	*1*	11			*Wilcox 6, 70, Smith 80*	*McBride*	*Orrell*	*Derbyshire*	*Tod*	*Hunter*	*McLean*	*Bourne*	*Bell*	*Wilcox*	*Smith P*	*Bond*
								Ref: H Shelton	The game opened at a quick pace and amid scenes of wild enthusiasm when Wilcox scored for Preston not long after the start. Against as polished a body of opponents as can be found, City, who were only slightly inferior, went further behind when Wilcox headed past Clay.										
12	H	GRIMSBY		4	W	4-0	3-0	Dean 8, Barnes 35, 45, Chambers 87	Clay	Gilson	Tuft	Jones	Hosie	Chambers	Dean	Morris	Corbett	Wombwell	Barnes
		21/11	8,000	*7*	13				*Spendiff*	*McConnell A*	*Gardner*	*Dunn*	*Roberts*	*McDiarmid*	*Nichol*	*Rouse*	*Long*	*Speight*	*Hodgkinson*
								Ref: A Green	There was not a weak link in this City side and, with Gilson improving with every match, there would appear no way that Bach will replace him. Dean's fine effort, in off the upright, gave City an early lead, then Barnes fired in number two before his header brought up the third.										
13	H	BLACKPOOL		4	W	5-0	3-0	Dean 10, Chambers 20, Fisher 30, [Corbett 55, Morris 70]	Clay	Gilson	Tuft	Jones	Hosie	Chambers	Dean	Morris	Corbett	Fisher	Wombwell
		5/12	5,000	*18*	15				*Hull*	*Anderson G*	*Scott*	*Threlfall*	*Parkinson*	*Wolstenholme*	*Miller*	*Rooke*	*Birket*	*Anderton*	*McEwan*
								Ref: W Weeks	Dean's first-half penalty failure, firing right at the keeper after Threlfall handled, scarcely mattered as City were 3-0 in front by that time. Corbett, who had an earlier effort disallowed, netted a lovely goal, whilst long-distance shooting was effective for both Chambers and Dean.										
14	H	BURTON UNITED		3	W	4-0	2-0	Morris 12, 60, Chambers 25, [Corbett 50]	Clay	Gilson	Tuft	Jones	Hosie	Chambers	Dean	Morris	Corbett	Fisher	Wombwell
		19/12	5,000	*13*	17				*Bromage*	*Ashby*	*Kirkland*	*Evans*	*Moir*	*Livingstone*	*Reynolds*	*Lewis*	*Hargreaves*	*Gilchrist*	*King*
								Ref: F Heath	Following their midweek exertions in the FA Cup, City took it easy after Chambers had given them a two-goal lead. A soft shot from Morris opened the scoring. The ref perplexed the fans, ruling out a first-half goal by Fisher, as well as efforts by Morris and Gilchrist after the break.										
15	A	BURSLEM PT VALE		4	L	1-3	0-3	Dean 70p	Clay	Gilson	Tuft	Jones !	Hosie	Chambers	Dean	Morris	Corbett	Fisher	Wombwell
		26/12	*4,000*	*9*	17			*Capes 15, 24, Simpson 20p*	*Cotton*	*Mullineux*	*Rowley*	*Croxton*	*Holyhead*	*Bradbury*	*Eardley*	*Price*	*Simpson T*	*Capes*	*Heames*
								Ref: J Pearson	Jones was ordered off five minutes from time for a foul on Capes, who had been City's scourge, after having waltzed through for the opener. Dean's spot-kick, following Mollineaux's trip on Morris, was scant reward for City, who had totally dominated the opening fifteen minutes.										
16	H	MANCHESTER U		5	D	1-1	1-0	Morris 30	Clay	Gilson	Tuft	Jones	Hosie	Chambers	Dean	Morris	Corbett	Fisher	Wombwell
		2/1	8,000	*6*	18			*Griffiths 52*	*Sutcliffe*	*Bonthron*	*Hayes*	*Bell*	*Griffiths*	*Robertson A*	*McCartney*	*Grassam*	*Robertson T*	*Arkesden*	*Wilkinson*
								Ref: J Adams	Despite the fact that United were short of five regulars due to cup injuries, they gave City a hard game. Morris opened the scoring with a fine shot, but Griffiths levelled matters with a long-distance drive shortly after the interval. Both sides squandered winning chances near the close.										
17	A	GLOSSOP		5	D	1-1	0-0	Corbett 80	Clay	Gilson	Tuft	Jones	Hosie	Chambers	Dean	Morris	Corbett	Fisher	Wombwell
		9/1	*800*	*18*	19			*Thornley 50*	*Clark*	*Hancock*	*Norgrove*	*Pell*	*Boden*	*Coates*	*Bainbridge*	*Thornley*	*Norton*	*Green*	*Murphy*
								Ref: G Capes	Facing the slope and a strong wind in the first half on the muddy North Road ground, City were miffed when the wind dropped a few minutes after the break. Thornley outstripped City's defence to fire in the opener, but Corbett shot in the rebound when Clarke spilled his first effort.										
18	H	BRADFORD CITY		6	D	1-1	0-1	Fisher 73	Clay	Gilson	Tuft	Hargett	Hosie	Chambers	Dean	Morris	Corbett	Fisher	Wombwell
		16/1	6,000	*9*	20			*Farnall 30*	*Seymour*	*Wilson*	*Halliday*	*Farnall*	*Robinson*	*Millar*	*Forrest*	*Beckram*	*Drain*	*McMillan*	*Graham*
								Ref: T Horn	A scrambling and somewhat uninteresting game at the Lane, where City had more than enough chances to have won comfortably. Fisher and Wombwell each had efforts disallowed before the equaliser, whilst Dean failed with a first-half spot-kick after a clumsy tackle by Wilson.										
19	H	BARNSLEY		6	W	2-0	2-0	Fisher 15, 30	Clay	Gilson	Tuft	Jones	Hosie	Chambers	Dean	Corbett	Wombwell	Fisher	Barnes
		30/1	2,500	*9*	22				*Hewitson*	*Welch*	*Edwards*	*Ward*	*Lees*	*Oxspring*	*Barnfather*	*Travers*	*Jones*	*Cornan*	*Kelly*
								Ref: A Millward	Despite the wretched weather, which led many to think that the game would be called off, fully 2,500 spectators turned up to see City play some exceedingly clever football. Sandwiched between Fisher's double strike, Wombwell had hard luck when his shot got stuck in the mud.										
20	H	STOCKPORT		6	W	6-0	4-0	Corbett 5, 10, 20, 35, Morris 60, [Jones 75]	Clay	Bach	Tuft	Jones	Hosie	Chambers	Dean	Corbett	Morris	Fisher	Wombwell
		13/2	1,700	*16*	24				*Butler*	*Ray*	*Allan*	*Brittleton*	*Hall*	*Codling*	*Stansfield*	*Pass*	*Kay*	*Raby*	*Sharpley*
								Ref: A Cooknell	With the wind blowing a half-hurricane and the rain falling incessantly, it was not surprising that so few ventured out to see this contest. Corbett fired in an early opener then, after registering again from long distance, he was unlucky when the referee ruled out his header.										
21	A	CHESTERFIELD		6	L	0-1	0-1		Clay	Bach	Tuft	Jones	Hosie	Chambers	Dean	Corbett	Morris	Fisher	Wombwell
		20/2	*4,000*	*11*	24			*Munday 9*	*Hardy*	*Marples*	*Unwin*	*Haig*	*Shuflebotham*	*Thacker*	*Walwin*	*Taylor*	*Newton*	*Munday*	*Earl*
								Ref: W Gilgryst	After Munday rounded the backs before steering the ball past Clay for Chesterfield's early opener, City had the chances to have saved the game. Hardy brought off a wonder save from Morris, though he excelled even this just before the end when he kept out Hosie's spot-kick.										

No	Date		Att	Pos	Pt	F-A	H-T	Scorers, Times, and Referees	1	2	3	4	5	6	7	8	9	10	11
22	A	LEICESTER FOSSE		6	L	0-1	0-1		Clay	Gilson	Tuft	Jones	Hosie	Chambers	Dean	Corbett	Morris	Fisher	Wombwell
	25/2		*3,000*	*14*	24			*Evenson 18*	*Smith*	*West*	*Robinson*	*Bell*	*Collins*	*Pollock*	*Hadley*	*Blessington*	*Warren*	*Evenson*	*Dilks*
								Ref: J Adams	In fine weather at Filbert Street, the early play was of a give-and-take nature. Shortly after Tuft had nearly put into his own net, Evenson gave the Fossils the lead with a pretty goal. In the second half City had more of the game, but found Smith, the Leicester custodian, in fine form.										
23	H	BOLTON		5	W	2-0	2-0	Dean 5, Corbett 35	Clay	Gilson	Tuft	Jones	Hosie	Chambers	Dean	Corbett	Morris	Fisher	Wombwell
	27/2		6,000	*4*	26				*Davies*	*Ostick*	*Brown*	*Clifford*	*Greenhaigh*	*Boyd*	*Leigh*	*Marsh*	*Yenson*	*White*	*Taylor*
								Ref: J Bailey	A fast and interesting game in the dull and cold conditions at St John's Lane. Dean's early long shot took effect as it went into goal in off of a post. Numerous offside decisions played havoc with City's attack, but Corbett was able to put away an easy chance to double their advantage.										
24	A	BURNLEY		5	W	3-2	1-1	Chambers 44, Hargett 62, 72	Clay	Gilson	Tuft	Jones	Hosie	Chambers	Dean	Morris	Hargett	Corbett	Wombwell
	5/3		*4,000*	*3*	28			*Hogan 7, Williams 49*	*Green*	*Ross*	*Dixon*	*Jenkinson*	*Walders*	*Taylor*	*Aspden*	*Hogan*	*Whittam*	*Bell*	*Williams*
								Ref: J Bailey	City's win was splendidly earned as in both combination and individual play they were supreme. After Chambers registered with a great shot, Clay saved Dixon's penalty following a push by Tuft. Shortly before City's second-half left-footed leveller, Hargett had a hot one disallowed.										
25	A	LINCOLN		4	W	6-2	2-1	Jones 11, Chambers 25, Morris 60,	Clay	Gilson	Tuft	Jones	Hosie	Chambers	Dean	Morris	Hargett	Corbett	Wombwell
	7/3		*4,000*	*12*	30			*Simpson C 40,80* [Dean 70p,Hosie 75],	*Webb*	*Groves*	*Pallister*	*Simpson W*	*McMillan*	*Blow*	*Hindson*	*O'Donnell D*	*Brown*	*Elmore*	*Simpson C*
								Ref: J Briggs [Hargett 85]	Jones opened the scoring with a magnificent long-distance shot; then Chambers drove in the second before Simpson beat Clay with a grounder. After the interval City were subjected to more pressure than hitherto, but the Imps only reward again came from Simpson with a close-in shot.										
26	H	PRESTON		3	W	3-1	2-1	Morris 20, Hosie 45, Chambers 65	Clay	Gilson	Tuft	Jones	Hosie	Chambers	Dean	Morris	Hargett	Corbett	Wombwell
	12/3		10,000	*1*	32			*Smith P 15*	*McBride*	*Derbyshire*	*Orrell*	*McLean*	*Hunter*	*Tod*	*Smith T*	*Maher*	*Smith P*	*Bell*	*Bourne*
								Ref: A Millward	City were much the superior side than the League leaders in this meeting, in glorious weather, at St John's Lane. Preston opened the scoring when Smith found the net in a very easy fashion, but Morris soon headed in an equaliser. Hosie registered with a fine shot right on the interval.										
27	A	WLCH ARSENAL		3	L	0-2	0-2		Clay	Gilson	Tuft	Jones	Hosie	Chambers	Dean	Morris	Hargett	Corbett	Wombwell
	14/3		*10,000*	*2*	32			*Coleman 4, 30*	*Ashcroft*	*Cross*	*Jackson*	*Dick*	*Sands*	*McEachrane*	*Briercliffe*	*Coleman*	*Gooing*	*Shanks*	*Linward*
								Ref: J Smith	It was as good as it got for City when Hargett kicked-off in lovely weather at the Manor Ground, as it wasn't long before the poor luck that dodges their meetings with the Gunners became apparent. With the game scarcely having started, Coleman secured a remarkably lucky goal.										
28	A	GRIMSBY		4	L	0-2	0-1		Clay	Gilson	Tuft	Jones	Hosie	Chambers	Dean	Morris	Hargett	Corbett	Wombwell
	19/3		*4,000*	*7*	32			*Rouse 40, Elkins 85*	*Spendiff*	*McConnell A*	*Gardner*	*Dunn*	*Nelmes*	*Harmsworth*	*Long*	*Rouse*	*Elkins*	*Wilkinson*	*Hodgkinson*
								Ref: T Campbell	Despite Nelmes taking the place of Roberts, whose mother was fatally burned on Friday, Grimsby had no trouble in maintaining their unbeaten home record. City were a big disappointment and there was no way back for them when Elkins scored from Long's centre just before the close.										
29	H	LEICESTER FOSSE		3	W	4-0	2-0	Dean 5, Hosie 35, Corbett 60, 87	Clay	Gilson	Tuft	Hales	Hosie	Chambers	Dean	Fisher	Hargett	Corbett	Wombwell
	26/3		5,000	*17*	34				*Smith*	*Cheater*	*Robinson*	*Pollock*	*Collins*	*Bell*	*Simpson*	*Blessington*	*Warren*	*Evenson*	*Barlow*
								Ref: J Adams	City were perhaps lucky with the opener, as the referee ignored Leicester's claims for hands when Dean breasted the ball into the net, but there was no doubt about the second. Hosie registered with a terrific shot that went in off the post. Corbett headed in the third, then fired in another.										
30	A	GAINSBOROUGH		4	L	1-3	0-2	Dean 78	Clay	Gilson	Tuft	Jones	Hosie	Chambers	Dean	Fisher	Hargett	Corbett	Wombwell
	1/4		*3,000*	*11*	34			*Dixon 25, Foxall F 26, Foxall A 85*	*Bagshaw*	*Thompson*	*Hempshall*	*Saul*	*Jenkinson*	*Turner*	*Langham*	*Greensill*	*Dixon*	*Foxall F*	*Foxall A*
								Ref: J Smith	A windy day at the Northolme ground, where Gainsborough were without the services of Hall and Jackson. The game opened even, but Trinity soon pressed, with Dixon and Frank Foxall scoring. In the second half Dean raised City hopes, but Trinity soon regained control of the contest.										
31	A	BLACKPOOL		4	W	1-0	1-0	Jones 30	Clay	Gilson	Tuft	Jones	Hosie	Chambers	Fisher	Morris	Hargett	Corbett	Wombwell
	2/4		*2,000*	*14*	36				*Hull*	*Birket*	*Scott*	*Threlfall*	*Parkinson*	*Wolstenholme*	*Anderton*	*Rooke*	*Bennett*	*Anderson T*	*McEwen*
								Ref: A Sutcliffe	Blackpool, who included new signing T Anderson (Clyde), as well as J Rooke (ex-Bristol East and brother of Stockport's half-back), turned out in white and blue so as not to clash with City's colours. The game was won by a short-range shot, which passed through a forest of legs.										

No	Venue	Opponent / Date	Att	Pos	Pts	Res	HT	Scorers, Times, Referees	1	2	3	4	5	6	7	8	9	10	11
32	H	GAINSBOROUGH		4		W	2-1	0-0 Corbett 53, Wombwell 70	Clay	Gilson	Tuft	Jones	Hosie	Chambers	Barnes	Fisher	Morris	Corbett	Wombwell
		9/4	4,000	8	38			*Turner 80*	*Bagshaw*	*Thompson*	*Hempshall*	*Saul*	*Jenkinson*	*Hall*	*Langham*	*Greensill*	*Dixon*	*Turner*	*Foxall A*
								Ref: A Cocknell	City's defence was to the fore in the first half when the high wind was against them. After the break, it didn't take them long to get going and Corbett headed them into the lead. Turner got the visitors back into the game; then Clay did well to keep out ex-City player Langham's shot.										
33	A	BURTON UNITED		4		W	3-2	0-2 Dean 60, 80, Fisher 70	Clay	Gilson	Hargett	Jones	Hosie	Chambers	Dean	Fisher	Morris	Barnes	Wombwell
		16/4	*2,000*	*11*	40			*Gilchrist 15, Lewis 17*	*Bromage*	*Ashby*	*Kirkland*	*Moir*	*Mann*	*Evans*	*Reynolds*	*Lewis*	*Hargreaves*	*Gilchrist*	*King*
								Ref: F Heath	City wound up their 'out' matches for the season with a brilliant display at Peel Croft after trailing to shots by Gilchrist and Lewis. Dean got City back into the contest with an excellent cross-shot; then Fisher fired in the leveller, before City's right-winger shot in the match winner.										
34	H	BURSLEM PT VALE		4		W	2-1	0-0 Fisher 56, Hosie 59	Clay	Gilson	Dean	Jones	Hosie	Hargett	Barnes	Fisher	Morris	Corbett	Wombwell
		23/4	4,000	*13*	42			*Loverseed 55*	*Cotton*	*Mullineux*	*Hamilton*	*Croxton*	*Holyhead*	*Perkins*	*Mountford*	*Price*	*Loverseed*	*Capes*	*Heames*
		Home / Away						Ref: J Jamieson	City, who won the toss, were the first to press, but didn't get far. The points were secured during a hectic five-minute spell in the second half after Loverseed had fired the visitors ahead. Fisher immediately levelled; then Hosie headed over the bar, before nodding City into the lead.										
		Ave 6,306 / 7,047																	

FRIENDLIES

No	Venue	Opponent / Date	Att	Res	Score	HT	Scorers, Times, Referees	1	2	3	4	5	6	7	8	9	10	11
1	A	BRISTOL ROV		W	1-0	1-0	Dean 20p	Clay	Tuft	**Gilson**	Jones	**Hosie**	Chambers	Dean	**Fisher**	**Corbett**	**Morris**	Wombwell
		2/9	*2,500*					*Cartlidge*	*Dunn*	*Pudan*	*Tait*	*Appleby*	*Gray*	*Robson*	*Elmore*	*Beats*	*Smith*	*Marriott*
							Ref: A Millward	The game opened briskly in a heavy storm of rain, though it was by no means easy to get a footing on the wet pitch. A trip allowed Dean to score from the spot with a fierce drive. The Rovers pressed strongly after the break, though Wombwell narrowly failed to increase City's lead.										
2	H	OXFORD UNIV		W	3-1	2-0	Fisher 35, 44, Barnes 80p	Demmery	Tuft	Bach	Jones	Hosie	Chambers	Dean	Fisher	Corbett	Wombwell	Barnes
		11/11	2,000				*Evans 65*	*Rogers R*	*Snell JE*	*Norris OT*	*Curwen WJH*	*Cheale R*	*McIver CD*	*Bence RE*	*M-Owen HM*	*Evans WHB*	*Goodcliffe GV*	*Simonds J*
							Ref: A Farrant	Except that Bence took the place of Rider, the University were at full strength. With City taking it much too easy early on, the amateur men squandered a number of opportunities before Fisher opened the scoring. Hands against Snell allowed Barnes to put away a late spot-kick.										
3	A	CLAPTON ORIENT		W	2-1	2-1	Fisher 5, Hosie 30	Clay	Gilson	Tuft	Jones	Hosie	Chambers	Dean	Morris	Corbett	Fisher	Barnes
		28/11	*2,000*				*Bush 15*	*Ward*	*Price*	*Chalkley*	*Berry*	*Simpson*	*McLelland*	*Bush*	*McGeorge R*	*Wallace*	*Seeley*	*Robertson*
								On the muddy Millfields Road pitch, City played their part in a rousing struggle. Fisher nabbed an easy goal early on, but Gilson's slip let Seeley through to centre for Bush's neat equaliser. Following Dean's good work, Hosie sent in a long-shot that proved to be City's winner.										
4	H	BRISTOL ROV		W	5-3	3-1	Hargett 15, 70, Jones 20, Dean 30,	Clay	Bach	Tuft	Jones	Hosie	Chambers	Dean	Fisher	Hargett A	Wombwell	Barnes
		25/12	7,500				*Wilson 10, Smith 60, Darke 85*	*Cartlidge*	*Hargett G*	*Pudan*	*Davies*	*Robertson*	*Gray*	*Jack*	*Wilson*	*Darke*	*Smith*	*Marriott*
							Ref: H Ward [Fisher 80]	After Wilson tucked away the visitors' easy opener, City found their form. Andrew Hargett raced onto a Chambers pass to level matters from close range; then Jones registered with a well-judged goal before Fisher had an effort disallowed. Smith neatly beat Clay for Rovers second.										
5	A	OXFORD UNIV		L	0-3	0-2	*[McIver 88]*	Clay	Bach	Hargett	Dean	Hosie	Chambers	Barnes	Corbett	Morris	Wombwell	Fisher
		8/2	*250*				*Simonds 15, Morgan-Owen 30,*	*Rogers R*	*Scothern AE*	*Norris OT*	*Todd AM*	*Boissier AP*	*Verney HC*	*Bird WS*	*B-Melville JE*	*McIver CD*	*M-Owen HM*	*Simonds J*
								Oxford were in good form at the Parks prior to Saturday's clash with Cambridge. City paid the price for spurning early chances when Simonds registered with a cross shot. Morgan-Owen then doubled Oxford's advantage with a judicious drive before a mix-up gave McIver his late goal.										
6	H	HIBERNIAN		W	3-1	2-1	Corbett 20, Dean 40p, Harrower 55og	Clay	Gilson	Hargett	Jones	Sims	Chambers	Dean	Fisher	Morris	Corbett	Wombwell
		5/4	2,000				*Buchanan 25*	*Divers*	*Gray*	*Glen*	*Harrower*	*McConnachie*	*Boyle*	*Stewart*	*McGlachan*	*Stoker*	*Callaghan*	*Buchanan*
							Ref: G Gay	The wind and rain kept the gate down for this attractive meeting with the Scottish Leaguers. The visitors were unlucky to have a goal struck off when, from Stewart's fine centre, Stoker completely beat Clay. Not long afterwards, Corbett produced a splendid shot to put City into the lead.										
7	A	WEYMOUTH		W	3-0	2-0	Jones 15, Barnes 40p, Morris 75	Clay	Dean	Gilson	Jones	Hosie	Chambers	Barnes	Fisher	Morris	Corbett	Wombwell
		20/4	*1,000*					*Anderson*	*Mitchell*	*Steadman*	*Bartlett*	*Barron*	*Cole*	*Sergeant*	*Hicks*	*Mabb*	*Brocklehurst*	*Grenham*
							Ref: S Major	This friendly, which had twice been postponed, was at last brought off as City looked to score their 100th goal of the season. Jones opened the scoring; then a foul by Barron allowed Barnes, from the penalty-spot, to notch up the century. A fine, straight drive took City's tally to 101.										
8	H	BRISTOL CITY RES		W	3-2	2-1	Fisher 35, Corbett 40, 60	Clay	Tuft	Gilson	Jones	Hosie	Chambers	Barnes	Fisher	Morris	Corbett	Wombwell
		30/4	1,500				*Harris 25, 75*	*Demmery*	*Hales*	*Hargett A*	*Burton*	*Rendall*	*Price*	*Stolz*	*Rowlands JA*	*Rowlands WH*	*Harris*	*Hawkins*
							Ref: C Neale	A fairly good attendance, in the congenial weather, for the last game on the St John's Lane ground before moving to Ashton Gate. Clay was injured early in the second half and was conveyed home in a cab. At the final whistle the band played *Auld Land Syne* as the fans filed away.										

FA Cup/Glos Cup						F-A	H-T	Scorers, Times, and Referees	1	2	3	4	5	6	7	8	9	10	11
IN	A	NEW BROMPTON		4	D	1-1	1-0	Wombwell 30	Clay	Gilson	Tuft	Jones	Hosie	Chambers	Dean	Morris	Corbett	Fisher	Wombwell
	12/12		*6,000 SL:18*					*Chambers 84og*	*Clutterbuck*	*McCurdy*	*White*	*Lloyd*	*Goldie*	*Elliott*	*Robertson*	*Raisbeck*	*Smith*	*Stevenson*	*Singleton*
								Ref: H Walker	City won the toss and New Brompton, for whom Smith was deputising for the injured Boucher, kicked off against the wind. Wombwell headed City into the lead, but near the finish Raisbeck struck the crossbar with a long shot and the ball went into the net off the back of Chambers.										
R	H	NEW BROMPTON		4	W	5-2	0-1	Hosie47,Fisher49,Morris70,Corbett75,	Clay	Gilson	Tuft	Jones	Hosie	Chambers	Dean	Morris	Corbett	Fisher	Wombwell
	16/12		5,000 *SL:18*					*Goldie 15,Stevenson 90*[McCurdy85og]	*Clutterbuck*	*McCurdy*	*White*	*Lloyd*	*Goldie*	*Elliott*	*Bradbury*	*Robertson*	*Raisbeck*	*Stevenson*	*Singleton*
								Ref: H Walker	Shortly after New Brompton had an effort disallowed, they took the lead when, following a corner, Goldie scored a grand goal. Despite all of their pressure, it wasn't until the second half that City levelled, when Hosie registered with a shot that went into the net off of the crossbar.										
1	H	SHEFFIELD U		6	L	1-3	1-2	Hosie 44	Clay	Gilson	Tuft	Jones	Hosie	Chambers	Dean	Corbett	Morris	Fisher	Wombwell
	6/2		17,909 *1:1*					*Priest 6, Johnson 38, Brown 84*	*Foulke*	*Boyle*	*Thickett*	*Needham E*	*Wilkinson*	*Johnson*	*Lipsham*	*Priest*	*Brown*	*Common*	*Bennett*
			(£754.11.9)					Ref: T Kirkham	A record crowd at the Lane for the visit of the Championship leaders, who scored in their first attack when Priest headed in. Corbett and Wombwell missed chances to level before Johnson lifted United's second into the net. Hosie headed in City's response before the interval.										
SF	N	BRISTOL EAST		4	W	4-0	0-0	Wombwell 50, Fisher 53, 58, Morris 60	Clay	Gilson	Tuft	Jones	Hosie	Chambers	Dean	Fisher	Morris	Corbett	Wombwell
GC	23/3		*500 WL:6*						*Frankham*	*Hulin*	*McKay*	*Stuart*	*Cook R*	*Perry*	*Veysey*	*Callender W*	*Godwin*	*Johnson*	*Cook P*
								Ref: A Farrant *(at 'Stapleton Road')*	Despite Dean firing his 35th-minute penalty hopelessly wide, after McKay's handling offence, this proved to be an easy win for City on neutral territory at Stapleton Road. Wombwell's headed opener not long after the break precipitated a goal-burst which put East out of contention.										
F	H	BRISTOL ROV		4	W	2-1	2-0	Corbett 22, Jones 35	Clay	Gilson	Hargett	Jones	Hosie	Chambers	Dean	Fisher	Morris	Corbett	Wombwell
GC	4/4		10,537 *SL:2*					*Beats 75*	*Cartlidge*	*Dunn*	*Pudan*	*Tait*	*Robertson*	*Gray*	*Wilson*	*Jacks*	*Beats*	*Smith*	*Marriott*
			(£296.2.1)					Ref: A Kingscott	A storm 30 minutes before the kick-off kept the crowd down, but those that stayed away missed a treat. A deft touch by Corbett against his old club gave City the lead; then a fine shot by Jones doubled their advantage. After the break Beats cleverly nipped the ball between Clay's legs.										

			Home					Away					
	P	W	D	L	F	A	W	D	L	F	A	Pts
1 Preston NE	34	13	4	0	38	10	7	6	4	24	14	50
2 Wlch Arsenal	34	15	2	0	67	5	6	5	6	24	17	49
3 Manchester U	34	14	2	1	42	14	6	6	5	23	19	48
4 BRISTOL C	34	14	2	1	53	12	4	4	9	20	29	42
5 Burnley	34	12	2	3	31	20	3	7	7	19	35	39
6 Grimsby T	34	12	5	0	39	12	2	3	12	11	37	36
7 Bolton Wndrs	34	10	3	4	38	11	2	7	8	21	30	34
8 Barnsley	34	10	5	2	25	12	1	5	11	13	45	32
9 Gainsboro' T	34	10	2	5	34	17	4	1	12	19	43	31
10 Bradford City	34	8	5	4	30	25	4	2	11	15	34	31
11 Chesterfield	34	8	5	4	22	12	3	3	11	15	33	30
12 Lincoln City	34	9	4	4	25	18	2	4	11	16	40	30
13 Burslem Pt V	34	10	3	4	44	20	0	6	11	10	32	29
14 Burton United	34	8	6	3	33	16	3	1	13	12	45	29
15 Blackpool	34	8	2	7	25	27	3	3	11	15	40	27
16 Stockport Co	34	7	7	3	28	23	1	4	12	12	49	27
17 Glossop	34	7	4	6	42	25	3	2	12	15	39	26
18 Leicester Fos'	34	5	8	4	26	21	1	2	14	16	61	22
	612	180	71	55	642	300	55	71	180	300	642	612

Odds & ends

Double wins: (4) Lincoln City, Burnley, Blackpool, Burton United.
Double losses: (1) Woolwich Arsenal.

Won from behind: Linc'n (h), Burnley (a), Preston (h), Burton (a), Vale (h).
Lost from in front: (0).

High spots: Beating Burnley 6-0 at 'St John's Lane' on 7 November.
A record home crowd v Sheffield United in the FA Cup.

Low spots: A trio of consecutive away defeats at Woolwich Arsenal, Grimsby and Gainsborough that put City out of the promotion race.

Player of the Year: Peter Chambers.
Ever-presents: (2) Harry Clay, Dickie Wombwell.
Hat-tricks: (2) Alf Dean, Fred Corbett.
Leading scorer: Overall: Fred Corbett (18). League: (14).

AGM (Temperance Hall, East Street, Bedminster, 21 June 1904):
Loss £416.17s.1d. Season Ticket Sales £200.6s.0d.

	Appearances			Goals			
	Lge	Cup	Fr	Lge	Cup	Fr	Tot
Bach, Phil	**3**		3				
Barnes, Charles	**11**		6	**3**		2	**5**
Chambers, Peter	**33**	5	8	**7**			**7**
Clay, Harry	**34**	5	7				
Corbett, Fred	**33**	5	7	**13**	2	3	**18**
Dean, Alf	**32**	5	7	**14**		3	**17**
Demmery, Bill			1				
Fisher, Albert	**24**	5	8	**8**	3	5	**16**
Gilson, Alf	**29**	5	5				
Hales, Billy	**1**						
Hargett, Andrew	**15**	1	3	**3**		2	**5**
Hosie, Jim	**32**	5	7	**5**	2	1	**8**
Jones, Billy	**32**	5	7	**4**	1	2	**7**
Morris, Jack	**29**	5	6	**11**	2	1	**14**
Sims			1				
Tuft, Billy	**32**	4	5				
Wombwell, Dickie	**34**	5	7	**5**	2		**7**
Opponents og					1	1	**2**
17 players used	**374**	55	88	**73**	**13**	**20**	**106**

No	Date		Att	Pos	Pt	F-A	H-T	Scorers, Times, and Referees	1	2	3	4	5	6	7	8	9	10	11
1	H	BOLTON			L	3-4	2-2	Dean 25, Gilligan 31, Wombwell 60	Clay	Gilson	Tuft	Jones	Hosie	Chambers	Dean	Corbett	Gilligan	Capes	Wombwell
	3/9		14,000					*Gilson 12og, Marsh 43, 82, Yenson 89*	*Davies*	*Ostick*	*Struthers*	*Clifford*	*Greenhaigh*	*Boyd*	*Stokes*	*Marsh*	*Yenson*	*White*	*Taylor R*
			(£300+)					Ref: A Cooknell	The visitors opened the scoring at City's new Ashton Gate ground, when Gilson, in attempting to clear Clifford's centre, put into his own net. Wombwell's great shot into the top corner deserved to win any game, but Bolton came back to snatch victory with City appealing for offside.										
2	A	MANCHESTER U			L	1-4	1-1	Wombwell 15 *[Robertson 80]*	Clay	Gilson	Tuft	Jones	Capes	Chambers	Dean	Corbett	Gilligan	Wombwell	**Fenton**
	10/9		*18,000*					*Williams 35, Peddie 60, Schofield 70,*	*Moger*	*Bonthron*	*Hayes*	*Downie*	*Roberts*	*Robertson*	*Schofield*	*Mackie*	*Allan*	*Peddie*	*Williams*
								Ref: C Liversedge	After starting brightly, City were quite outplayed at Clayton where they lost to United for the first time ever. Wombwell's shot hit the inside of the post before rebounding into the net for City's goal, but it was easy for United after Williams dribbled through and banged in the equaliser.										
3	H	GLOSSOP		15	W	2-0	1-0	Gilligan 23, 75	Clay	Tuft	Gilson	Jones	Hosie	Chambers	Dean	Capes	Gilligan	Wombwell	Fenton
	17/9		7,000	*16*	2				*Davies*	*Synott*	*Orr*	*Phillips*	*Boden*	*Maginnis*	*Gall*	*Cairns*	*Goodall*	*Murphy*	*Lawrence*
			(£200)					Ref: W Weeks	The City forwards were full of dash, but were let down by their extremely poor marksmanship. Clay had little to do between the sticks as his side monopolised the play. Fortunately Gilligan was able to find the target, firstly with a long-distance shot, then a header after the interval.										
4	A	CHESTERFIELD		10	W	3-0	1-0	Dean 23, 81, Hosie 46	Clay	Thickett	Tuft	Jones	Hosie	Chambers	Dean	Corbett	Gilligan	Capes	Wombwell
	24/9		*4,000*	*14*	4				*Hardy*	*Gadsby W*	*Ray*	*Haig*	*Banner*	*Thacker*	*Tomlinson*	*Smith F*	*Newton*	*Munday*	*Kelly*
								Ref: W Chadwick	Clay needed to be on his mettle early on when Chesterfield pressed, but a mis-kick by Haig allowed Dean to drive in the opener. Thereafter it was easy for City who completely outclassed the homesters. Hosie's splendid shot and a header from Dean brought City a well-deserved win.										
5	H	BRADFORD CITY		4	W	1-0	1-0	Wilson 25og	Clay	Thickett	Tuft	Jones	Hosie	Chambers	Dean	Corbett	Gilligan	Capes	Wombwell
	1/10		8,000	*12*	6				*Mearns*	*Wilson W*	*Halliday*	*McLean*	*Robinson*	*Millar*	*Graham*	*Henderson*	*Forrest*	*Drain*	*Conlin*
								Ref: F Kirkham	Bradford were handicapped by the 35th-minute departure of Graham, following a collision with the burly, thick-set Thickett, but there was no doubt that City were the better side. A fortunate winner, however, as Wilson's foot deflected Wombwell's cross into the corner of the net.										
6	A	LINCOLN		3	W	3-1	3-1	Dean 20p, Hosie 21, Gilligan 35	Clay	Thickett	Tuft	Jones	Hosie	Chambers	Dean	Capes	Gilligan	Corbett	Wombwell
	8/10		*7,000*	*10*	8			*O'Donnell M 10*	*Buist*	*Laverick*	*Pallister*	*Fraser*	*Simpson W*	*Wield*	*Watson*	*Brown*	*O'Donnell D*	*O'Donnell M*	*Simpson C*
								Ref: F Dickenson	City's rich vein of form continued with this win over the Cathedralites, despite falling behind when Magnus O'Donnell ran onto Brown's pass to slot the ball into an open net. Fraser's handling offence brought Dean his spot-kick, before Hosie fired in off the bar from long distance.										
7	H	LEICESTER FOSSE		3	W	3-0	0-0	Gilligan 48, 58, Pollock 80og	Clay	Thickett	Tuft	Jones	Hosie	Chambers	Dean	Capes	Gilligan	Corbett	Wombwell
	15/10		9,000	*9*	10				*Smith*	*Bennett*	*Robinson*	*Morgan*	*Bannister*	*Pollock*	*Durrant*	*Blessington*	*Mounteney*	*Evenson*	*Allsopp*
								Ref: J Jamieson	City started towards the Covered End, but despite much admired play they didn't open the scoring until after the break when Gilligan headed the leather in. City's centre-forward dribbled through to double the advantage before a fierce drive by Chambers was turned in by Pollock.										
8	A	BARNSLEY		6	L	0-1	0-1		Clay	Thickett	Tuft	Jones	Hosie	Chambers	Dean	Capes	Gilligan	Corbett	Wombwell
	22/10		*4,000*	*4*	10			*Beech 42*	*Hewitson*	*Gill*	*Edwards*	*Donagher*	*Cornan*	*Oxspring*	*Birtles*	*Hellewell Alec*	*Beech*	*Heppinstall*	*Wall*
								Ref: J Sykes	Despite being reduced to nine men for the last 25 minutes, with Beech and Cornan off injured, Barnsley had no trouble in holding onto the lead given them by their centre-forward's close-in shot just before the interval. Towards the close, City rarely attacked without being caught offside.										
9	H	WEST BROM		5	W	2-1	1-0	Gilligan 15, Fisher 55	Clay	Thickett	Tuft	Jones	Hosie	Chambers	Dean	Fisher	Gilligan	Capes	Wombwell
	29/10		10,795	*11*	12			*Jack 87*	*Webb*	*Adams*	*Pennington*	*Edwards*	*Bowden*	*Randle*	*Davies*	*Jack*	*Brown*	*Lewis*	*Dorsett*
								Ref: P Harrower	City were all-round better than their opponents, who played a very ragged game. Gilligan charged down Webb's clearance for the opener; then, after the interval, he gave the pass from which Fisher scored with a low, well-directed, shot. Jack had a clear run for Albion's late consolation										
10	A	BURNLEY		4	W	3-2	1-1	Dean 5, 75p, Chambers 85	Clay	Thickett	Tuft	Jones	Gilson	Chambers	Dean	Fisher	Gilligan	Capes	Wombwell
	5/11		*3,000*	*17*	14			*Macfarlane 44, Barron 65p*	*Green*	*Dixon*	*Moffat*	*Barron*	*Walders D*	*Taylor*	*Atkinson*	*Hogan*	*Smith R*	*Macfarlane*	*Smith J*
								Ref: I Garner	City, the less impressive of two under-par sides, had the luck that enabled them to win this game. Green's misjudgement of a long distance shot by Capes allowed Dean to slip in the opener, but Macfarlane's great 15-yarder brought Burnley level. Clay had a busy time between the sticks.										

No	Venue	Opponent / Date	Att	Pos	Pts	Res	HT	Scorers, Times, Referee	1	2	3	4	5	6	7	8	9	10	11
11	H	GRIMSBY		4	W	5-0	2-0	Fisher 30, 35, Capes 65, 90, Gilligan 88	Clay	Thickett	Tuft	Jones	Gilson	Chambers	Dean	Fisher	Gilligan	Capes	Wombwell
		12/11	10,000	*9*	16				*Spendiff*	*McGregor*	*Morley*	*McDiarmid*	*Coles*	*Nelmes*	*Reynolds*	*Higgins*	*Elkins*	*Turner*	*Ross*
								Ref: G Capes	Gilligan kicked off towards the Covered End and, with City having the lions' share of the play, it was no surprise when Fisher banged in the opener. With the forwards showing their best form, the goals flowed, despite Dean missing the second half with a serious injury to his left eye.										
12	A	BLACKPOOL		4	W	4-2	2-2	Chambers 10, Capes 31, 60, Fisher 80	Clay	Thickett	Tuft	Jones	Gilson	Chambers	Wombwell	Fisher	Gilligan	Capes	Fenton
		19/11	*4,000*	*14*	18			*Scott 3, Hogg 30*	*Dorrington*	*Birket*	*Scott*	*Crewdson*	*Parkinson*	*Wolstenholme*	*Waddington*	*Morgan*	*Hogg*	*Chadwick*	*McEwan*
								Ref: J Pearson	City made good use of their chances and came through an often-trying ordeal triumphant. The Pool players paid the price of thinking the ball was going out of play when Capes turned the leather into the net early in the second half. Fisher tied up City's success when he headed in.										
13	H	DONCASTER		3	W	4-1	0-1	Jones 57, Capes 60, Wombwell 75,	Clay	Thickett	Tuft	Jones	Gilson	Chambers	Wombwell	Fisher	Gilligan	Capes	Fenton
		26/11	5,000	*18*	20			*Carnegie 2* [Gilligan 80]	*Thorpe*	*Birch*	*Davies*	*Tomkins*	*Moralee*	*Norris*	*Hyde*	*Hanson*	*Carnegie*	*Shinner*	*Law*
								Ref: J Lewis	Despite Fisher shooting wide from the penalty-spot right on the interval, City had no difficulty in winning this game in the second half. After Jones levelled matters with a capital shot at the Open End, it was easy for City. Wombwell's brilliant run and shot was the game's highlight.										
14	A	GAINSBOROUGH		4	L	1-4	1-1	Jones 40 *[Langham 75]*	Clay	Thickett	Tuft	Jones	Hosie	Chambers	Dean	Fisher	Gilligan	Capes	Wombwell
		3/12	*3,000*	*6*	20			*Foxall A 35, Foxall F 55, Twigg 60p,*	*Bagshaw*	*Ashton*	*Floyd*	*Hall*	*Greenhaigh*	*Hempshall*	*Langham*	*Milsom*	*Twigg*	*Foxall F*	*Foxall A*
								Ref: W Gilgryst	With a full side available it was expected that City would at least get a point from this encounter. The form that they showed before the interval justified hopes of something even better, but they fell to pieces thereafter. Ex-City player Billy Langham was able to complete the humiliation.										
15	H	BURTON UTD		4	W	5-0	2-0	Dean 40, 65p, Capes 45, Hosie 48, [Fisher 60]	Clay	Gilson	Tuft	Jones	Hosie	Chambers	Dean	Fisher	Gilligan	Capes	Fenton
		10/12	4,000	*17*	22				*Bromage*	*Aston C*	*Kirkland*	*Wildin*	*Evans*	*Frost*	*Beddow*	*Gould*	*Hargreaves F*	*Moore*	*King*
								Ref: F Heath	Burton offered little in what was an easy win for City after Dean's low shot found the net, in off an upright. Capes fired in the second; then after the interval Dean's penalty, following a foul by Kirkland, tied up a convincing success. On three occasions City had goals disallowed.										
16	A	LIVERPOOL		4	L	1-3	1-2	Hosie 40	Clay	Gilson	Tuft	Jones	Hosie	Chambers	Dean	Wombwell	Gilligan	Fisher	Fenton
		17/12	*12,000*	*2*	22			*Raisbeck 3, Parkinson 15, 85*	*Doig*	*Murray*	*Dunlop*	*Parry*	*Raisbeck*	*Fleming*	*Goddard*	*Robinson*	*Parkinson*	*Raybould*	*Cox*
								Ref: T Kirkham	City's hopes were jolted when Raisbeck netted Liverpool's early opener with a long-distance oblique drive. Parkinson then doubled the Pool's advantage when Clay misjudged his shot. A corner led to Hosie getting City back into the game, but they were unable to break through again.										
17	H	BURSLEM PT VALE		4	W	4-2	2-1	Hosie 15, Jones 25, Corbett 65,	Clay	Dean	Tuft	Jones	Gilson	Hosie	Wombwell	Fisher	Gilligan	Corbett	Fenton
		24/12	6,000	*15*	24			*Allman 30, 86* [Dean 70p]	*Cotton*	*Hamilton*	*Cope*	*Whittingham*	*Holyhead*	*Croxton*	*Mountford*	*Price*	*Allman*	*Capes*	*Eardley*
								Ref: P Harrower	Hosie's terrific drive, which carried the keeper over the line, put City in front. Jones doubled the advantage with a low shot before Allman fired in Vale's response. Cope's handling offence brought the penalty; then Allman beat Clay from long distance to produce a misleading score-line.										
18	A	GLOSSOP		4	W	1-0	0-0	Gilligan 51	Clay	Dean	Tuft	Jones	Hosie	**Spear**	Wombwell	Fisher	Gilligan	Corbett	Fenton
		27/12	*1,500*	*16*	26				*Davies*	*Synott*	*Orr*	*Phillips*	*Boden*	*Brown*	*Gall*	*Claugh*	*Goodall*	*Lawrence*	*Irvine*
								Ref: W Weeks	City gave the home custodian a hot time early on, but were unable to beat him before the interval. In the second half Gilligan broke through to register with a rasper, but thereafter Davies regained his previously unbeatable form to deny City the much greater victory their play deserved.										
19	A	BOLTON		4	L	1-3	1-2	Gilligan 6	Clay	Dean	Tuft	Jones	Hosie	Spear	Wombwell	Fisher	Gilligan	Corbett	Fenton
		31/12	*16,000*	*1*	26			*Shepherd 30, 33, Marsh 85*	*Davies*	*Eccles*	*Struthers*	*Clifford*	*Greenhaigh*	*Boyd*	*Stokes*	*Marsh*	*Shepherd*	*White*	*Taylor A*
								Ref: J Mason	With the recent extensions at Burnden Park, there was plenty of room for the City fans who travelled to the game in the two 'special' trains. Gilligan obtained the early opener from Wombwell's corner, but Shepherd fired in a double to put the Trotters in front before the interval.										
20	H	MANCHESTER U		4	D	1-1	1-1	Fisher 13	Clay	Gilson	Tuft	Jones	Hosie	Capes	Dean	Fisher	Gilligan	Corbett	Wombwell
		7/1	18,000	*2*	28			*Arkesden 40*	*Moger*	*Bonthron*	*Blackstock*	*Downie*	*Roberts*	*Bell*	*Schofield*	*Grassam*	*Peddie*	*Arkesden*	*Williams*
			(£335)					Ref: J Adams	Despite Fisher putting City in front with a screw shot, the homesters often proved over eager in this game. United, hit by injuries to Roberts and Peddie, which necessitated them going off for treatment, played like terriers and thoroughly deserved the point earned by Arkesden's shot.										
21	H	CHESTERFIELD		4	W	2-1	1-0	Fisher 5, Darke 70	Clay	Thickett	**Hargett G**	Jones	Spear	Capes	Wombwell	Fisher	Gilligan	**Darke**	Fenton
		21/1	5,000	*7*	30			*Evans 65*	*Hardy*	*Marples*	*Ray*	*Tye*	*Banner*	*Thacker*	*Tomlinson*	*Newton*	*Taylor*	*Munday*	*Evans*
								Ref: F Brunt *(Peter Chambers' Benefit)*	City squandered many chances in this game that was set apart for their Captain's benefit. Fine passing between Gilligan and Fisher led to the latter notching the opener with a low shot. An oblique drive brought Chesterfield level, but from a rebound Darke was able to grab the winner.										

No	Date		Att	Pos	Pt	F-A	H-T	Scorers, Times, and Referees	1	2	3	4	5	6	7	8	9	10	11
22	A	BRADFORD CITY		4	W	3-2	0-1	Gilligan 70, Fisher 80, Dean 85p	Clay	Thickett	Tuft	Jones	Spear	Capes	Dean	Fisher	Gilligan	Corbett	Fenton
	28/1		*14,000*	*14*	32			*McGeachen 45, Jefferson 90*	*Mearns*	*Wilson W*	*Halliday*	*Millar*	*Robinson*	*McLean*	*Jefferson*	*McGeachan*	*Wilson D*	*McMillan*	*Conlin*
								Ref: J Lewis	Fisher is at the heart of City's late show at Valley Parade, after Gilligan rushed in and scored when Mearns failed to fly-kick the ball away. He finished his lengthy run by shooting City into the lead, then was brought down by McLean for Dean to register from the subsequent penalty.										
23	A	LEICESTER FOSSE		4	L	1-2	1-1	Gilson 32	Clay	Hargett A	Tuft	Spear	Gilson	Capes	Wombwell	Fenton	Corbett	Fisher	Turner
	11/2		*6,000*	*13*	32			*Durrant 40, Mounteney 69p*	*Smith*	*Bennett*	*Robinson*	*Pollock*	*Bannister*	*Collins*	*Durrant*	*Blessington*	*Evenson*	*Mounteney*	*Allsopp*
								Ref: J Lewis	In view of their forthcoming cup-tie, City fielded a weakened line-up – that included ex-Nottingham Forest amateur Turner – against the Fosse. After Gilson's magnificent long-distance drive put City in front, they were undone by Durrant's hot-shot and Mounteney's fierce spot-kick.										
24	A	WEST BROM		4	D	0-0	0-0		Clay	Gilson	Tuft	Jones	Hosie	Price	Fenton	Fisher	Gilligan	Capes	Wombwell
	25/2		*4,172*	*10*	33				*Cooke*	*Kifford*	*Adams*	*Randle*	*Pheasant*	*Manners*	*Bradley*	*Bell*	*Aston*	*Jack*	*Lewis*
								Ref: J Mason	Football interest is at a low ebb at West Bromwich just now, and consequently there was a very poor gate at the Hawthorns. Those that stayed away missed an entertaining game, despite the goalless scoreline. Clay had to be at his best as the Albion gave their best display for some time.										
25	H	BURNLEY		4	D	0-0	0-0		Clay	Gilson	Tuft	Jones	Hosie	Price	Dean	Fisher	Corbett	Capes	Wombwell
	4/3		4,000	*9*	34				*Green*	*Dixon*	*Moffat*	*Barron*	*Walders D*	*Taylor*	*Marshall*	*Hogan*	*Macfarlane*	*Ross*	*Walders J*
								Ref: H Ward	The highlight of this poor game at a wet Ashton Gate was Fisher's run half the length of the field, beating all opponents, before passing to Corbett, who fired just wide of a post. City had the chances to have won this game easily, but after the break became bogged down in the mud.										
26	A	GRIMSBY		4	L	0-4	0-1		Clay	Thickett	Tuft	Jones	Gilson	Chambers	Dean	Fisher	Corbett	Capes	Wombwell
	11/3		*4,000*	*13*	34			*Reynolds 44, Butler 65, 80, Baker 75*	*Spendiff*	*Morley*	*McConnell J*	*McGregor*	*McDiarmid*	*Nelmes*	*Reynolds*	*Baker*	*Butler*	*Higgins*	*Ross*
								Ref: G Capes	It wasn't expected that City would lose this game, but lose it they did, and heavily at that. Despite the advantage of a strong wind before the interval, City fell behind when a cross from Reynolds went into the net. Give and take play characterised the early part of the second half.										
27	H	BLACKPOOL		4	W	2-0	1-0	Capes 5, Fisher 75	Clay	Tuft	Gilson	Jones	Spear	Chambers	Dean	Fisher	Corbett	Capes	Fenton
	18/3		7,000	*10*	36				*Hull*	*Birket*	*Scott*	*Crewdson*	*Parkinson*	*Wolstenholme*	*Kearns*	*Hogg*	*Morgan*	*Chadwick*	*Waddington*
								Ref: J Adams	A fast and exciting game in which the football was bright from the start until the finish. Early on, Fisher passed for Capes to bang in City's opener, but the visitors were not dismayed and responded with determination. After the break, Fisher fired into the net in no uncertain fashion.										
28	A	DONCASTER		4	W	2-0	1-0	Fenton 15, Dean 80p	Clay	Gilson	Tuft	Jones	Spear	Hosie	Dean	Fisher	Gilligan	Capes	Fenton
	25/3		*1,600*	*18*	38				*Thorpe*	*Burn*	*Davies*	*Wright*	*Moralee*	*Gordon*	*Hyde*	*Magee*	*Norris*	*McIntyre*	*Bradley*
								Ref: J Lewis	With Doncaster rooted at the bottom of the table with just six points, it was expected that City would have done better than this. Against dogged opponents, there was no doubting their superiority however, even if it did take a late penalty to make sure they claimed both points.										
29	H	BARNSLEY		4	W	3-0	1-0	Gilligan 2, Fisher 60, 85	Clay	Gilson	Tuft	Jones	Spear	Hosie	Dean	Fisher	Gilligan	Capes	Fenton
	29/3		3,000	*8*	40				*Rounds*	*Hay*	*Edwards*	*McGuire*	*Donagher*	*Oxspring*	*Brooks*	*Beech*	*Jones*	*Cornan*	*Wall*
								Ref: J Sykes	City won this game with something to spare after taking an early lead when Gilligan put away a rebound off the bar from Hosie's fine shot. Fisher was the star in the second half, netting with low drive, then notching a fine individual goal before having another effort ruled offside.										
30	H	GAINSBOROUGH		4	D	1-1	1-1	Dean 7	Clay	Hargett G	Tuft	Jones	Spear	Hosie	Dean	Fisher	Gilligan	Darke	Fenton
	1/4		6,000	*5*	41			*Twigg 30*	*Bagshaw*	*Thompson*	*Floyd*	*Westwood*	*Jenkinson*	*Hall G*	*Langham*	*Jacklin*	*Milsom*	*Twigg*	*Foxall F*
								Ref: W Gilgryst	After Jones won the toss and elected to play towards the Entrance End, City had the better of the first half. It was a different story following the break, though, as the visitors did much pressing. Clay brought off a couple of fortunate saves near the finish to preserve a point for City.										
31	A	BURTON UTD		4	L	0-2	0-2		Clay	Hargett G	Tuft	Jones	Spear	Chambers	Stolz	Fisher	Gilligan	Capes	Fenton
	8/4		*2,000*	*17*	41			*Mann 25, Gould 35*	*Bromage*	*Aston C*	*Kirkland*	*Evans*	*Mann*	*Wildin*	*Hargreaves F*	*Hargreaves W*	*Aston A*	*Gould*	*King*
								Ref: F Heath	City were not strongly represented and paid the price by going down to their first ever defeat at Peel Croft. Mann headed in United's opener, and this was soon followed by another from the foot of Gould. After the break, City's defence was sorely tested, but wasn't breached again.										

No	Venue	Opponent	Att	Pos	Pts	Res	HT	Scorers	1	2	3	4	5	6	7	8	9	10	11
32	H	LIVERPOOL		4	L	0-1	0-0		Clay	Tuft	Dean	Jones	Hosie	Chambers	**Bennett**	Fisher	Gilligan	Capes	Fenton
	15/4		10,000	*7*	41			*Cox 80*	*Doig*	*Chorlton*	*Dunlop*	*Parry*	*Raisbeck*	*Fleming*	*Hewitt*	*Robinson*	*Parkinson*	*Raybould*	*Cox*
								Ref: F Kirkham	The leaders didn't particularly impress in this keen game at Ashton Gate, where City's poor finishing let them off the hook. Bennett, City's new outside-right from Sheffield United, impressed the fans with some brilliant play, but he couldn't prevent Cox firing in Pool's late winner.										
33	A	BURSLEM PT VALE		4	L	2-3	2-2	Fisher 20, Gilligan 40	Clay	Dean	Tuft	Jones	Spear	Chambers	Bennett	Fisher	Gilligan	Capes	Fenton
	22/4		*2,000*	*16*	41			*Allman 5, Capes 35, Carter 70*	*Box*	*Cope*	*Hamilton*	*Croxton*	*Holyhead*	*Whittingham*	*Carter*	*Price*	*Allman*	*Capes*	*Horrocks*
								Ref: H Ward	City experienced their usual defeat on the Cobridge enclosure. They fell behind early on, when Allman slammed the ball past Clay, but a beauty from Fisher brought City level, before Capes headed Vale back in front. Carter fired in Vale's winning goal through a forest of legs.										
34	H	LINCOLN		4	W	2-0	0-0	Fisher 50, Darke 70	Clay	Capes	Tuft	Spear	Gilligan	Price	Bennett	Fisher	Darke	**Wadley**	Fenton
	25/4		4,000	*9*	43				*Buist*	*Laverick*	*Simpson W*	*Fraser*	*Hood*	*Blow*	*Watson*	*O'Donnell D*	*Martin*	*Sharp*	*Simpson C*
		Home	Away					Ref: F Dickenson	Dull and damp weather prevailed at Ashton Gate when City started play from the Park End. After a keen first half, a scramble around the visitors' goalkeeper lead to Fisher netting the opener, before Darke rushed up with a fine effort to make sure of City taking both points.										
	Ave	7,694	6,251																

FRIENDLIES

No	Venue	Opponent	Att	Res	Score	HT	Scorers	1	2	3	4	5	6	7	8	9	10	11
1	A	WLCH ARSENAL		L	2-3	2-2	Capes 25, Gilligan 40	Clay	**Thickett**	Tuft	Jones	Hosie	Chambers	Dean	Corbett	**Gilligan**	Capes	Wombwell
	1/9		*6,000*				*Satterthwaite 3, 35p, Coleman 90*	*Ashcroft*	*Gray*	*Cross*	*Bigden*	*Theobald*	*McEachrane*	*Briercliffe*	*Coleman*	*Crowe*	*Hunter*	*Satterthwaite*
							Ref: A Millward	As the normal season starter versus the Rovers has been postponed until after the opening of the new ground, City accepted a handsome guarantee to visit Arsenal. Satterthwaite put away a lovely goal when Crowe's effort hit the crossbar, but Capes levelled with an artistic shot.										
2	H	BRISTOL ROV		W	4-2	2-2	Gilligan 42, Dean 44p, Corbett 80, [Capes 90]	Clay	Thickett	Tuft	Jones	Hosie	Chambers	Dean	Corbett	Gilligan	Capes	Wombwell
	5/9		4,000				*Griffiths 12, Wilson 30*	*Cartlidge*	*Dunn*	*Wassell*	*Tait*	*Jarvie*	*Hales*	*Clark*	*Lewis*	*Beats*	*Wilson*	*Smith*
							Ref: A Hines	Even though the weather was fine, there were not more than 4,000 present for this derby clash. Gilligan inspired City's fight-back when, from a nicely taken corner-kick, he placed the ball beyond the reach of Cartlidge. Thickett's poor display wasn't to the liking of the City fans.										
3	H	OXFORD UNIV		W	6-1	3-1	Corbett 2, 5, Rowlands 43, 80, 89, [Fisher 70]	Demmery	Thickett	Tuft	**Spear**	Gilson	Capes	Dean	Fisher	**Rowlands**	Corbett	Fenton
	9/11		300				*Goodliffe 40*	*Rogers R*	*Branston T*	*Snell JE*	*Craig JD*	*Scothern AE*	*Curwen WH*	*B-Melville JE*	*Foster GN*	*Coleby AT*	*Goodliffe GV*	*Guy EM*
							Ref: A Farrant	The wind and rain spoilt the possibility of an interesting contest as the muddy conditions handicapped the much lighter visitors. Corbett gave his best display of the season as he showed that he hasn't completely lost form. He opened the scoring with a low shot and soon added another.										
4	A	BRISTOL ROV		L	2-5	1-2	Corbett 10, Darke 50	Demmery	Dean	Hargett G	Spear	**Rendall**	Price	**Stolz**	Fisher	Darke	Corbett	Wombwell
	26/12		*14,000*				*Wilson 20, Lewis 35, 60, 80, Beats 78*	*Cartlidge*	*Dunn*	*Hales*	*Tait*	*Appleby*	*Jarvie*	*Wilson*	*Lewis*	*Beats*	*Griffiths*	*Smith*
							Ref: A Neale	After Beats had his oblique shot ruled offside, Corbett put City in front with a shot that went in off the underside of the bar. Wilson headed the Rovers level, then Lewis failed with a spot-kick, before finding the net from long distance. For most of the second half City were outplayed.										
5	A	ABERDARE		W	1-0	1-0	Fisher 42	Clay	Tuft	**Cottle**	Spear	Capes	Price	Bennett	Fisher	Darke	Wadley	Fenton
	27/4		*500*					*Seward*	*Golding*	*Jones*	*Reed*	*Wedlock*	*Shenton*	*McKiernan*	*Ingham*	*Grant*	*Lloyd P*	*Roberts*
							Ref: Mr Rowlands	Thanks to Fisher kicking the ball in when Darke's hot-shot was only partially cleared, City notched up a narrow win against an Aberdare side with five Bristolians in their ranks. The fact that Aberdare lost the Welsh Cup final 0-3 on Monday served to keep the size of the crowd down.										
6	H	CORINTHIANS		L	0-1	0-1		Clay	Tuft	Cottle	Spear	Darke	Capes	**Turner AD**	Bennett	Fisher	**Lee**	Fenton
	29/4		2,000				*Vassall 40*	*Day HP*	*Wither'gt'n JG*	*Timmis WV*	*Norris O*	*Morg'-Ow'n M*	*Vicars H*	*Corbett B*	*Vassall G*	*McIver CD*	*Birks AH*	*Wright E*
							Ref: A Farrant	The amateurs, who arrived with but one victory on their South-West tour, were able double their success rate as a result of Vassall's shot on the run. The play fluctuated in a remarkable manner, but overall the famous Corinthians were deserving of their success over depleted City.										

FA Cup/Glos Cup					F-A	H-T	Scorers, Times, and Referees	1	2	3	4	5	6	7	8	9	10	11
IN	H	BLACKPOOL	4	W	2-1	2-1	Jones 15, Gilligan 40	Clay	Dean	Tuft	Jones	Hosie	Capes	Wombwell	Fisher	Gilligan	Corbett	Fenton
	14/1	8,607 *12*					*Morgan 10*	*Hull*	*Birket*	*Scott*	*Threlfall*	*Parkinson*	*Wolstenholme*	*Cook*	*Waddington*	*Morgan*	*Chadwick*	*McEwan*
		(£214)					Ref: A Cooknell	Stung by the early reverse when Morgan's fierce long-distance drive found the net, Jones quickly banged in City's leveller. Gilligan's fine low shot put City in front just before the interval, a lead which they were decidedly lucky to hang onto until the finish, and so enter the first round.										
1	A	WLCH ARSENAL	4	D	0-0	0-0		Clay	Thickett	Tuft	Jones	Hosie	Chambers	Dean	Fisher	Gilligan	Capes	Wombwell
	4/2	*26,197* *1:10*						*Ashcroft*	*Gray*	*Jackson*	*Dick*	*Sands*	*McEachrane*	*Briercliffe*	*Coleman*	*Gooing*	*Satterthwaite*	*Templeton*
		(£718)					Ref: J Brodie	A typical cup-tie on the awkwardly situated Manor Ground, where Arsenal, aided by a strong wind, had the best of things in the first half. After the break, however, it was City who looked the more likely winners, and they could have had a penalty when Dick fouled Gilligan in the box.										
R	H	WLCH ARSENAL	4	W	1-0	0-0	Dean 53	Clay	Thickett	Tuft	Jones	Hosie	Chambers	Dean	Fisher	Gilligan	Capes	Wombwell
	8/2	11,176 *1:10*						*Ashcroft*	*Gray*	*Jackson*	*Dick*	*Sands*	*McEachrane*	*Briercliffe*	*Coleman*	*Watson*	*Satterthwaite*	*Templeton*
		(£298.19.3)					Ref: J Howcroft	City, playing in green, beat Woolwich handsomely in this replay at Ashton Gate. For all but the opening 20 minutes, City had the full measure of their opponents and fully deserved the victory earned by Dean's hot shot, even though Coleman had an effort disallowed for offside.										
2	H	PRESTON	4	D	0-0	0-0		Clay	Thickett	Tuft	Jones	Gilson	Chambers	Dean	Fisher	Gilligan	Capes	Wombwell
	18/2	19,371 *1:11*						*McBride*	*Derbyshire*	*Rodway*	*McLean*	*Hunter*	*Lyon*	*Bond*	*Brown*	*Smith P*	*Bell*	*Bourne*
		(£742)					Ref: A Barker	A thrice-taken penalty early in the second half suggests that City were a trifle fortunate to earn a replay. Following Thickett's tackle on Smith, the spot-kick was saved after Bond had twice beaten Clay. Thereafter, City had the chances to have won this somewhat disappointing clash.										
R	A	PRESTON	4	L	0-1	0-0		Clay	Thickett	Tuft	Jones	Gilson	Chambers	Dean	Fisher	Gilligan	Capes	Wombwell
	23/2	*15,000* *1:11*					*Bourne 90*	*McBride*	*Derbyshire*	*Rodway*	*McLean*	*Hunter*	*Lyon*	*Bond*	*Wilcox*	*Smith P*	*Bell*	*Bourne*
		(£466)					Ref: A Barker	After training at Southport, City were often the better side in this rousing replay. Cruelly, they bowed out at the very last gasp when, from a scrimmage, Bourne netted the only goal. Even the watching League President, Mr Bentley, said 'the result wasn't what it should have been'.										
SF	H	BRISTOL EAST	4	W	5-1	1-1	Hosie 30, Gilligan 51, 75, Fisher 55, [Dean 89]	Clay	Tuft	Hargett G	Jones	Hosie	Chambers	Dean	Fisher	Gilligan	Capes	Fenton
GC	3/4	300 *WL:5*					*Palmer 44*	*Frankham*	*Carter*	*Boulton*	*Smart*	*Rooke W*	*Hendy*	*Sweet*	*Rooke J*	*McKay*	*Palmer*	*Tout*
							Ref: A Farrant	Despite a lively start, it wasn't until the half-hour mark that Hosie put City in front with a long dropping shot. Palmer poked in East's equaliser from a scrimmage shortly before half-time, but soon after the break Gilligan's neat goal, and a fine high shot by Fisher, put City firmly on top.										
F	A	BRISTOL ROV	4	D	2-2	2-1	Capes 1, Fenton 3	Clay	Dean	Tuft	Jones	Spear	Chambers	Stolz	Fisher	Gilligan	Capes	Fenton
GC	24/4	*10,610* *SL:1*					*Beats 8, Smith 53*	*Cartlidge*	*Dunn*	*Pudan*	*Tait*	*Appleby*	*Jarvie*	*Clark*	*Lewis*	*Beats*	*Smith*	*Dunkley*
		(£306.9.0)					Ref: H Ward	City started as though they meant to go for a record score, with shots from Capes and Fenton registering almost before play had started. Beats got Rovers back into the contest with a grounder that beat Clay; then, following the interval, Smith's fine shot ensured there would be a replay.										
R	H	BRISTOL ROV	4	L	1-3	1-1	Fisher 32	Clay	Thickett	Tuft	Spear	Hosie	Chambers	Stolz	Fisher	Capes	Wadley	Fenton
GC	28/4	3,916 *SL:1*					*Beats 35, Dunkley 70, Lewis 75*	*Cartlidge*	*Dunn*	*Pudan*	*Tait*	*Appleby*	*Jarvie*	*Clark*	*Lewis*	*Beats*	*Smith*	*Dunkley*
		(£110.0.10)					Ref: J Howcroft	Injury-hit City, who lost Chambers early in the second half, were down to nine men when Hosie had to go off shortly after Lewis headed in for Rovers. City made a good start with Fisher's headed opener but, after Beats blasted in an equaliser, Dunkley fired the Rovers into the lead.										

		Home						Away					
		P	W	D	L	F	A	W	D	L	F	A	Pts
1	Liverpool	34	14	3	0	60	12	13	1	3	33	13	58
2	Bolton Wndrs	34	15	0	2	53	16	12	2	3	34	16	56
3	Manchester U	34	16	0	1	60	10	8	5	4	21	20	53
4	BRISTOL C	34	12	3	2	40	12	7	1	9	26	33	42
5	Chesterfield	34	9	6	2	26	11	5	5	7	18	24	39
6	Gainsboro' T	34	11	4	2	32	15	3	4	10	29	43	36
7	Barnsley	34	11	4	2	29	13	3	1	13	9	43	33
8	Bradford City	34	8	5	4	31	20	4	3	10	14	29	32
9	Lincoln City	34	9	4	4	31	16	3	3	11	11	24	31
10	West Brom	34	8	2	7	28	20	5	2	10	28	28	30
11	Burnley	34	10	1	6	31	21	2	5	10	12	31	30
12	Glossop	34	7	5	5	23	14	3	5	9	14	32	30
13	Grimsby T	34	9	3	5	22	14	2	5	10	11	32	30
14	Leicester Fos'	34	8	3	6	30	25	3	4	10	10	30	29
15	Blackpool	34	8	5	4	26	15	1	5	11	10	33	28
16	Burslem Pt V	34	7	4	6	28	25	3	3	11	19	47	27
17	Burton United	34	7	2	8	20	29	1	2	14	10	55	20
18	Doncaster R	34	3	2	12	12	32	0	0	17	11	49	8
		612	172	56	78	582	320	78	56	172	320	582	612

Odds & ends

Double wins: (6) Glossop, Chesterfield, Bradford City, Lincoln City, Blackpool, Doncaster Rovers.
Double losses: (2) Bolton Wanderers, Liverpool.

Won from behind: Lincoln (a), Blackpool (a), Doncaster (h), Brad C (a).
Lost from in front: Manchester U (a), Bolton (a), Leicester (a).

High spots: Beating Woolwich Arsenal in the FA Cup.
The playing of an International Trial at 'Ashton Gate' on 13 February when the South lost 1-3 against the North.

Low spots: The official opening of the new 'Ashton Gate' being marred by two late goals that snatched victory from City's grasp.
Losing 1-4 on the 'Bank Street' ground, Clayton, on 10 September.
The heavy 4-0 defeat at Grimsby on 11 March.
Going out of the FA Cup in a replay at Preston.
Losing 1-3 to Bristol Rovers in the Gloucestershire Cup final on 28 April.

Player of the Year: Sammy Gilligan.
Ever-presents: (1) Harry Clay.
Hat-tricks: (0).
Leading scorer: Overall: Sammy Gilligan (19). League: Gilligan (14).

Pre-Season Trial Match:
27 Aug Probables 9(2) Possibles 0 Ref: A Found
5,000 Corbett 30, Chambers 32, Jones 50, Gilligan 51, 65, 75, Capes 70, 80, Hosie 89

AGM (Temperance Hall, East Street, Bedminster, 5 July 1905):
Profit £71.5s.0d. Season Ticket Sales £272.2s.11d.

	Appearances			Goals			
	Lge	Cup	Fr	Lge	Cup	Fr	Tot
Bennett, Walter	**3**		2				
Capes, Arthur	**29**	8	5	**7**	1	2	**10**
Chambers, Peter	**21**	7	2	**2**			**2**
Clay, Harry	**34**	8	4				
Corbett, Fred	**16**	1	4	**1**		4	**5**
Cottle, Joe			2				
Darke, Tom	**3**		3	**2**		1	**3**
Dean, Alf	**27**	7	4	**12**	2	1	**15**
Demmery, Bill			2				
Fenton, Freddie	**21**	4	3	**1**	1		**2**
Fisher, Albert	**26**	8	4	**13**	2	2	**17**
Gilligan, Sammy	**30**	7	2	**14**	3	2	**19**
Gilson, Alf	**18**	2	1	**1**			**1**
Hargett, Andrew	**1**						
Hargett, George	**3**	1	1				
Hosie, Jim	**21**	5	2	**5**	1		**6**
Jones, Billy	**32**	7	2	**3**	1		**4**
Lee			1				
Price, Alf	**3**		2				
Rendall			1				
Rowlands, WH			1			3	**3**
Spear, Arthur	**12**	2	4				
Stolz, Bill	**1**	2	1				
Thickett, Harry	**14**	5	3				
Tuft, Billy	**33**	8	5				
Turner, Arthur	**1**		1				
Wadley, HE	**1**	1	1				
Wombwell, Dickie	**24**	5	3	**3**			**3**
Opponents og				**2**			**2**
28 players used	**374**	**88**	**66**	**66**	**11**	**15**	**92**

No	Date		Att	Pos	Pt	F-A	H-T	Scorers, Times, and Referees	1	2	3	4	5	6	7	8	9	10	11
1	A	MANCHESTER U			L	1-5	0-2	Maxwell 89	Clay	**Annan**	Tuft	Jones	Wedlock	Chambers	Bennett	**Maxwell**	Gilligan	**Burton**	Fenton
	2/9		25,000					Picken 25, 75, Sagar 35, 70, [Beddow 80]	Moger	Bonthron	Blackstock	Downie	Roberts	Bell	Beddow	Picken	Sagar	Peddie	Arkesden
								Ref: A Green	Despite the score, City are far from being outplayed at Clayton, but they didn't have the best of luck. Their captain, Chambers, was twice knocked out in the first half, and a knee-injury prevented him returning after the break. Sagar's brilliant long-range shot put United two up.										
2	H	GLOSSOP			W	2-1	1-0	Maxwell 15, Bennett 55	Clay	Annan	Tuft	Jones	Wedlock	Spear	Bennett	Maxwell	Gilligan	Burton	Fenton
	9/9		4,000		2			Ross 65	Davis	Kier	Orr	Phillips	McNab	Mair	Callaghan	Whitehouse	Cameron	Chadwick	Ross
								Ref: N Whittaker	In the pouring rain, Glossop, clad in black and white hoops, elected to kick towards the Club House, but it was City who took an early lead. Maxwell raced in to find the net after Davis was only able to scoop the ball out. Bennett notched the second from Fenton's well-placed corner.										
3	A	STOCKPORT		9	W	3-2	2-1	Maxwell 10, Bennett 22, 75	Clay	Annan	Tuft	Jones	Wedlock	Spear	Bennett	Maxwell	Gilligan	Burton	Fenton
	16/9		5,400	11	4			Manson 7, Bardsley 65	Pemble	Heywood	Waters	Suart	Hall	Hancock	Scofield	Crump	Manson	Dodd G	Bardsley
								Ref: J Ibbotson	In brilliant weather at Edgeley Park, City took Stockport's unbeaten record after Annan's slip had allowed Manson to fire in the homesters' brilliant opener. City soon levelled, however, as Maxwell was on hand to head the ball in when Fenton's shot rebounded off the crossbar.										
4	H	BRADFORD CITY		3	W	1-0	0-0	Gilligan 65	Clay	Annan	Tuft	Jones	Wedlock	Spear	Bennett	Maxwell	Gilligan	Burton	Fenton
	20/9		5,000	2	6				Garvey	Easton	Halliday	Robinson	O'Rourke	Millar	Clarke	McGeachan	Smith	McMillan	Conlin
								Ref: F Kirkham	Gilligan consigned the visitors to their first defeat of the season by putting the ball away, following Garvey's failure to hold Bennett's shot. A deserved success, as City dominated after the break, though they were perhaps fortunate that Bradford had a goal disallowed in the last minute.										
5	H	BLACKPOOL		2	W	2-1	1-0	Bennett 15p, Burton 88	Clay	Annan	Tuft	Jones	Wedlock	Spear	Bennett	Maxwell	Gilligan	Burton	Fenton
	23/9		9,000	9	8			Bennett 89	Hull	Birket	Scott	Threlfall	Parkinson	Raisbeck	Gow	Connor	Hancock	Bennett	Bate
			(£197.10.0)					Ref: G Capes	The City players wore crepe armlets in respect for AE Denby, one of the club's founders, who died during the week. City attacked the entrance goal at the start, and took the lead from the spot following a handling offence. Tuft's knee injury had City down to ten men for the second half.										
6	A	BRADFORD CITY		2	W	2-1	1-1	Gilligan 36, Bennett 80	Clay	Annan	**Cottle**	Jones	Wedlock	**Hanlin**	Bennett	Maxwell	Gilligan	Burton	Fenton
	30/9		16,000	4	10			McMillan 30p	Garvey	Easton	Halliday	Robinson	O'Rourke	Millar	Clarke	McGeachan	Forrest	McMillan	Conlin
								Ref: J Mason	McMillan put Bradford ahead from the spot following Cottle's handball, but three minutes later he missed with another penalty after Jones had brought him down. Gilligan screwed in City's equaliser; then, after the break, Fenton's subtle pass allowed Bennett to notch the late winner.										
7	H	WEST BROM		2	W	1-0	0-0	Gilligan 60	Clay	Annan	Cottle	Jones	Wedlock	Spear	Bennett	Maxwell	Gilligan	Burton	Fenton
	7/10		10,000	11	12				Stringer	Young	Pennington	Heywood T	Pheasant	Randle	Haycock	Simmons	Shinton	Heywood A	Perkins
								Ref: J Bailey	Good work by Maxwell set up the chance for Gilligan to beat Stringer from close in. City were fortunate that Wedlock was on top of his form early on as the Baggies applied the pressure, but after the break City responded in full measure in this incident filled, rushing, bustling game.										
8	A	LEICESTER FOSSE		1	W	2-1	1-1	Bennett 40p, 88	Clay	Annan	Cottle	Jones	Wedlock	Spear	Bennett	Maxwell	Gilligan	Burton	Fenton
	14/10		7,000	13	14			Hubbard 35	Smith	Oakes	Ashby	Trueman	Bannister	Morgan	Hodgkinson	Moody	Hubbard	Blessington	Durrant
								Ref: T Kirkham	The City were the first to be aggressive, but the Fosse took the lead when Hubbard slipped past Cottle to deposit the ball in the net. Fortunately Bennett was able to level from the spot, before firing in a late winner that took City to the top of the League with the best record in the country.										
9	H	HULL		1	W	2-1	1-1	Bennett 40, Maxwell 60	Clay	Annan	Cottle	Jones	Wedlock	Chambers	Bennett	**Ingham**	Maxwell	Burton	Fenton
	21/10		10,000	7	16			Smith 8	Spendiff	Langley	Jones	Browell	Robinson	Gordon	Simmon	Wilson	Smith Joe	Howe	Raisbeck
			(£240)					Ref: F Gardner	Smith soon put the home fans out of sorts when he netted from a scrimmage. Fortunately, City equalised when the referee ruled that Bennett's corner had been deflected in off one of the backs. Maxwell needed two attempts at Bennett's centre before being able to put away the winner.										
10	A	LINCOLN		2	W	3-0	1-0	Bennett 20, 83p, Maxwell 86	Clay	Annan	Cottle	Jones	Wedlock	Chambers	Bennett	Maxwell	Gilligan	Burton	**Hilton**
	28/10		3,000	18	18				Buist	Laverick	Simpson W	Fraser	Hood	Blow	Watson	Dixon	Martin	O'Donnell M	Simpson C
								Ref: F Bye	Despite the loss of the injured Laverick early in the second half, Lincoln gave City a hard game. Bennett's fast drive gave City the advantage; then, near the finish, he increased the score from the spot. Maxwell put through from the rebound when Hilton hit the post with a terrific shot.										

No	Venue	Opponent	Pos	Res	F-A	H-T	Scorers, Times, and Referees	1	2	3	4	5	6	7	8	9	10	11
11	H	CHESTERFIELD	2	W	3-1	1-0	Maxwell 20, 65, Bennett 50	Clay	Annan	Cottle	Jones	Wedlock	Chambers	Bennett	Maxwell	Gilligan	Burton	Hilton
	4/11	10,000	*9*	20			*Lunn 51*	*Cope*	*Marples*	*Baker*	*Haig*	*Banner*	*Thacker*	*Dyal*	*Lunn*	*Taylor*	*Munday*	*Ball*
							Ref: F Gardner	City gave one of their best displays for sometime as they chalked up their tenth successive victory. Maxwell cleverly beat Cope for the opener; then, after the break, Bennett's magnificent shot doubled the advantage. Lunn responded immediately, but Maxwell made sure of City's win.										
12	A	BURSLEM PT VALE	1	W	1-0	0-0	Maxwell 80	Clay	Annan	Cottle	Jones	Wedlock	Chambers	Bennett	Maxwell	Gilligan	Burton	Hilton
	11/11	*3,000*	*14*	22				*Box*	*Cope*	*Hamilton*	*Holyhead*	*Boullimier*	*Bradbury*	*Carter*	*Price*	*Mountford*	*Capes*	*Horrocks*
							Ref: A Sutcliffe	City confounded their fears by achieving their first ever win on their unlucky ground at Cobridge. The defences on both sides held the upper hand throughout this contest, but City made the breakthrough when Maxell gained possession close in and gave Box no chance with his shot.										
13	H	BARNSLEY	1	W	3-0	1-0	Wedlock 10, Hay 46og, Maxwell 80	Clay	Annan	Cottle	Jones	Wedlock	Chambers	Bennett	Maxwell	Gilligan	Burton	Hilton
	18/11	10,000	*13*	24				*Thorpe*	*Hay*	*Stacey*	*Robertson*	*Donagher*	*Oxspring*	*Ryalls*	*Owen*	*Hellew'll Alec*	*Bell*	*Wall*
							Ref: J Bailey	After Wedlock ended his fine dribble with a magnificent low shot which completely beat Thorpe, the City were grateful for the boot of Hay, who diverted Maxwell's off-target effort into his own net. Maxwell eventually registered when putting away a rebound from Burton's shot.										
14	A	CLAPTON ORIENT	1	W	2-0	2-0	Maxwell 10, Bennett 40p	Clay	Annan	Cottle	Jones	Wedlock	Chambers	Bennett	Maxwell	Gilligan	Burton	Hilton
	25/11	*7,000*	*20*	26				*Butler*	*Lamberton J*	*Reason*	*Proudfoot*	*Boden*	*Codling*	*Bourne*	*Evenson*	*Leigh*	*Lamberton G*	*Kingaby*
							Ref: A Green	Bennett quickly made amends for failing from the spot, following Lamberton's foul on Gilligan. Just a minute later, Proudfoot brought down Hilton, and Bennett had no trouble this time in putting away another penalty. Maxwell neatly headed City into the lead from Hilton's flag-kick.										
15	H	BURNLEY	1	W	2-0	1-0	Dixon 10og, Maxwell 52	Clay	Annan	Cottle	Jones	Wedlock	Chambers	Fenton	Maxwell	Gilligan	Burton	Hilton
	2/12	8,000	*5*	28				*Green*	*Campbell*	*Dixon*	*Barron*	*Walders D*	*Moffat*	*Walders J*	*Davidson*	*Smith R*	*Cretney*	*Bell*
							Ref: F Kirkham	Burnley were at full strength, but City were without Bennett, whose father died the previous day. The visitors didn't play as well as expected and City didn't have any real trouble in equalling the League record of 14 successive wins. Dixon deflected Burton's shot into his own net.										
16	A	LEEDS CITY	1	D	1-1	1-0	Maxwell 25	Clay	Annan	Cottle	Jones	Wedlock	Spear	Bennett	Maxwell	Gilligan	Burton	Hilton
	9/12	*15,000*	*12*	29			*Morgan 85*	*Bromage*	*Murray*	*Ray*	*Morgan*	*Stringfellow*	*Henderson*	*Parnell*	*Watson*	*Hargraves*	*Morris R*	*Singleton*
							Ref: N Hammond	All good things come to an end, as a late goal deprives City of setting a new FL benchmark. Maxwell fired in an easy chance for the opener; then Gilligan wasted a good opportunity just before the interval. Morgan's header brought Leeds reward for their second-half improvement.										
17	H	BURTON UTD	1	W	4-0	3-0	Burton 15, Maxwell 30, 40, 55	Clay	Annan	Cottle	Hanlin	Wedlock	Chambers	Bennett	Maxwell	Gilligan	Burton	Hilton
	16/12	8,000	*11*	31				*Starbuck*	*Shreeve*	*Kirkland*	*Robinson*	*Davis*	*Battles*	*Bradshaw*	*W Hunt*	*Aston*	*Burton*	*King*
							Ref: R Johns	An early Christmas treat for City fans at Ashton Gate, where the Burton citadel was under almost constant siege. Maxwell's headed goal, sandwiched between a couple of shots, put City firmly in control; then after the break his magnificent drive made things even easier.										
18	A	CHELSEA	1	D	0-0	0-0		Clay	Annan	Cottle	Hanlin	Wedlock	Chambers	Bennett	Maxwell	Gilligan	Burton	Hilton
	23/12	*25,000*	*3*	32				*Foulke*	*Mackie*	*Miller*	*Key*	*McRoberts*	*Watson*	*Moran*	*Roberts'n JT*	*Copeland*	*McDermott*	*Kirwan*
							Ref: A Green	City fulfilled the expectations of their fans by drawing at Stamford Bridge, but they should have won. They had the better chances but were let down by some poor shooting. Chelsea were kept at bay by the quick-tackling of Wedlock, Cottle and Chambers, allied to Clay's form in goal.										
19	A	GAINSBOROUGH	1	W	3-1	1-1	Burton 15, 83, Bennett 70	Clay	Annan	Cottle	Hanlin	Wedlock	Chambers	Bennett	Maxwell	Gilligan	Burton	Hilton
	26/12	*5,000*	*19*	34			*Taylor 38*	*Bagshaw*	*Prescott*	*Betts*	*Dixon*	*Jenkinson*	*Westwood*	*Langham*	*Taylor*	*Morley*	*Nicholson*	*Foxall F*
							Ref: H Ward	City had the better of the early play with Gilligan and Wedlock getting in good efforts before Burton registered with a fine shot. Taylor's fierce drive brought the Trinity level, but after the break Bennett drove in from close range to restore City's advantage, before Westwood retired hurt.										
20	A	GRIMSBY	1	D	1-1	1-0	Gilligan 38	Clay	Annan	Cottle	Jones	Wedlock	Chambers	Bennett	Maxwell	Gilligan	Burton	Hilton
	27/12	*6,000*	*10*	35			*Fletcher 80*	*Cartledge*	*Morley*	*McConnell*	*McGregor*	*Milnes*	*Higgins*	*Fletcher*	*Robinson*	*Burnett*	*Swarbrick*	*Johnson*
							Ref: W Gilgryst	The play was in City's favour during the first half, when they should have managed more than Gilligan heading through from a goalmouth scramble. After Fletcher brought Grimsby level, with a low drive from out wide, a ding-dong struggle ensued as both teams sought a winner.										
21	H	MANCHESTER U	1	D	1-1	0-0	Gilligan 60	Demmery	Annan	Cottle	Spear	Wedlock	Chambers	Bennett	Maxwell	Gilligan	Burton	Hilton
	30/12	18,959	*2*	36			*Roberts 75*	*Moger*	*Bonthron*	*Holden*	*Downie*	*Roberts*	*Bell*	*Schofield*	*Peddie*	*Beddow*	*Picken*	*Williams*
		(£726.4.3)					Ref: T Armitt	If City had been able rest like their opponents, instead of taking part in matches at Gainsborough and Grimsby, the feeling was that they would have won this thrilling top-of-the-table contest. Gilligan easily drove the opener past Mogg, but Roberts shot in United's well-placed leveller.										

No	Date	Att	Pos	Pt	F-A	H-T	Scorers, Times, and Referees	1	2	3	4	5	6	7	8	9	10	11
22	A GLOSSOP		1	W	5-1	3-0	Gilligan 7, 30, 40, 65, Bennett 80p	Demmery	Annan	Cottle	Jones	Wedlock	Chambers	Bennett	Maxwell	Gilligan	Burton	Hilton
	6/1	*1,500*	*15*	38			*Demmery 70og*	*Davis*	*Orr*	*Cuffe*	*Brown*	*McNab*	*Mair*	*Callaghan*	*Chadwick*	*Cameron*	*Darque*	*Irvine*
							Ref: A Hargreaves	The gale, which had broken down telephonic and telegraphic communications, had not expended itself by kick-off time, but this bothered City not a jot. With the wind at their backs, City took an early lead when, from Wedlock's centre, Gilligan shot into the left corner of Glossop's net.										
23	H STOCKPORT		1	W	7-0	4-0	Maxwell 10, 40, 80, [Gilligan 20, 30, 60, 70]	Clay	Annan	Cottle	Spear	Wedlock	Chambers	Bennett	Maxwell	Gilligan	Stevens	Fenton
	20/1	*7,000*	*12*	40				*Frail*	*Heywood*	*Waters*	*Suart*	*Dodd*	*Butterworth*	*Schofield*	*Pass*	*Crump*	*Farrant*	*Bardsley*
							Ref: J Ibbotson	Wedlock was the only man on the pitch who didn't seem to mind the mud. Despite the terrible state of the Ashton Gate pitch, City notched up their record League success, the goals flowing regularly throughout after Maxwell's clever use of his head in putting away Fenton's centre.										
24	A BLACKPOOL		1	W	3-1	3-0	Gilligan 10, Maxwell 15, 75	Clay	Annan	Cottle	Spear	Wedlock	Chambers	Bennett	Maxwell	Gilligan	Burton	Hilton
	27/1	*4,000*	*16*	42			*Gow 80*	*Hull*	*Birket*	*Scott*	*Threlfall*	*Parkinson*	*Johnson*	*Gow*	*Hancock*	*Francis*	*Connor*	*Hollingworth*
							Ref: M McQueen	Blackpool, who had done most of the early attacking, were shocked when Gilligan, on receiving Bennett's centre, neatly put the ball past the home keeper. Maxwell's header then doubled the seasiders' misfortune, which was made complete soon after by the loss of the injured Birkett.										
25	A WEST BROM		1	W	3-1	2-0	Gilligan 6, Bennett 12, Maxwell 70	Clay	Annan	Cottle	Spear	Wedlock	Chambers	Bennett	Maxwell	Gilligan	Burton	Hilton
	10/2	*6,400*	*4*	44			*Pheasant 60*	*Stringer*	*Williams*	*Pennington*	*Randle*	*Pheasant*	*Manners*	*Rankin*	*Simmons*	*Bradley*	*Heywood A*	*Perkins*
							Ref: J Bailey	The Albion fans were not amused by the referee, who ruled out five of their goals (four clearly offside and one direct from a corner). The goal that did count came from a dubious penalty award. After Clay had palmed out Pheasant's spot-kick, the centre-half followed up to score.										
26	H LEICESTER FOSSE		1	L	1-2	0-2	Gilligan 75	Clay	Annan	Cottle	Spear	Wedlock	Chambers	Bennett	Maxwell	Gilligan	Burton	Hilton
	17/2	8,000	*5*	44			*Bannister 15, Blessington 30*	*Smith*	*Ashby*	*Oakes*	*Morgan*	*Bannister*	*Pollock*	*Durrant*	*Blessington*	*Moody*	*Hubbard*	*Hodgkinson*
							Ref: J Ibbotson	This defeat came as a surprise, though Leicester's impressive away record should have made City wary. Given the overall run of the play it is difficult to understand how the visitors won. Two fine shots put them in the driving seat, and the solidarity of their fine defence did the rest.										
27	A HULL		1	W	3-0	1-0	Maxwell 9, Hilton 85, Bennett 87p	Clay	Annan	Cottle	Spear	Wedlock	Chambers	Bennett	Maxwell	Gilligan	Burton	Hilton
	24/2	*8,000*	*6*	46				*Spendiff*	*Davies*	*Langley*	*Browell*	*Robinson*	*Simmon*	*Manning*	*Smith Jack*	*Smith Joe*	*Gordon*	*Raisbeck*
							Ref: W Gilgryst	City responded to the fears that last week's defeat would herald a bad patch with this fine display on the Circle Ground. Maxwell headed in the early opener; then near the end of the game Hilton's low drive, followed by Spendiff's foul on Bennett, improved City's goal-average.										
28	H LINCOLN		1	W	1-0	1-0	Hilton 15	Clay	Annan	Cottle	Spear	Wedlock	Chambers	Bennett	Maxwell	Gilligan	Burton	Hilton
	3/3	10,000	*15*	48				*Buist*	*Laverick*	*Simpson W*	*Fraser*	*Hood*	*Blow*	*Watson*	*Machin*	*Martin*	*Kelly*	*Fairgray*
							Ref: A Hines	City were disrupted by the early loss of their captain, Chambers, with a wrenched right knee, but they still had the resilience to hang on to the lead. Bennett's shot rebounded off a post, right to the feet of Hilton, who had no trouble at all in firing the ball past Buist in the Imps' goal.										
29	A CHESTERFIELD		1	W	2-1	0-1	Maxwell 60, Burton 84	Clay	Annan	Cottle	Spear	Wedlock	Hanlin	Bennett	Maxwell	Gilligan	Burton	Hilton
	10/3	*4,000*	*14*	50			*Lunn 30*	*Cope*	*Marples*	*Baker*	*Haig*	*Banner*	*Milnes*	*Taylor*	*Thacker*	*Lunn*	*Munday*	*Ball*
							Ref: F Gardner	This success was achieved after one of the most exciting games City have been engaged in this season, after finding themselves trailing to Lunn's drive at the break. Maxwell fired in the leveller from close range, before Burton found the far corner with a shot from out on the left.										
30	H BURSLEM PT VALE		1	W	4-0	2-0	Bennett 20, 35, 85, Gilligan 75	Clay	Annan	Cottle	Spear	Wedlock	Hanlin	Bennett	Maxwell	Gilligan	Burton	Hilton
	17/3	10,000	*17*	52				*Box*	*Cope*	*Hamilton*	*Eardley*	*Holyhead*	*Whittingham*	*Carter*	*Smith*	*Mountford*	*Price*	*Hall*
							Ref: J Adams	Bennett began by failing to net a penalty, but after beating Box with a truly grand shot he was unstoppable. He added a second from a trifle shorter range, then put on a third from a free-kick just outside the penalty area. The ball ran out before Maxwell crossed for Gilligan's goal.										
31	A BARNSLEY		1	D	2-2	1-1	Maxwell 29, Bennett 49p	Clay	Annan	Cottle	Spear	Wedlock	Hanlin	Bennett	Maxwell	Gilligan	Burton	Hilton
	24/3	*6,000*	*15*	53			*Owen 30, Birtles 75*	*Thorpe*	*Hay*	*Stacey*	*Donagher*	*Wilkinson*	*Oxspring*	*Birtles*	*Owen*	*Hellew'll Alec*	*Beech*	*Wall*
							Ref: J Bailey	Played in a fierce gale, the players were also subjected to heavy snow in the bitterly cold conditions. Playing against the wind in the second half, City were boosted by Bennett's spot-kick. Barnsley, who thereafter were the aggressors, deserved the point achieved by a Birtles header.										

No	Venue	Opponent / Date	Att			FT	HT	Scorers, Times, Referees											
32	H	CLAPTON ORIENT		1	W	1-0	0-0	Hilton 49	Clay	Annan	Cottle	Spear	Wedlock	Hanlin	Bennett	Maxwell	Gilligan	Burton	Hilton
		31/3	8,000	*20*	55				*Bower*	*Lamberton*	*J Holmes*	*Proudfoot*	*McGeorge*	*Evenson*	*Dougall*	*Orton*	*Hunt*	*Leigh*	*Bourne*
								Ref: A Green	For the first time this year the ground was hard and in consequence both sides found the lively ball difficult to control. A scrappy and generally uninteresting game was won by Hilton, after Burton was blocked by Bower, managing to put the ball away from Bennett's well-placed corner.										
33	A	BURNLEY		1	D	2-2	0-0	Burton 56, Gilligan 70	Clay	Annan	Cottle	Spear	Wedlock	Hanlin	Bennett	Maxwell	Gilligan	Burton	Hilton
		7/4	*10,000*	*9*	56			*Smith R 66, Davidson 67*	*Green*	*Barron*	*Moffat*	*Cretney*	*Walders D*	*Taylor*	*Walders J*	*Davidson*	*Smith R*	*Bell*	*Smith A*
								Ref: F Kirkham	A draw was a fair result of this interesting game, even though Burnley were unfortunate to lose the services of the injured Cretney for the last half-hour. After Burton drove in the opener it needed Gilligan's shot to save the day, as Smith and Davidson got through for the homesters.										
34	H	GAINSBOROUGH		1	W	2-0	2-0	Bennett 35, Burton 44	Clay	Annan	Cottle	Spear	Wedlock	Hanlin	Bennett	Maxwell	Gilligan	Burton	Fenton
		13/4	11,000	*19*	58				*Bagshaw*	*Thompson*	*Taylor*	*Westwood*	*Hall*	*Turner*	*Smith*	*Langham*	*Dixon*	*Foxall A*	*Foxall F*
			(£280)					Ref: H Ward	The large Ashton Gate crowd included a fair number of excursionists from Gainsborough, who saw their side put up a good performance. Fenton's centre allowed Bennett to head in City's opener; then Burton dashed through to score a magnificent goal just before the interval.										
35	H	LEEDS CITY		1	W	2-0	0-0	Spear 46, Wedlock 75	Clay	Annan	Cottle	Spear	Wedlock	Hanlin	Bennett	Maxwell	Gilligan	Burton	Fenton
		14/4	13,000	*7*	60				*Bromage*	*McDonald*	*Murray*	*George*	*Walker*	*Henderson*	*Parnell*	*Morris R*	*Hargraves*	*Lavery*	*Singleton*
			(£300)					Ref: F Heath	After an anxious opening quarter of an hour, City made sure of promotion with this deserved victory. With Murray winded from being struck by Maxwell's shot, Spear dashed up to fire in City's opener. Wedlock, on receiving from a corner, beat Bromage to make sure of the points.										
36	H	GRIMSBY		1	W	2-0	1-0	Maxwell 10, Hilton 59	Clay	Annan	Cottle	Spear	Wedlock	Hanlin	Bennett	Maxwell	Gilligan	Burton	Hilton
		17/4	7,000	*8*	62				*Cartledge*	*Morley*	*McConnell*	*McGregor*	*Milnes*	*Nelmes*	*Hooper*	*Baker*	*Burnett*	*Robinson*	*Swarbrick*
								Ref: E Case	City played towards the Pavilion End in the first half, and took the lead when Maxwell registered with a magnificent drive. In spite of the wet weather a fair-sized crowd were present and they saw Hilton turn in City's second after the visitors had started the better following the interval.										
37	A	BURTON UTD		1	W	1-0	1-0	Hilton 19	Clay	Annan	Cottle	Spear	Wedlock	Hanlin	Bennett	Maxwell	Gilligan	Burton	Hilton
		21/4	*5,000*	*19*	64				*Starbuck*	*Shreeve*	*Kirkland*	*Stanley*	*Davis*	*Robinson*	*Aston*	*Hunt*	*Axcell*	*King*	*Tooth*
								Ref: E Case	Despite their lowly position, Burton gave City a tough game at Peel Croft. Thankfully Hilton scored, receiving the ball wide from Maxwell; he swerved in towards goal at a great rate and fired in an oblique shot just under the bar. An important goal this, as it clinched the Championship.										
38	H	CHELSEA		1	W	2-1	1-0	Gilligan 10, Burton 65	Clay	Annan	Cottle	Spear	Wedlock	Hanlin	Bennett	Maxwell	Gilligan	Burton	Hilton
		28/4	14,050	*3*	66			*Pearson 89*	*Whiting*	*Mackie*	*Miller*	*Henderson*	*McRoberts*	*Proudfoot*	*Moran*	*McDermott*	*Pearson*	*Copeland*	*Kirwan*
		Home	Away					Ref: A Green	A well-contested game, despite a strong wind as well as intermittent rain and hailstorms. Gilligan opened the scoring when he put away Bennett's centre; then after the interval Burton shot in a second before Pearson got in on the act for Chelsea by firing in off the crossbar.										
	Ave	9,527	8,542																

CUP-TIES

FA Cup/Glos Cup		F-A	H-T	Scorers, Times, and Referees	1	2	3	4	5	6	7	8	9	10	11	12 sub used
1 A BRENTFORD 1	L	1-2	1-0	Maxwell 8	Clay	Annan	Cottle	Jones	Wedlock	Chambers	Bennett	Maxwell	Gilligan	Burton	Hilton	
13/1 *10,112 SL:7*				*Corbett 60, 78*	*Whittaker*	*Watson*	*Riley*	*Jay*	*Parsonage*	*Robotham*	*Hartley*	*Shanks*	*Corbett*	*Hobson*	*Underwood*	
(£333)				Ref: F Heath	Maxwell's low cross-shot gave City false expectations against their Southern League opponents. Brentford soon disillusioned them as ex-City man Corbett ensured that the homesters extended their unbeaten run to six games by twice firing in as well as having a great shot disallowed.											
F H BRISTOL ROV 1	W	4-0	2-0	Bennett 36p, Burton 44, Gilligan 55,	Clay	Annan	Cottle	Spear	Wedlock	Hanlin	Bennett	Maxwell	Gilligan	Burton	Hilton	
GC 16/4 8,836 *SL:7*				[Wedlock 80]	*Cartlidge*	*Hales*	*Pudan*	*Tait*	*Appleby*	*Taylor*	*Clark*	*Lewis*	*Beats*	*Walker*	*Bennett*	
(£248.5.11)				Ref: J Pearson	City kicked off in brilliant weather at Ashton Gate but had to wait until a foul on Hilton allowed them to take the lead from the spot. Prior to the interval Burton shot in the second; then after the break Gilligan drove in another before Wedlock's low drive tied up what was an easy win.											

FRIENDLIES

		F-A	H-T	Scorers, Times, and Referees	1	2	3	4	5	6	7	8	9	10	11	12 sub used
1 A BRISTOL ROV	W	6-0	1-0	Maxwell 35, 60, 70, Burton 48,	Clay	Annan	Tuft	Jones	Wedlock	Spear	Bennett	Maxwell	Gilligan	Burton	Fenton	
6/9 *5,000*				[Gilligan 65, Bennett 85]	*Cartlidge*	*Dunn*	*Taylor*	*Tait*	*Appleby*	*Jarvie*	*Haxten*	*Lewis*	*Beats*	*Walker*	*Dunkley*	
				Ref: A Farrant	Play was fairly even initially, though City missed the better chances, but after Maxwell opened the scoring with a beauty late in the first half the floodgates burst open. City's play was a revelation, their passing, shooting and tackling was irreproachable as the Rovers were swept aside.											
2 A PLYMOUTH	W	3-1	1-1	Gilligan 30, Burton 75, Ingham 89	Clay	Gilson	Cottle	Hanlin	Wedlock	Chambers	Bennett	Ingham	Gilligan	Burton	Hilton	
18/10 *3,000*				*Jack 10*	*Horne*	*Saul*	*McNeil*	*Tapson*	*Clark C*	*Buchanan*	*Birch*	*Bauchop*	*Wilcox*	*Reid*	*Jack*	
					Despite City being the first to settle down, it was the Argyle who took the lead at Home Park. Clever passing between Jack, Reid and Bauchop, ended with the latter sending across to Jack, who found the net. Hilton had a goal disallowed shortly before Gilligan fired in City's equaliser.											
3 H BRISTOL ROV	W	2-0	0-0	McKay 60, Stevens 75	Demmery	Gilson	Tuft*	Jones	McKay	Price	Ingham	Radford	Jacobs	Stevens	Fenton	Rowlands
25/12 7,000					*Cartlidge*	*Taylor*	*Gerrish*	*Hales*	*Appleby*	*Evans*	*Walker*	*Smith*	*Huxtable*	*Orr*	*Dunkley*	
				Ref: A Farrant	Tuft's return, after nearly three months absence with a knee-injury, is spoilt by him having to go off just before the interval with an unrelated problem. City improved in the second half and McKay opened the scoring from a corner before Stevens fired in to double their advantage.											
4 H BRISTOL ROV	L	0-3	0-2		Clay	Gilson	Tuft	Spear	Jones	Hanlin	Ingham	Maxwell	Rowlands	Stevens	Fenton	
3/2 *4,000*				*Clark 20, Walker 35, Lewis 75*	*Clarke D*	*Taylor*	*Hales*	*Tait*	*Appleby*	*Jarvie*	*Clark W*	*Lewis*	*Beats*	*Walker*	*Dunkley*	
				Ref: C Fallowfield	The Rovers experienced little difficulty in winning this encounter. Although facing a strong wind, they opened the scoring thanks to Clark registering with a grand shot. Walker then doubled their advantage before, in a decidedly tame second half, Lewis made victory complete.											

		Home					Away					
	P	W	D	L	F	A	W	D	L	F	A	Pts
1 BRISTOL C	38	17	1	1	43	8	13	5	1	40	20	66
2 Manchester U	38	15	3	1	55	13	13	3	3	35	15	62
3 Chelsea	38	13	4	2	58	16	9	5	5	32	21	53
4 West Brom	38	13	4	2	53	16	9	4	6	26	20	52
5 Hull City	38	10	5	4	38	21	9	1	9	29	33	44
6 Leeds City	38	11	5	3	38	19	6	4	9	21	28	43
7 Leicester Fos'	38	10	3	6	30	21	4	9	6	21	28	40
8 Grimsby T	38	11	7	1	33	13	4	3	12	13	33	40
9 Burnley	38	10	4	5	27	21	6	4	9	16	30	40
10 Stockport Co	38	11	6	2	36	16	2	3	14	8	40	35
11 Bradford City	38	7	4	8	21	22	6	4	9	25	38	34
12 Barnsley	38	11	4	4	45	17	1	5	13	15	45	33
13 Lincoln City	38	10	1	8	46	29	2	5	12	23	43	30
14 Blackpool	38	8	3	8	22	21	2	6	11	15	41	29
15 Gainsboro' T	38	10	2	7	35	22	2	2	15	9	35	28
16 Glossop	38	9	4	6	36	28	1	4	14	13	43	28
17 Burslem Pt V	38	10	4	5	34	25	2	0	17	15	57	28
18 Chesterfield	38	8	4	7	26	24	2	4	13	14	48	28
19 Burton United	38	9	4	6	26	20	1	2	16	8	47	26
20 Clapt' Orient	38	6	4	9	19	22	1	3	15	16	56	21
	760	209	76	95	721	394	95	76	209	394	721	760

Odds & ends

Double wins: (12) Glossop, Stockport, Brad C, Blackpool, West Brom, Hull, Lincoln, Chesterfield, P Vale, Orient, Burton, Gainsborough.
Double losses: (0).

Won from behind: (4) Stockport (a), Brad C (a), Leicester (a), Hull (h).
Lost from in front: (1) Brentford (a).

High spots: Notching new Football League record with 66 points.
Becoming the first ever FL club to win 30 games in a season.
A Club record of scoring in all but one League game, 18 blank sheets.
A record 7-0 League success versus Stockport County on 20 January.
Beating Bristol Rovers 4-0 in the Gloucestershire Cup Final on 16 April.

Low spots: The opening day hammering at Manchester United.

Player of the Year: Walter Bennett & Billy Maxwell.
Ever-presents: (3) Archie Annan, Billy Wedlock, William Maxwell.
Hat-tricks: (5) Billy Maxwell (2), Sammy Gilligan (2), Walter Bennett.
Leading scorer: Overall: Billy Maxwell (29). League: Billy Maxwell (25).

Pre-Season Trial Match:
23 Aug Greens 2(2) Reds 1(1) Ref: H Thickett
4,000 Bennett 25, Gilligan 30 / *Ingham 40*

AGM (Temperance Hall, East Street, Bedminster, 25 July 1906):
Profit £257.3s.10d. Season Ticket Sales £250.10s.4d.

	Appearances				Goals			
	Lge	Cup	Fr	*Sub*	Lge	Cup	Fr	Tot
Annan, Archie	**38**	2	1					
Bennett, Walter	**37**	2	2		**21**	1	1	**23**
Burton, Andy	**37**	1	2		**8**	1	2	**11**
Chambers, Peter	**20**	1	1					
Clay, Harry	**36**	2	3					
Cottle, Joe	**33**	2	1					
Demmery, Bill	**2**		1					
Fenton, Freddie	**13**	1	3					
Gilligan, Sammy	**37**	2	2		**19**	1	2	**22**
Gilson, Alf			3					
Hanlin, Pat	**14**	1	2					
Hilton, Frank	**26**	2	1		**5**			**5**
Ingham, Billy	**1**		3				1	**1**
Jacobs			1					
Jones, Billy	**18**	1	3					
McKay			1				1	**1**
Maxwell, Billy	**38**	2	2		**25**	1	3	**29**
Price, Alf			1					
Radford, Tom			1					
Rowlands, WH			1	*1*				
Spear, Arthur	**24**	1	2		**1**			**1**
Stevens, Charles	**1**		2				1	**1**
Tuft, Billy	**5**		3					
Wedlock, Billy	**38**	2	2		**2**	1		**3**
Opponent og					**2**			**2**
24 players used	**418**	**22**	**44**	*1*	**83**	**5**	**11**	**99**

No	Date	Att	Pos	Pt	F-A	H-T	Scorers, Times, and Referees	1	2	3	4	5	6	7	8	9	10	11
1	H MANCHESTER U			L	1-2	1-2	Bennett 3p	Clay	Annan	Cottle	Spear	Wedlock	Hanlin	Bennett	Maxwell	Gilligan	Burton	Hilton
	1/9	21,000					*Roberts 10, Picken 32*	*Moger*	*Bonthron*	*Holden*	*Downie*	*Roberts*	*Bell*	*Schofield*	*Peddie*	*Sagar*	*Picken*	*Wall*
		(£485)					Ref: J Adams	In the sweltering heat City took the lead after the referee had deliberated over Bonthron's handball, but United fought back and it didn't take long before Roberts levelled from the edge of the area. Picken nipped in to poke home the winner when Clay knocked down Schofield's shot.										
2	A BIRMINGHAM			D	2-2	2-2	Gilligan 22, Glover 42og	Clay	Annan	Cottle	**Marr**	Wedlock	Hanlin	Bennett	Maxwell	Gilligan	Burton	Hilton
	3/9	*10,000*		1			*Jones 20, Mounteney 40*	*Robinson*	*Glover*	*Stokes*	*Beer*	*Wigmore*	*Dougherty*	*Tickle*	*Green*	*Jones W*	*Mounteney*	*Anderson*
							Ref: J Howcroft	City received good reviews in the national press for their performance in this game, in which it took Hanlin's effort, which went in off Glover, to save the day. Jones opened the scoring for Brum with a fine goal, but a brilliant low shot by Gilligan brought City level almost immediately.										
3	A STOKE		10	W	3-0	1-0	Gilligan 35, Maxwell 70, [Bennett 90]	Clay	Annan	Cottle	Marr	Wedlock	Hanlin	Bennett	Maxwell	Gilligan	Burton	Hilton
	8/9	*8,000*	*20*	3				*Roose*	*Burgess*	*Cook Albert*	*Croxton*	*Sturgess*	*Baddeley*	*Fielding*	*Rouse*	*Chalmers*	*Gallimore*	*Miller*
							Ref: C Fallowfield	Gilligan notched the opener, firing in the rebound when Hilton's acute angled shot hit a post. Roose then kept the visitors out until near the end, when he could do little about the two headers which beat him as City, somewhat comfortably, achieved their first ever top-flight win.										
4	H BLACKBURN		8	W	3-0	0-0	Maxwell 61, Hilton 72, Burton 73	Clay	Annan	Cottle	Marr	Wedlock	Hanlin	Bennett	Maxwell	Gilligan	Burton	Hilton
	15/9	18,000	*18*	5				*Evans*	*Crompton*	*Cowell*	*Wolst'nholme*	*Houlker*	*Bradshaw*	*Whittaker*	*Davies*	*Martin*	*Bowman*	*Dawson*
		(£405)					Ref: F Heath	City have never played better, though they were helped when the visitors lost the services of Houlker with an injured knee-cap not long after the interval. Maxwell promptly steered the ball in from Hilton's pass, then the left-winger got on the scoresheet himself by firing in the second.										
5	A SUNDERLAND		7	D	3-3	1-1	Maxwell 7, 76, Burton 77	Clay	Annan	Cottle	Marr	Wedlock	Hanlin	Bennett	Maxwell	Gilligan	Burton	Hilton
	22/9	*28,000*	*11*	6			*Hogg 36, Bridgett 75, Shaw 80*	*Ward*	*Rhodes*	*Watson*	*Tait*	*McGhie*	*McConnell*	*Hogg*	*Gemmell*	*Shaw*	*Hall*	*Bridgett*
							Ref: T Armitt	After Burton's 20-yarder, it took Shaw's brilliant shot to deprive City of another win as they continued to create a stir amongst the top clubs in the country. Maxwell fired in their early opener, but Hogg headed through Sunderland's equaliser when Gilligan was temporarily off the field.										
6	H BIRMINGHAM		7	D	0-0	0-0		Clay	Annan	Cottle	Marr	Wedlock	Hanlin	Bennett	Maxwell	Gilligan	Burton	Hilton
	29/9	17,000	*16*	7				*Robinson*	*Kearns*	*Stokes*	*Beer*	*Wigmore*	*Dougherty*	*Harper*	*Green*	*Jones WH*	*Mounteney*	*Anderson*
		(£472)					Ref: J Howcroft	In all respects save one, City played well enough to have won this game. Where they fell short was in the all-important matter of shooting, and their failure was not wholly due to the efforts of the opposition. City lacked the finishing ability to turn their many scoring chances to account.										
7	A EVERTON		9	L	0-2	0-2		Clay	Annan	Cottle	Spear	Wedlock	Hanlin	**Staniforth**	Maxwell	Gilligan	Burton	Hilton
	6/10	*20,000*	*4*	7			*Bolton 1, Sharp 40*	*Scott*	*Balmer W*	*Crelley*	*Makepeace*	*Taylor*	*Abbott*	*Sharp*	*Bolton*	*Young*	*Wilson G*	*Hardman H*
							Ref: N Whittaker	After falling behind when Bolton ran through onto Young's pass to fire in the early opener, City were unfortunate when a defender cleared Gilligan's shot off the line. Sharp made sure of ending City's remarkable thirteen-month unbeaten away run by netting with a real swerver.										
8	H WLCH ARSENAL		10	L	1-3	0-2	Wedlock 77	Clay	Annan	Cottle	Marr	Wedlock	Hanlin	Staniforth	Bennett	Gilligan	Burton	Hilton
	13/10	**22,000**	*1*	7			*Ducat 11, Bidgen 22, Neave 62*	*Ashcroft*	*Gray*	*Sharp*	*Bigden*	*Theobald*	*McEachrane*	*Bellamy*	*Ducat*	*Kyle*	*Sat'rthwaite*	*Neave*
		(£621.14.8)					Ref: F Gardner	The Gunners' illustrated the extent to which science may overcome dash in football. Taking the game as a whole they did not attack as much as the City, but near goal their methods were far more effective. Ashcroft was frequently blessed by good fortune in getting himself out of trouble.										
9	A THE WEDNESDAY		13	L	**0-3**	0-1		Demmery	Annan	Cottle	Marr	Wedlock	Hanlin	Bennett	Maxwell	Gilligan	Burton	Hilton
	20/10	*20,000*	*2*	7			*Davis 23, 84, Wilson 90*	*Lyall*	*Burton*	*Layton*	*Brittleton*	*Crawshaw*	*Bartlett*	*Davis*	*Simpson V*	*Wilson*	*Malloch*	*Tummon*
							Ref: F Gardner	Poor finishing again proves costly for City, as they slip to a third successive defeat. Give-and-take play characterised the first half, but Davis gave Wednesday the advantage with a fine shot. After the break City had most of the game, but two late goals produced an unjust score-line.										
10	H BURY		10	W	2-0	1-0	Burton 28, Maxwell 75	Demmery	Annan	Cottle	Marr	Wedlock	Hanlin	**Gilligan**	Maxwell	**Smith**	Burton	Hilton
	27/10	**12,000**	*14*	9				*Mearns*	*Lindsay*	*Leeming*	*Johnston*	*Dewhurst*	*Davidson*	*Kilbourne*	*Hibbert*	*Bevan*	*Kay*	*Bradley*
							Ref: F Bye	After six weeks without a win, City's superior play brought success, despite the loss of the injured Gilligan for the final half-hour. Burton shot in the opener; then after the break the seal was set on City's victory when new man Smith set Maxwell clear to run through and beat Mearns.										

No	Venue	Opponent	Att	Pos	Res / Pts	FT	HT	Scorers	1	2	3	4	5	6	7	8	9	10	11
11	A	MANCHESTER C		10	W	1-0	1-0	Maxwell 40	Demmery	Annan	Cottle	Marr	Wedlock	Hanlin	Smith	Maxwell	Gilligan	Burton	Hilton
	3/11		*16,000*	*17*	11				*Hall*	*Christie*	*Norgrove*	*Steel*	*Eadie*	*Banks*	*Stewart*	*Dorsett*	*Thornley*	*Jones*	*Conlin*
								Ref: J Adams	The homesters, despite having most of the play after an even first half, lost out to a City side who took their chance for victory. Demmery starred between the sticks, whilst Thornley missed with four far easier chances than that which Maxwell was able to drive in for City's winner.										
12	H	MIDDLESBROUGH		9	W	3-0	2-0	Hanlin 21, Gilligan 44, Smith 47	Demmery	Annan	Cottle	Marr	Wedlock	Hanlin	Smith	Maxwell	Gilligan	Burton	Fenton
	10/11		14,000	*20*	13				*Williamson*	*Tildesley*	*Campbell*	*Aitken S*	*Aitken A*	*Harkins*	*Brawn*	*Common*	*Tucker*	*Wilcox*	*Priest*
								Ref: C Fallowfield	The visitors were the early aggressors, but Hanlin's long drive put City into the lead after Williamson had repelled shots from Maxwell and Gilligan. From Fenton's corner, Tildesley turned the ball towards his own net to set up Gilligan. Smith's acute angled volley tied up a fine win.										
13	A	PRESTON		9	L	1-3	0-2	Maxwell 70	Demmery	Annan	Cottle	Marr	Wedlock	Hanlin	Smith	Maxwell	Gilligan	Burton	Hilton
	17/11		*7,000*	*14*	13			*Cottle 39og, Wilson 40, 55*	*Taylor*	*Lavery*	*Rodway*	*McLean*	*Hunter*	*Lyon*	*Dawson*	*Wilson*	*Smith P*	*Bell*	*Danson*
								Ref: J Brodie	City suffered on the rain-saturated pitch against a much-changed Preston side following their 1-6 mauling at Liverpool last week. Cottle's mis-kick sent the ball flying into the top corner of the net; then Wilson twice shot past Demmery, before Maxwell fired in City's only success.										
14	H	NEWCASTLE		8	W	2-1	1-1	Wedlock 25, Burton 65	Demmery	Annan	Cottle	Marr	Wedlock	Hanlin	Smith	Maxwell	Gilligan	Burton	Hilton
	24/11		20,000	*4*	15			*Brown 15*	*Lawrence*	*McCombie*	*Carr*	*Gardner*	*Veitch*	*McWilliam*	*Rutherford*	*Howie*	*Brown*	*Speedie*	*Gosnell*
								Ref: T Kirkham	City deserved the points, thanks to Burton finishing off his fine run with a shot past Lawrence, even though they were much helped by polished Newcastle's poor finishing. After Brown fired in from close range, City levelled when Wedlock's long, low shot was deflected in off Gilligan.										
15	A	ASTON VILLA		9	L	2-3	0-2	Gilligan 70, Burton 82	Demmery	Annan	Cottle	Marr	Wedlock	Hanlin	Smith	Maxwell	Gilligan	Burton	Hilton
	1/12		*27,000*	*6*	15			*Cantrell 30, Millington 44, Bache 49*	*George*	*Miles*	*Logan J*	*Greenhaigh*	*Leake*	*Codling*	*Walters*	*Cantrell*	*Millington*	*Bache*	*Hall*
								Ref: T Campbell (*Joe Bache Benefit*)	When Bache's grounder found the net, City seemed well beaten. However they recovered to play with great determination and nearly saved the game. Unfortunately, after Burton registered with a screw-shot following on from Gilligan's earlier drive, the equaliser just wouldn't come.										
16	H	LIVERPOOL		8	W	3-1	0-1	Burton 49, 87, Gilligan 70	Demmery	Annan	Cottle	Marr	Wedlock	Hanlin	Smith	Maxwell	Gilligan	Burton	Hilton
	8/12		18,000	*9*	17			*Robinson 30*	*Hardy*	*Saul*	*Chorlton*	*Lathom*	*Raisbeck*	*Bradley*	*Goddard*	*Robinson*	*Raybould*	*McPherson*	*Hewitt*
								Ref: S Carr	Shortly after the concussed Robinson's retirement, Burton beat Hardy with a splendid shot to level matters. City then lost Smith with an injury sustained in the movement that lead to Gilligan firing in another, before Saul, in trying to be clever, was robbed by Burton for City's third.										
17	H	DERBY		6	W	3-0	1-0	Burton 35, 60, Gilligan 80	Demmery	Annan	Cottle	Marr	Wedlock	Hanlin	Staniforth	Maxwell	Gilligan	Burton	Hilton
	15/12		**12,000**	*16*	19				*Maskrey*	*Nicholas*	*Morris*	*Bagshaw*	*Hall*	*Wood A*	*Davies J*	*Long*	*Warren*	*Wood J*	*Davis G*
								Ref: J Adams	City's nippy forward play was the feature of this well-deserved win. When Maskrey pushed out Maxwell's drive, an alert Burton snapped up the chance to score the opener; then after the break he headed in to double City's advantage, before Gilligan registered with a clever shot.										
18	A	NOTTS CO		6	W	3-2	1-1	Staniforth 20, Hilton 75, Maxwell 89	Demmery	Annan	Cottle	Marr	Wedlock	Hanlin	Staniforth	Maxwell	Gilligan	Burton	Hilton
	22/12		*10,000*	*19*	21			*Jones 5, Gee 60*	*Iremonger*	*Griffiths*	*Montgomery*	*Emberton*	*Watts*	*Craythorne*	*Dean*	*Humphreys*	*Jones Aaron*	*Matthews*	*Gee*
								Ref: W Gilgryst	Notts' hopes of their first home win were raised when Jones, a new signing from Birmingham, hooked in the opener. City, however, had other ideas after Staniforth ran through and fired in an equaliser. Maxwell, from the right-hand side of the box, screwed in City's last-gasp winner.										
19	H	SHEFFIELD U		6	D	3-3	2-2	Gilligan 10, Burton 23, 90	Demmery	Annan	Cottle	Marr	Wedlock	Hanlin	Staniforth	Maxwell	Gilligan	Burton	Hilton
	24/12		17,500 (£507)	*7*	22			*Bromage 8, Bluff 33, 65*	*Lievesley*	*Johnson W*	*Benson*	*Needham*	*Wilkinson B*	*McGuire*	*Croot*	*Bromage*	*Brown*	*Bluff*	*Lang*
								Ref: A Barker	After Bluff's second-half shot gave United the advantage, Burton salvaged a point for City when, in the dying seconds, he fired home from Wedlock's pass. The thrills started early with Bromage and Gilligan exchanging headers, before Burton's brilliant shot put City into the lead.										
20	A	MANCHESTER U		6	D	0-0	0-0		Demmery	Annan	Cottle	Marr	Wedlock	Hanlin	Staniforth	Maxwell	Gilligan	Burton	Hilton
	29/12		*16,000*	*15*	23				*Moger*	*Bonthron*	*Holden*	*Downie*	*Duckworth*	*Bell*	*Wombwell*	*Berry*	*Menzies*	*Picken*	*Wall*
								Ref: J Adams	It took 60 men to clear the pitch of 18 inches of snow before the game could go ahead. Even then it was threatened throughout by fog that made it impossible to see the full length of the pitch. City had a goal disallowed for offside, but an even contest ended with the points shared.										
21	A	SHEFFIELD U		6	D	1-1	0-1	Maxwell 78	Demmery	Annan	Cottle	Marr	Wedlock	Spear	Staniforth	Maxwell	Gilligan	Burton	Hilton
	31/12		*10,873* (£307)	*7*	24			*McGuire 30*	*Lievesley*	*Benson*	*Johnson C*	*McGuire*	*Wilkinson B*	*Parker*	*Donnelly*	*Bluff*	*Brown*	*Wilkinson W*	*Lipsham*
								Ref: A Barker	A long shot from McGuire completely beat Demmery to give United the advantage. As the game wore on, City looked likely to pay for their hesitation in shooting when well placed, but Maxwell got them some reward when he cleverly beat Lievesley after receiving Gilligan's pass.										

No	Date		Att	Pos	Pt	F-A	H-T	Scorers, Times, and Referees	1	2	3	4	5	6	7	8	9	10	11
22	H	STOKE		6	W	**4-0**	2-0	Maxwell 23, Hilton 24, Marr 71,	Demmery	Annan	Cottle	Marr	Wedlock	Spear	Staniforth	Maxwell	Gilligan	Burton	Hilton
	5/1		**12,000**	*19*	26			[Gilligan 88]	*Turner*	*Burgess*	*Mullineux*	*Baddeley*	*Holford*	*Sturgess*	*Griffiths*	*Arrowsmith*	*Chalmers*	*Gallimore*	*Miller*
								Ref: C Fallowfield	City, in blue, started from the Station end against opponents with Turner (ex-Kidderminster) in goal for the injured Welsh international Roose, and new signing Mullineux (ex-Burslem and Bury) at back. The Potters proved no match for City who recorded their best top-flight win so far.										
23	A	BLACKBURN		4	W	1-0	0-0	Gilligan 75	Demmery	Annan	Cottle	Marr	Wedlock	Hanlin	Staniforth	Maxwell	Gilligan	Burton	Hilton
	19/1		*15,000*	*12*	28				*Evans*	*Crompton*	*Cowell*	*Wolst'nholme*	*Robertson*	*Bradshaw*	*Whittaker*	*Latheron*	*Martin*	*Aitkenhead*	*Bracegirdle*
			(£360)					Ref: F Heath	Following two successive away wins, the home fans were expecting Rovers to have won this game. However, their forwards were off form and City took full advantage. Gilligan, after having missed two chances from close in, sent in a long-distance shot which completely beat Evans.										
24	H	SUNDERLAND		5	D	1-1	1-1	Gilligan 7	Demmery	Annan	Cottle	Marr	Wedlock	Hanlin	Staniforth	Maxwell	Gilligan	Burton	Hilton
	26/1		14,000	*14*	29			*Holley 18*	*Ward*	*Rhodes*	*Daykin*	*Tait*	*McGhie*	*McConnell*	*Raine*	*Gemmell*	*McIntosh*	*Holley*	*Bridgett*
			(£350)					Ref: T Armitt	The sides were evenly matched on the frost-bound pitch, but Sunderland would have won but for Demmery saving a Rhodes penalty four mins from time following Marr's injudicious charge. After Gilligan burst through to give City the lead, Holley levelled by converting Raine's centre.										
25	H	EVERTON		5	W	2-1	2-0	Maxwell 24, Gilligan 38	Demmery	Annan	Cottle	Spear	Wedlock	Hanlin	Staniforth	Maxwell	Gilligan	Burton	Hilton
	9/2		20,000	*2*	31			*Young 87*	*Scott*	*Balmer W*	*Balmer R*	*Black*	*Booth*	*Abbott*	*Sharp*	*Settle*	*Young*	*Rouse*	*Donnachie*
								Ref: N Whittaker	In brilliant weather the fans saw City win an exciting game against the cup holders. Maxwell scrimmaged in the opener, then Gilligan doubled City's advantage when putting away a centre from Staniforth. After the break, a clever shot by Young brought Everton their solitary reward.										
26	A	WLCH ARSENAL		4	W	2-1	1-0	Marr 6, Hilton 87	Demmery	Annan	Cottle	Marr	Spear	Hanlin	Staniforth	Maxwell	Gilligan	Burton	Hilton
	16/2		*18,000*	*7*	33			*Satterthwaite 65*	*Ashcroft*	*Gray*	*Sharp*	*Bigden*	*Hynds*	*McEachrane*	*Garbutt*	*Ducat*	*Freeman*	*Sat'rthwaite*	*Neave*
								Ref: F Gardner	City, with Spear at centre-half for Wedlock (on international duty), turned in a strong cohesive performance at Plumstead. They were stronger than Woolwich in all departments and took the points thanks to Hilton's late drive, after Marr's acute angled shot had opened the proceedings.										
27	A	BURY		5	D	1-1	0-0	Smith 55	Demmery	Annan	Cottle	Spear	Wedlock	Hanlin	Staniforth	Smith	Maxwell	Burton	Hilton
	2/3		*8,551*	*17*	34			*Hibbert 84*	*Raeside*	*Lindsay*	*Leeming*	*Bell*	*Dewhurst*	*Davidson*	*Gildea*	*Kilbourne*	*Hibbert*	*Plant*	*Booth*
								Ref: F Bye	Smith's 25-yarder, which gave City the lead, produced a terrific response from Bury. City struggled to contain the Shakers' relentless attacks and it was no surprise when Hibbert netted a leveller. Fortunately, City were able to survive a hectic time to the close and escape with a point.										
28	H	MANCHESTER C		4	W	2-0	0-0	Hanlin 78, Staniforth 83	Demmery	Annan	Cottle	Marr	Wedlock	Hanlin	Staniforth	Maxwell	Gilligan	Burton	Hilton
	9/3		**12,000**	*16*	36				*Smith*	*Hill*	*Kelso*	*Dorsett*	*Eadie*	*Buchan*	*Stewart*	*Grieve*	*Thornley*	*Ross*	*Conlin*
								Ref: A Barker	At times the superiority of the visitors was remarkable and if it hadn't been for Wedlock then City would surely have lost. After Hanlin had netted with a high shot, Staniforth made sure of a rather fortunate win when, from near the touchline, he swung at the ball in Bassett-fashion.										
29	A	MIDDLESBROUGH		5	L	0-1	0-1		Demmery	Annan	Cottle	Marr	Spear	Hanlin	Staniforth	Maxwell	Gilligan	Burton	Fenton
	16/3		*10,000*	*12*	36			*Thackeray 33*	*Williamson*	*Tildesley*	*Campbell*	*Aitken S*	*Aitken A*	*Harkins*	*Brawn*	*Bloomer*	*Common*	*Wilcox*	*Thackeray*
								Ref: H Pollitt	With Wedlock absent on international duty, City's three-month immunity from League defeat came to an end at Ayresome Park. Whilst City lost chances of scoring in the wretched weather, Middlesbrough deserved the victory brought about when Thackeray fired in Brown's pass.										
30	H	PRESTON		4	W	1-0	1-0	Staniforth 20	Demmery	Annan	Cottle	Marr	Wedlock	Spear	Staniforth	Maxwell	Gilligan	Burton	Hanlin
	23/3		15,000	*10*	38				*McBride*	*Lockett*	*Rodway*	*Stringfellow*	*Hunter*	*Lyon*	*Becton*	*Wilson*	*Smith P*	*Bell*	*Danson*
								Ref: J Brodie	The brilliant sunny conditions matched City's optimism as their win over Preston, coupled with Newcastle's 1-4 defeat at Liverpool, much improved their Championship prospects. Staniforth's shot from near the corner flag twisted over the hands of McBride to give City the points.										
31	A	BOLTON		3	W	2-1	1-1	Maxwell 40, Burton 69	Demmery	Annan	Cottle	Spear	Wedlock	Hanlin	Staniforth	Maxwell	Gilligan	Burton	Smith
	29/3		20,000	*6*	40			*White 30*	*Edmondson*	*Baverstock*	*Stanley*	*Gaskell*	*Clifford*	*Boyd*	*Stokes*	*Owen*	*Shepherd*	*White*	*McEwan*
								Ref: A Millward	Stokes placed a corner perfectly for White to head through the opener, but City, who had sojourned at Matlock, were not dismayed. Maxwell did the necessary from a corner, before Burton, after Stokes had an effort disallowed for offside, fired in the winner through a forest of legs.										

No	Venue	Opponent	Att	Pos	Res	F-A	H-T	Scorers, Times, and Referees	1	2	3	4	5	6	7	8	9	10	11
32	A	NEWCASTLE		4	L	**0-3**	0-1		Demmery	Annan	Cottle	Spear	Wedlock	Hanlin	Staniforth	Maxwell	Gilligan	Burton	Smith
30/3			*40,000*	*1*	40			*Howie 5, Rutherford 60, 89*	*Sinclair*	*Carr*	*McCracken*	*McWilliam*	*Speedie*	*Gardner*	*Rutherford*	*Howie*	*Appleyard*	*Orr*	*Duffy*
								Ref: T Kirkham	With both sides chasing the Championship, 350 excursionists from Bristol were in the large crowd. Unfortunately, City were out of sorts in the hot weather and they fell behind early on when Howie shot in the opener after beating three men. Demmery was under siege in the second half.										
33	H	BOLTON		4	L	1-2	1-0	Maxwell 41	Demmery	Annan	Cottle	Marr	Spear	Hanlin	Staniforth	Maxwell	Gilligan	Burton	Smith
2/4			14,000	*6*	40			*Marsh 51, Boyd 83*	*Edmondson*	*Baverstock*	*Stanley*	*Gaskell*	*Clifford*	*Boyd*	*Stokes*	*Marsh*	*Owen*	*Ryder*	*Weaver*
								Ref: A Millward	With several City players turning out with bandages on ankles and limbs, the heavyweight tactics of Bolton were soon apparent. Shortly after failing from just a yard out, Maxwell fired in the opener, but a fine run by Stokes set up Marsh's equaliser, before Boyd hit a brilliant winner.										
34	H	ASTON VILLA		5	L	2-4	0-2	Maxwell 55p, Burton 65	Demmery	Annan	Cottle	Marr	Spear	Hanlin	Staniforth	Maxwell	Gilligan	Burton	Hilton
6/4			18,000	*3*	40			*Hampton 25, 35, 75, 85, Bache 60*	*George*	*Logan J*	*Corbett*	*Greenhaigh*	*Leake*	*Codling*	*Millington*	*Cantrell*	*Hampton*	*Bache*	*Hall*
								Ref: J Ibbotson	Three successive defeats have extinguished City's Championship hopes as, with two games in hand, they are now ten points behind Newcastle. In the stormy conditions they couldn't complain about this loss as Villa, despite losing Greenhaigh with an injury, were much the superior side.										
35	A	LIVERPOOL		5	W	4-2	2-1	Connelly 20, Maxwell 30, 75,	Demmery	Annan	Cottle	Marr	Wedlock	Hanlin	Staniforth	Maxwell	Gilligan	Connelly	Hilton
13/4			*12,000*	*13*	42			*Annan 35og, Raybould 60*	*Hardy*	*Saul*	*Dunlop*	*Parry*	*Gorman*	*Bradley*	*Goddard*	*McPherson*	*Blanthorne*	*Raybould*	*Cox*
								Ref: T Kirkham [Gilligan 50]	City's return to form was acknowledged by the Liverpool supporters, who were unanimous in their opinion that the best side won. Connelly opened the scoring when he raced round Saul and fired in an oblique left-footer; then Maxwell doubled City's advantage with a clear shot.										
36	A	DERBY		4	W	3-1	2-1	Gilligan 7, Maxwell 35, Hanlin 75	Demmery	Annan	Gale	Marr	Wedlock	Hanlin	Staniforth	Maxwell	Gilligan	Connelly	Hilton
20/4			***6,000***	*19*	44			*Armstrong 4*	*Smith*	*Nicholas*	*Moore*	*Warren*	*Hall*	*Bagshaw*	*Armstrong*	*Long*	*Bentley*	*Wheatcroft*	*Davis G*
								Ref: J Carr	This game, which the Rams needed to win to escape relegation, started sensationally when Armstrong popped the ball in after Warren had shot against Gale's legs. It then all went wrong for Derby as, shortly after Maxwell had fired City into the lead, Warren failed from the penalty spot.										
37	H	THE WEDNESDAY		2	W	2-0	0-0	Gilligan 65, Connelly 85	Demmery	Annan	Cottle	Spear	Wedlock	Hanlin	Staniforth	Maxwell	Gilligan	Connelly	Hilton
24/4			15,000	*13*	46				*Lyall*	*Layton*	*Brittleton*	*Hemmingf'ld*	*Crawshaw*	*Bartlett*	*Chapman*	*Bradshaw*	*Wilson*	*Stewart*	*Simpson G*
			(£365)					Ref: J Howcroft	This win over Saturday's cup winners, who brought the trophy with them, took City into the runners-up spot. Hilton, with his dashing runs, opened up the game wonderfully in the second half, when Gilligan raced through to place in the opener, and Connelly drove in the second.										
38	H	NOTTS CO		2	W	1-0	0-0	Gilligan 65	Demmery	Annan	Cottle	Spear	Wedlock	Hanlin	Staniforth	Maxwell	Gilligan	Connelly	Hilton
27/4			**12,000**	*18*	48				*Iremonger*	*Morley*	*Griffiths*	*Emberton*	*Clamp*	*Craythorne*	*Dean*	*Tarplin*	*Jones Aaron*	*Poppitt*	*Waterall*
		Home	Away					Ref: W Gilgryst	A solitary goal, when Hilton's centre was returned by Staniforth for Gilligan to slip over the line, proved enough to beat the impressive visitors. On a muddy pitch, both goals had remarkable escapes, and had Notts been able to share the spoils few would have begrudged them.										
Ave		15,974	15,917																

CUP-TIES

FA Cup/Glos Cup				F-A	H-T	Scorers, Times, and Referees	1	2	3	4	5	6	7	8	9	10	11
1 H LEEDS CITY	6	W		4-1	3-0	Maxwell 1, Burton 3, Gilligan 32, 77	Demmery	Annan	Cottle	Marr	Wedlock	Hanlin	Staniforth	Maxwell	Gilligan	Burton	Hilton
12/1	14,324 *2:16*					*McLeod 70*	*Bromage*	*Murray*	*Ray*	*Hargreaves*	*Kirk*	*Kennedy*	*Jefferson*	*Watson*	*McLeod*	*Lavery*	*Wilson*
(£427.0.9)						Ref: J Adams	Despite a week's preparation at Clevedon, Leeds were soon in trouble against a City side who completed their preparations in Portishead. Even though McLeod managed to score for Leeds, there proved no way back for them as Gilligan twice shot into the net to tie up City's easy victory.										
2 A WLCH ARSENAL	6	L		1-2	0-1	Gilligan 51	Demmery	Annan	Cottle	Spear	Wedlock	Hanlin	Staniforth	Maxwell	Gilligan	Burton	Hilton
2/2	*31,300* *4*					*Kyle 30, Hynds 75*	*Ashcroft*	*Cross*	*Sharp*	*Bigden*	*Hynds*	*McEachrane*	*Garbutt*	*Coleman*	*Kyle*	*Sat'rthwaite*	*Neave*
(£1,066)						Ref: J Howcroft	Over 3,000 City fans, who travelled to London on the GWR excursion, saw their favourites go down to their usual defeat against the Arsenal, despite having most of the play. Kyle headed the Gunners in front from a difficult angle, but Gilligan fired in a delightful second-half leveller.										
F A BRISTOL ROV	4	W		2-0	1-0	Gilligan 25, 50	Demmery	Annan	Cottle	Spear	Wedlock	Marr	Hanlin	Burton	Gilligan	Maxwell	Staniforth
GC 1/4	*12,629* *SL:13*						*Cartlidge*	*Hales*	*Ovens*	*Hutchinson*	*Jarvie*	*Smart*	*Clark*	*Young*	*Walker*	*Gerrish*	*Gould*
(£318.17.3)						Ref: J Ibbotson	Given the hot weather and the hard pitch, as well as the fact that both teams have been fully occupied recently, the play had much to commend it. Gilligan fired in the opener from close range; then he later made sure of City's success by putting the ball away from Staniforth's corner.										

FRIENDLIES

Match	Att	Res	F-A	H-T	Scorers, Times, and Referees	1	2	3	4	5	6	7	8	9	10	11
1 A SOUTHAMPTON		L	1-2	0-1	Bennett 88	Demmery	Annan	Tuft	Spear	Wedlock	Chambers	Bennett	Maxwell	**Connelly**	Burton	Hilton
10/12	*3,000*				*Harrison 10, 70*	*Clawley*	*Clarke*	*Glover*	*Hogg*	*Robertson*	*Gray*	*Jefferies*	*Glen*	*Harrison*	*Harris*	*Mouncher*
					(Fred Harrison Benefit)	At the frost-bound Dell, Harrison marked his benefit by opening the scoring from a pass by Jefferies, before getting past Spear to notch the winner. Shortly before Bennett scored for City, despite appeals for offside, Demmery pulled off a sensational save from a Jefferies cross-drive.										
2 H BIRMINGHAM		W	3-2	3-1	Gilligan 10, 17, Connelly 16	Demmery	Annan	Cottle	Spear	Wedlock	Hanlin	Smith	Bennett	Gilligan	Connelly	Hilton
23/2	6,000				*Jones 38, 65*	*Robinson*	*Kearns*	*Stokes*	*Green*	*Shuf'botham*	*Cornan*	*Kirby*	*Smith*	*Jones W*	*Morris*	*Anderson*
					Ref: H Ward	Whilst there was much that marked this game down as being a friendly, there were patches of good play. For City, Connelly was frequently conspicuous, firing in one of the goals and displaying a good turn of speed. Hinton was also in good form, producing many accurate centres.										
3 H SOUTHAMPTON		L	2-4	0-1	Fenton 75, Connelly 85 *[Harrison 70]*	Clay	**Gale**	Tuft	Spear	Wedlock	Chambers	Staniforth	Bennett	Smith	Connelly	Fenton
25/2	2,000				*Glen 20, 60, Mouncher 46,*	*Burrows*	*Clark*	*Glover*	*Robertson*	*Bowden*	*Gray*	*Everist*	*Glen*	*Harrison*	*Harris*	*Mouncher*
					Ref: C Neale *(Billy Tuft Benefit)*	Glen opened the scoring in Tuft's Benefit with a fine shot. After the break, Tuft was often noticed and on one occasion he got Gale out of difficulty with an overhead kick. Glen's long shot put on Soton's third and Harrison added a fourth before Fenton fired in a reply for City.										

		Home						Away					
		P	W	D	L	F	A	W	D	L	F	A	Pts
1	Newcastle U	38	18	1	0	51	12	4	6	9	23	34	51
2	BRISTOL C	38	12	3	4	37	18	8	5	6	29	29	48
3	Everton	38	16	2	1	50	10	4	3	12	20	36	45
4	Sheffield Utd	38	13	4	2	36	17	4	7	8	21	38	45
5	Aston Villa	38	13	4	2	51	19	6	2	11	27	33	44
6	Bolton Wndrs	38	10	4	5	35	18	8	4	7	24	29	44
7	Wlch Arsenal	38	15	1	3	38	15	5	3	11	28	44	44
8	Manchester U	38	10	6	3	33	15	7	2	10	20	41	42
9	Birmingham	38	13	5	1	41	17	2	3	14	11	35	38
10	Sunderland	38	10	4	5	42	31	4	5	10	23	35	37
11	Middesbrough	38	11	2	6	33	21	4	4	11	23	42	36
12	Blackburn R	38	10	3	6	40	25	4	4	11	16	34	35
13	Wednesday	38	8	5	6	33	26	4	6	9	16	34	35
14	Preston NE	38	13	4	2	35	19	1	3	15	9	38	35
15	Liverpool	38	9	2	8	45	32	4	5	10	19	33	33
16	Bury	38	9	4	6	30	23	4	2	13	28	45	32
17	Manchester C	38	7	7	5	29	25	3	5	11	24	52	32
18	Notts Co	38	6	9	4	31	18	2	6	11	15	32	31
19	Derby Co	38	8	6	5	29	19	1	3	15	12	40	27
20	Stoke	38	7	6	6	27	22	1	4	14	14	42	26
		760	218	82	80	746	402	80	82	218	402	746	760

Odds & ends

Double wins: (6) Stoke, Blackburn, Man C, Liverpool, Derby, Notts Co.
Double losses: (1) Aston Villa.

Won from behind: (5) New', (h), L'pool (h), Shef U (h), Bolt' (a), Derby (a).
Lost from in front: (2) Manchester United (h), Bolton Wanders (h).

High spots: Becoming the first Southern club to finish in the top two.
A new record of the highest placing for a newly promoted club.
Billy Wedlock's England debut at Goodison Park, where Ireland lost 0-1.

Low spots: The two defeats over Easter that cost the Championship.

Player of the year: Billy Wedlock.
Ever-presents: (1) Archie Annan.
Hat-tricks: (0).
Leading scorer: Overall: Sammy Gilligan (22). League: Maxwell (17)

Pre-Season Trial Match: 20 Aug Reds 8(2) Blues 0 Ref: A Farrant
2,500 Jones (4), Staniforth, Critchley, Wedlock, Connelly.

AGM (Temperance Hall, East Street, Bedminster, 24 June 1907):
Profit £2,879.17s.4d. Season Ticket Sales £464.16s.9d.

	Appearances			Goals			
	Lge	**Cup**	**Fr**	**Lge**	**Cup**	**Fr**	**Tot**
Annan, Archie	**38**	3	2				
Bennett, Walter	**8**		3	**2**		1	**3**
Burton, Andy	**34**	3	1	**13**	1		**14**
Chambers, Peter			2				
Clay, Harry	**8**		1				
Connelly, Fred	**4**		3	**2**		2	**4**
Cottle, Joe	**37**	3	1				
Demmery, Bill	**30**	3	2				
Fenton, Freddie	**2**		1			1	**1**
Gale, Tom	**1**		1				
Gilligan, Sammy	**37**	3	1	**15**	5	2	**22**
Hanlin, Pat	**36**	3	1	**3**			**3**
Hilton, Frank	**32**	2	2	**4**			**4**
Marr, Reuben	**30**	2		**2**			**2**
Maxwell, Billy	**37**	3	1	**17**	1		**18**
Smith, George	**11**		2	**2**			**2**
Spear, Arthur	**15**	2	3				
Staniforth, Fred	**24**	3	1	**3**			**3**
Tuft, Billy			2				
Wedlock, Billy	**34**	3	3	**2**			**2**
Opponent og				**1**			**1**
20 players used	**418**	**33**	**33**	**66**	**7**	**6**	**79**

No	Date	Opponent	Att	Pos	Pt	F-A	H-T	Scorers, Times, and Referees	1	2	3	4	5	6	7	8	9	10	11
1	H	EVERTON			W	3-2	2-2	Staniforth 9, Maxwell 18, Gilligan 85	Demmery	Annan	Cottle	Marr	Wedlock	Hanlin	Staniforth	Maxwell	Gilligan	Burton	Hilton
	2/9		14,000		2			*Bolton 3, Hardman 25*	*Scott*	*Balmer R*	*Balmer W*	*Booth*	*Taylor*	*Abbott*	*Donnachie*	*Bolton*	*Young*	*Rouse*	*Hardman*
			(£371)					Ref: T Armitt	In spite of the threatening character of the weather, there was a good-sized crowd at the Gate who saw some excellent play in the opening half, when all four goals were the result of good combination play. City secured the points thanks to Gilligan's lobbed in winner near the finish.										
2	A	WLCH ARSENAL			W	**4-0**	1-0	Connelly 9, 89, Maxwell 70, 73	Demmery	Gale	Cottle	Marr	Wedlock	Hanlin	Staniforth	Maxwell	Gilligan	Connelly	Hilton
	7/9		*17,000*		4				*Ashcroft*	*Gray*	*Sharp*	*Bigden*	*Sands*	*McEachrane*	*Lee*	*Coleman*	*Freeman*	*Mordue*	*Neave*
								Ref: H Pollitt	Connelly put City, who were weakened by the absence of Annan and Burton, on course for this great win by netting the opener with a fine cross-shot. Arsenal, missing forwards Satterthwaite and Garbutt (injured versus Notts), wasted their chances before Maxwell drove in his pair.										
3	H	THE WEDNESDAY		5	L	0-2	0-0		Demmery	Gale	Cottle	Marr	Wedlock	Hanlin	Staniforth	Maxwell	Gilligan	Burton	Hilton
	14/9		**20,000**	*4*	4			*Chapman 50, Wilson 68*	*Lyall*	*Layton*	*Burton*	*Brittleton*	*Crawshaw*	*Bartlett*	*Maxwell*	*Chapman*	*Wilson*	*Bradshaw*	*Simpson*
								Ref: J Howcroft/C Crisp	Receiving the full force of the ball to the side of his head just before the break, the referee retired from the fray for a quarter of an hour. City opened with all their customary dash, but Gale faded after his bright start and was often beaten in the second half as the Reds slipped to defeat.										
4	H	NEWCASTLE		9	D	1-1	1-1	Hilton 5	Demmery	**Young**	Cottle	Marr	Wedlock	Hanlin	Staniforth	Maxwell	Gilligan	Connelly	Hilton
	21/9		**20,000**	*15*	5			*Orr 30*	*Lawrence*	*McCracken*	*McCombie*	*Gardner*	*Speedie*	*McWilliam*	*Rutherford*	*Orr*	*Hall*	*Brown*	*Duffy*
								Ref: N Whittaker	City were the better side up to the interval, but Newcastle were superior thereafter and would have won but for some erratic finishing. Hilton opened the scoring with a brilliant shot into the top corner of the net, but Orr's terrific drive from Rutherford's pass brought the visitors level.										
5	A	THE WEDNESDAY		9	L	3-5	0-1	Bartlett 69og, Connelly 72, Maxwell 76	Demmery	Young	Cottle	Marr	Wedlock	Hanlin	Staniforth	Maxwell	Gilligan	Connelly	Hilton
	23/9		*10,000*	*1*	5			*Chapman 10, Wilson 50, 65, 80,*	*Lyall*	*Layton*	*Burton*	*Brittleton*	*Crawshaw*	*Bartlett*	*Maxwell*	*Chapman*	*Wilson*	*Stewart*	*Simpson*
								Ref: J Howcroft *[Stewart 60]*	Glorious weather attended this exciting affair at Owlerton, where Wilson extinguished City's fine recovery. Chapman started the goal feast when he converted Simpson's centre. Bartlett sparked City's fight-back when, under pressure from Maxwell, he put through his own goal.										
6	A	NOTTS CO		13	L	1-3	1-1	Gilligan 21	Clay	Young	Cottle	Marr	Wedlock	Hanlin	Staniforth	Maxwell	Gilligan	Connelly	**Copestake**
	28/9		*12,000*	*9*	5			*Dean 40p, O'Donnell 70, Craythorne 87*	*Iremonger*	*Morley*	*Griffiths*	*Emberton*	*Bemment*	*Craythorne*	*Dean*	*Matthews*	*O'Donnell*	*Jones A*	*Waterall*
								Ref: A Briggs	Even though they fell behind to Gilligan's slipped in opener, Notts had no problems in winning this contest. Marr's handling offence, just after Clay's challenge, which had left Aaron Jones with a broken leg, brought about the spot-kick leveller; then O'Donnell fired them into the lead.										
7	H	MANCHESTER C		12	W	2-1	2-0	Hilton 25, Staniforth 35	Clay	Young	Cottle	Marr	Wedlock	Spear	Staniforth	**Rippon**	Gilligan	Connelly	Hilton
	5/10		15,000	*13*	7			*Grieve 52*	*Smith*	*Hill*	*Kelso*	*Buchan*	*Eadie*	*Blair*	*Dorsett*	*Grieve*	*Thornley*	*Ross*	*Conlin*
								Ref: A Millward	Wedlock took advantage of Buchan's absence for treatment on his injured ankle by pushing the ball across for Hilton to dash in and beat Smith for City's opener. Staniforth's power-drive doubled the advantage after Thornley had been unfortunate in having a shot disallowed for offside.										
8	A	PRESTON		14	L	0-3	0-1		Lewis	Young	Cottle	Marr	Wedlock	Spear	Staniforth	Rippon	Gilligan	Connelly	Hanlin
	12/10		*9,000*	*15*	7			*Barlow 43, Smith 61, Derbyshire 85p*	*McBride*	*Derbyshire*	*Rodway*	*McLean*	*Hunter*	*Lyon*	*Sanderson*	*Carlin*	*Smith P*	*Bell*	*Barlow*
								Ref: S Carr	City, with Hanlin in for Hilton (playing for the League), were indebted to their defence. Even though Preston attacked almost continuously it wasn't until almost on the break that Barlow rushed the ball in. Smith headed in the second; then a handling offence resulted in the penalty.										
9	H	BURY		13	D	1-1	1-0	Rippon 20	Lewis	Young	Cottle	Marr	Wedlock	Spear	Staniforth	Maxwell	Rippon	Burton	Hilton
	19/10		12,000	*4*	8			*Davidson 50*	*Raeside*	*Lindsay*	*Leeming*	*Dewhurst*	*Davidson*	*Bullen*	*Gildea*	*Tufnell*	*Hibbert*	*Kay*	*Booth*
								Ref: N Whittaker	Controversy over City's goal, which didn't appear to have crossed the line before being cleared. The referee had no doubts and immediately pointed to the centre, though in the second half he disallowed Maxwell's headed effort. Davidson's fierce shot, in off a post, levelled matters.										
10	A	ASTON VILLA		11	D	4-4	1-3	Gilligan 23, Wedlock 54, Maxwell 65,	Lewis	Young	Cottle	Marr	Wedlock	Hanlin	Staniforth	Maxwell	Gilligan	Burton	Hilton
	26/10		*22,000*	*12*	9			*Hampton 3, 25, Bache 11, 52*	*Turner*	*Leake*	*Miles*	*Tranter*	*Logan J*	*Codling*	*Wallace*	*Logan A*	*Hampton*	*Bache*	*Hall*
								Ref: S Peers [Hilton 67]	Following a free-kick, Wedlock sparked City's fight-back against a Villa side that appeared to have shot their bolt after Bache's cross-shot had given them a three-goal advantage. Maxwell headed in from a corner, then Hilton dribbled through from halfway to fire in a great equaliser.										

No	H/A	Opponents / Date	Att	Pos	Res	Pts	F-A	H-T	Scorers, Times, and Referees	1	2	3	4	5	6	7	8	9	10	11	Notes
11	H	LIVERPOOL 2/11	12,000	8 *6*	W	11	2-0	1-0	Wedlock 10, Gilligan 70 Ref: J Bailey	Lewis *Hardy*	Young *West*	Cottle *Rogers*	Marr *Robinson*	Wedlock *Gorman*	Hanlin *Bradley*	Staniforth *Goddard*	Maxwell *Hewitt C*	Gilligan *Hewitt J*	Burton *Fitzpatrick*	Hilton *Cox*	Liverpool played better than they did against City last season, but it still needed a great performance from keeper Sam Hardy to keep the score down. After Wedlock gave City the lead with a powerful shot, Hardy's only mistake was to be caught out of his charge when Gilligan netted.
12	A	MIDDLESBROUGH 9/11	*12,000*	7 *14*	W	13	2-0	0-0	Staniforth 51, Maxwell 88 Ref: R Horrocks	Lewis *Williamson*	Young *Brown*	Cottle *Watson*	Marr *Aitken S*	Wedlock *Aitken A*	Hanlin *Barker*	Staniforth *Brawn*	Maxwell *Bloomer*	Gilligan *Common*	Burton *Wilcox*	Hilton *Thackeray*	City's defence proved too good despite all the efforts of Middlesbrough's front rank. Williamson had no chance with Maxwell's shot, which tied up the Westerners' victory, but he appeared to have had the time to stop Staniforth's hard-driven opener into the corner to the keeper's left.
13	H	SHEFFIELD U 16/11	14,000	6 *12*	W	15	3-2	2-1	Maxwell 13, Gilligan 20, Burton 56 *Wilkinson 15, Needham 55* Ref: C Fallowfield	Lewis *Lievesley*	Young *Benson*	Cottle *Brooks*	Marr *Johnson C*	Wedlock *Wilkinson B*	Hanlin *Needham*	Staniforth *Thompson*	Maxwell *Levick*	Gilligan *Brown*	Burton *Bluff*	Hilton *Bromage*	On their performance in this match, it is doubtful if there is a finer half-back line in the country than that of the City's. A deserved win, thanks to Burton's fired-in effort immediately after Needham had brought United level with a 25-yarder over the outstretched hands of Talbot-Lewis.
14	A	CHELSEA 23/11	***30,000***	7 *19*	L	15	**1-4**	0-3	Burton 75 *Hilsdon 3, 35, 38, 60* Ref: A Barker	Lewis *Whiting*	Young *Cameron*	Cottle *Miller*	Marr *Henderson*	Wedlock *Stark*	Hanlin *Birnie*	Staniforth *Brawn*	Maxwell *Rouse*	Gilligan *Hilsdon*	Burton *Windridge*	Hilton *Fairgray*	City received a shock at Stamford Bridge, where a rampant Chelsea, with new acquisitions, Brawn (Middlesbrough) and Rouse (Everton), got off the bottom of the table. Wedlock found Hilsdon in fine form, leaping a great height into the air to meet Brawn's centre for his second goal.
15	H	NOTTINGHAM F 30/11	15,000	4 *17*	W	17	3-0	3-0	Maxwell 15p, Hilton 30, Burton 40 Ref: J Mason *(Harry Clay Benefit)*	Lewis *Linacre*	Annan *Iremonger*	Cottle *Maltby*	Marr *Hughes*	Wedlock *Needham*	Hanlin *Armstrong*	Staniforth *Shearman*	Maxwell *Marrison*	Gilligan *West*	Burton *Green*	Hilton *Spouncer*	Against a Forest side, for whom Iremonger made a return after two years' inactivity, City had it easy before losing Marr with a leg injury at the break. Iremonger's handball on the goal-line gave Maxwell his penalty opener, before both Hilton and Burton registered with grand drives.
16	A	MANCHESTER U 7/12	*15,000*	5 *1*	L	17	1-2	1-1	Hilton 5 *Wall 35, 75* Ref: J Mason	Lewis *Moger*	Annan *Holden*	Cottle *Stacey*	Spear *Duckworth*	Wedlock *Roberts*	Hanlin *Bell*	Staniforth *Meredith*	Maxwell *Bannister*	Gilligan *Turnbull J*	Burton *Turnbull A*	Hilton *Wall*	Spurred on by a second-half penalty failure, when Meredith shot wide, United played a fierce game and deservedly took the points, thanks to Wall's brilliant shot shortly before the close. City, who played a sterling game in the heavy going, proved unable to build on their gift opener.
17	H	BLACKBURN 14/12	**10,000**	6 *14*	D	18	2-2	2-0	Burton 32, Maxwell 39 *Davies 80, Latheron 82* Ref: T Armitt	Lewis *McIver*	Annan *Crompton R*	Cottle *Suttie*	Young *Walmsley*	Wedlock *Wilson*	Spear *Stevenson*	Staniforth *Whittaker*	Maxwell *Manson*	Gilligan *Davies*	Burton *Latheron*	Hilton *Bradshaw*	An unpleasant surprise for City after having the game well in hand at the interval. The loss of Hilton with an ankle injury early in the second half saw Blackburn grab an undeserved share of the spoils. A smart-combined movement, initiated by Wedlock, lead to Burton's fine opener.
18	A	BOLTON 21/12	*10,000*	5 *14*	W	20	2-1	0-1	Burton 46, 57 *Shepherd 36* Ref: R Pitchford	Lewis *Edmondson*	Annan *Baverstock*	Cottle *Stanley*	Marr *Greenhaigh*	Wedlock *Clifford*	Spear *Boyd*	Staniforth *Stokes*	Maxwell *Owen*	Gilligan *Shepherd*	Connelly *White*	Burton *McEwan*	City were not discouraged to be trailing to Shepherd's terrific shot from a clearly offside position some three yards beyond the backs and with no one, other than the City keeper, in front of him. Keeping up their good play they well deserved the points secured by Burton's double strike.
19	A	SUNDERLAND 25/12	*10,000*	5 *19*	D	21	3-3	3-2	Staniforth 3, Gilligan 10, Maxwell 22 *Hogg 17, Holley 44, Bridgett 63p* Ref: H Pollitt	Lewis *Allan*	Annan *Bonthron*	Cottle *Rhodes*	Spear *Tait*	Wedlock *Low*	Hanlin *Jarvie*	Staniforth *Hogg*	Maxwell *Holley*	Gilligan *Foster*	Connelly *Raybould*	Burton *Bridgett*	The weather was dull, but the pitch in good condition as City opened brilliantly with two early goals. Rhodes let in Staniforth, who easily beat Allan, who soon allowed a simple shot from Gilligan to roll into the net. Hogg then banged in a response which set up an exciting contest.
20	A	EVERTON 26/12	*15,000*	5 *7*	D	22	0-0	0-0	Ref: T Armitt	Lewis *Scott*	Annan *Balmer W*	Cottle *Stevenson*	Spear *Adamson*	Wedlock *Maconnachie*	Hanlin *Makepeace*	Stainiforth *Sharp*	Maxwell *Bolton*	Gilligan *Young*	Burton *Settle*	**Nixon** *Hardman*	After City won the toss the teams played out a grandly contested first half at Goodison Park. After the break, City showed their staying power by making further inroads into home quarters, but unfortunately they continued to be thwarted by Scott and the rest of Everton's fine defence.
21	H	BIRMINGHAM 28/12	12,000	5 *19*	D	23	0-0	0-0	Ref: W Gilgryst	Lewis *Dorrington*	Annan *Corbett*	Cottle *Kearns*	Spear *Beer*	Wedlock *Wigmore*	Hanlin *Dougherty*	Staniforth *Peplow*	Maxwell *Tickle*	Gilligan *Jones W*	Burton *Drake*	Nixon *Eyre*	Nixon (ex-Hibernian) continued in City's team in place of Hilton, but he was unable to inspire his colleagues in a biting wind on a bone-hard pitch. The Birmingham defence, in which Dorrington, Corbett and Kearns were outstanding, were not often troubled by a lacklustre City side.

No	Date		Att	Pos	Pt	F-A	H-T	Scorers, Times, and Referees	1	2	3	4	5	6	7	8	9	10	11
22	H	WLCH ARSENAL		6	L	1-2	0-1	Gilligan 60	Lewis	Annan	Cottle	Spear	Wedlock	Hanlin	Staniforth	Maxwell	Gilligan	Burton	Nixon
	4/1		15,000	*12*	23			*Coleman 5, Freeman 88*	*Ashcroft*	*Sharp*	*Gray*	*Ducat*	*Dick*	*McEachrane*	*Mordue*	*Coleman*	*Freeman*	*Kyle*	*Neave*
								Ref: H Pollitt	On a hard pitch, Arsenal regained form to notch up their customary win at Bristol, thanks to a failed offside appeal over Freeman's late strike. Gilligan rushed in Staniforth's centre to bring City level, after Coleman had concluded his fine run with a high shot to put Arsenal in front.										
23	A	NEWCASTLE		7	L	0-2	0-1		Lewis	Young	Cottle	Marr	Wedlock	Hanlin	Staniforth	Maxwell	Gilligan	Burton	Hilton
	18/1		***30,000***	*2*	23			*Soye 2, McClarence 50*	*Lawrence*	*McCracken*	*Pudan*	*Gardner*	*McWilliam*	*Willis*	*Rutherford*	*Higgins*	*McClarence*	*Soye*	*Wilson*
								Ref: N Whittaker	City wasted many chances at St James' Park where, even though Newcastle had two goals (one in each half) disallowed, they had much the better of the play. Rutherford took advantage of City's early hesitancy and put in a fine centre from which Soye beat Lewis with a rising shot.										
24	H	NOTTS CO		6	W	2-1	2-0	Gilligan 5, 30	Lewis	Young	Cottle	Marr	Wedlock	Hanlin	Staniforth	Maxwell	Gilligan	Burton	Hilton
	25/1		12,000	*11*	25			*Dean 70p*	*Iremonger*	*Morley*	*Montgomery*	*Emberton*	*Clamp*	*Craythorne*	*Dean*	*Matthews*	*Tarplin*	*Jones A*	*Munro*
								Ref: A Briggs	City recovered some of their old form against Notts, and emerged victorious after a vigorous game. A hot pace was kept up throughout and the visitors were rather fortunate to escape so lightly as City were much livelier and more enterprising than they have been for many weeks past.										
25	H	PRESTON		8	L	1-3	1-2	Maxwell 10	Demmery	Young	Cottle	Marr	**Chapman**	Hanlin	Staniforth	Maxwell	Gilligan	Burton	Hilton
	8/2		**10,000**	*5*	25			*Wilson 20, Smith 35, Gillibrand 70*	*McBride*	*McFadyen*	*Rodway*	*McLean*	*Stringfellow*	*Lyon*	*Gillibrand*	*Wilson*	*Smith P*	*Dawson H*	*Dawson G*
								Ref: T Rowbotham	Unlike many other times this season, City's forward line didn't lack for cohesion or shooting power, but were constantly foiled by the visiting keeper, who turned in a performance that has never been surpassed at the Gate. Burton fired in the opener to set the scene for a virtual siege.										
26	A	BURY		10	D	1-1	0-1	Gilligan 63	Clay	Young	Cottle	Marr	Spear	Hanlin	Staniforth	Maxwell	Gilligan	Burton	Hilton
	15/2		*7,231*	*5*	26			*Hibbert 7*	*Raeside*	*Lindsay*	*McMahon*	*Bullen*	*Rae*	*Dewhurst*	*Richards*	*Currie*	*Hibbert*	*Kay*	*Booth*
								Ref: N Whittaker	City turned in a splendid performance at Gigg Lane, where they were much the better side for the majority of the game. Hibbert opened the scoring by turning the ball in with his left leg as Clay came out, but City fought back to deservedly level thanks to Gilligan's shot in off a post.										
27	A	LIVERPOOL		13	L	1-3	0-2	Gilligan 60	Lewis	Young	Cottle	Marr	Spear	Hanlin	Staniforth	Maxwell	Gilligan	Burton	Hilton
	29/2		*12,000*	*9*	26			*Robinson 30, Hanlin 40og, Hewitt 80*	*Doig*	*West*	*Saul*	*Parry*	*Raisbeck*	*Bradley*	*Goddard*	*Robinson*	*Hewitt J*	*McPherson*	*Cox*
								Ref: J Bailey	Despite Liverpool's regular keeper Sam Hardy, together with City's Wedlock, turning out at Villa Park for the Football League in their 2-0 success over their Scottish counterparts, the homesters deserved this victory. Robinson opened the scoring by turning in Cox's low, level pass.										
28	H	MIDDLESBROUGH		14	L	0-1	0-1		Lewis	Marr	Cottle	Spear	Wedlock	Hanlin	Staniforth	Maxwell	Gilligan	Burton	Hilton
	7/3		**10,000**	*7*	26			*Bloomer 2*	*Wilson*	*Groves*	*Watson*	*Aitken S*	*Aitken A*	*Verrill*	*Bloomer*	*Common*	*Cail*	*Wilcox*	*Thackeray*
								Ref: R Horrocks	City were not discouraged when Bloomer gave Borough the early lead by converting the rebound, when Verrell's well-placed free-kick struck the crossbar. Unfortunately, despite their best efforts, they had only sympathy at the finish, as Hilton, Burton and Gilligan each hit a goal-post.										
29	H	ASTON VILLA		11	D	2-2	2-1	Copesake 12, Connelly 35	Lewis	Marr	Cottle	Spear	Wedlock	Hanlin	Stainiforth	Rippon	Connelly	Burton	Copestake
	11/3		**10,000**	*6*	27			*Hampton 5, 60*	*George*	*Lyons*	*Kimberly*	*Tranter*	*Garraty*	*Codling*	*Wallace*	*Reeves*	*Hampton*	*Walters*	*Hall*
								Ref: S Peers	The play was fast and exciting on the wet surface with Copestake equalising from Staniforth's low centre following Hampton's early opener. A corner, gained in dashing style off of Lyons, allowed Connelly to put City in front, but a Wallace centre gave Hampton his second-half leveller.										
30	A	SHEFFIELD U		14	L	0-2	0-1		Lewis	Young	Cottle	Spear	Wedlock	Hanlin	Staniforth	Marr	Rippon	Burton	Hilton
	14/3		*12,000*	*8*	27			*Benson 44p, Peart 75*	*Lievesley*	*Benson*	*Brooks*	*Wilkinson W*	*Wilkinson B*	*Needham*	*Thompson*	*Featherstone*	*Peart*	*Hardinge*	*Bromage*
								Ref: C Fallowfield	Despite Marr being a limping passenger for all but the first quarter of an hour, City – who had many chances – didn't deserve to lose this keen encounter. Many thought the penalty decision against Cottle was harsh, whilst Peart appeared offside when he headed in Thompson's centre.										
31	H	CHELSEA		15	D	0-0	0-0		Clay	Young	Annan	Spear	Wedlock	Hanlin	Nixon	Staniforth	Maxwell	Burton	Hilton
	21/3		12,000	*11*	28				*Whitley*	*Cameron*	*Miller*	*McRoberts*	*Stark*	*Birnie*	*Brawn*	*Humphreys*	*Hilsdon*	*Windridge*	*Fairgray*
								Ref: A Barker	A creditable City performance, considering the absence of Lewis, Cottle, Marr and Gilligan. Against fast and clever opponents, City compared unfavourably in all except the earnestness of their display, which brought them what might prove to be a crucial point at the season's finish.										

No	Date	Venue	Opponent	Att	Pos	Pts	Res	F-A	H-T	Scorers, Times, and Referees	1	2	3	4	5	6	7	8	9	10	11
32	28/3	A	NOTTINGHAM F	*12,000*	17 *12*	28	L	1-3	1-2	Gilligan 5	Clay	Young	Annan	Spear	Wedlock	Hanlin	Staniforth	Maxwell	Gilligan	Burton	Hilton
										West 6, 45, Morris 50	*Linacre*	*Dudley*	*Maltby*	*Hughes*	*Wolfe*	*Armstrong*	*Hooper*	*Marrison*	*West*	*Morris*	*Spouncer*
										Ref: A Hargreaves	City's fluid forward play was disrupted when Gilligan had to move into defence to replace Young, who had to retire with a hip injury shortly before Morris scored Forest's third goal. Early headers were traded, before West's brilliant low shot brought Forest the half-time advantage.										
33	4/4	H	MANCHESTER U	15,000	17 *1*	29	D	1-1	0-1	Maxwell 70	Clay	Annan	Cottle	Spear	Gilligan	Hanlin	Staniforth	Maxwell	Rippon	Burton	Hilton
										Wall 35	*Broomfield*	*Stacey*	*Burgess*	*Duckworth*	*Roberts*	*Bell*	*Meredith*	*Bannister*	*Halse*	*Turnbull A*	*Wall*
										Ref: Lieut W Clover	City continued their recent improved form, but still proved unable to obtain an elusive win as they missed their chances. A welcome point, nevertheless, against the leaders, who looked a well-balanced side. Billy Meredith was brilliant, as quick as ever, the ball always under control.										
34	11/4	A	BLACKBURN	*8,000*	19 *16*	29	L	**1-4**	1-2	Gilligan 37	Clay	Annan	Cottle	Spear	Wedlock	Hanlin	Staniforth	Maxwell	Gilligan	Burton	Hilton
										Crompton E 30, 44, Latheron 65, 75	*McIver*	*Crompton R*	*Suttie*	*Walmsley*	*Stevenson*	*Houlkner*	*Whittaker*	*Latheron*	*Crompton E*	*Wombwell*	*Anthony*
										Ref: T Armitt	Matters got no better for City at Ewood Park, where Gilligan had a first-half goal disallowed for offside. They held their own before Clay let in Crompton's weak shot just before the break. Latheron netted with unstoppable shot; then headed in another before missing an open goal.										
35	18/4	H	BOLTON	15,000	18 *17*	31	W	2-0	0-0	Gilligan 55, 75	Clay	Young	Cottle	Spear	Wedlock	Hanlin	Nixon	Maxwell	Gilligan	Burton	Hilton
											Davies	*Slater*	*Stanley*	*Gaskell*	*Clifford*	*Boyd*	*Stokes*	*McClarence*	*Shepherd*	*White*	*McEwan*
										Ref: J Mason	Victory at last enabled City to haul themselves out of the relegation zone. Davies starred for the visitors, but he could do little about Gilligan's two shots that beat him. Perhaps City were fortunate that the Trotters had been engaged in a hard game with Aston Villa the previous day.										
36	20/4	H	SUNDERLAND	19,500 (£529)	17 *13*	33	W	3-0	2-0	Burton 13, Gilligan 26, Maxwell 72	Clay	Young	Cottle	Spear	Wedlock	Hanlin	Nixon	Maxwell	Gilligan	Burton	Hilton
											Roose	*Marples*	*Forster*	*Tait*	*Low*	*Jarvie*	*McIntosh*	*Hogg*	*Raybould*	*Holley*	*Bridgett*
										Ref: H Pollitt	In a strong wind City, who played well on the hard ground, took charge early on. They never looked threatened by opponents who lost the services of the injured Hogg just before the break. Burton's cross-shot gave City the lead; then Gilligan scrambled the second over the line.										
37	21/4	A	MANCHESTER C	***5,000***	17 *3*	34	D	0-0	0-0		Clay	Young	Cottle	Spear	Wedlock	Hanlin	Nixon	Maxwell	Gilligan	Burton	Hilton
											Smith	*Jackson*	*Norgrove*	*Buchan*	*Holford*	*Blair*	*Dorsett*	*Wood*	*Thornley*	*Jones*	*Conlin*
										Ref: T Armitt	With this point at Hyde Road, City practically secured their First Division status. Despite their exertions of the previous day, City did the majority of the first-half attacking. In the fading light after the break, the homesters were awarded a penalty, but Clay preserved City's point.										
38	25/4	A	BIRMINGHAM	***5,000***	10 *20*	36	W	**4-0**	1-0	Burton 20,65, Rippon 80, Kearns 85og	Clay	Young	Cottle	Spear	Wedlock	Hanlin	Staniforth	Maxwell	Rippon	Burton	Hilton
											Dorrington	*Kearns*	*Stokes*	*Beer*	*Wigmore*	*Cornan*	*Green*	*Moore*	*Jones W*	*Mounteney*	*Anderson*
			Home	Away						Ref: W Gilgryst	City had it easy against opponents who, without Cornan from the first half, were further handicapped when Wigmore had to retire just before Rippon's headed effort. Burton's fine drive gave City the lead, then Wedlock got in some excellent shots, before Burton hooked in the second.										
	Ave		13,816	13,328																	

CUP-TIES

FA Cup/Glos Cup						F-A	H-T	Scorers, Times, and Referees	1	2	3	4	5	6	7	8	9	10	11
1	H	GRIMSBY		6	D	0-0	0-0		Lewis	Annan	Cottle	Marr	Wedlock	Hanlin	Staniforth	Maxwell	Gilligan	Burton	Hilton
	11/1		11,740 *2:19*						*Scott*	*Wheelhouse*	*Vincett*	*Lee*	*Higgins*	*Hatton*	*Stokes*	*Kilbourne*	*Blanthorne*	*Hakin*	*Fletcher*
			(£350)					Ref: A McQue	City, the hottest favourites of the first round, are thwarted by a combination of the frost-bound pitch and the inspired play of the visiting keeper. After the break, the game developed into virtually a contest between the City and Scott, who was well backed up by his colleagues.										
R	A	GRIMSBY		6	L	1-2	1-2	Hilton 43	Lewis	Annan	Cottle	Spear	Wedlock	Hanlin	Staniforth	Maxwell	Gilligan	Burton	Hilton
	15/1		*6,000 2:19*					*Lee 18, Blanthorne 30*	*Scott*	*Wheelhouse*	*Vincett*	*Lee*	*Higgins*	*Hatton*	*Stokes*	*Kilbourne*	*Blanthorne*	*Hakin*	*Fletcher*
			(£203)					Ref: A McQue/J Benson	Lee swung at the ball and completely beat Lewis for Grimsby's opener; then Blanthorne turned in a second before Hilton gave City hope just before the interval. Early in the second half the referee had to retire from the fray on sustaining an injured ankle in a collision with a player.										
F	H	BRISTOL ROV		10	W	2-0	2-0	Burton 6, Maxwell 35	Clay	Young	Cottle	Spear	Wedlock	Hanlin	Staniforth	Maxwell	Gilligan	Burton	Hilton
GC	29/4		8,186 *SL:5*						*Cartlidge*	*Appleby*	*Ovens*	*Smart*	*Strang*	*Handley*	*Clark*	*Gerrish*	*Smith*	*Roberts*	*Buckle*
			(£230)					Ref: T Kirkham	With both sides at practically full-strength, a keen game was anticipated. After Rovers won the toss, both goals were early in danger before Burton raced through to put City into the lead with a fine shot. Against the run of play, Maxwell's great drive doubled City's advantage.										

FRIENDLIES

					F-A	H-T	Scorers, Times, and Referees	1	2	3	4	5	6	7	8	9	10	11
1	A	BRENTFORD		W	3-1	1-0	Maxwell 15, Gilligan 50, 75	Lewis	Young	Cottle	Marr	Wedlock	Hanlin	Staniforth	Maxwell	Gilligan	Burton	Hilton
	1/2		*4,000*				*Underwood 65*	*Williams*	*Watson*	*Clark*	*Jay*	*Hamilton*	*McAllister*	*Brown*	*Parsonage*	*Corbett*	*Bowman*	*Underwood*
							Ref: A Barton	Southern Leaguers Brentford missed two early chances before Maxwell opened the scoring when his grand shot gave City the lead. Gilligan then appeared an almost certain scorer, but was frustrated by a remarkable save by Williams, before eventually registering after the interval.										
2	A	SWANSEA EAST		W	3-2	1-2	Gould 15, 75, Connelly 50	**Clegg**	**Shinner**	**Nash**	**Cross**	Radford	**Nash R**	**Connelly**	Dumble	Copestake	**Gould**	**Cranfield**
	2/4		*1,600*				*Baxter 30, Turvey 40*	*Fisher*	*Savage*	*Kift J*	*Morgan*	*Arnold*	*Rowe*	*Turvey*	*Williams*	*Ford*	*Glover*	*Baxter*
							Ref: D Sanbrook	The East Side club created much interest by putting together a representative Swansea XI for this game on the St Thomas Athletic ground. The City were much the superior combination, but found Fisher in such magnificent form that they were only able to win by the odd goal in five.										
3	A	ABERDARE		W	1-0	1-0	Staniforth 43	Clay	Spear	Cottle	Nash R	Wedlock	Hanlin	Copestake	Staniforth	Gilligan	Connelly	Hilton
	30/4		*1,000*					*Roose*	*Lewis*	*Goodwin*	*Parker*	*Griffiths*	*Shields*	*Powell*	*Bowell*	*Farr*	*Smith*	*Holland*
							Ref: M Morgan	Aberdare had the assistance of Roose, the Welsh international goalkeeper, but he wasn't severely tested. Clay saved splendidly from Farr, then Bowell threw away a chance before Staniforth scored. After the break, Gilligan wasted a fine opening set up by Wedlock's effective headwork.										

		Home						Away					
	P	W	D	L	F	A	W	D	L	F	A	Pts
1 Manchester U	38	15	1	3	43	19	8	5	6	38	29	52
2 Aston Villa	38	9	6	4	47	24	8	3	8	30	35	43
3 Manchester C	38	12	5	2	36	19	4	6	9	26	35	43
4 Newcastle U	38	11	4	4	41	24	4	8	7	24	30	42
5 Wednesday	38	14	0	5	50	25	5	4	10	23	39	42
6 Middlesbro'	38	12	2	5	32	16	5	5	9	22	29	41
7 Bury	38	8	7	4	29	22	6	4	9	29	39	39
8 Liverpool	38	11	2	6	43	24	5	4	10	25	37	38
9 Nottm Forest	38	11	6	2	42	21	2	5	12	17	41	37
10 BRISTOL C	38	8	7	4	29	21	4	5	10	29	40	36
11 Everton	38	11	4	4	34	24	4	2	13	24	40	36
12 Preston NE	38	9	7	3	33	18	3	5	11	14	35	36
13 Chelsea	38	8	3	8	30	35	6	5	8	23	27	36
14 Blackburn R	38	10	7	2	35	23	2	5	12	16	40	36
15 Wlch Arsenal	38	9	8	2	32	18	3	4	12	19	45	36
16 Sunderland	38	11	2	6	53	31	5	1	13	25	44	35
17 Sheffield Utd	38	8	6	5	27	22	4	5	10	25	36	35
18 Notts Co	38	9	3	7	24	19	4	5	10	15	32	34
19 Bolton Wndrs	38	10	3	6	35	26	4	2	13	17	32	33
20 Birmingham	38	6	6	7	22	28	3	6	10	18	32	30
	760	202	89	89	717	459	89	89	202	459	717	760

Odds & ends

Double wins: (1) Bolton Wanderers.
Double losses: (2) The Wednesday, Preston North End.

Won from behind: (2) Everton (h), Bolton Wanderers (a).
Lost from in front: (3) Notts Co (a), Manchester United (a), Preston (h).

High spots: Beating Everton at 'Ashton Gate' on the opening day.
Pat Hilton making a scoring debut for the Football League XI in a 6-3 success against the Irish League at 'Roker Park' on 12 October.
Billy Wedlock scoring for England in a 7-1 win over Wales at Wrexham.

Low spots: Losing 0-3 at Preston on 12 October.
The death of ex-player Walter Bennett following a cave in at Denaby Main Colliery on 6 April.

Player of the Year: Sammy Gilligan.
Ever-presents: (0).
Hat-tricks: (0).
Leading scorer: Overall: Sammy Gilligan (18). League: Gilligan (16)

Pre-Season Trial Match:
21 Aug Blues 2(0) Reds 0
3,000 (£40) Burton 50, Maxwell 75

AGM (Temperance Hall, East Street, Bedminster, 29 June 1908):
Profit £573.2s.7d. Season Ticket Sales £429.3s.11d.

	Appearances			Goals			
	Lge	**Cup**	**Fr**	**Lge**	**Cup**	**Fr**	**Tot**
Annan, Archie	**13**	2					
Burton, Andy	**32**	3	1	**9**	1		**10**
Chapman, Bert	**1**						
Clay, Harry	**11**	1	1				
Clegg, John			1				
Connelly, Fred	**9**		2	**4**		1	**5**
Copestake, Levi	**2**		2	**1**			**1**
Cottle, Joe	**36**	3	2				
Cranfield, M			1				
Cross, W			1				
Demmery, Bill	**6**						
Dumble			1				
Gale, Tom	**2**						
Gilligan, Sammy	**33**	3	2	**16**		2	**18**
Gould, Charlie			1			2	**2**
Hanlin, Pat	**34**	3	2				
Hilton, Frank	**30**	3	2	**5**	1		**6**
Marr, Reuben	**24**	1	1				
Maxwell, Billy	**34**	3	1	**13**	1	1	**15**
Nash, R			2				
Nash			1				
Nixon, John	**7**						
Radford, Tom			1				
Rippon, Willis	**7**			**2**			**2**
Shinner			1				
Spear, Arthur	**23**	2	1				
Staniforth, Fred	**35**	3	2	**4**		1	**5**
Talbot-Lewis, Albert	**21**	2	1				
Wedlock, Billy	**34**	3	2	**2**			**2**
Young, Bob	**24**	1	1				
Opponents og				**2**			**2**
30 players used	**418**	**33**	**33**	**58**	**3**	**7**	**68**

LEAGUE DIVISION 1 — Manager: Harry Thickett — SEASON 1908-09

No	Date		Att	Pos	Pt	F-A	H-T	Scorers, Times, and Referees	1	2	3	4	5	6	7	8	9	10	11
1	A	BLACKBURN			D	1-1	0-0	Maxwell 60	Clay	Young	Cottle	Spear	Wedlock	Hanlin	Staniforth	Maxwell	Gilligan	Burton	Hilton
	1/9		*10,000*		1			*Kyle 50*	*Ashcroft*	*Crompton R*	*Suttie*	*Walmsley*	*Chapman*	*Cameron*	*Garbutt*	*Ellis*	*Davies*	*Kyle*	*Anthony*
			(£228)					Ref: A Adams	City produce a fine display at Ewood Park, where the homesters were fortunate to share the spoils as towards the finish Maxwell's low shot hit a post. After Kyle followed up his powerful-drive, which hit the bar, to force the ball over the line, Maxwell brought City level with a fine shot.										
2	H	EVERTON			L	0-2	0-1		Clay	Young	Cottle	Spear	Wedlock	Hanlin	Staniforth	Maxwell	Gilligan	Burton	Hilton
	5/9		15,000		1			*Freeman 26, 70*	*Scott*	*Balmer R*	*Maconnachie*	*Harris*	*Taylor*	*Makepeace*	*Sharp*	*Coleman*	*Freeman*	*Bolton*	*Donnachie*
			(£400+)					Ref: C Fallowfield	Despite taking the lead when Freeman followed up after Clay had palmed away his first effort, the half-time whistle came as a relief to Everton who were under much pressure. After the break, Freeman made the game safe for the visitors when he beat Clay at the end of his speedy run.										
3	A	NEWCASTLE		18	L	1-2	1-0	Gilligan 30	Clay	Young	Cottle	Marr	Wedlock	Hanlin	Staniforth	Rippon	Gilligan	Burton	Hilton
	9/9		*22,000*	*1*	1			*Howie 53, 90*	*Lawrence*	*McCracken*	*Whitson*	*Gardner*	*Veitch*	*McWilliam*	*Rutherford*	*Howie*	*Allan*	*Stewart*	*Wilson*
								Ref: Lieut W Clover	City often looked likely winners of this sparkling contest, but ended up succumbing to Howie's last-gasp winner. After putting City in front, Gilligan had a first-half shot disallowed for offside, but Newcastle fought back to secure the points with practically the final kick of the game.										
4	A	LEICESTER FOSSE		18	D	1-1	1-1	Burton 8	Clay	Young	Cottle	Marr	Wedlock	Hanlin	Staniforth	Rippon	Gilligan	Burton	Hilton
	12/9		*17,000*	*19*	2			*Shanks 30*	*Bailey*	*Hedley*	*Blackett*	*Randle*	*Bannister*	*Goldie*	*Donnelly*	*Walker*	*Garraty*	*Shanks*	*Turner RF*
								Ref: A Neale	City, who travelled from their overnight base at Matlock, were greeted by a heavy thunderstorm. Burton dashed in to give City the lead in this fast and exciting encounter in which science gave way to keenness, but by the finish they were indebted to Clay's fine form between the sticks.										
5	H	WLCH ARSENAL		13	W	2-1	1-0	Gilligan 3, Hilton 50	Clay	Young	Cottle	Spear	Wedlock	Hanlin	Staniforth	**Hardy**	Gilligan	Burton	Hilton
	19/9		12,000	*17*	4			*Greenaway 70*	*McDonald*	*Gray*	*Cross*	*Dick*	*Sands*	*McEachrane*	*Greenaway*	*Lewis*	*Lee*	*Raybould*	*Neave*
								Ref: J Smith	Arsenal experienced their usual portion of good fortune at Ashton Gate, where the score should have been 5-3 if all the chances had been taken. However, this time it proved not enough to save them as City were able to achieve a rare home success against the lowly Gunners.										
6	A	NOTTS CO		9	W	1-0	0-0	Burton 79	Clay	Young	Cottle	Marr	Wedlock	Hanlin	Staniforth	Hardy	Gilligan	Burton	Hilton
	26/9		*13,000*	*20*	6				*Iremonger*	*Morley*	*Montgomery*	*Emberton*	*Clamp*	*Craythorne*	*Dean*	*Matthews*	*Walker*	*Cantrell*	*Dodd*
								Ref: A McQue	Magnificent weather prevailed at Trent Bridge where City, though playing the brighter and cleaner football, most unexpectedly captured both points. Marr's pass, following a corner, set up Burton to do the business and beat Iremonger with a shot that glanced into the net off the post.										
7	H	NEWCASTLE		8	D	3-3	1-0	Burton 6, Gilligan 55, 76	Clay	Young	Cottle	Marr	Wedlock	Hanlin	Staniforth	Hardy	Gilligan	Burton	Hilton
	3/10		16,000	*2*	7			*Veitch 60p, 85, Higgins 75*	*Lawrence*	*McCracken*	*Whitson*	*Gardner*	*Veitch*	*Willis*	*Rutherford*	*Howie*	*Higgins*	*Stewart*	*Wilson*
								Ref: Lieut W Clover	Entertainment aplenty at Ashton Gate, where Newcastle do well, seeing as they lost Gardner with a leg injury soon after Burton headed in City's opener. In heat-wave conditions, Wedlock won the toss and elected to face the Ashton Road End at the start of this extraordinary game.										
8	A	THE WEDNESDAY		12	L	0-2	0-2		Clay	Annan	Cottle	Young	**Penman**	Spear	Staniforth	Hardy	Gilligan	Burton	Hilton
	10/10		*15,000*	*4*	7			*Rollinson 10, Lloyd 25*	*Davison*	*Layton*	*Holbem*	*Brittleton*	*McConnell*	*Bartlett*	*Lloyd*	*Chapman*	*Wilson*	*Rollinson*	*Foxall*
								Ref: A Barker	The Wednesday started off like a team determined to win, and Clay brought off three saves in quick succession before Rollinson headed in the early opener. City were unfortunate enough to have Young off the field when Lloyd's unstoppable shot doubled the homesters' advantage.										
9	A	PRESTON		15	L	1-2	0-2	Burton 65	Clay	Young	Cottle	Spear	Wedlock	Hanlin	Staniforth	Hardy	Gilligan	Burton	Hilton
	17/10		*6,000*	*9*	7			*Sanderson 1, 38*	*McBride*	*Lavery*	*Rodway*	*Chadwick*	*McCall*	*Lyon*	*Main*	*Carlin*	*Smith P*	*Dawson*	*Sanderson*
								Ref: J Rowbotham	City didn't get the reward they deserved from a much-improved display. Trailing to Sanderson's two great rising shots, the first from an acute-angle following a disputed free-kick soon after the kick-off, it wasn't until the second half that Burton's long shot brought City some success.										
10	H	MIDDLESBROUGH		15	D	1-1	1-0	Hardy 8	Clay	Young	Cottle	Spear	Wedlock	Hanlin	Staniforth	Hardy	Gilligan	Burton	Hilton
	24/10		12,000	*17*	8			*Common 68*	*Williamson*	*McLeod*	*Watson*	*Aitken S*	*Aitken A*	*Wilcox*	*Common*	*Bloomer*	*Cail*	*Hall*	*Thackeray*
								Ref: A Briggs *(Bill Demmery Benefit)*	With the Ironsides playing bright and open football, the fans were treated to an exhilarating game at Ashton Gate. From Hinton's corner-kick Hardy put City in front with a fine header, but Common restored parity after the break by neatly sliding the ball in from Thackeray's flag-kick.										

No	Venue	Opponent	Pos	Res	F-A	H-T	Scorers, Times, Referees	1	2	3	4	5	6	7	8	9	10	11
11	A	MANCHESTER C	17	L	**1-5**	0-1	Wedlock 85 *[Dorsett 70]*	Clay	Young	Cottle	Hanlin	Wedlock	Spear	Staniforth	Hardy	Maxwell	Burton	Hilton
31/10		*20,000*	12	8			*Thrnley25,60,Wood 59,Cottle 65og,*	*Smith*	*Kelso*	*Burgess*	*Buchan*	*Eadie*	*Buckley*	*Webb*	*Wood*	*Thornley*	*Jones*	*Dorsett*
							Ref: T Armitt	Trailing to Thornley's rather soft goal at the interval, City fell away during the second half as the light blues went on the rampage. Wood started the carnage by heading Dorsett's splendidly placed corner. Thornley then scrambled in another before injury forced his departure.										
12	H	LIVERPOOL	15	W	1-0	0-0	Burton 75	Clay	Annan	Cottle	Marr	Wedlock	Spear	Staniforth	Gilligan	**Latham**	Burton	Hardy
7/11		12,000	*8*	10				*Hardy*	*Saul*	*Chorlton*	*Bradley*	*Harrop*	*Parry*	*Cox*	*Goode*	*Hewitt*	*Robinson*	*Goddard*
							Ref: A Green	A penalty against Saul led to City's well-merited winner, as Burton put away the rebound when Hardy beat away his spot-kick. Liverpool were at their best before the interval, but in the second half they had no answer to City's determined display, despite Latham's notably quiet debut.										
13	A	BURY	12	W	2-1	0-1	Burton 60, Rippon 70	Clay	Annan	Cottle	Young	Wedlock	Spear	Staniforth	Gilligan	Rippon	Burton	Hardy
14/11		*5,625*	*19*	12			*Hibbert 25*	*Raeside*	*Lindsay*	*McMahon*	*Dewhurst*	*Currie*	*Bullen*	*Gibson*	*Hughes*	*Hibbert*	*Kay*	*Duffy*
							Ref: J Smith	Trailing to Hibbert's rising drive at the break, City seemed unlikely winners. Fortunately, a bad miss by Hibbert at the start of the second half changed the course of this game. Taking command of the proceedings, Burton hooked in an equaliser, before Rippon put away Hardy's centre.										
14	H	SHEFFIELD U	12	D	1-1	1-0	Gilligan 37	Clay	Annan	Cottle	Marr	Wedlock	Spear	Staniforth	Rippon	Gilligan	Burton	Hardy
21/11		10,000	*18*	13			*Benson 70p*	*Lievesley*	*Benson*	*Brooks*	*Parker*	*Wilkinson B*	*Needham*	*Lang*	*Featherstone*	*Peart*	*Hardinge*	*Evans*
							Ref: J Ibbotson	Whilst City's lead, courtesy of Burton's run in, was ill-deserved at the break, they played so much better in the second half that they should have won. Unfortunately, Annan gifted United a share of the spoils by handling the ball in the box and Benson made no mistake from the spot.										
15	A	ASTON VILLA	11	D	1-1	1-0	Gilligan 8	Clay	Annan	Cottle	Marr	Wedlock	Spear	Staniforth	Gilligan	Rippon	Burton	Hardy
28/11		*18,000*	*5*	14			*Bache 65*	*George*	*Lyons*	*Miles*	*Tranter*	*Buckley*	*Logan J*	*Wallace*	*Reeves*	*Hampton*	*Bache*	*Hall*
							Ref: A Adams	Following Cottle's handling offence on the half-hour mark, City were fortunate that Hall drove Villa's spot-kick high over the bar. A draw was however the least that City deserved for their fine display. Gilligan shot in the opener during a melee, but Bache fired in Villa's fierce leveller.										
16	H	NOTTM FOREST	9	W	2-1	1-0	Hilton 14, 65	Clay	Annan	Cottle	Marr	Wedlock	Spear	Staniforth	Gilligan	Rippon	Burton	Hilton
5/12		11,000	*15*	16			*Green 80*	*Linacre*	*Dudley*	*Gibson*	*Hughes*	*Wolfe*	*Armstrong*	*Hooper*	*Shearman*	*Green*	*Morris*	*Spouncer*
							Ref: C Fallowfield	By far the best football in this game was played during the early stages, when Hilton put City in front with a fierce shot. After City had missed a remarkable number of chances, Gilligan's pass set up Hilton to secure the second, before Spouncer's centre allowed Green to net for Forest.										
17	A	SUNDERLAND	8	W	2-0	1-0	Rippon 1, Hilton 65	Clay	Annan	Cottle	Marr	Wedlock	Spear	Staniforth	Maxwell	Rippon	Burton	Hilton
12/12		*10,000*	*6*	18				*Roose*	*Montgomery*	*Forster*	*Tait*	*Thompson*	*Jarvie*	*Mordue*	*Hogg*	*Brown*	*Holley*	*Bridgett*
							Ref: M McQueen	A sensation at Roker Park, where City put on a great display to beat the side, who had won 9-1 at Newcastle last week. Rippon gave City the best possible start when he drove the ball in under the bar right at the start. Hilton made sure of the points by netting from Maxwell's pass.										
18	H	CHELSEA	5	W	1-0	1-0	Hilton 13	Clay	Annan	Cottle	Marr	Wedlock	Spear	Staniforth	Maxwell	Rippon	Burton	Hilton
19/12		12,000	*17*	20				*Whitley*	*Cameron*	*Miller*	*Kennedy*	*Warren*	*Birnie*	*Brawn*	*Humphreys*	*Hilsdon*	*Windridge*	*Bridgeman*
							Ref: J Mason	Despite the depressing rain, a good crowd were in attendance to witness City win a game in which the play was of a high order. Hilton settled matters early on when, from Staniforth's cross, he rushed in the only goal. Chelsea lost the services of Hilsdon for 20 minutes in the first half.										
19	A	BRADFORD C	5	W	1-0	1-0	Hilton 30	Clay	Annan	Cottle	Marr	Wedlock	Spear	Staniforth	Radford	Rippon	Burton	Hilton
25/12		***36,000***	*20*	22				*Spendiff*	*Campbell*	*Farren*	*Robinson*	*Lintott*	*Hanger*	*Grimes*	*Whittaker*	*O'Rourke*	*Smith Wally*	*Gould*
		(£1,000+)					Ref: A Briggs	Hilton's shot, which went in off the crossbar, allowed City to escape from Valley Parade with both points. The homesters, especially in the first half, squandered many chances, but Rippon, after beating the defence, missed two good opportunities for City by shooting much too high.										
20	H	BRADFORD C	5	L	0-1	0-0		Clay	Annan	Cottle	Marr	Wedlock	Spear	Staniforth	Maxwell	Rippon	Hilton	Hardy
26/12		**23,000**	*19*	22			*O'Rourke 88*	*Spendiff*	*Campbell*	*Farren*	*Williams*	*Lintott*	*Hanger*	*Grimes*	*Smith W*	*O'Rourke*	*Smith Wally*	*Gould*
		(£660.11.9)					Ref: A Briggs	The visitors' aggressive centre-forward secured quick revenge by driving in the winner in the dying minutes of this fast and entertaining game. On this form it is hard to understand Bradford's lowly position. A savage blow for City, whose strong defence never looked likely to concede.										
21	A	EVERTON	9	L	2-5	1-4	Rippon 25, Staniforth 80	Clay	Annan	Cottle	Marr	Wedlock	Spear	**Brown**	Staniforth	Rippon	Gilligan	Hilton
2/1		*16,000*	*1*	22			*Young10,35,White17,Freem'n 40,65*	*Scott*	*Strettle*	*Maconnachie*	*Harris*	*Clifford*	*Makepeace*	*Jones*	*White*	*Freeman*	*Young*	*Dawson*
							Ref: C Fallowfield	Everton reserve Jones, a local lad from Warrington deputising for the injured Sharp, was the architect of City's downfall. Although the scorer of 24 goals for the stiffs didn't get on the score-sheet himself, he set up the first three goals for his side and was a constant menace throughout.										

No	Date		Att	Pos	Pt	F-A	H-T	Scorers, Times, and Referees	1	2	3	4	5	6	7	8	9	10	11
22	H	LEICESTER FOSSE		10	D	1-1	0-0	Gilligan 51	Clay	Annan	Cottle	Spear	Wedlock	Hanlin	Hardy	Rippon	Gilligan	Burton	Hilton
	9/1		10,000	*20*	23			*Shinton 59*	*Bailey*	*Hedley*	*Mackie*	*Randle*	*Webster*	*Pollock*	*Durrant*	*Shinton*	*Hubbard*	*Smith*	*Turner RF*
								Ref: A Neale	The fans were but poorly entertained by this encounter at Ashton Gate, where both sides netted from an offside position in the goalless first half. Straight after the break, the Fosse goal had a miraculous escape, but it wasn't long before Gilligan registered with a shot in off the post.										
23	A	WLCH ARSENAL		7	D	1-1	1-1	Rippon 30	Clay	Annan	Cottle	Hanlin	Wedlock	Spear	Staniforth	Gilligan	Rippon	Burton	Hardy
	23/1		*10,000*	*16*	24			*Hoare 25*	*McDonald*	*Shaw*	*Gray*	*Ducat*	*Sands*	*McEachrane*	*Greenaway*	*Raybould*	*Hoare*	*Fitchie*	*Neave*
								Ref: J Smith	City had to settle for a draw on the Manor Ground at Plumstead, although they enjoyed the majority of the play after a very even first half. Arsenal's amateur centre-forward, Hoare, headed the Gunners into the lead, but an offside-looking Rippon drove in a fierce equaliser for City.										
24	H	NOTTS CO		7	W	1-0	1-0	Staniforth 11	Clay	Annan	Cottle	Spear	Wedlock	Hanlin	Staniforth	Gilligan	Rippon	Burton	Hardy
	30/1		10,000	*13*	26				*Iremonger*	*Morley*	*Montgomery*	*Emberton*	*Clamp*	*Craythorne*	*Dean*	*Matthews*	*Cantrell*	*Dodd*	*Walker*
								Ref: A McQue	Notts didn't play a clean game, but that didn't excuse the fans who threw stones at the visitors' keeper, the one man on the pitch who was scrupulously fair. For a City side, scarcely any better behaved than their opponents, Rippon crashed in the winner from Hardy's corner.										
25	H	THE WEDNESDAY		6	D	1-1	0-0	Burton 64	Clay	Annan	Brown	Marr	Spear	Hanlin	Staniforth	Gilligan	Rippon	Burton	Hilton
	13/2		10,000	*3*	27			*Rollinson 49*	*Lyall*	*Layton*	*Holbem*	*Brittleton*	*Spoors*	*Bartlett*	*Lloyd*	*Chapman*	*Wilson*	*Rollinson*	*Simpson*
								Ref: A Barker	City tackled hard and well to keep Wednesday out in the first half, but after the break Lloyd broke through, despite appeals for offside. Clay was unable to hold his acute-angled shot and Rollinson was able to slip in the opener. Fortunately Burton's well-placed shot saved a point.										
26	A	MIDDLESBROUGH		10	L	0-4	0-2		Clay	Annan	Brown	Hanlin	Wedlock	Spear	Staniforth	Gilligan	Rippon	Burton	Hilton
	27/2		*10,000*	*14*	27			*Cail 18, Bloomer 30, Hall 47, 85*	*Williamson*	*McLeod*	*Watson*	*Aitken S*	*Wilcox*	*Verrill*	*Pentland*	*Bloomer*	*Hall*	*Cail*	*Thackeray*
								Ref: A Briggs *(Sam Aitken Benefit)*	Middlesbrough were such easy masters at Ayresome Park that it was a wonder that City were able to escape so lightly. The brave, pale-faced, Steve Bloomer made a starring return after his serious illness, displaying all his characteristic delightful touches with deft head and footwork.										
27	A	LIVERPOOL		9	W	2-1	1-0	Rippon 25p, 50	Clay	Young	Cottle	Marr	Spear	Hanlin	Staniforth	Gilligan	Rippon	Burton	Hardy
	13/3		*8,000*	*5*	29			*Chorlton 70p*	*Hardy*	*Chorlton*	*West*	*Allman*	*Harrop*	*Hughes*	*Goddard*	*Robinson*	*Parkinson*	*Orr*	*Cox*
								Ref: A Green	A penalty against Chorlton was City's sole reward for their brilliant first-half display, during which Hardy had a goal disallowed. Soon after the re-start, Rippon doubled the advantage from close in, but a handball offence allowed Chorlton to have the final say from the penalty spot.										
28	H	PRESTON		10	L	2-3	1-2	Hardy 37, Rippon 56	Clay	Young	Cottle	Marr	Spear	Hanlin	Staniforth	Gilligan	Rippon	Burton	Hardy
	17/3		**5,000**	*11*	29			*Derbyshire 21p, 60p, Smith 39*	*McBride*	*Derbyshire*	*McFadyen*	*Holdsworth*	*McCall*	*Henderson*	*Bond*	*Wilson*	*Smith P*	*Danson*	*Winterhalder*
								Ref: J Sykes	The start of this game gave promise of great things as City bombarded the Preston citadel. Unfortunately, Young virtually handed victory to the visitors by giving away penalties. First with an unnecessary challenge on Danson, then handling inside the area shortly after the interval.										
29	H	BURY		8	W	**4-2**	3-1	Hardy 15, Rippon 25, Maxwell 40, [Staniforth 55]	Clay	Annan	Cottle	Marr	Wedlock	Young	Staniforth	Maxwell	Rippon	Burton	Hardy
	20/3		8,000	*18*	31			*Kay 35, Hibbert 75*	*Raeside*	*Lindsay*	*Parkin*	*Humphreys*	*Currie*	*Bullen*	*Birnie*	*McIntosh*	*Hibbert*	*Kay*	*Duffy*
								Ref: J Smith	City's exhilarating display gives cause for optimism in regard to next Saturday's cup semi-final. Hardy has never given a better display than that in the first half and he opened the scoring by heading in from Staniforth's flag-kick. Just on time Rippon hit the post from a free-kick.										
30	H	ASTON VILLA		12	D	0-0	0-0		Clay	Annan	Cottle	Marr	Spear	Hanlin	Staniforth	Gilligan	Rippon	Burton	Hardy
	3/4		14,000	*11*	32				*Turner*	*Kearns*	*Miles*	*Hunter*	*Logan J*	*Cornan*	*Wallace*	*Hampton*	*Bache*	*Walters*	*Eyre*
								Ref: A Adams	The scrappy nature of the play asserted itself almost from the start of this game in which there was too much keen tackling for the referee's fancy. In the second half, Villa hit a post and several players were injured, including Marr, who had to retire at about three-quarter time.										
31	A	SHEFFIELD U		13	L	1-3	1-1	Maxwell 35	Clegg	Annan	Cottle	Young	Spear	Hanlin	Staniforth	Hardy	Rippon	Maxwell	Hilton
	5/4		***4,000***	*12*	32			*Gallimore 40, Kitchen 70, Lang 71*	*Lievesley*	*Benson*	*Brooks*	*Sturgess*	*Wilkinson B*	*Needham*	*Lang*	*Featherstone*	*Kitchen*	*Gallimore*	*Evans*
								Ref: J Ibbotson	Clegg impressed on his League debut in front of his home-town crowd, but he was unable to prevent defeat. Maxwell's capped his brilliant run with an equally brilliant shot to give City the advantage, but Gallimore soon equalised and Evans headed against the bar right on the interval.										

No	Venue	Date / Opponent	Att	Pos	Res / Pts	F-A	H-T	Scorers, Times, Referees	1	2	3	4	5	6	7	8	9	10	11
32	A	MANCHESTER U		8	W	1-0	1-0	Burton 35	Clay	Annan	Cottle	Hanlin	Wedlock	Spear	Staniforth	Maxwell	Gilligan	Burton	Hardy
		9/4	*18,000*	*11*	34				*Moger*	*Hayes*	*Stacey*	*Duckworth*	*Roberts*	*Downie*	*Meredith*	*Bannister*	*Halse*	*Livingstone*	*Wall*
								Ref: J Pearson	In glorious weather, City beat their cup opponents thanks to Burton's first-half cross-drive, which left Moger powerless. City's shooting left a lot to be desired, and if it hadn't been for Wedlock's dominance and Clay's 75th-minute save of Halse's penalty they would probably have lost.										
33	A	NOTTINGHAM F		7	D	1-1	0-1	Gilligan 89	Clay	Annan	Cottle	Hanlin	Wedlock	Spear	Staniforth	Hardy	Gilligan	Burton	Hilton
		10/4	*10,000*	*15*	35			*Morris 23*	*Linacre*	*Dudley*	*Maltby*	*Hughes*	*Wolfe*	*Armstrong*	*Hooper*	*Marrison*	*West*	*Morris*	*Spouncer*
								Ref: C Fallowfield	Losing the toss and facing both the wind and the sun at the outset, City were fortunate to save a point right at the end of this lethargic display. Trailing to a first-half drive from Morris after Clay had thrice fisted away, City saved themselves from defeat thanks to Gilligan's flying shot.										
34	H	MANCHESTER U		6	D	0-0	0-0		Clay	Annan	Cottle	Young	Wedlock	Spear	Hardy	Gilligan	Rippon	Burton	Hilton
		12/4	20,000	*8*	36				*Moger*	*Stacey*	*Linkson*	*Duckworth*	*Roberts*	*Downie*	*Meredith*	*Livingstone*	*Turnbull J*	*Picken*	*Wall*
			(£780.9.3)					Ref: J Pearson	Whatever suspicion may have existed that City's Good Friday win at Clayton was faked for the sake of this gate was dispelled as both teams fought out an exciting goalless draw. Wall could have won the game for United towards the finish, but his fierce shot was repelled by the post.										
35	H	BLACKBURN		9	L	1-4	0-1	Hardy 63	Clay	Annan	Cottle	Young	Wedlock	Spear	Hardy	Maxwell	Rippon	Burton	Hilton
		13/4	8,000	*5*	36			*Davies 38, 62, 75, 77*	*Ashcroft*	*Crompton R*	*Cowell*	*Walmsley*	*Chapman*	*Bradshaw*	*Garbutt*	*Latheron*	*Davies*	*Kyle*	*Anthony*
								Ref: A Adams	The absence of the injured Rippon from just before the interval proved costly, though by then City were already trailing to a drive by Davies that went in off the bar. City's goal was allowed, even though the referee appeared to have whistled for a penalty before Hardy fired in his shot.										
36	H	SUNDERLAND		11	L	2-4	2-0	Gilligan 10, Hilton 25	Clay	Annan	Cottle	Young	Wedlock	Spear	Hardy	Maxwell	Gilligan	Burton	Hilton
		17/4	7,000	*3*	36			*Holley 50, 60, Brown 75, 80*	*Roose*	*Forster*	*Milton*	*Tait*	*Thompson*	*Jarvie*	*Low*	*Hogg*	*Brown*	*Holley*	*Bridgett*
								Ref: M McQueen	Whilst Cup finalists often take things somewhat leisurely prior to the great day, it seemed in this game that City went to sleep. Holding a two-goal lead, thanks to shots by Gilligan and Hilton, City switched off after the break. Holley started the Wearside comeback by firing past Clay.										
37	A	CHELSEA		15	L	1-3	0-2	Staniforth 52	Clay	Annan	Cottle	Young	Wedlock	Spear	Staniforth	Hanlin	Hardy	Burton	Hilton
		26/4	*12,000*	*16*	36			*Hilsden 30, 65, Humphreys 35*	*Whitley*	*Cameron*	*Walton*	*Warren*	*Downing*	*Birnie*	*Brawn*	*Humphreys*	*Hilsdon*	*Windridge*	*Holden*
								Ref: R Pitchford	City's were no match for a Chelsea side needing the points to escape the threat of relegation. The brilliant Clay kept them at bay for a good while, before Hilsden registered with a cross-shot. City's goal was rather fortunate as Whitley fumbled Staniforth's centre into his own net.										
38	H	MANCHESTER C		8	W	1-0	0-0	Kelso 88og	Clay	Annan	Cottle	Hanlin	Wedlock	Spear	Staniforth	Gilligan	**Cowell**	Burton	Hilton
		28/4	**5,000**	*17*	38				*Smith*	*Burgess*	*Kelso*	*Buchan*	*Eadie*	*Blair*	*Dorsett*	*Jones*	*Thornley*	*Ross*	*Conlin*
		Home / Ave 11,579	Away 13,717					Ref: T Armitt	Calamity befell the relegation-threatened visitors just before the finish of this fiercely competitive game, which was played at a terrific pace. Following Staniforth's characteristic dash, Kelso, in dealing with the wing-man's centre, had the misfortune to turn the ball into his own net.										

FA Cup	F-A	H-T	Scorers, Times, and Referees	1	2	3	4	5	6	7	8	9	10	11
1 H SOUTHAMPTON 10 D	1-1	1-1	Rippon 35	Clay	Annan	Cottle	Marr	Wedlock	Spear	Staniforth	Gilligan	Rippon	Burton	Hardy
16/1 *18,531 SL:2*			*Jordan 10*	*Lock*	*Eastham*	*Glover*	*Johnson*	*Trueman*	*Jepp*	*Bainbridge*	*Jefferies*	*Costello*	*Jordan*	*Blake*
(£670)			Ref: A Barker	City gave a sparkling display, but were deprived of victory by the brilliant form of the visiting keeper. Lock thwarted City time and time again and then five minutes before the close he saved Burton's spot-kick. Rippon fired in City's leveller after Jordan's shot had opened proceedings.										
R A SOUTHAMPTON 10 W	2-0	1-0	Rippon 35p, Hardy 80	Clay	Annan	Cottle	Marr	Wedlock	Spear	Staniforth	Gilligan	Rippon	Burton	Hardy
20/1 *18,800 SL:2*				*Lock*	*Eastham*	*Glover*	*Johnson*	*Trueman*	*Jepp*	*Bainbridge*	*Jefferies*	*Hughes*	*Jordan*	*Blake*
(£962)			Ref: A Barker	The '6d' end was full well before the start, which saw So'ton kick off facing the bright sun. Offside ruled out Bainbridge's early effort, before Rippon put City in front from the spot after Johnson had handled to keep out a header. A deflection, off a shot by Hardy, clinched matters.										
2 H BURY 7 D	2-2	2-0	Gilligan 6, Burton 19	Clay	Annan	Cottle	Marr	Wedlock	Spear	Staniforth	Hardy	Gilligan	Burton	Hilton
6/2 23,528 *18*			*Hibbert 62, 64*	*Raeside*	*Lindsay*	*Parkin*	*Humphreys*	*Currie*	*Bullen*	*Pearson*	*McIntosh*	*Hibbert*	*Millington*	*Duffy*
(£817.4.4)			Ref: J Pearson	City, who outclassed Bury for the first hour and had the advantage of a two-goal lead, thanks to shots by Gilligan and Burton, were shocked by a quick double salvo from the head of Hibbert. Play was fairly even thereafter, but near the close Burton's great drive was kept out by the post.										
R A BURY 7 W	1-0	1-0	Gilligan 17	Clay	Annan	Cottle	Marr	Wedlock	Spear	Staniforth	Gilligan	Rippon	Burton	Hilton
10/2 9,895 *18*				*Raeside*	*Lindsay*	*Parkin*	*Humphreys*	*Hughes*	*Bullen*	*Pearson*	*McIntosh*	*Hibbert*	*Millington*	*Duffy*
(£353)			Ref: J Pearson	City's defence proved more than a match for Bury's efforts. A drive by Burton was kept out by the crossbar early on, but it wasn't long before City scored what proved to be the winner. A mix-up between Parkin and Raeside allowed Gilligan to nip in and almost run the ball into the net.										
3 H NORWICH 6 W	2-0	1-0	Burton 21, Rippon 65	Clay	Annan	Cottle	Marr	Wedlock	Spear	Staniforth	Gilligan	Rippon	Burton	Hilton
20/2 24,009 *SL:13*				*Roney*	*French*	*Craig*	*Newlands*	*Wagstaffe*	*Whiteman*	*Long*	*Flanagan*	*Tomlinson*	*Smith*	*Allsopp*
(£868.0.9)			Ref: J Schumacher	The conquerors of Liverpool were outclassed in the bright sunshine, even though City could only manage to beat the brilliant Roney on two occasions. Burton headed in the opener, but this goal was completely eclipsed by Rippon's thunderous drive, which doubled City's advantage.										
4 A GLOSSOP 10 D	0-0	0-0		Clay	Annan	Cottle	Marr	Wedlock	Spear	Staniforth	Gilligan	Rippon	Burton	Hardy
6/3 *4,500 2:14*				*Butler*	*Hofton*	*Cuffe*	*McGregor*	*Morrison*	*Wilson*	*Robertson*	*Stapley H*	*Raine*	*Greechan*	*Underwood*
(£238)			Ref: T Campbell	The City kicked-off against the full force of the blizzard which was sweeping the country. The farcical conditions increased the chances of an upset and Stapley headed against the post early on. After the break City had the better chances and Gilligan crashed a shot against the crossbar.										
R H GLOSSOP 10 W	1-0	0-0	Gilligan 84	Clay	Annan	Cottle	Marr	Wedlock	Spear	Staniforth	Gilligan	Rippon	Burton	Hardy
10/3 15,932 *2:14*				*Butler*	*Hofton*	*Cuffe*	*McGregor*	*Morrison*	*Wilson*	*Raine*	*Robertson*	*Stapley H*	*Greechan*	*Underwood*
(£586)			Ref: T Campbell	The home fans, who expected an easy City win, were surprised by Glossop's brilliant defending. It wasn't until the loss of the injured Robertson some 20 minutes before the finish that a breakthrough appeared likely. Gilligan fired in City's late winner from Staniforth's centre.										
SF N DERBY 11 D	1-1	0-0	Rippon 90p	Clay	Annan	Cottle	Marr	Wedlock	Spear	Staniforth	Gilligan	Rippon	Burton	Hardy
27/3 *33,878 2:6*			*Garry 55*	*Maskrey*	*Nicholas*	*Morris*	*Barbour*	*Hall*	*Richards*	*Thompson*	*Garry*	*Bentley*	*Barnes*	*Davis J*
(£2,056)			Ref: H Bamlett (at 'Stamford Bridge')	City appeared guilty of underestimating the opposition and but for Rippon's spot-kick they would have paid the price. Trailing to Garry's scrambled effort, and with the referee ready to signal full-time, Hardy sent in a shot that looked finding the net if Nicholas hadn't handled.										
R N DERBY 11 W	2-1	1-0	Rippon 43p, Hardy 54	Clay	Annan	Cottle	Marr	Wedlock	Spear	Staniforth	Gilligan	Rippon	Burton	Hardy
31/3 *27,600 2:6*			*Davis 48*	*Maskrey*	*Nicholas*	*Morris*	*Barbour*	*Hall*	*Richards*	*Thompson*	*Garry*	*Bentley*	*Barnes*	*Davis J*
(£962.8.6)			Ref: H Bamlett (at 'St Andrews', Birmingham)	City took the game to their opponents right from the off. Rippon's penalty, following a handball by Nicholas, was fitting reward for their first-half display, which had seen Staniforth fire against the post. Davis drove in Derby's acute-angled leveller, but Hardy banged in City's winner.										
F N MANCHESTER U 15 L	0-1	0-1		Clay	Annan	Cottle	Hanlin	Wedlock	Spear	Staniforth	Hardy	Gilligan	Burton	Hilton
24/4 *71,401 8*			*Turnbull A 22*	*Moger*	*Stacey*	*Hayes*	*Duckworth*	*Roberts*	*Bell*	*Meredith*	*Halse*	*Turnbull J*	*Turnbull A*	*Wall*
(£6,434)			Ref: J Mason (at 'The Crystal Palace')	The English Cup final – for that is what it is and ever will be whatever the official title – is over, and over with it are the hopes that the Cup would be brought to Bristol. Sandy Turnbull spoilt all City hopes by firing the ball into the net after Halse's shot hit the underside of the bar.										

		Home					Away					
	P	W	D	L	F	A	W	D	L	F	A	Pts
1 Newcastle U	38	14	1	4	32	20	10	4	5	33	21	53
2 Everton	38	11	3	5	51	28	7	7	5	31	29	46
3 Sunderland	38	14	0	5	41	23	7	2	10	37	40	44
4 Blackburn R	38	6	6	7	29	26	8	7	4	32	24	41
5 Wednesday	38	15	0	4	48	24	2	6	11	19	37	40
6 Wlch Arsenal	38	9	3	7	24	18	5	7	7	28	31	38
7 Aston Villa	38	8	7	4	31	22	6	3	10	27	34	38
8 BRISTOL C	38	7	7	5	24	25	6	5	8	21	33	38
9 Middlesbro'	38	11	2	6	38	21	3	7	9	21	32	37
10 Preston NE	38	8	7	4	29	17	5	4	10	19	27	37
11 Chelsea	38	8	7	4	33	22	6	2	11	23	39	37
12 Sheffield Utd	38	9	5	5	31	25	5	4	10	20	34	37
13 Manchester U	38	10	3	6	37	33	5	4	10	21	35	37
14 Nottm Forest	38	9	2	8	39	24	5	6	8	27	33	36
15 Notts Co	38	9	4	6	31	23	5	4	10	20	25	36
16 Liverpool	38	9	5	5	36	25	6	1	12	21	40	36
17 Bury	38	9	6	4	35	27	5	2	12	28	50	36
18 Bradford City	38	7	6	6	27	20	5	4	10	20	27	34
19 Manchester C	38	12	3	4	50	23	3	1	15	17	46	34
20 Leicester Fos'	38	6	6	7	32	41	2	3	14	22	61	25
	760	191	83	106	698	487	106	83	191	487	698	760

Odds & ends

Double wins: (3) Notts County, Liverpool, Bury.
Double losses: (2) Everton, Preston North End.

Won from behind: (1) Bury (a).
Lost from in front: (3) Newcastle (a), Sheffield U (a), Sunderland (h).

High spots: Reaching the Final of what was commonly known as the English Cup and soaking up the atmosphere at Crystal Palace.
Joe Cottle and Billy Wedlock playing for England in a 4-0 win versus Ireland 4-0 at Bradford Park Avenue on 13 February.

Low spots: 'Sandy' Turnbull's goal that won the FA Cup for Man Utd.
The death of City director Billie Burland at only 37 on 5 March.

Player of the Year: Andy Burton and Joe Cottle.
Ever-presents: (0).
Hat-tricks: (0).
Leading scorer: Overall: Willis Rippon (13). League: Sammy Gilligan (9).

Pre-Season Trial Match: 26 Aug Blues 3(1) Reds 2(2)
1,000 Dumble (2), Hardy / *Burton, Maxwell*
AGM (Temperance Hall, East Street, Bedminster, 30 June 1909):
Profit £3,133.18s.11d. Season Ticket Sales £430.0s.10d.

	Appearances		Goals		
	Lge	Cup	Lge	Cup	Tot
Annan, Archie	**26**	10			
Brown, John	**3**				
Burton, Andy	**35**	10	**8**	2	**10**
Clay, Harry	**37**	10			
Clegg, John	**1**				
Cottle, Joe	**36**	10			
Cowell, John	**1**				
Gilligan, Sammy	**29**	10	**9**	3	**12**
Latham, Frank	**1**				
Hanlin, Pat	**23**	1			
Hardy, Bob	**26**	8	**4**	2	**6**
Hilton, Frank	**27**	4	**7**		**7**
Marr, Reuben	**18**	9			
Maxwell, Billy	**11**		**3**		**3**
Penman, Tom	**1**				
Radford, Tom	**1**				
Rippon, Willis	**23**	8	**8**	5	**13**
Spear, Arthur	**33**	10			
Staniforth, Fred	**34**	10	**4**		**4**
Wedlock, Billy	**32**	10	**1**		**1**
Young, Bob	**20**				
Opponent og			**1**		**1**
21 players used	**418**	**110**	**45**	**12**	**57**

No	Date	Att	Pos	Pt	F-A	H-T	Scorers, Times, and Referees	1	2	3	4	5	6	7	8	9	10	11
1	A BRADFORD C			L	1-3	0-3	Rippon 55	Clay	Annan	Cottle	Marr	Wedlock	Spear	Staniforth	Gilligan	Rippon	**Foster**	**Shearman**
	4/9	*24,000*					*O'Rourke 13, 18, 23*	*Spendiff*	*Chaplin*	*Campbell*	*Lintott*	*Comrie*	*Robinson*	*Hardman*	*Spiers*	*O'Rourke*	*Whittingham*	*Bond*
							Ref: J Bailey	Last season's FA Cup runners-up are torn apart, as O'Rourke, aided by a fortunate second when Clay's clearance struck him and re-bounded into the net, grabs a hat-trick. Fortunately, matters then settled down and Rippon's header saved some pride by putting City on the score-sheet.										
2	H BURY			D	1-1	0-0	Cowell 90	Clay	Annan	Cottle	Marr	Wedlock	Hanlin	Staniforth	Gilligan	Cowell	Foster	Shearman
	8/9	5,000		1			*McIntosh 78*	*Raeside*	*Lindsay*	*Parkin*	*Humphreys*	*Dewhurst*	*Jarvis*	*Birnie*	*McIntosh*	*Hibbert*	*Currie*	*Bradley*
							Ref: J Sykes	Trailing to McIntosh's low shot, City managed to salvage a point in the dying moments of this evenly contested game. Cowell received the ball on the halfway line and, despite the attentions of the Bury defenders, ran right through to place the ball into the net from a few yards out.										
3	H THE WEDNESDAY		14	D	1-1	1-1	Cowell 10	Clay	Annan	Cottle	Marr	Wedlock	Hanlin	Staniforth	Gilligan	Cowell	Foster	Shearman
	11/9	9,000	*15*	2			*Bradshaw 23*	*Davison*	*Layton*	*Holbem*	*Brittleton*	*Spoors*	*Bartlett*	*Hunter*	*Chapman*	*Wilson*	*Bradshaw*	*Foxall*
							Ref: A McQue	Whilst this result still leaves City seeking their first win, victory will not be long in coming if they continue to perform as well as they did in this excellent game. Cowell fired City in front, but they were pegged back when, from Foxall's centre, Bradshaw crashed in the Owls' leveller.										
4	A BLACKBURN		15	L	2-5	1-3	Sherman 44, Foster 75	Clay	Annan	Cottle	Marr	Wedlock	Hanlin	Staniforth	Gilligan	Cowell	Foster	Shearman
	13/9	*8,000*	*9*	2			*Anthony 2, Aitk'head 20, Latheron 40,*	*Murray*	*Crompton R*	*Cowell*	*Walmsley*	*Chapman*	*Bradshaw*	*Bracegirdle*	*Latheron*	*Crompton E*	*Aitkenhead*	*Anthony*
							Ref: J Ibbotson *[Bracegirdle 49, Clay 90og]*	The only bad luck City experienced was when offside ruled out Wedlock's goal shortly after Foster's low six-yarder had revived their hopes. Anthony finished his dazzling run by firing in an angled opener for a Blackburn side, who had keeper Murray making his First League debut.										
5	H MIDDLESBROUGH		12	W	4-1	2-0	Cowell 2, 7, 86, Staniforth 70	Clay	Annan	Cottle	Spear	Wedlock	Hanlin	Staniforth	Hardy	Cowell	Burton	Shearman
	18/9	12,000	*11*	4			*Bloomer 85*	*Williamson*	*McLeod*	*Watson*	*Aitken S*	*Common*	*Verrill*	*Pentland*	*Bloomer*	*Hall*	*Dixon*	*Jones*
							Ref: D Hammond	City found their form against the Ironsides who, despite displaying splendid combination, failed in front of goal. Cowell, after breaking clear and crashing home the opener, claimed two more, but the best strike was Staniforth's fierce shot that crashed in off the underside of the bar.										
6	A BURY		11	W	2-1	0-1	Hardy 60, Cowell 65	Clay	Annan	Cottle	Spear	Wedlock	Hanlin	Staniforth	Hardy	Cowell	Burton	Shearman
	25/9	*10,457*	*16*	6			*Birnie 19*	*Raeside*	*McMahon*	*Parkin*	*Humphreys*	*Dewhurst*	*Jarvis*	*Birnie*	*McIntosh*	*Kay*	*Smith*	*Bradley*
							Ref: J Sykes	The legitimacy of Bury's goal was in doubt as Clay was insistent that Birnie's shot, after hitting the junction twixt bar and post, had not gone in. Still, all was well at the finish, as from Shearman's pass Cowell secured the points after Hardy's close-in shot had brought matters level.										
7	H TOTTENHAM		11	D	0-0	0-0		Clay	Annan	Cottle	Spear	Wedlock	Hanlin	Staniforth	Hardy	Cowell	Burton	Shearman
	2/10	**18,000**	*17*	7				*Boreham*	*Coquet*	*Burton*	*Macfarlane*	*Steel D*	*Darnell*	*Curtis*	*Tull*	*Minter*	*Steel R*	*Middlemiss*
							Ref: A Adams	This meeting with old rivals after a lapse of many years attracted City's largest crowd of the season so far. A hard and vigorous game was witnessed but, despite the absence of the injured Darnell for a while in the first half, no goals were scored as the defences took the honours.										
8	A PRESTON		13	L	0-3	0-1		Clay	Annan	Cottle	Marr	Spear	Hanlin	Staniforth	Hardy	Cowell	Burton	Shearman
	9/10	*11,000*	*19*	7			*Smith 4, Mouteney 52, Platt 54*	*McBride*	*McFadyen*	*Rodway*	*Holdsworth*	*Smith P*	*Lyon*	*Winterhalder*	*Platt*	*Mounteney*	*Danson*	*Sanderson*
							Ref: Lieut W Clover	The dull weather that prevailed was matched by City's performance after they fell behind to Smith's header and had a claim for a spot-kick refused when Gilligan was brought down by McFayden. After the interval, Clay had no chance with either Mounteney's header or Platt's shot.										
9	H NOTTS CO		11	W	3-1	1-1	Hardy 30, 60, Cowell 55	Clay	Annan	Cottle	Marr	Wedlock	Spear	Staniforth	Hardy	Cowell	Burton	Shearman
	16/10	10,000	*14*	9			*Cantrell 35*	*Iremonger*	*Morley*	*Montgomery*	*Emberton*	*Clamp*	*Griffiths*	*Waterall*	*Walker*	*Cantrell*	*Jones*	*Dodd*
							Ref: C Fallowfield	County, who had Walker's 17th-minute strike disallowed for offside, didn't resort to last season's rough-house tactics, even though they gave away a penalty that Cowell fired wildly wide shortly before the finish. Hardy's header, from Shearman's centre, tied up City's convincing win.										
10	A NEWCASTLE		12	L	1-3	1-1	Cowell 30	Clay	Annan	Cottle	Marr	Wedlock	Spear	Staniforth	Hardy	Cowell	Burton	Hilton
	23/10	*10,000*	*4*	9			*Shepherd 12, 75, Anderson 46*	*Lawrence*	*McCracken*	*Carr*	*Jobey*	*Liddell*	*McWilliam*	*Rutherford*	*Stewart*	*Shepherd*	*Wilson*	*Anderson*
							Ref: M McQueen	Cowell threaded himself through from Hardy's pass for the equaliser after Shepherd's rising drive had brought Newcastle the early lead. The heavy pitch took its toll on City's lightly built forwards, and after the break they succumbed to Anderson's fine effort and Shepherd's header.										
11	H LIVERPOOL		13	L	0-1	0-0		Clay	Annan	Cottle	Marr	Wedlock	Spear	Staniforth	Foster	Cowell	Burton	Hardy
	30/10	12,000	*2*	9			*Robinson 60*	*Hardy*	*Chorlton*	*Crawford*	*Robinson*	*Harrop*	*Bradley*	*Goddard*	*Stewart*	*Parkinson*	*Orr*	*Uren*
							Ref: J Sharpe	After City's trainer, Dick Batten, was the recipient of a half-time collection made by the bandsmen, this well-contested game was settled by Robinson's chance shot from out near the touchline. The burly, light-haired half-back deceived City keeper Clay with the flight of the ball.										

No	Date		Att	Pos	Pt	F-A	H-T	Scorers, Times, and Referees	1	2	3	4	5	6	7	8	9	10	11
12	A	ASTON VILLA		15	L	0-1	0-1		Clay	Annan	Cottle	Marr	Wedlock	Spear	Staniforth	Hardy	Cowell	Burton	Shearman
	6/11		*25,000*	*7*	9			*Gerrish 28*	*Cartlidge*	*Lyons*	*Miles*	*Logan*	*Buckley*	*Tranter*	*Walters*	*Gerrish*	*Hampton*	*Bache*	*Hall*
								Ref: T Campbell	A keen game at Villa Park where, due mainly to City's magnificent defence, the issue was in doubt throughout. Hampton had the misfortune to have his shot strike the inside of both posts early on. It wasn't long, however, before Hall set up Gerrish to fire past Clay from close range.										
13	H	SHEFFIELD U		15	L	0-2	0-1		Clay	Annan	Cottle	Hanlin	Wedlock	Spear	Staniforth	Burton	Cowell	Foster	Hardy
	13/11		10,000	*3*	9			*Simmons 20, 65*	*Lievesley*	*Benson*	*Brooks*	*Brelsford*	*Wilkinson*	*Sturgess*	*Walton*	*Simmons J*	*Kitchen*	*Batty*	*Evans*
								Ref: H Pollitt	City were neither heavy nor sufficiently clever enough to overcome the powerful Blades defence. Only Staniforth showed to advantage as City gave their worst display of the season so far. From Walton's centre, Clay's poor punch that dropped at the feet Simmons led to the opener.										
14	A	WLCH ARSENAL		13	D	2-2	2-1	Rippon 4, 6	Clay	Annan	Cottle	Hanlin	Wedlock	Spear	Hardy	Gilligan	Rippon	Burton	Shearman
	20/11		*8,000*	*20*	10			*Buckenham 42, Greenaway 89*	*McDonald H*	*McDonald D*	*Gray*	*Ducat*	*Sands*	*McEachrane*	*Greenaway*	*Stevens*	*Buckenham*	*Lawrence*	*Heppinstall*
								Ref: J Smith	The ground was enveloped in fog when Rippon started and it wasn't long before he had given City a two-goal advantage. He put on the opener with a fine shot, then doubled the tally when, from Hardy's cross, he fired in an effort that cannoned into the net off the inside of the upright.										
15	H	BOLTON		14	W	1-0	0-0	Burton 65	Clay	Annan	Cottle	Marr	Wedlock	Spear	Hardy	Gilligan	Rippon	Burton	Shearman
	27/11		8,000	*20*	12				*Edmondson*	*Baverstock*	*Slater*	*Gaskell*	*Greenhaigh*	*Barber*	*Whiteside J*	*Lockett*	*Hunter*	*Hogan*	*McEwan*
								Ref: A Neale	Although the sun shone brilliantly, there was but a small crowd for this game, which only rose above the mediocre in the latter stages. Burton's header from Shearman's centre caused Bolton to bestir themselves, but despite all their best endeavours they were unable to level matters.										
16	A	CHELSEA		14	L	1-4	0-0	Rippon 76p	Clegg	Annan	Cottle	Marr	Wedlock	Spear	Hardy	Gilligan	Rippon	Burton	Shearman
	4/12		*20,000*	*15*	12			*Woodward 46, 50, Bradshaw 85, 87*	*Whitley*	*Cartwright*	*Cameron*	*Warren*	*Birnie*	*Downing*	*Brawn*	*Woodward*	*Jones*	*Bradshaw*	*Mair*
								Ref: W Chadwick	The irresistible play of Woodward and Mair, coupled with City's failure to put away their first-half chances, brought about this heavy defeat. After the break, Woodward quickly put on two goals from centres by Mair and Jones, before a trip on Rippon allowed City to pull one back.										
17	H	BLACKBURN		14	D	2-2	1-1	Marr 44, Hardy 55	Clegg	Annan	Cottle	Marr	Wedlock	Spear	Hardy	Gilligan	Rippon	Burton	Shearman
	11/12		**4,000**	*2*	13			*Aitkenhead 20, Compton 87*	*Murray*	*Suttie*	*Cowell*	*Walmsley*	*Chapman*	*Bradshaw*	*Garbutt*	*Latheron*	*Crompton E*	*Aitkenhead*	*Bracegirdle*
								Ref: J Ibbotson	An exciting contest in the mud after the visitors had taken the lead with a swerving shot from beyond the penalty line. City outplayed Rovers after the break, but Annan's slip deprived them of a deserved success. Crompton took advantage by smashing in the late close-range leveller.										
18	A	NOTTM FOREST		13	D	0-0	0-0		Clegg	Annan	Cottle	Marr	Wedlock	Spear	Hardy	Gilligan	Cowell	Burton	Shearman
	18/12		*8,000*	*9*	14				*Smith*	*Dudley*	*Maltby*	*Hughes*	*Wolfe*	*Needham*	*Hooper*	*Marrison*	*West*	*Morris*	*Horrocks*
								Ref: J Howcroft	Those witnessing this match, whether with Bristol or Nottingham bias, agreed that both points instead of one should have been City's fortune. Encouraged by brilliant half-back play, City made countless raids and it is a mystery why a victory of sensational dimensions wasn't recorded.										
19	H	EVERTON		13	W	3-1	1-0	Cowell 3, Gilligan 60, Staniforth 70	Clegg	Annan	Cottle	Hanlin	Wedlock	Spear	Staniforth	Gilligan	Cowell	Burton	Shearman
	25/12		15,000	*11*	16			*Freeman 50*	*Scott*	*Clifford*	*Maconnachie*	*Harris*	*Borthwick*	*Makepeace*	*Sharp*	*Coleman*	*Freeman*	*White*	*Barlow*
								Ref: H Bamlett	With heavy rain overnight, following a sharp frost, the muddy conditions proved not to the liking of an Everton side who failed to adapt. From Shearman's centre, Cowell opened the scoring, but after the break Freeman equalised by finishing his 50-yard dribble with a shot past Clegg.										
20	A	EVERTON		13	L	0-1	0-1		Clegg	Annan	Cottle	Hanlin	Wedlock	Spear	Staniforth	Gilligan	Cowell	Burton	Shearman
	27/12		*30,000*	*10*	16			*Sharp 20*	*Scott*	*Clifford*	*Stevenson*	*Harris*	*Taylor*	*Makepeace*	*Sharp*	*Coleman*	*Freeman*	*White*	*Young*
								Ref: H Bamlett	Both sides put in some good work in this encounter at Goodison Park, but Everton took the spoils thanks to Sharp's first-half shot. City had their chances before the break, but Clegg was much the busier keeper and received a warm ovation when on his return after the half-time break.										
21	H	SUNDERLAND		13	L	2-3	0-1	Cowell 70p, 87p	Clegg	Annan	Cottle	Hanlin	Wedlock	Spear	Staniforth	Gilligan	Cowell	Burton	Shearman
	28/12		**18,000**	*7*	16			*Holley 44, 85, Low 48*	*Allan*	*Troughear*	*Agnew*	*Tait*	*Thompson*	*Jarvie*	*Clark*	*Low*	*Holley*	*Bridgett*	*Mordue*
								Ref: C Neale	Holley's tap-in and Low's shot shortly after put Sunderland in the ascendancy before a trip on Burton allowed Cowell to give City some hope by scoring from the spot. Holley placed in the visitors' third, but there was a tense finish after a trip on Cowell brought City another penalty.										
22	A	SUNDERLAND		15	L	**0-4**	0-0		Clegg	Annan	Cottle	Marr	Wedlock	Spear	Hardy	Gilligan	Cowell	Burton	Shearman
	1/1		*20,000*	*7*	16			*Bridgett 51, Mordue 52, 57, Low 75*	*Roose LR*	*Troughear*	*Agnew*	*Tait*	*Thompson*	*Forster*	*Clark*	*Low*	*Holley*	*Bridgett*	*Mordue*
								Ref: H Taylor	City were on top prior to the break, but thereafter Sunderland were much superior. However, the score, which was in no way representative of the play, rather flattered the homesters. Three goals, of which Mordue's hard drive for his first was the best, in a six-minute spell did for City.										
23	H	BRADFORD C		14	W	2-0	1-0	Burton 25, 65	Clegg	Annan	Cottle	Marr	Wedlock	Spear	Hardy	Gilligan	Cowell	Burton	Shearman
	8/1		8,000	*7*	18				*Maskrey*	*Torrance*	*Campbell*	*Robinson*	*Comrie*	*Lintott*	*Logan*	*McDonald*	*O'Rourke*	*Spiers*	*Bond*
								Ref: J Bailey	City played well against opponents who badly missed their prolific scorer Whittingham. Burton rushed in the opener from Marr's pass, then after the break he produced a great shot to complete a well-deserved success over the side who had won 7-3 at Middlesbrough on Boxing Day.										

LEAGUE DIVISION 1

Manager: Harry Thickett

SEASON 1909-10

No	Date		Att	Pos	Pt	F-A	H-T	Scorers, Times, and Referees	1	2	3	4	5	6	7	8	9	10	11
24	A	THE WEDNESDAY		15	L	0-2	0-2		Clegg	Annan	Cottle	Marr	Wedlock	Spear	Hardy	Gilligan	Rippon	Burton	Shearman
	22/1		*8,000*	*10*	18			*Rollinson 30, Cottle 40og*	*Davison*	*Spoors*	*Holbem*	*Lloyd*	*McConnell*	*Bartlett*	*Kirkman*	*Chapman*	*Hamilton*	*Rollinson*	*Tummon*
								Ref: A McQue	There was no disputing the Owls' superiority, but it was disappointing for the City fans to see their side go down at Owlerton where, but two days previously, Northampton had succeeded. Wednesday were full value for their goals, even though they were somewhat luckily obtained.										
25	A	TOTTENHAM		16	L	2-3	1-2	Gilligan 30, Marr 68 *[Minter 80]*	Clay	Annan	Cottle	Hanlin	Young	Spear	Staniforth	Gilligan	Marr	Burton	Shearman
	12/2		*25,000*	*15*	18			*Middlesmiss 34, Humphreys 36,*	*Joyce*	*Coquet*	*Leslie*	*Morris*	*Steel D*	*Darnell*	*Curtis*	*Minter*	*Humphreys*	*Steel R*	*Middlemiss*
								Ref: A Adams	At the end of this fast and exciting tussle, decided by Minter's shot, one of the City players commented: 'We shall never work so hard again without getting a point.' Gilligan drove in the opener, but a cross-drive by Middlemiss and Humphrey's tap-in put Spurs in the ascendancy.										
26	H	PRESTON		15	W	2-0	1-0	Shearman 27, Cowell 75	Clay	Young	Cottle	Marr	Wedlock	Hanlin	Hardy	Gilligan	Cowell	Burton	Shearman
	19/2		7,000	*13*	20				*McBride*	*McFadyen*	*Rodway*	*McLean J*	*McCall*	*Roche*	*Galbraith*	*Bannister*	*McLean D*	*Mounteney*	*Winterhalder*
								Ref: Lieut W Clover	City started against a breeze, which soon became a gale. Preston made little headway despite the wind being in their favour and Shearman gave City the lead with a hard rising shot. After the break, Cowell rushed the ball out of the keeper's hands to tie up City's well-deserved victory.										
27	A	NOTTS CO		15	W	2-0	0-0	Cowell 82, 85	Clay	Young	Cottle	Marr	Wedlock	Hanlin	Hardy	Gilligan	Cowell	Burton	Shearman
	26/2		*8,000*	*2*	22				*Iremonger*	*Morley*	*Montgomery*	*Mosley*	*Clamp*	*Craythorne*	*Dean*	*Matthews*	*Flint*	*Jones*	*Walker*
								Ref: C Fallowfield	A persistent downpour throughout made conditions unpleasant at Trent Bridge. City, however, were not dismayed as Cowell's late double (a header and a well-placed shot) cost County, for whom Flint and Morley were but poor replacements for Cantrell and Emberton, their top spot.										
28	A	LIVERPOOL		15	W	1-0	0-0	Gilligan 80	Clay	Young	Cottle	Marr	Wedllock	Spear	Hardy	Gilligan	Cowell	Burton	Shearman
	12/3		*15,000*	*5*	24				*Hardy*	*Crawford*	*Chorlton*	*Robinson*	*Peake*	*Bradley*	*Goddard*	*Stewart*	*Parkinson*	*Orr*	*McDonald*
								Ref: J Sharpe	This fine win enhanced the considerable reputation City already had at Anfield. A lively open game was won by Gilligan's magnificent shot, after he had rounded Chorlton. Whilst City's defence was superb, it was Cowell who made victory possible by unsettling the Pool defence.										
29	H	ASTON VILLA		15	D	0-0	0-0		Clay	Young	Cottle	Marr	Wedlock	Spear	Hardy	Gilligan	Cowell	Burton	Shearman
	19/3		16,000	*1*	25				*Cartlidge*	*Lyons*	*Layton*	*Tranter*	*Buckley*	*Hunter*	*Wallace*	*Gerrish*	*Hampton*	*Bache*	*Eyre*
			(£456.16.6)					Ref: T Campbell *(Sammy Gilligan Benefit)*	There was rather too much vigour in this keenly fought-out encounter, but little in the way of goalmouth action. The teams have never played a less impressive match during their eight meetings and by early in the second half the contest had resolved itself into just playing out time.										
30	A	MANCHESTER U		15	L	1-2	0-1	Staniforth 75	Clay	Young	Cottle	Marr	Wedlock	Spear	Staniforth	Hardy	Cowell	Burton	Shearman
	25/3		***50,000***	*7*	25			*Turnbull 15, Picken 55*	*Moger*	*Hayes*	*Stacey*	*Duckworth*	*Whalley*	*Bell*	*Meredith*	*Halse*	*Turnbull J*	*Picken*	*Wall*
								Ref: C Gillett	Two rather fortunate goals brought United victory in a well-contested game that City were fully entitled to draw. Clay was unsighted when Turnbull put United in front, and he was caught off-guard by Picken's long, high shot. Staniforth's long-distance effort was City's sole reward.										
31	A	SHEFFIELD U		15	L	**0-4**	0-2	*[Burgess 80p]*	Clay	Young	Cottle	Hanlin	Wedlock	Spear	Staniforth	Hardy	Cowell	Burton	Shearman
	26/3		*12,000*	*2*	25			*Evans 37, Simmons 43, Hardinge 50,*	*Lievesley*	*Benson*	*Brooks*	*Brelsford*	*Wilkinson*	*Sturgess*	*Kitchen*	*Simmons J*	*Peart*	*Hardinge*	*Evans*
								Ref: H Pollitt	City, who lost the injured Spear early on, suffered at Bramall Lane. Stopping for offside when Kitchen crossed for Evans to shoot in the opener, Hardinge also looked illegally placed when notching the third. Wedlock gave away his first ever spot-kick to complete the tale of woe.										
32	H	MANCHESTER U		14	W	2-1	1-1	Cowell 25, Wedlock 75	Clay	Young	Cottle	Marr	Wedlock	Hanlin	Staniforth	Gilligan	Cowell	Burton	Shearman
	28/3		16,000	*8*	27			*Meredith 20*	*Moger*	*Duckworth*	*Hayes*	*Blott*	*Whalley*	*Bell*	*Meredith*	*Halse*	*Turnbull J*	*Picken*	*Wall*
								Ref: C Gillett	Judging City by the final 15 minutes, they were easily the better side, but overall their one-goal advantage, secured by Wedlock's splendid low drive, was fair reward. Cowell ran between the backs to fire in City's equaliser after Meredith had lobbed in the opener over the head of Clay.										
33	H	WLCH ARSENAL		16	L	0-1	0-1		Clay	Young	Cottle	Marr	Chapman	Hanlin	Staniforth	Gilligan	Cowell	Burton	Shearman
	2/4		8,000	*17*	27			*Lawrence 30*	*McDonald H*	*McDonald D*	*Shaw*	*McKinnon*	*Thomson*	*McEachrane*	*Greenaway*	*Lewis*	*Buckenham*	*Lawrence*	*Heppinstall*
								Ref: J Smith	Well led by Bombardier Buckenham, who was denied by a post early on, the visitors played bright football to delight the good number of Woolwich excursionists among the crowd. Despite City's attempts to equalise the Gunner's hung onto the lead given them by Lawrence's shot.										
34	A	BOLTON		18	L	2-4	2-3	Cowell 4, Hardy 10	Clay	Annan	Cottle	Young	Wedlock	Hanlin	Hardy	**Batty**	Cowell	Foster	Shearman
	9/4		***5,000***	*20*	27			*Jones 2, Hughes 20, 70, Stokes 43*	*Edmondson*	*Baverstock*	*Feebury*	*Owen*	*Greenhaigh*	*Whiteside E*	*Stokes*	*Jones*	*Hughes*	*Hilton*	*Smith*
								Ref: A Neale	City's failure, despite Hardy's header putting them in front after two earlier shots had accrued to each side, raises the spectre of relegation. After a fierce drive by Stokes put Bolton back in front, Hughes tied matters up by ending his sprint from halfway with a crisp shot past Clay.										

No	H/A	Opponent / Date	Att	Pos		Res	FT	HT	Scorers / Ref											
35	H	CHELSEA		17		W	1-0	1-0	Marr 40	Clay	Young	Cottle	Marr	Wedlock	Hanlin	Hardy	Batty	Cowell	Burton	Shearman
		16/4	14,000	*19*	29					*Whitley*	*Cameron*	*Cartwright*	*Taylor*	*McConnell*	*Downing*	*Brown*	*Whittingham*	*Smith*	*Windridge*	*McEwan*
									Ref: W Chadwick	By defeating a Chelsea side containing costly signings, McConnell, Whittingham and Smith, City should now escape relegation. A fitting reward for the Reds, who played with marvellous keenness and dash. Marr, whose first-time drive secured the points, was quite brilliant.										
36	A	MIDDLESBROUGH		17		D	0-0	0-0		Clay	Annan	Cottle	Young	Wedlock	Hanlin	Hardy	Batty	Cowell	Burton	Shearman
		20/4	*12,000*	*16*	30					*Williamson*	*Watson*	*McLeod*	*Verrill*	*Young*	*Aitken S*	*Thackeray*	*Cail*	*Common*	*Elliott*	*Pentland*
									Ref: D Hammond	The play was fairly interesting, though little good shooting was performed by either side. With Young off the pitch for half an hour prior to the break, Common failed from the spot after being fouled by Annan. In the second half, the Ironsides did most of the pressing without success.										
37	H	NEWCASTLE		18		L	0-3	0-1		Clay	Young	Cottle	Marr	Wedlock	Hanlin	Hardy	Batty	Cowell	Burton	Shearman
		25/4	5,000	*4*	30				*Young 20og, Stewart 60, 75*	*Blake*	*Waugh*	*Carr*	*Willis*	*Liddell*	*Finlay*	*Duncan*	*Metcalf*	*Stewart*	*Randall*	*Anderson*
									Ref: C Gillett	With the 1st XI going to Saltburn-on-Sea following their drawn FA Cup final, the Toon fielded their reserves at Ashton Gate. Against a City side giving their most impotent display of the season, Stewart tied up an easy victory by kicking in the third goal from Anderson's clever pass.										
38	H	NOTTM FOREST		16		W	**4-0**	1-0	Cowell 19, 70, 75p, 85	Clay	Annan	Cottle	Young	Wedlock	Hanlin	Staniforth	Hardy	Cowell	Burton	Shearman
		30/4	11,000	*14*	32					*Hassell*	*Gibson*	*Maltby*	*Hughes*	*Wolfe*	*Needham*	*Hooper*	*Armstrong*	*West*	*Whitchurch*	*Horrocks*
		Home / Ave 10,842	Away / 16,287						Ref: J Howcroft	Whilst Forest showed plenty of speed and played much attractive football, they were beaten by a City side determined to make sure of retaining top-flight status. After Cowell drove in the opener, no one in the crowd could have possibly had anything but praise for the team.										

FRIENDLIES

No	H/A	Opponent / Date	Att	Res	FT	HT	Scorers											
1	H	THE BUTTERFLIES		W	7-2	3-0	Cottle 15, 25, Spear 35, 85,	Wedlock	Hardy	Burton	Foster	Young	Clay	Annan	**Stock**	Cottle	Spear	**Brewer**
		6/10	250				*Welsh 55, Mudie 80* [Stock 60, 65, 70]	*Edwards A*	*Weighall R*	*Wren F*	*Williams F*	*Dunn R*	*Douglas J*	*Abbott W*	*Wallace A*	*Welsh SC*	*Kibble W*	*Mudie A*
							(Unemployed Benefit)	City turned out with many of their players out of position, in order to give the musical comedy company from the Princes Theatre a chance in this game played for the benefit of the local unemployed. The ploy didn't work, however as, after Miss Ada Reeve kicked off, it was a rout.										
2	A	EXETER		L	1-4	1-2	Gilligan 20	Clegg	Young	Cottle	Marr	Wedlock	Hanlin	Staniforth	Gilligan	Rippon	Burton	Hardy
		3/11	*4,000*				*Bell 8, 44, Garside 65, 80*	*Crossthwaite*	*Jones*	*Crelly*	*Hartley*	*Tierney*	*Atkinson*	*Garside*	*Bell*	*Harrison*	*Watson*	*Green*
								City, without Clay, Annan, Spear, Cowell and Shearman, came a cropper in this friendly at St James Park against a home side short of Chadwick at centre-half. Young was at fault for Exeter's second, whilst the way that Rippon failed in front of the posts was remarkable.										
3	A	CARDIFF		W	7-0	3-0	Rippon 30, 55, 75, Hardy 32, [Shearman 40, 70, Wedlock 85]	Clegg	Young	Cottle	Hanlin	Wedlock	Spear	Hardy	Gilligan	Rippon	Burton	Shearman
		17/11	*2,000* (£50)				*(at the 'Arms Park')*	*Simmonds F*	*Milford E*	*Nash L*	*Wilson N*	*Johnston W*	*Stone A*	*Huxtable T*	*Boon W*	*Evans*	*Jones TD*	*Vizard ET*
								City, as expected, exerted most of the pressure, but Clegg had to be alert in dealing with efforts from Huxstable and Boon. Rippon opened the scoring with a fine low shot, then Hardy headed in a second before Shearman's terrific drive had City cruising by the time ends were changed.										
4	A	PLYMOUTH		D	1-1	1-1	Staniforth 20	**Demmery**	Young	Cottle	Gilligan	Wedlock	Hanlin	Staniforth	Hardy	Cowell	Stock	Shearman
		5/3	*5,000* (£129)				*Raymond 30*	*Sutcliffe*	*Butler*	*Fagan*	*McCormick*	*Evenson*	*Baker*	*Leavey*	*Raymond*	*Hindmarsh*	*Burch*	*Lamb*
								Staniforth gave City the lead with a fine shot in this vigorous encounter at Home Park. Demmery (Kingswood Rovers) a cousin of the ex-City keeper, kept a good goal and had no chance with the equaliser from the amateur Raymond, whose high lob found its way in just under the bar.										

FA Cup

					F-A	H-T	Scorers, Times, and Referees	1	2	3	4	5	6	7	8	9	10	11
1	H	LIVERPOOL	14	W	2-0	1-0	Burton 26, Rippon 48	Clegg	Annan	Cottle	Marr	Wedlock	Spear	Hardy	Gilligan	Rippon	Burton	Shearman
15/1		16,181	*5*					*Hardy*	*Chorlton*	*Rogers*	*McConnell*	*Harrop*	*Robinson*	*McDonald*	*Bowyer*	*Parkinson*	*Stewart*	*Goddard*
		(£552)					Ref: A McQue											

Somewhat surprisingly, City, who had done their cup-tie training in Portishead, controlled this game against high-riding Liverpool, who had prepared at Clevedon. Burton ran in and fired home the opener; then early in the second half Rippon clinched matters with a shot past Hardy.

					F-A	H-T	Scorers, Times, and Referees	1	2	3	4	5	6	7	8	9	10	11
2	H	WEST BROM	15	D	1-1	1-1	Gilligan 42	Clegg	Annan	Cottle	Marr	Wedlock	Spear	Hardy	Gilligan	Cowell	Burton	Shearman
5/2		16,885	*2:9*				*Pailor 22*	*Pearson*	*Burton*	*Pennington*	*Garraty*	*Waterhouse*	*Manners*	*Hewitt*	*Bowser*	*Pailor*	*Buck*	*Simpson*
		(£576)					Ref: C Fallowfield											

A deserved replay for the Baggies in the drizzle at Ashton Gate. They took the lead when Pailor controlled Garraty's long pass and beat Clegg with a low shot from close range. City equalised when Gilligan fired in after the keeper Pearson was only able to push out Burton's fine shot.

					F-A	H-T	Scorers, Times, and Referees	1	2	3	4	5	6	7	8	9	10	11
2R	A	WEST BROM	15	L	2-4	1-2	Gilligan 30, Staniforth 70	Clegg	Annan	Cottle	Marr	Wedlock	Spear	Staniforth	Hardy	Gilligan	Burton	Shearman
9/2		*14,870*	*2:9*				*Simpson 11, Pailor 44, Hewitt 58, 82*	*Pearson*	*Burton*	*Pennington*	*Garraty*	*Waterhouse*	*Manners*	*Hewitt*	*Bowser*	*Pailor*	*Buck*	*Simpson*
		(£560)					Ref: T Campbell											

Whilst Pailor was off the field receiving treatment, Simpson opened the scoring from Garraty's free-kick. City, who twice netted with headers, went to sleep when Pennington placed the ball into the area for Hewitt to shoot in the goal that make sure of Albion's well deserved success.

1908-09 Glos Cup final *(postponed until this season in consequence of City's FA Cup run)*

					F-A	H-T	Scorers, Times, and Referees	1	2	3	4	5	6	7	8	9	10	11
F	A	BRISTOL ROV	FL	D	1-1	1-1	Burton 21	Clay	Annan	Cottle	Marr	Wedlock	Spear	Staniforth	Gilligan	Rippon	Burton	Hardy
1/9		*9,521*	*SL*				*Corbett 42*	*Roney*	*McKenzie*	*Westwood*	*Smart*	*Williams*	*Handley*	*Peplow*	*Mason*	*Corbett*	*Riddell*	*Lawrie*
		(£275)					Ref: F Heath											

On actual chances, City should have won as Rippon hit the underside of the bar and Gilligan was denied by a post. As it was, they had to be satisfied with a draw as, following Burton's right-footer past a hesitant Roney, Corbett was able to grab a leveller from Riddell's short pass.

					F-A	H-T	Scorers, Times, and Referees	1	2	3	4	5	6	7	8	9	10	11
R	H	BRISTOL ROV	11	D	1-1	1-0	Cowell 15	Clay	Annan	Cottle	Marr	Wedlock	Spear	Staniforth	Hardy	Cowell	Burton	Shearman
13/10		3,000	*SL:13*				*Corbett 75*	*Roney*	*McKenzie*	*Westwood*	*Smart*	*Williams*	*Handley*	*Peplow*	*Corbett*	*Mason*	*Roberts*	*Lawrie*
							Ref: A Adams											

Play was fairly interesting, but there wasn't the keenness that had characterised the first encounter. After Cowell's fired-in effort, Corbett's tapped-in leveller should have lead to extra-time, but with Rovers disadvantaged by the loss of the injured Smart, it wasn't insisted upon.

					F-A	H-T	Scorers, Times, and Referees	1	2	3	4	5	6	7	8	9	10	11
R2	A	BRISTOL ROV	15	W	2-1	2-0	Cowell 20, Radford 35	Clay	**Padfield**	Young	**Mason**	**Chapman**	Hanlin	Staniforth	Radford	Cowell	Foster	Hilton
26/1		*2,000*	*SL:12*				*Roberts 82*	*Roney*	*Ovens*	*Westwood*	*Williams*	*Shaw*	*Handley*	*Peplow*	*Roberts*	*Corbett*	*McColl*	*Laurie*
							Ref: J Ibbotson											

City surprised the FA Cup conquerors of Grimsby by winning this second replay of the delayed 1908-09 final with their reserve XI. However, the Rovers, but for spurning many chances including a second-half penalty, which Peplow fired straight at Clay, would have been easy victors.

1909-10 Glos Cup final

					F-A	H-T	Scorers, Times, and Referees	1	2	3	4	5	6	7	8	9	10	11
F	H	BRISTOL ROV	16	W	2-0	1-0	Foster 20, 47	Clay	Annan	Cottle	Young	Wedlock	Hanlin	Hardy	Staniforth	Cowell	Foster	Shearman
6/4		1,175	*SL:14*					*Roney*	*Ovens*	*Westwood*	*Williams*	*Shaw*	*Handley*	*Peplow*	*Rodgers*	*Corbett*	*McColl*	*Laurie*
		(£33)																

On the sodden pitch, City shaped much better than their counterparts. They secured the county trophy thanks to two headers, the second of which saw Foster throwing himself at the ball and, sprawling on all fours in the mud, going into the net with the leather practically on his head.

		Home						Away					
		P	W	D	L	F	A	W	D	L	F	A	Pts
1	Aston Villa	38	17	2	0	62	19	6	5	8	22	23	53
2	Liverpool	38	13	3	3	47	23	8	3	8	31	34	48
3	Blackburn R	38	13	6	0	47	17	5	3	11	26	38	45
4	Newcastle U	38	11	3	5	33	22	8	4	7	37	34	45
5	Manchester U	38	14	2	3	41	20	5	5	9	28	41	45
6	Sheffield Utd	38	10	5	4	42	19	6	5	8	20	22	42
7	Bradford City	38	12	3	4	38	17	5	5	9	26	30	42
8	Sunderland	38	12	3	4	40	18	6	2	11	26	33	41
9	Notts Co	38	10	5	4	41	26	5	5	9	26	33	40
10	Everton	38	8	6	5	30	28	8	2	9	21	28	40
11	Wednesday	38	11	4	4	38	28	4	5	10	22	35	39
12	Preston NE	38	14	2	3	36	13	1	3	15	16	45	35
13	Bury	38	8	3	8	35	30	4	6	9	27	36	33
14	Nottm Forest	38	4	7	8	19	34	7	4	8	35	38	33
15	Tottenham H	38	10	6	3	35	23	1	4	14	18	46	32
16	BRISTOL C	38	9	5	5	28	18	3	3	13	17	42	32
17	Middlesbro'	38	8	4	7	34	36	3	5	11	22	37	31
18	Wlch Arsenal	38	6	5	8	17	19	5	4	10	20	48	31
19	Chelsea	38	10	4	5	32	24	1	3	15	15	46	29
20	Bolton Wndrs	38	7	2	10	31	34	2	4	13	13	37	24
		760	207	80	93	726	468	93	80	207	468	726	760

Odds & ends

Double wins: (1) Notts County.
Double losses: (3) Newcastle United, Sheffield United, Sunderland.

Won from behind: (2) Bury (a), Manchester United (h).
Lost from in front: (1) Tottenham Hotspur (a).

High spots: Beating Middlesbrough 4-1 on 18 September.
Achieving First Division survival with a 1-0 success over Chelsea.
John Cowell's great display in scoring all the goals that beat Nottingham Forest 4-0 on the last day of the season.
Beating Rovers in the 1908-09 Glos Cup final and the current tournament.

Low spots: Commencing the campaign by losing at Bradford City.
The abuse, reported by the 'Football Star', to be *'lower than that of a Billingsgate Porter'*, hurled at the black Spurs player Walter Tull.
The embarrassment of losing 0-3 to a virtual Newcastle reserve side.
Going out of the FA Cup to Second Division West Brom on 9 February.

Player of the Year: John Cowell.
Ever-presents: (1) Joe Cottle.
Hat-tricks: (2) John Cowell (2).
Leading scorer: Overall: John Cowell (22). League: John Cowell (20).

Pre-Season Trial Match: 25 Aug Blues 3(1) Reds 2(1) Ref: F Curtis
4,000 Gilligan 30, Foster 53, Rippon 70 / *Cowell 20, 47*

AGM (Temperance Hall, East Street, Bedminster, 30 June 1910):
Loss £78.0s.10d. Season Ticket Sales: £327.3s.6d.

	Appearances			Goals			
	Lge	**Cup**	**Fr**	**Lge**	**Cup**	**Fr**	**Tot**
Annan, Archie	**28**	6	1				
Batty, Billy	**4**						
Brewer			1				
Burton, Andy	**33**	5	3	**3**	2		**5**
Chapman, Bert	**1**	1					
Clay, Harry	**29**	4	1				
Clegg, John	**9**	3	2				
Cowell, John	**31**	4	1	**20**	2		**22**
Cottle, Joe	**38**	6	4			2	**2**
Demmery, A*			1				
Foster, Allan	**7**	2	1	**1**	2		**3**
Gilligan, Sammy	**22**	4	3	**3**	2	1	**6**
Hanlin, Pat	**23**	2	3				
Hardy, Bob	**28**	6	4	**5**		1	**6**
Hilton, Frank	**1**	1					
Marr, Reuben	**26**	5	1	**3**			**3**
Mason, SR		1					
Padfield, W		1					
Radford, Tom		1			1		**1**
Rippon, Willis	**6**	2	2	**4**	1	3	**8**
Shearman, Ben	**35**	5	2	**2**		2	**4**
Spear, Arthur	**26**	5	2			2	**2**
Staniforth, Fred	**22**	5	2	**3**	1	1	**5**
Stock			2			3	**3**
Wedlock, Billy	**35**	6	4	**1**		1	**2**
Young, Bob	**14**	2	4				
26 players used	**418**	**77**	**44**	**45**	**11**	**16**	**72**

* Cousin of ex-keeper Bill Demmery.

No	Date		Att	Pos	Pt	F-A	H-T	Scorers, Times, and Referees	1	2	3	4	5	6	7	8	9	10	11
1	A	NEWCASTLE			W	1-0	0-0	Hardy 84	Clegg	Young	Cottle	Marr	Wedlock	Hanlin	Staniforth	Hardy	Cowell	Burton	Shearman
	3/9		*26,000*		2				*Lawrence*	*McCracken*	*Carr*	*Finlay*	*Low*	*McWilliam*	*Duncan*	*Stewart*	*Shepherd*	*Higgins*	*Wilson*
								Ref: A Briggs	A dream start for City, as they notch up their first-ever success at St James' Park. In truth, though, they hardly ever looked likely winners, but their defence gave a sterling display and near the finish Hardy won the game when he ran through to fire the ball into the net from close range.										
2	H	TOTTENHAM			L	0-2	0-0		Clegg	Young	Cottle	Marr	Wedlock	Hanlin	Staniforth	Hardy	Cowell	Burton	Shearman
	10/9		18,000		2			*Middlemiss 65, 75*	*Lunn*	*Elkin*	*Wilkes*	*Morris*	*Steel D*	*Darnell*	*Curtis*	*Minter*	*Humphreys*	*Steel R*	*Middlemiss*
								Ref: T Rowbotham	During the opening half-hour, with their forwards displaying excellent combination, City gave an admirable display. After the break, a Curtis free-kick lead to Middlemiss firing in the opener. The winger made sure of victory with an angled effort to finish off his run from halfway.										
3	A	MIDDLESBROUGH		17	L	0-3	0-1	*[Williamson 82p]*	Clegg	Young	Cottle	Marr	Wedlock	Hanlin	Staniforth	Hardy	Cowell	Burton	Shearman
	17/9		*20,000*	*4*	2			*Pentland 37, Gibson 50,*	*Williamson*	*McLeod*	*Weir*	*Barker*	*Jackson*	*Verrill*	*Gibson*	*Elliott*	*Pentland*	*McClure*	*Nicholl*
								Ref: J Howcroft	Although the sun shone on Teesside, the scoreline failed to reflect City's bright performance. Pentland trapped a high ball, turned round and drove in the opener off of a post. During the interval the appearance of a rabbit, followed by a whippet, brought about a coursing session.										
4	H	PRESTON		18	D	0-0	0-0		Clay	Young	Cottle	Marr	Wedlock	Hanlin	Staniforth	Hardy	**Owers**	Burton	Shearman
	24/9		15,000	*20*	3				*McBride*	*McFadyen*	*Rodway*	*Wareing*	*McCall*	*Lyon*	*Thompson J*	*Bannister*	*McLean D*	*Mounteney*	*Danson*
								Ref: L Bullimer	A poorer exhibition has rarely, if ever, been seen at Ashton Gate, as two impotent sides shared the spoils. If this is the best that City can produce, then the outlook is alarming indeed. Rarely can there have been a match in which mediocrity was so completely conspicuous.										
5	A	NOTTS CO		20	L	0-2	0-1		Clay	Young	Cottle	Marr	Wedlock	Hanlin	Hardy	Cowell	Burton	Foster	Shearman
	1/10		*14,000*	*3*	3			*Richards 38, Waterall 65*	*Iremonger*	*Griffiths*	*Montgomery*	*Emberton*	*Clamp*	*Craythorne*	*Dean*	*Matthews*	*Flint*	*Richards*	*Waterall I*
								Ref: Rev J Marsh	City's drawing-room football availed them nothing. They fell behind to a header shortly after the action had stopped when M. de Lesseps passed over Meadow Lane in his aeroplane. Dean appeared to have taken the ball out of play before crossing for Waterall to drive in his goal.										
6	H	MANCHESTER U		20	L	0-1	0-1		Clay	**Fagan**	Cottle	Mason	Wedlock	Hanlin	Hardy	Cowell	Owers	Burton	Foster
	8/10		**20,000**	*2*	3			*Halse 10*	*Moger*	*Holden*	*Stacey*	*Livingstone*	*Roberts*	*Bell*	*Meredith*	*Halse*	*West*	*Picken*	*Wall*
			(£462.16.10)					Ref: A Shallcross	City did their best, but the superior skill of the United forwards was too much for them. Clay was outstanding and, but for him, more than										
								(Billy Wedlock Benefit)	Halse's shot would have accrued to the visitors' account. It was quite extraordinary when Foster failed to net, not long before the interval.										
7	A	LIVERPOOL		20	L	**0-4**	0-1	*[Parkinson 60, 80]*	Clay	Young	Cottle	Mason	Wedlock	Hanlin	Staniforth	Hardy	Owers	Foster	Shearman
	15/10		*15,000*	*14*	3			*Brough 31, Harrop 51,*	*Hardy*	*Longworth*	*Crawford*	*Robinson*	*Peake*	*Harrop*	*Goddard*	*Brough*	*Parkinson*	*Orr*	*Uren*
								Ref: F Heath	Cottle's decision to leave the ball for Clay allowed Parkinson to nip in and set up Brough to prod in the close-range opener. City, who had been the better side up to then, fell away and their defeat could have been worse as Parkinson had a second-half goal disallowed for offside.										
8	H	BURY		19	W	2-0	1-0	Owers 3, Burton 65	Clay	Young	Cottle	Marr	Wedlock	Hanlin	**Clark**	Hardy	Owers	Burton	Shearman
	22/10		12,000	*12*	5				*Holt*	*Fenner*	*Parkin*	*Humphreys*	*Dewhurst*	*Bullen*	*Lee*	*Kay*	*Hibbert*	*Currie*	*Walker*
								Ref: J Bailey	Owers, who had already missed two chances, notched the opener by beating Holt with the game but three minutes old. Despite playing second fiddle to Bury for 20 minutes after the interval, Burton fired in another to make victory secure. Clark, from Sunderland, enjoyed a good debut.										
9	A	SHEFFIELD U		18	W	4-0	1-0	Burton 26, Hardy 65, 80, Owers 75	Clay	Young	Cottle	Marr	Wedlock	Hanlin	Clark	Hardy	Owers	Burton	Sherman
	29/10		*10,000*	*17*	7				*Lievesley*	*Benson*	*Brooks*	*Brelsford*	*Wilkinson*	*Sturgess*	*Walton*	*Simmons J*	*Kitchen*	*Hardinge*	*Evans*
								Ref: R Eccles	There was little to choose between the sides before the interval, but City held the lead thanks to Burton's brilliant left-footed drive. Hardy doubled the advantage with a shot into the left-hand corner of the net as City went on to to achieve their first ever victory at Bramall Lane.										
10	H	ASTON VILLA		19	L	1-2	1-2	Owers 30	Clay	Fagan	Cottle	Marr	Young	Hanlin	Clark	Hardy	Owers	Burton	Shearman
	5/11		18,000	*4*	7			*Bache 12, Walters 15*	*Cartlidge*	*Lyons*	*Miles*	*Tranter*	*Buckley*	*Hunter*	*Wallace*	*Walters*	*Hampton*	*Bache*	*Eyre*
			(£421.19.0)					Ref: C Gillett	A vigorous, clever game, in which the lightweight City forwards were overpowered. Bache's header and a close-in drive from Walters put										
								(Andy Burton Benefit)	Villa in charge, and City, without Wedlock, following his concussion at Sheffield, were only able to respond when Owers fired the ball home.										

No	H/A	Opponent	Pos	Res	F-A	H-T	Scorers, Times, and Referees	1	2	3	4	5	6	7	8	9	10	11
11	A	SUNDERLAND	19	L	1-3	0-2	Owers 60	Clay	Fagan	Cottle	Marr	Young	Hanlin	Clark	Hardy	Owers	Burton	Shearman
	12/11	*15,000*	*1*	7			*Coleman 23, 90, Cowell 25*	*Roose*	*Troughear*	*Forster*	*Tait*	*Thomson*	*Low*	*Mordue*	*Coleman*	*Cowell*	*Gemmell*	*Bridgett*
							Ref: T Field	Against the only unbeaten side in the League, there was a period, after Owers had scored, that a draw seemed quite within the bounds of possibility. After Coleman had opened the scoring from Gemmell's pass, ex-City man Cowell soon doubled the Weirsiders' advantage.										
12	H	WLCH ARSENAL	20	L	0-1	0-0		Clay	Young	Cottle	Marr	Wedlock	Hanlin	Clark	Hardy	Owers	Burton	Shearman
	19/11	8,000	*10*	7			*Chalmers 48*	*Bateup*	*Gray*	*Shaw*	*Ducat*	*Thomson*	*McEachrane*	*Lewis*	*Rippon*	*Chalmers*	*Common*	*Neave*
							Ref: J Mason	A moderate game in which City's forwards were easily held by the Woolwich defence. Chalmers settled the outcome with a shot of such speed that Clay was unable to properly stop the ball. This defeat, coupled with Man City's success against Forest, deposits City at the foot of affairs.										
13	A	BRADFORD C	20	L	1-3	1-3	Owers 25	Clay	Fagan	Cottle	Marr	Wedlock	**Osborne**	Staniforth	Clark	Owers	Foster	Shearman
	26/11	*10,000*	*4*	7			*O'Rourke 5, 14, Speirs 27*	*Mellors*	*Campbell*	*Chaplin*	*Robinson*	*Taylor*	*Hampton*	*Bond*	*Speirs*	*O'Rourke*	*Devine*	*Handley*
							Ref: D Hammond	Despite their forwards demonstrating an unaccustomed fire, City still struggled throughout at Valley Parade. Osborne's tackling impressed on a fine debut, but he could do little about Bradford's rampant forwards, who kept up the offensive even though they had their keeper carried off.										
14	H	BLACKBURN	20	W	1-0	1-0	Burton 15	Clay	Young	Cottle	Marr	Wedlock	Hanlin	Clark	**Date**	Owers	Burton	Hardy
	3/12	10,000	*15*	9				*Ashcroft*	*Crompton R*	*Cowell*	*Walmsley*	*Smith*	*Bradshaw*	*Garbutt*	*Latheron*	*Davies*	*Aitkenhead*	*Smethams*
							Ref: H Lewis	City's defence carried the team through a severe ordeal as the forwards squeezed out one goal from the highly skilled Blackburn defence. The visitors played well, but they found the City defence in an uncompromising mood. Date, the Frome amateur, did nothing of note on his debut.										
15	A	NOTTM FOREST	20	D	3-3	2-1	Owers 10, 30, Logan 75	Clay	Young	Cottle	Marr	Wedlock	Hanlin	Clark	Hardy	Owers	**Logan**	Shearman
	10/12	*8,000*	*7*	10			*Hooper 26, Morris 47, Needham 50*	*Smith*	*Gibson*	*Maltby*	*Armstrong*	*Wolfe*	*Needham*	*Hooper*	*Lockett*	*Marrison*	*Morris*	*Ford*
							Ref: A McQue	Logan, the newly signed recruit from Falkirk, brought City a deserved point when he cleverly shot in the leveller after Clark's delightful work. Wedlock set up City's opener with a skilful pass to Owers, who turned and sent the ball inside the post. Clay's slip gave Morris his open goal.										
16	H	MANCHESTER C	18	W	2-1	1-1	Logan 4, Wedlock 49	Clay	Young	Cottle	Marr	Wedlock	Hanlin	Clark	**Gadsby**	Owers	Logan	Shearman
	17/12	10,000	*20*	12			*Smith J 32*	*Smith W*	*Humphreys*	*Chaplin*	*Bottomley*	*Eadie*	*Holford*	*Dorsett J*	*Dorsett G*	*Smith J*	*Wall*	*Conlin*
							Ref: A Neale	Although they produced little in the way of fantastic football, City's forward line was effective and should improve when they have played together more. The visitors belied their lowly position with some enterprising soccer, but Wedlock's keenness made sure of the points.										
17	A	EVERTON	20	L	3-4	1-1	Logan 30, Owers 55, Wedlock 75	Clay	Young	Cottle	Marr	Wedlock	Hanlin	Clark	Gadsby	Owers	Logan	Shearman
	24/12	*8,000*	*3*	12			*Young R 10, Berry 46, 49, Lacey 53*	*Scott*	*Stevenson*	*Balmer R*	*Harris*	*Young R*	*Allen*	*Berry*	*Lacey*	*Young A*	*Gourlay !*	*Beare*
							Ref: T Kirkham	City got off to a bad start in this exciting contest when Clay misjudged a thirty-yarder. Logan levelled with a grand drive, but straight after the interval Berry's shot was ruled to have crossed the line before Young cleared the ball. Shortly before Wedlock fired in, Gourlay was sent off.										
18	H	THE WEDNESDAY	20	D	2-2	2-1	Shearman 32, Gadsby 40p	**Bailiff**	Young	Cottle	Marr	Wedlock	Spear	Clark	Gadsby	Owers	Logan	Shearman
	26/12	**20,000**	*16*	13			*Chapman 30, Weir 50*	*Kinghorn*	*Spoors*	*Holbein*	*Lloyd*	*O'Connell*	*Weir*	*Kirkman*	*Chapman*	*Wilson*	*Rollinson*	*Robertson*
							Ref: J Sykes	The large Ashton Gate crowd were treated to a spirited game. Chapman nodded in Kirkham's centre to put Wednesday in front, but a shot by Shearman and Gadsby's spot-kick saw City in front by half-time. Unfortunately Weir beat Bailiff from close range to earn the visitors a point.										
19	H	OLDHAM	15	W	3-2	2-1	Owers 25, Shearman 40, Wedlock 90	Bailiff	Young	Cottle	Marr	Wedlock	Fagan	Staniforth	Gadsby	Owers	Logan	Shearman
	27/12	16,500	*10*	15			*Wilson 7, Woodger 60*	*McDonald*	*Cook*	*Cope*	*Moffat*	*Walders*	*Wilson*	*McTavish*	*Donnachie*	*Fay*	*Woodger*	*Miller*
							Ref: F Heath	This Ashton Gate thriller is settled in the dying seconds when Wedlock hurled himself into a mass of players to obtain a splendid winner. After Wilson had headed in an early opener, a rushed centre from Owers and a well-considered shot by Shearman had City in front by the interval.										
20	H	NEWCASTLE	14	W	1-0	1-0	Logan 26	Bailiff	Young	Fagan	Spear	Wedlock	Cottle	Staniforth	Gadsby	Owers	Logan	Shearman
	31/12	15,000	*8*	17				*Lawrence*	*McCracken*	*Hudspeth*	*Veitch*	*Low*	*McWilliam*	*Duncan*	*Higgins*	*Shepherd*	*Stewart*	*Wilson*
							Ref: A Briggs	Logan's header allowed City to conclude the holiday period with a points tally of five from their four games. McCracken was the star of this excellent match, in which Newcastle, faced by the uncanny alertness of Bailiff, were let down by a combination of bad luck and poor finishing.										
21	A	THE WEDNESDAY	16	L	1-2	0-2	Logan 79	Bailiff	Young	Fagan	Mason	Wedlock	Cottle	Staniforth	Gadsby	Owers	Logan	Shearman
	2/1	*5,000*	*15*	17			*Glennon 7, Fagan 12og*	*Davison*	*Spoors*	*Holbein*	*Brittleton*	*O'Connell*	*Weir*	*Kirkman*	*Stringfellow*	*Glennon*	*Wilson*	*Robertson*
							Ref: J Sykes	Logan beat three men before scoring in brilliant fashion in the second half, but City were unable to recover from earlier mistakes. Fagan completely missed his kick when Glennon ran through to notch the opener; then he deflected in a shot, which Bailiff would have saved.										

No	Date		Att	Pos	Pt	F-A	H-T	Scorers, Times, and Referees	1	2	3	4	5	6	7	8	9	10	11
22	A	TOTTENHAM		18	L	2-3	1-2	Owers 35, 79	Bailiff	Young	Fagan	Spear	Wedlock	Cottle	Clark	Gadsby	Owers	Logan	Shearman
	7/1		*20,000*	*17*	17			*Minter 8, 13, 60*	*Lunn*	*Collins*	*Wilkes*	*Steel D*	*Kennedy*	*Darnell*	*Curtis*	*Minter*	*Crompton*	*McTavish*	*Gosnell*
								Ref: T Rowbotham	After a game of curious fluctuations, City had to return beaten from White Hart Lane, when all things considered they deserved at least to have shared the points. Four of the goals were headers, the exception being Minter's shot when he followed up Crompton's fierce second-half drive.										
23	H	MIDDLESBROUGH		15	W	3-2	1-2	Owers 1, 46, 75	Bailiff	Fagan	Cottle	Young	Wedlock	Hanlin	Clark	Staniforth	Owers	Logan	Hardy
	21/1		6,000	*8*	19			*Elliott 3, Wedlock 43og*	*Williamson*	*Wardrope*	*Weir*	*Barker*	*Jackson*	*Verrill*	*Gibson*	*Elliott*	*Pentland*	*Cail*	*Davidson*
								Ref: J Howcroft	After last week's cup flop, drastic changes were made to City's line-up, but Cottle, who had been dropped, turned out at the last moment. A sensational game, which started with Owers and Elliott exchanging goals, ended with both sides spurning excellent chances in the last minute.										
24	A	PRESTON		18	L	**0-4**	0-1	*[McCall 75]*	Bailiff	Fagan	Cottle	Young	Wedlock	Hanlin	Clark	Staniforth	Owers	Logan	Hardy
	28/1		*12,000*	*11*	19			*Bannister 15, 65, Mounteney 55,*	*McBride*	*McFadyen*	*Rodway*	*Holdsworth*	*McCall*	*Wareing*	*Thompson J*	*Bannister*	*Mounteney*	*Danson*	*Winterhalder*
								Ref: L Bullimer	City were soon up against it at Deepdale as, shortly after Bannister's splendidly fired-in opener, Cottle suffered a fractured right leg as he endeavoured to stop McFayden. Defending with a rare pertinacity, City held out until the second half, when their citadel fell thrice more.										
25	H	NOTTS CO		15	W	1-0	0-0	Owers 73	Clay	Padfield	Fagan	Young	Wedlock	Hanlin	Clark	Staniforth	Owers	Logan	Hardy
	4/2		*10,000*	*12*	21				*Iremonger*	*Morley*	*Montgomery*	*Emberton*	*Garrett*	*Craythorne*	*Waterall I*	*Matthews*	*Cantrell*	*Flint*	*Dodd*
								Ref: Rev J Marsh	Owers clinched another important win for City when he took Hardy's swift centre and lashed the ball in under the bar in convincing fashion. An extremely vigorous game in which, despite being injured, Owers did much to play up to the honour of being selected as an England reserve.										
26	A	MANCHESTER U		17	L	1-3	0-2	Sweet 70	Clay	Young	Padfield	Marr	**Sweet**	Hanlin	Clark	Hardy	Owers	Logan	Shearman
	11/2		*17,000*	*1*	21			*Picken 30, West 33, Homer 75*	*Edmonds*	*Donnelly*	*Stacey*	*Duckworth*	*Roberts*	*Bell*	*Meredith*	*Homer*	*West*	*Picken*	*Wall*
								Ref: A Shallcross	Against the leaders, City were dealt a cruel blow by the loss of Owers with an injured left knee after being hooked down by Stacey. The award of a free-kick was hardly adequate, especially as United went on to score twice before half-time. City's only reward came from Sweet's head.										
27	H	LIVERPOOL		18	D	1-1	1-1	Hardy 5	Clay	Young	**Jones**	Marr	Wedlock	Hanlin	Clark	Hardy	Logan	Gadsby	Shearman
	18/2		10,000	*14*	22			*Parkinson 43*	*Hardy*	*Longsworth*	*Crawford*	*Robinson*	*Harrop*	*McConnell*	*Goddard*	*Gilligan*	*Parkinson*	*Orr*	*McDonald*
								Ref: F Heath	With rain falling throughout, the treacherous conditions, combined with disjointed forward play, kept the City fans in a continuous state of anxiety. Hardy headed in the opener from Clark's corner, but Parkinson ran though and shot in the equaliser as Clay advanced off his line.										
28	A	BURY		18	L	1-2	1-1	Owers 27	Clay	Young	Jones	Marr	Wedlock	Hanlin	Clark	Logan	Owers	Gadsby	Shearman
	25/2		***4,616***	*19*	22			*Walker 7, Hibbert 75*	*Raeside*	*Fenner*	*Millington*	*Jarvis*	*Dewhurst*	*Bullen*	*Walker*	*Currie*	*Hibbert*	*Lomas*	*Birnie*
								Ref: J Bailey	For the first time, City lost at Gigg Lane, where the wind swept Walker's centre into the net for the opener. Owers equalised by firing in a rebound shortly before Clay saved Raeside's spot-kick. Walker's centre set up Hibbert for Bury's winner, just after Owers had been thwarted.										
29	H	SHEFFIELD U		18	L	0-2	0-1		Clay	Young	Fagan	Marr	Wedlock	Hanlin	Clark	Staniforth	Owers	Logan	Hardy
	4/3		**5,000**	*6*	22			*Kitchen 17, 75*	*Mitchell*	*Benson*	*Brooks*	*Brelsford*	*Wilkinson*	*Sturgess*	*Walton*	*Simons T*	*Kitchen*	*Simmons J*	*Evans*
								Ref: R Eccles	United merely played a safe, methodical game, without brilliance, but it was too much for a feeble City side who look unlikely to claim many more points this season. Clay didn't have an enviable task after Kitchen raced through to toe-poke in the opener, which trickled over the line.										
30	A	ASTON VILLA		20	L	0-2	0-2		Clay	Young	Fagan	Marr	Wedlock	Hanlin	Clark	Logan	Owers	Burton	Foster
	11/3		*20,000*	*2*	22			*Stephenson 18, Wallace 25*	*George*	*Layton*	*Kearns*	*Tranter*	*Buckley*	*Hunter*	*Wallace*	*Stephenson*	*Hampton*	*Walters*	*Henshall*
								Ref: C Gillett	City, helped by the fact that Buckley was off injured for a good hour of the game, were thwarted by poor marksmanship. The tone was set before Villa got off the mark when, following Layton's handball on the line, Owers put the resultant spot-kick much too close to the keeper.										
31	H	SUNDERLAND		20	D	1-1	0-1	Logan 47p	Clay	Young	Padfield	Marr	Wedlock	Hanlin	Staniforth	Logan	Owers	Burton	Foster
	18/3		**5,000**	*3*	23			*Coleman 30*	*Worrall*	*Throughear*	*Milton*	*Tait*	*Cuggy*	*Jarvie*	*Mordue*	*Coleman*	*Low*	*Gemmell*	*Bridgett*
								Ref: T Field	City put up a good performance against Sunderland, which should have secured them both points. Unfortunately, they again failed in front of goal and only managed to score from the spot after Burton was fouled. Padfield's slip allowed Coleman to shoot in the Weirsiders' opener.										

No	Venue	Date / Opponent	Att	Pos	Pts	Res	F-A	H-T	Scorers, Times, and Referees	1	2	3	4	5	6	7	8	9	10	11
32	A	WLCH ARSENAL		20		L	0-3	0-3		Clay	Young	Padfield	Marr	Wedlock	Hanlin	Staniforth	Clark	Owers	Burton	Shearman
		25/3	*10,977*	*16*	23				*Common 10, 15, Flanagan 20*	*Bateup*	*Shaw*	*Peart*	*Ducat*	*Sands*	*McEachrane*	*Greenaway*	*Flanagan*	*Chalmers*	*Common*	*Neave*
			(£282.10.6)						Ref: I Baker	This match was really lost when Wedlock lost the toss, as no team could battle successfully against the hurricane. City might have held out but for the vagaries of the wind and the storm of sleet that passed over the ground, and were blown away by the bewildering rapidity of the goals.										
33	H	BRADFORD C		20		L	0-2	0-0		Clay	Young	Jones	Marr	**Sweet**	Hanlin	Staniforth	Logan	Owers	Burton	Shearman
		1/4	8,000	*4*	23				*Devine 60, 65*	*Mellors*	*Campbell*	*Taylor*	*Hampton*	*Gildea*	*McDonald*	*Logan*	*Fox*	*O'Rourke*	*Devine*	*Handley*
									Ref: D Hammond	In anticipation of seeing City make a bold bid for victory against the cup finalists, there were rather more spectators present than has lately been the case. Unfortunately, the Reds lacked cohesion and, after failing to put away their chances, they succumbed to Devine's capital pair.										
34	A	BLACKBURN		20		L	0-2	0-0		Clay	Young	Fagan	Marr	Wedlock	Hanlin	Clark	**Gildea**	Owers	**Batty**	Burton
		8/4	*7,000*	*11*	23				*Bradshaw 60p, Cameron 70*	*Ashcroft*	*Crompton R*	*Cowell*	*Walmsley*	*Smith*	*Bradshaw*	*Simpson*	*Latheron*	*Cameron*	*Aitkenhead*	*Dennison*
									Ref: H Lewis	In their fight against relegation, this game was looked upon as providing City with their last chance. Unfortunately, so far from taking it, they were outplayed by a team with but a moderate attack. Hanlin was unlucky that his tackle on Simpson brought the award of the spot-kick.										
35	A	OLDHAM		20		L	0-1	0-1		Clay	Young	Fagan	Marr	Wedlock	Hanlin	Clark	Gadsby	Chapman	Burton	**Copestake**
		14/4	*11,030*	*8*	23				*Woodger 12*	*McDonald*	*Hodson*	*Cope*	*Moffat*	*Walders*	*Wilson*	*Pilkington*	*Fay*	*Jones*	*Woodger*	*Donnachie*
									Ref: Lieut W Clover	After winning the toss, City held the early advantage in front of a disappointing holiday crowd. After Jones put a fine drive just over the bar, Oldham came away and debutant Pilkington sent in a hard shot which Clay could only palm out to Fay, who put over for Woodger to head in.										
36	H	NOTTM FOREST		20		W	**5-1**	1-1	Clark 15, Burton 50, Fisher 68og	Clay	Young	Fagan	Marr	Wedlock	Hanlin	Staniforth	Clark	Chapman	Burton	Copestake
		15/4	**5,000**	*19*	25				*Derrick 44* [Chapman 69, Marr 74p]	*Drabble*	*Dudley*	*Gibson*	*Fisher*	*Mercer*	*Armstrong*	*Hooper*	*Marrison*	*Derrick*	*Bailey*	*Ford*
									Ref: A McQue	City, in notching up their best score since gaining promotion, consigned Forest to relegation. Clark charged the keeper into the net for the opener, but Derrick levelled with a splendid shot past Clay. Taking advantage of Dudley's temporary absence, Burton fired City back in front.										
37	A	MANCHESTER C		19		W	2-1	1-1	Logan 37p, Marr 67p	Clay	Young	Fagan	Marr	Wedlock	Hanlin	Staniforth	Logan	Owers	Burton	Copestake
		22/4	***34,000***	*17*	27				*Wynn 35*	*Smith W*	*Kelso*	*Norgrove*	*Dorsett G*	*Eadie*	*Holford*	*Nelson*	*Wynn*	*Thornley*	*Jones*	*Salt*
			(£689)						Ref: A Neale *(George Dorsett Benefit)*	It was expected that the Light Blues would extract revenge for a defeat two years ago, which brought about their demotion, by doing likewise against City. However, it didn't work out that way as, despite falling behind to Wynn's shot, City survived to bring off a thrilling victory.										
38	H	EVERTON		19		L	0-1	0-1		Clay	Young	Fagan	Marr	Wedlock	Hanlin	Staniforth	Logan	Owers	Burton	Copestake
		29/4	8,000	*4*	27				*Jefferies 12*	*Scott*	*Maconnachie*	*Balmer R*	*Weller*	*Fleetwood*	*Makepeace*	*Beare*	*Jefferies*	*Gracie*	*Gourlay*	*Lacey*
		Home / Ave 11,553	Away / 14,085						Ref: T Kirkham *(Annan & Spear Joint Benefit)*	With only a small crowd in attendance, it was obvious that many City fans were not convinced that their side had the ability to beat Everton. Unfortunately the stay-aways were proved correct as the win – that would have brought escape from relegation's jaws – never looked likely.										

FA Cup/Glos Cup		F-A	H-T	Scorers, Times, and Referees	1	2	3	4	5	6	7	8	9	10	11
1 H CREWE	18 L	0-3	0-1		Bailiff	Young	Cottle	Mason	Wedlock	Hanlin	Clark	Gadsby	Owers	Burton	Shearman
14/1	11,600 *BL:8*			*King 30, Mason 75, Chapple 80*	*Coventry*	*Fletcher*	*Spittle*	*Peters*	*Haywood*	*Stanley*	*Mason*	*Davies*	*King*	*Chapple*	*Whalley*
	(£370)			Ref: W Archer	The netting of the ball by Davies when offside was the preliminary to King's opener. In the second half, Bailiff allowed Mason's tame shot to slip through his hands, before Chapple headed in as Crewe eclipsed the sensation of City's defeat at the hands of Grimsby a few seasons ago.										
F A BRISTOL ROV	20 W	1-0	1-0	Foster 15	**Davis**	Annan	Fagan	Mason	Sweet	Osborne	Copestake	Gildea	Foster	Batty	Shearman
GC 19/4	*4,466 SL:17*				*Roney*	*Harvie*	*Gange*	*Alden*	*Shaw*	*Phillips*	*McColl*	*Shervey*	*Jones*	*Hughes*	*Rankin*
	(£129)			Ref: F Kirkham	In view of the important match at Hyde Road, City relied solely upon their reserves at Eastville, while Rovers were without the injured trio of Peplow, Williams and Westwood. Had the City won by more than Foster's shot, it would scarcely have been inconsistent with their superiority.										

		P	W	D	L	Home F	Home A	W	D	L	Away F	Away A	Pts
1	Manchester U	38	14	4	1	47	18	8	4	7	25	22	52
2	Aston Villa	38	15	3	1	50	18	7	4	8	19	23	51
3	Sunderland	38	10	6	3	44	22	5	9	5	23	26	45
4	Everton	38	12	3	4	34	17	7	4	8	16	19	45
5	Bradford City	38	13	1	5	33	16	7	4	8	18	26	45
6	Wednesday	38	10	5	4	24	15	7	3	9	23	33	42
7	Oldham Ath	38	13	4	2	30	12	3	5	11	14	29	41
8	Newcastle U	38	8	7	4	37	18	7	3	9	24	25	40
9	Sheffield Utd	38	8	3	8	27	21	7	5	7	22	22	38
10	Wlch Arsenal	38	9	6	4	24	14	4	6	9	17	35	38
11	Notts Co	38	9	6	4	21	16	5	4	10	16	29	38
12	Blackburn R	38	12	2	5	40	14	1	9	9	22	40	37
13	Liverpool	38	11	3	5	38	19	4	4	11	15	34	37
14	Preston NE	38	8	5	6	25	19	4	6	9	15	30	35
15	Tottenham H	38	10	5	4	40	23	3	1	15	12	40	32
16	Middlesbro'	38	9	5	5	31	21	2	5	12	18	42	32
17	Manchester C	38	7	5	7	26	26	2	8	9	17	32	31
18	Bury	38	8	9	2	27	18	1	2	16	16	53	29
19	BRISTOL C	38	8	4	7	23	21	3	1	15	20	45	27
20	Nott'm Forest	38	5	4	10	28	31	4	3	12	27	44	25
		760	199	90	91	649	379	91	90	199	379	649	760

Odds & ends

Double wins: (2) Newcastle United, Manchester City.
Double losses: (6) Tottenham Hotspur, Manchester United, Aston Villa, Woolwich Arsenal, Bradford City, Everton.

Won from behind: (2) Oldham Athletic (h), Manchester City (a).
Lost from in front: (0).

High spots: The opening day win versus Newcastle at St James' Park.
Beating Sheffield United 4-0 at 'Bramall Lane' on 29 October.
A 3-2 thriller at Middlesbrough on 21 January.
Alec Logan's promising debut in a 3-3 draw with Nottingham Forest.
Winning 2-1 against Manchester City at Hyde Road on 22 April.
Beating Oldham Athletic 3-2 at 'Ashton Gate' on 27 December.
The 1-0 home success over Newcastle United on New Year's Eve.

Low spots: Losing 0-4 at 'Anfield' on 15 October.
Joe Cottle's fractured leg in a 0-4 defeat at 'Deepdale' on 28 January.
Failure to muster a good performance in the last game of the season when a win against Everton at 'Ashton Gate' would have prevented relegation.
Being at the wrong end of the biggest FA Cup shock of the season - losing 0-3 at home to Crewe Alexandra on 14 January.

Player of the Year: Ebenezer 'Ginger' Owers.
Ever-presents: (0).
Hat-tricks: (0).
Leading scorer: Ebenezer 'Ginger' Owers (16).

Pre-Season Trial Match:
24 Aug Reds 1(0) Blues 1(1)
4,000 Owers / *Cowell*

AGM (Temperance Hall, East Street, Bedminster, 30 June 1911):
Loss £3,842.5s.4d. Season Ticket Sales £359.11s.8d.

	Appearances Lge	Appearances Cup	Goals Lge	Goals Cup	Tot
Annan, Archie		1			
Bailiff, William	**7**	1			
Batty, Billy	**1**	1			
Burton, Andy	**21**	1	**4**		**4**
Chapman, Bert	**2**		**1**		**1**
Clay, Harry	**28**				
Clark, Willie	**24**	1	**1**		**1**
Clegg, John	**3**				
Copestake, Levi	**4**	1			
Cottle, Joe	**24**	1			
Cowell, John	**5**				
Date, Marmy	**1**				
Davis, W		1			
Fagan, Stephen	**18**	1			
Foster, Allan	**6**	1		1	**1**
Gadsby, Ernie	**10**	1	**1**		**1**
Gildea, Harry	**1**	1			
Hanlin, Pat	**32**	1			
Hardy, Bob	**20**		**4**		**4**
Jones, Edwin	**3**				
Logan, Alec	**20**		**7**		**7**
Marr, Reuben	**30**		**2**		**2**
Mason, SR	**3**	2			
Osborne, Albert	**1**	1			
Owers, Ebenezer	**31**	1	**16**		**16**
Padfield, W	**4**				
Shearman, Ben	**25**	2	**2**		**2**
Spear, Arthur	**3**				
Staniforth, Fred	**19**				
Sweet, Frank	**2**	1	**1**		**1**
Wedlock, Billy	**34**	1	**3**		**3**
Young, Bob	**36**	1			
Opponent og			**1**		**1**
32 players used	**418**	**22**	**43**	**1**	**44**

LEAGUE DIVISION 2

Manager: Sam Hollis

SEASON 1911-12

No		Date	Att	Pos	Pt	F-A	H-T	Scorers, Times, and Referees	1	2	3	4	5	6	7	8	9	10	11
1	H	FULHAM			W	1-0	1-0	Butler 17	**Anderson**	Young	Jones	Marr	Wedlock	**Nicholson**	**Brand**	**Cairns**	**Butler**	Logan	**Forbes**
		2/9	12,000		2				*Reynolds*	*Charlton*	*Sharp*	*Collins*	*Mavin*	*Marshall*	*Smith*	*Coleman*	*Pearce*	*White*	*Walker*
								Ref: J Sharpe	Back in the lower division, City gave every reason to suggest that they will prove strong opponents. The forward line, which proved to be so unsatisfactory last season, looked much improved, even though Brand missed two good chances before Butler notched the solitary goal.										
2	A	WOLVES			L	1-3	1-2	Cairns 40 *[Needham 85]*	Anderson	Fagan	Jones	Marr	Wedlock	Nicholson	Brand	Cairns	Butler	Logan	Forbes
		4/9	*8,000*		2			*Yule 32, Parsonage 37,*	*Boxley*	*Garratly*	*Fownes*	*Groves*	*Collins*	*Bishop*	*Harrison*	*Halligan*	*Parsonage*	*Needham*	*Yule*
								Ref: J Mason	All thoughts that City had about making an easy return to the top flight were dispelled in this game at Molineux, where they were savaged by the Wolves. After Yale's swift shot opened the scoring, City's only reward came shortly before the interval when Cairns outwitted Boxley.										
3	A	DERBY		17	L	0-3	0-0		Anderson	Young	Jones	Marr	Wedlock	Nicholson	**Gould**	Cairns	Butler	Logan	Forbes
		9/9	*8,000*	*11*	2			*Donald 54, Barnes 68, 72*	*Scattergood*	*Atkin*	*Barbour*	*Garry*	*Bagshaw*	*Richards*	*Grimes*	*Bloomer*	*Bauchop*	*Barnes*	*Donald*
								Ref: L Bullimer	City will not forget this experience in a hurry as, after putting together a good first-half performance, they were beaten fore and aft. They were overwhelmed by a Rams side, for whom the giant Atkin was insurmountable at the back, whilst Bagshaw was excellent as Buckley's deputy.										
4	H	STOCKPORT		11	W	2-1	2-1	Marr 12p, Butler 34	Anderson	Young	Fagan	Marr	Wedlock	Nicholson	Gould	Cairns	Butler	Logan	Forbes
		16/9	10,000	*14*	4			*O'Brien 18*	*McIver*	*Goodwin*	*Graham*	*Melville*	*Russell*	*Hindmarsh*	*Charlton*	*Devlin*	*Prout*	*Lomax*	*O'Brien*
								Ref: J Adams	City came out on top in this exciting game, which featured much charging and tackling. Stockport's performance belied their lowly position and suggested that they are capable of surprising many before the season ends. A handball offence brought Marr his successful spot-kick.										
5	A	LEEDS CITY		15	L	1-3	1-1	Logan 25	Anderson	Young	Fagan	Marr	Wedlock	Nicholson	Gould	Cairns	Butler	Logan	Forbes
		23/9	*12,000*	*16*	4			*Croot 9, Enright 47, McLeod 88*	*Murphy*	*Affleck*	*Creighton*	*Harkins*	*Morris*	*Cubberley*	*Roberts*	*Mulholland*	*McLeod*	*Enright*	*Croot*
								Ref: A McQue	Although Leeds delighted their supporters at Elland Road, they did little to suggest they are other than a poor side. The causes of City's defeat, Anderson, Fagan and Butler, were distinct failures, lacking the necessary qualities for their positions. Logan's drive was the game's highlight.										
6	H	WOLVES		16	L	0-3	0-0		Anderson	Young	Fagan	Marr	Wedlock	Nicholson	Gould	Cairns	Butler	Logan	Forbes
		30/9	10,000	*8*	4			*Yule 60, Halligan 75, Needham 80*	*Boxley*	*Collins*	*Garratly*	*Groves*	*Perrett*	*Bishop*	*Harrison*	*Hedley*	*Halligan*	*Needham*	*Yule*
								Ref: J Mason	Both goals had narrow escapes in the first half, but after the break the faster Wolves forwards broke through and Needham's header completed their well-deserved success. City, who found Harrison and Headley formidable opponents, gave try-outs to Cairns and Marr at centre-forward.										
7	A	LEICESTER FOSSE		17	L	0-2	0-2		Clay	Jones	**Gechern**	Young	Wedlock	Osborne	Gould	Logan	Marr	**Wilson**	Forbes
		7/10	*12,000*	*11*	4			*Benfield 10, Humphreys 37*	*Mearns*	*Henry*	*Currie*	*Randle*	*Hall*	*Butler*	*Benfield*	*Hubbard*	*Humphreys*	*Rollinson*	*Bauchop*
								Ref: T Kirkham	City re-arranged their side to a surprising extent, but the experiment didn't work as they gave an exhibition difficult to classify. Clay, who was unsighted when Benfield fired in the opener, can however be satisfied following his midweek re-signing, as he saved a second-half spot-kick.										
8	H	GAINSBOROUGH		15	W	2-0	1-0	Copestake 40, Forbes 70	Clay	Young	Fagan	Marr	Wedlock	Nicholson	Gould	Cairns	Logan	Forbes	**Copestake**
		14/10	*7,000*	*20*	6				*Sewell*	*Gunton*	*Spilman*	*Allsop*	*Tellum*	*Cretney*	*Tummon*	*Jex*	*Coulbeck*	*Foxall*	*Tooth*
								Ref: J Bailey	City's changed side served to produce much lively and enterprising soccer. They created many chances, but the two that they took were somewhat unexpected. Copestake bobbed up from nowhere to breast in a cross-field drive, whilst Forbes lashed the ball in from Logan's pass.										
9	A	GRIMSBY		17	L	0-3	0-2		Clay	Young	Fagan	Marr	Wedlock	Nicholson	Gould	Butler	Logan	Forbes	Copestake
		21/10	*6,000*	*9*	6			*Gordon 30, Hubbard 33, 70p*	*Lonsdale*	*Wheelhouse*	*Arrowsmith*	*Seeburgh*	*Gordon*	*Martin*	*Staniforth*	*Hubbard*	*Mounteney*	*Mayson*	*Huxford*
								Ref: S Peers	Despite having the wind in their favour, Hubbard's high drive, shortly after Gordon had put Grimsby in front, saw City with a mountain to climb at the break. City made many raids in the second half before Fagan's foul on Martin brought the Mariner's their successful spot-kick.										
10	H	NOTTM FOREST		16	D	2-2	1-0	Forbes 3, 78	Clay	Young	Jones	Marr	Wedlock	Nicholson	Gould	Logan	Butler	Forbes	Copestake
		28/10	8,000	*9*	7			*Banks 70, Ford 88*	*Hanna*	*Gibson*	*Maltby*	*Fisher*	*Mercer*	*Needham*	*Firth*	*Derrick*	*Saunders*	*Ford*	*Banks*
								Ref: A McQue	City held firm in the face of some fast and accurate play, and took the lead when, from Gould's fine centre, Forbes glanced the ball just inside the upright. Banks levelled with a clever drive after the break, but Forbes tapped City back in front before Ford's quick shot restored parity.										

No	Venue / Date	Opponent / Att	Pos	Res / Pts	FT	HT	Scorers, Times, Referees	1	2	3	4	5	6	7	8	9	10	11
11	A	CHELSEA	18	D	2-2	1-2	Logan 4, Wedlock 65	Clay	Young	Jones	Marr	Wedlock	Nicholson	Gould	Forbes	Logan	Wilson	Copestake
	4/11	***25,000***	5	8			*Whittingham 25, 35*	*Whitley*	*Cameron*	*Buchanan*	*Taylor*	*Ormiston*	*Downing*	*Douglas*	*Whittingham*	*Thompson*	*Dodd*	***Bridgeman***
							Ref: T Kirkham	Wedlock drove in City's point-saver against a Chelsea side which had won 4-1 at high-riding Orient last week. Despite Marr putting his spot-kick too close to the keeper, shortly after Whittingham fired Chelsea in front, City's cause was helped by the Pensioners' erratic shooting.										
12	H	CLAPTON ORIENT	16	W	1-0	1-0	Wedlock 7	Clay	Young	Jones	Marr	Wedlock	Nicholson	Gould	Forbes	Butler	Wilson	Copestake
	11/11	6,000	*9*	10				*Bower*	*Johnston*	*Johnson*	*Hind*	*Liddell*	*Scott*	*Parker*	*Dalyrymple*	*Bevan*	*McFadden*	*Dix*
							Ref: A Shallcross	Billy 'Fatty' Wedlock, City's famous captain, showed he has developed a taste for scoring, as, following on from last week's effort, he settled this exciting game early on. On seeing his side dispossessed at the end of a promising attack, he rushed forward and shot grandly into the net.										
13	A	BURNLEY	16	L	2-4	1-2	Copestake 35, 75 *[Hodgson 70]*	Clay	Young	Jones	Marr	Wedlock	Nicholson	Gould	Forbes	Logan	Wilson	Copestake
	18/11	*11,000*	*1*	10			*Harris 20, Freeman 44, 49p,*	*Dawson*	*Reid*	*Bamford*	*Swift*	*Boyle*	*Watson*	*Snowden*	*Lindley*	*Freeman*	*Hodgson*	*Harris*
							Ref: J Pearson	Both sides were strongly represented at Turf Moor, where Clay rather fortunately cleared from Freeman and Hodgson early on. The crossbar thwarted efforts by both Hodgson (shortly before Harris scrambled in the opener) and Copestake (not long before he ran home the equaliser).										
14	A	BIRMINGHAM	15	D	0-0	0-0		Clay	Young	Jones	Marr	Wedlock	Nicholson	Gould	Forbes	Logan	Wilson	Copestake
	25/11	*12,000*	*17*	11				*Bailey*	*Daykin*	*Womack*	*Bumphrey*	*Gildea*	*Robertson*	*Millington*	*Gibson*	*Hall*	*Jones*	*Conlin*
							Ref: W Chadwick	The Brummies showed promise of a complete revival in form, delighting their supporters with their keenness and dash. The City, for whom Wedlock was denied by the crossbar before the interval, resisted marvellously, however, and plunged into the fray regardless to earn a point.										
15	H	HUDDERSFIELD	13	W	3-2	1-1	Butler 35, 66, 68	Anderson	Gechren	Jones	Marr	Wedlock	Nicholson	Gould	Forbes	Butler	Wilson	Copestake
	2/12	5,000	*12*	13			*Blackburn 25, Howie 65*	*Brebner*	*Blackman*	*Bullock*	*Beaton*	*Hall*	*Bartlett*	*Blackburn*	*Howie*	*Richardson*	*Macauley*	*Jee*
							Ref: F Heath	The visitors took the lead in this entertaining encounter with a fine cross-shot. Butler headed in City's equaliser, but after the break Hewie heralded a three goals in a three-minute spell when he ran in to score after Anderson had spilled Blackburn's shot. Both sides missed chances.										
16	A	BLACKPOOL	14	L	0-1	0-0		Davis	Gechren	Jones	Marr	Wedlock	Nicholson	Gould	Logan	Butler	Wilson	Copestake
	9/12	*2,400*	*13*	13			*Milne 57*	*Fiske*	*Crewdson*	*Gladwin*	*Thorpe*	*Connor*	*Bradshaw*	*Nesbitt*	*Wolstenh'lme*	*Milne*	*Quinn*	*Cahill*
							Ref: T Rowbotham	An error by Davis, who had played soundly between the sticks, brought defeat for City at Bloomfield Road. After a hectic first half, which did not produce any goals, Davis was penalised for running the ball quite twenty yards. From the resultant free-kick Milne scrambled the ball in.										
17	H	GLOSSOP	13	W	2-0	1-0	Forbes 44, Copestake 61	Clay	Young	Jones	Marr	Wedlock	Nicholson	Gould	Forbes	Butler	Wilson	Copestake
	16/12	5,000	*19*	15				*Butler*	*Hampton*	*Cuffe*	*Heywood*	*Goldie*	*Carney*	*Law*	*Berwick*	*Stapley*	*Fitchie*	*Hodgkinson*
							Ref: Lieut W Clover	In an interesting game of numerous scoring opportunities, Berwick squandered a late penalty for the visitors by shooting into Clay's arms. Forbes ran through in grand style to beat the Glossop custodian for the opener; then, after the interval, Copestake shot just inside the far post.										
18	A	HULL	14	L	0-3	0-1		**Ware**	Young	Jones	Marr	Wedlock	Nicholson	**Cook**	Cairns	Forbes	Wilson	Copestake
	23/12	*9,000*	*3*	15			*Temple 28, 55, Wright 88*	*Roughley*	*Nevins*	*McQuillan*	*Wright W*	*Browell A*	*Gordon*	*Best*	*Chapman*	*Browell T*	*Temple*	*Wright E*
							Ref: T Campbell	City got no satisfaction out of their visit to Hull, where further experiments with the forwards tended to weaken, rather than strengthen the side. Ware however, deputising in goal for Clay who is still suffering the effects of injury sustained at Birmingham, gave a rather promising display.										
19	A	BARNSLEY	14	L	1-4	0-0	Gechern 85 *[Leavey 63]*	Ware	Young	Jones	Marr	Wedlock	Nicholson	Cook	Logan	Gechern	Forbes	Copestake
	25/12	*12,000*	*6*	15			*Lillycrop 54, Utley 58, Travers 61,*	*Cooper*	*Downs*	*Taylor*	*Glendenning*	*Bratley*	*Utley*	*Bartrop*	*Tuftnell*	*Lillycrop*	*Travers*	*Leavey*
							Ref: L Bullimer	After experiencing hard luck when Logan was bowled over by Downie when in the act of shooting, City fell away at Oakwell. Barnsley went in front shortly after the break, when Lillycrop put the finishing touch to a shot by Tuftnell, which Ware had found much too hot to hold.										
20	H	BARNSLEY	14	L	0-1	0-0		Clay	Young	Jones	Marr	Wedlock	Nicholson	Cook	Logan	Brand	Forbes	Copestake
	26/12	5,000	*6*	15			*Tuftnell 46*	*Cooper*	*Downs*	*Taylor*	*Hall*	*Bratley*	*Utley*	*Bartrop*	*Tuftnell*	*Lillycrop*	*Travers*	*Leavey*
							Ref: L Bullimer	Clay was called upon to save but a few shots during the course of this game, in which the players found it difficult to gain a firm foothold. Straight after the interval, Tuftnell netted from close range, and thereafter it was a struggle between City's forwards and the visitors' defence.										
21	A	FULHAM	15	L	1-2	0-1	Forbes 90	Ware	Young	Jones	Logan	Sweet	Nicholson	Gould	Forbes	Brand	Wilson	Copestake
	30/12	*10,000*	*9*	15			*Coleman 4, 75*	*Reynolds*	*Charlton*	*Sharp*	*Clifford*	*Mavin*	*White*	*Smith*	*Coleman*	*Pearce*	*Brown*	*McIntosh*
							Ref: J Sharpe	Even with a side containing many juniors, City might have easily won at Craven Cottage had their shooting been more accurate. As it was their only reward came from Forbes at the finish against a Fulham team who were somewhat lackadaisical after Coleman gave them the early lead.										

No	Date		Att	Pos	Pt	F-A	H-T	Scorers, Times, and Referees	1	2	3	4	5	6	7	8	9	10	11
22	H	DERBY		14	D	1-1	0-1	Ball 60	Ware	Young	Jones	Marr	Wedlock	Nicholson	Gould	**Ball**	Brand	Forbes	Copestake
	6/1		**4,000**	*1*	16			*Bauchop 20*	*Scattergood*	*Atkin*	*Betts*	*Garry*	*Bagshaw*	*Richards*	*Grimes*	*Bloomer*	*Leonard*	*Bauchop*	*Donald*
								Ref: L Bullimer	By drawing with the leaders, City gained more credit than the majority of their victories have brought them this season. Against clearly the best team in the League, City fought back after the interval to secure a division of the spoils, thanks to Ball shooting the leather past Scattergood.										
23	A	STOCKPORT		14	L	0-1	0-1		Ware	Young	Fagan	Marr	Wedlock	Nicholson	Gould	Ball	Butler	Brand	Copestake
	20/1		*5,000*	*15*	16			*O'Brien 13*	*McIver*	*Goodwin*	*Houghton*	*Rourke*	*Melville*	*Hindmarsh*	*Charlton*	*Devlin*	*Smith*	*Lomax*	*O'Brien*
								Ref: J Adams	Yet another City display entirely in keeping with the majority of their away performances this season. One goal again decided the issue, and once more it wasn't scored by City. O'Brien it was who brought County their deserved success, heading in from Charlton's well-placed corner.										
24	H	LEEDS CITY		14	W	**4-1**	3-1	Wedlock 5, Butler 12, 55,	Clay	Young	Jones	Marr	Wedlock	Nicholson	Gould	**Brough**	Butler	Brand	Copestake
	27/1		8,000	*15*	18			*Croot 20p* [Brough 15]	*Reinhardt*	*Affleck*	*Moran*	*Harkins*	*Morris*	*Johnson*	*Roberts*	*Mulholland*	*McLeod*	*Enright*	*Croot*
								Ref: A McQue	The introduction of Brough, the new signing from Liverpool, helped bring about this comprehensive success against the team with the weakest defence in the League. After Wedlock drove in the opener, a rebound off Affleck's chest allowed Butler to shoot the second past Dr Reinhardt.										
25	H	LEICESTER FOSSE		17	L	0-1	0-0		Clay	Fagan	Jones	Marr	Sweet	Nicholson	Gould	Brough	Butler	Forbes	Copestake
	10/2		6,000	*18*	18			*Sparrow 60*	*Starbuck*	*Clay*	*Currie*	*Randle*	*Hanger*	*King E*	*Benfield*	*Osborn*	*Sparrow*	*Hubbard*	*Harrison*
								Ref: T Kirkham	Never before has the value of Wedlock, away helping England defeat Ireland, been better illustrated than after Sparrow fired in Leicester's winner. Without him, City completely lost all idea of unity, after having been kept at bay by Starbuck's brilliant display between the sticks.										
26	A	GAINSBOROUGH		16	W	3-2	1-0	Marr 15, Bowyer 47, Butler 75	Clay	Fagan	Jones	Marr	Wedlock	Nicholson	Gould	Brough	Butler	**Bowyer**	Copestake
	17/2		*5,000*	*19*	20			*Foxall 70, Young 83p*	*Sewell*	*Gunton*	*Smith*	*Spilman*	*Coe*	*Tellum*	*Lounds*	*Coulbeck*	*Young*	*Foxall*	*Tummon*
								Ref: J Bailey	With Bowyer (ex-Liverpool) in their ranks, City secured their first away success. Marr was at the heart of the action, opening the scoring with a 30-yard cross-shot, then setting up Bowyer to shoot in the second before his handling offence brought about a tense and exciting finish.										
27	H	GRIMSBY		15	W	3-0	2-0	Butler 25, Copestake 35, [Bowyer 70]	Clay	Young	Jones	Marr	Wedlock	Nicholson	Gould	Brough	Butler	Bowyer	Copestake
	24/2		8,000	*7*	22				*Lonsdale*	*Wheelhouse*	*Arrowsmith*	*Browell*	*Fullames*	*Martin*	*Staniforth*	*Rippon*	*Mounteney*	*Mayson*	*Worth*
								Ref: F Heath	If City go on playing as well as they did in this game, then their reputation will be speedily restored. The score didn't flatter them in the least, indeed they would have deserved the fourth goal from a penalty right on time, but the final whistle blew just as Bowyer put away the rebound.										
28	A	NOTTM FOREST		16	L	0-2	0-1		Clay	Young	Jones	Marr	Wedlock	Nicholson	Gould	Chapman	Butler	Bowyer	Copestake
	2/3		*7,000*	*10*	22			*Morris 9, Gibson 63p*	*Hanna*	*Dudley*	*Gibson*	*Armstrong*	*Mercer*	*Needham*	*Firth*	*Derrick*	*Saunders*	*Morris*	*Banks*
								Ref: A McQue	Forest took an early lead when Morris splendidly headed in a flag-kick well out of Clay's reach. City improved after the break, but a foul on Frith allowed Gibson to score from the spot. Despite much endeavour thereafter, City were unable to turn any of their chances to good effect.										
29	H	CHELSEA		17	D	1-1	0-1	Bowyer 73	Clay	Young	Jones	Marr	Wedlock	Nicholson	Gould	Bowyer	Butler	Forbes	Copestake
	9/3		9,750	*2*	23			*Whittingham 18*	*Molyneux*	*Bettridge*	*Cameron*	*Taylor*	*Ormiston*	*Harrow*	*Douglas*	*Whittingham*	*Hilsdon*	*Woodward*	*Bridgeman*
								Ref: T Kirkham	After Whittingham secured the Pensioners' lead, there seemed no way back for City, as their unconvincing forwards made little impression on the visiting defence. In the second half, however, Bowyer cleverly set up Copestake to centre the ball for the No 8 to deftly put it into the net.										
30	A	CLAPTON ORIENT		17	L	**0-4**	0-2	*[McFadden 55p, Hind 57]*	Clay	Young	Jones	Marr	Wedlock	Nicholson	Gould	Brand	Butler	Bowyer	Copestake
	16/3		*8,000*	*5*	23			*Dalyrymple 12, Bevan 30,*	*Hugall*	*Holmes*	*Johnston*	*Hind*	*Stonehouse*	*Willis*	*Prior*	*Dalrymple*	*Bevan*	*McFadden*	*Dix*
								Ref: A Shallcross	In marked contrast to the City, Orient made the most of their chances at Homerton. Dalrymple opened the scoring by finishing off his fine dash with a shot that bounced down over the line after hitting the corner of the upright. Marr's foul on Bevan gave McFadden his goal from the spot.										
31	H	BURNLEY		17	L	0-3	0-2		Clay	Fagan	Jones	Marr	Young	Nicholson	Gould	Butler	Owers	Bowyer	Copestake
	23/3		10,000	*1*	23			*Picken 40, 75, Nesbitt 43*	*Dawson*	*Reid*	*Taylor*	*McLaren*	*Boyle*	*Watson*	*Nesbitt*	*Lindley*	*Picken*	*Hodgson*	*Harris*
								Ref: J Pearson	Apart from the opening half-hour, City are outclassed in this heavy defeat which increased the prospect of their having to apply for re-election. Despite having Owers, on his return from Darlington, back in their ranks, they could make little impression due to Boyle's outstanding display.										

32	H	BIRMINGHAM	17	W	2-1	2-0	Butler 28, Marr 30p	Clay	Young	Jones	Marr	Wedlock	Nicholson	Butler	Brough	Owers	Bowyer	Copestake
30/3		8,000	*13*	25			*Hastings 83*	*Crossthwaite*	*Ball*	*Womack*	*Gardner*	*Tinkler*	*Bumphrey*	*Gibson*	*Jones*	*Hall*	*Robertson*	*Hastings*
							Ref: H Thompson	A most welcome success, but City were never sure of victory until the final whistle. Owers twice netted from clever play, but the goals were disallowed. Those that counted came from Butler, who played a forceful game on the wing, and Marr, who made no mistake from the spot.										
33	A	BRADFORD PA	17	W	1-0	1-0	Owers 12	Clay	Fagan	Jones	Marr	Wedlock	Nicholson	Butler	Brough	Owers	Bowyer	Copestake
5/4		*8,000*	*11*	27				*Wallace*	*Watson*	*Blackham*	*Halley*	*Dainty*	*Howie*	*Kivlichan*	*Simpson*	*Turnbull*	*McCandless*	*Buchanan*
							Ref: J Bailey	Having the advantage of a pretty stiff breeze, City took an early lead when Owers netted with a fierce shot, whilst Wedlock had to be at his best to hold Turnbull in check. Despite the conditions being in their favour after the break, the Park Avenue side were unable to level matters.										
34	A	HUDDERSFIELD	16	W	2-1	2-1	Owers 10, Bowyer 40	Clay	Fagan	Jones	Marr	Wedlock	Nicholson	Butler	Forbes	Owers	Bowyer	Copestake
6/4		***2,000***	*17*	29			*Howie 25*	*Mutch*	*Blackman*	*Thomson*	*Dinnie*	*Fayers*	*Bartlett*	*Armour*	*Howie*	*Richardson*	*Macauley*	*Jee*
							Ref: F Heath	A tale of errors at Leeds Road, where Thomson's mis-kick allowed Owers to run in and put City in front with a grand shot which went in off a post. Owers set up Bowyer to put City back in front after another mis-kick, this time by Jones, had enabled Howie's weak shot to find the net.										
35	H	BRADFORD PA	13	W	1-0	0-0	Owers 80	Clay	Fagan	Jones	Marr	Wedlock	Nicholson	Butler	Chapman	Owers	Bowyer	Forbes
8/4		10,000	*11*	31				*McDonald*	*Watson*	*Dixon*	*Halley !*	*Dainty*	*Scott*	*Kivlichan*	*Little*	*Reeves*	*Howie*	*Munroe*
							Ref: J Bailey	Facing the strong wind after the interval, City's position in Second Division affairs was secured by a smart low drive from Owers. Having lost the services of Marr with a 15th-minute ankle injury, City were helped by Halley's dismissal on the hour mark for his running kick on Butler.										
36	H	BLACKPOOL	10	W	2-0	0-0	Bowyer 48, Butler 49	Clay	Fagan	Jones	Chapman	Wedlock	Nicholson	Butler	Forbes	Owers	Bowyer	Copestake
13/4		9,750	*17*	33				*Fiske*	*Crewdson*	*Dale*	*Thorpe*	*Connor*	*Evans*	*Cahill*	*Wolstenh'lme*	*Milne*	*Wilson*	*Quinn*
							Ref: T Rowbotham	A keenly contested game, which saw City clinch their fifth consecutive win. Early after the break, Bowyer dribbled through to score the opener with a brilliant shot. Almost immediately, Butler's long-distance left-footer doubled the advantage before the bar thwarted a drive by Milne.										
37	A	GLOSSOP	13	L	0-3	0-2		Clay	Fagan	Jones	Cairns	Wedlock	Nicholson	Butler	Brough	Owers	Bowyer	Copestake
20/4		*3,000*	*18*	33			*Littlewort 10, Hoare 40, 85*	*Butler*	*Hampton*	*Cuffe*	*Littlewort*	*Goldie*	*Carney*	*Law*	*Berwick*	*Hoare*	*Moore*	*Hodgkinson*
							Ref: Lieut W Clover	Despite fielding their strongest available forward line, City never got going at Glossop, where the homesters played at the top of their form. They was little between the sides until Littlewort put Glossop in front; then shortly before the break Hoare headed in the Peakmen's second.										
38	H	HULL	13	D	0-0	0-0		Clay	Fagan	**Banfield**	Cairns	Wedlock	Nicholson	Butler	Brough	Owers	Bowyer	Forbes
27/4		5,000	*6*	34				*Roughley*	*Houghton*	*McQuinlan*	*Wright W*	*Temple*	*McIntosh*	*McDonald*	*Chapman*	*Best*	*Fazackerley*	*Shaw*
	Home	Away					Ref: T Campbell	This game against the Third Porters, which started with the promise of being a keen struggle, deteriorated into an aimless exhibition. A poor end to a difficult season as, apart from an Owers effort which skimmed the bar, neither side made much of an effort to end the stalemate.										
Ave	7,711	8,705																

CUP-TIES

FA Cup/Glos Cup		F-A	H-T	Scorers, Times, and Referees	1	2	3	4	5	6	7	8	9	10	11
1 A NORTHAMPTON 14	L	0-1	0-0		Ware	Young	Jones	Marr	Wedlock	Nicholson	Gould	Ball	Butler	Forbes	Copestake
13/1 *16,000 SL:3*				*Lewis 75*	*Thorpe*	*Clipston*	*Davies*	*Manning*	*Hampson*	*Tomkins*	*Walden*	*King*	*Lessons*	*Lewis*	*Freeman*
(£529)				Ref: A Oakley	City made a gallant fight at the County ground, where Northampton have not been beaten so far this season. Had City shown but reasonable thrustfulness they would have survived to fight another day, but, as it was, Lewis drove in Walden's centre to bring Northampton victory.										
F H BRISTOL ROV 14	W	1-0	1-0	Copestake 7	Clay	Young	Jones	Marr	Wedlock	Nicholson	Gould	Brough	Butler	Ball	Copestake
GC 3/2 8,966 *SL:12*					*Roney*	*Harvie*	*Bennett*	*Williams*	*Morris*	*Shaw*	*Peplow*	*Hughes*	*Jones*	*Walker*	*Rankin*
(£251.16.3)				Ref: J Mason	Copestake secured City's victory when he lifted the ball over Roney's head, just as the keeper had got back into position after dashing out and knocking the leather away from Ball. Overall the Rovers had a fair share of the game but, on the frost-bound pitch, they failed in front of goal.										

FRIENDLIES

Match		F-A	H-T	Scorers, Times, and Referees	1	2	3	4	5	6	7	8	9	10	11
1 A CARDIFF	L	0-2	0-2		Ware	Gechern	Fagan	Young	Cairns	Nicholson	Copestake	Logan	**Broad**	Butler	Forbes
1/1 *7,000*				*Featherstone 20, Tracey 35p*	*Germaine*	*Duffy*	*Walters*	*Abley*	*Lawrie*	*Hardy*	*Latham G*	*Burton J*	*Featherstone*	*Burton G*	*Tracey*
				Ref: A Farrant	City paid the price for their over-indulgence in gallery work at Ninian Park. Featherstone's nice drive, from Latham's centre, gave Cardiff the lead; then Tracey converted a penalty following Fagan's foul on Jack Burton. After the break Featherstone had an effort disallowed for offside.										
2 H BRISTOL ROV	W	3-1	1-1	Gould 45, Owers 65, Wedlock 80	Davis	Banfield	Jones	**Morgan**	Wedlock	Sweet	Gould	**Johnson**	Owers	Chapman	**Rose**
4/5 1,500				*Hurley 40*	*Roney*	*Gange*	*Bennett*	*Phillips*	*Guest*	*Mason*	*Long*	*Hurley WE*	*Richards*	*Roe*	*Lines*
(£47)				Ref: F Curtis *(Titanic Disaster Fund)*	Following quickly on Hurley's hooked-in opener, City levelled right on the half-time whistle when Gould's shot from near the touchline found the net. After the break Rose galloped down the wing before crossing for Owers to double City's advantage before Wedlock fired in the third.										

		Home						Away					
	P	W	D	L	F	A	W	D	L	F	A	Pts
1 Derby Co	38	15	2	2	55	13	8	6	5	19	15	54
2 Chelsea	38	15	2	2	36	13	9	4	6	28	21	54
3 Burnley	38	14	5	0	50	14	8	3	8	27	27	52
4 Clapt' Orient	38	16	0	3	44	14	5	3	11	17	30	45
5 Wolves	38	12	3	4	41	10	4	7	8	16	23	42
6 Barnsley	38	10	5	4	28	19	5	7	7	17	23	42
7 Hull City	38	12	3	4	36	13	5	5	9	18	38	42
8 Fulham	38	10	3	6	42	24	6	4	9	24	34	39
9 Grimsby T	38	9	6	4	24	18	6	3	10	24	37	39
10 Leicester Fos'	38	11	4	4	34	18	4	3	12	15	48	37
11 Bradford PA	38	10	5	4	30	16	3	4	12	14	29	35
12 Birmingham	38	11	3	5	44	29	3	3	13	11	30	34
13 BRISTOL C	38	11	4	4	27	17	3	2	14	14	43	34
14 Blackpool	38	12	4	3	24	12	1	4	14	8	40	34
15 Nott'm Forest	38	9	3	7	26	18	4	4	11	20	30	33
16 Stockport Co	38	8	5	6	31	22	3	6	10	16	32	33
17 Huddersfield	38	8	5	6	30	22	5	1	13	20	42	32
18 Glossop	38	6	8	5	33	23	2	4	13	9	33	28
19 Leeds City	38	7	6	6	21	22	3	2	14	29	56	28
20 Gainsboro' T	38	4	6	9	17	22	1	7	11	13	42	23
	760	210	82	88	673	359	88	82	210	359	673	760

Odds & ends

Double wins: (3) Gainsborough Trinity, Huddersfield Town, Bradford PA.
Double losses: (3) Wolves, Leicester Fosse, Burnley, Barnsley.

Won from behind: (1) Huddersfield Town (h).
Lost from in front: (0).

High spots: Starting the season with a 1-0 win over Fulham.
Billy Wedlock's record breaking 25th consecutive England appearance in a 1-1 draw with Scotland in Glasgow on 23 March.

Low spots: Having to struggle at the wrong end of the table following relegation from the top flight.
Losing 1-4 at Barnsley on Christmas Day.
Barnsley's completing of the double with a 1-0 Boxing Day success at 'Ashton Gate'.
City's failure to take their chances in a 0-4 defeat at 'Homerton' on 16 March.
Losing 0-3 at Glossop on 20 April.
Going out of the FA Cup to Southern League Northampton Town, managed by Herbert Chapman, destined to set up both Huddersfield and Arsenal for their consecutive trio of League Championships.

Player of the Year: 'Jock' Nicholson.
Ever-presents: (0).
Hat-tricks: (1) Jack Butler.
Leading scorer: Jack Butler (11).

Pre-Season Trial Match:
26 Aug Reds 2(1) Blues 1(0)
2,500 Brand, Forbes / *Ball*

AGM (Temperance Hall, East Street, Bedminster, 26 June 1912):
Loss £817.0s.0d. Season Ticket Sales £199.15s.6d.

	Appearances			Goals			
	Lge	Cup	Fr	Lge	Cup	Fr	Tot
Anderson, Fergus	**7**						
Ball, Henry	**2**	2		**1**			**1**
Banfield, Laurie	**1**		1				
Bowyer, Sam	**13**			**5**			**5**
Brand, Tom	**8**						
Broad, Tommy			1				
Brough, Joe	**8**	1		**1**			**1**
Butler, Jack	**28**	2	1	**11**			**11**
Cairns, Tommy	**10**		1	**1**			**1**
Chapman, Bert	**3**		1				
Clay, Harry	**25**	1					
Cook, W	**3**						
Copestake, Levi	**29**	2	1	**5**	1		**6**
Davis, W	**1**		1				
Fagan, Stephen	**16**		1				
Forbes, Johnny	**27**	1	1	**5**			**5**
Gechern, Pat	**4**		1	**1**			**1**
Gould, Charlie	**26**	2	1			1	**1**
Johnson			1				
Jones, Edwin	**31**	2	1				
Logan, Alec	**17**		1	**2**			**2**
Marr, Reuben	**34**	2		**3**			**3**
Morgan, Jerry			1				
Nicholson, 'Jock'	**37**	2	1				
Osborne, Albert	**1**						
Owers, Ebenezer	**8**		1	**3**		1	**4**
Rose, Leslie			1				
Sweet, Frank	**2**		1				
Ware, Tommy	**5**	1	1				
Wedlock, Billy	**35**	2	1	**3**		1	**4**
Wilson, Peter	**10**						
Young, Bob	**27**	2	1				
32 players used	**418**	**22**	**22**	**41**	**1**	**3**	**45**

No	Date		Att	Pos	Pt	F-A	H-T	Scorers, Times, and Referees	1	2	3	4	5	6	7	8	9	10	11
1	H	BRADFORD PA			D	0-0	0-0		Clay	**Kearns**	Jones	Marr	Wedlock	Nicholson	Broad	**Marrison**	Owers	Bowyer	**Harris**
	4/9		10,000		1				*McDonald*	*Watson*	*Blackham*	*Howie*	*Dainty*	*Scott*	*Kivlichan*	*Simpson*	*Little T*	*McCandless*	*Buchanan*
								Ref: L Bullimer	Whilst it was disappointing to start the term without a goal, it was encouraging that City, who were on top throughout, had no difficulty in preventing Avenue from scoring. Owers thought he broke the deadlock towards the close, but the goal was disallowed because he handled.										
2	A	WOLVES			D	1-1	1-0	Owers 20	Clay	Jones	Kearns	Marr !	Wedlock	Nicholson	Broad	Marrison	Owers	Bowyer	Harris
	7/9		*14,000*		2			*Jordan 89*	*Peers*	*Garratly*	*Collins*	*Groves*	*Young*	*Bishop*	*Harrison*	*Jordan*	*Halligan*	*Needham*	*Brooks*
								Ref: J Sharpe	Battling City, who had taken the lead when Owers headed in Broad's centre, were pegged back at the finish by the Reverend Jordan's late equaliser. A cruel fate for a City side down to ten men for the final twenty minutes, due to Marr's dismissal for nails protruding from his studs.										
3	H	LEICESTER FOSSE		7	W	1-0	1-0	Owers 10	Clay	Kearns	Jones	Marr	Wedlock	Nicholson	Broad	Marrison	Owers	Bowyer	Harris
	14/9		13,000	*11*	4				*Mearns*	*Currie*	*Thompson*	*McWhirter*	*Hanger*	*King*	*Benfield*	*Noble*	*Sparrow*	*Osborn*	*Harrison*
								Ref: A Adams	At the start, the football was of an unusually high class, but after City scored there was a steady falling off until, by the end, the exchanges were little short of scrambling. Bowyer won the game when, from Thompson's faulty clearance, he was able to walk the ball into the net.										
4	A	STOCKPORT		2	W	1-0	0-0	Bowyer 70	Clay	Kearns	Jones	Marr	Wedlock	Nicholson	Broad	Marrison	Owers	Bowyer	Harris
	21/9		*7,000*	*20*	6				*McIver*	*Goodwin*	*Fagan*	*Tattersall*	*Garratt*	*Houghton*	*Charlton*	*Rodgers*	*Smith*	*Blair*	*O'Brien*
								Ref: I Baker	Bowyer who, when he had only the keeper to beat in the first half, had skied the ball over the bar, made amends with the winner following the interval. Not long after Owers had headed against the crossbar, Bowyer was able to dribble through and beat the custodian from close in.										
5	H	PRESTON		4	D	1-1	0-0	Owers 75	Clay	Kearns	Jones	Marr	Wedlock	Nicholson	Broad	Marrison	Owers	Bowyer	Harris
	28/9		12,000	*12*	7			*Morley 48*	*Toone*	*McFadyen*	*Rodway*	*Holdsworth*	*McCall*	*Galloway*	*Morley*	*Green*	*Wareing*	*Gerrish*	*Kirby*
								Ref: J Pearson	A rather fortunate point for City as, for only the second time in their Football League career, they got through the opening month of a season undefeated. Following Green's retirement with a badly cut head, a header by Owers was carried over the line when Toone lost his balance.										
6	A	BURNLEY		5	D	2-2	1-0	Owers 38, Bowyer 81	Clay	Kearns	Banfield	Marr	Wedlock	Nicholson	Broad	Marrison	Owers	Bowyer	Harris
	5/10		*15,000*	*6*	8			*Boyle 47, Husband 86*	*Dawson*	*Reid*	*Taylor*	*Swift*	*Boyle*	*Watson*	*Mosscrop*	*Lindley*	*Freeman*	*Hodgson*	*Husband*
								Ref: A Wilkes	An exciting affair at Turf Moor, which ended with Husband being carried unconscious from the pitch after heading in Burnley's late point-saver. With Harris playing against his old club, City took the lead shortly before half-time, when Owers beat Dawson with a magnificent shot.										
7	H	HULL		6	D	1-1	0-0	Marr 50p	Clay	Kearns	Jones	Marr	Wedlock	Nicholson	Broad	Marrison	Owers	Harris	Butler
	12/10		**20,000** (£478)	*1*	9			*Fazackerley 83*	*Hendry*	*Nevins*	*McQuillan*	*Fenwick*	*McIntosh*	*Gordon*	*Best*	*Goode*	*Stevens*	*Fazackerley*	*Wright E*
								Ref: S Peers	The only disappointment for City fans in the big crowd was Hull's driven late leveller, which allowed both sides to keep their unbeaten tags. Justice perhaps for a Hull side who were deprived of a first-half goal when, after Kearns had fisted out a shot, Goode fired wide from the spot.										
8	A	GLOSSOP		10	L	1-3	1-2	Wedlock 33	Clay	Kearns	Jones	Marr	Wedlock	Nicholson	Broad	Marrison	Owers	Harris	Copestake
	19/10		*3,000*	*20*	9			*Hodkinson 5, Cooper 20, Hoare 62*	*Causer*	*Spittle*	*Cuffe*	*Littlewort*	*Brennan*	*Carney*	*Cooper*	*Hoare*	*Williams*	*Moore*	*Hodkinson*
								Ref: A Shallcross	After last week's magnificent game, all City could manage at bottom-of-the-table Glossop was a shot of Wedlock's that went in just under the crossbar. Glossop swung the ball about well in the muddy conditions and Hoare's header served to set the seal on their fully deserved victory.										
9	H	CLAPTON ORIENT		8	W	1-0	1-0	Owers 7	Clay	Kearns	Jones	Marr	Wedlock	Nicholson	Broad	Owers	**Nichol**	Bowyer	Harris
	26/10		11,000	*3*	11				*Bower*	*Johnston*	*Evans*	*Scott*	*Liddell*	*Willis*	*Parker*	*Dalrymple*	*Bevan*	*McFadden*	*Dix*
								Ref: S Peers	City's experiment of playing twin centre-forwards in Owers and Nichol was somewhat a failure after promising much at the start. For a considerable time at the outset, City's forwards overran the Clapton defence, but subsequent to the goal they never looked likely again.										
10	A	LINCOLN		10	L	0-2	0-1		Clay	Kearns	Jones	**Moss**	Wedlock	Nicholson	Broad	Nichol	Owers	Bowyer	Harris
	2/11		*9,000*	*1*	11			*Miller 30, Barrell 78*	*Fern*	*Wilson*	*Meunier*	*Wield*	*Gardner*	*Robson*	*Brindley*	*Barrell*	*Miller*	*McCubbin*	*Manning*
								Ref: A Pellowe	On the run of play, the leaders deserved their win, but City might well have snatched a point had not Owers missed an open goal, not long after the interval, when Bowyer's shot rebounded off a post. They soon paid the price as Barrell flung himself at a centre to double Lincoln's lead.										

No	Venue	Opponent / Date	Att	Pos	Pts	F-A	H-T	Scorers, Times, Referees	1	2	3	4	5	6	7	8	9	10	11
11	H	NOTTM FOREST		13	L	1-2	1-0	Marrison 15	Clay	Kearns	Jones	Moss	Wedlock	Nicholson	Broad	Marrison	Nichol	Bowyer	Harris
		9/11	10,000	*3*	11			*Morris 65, 80*	*Hanna*	*Dudley*	*Maltby*	*Armstrong*	*Mercer*	*Needham*	*Firth*	*Derrick*	*Gibson*	*Morris*	*Ford*
								Ref: J Hornby/C Knight-Coutts	Many in the crowd were amused when the referee was knocked out on the hour. He was replaced for a time by his senior linesman, whilst a Forest Committee member, who tossed with E Hall, filled the vacancy on the line. Clay's brilliant display kept down City's margin of defeat.										
12	H	BLACKPOOL		10	D	0-0	0-0		Clay	Kearns	Jones	Moss	Wedlock	Nicholson	Broad	Brough	Owers	Bowyer	Harris
		16/11	8,000	*18*	12				*Kidd*	*Crewdson*	*Jones*	*Bainbridge*	*Thorpe*	*Booth*	*Charles*	*Heslop*	*Wilson*	*Gillow*	*Quinn*
								Ref: A Adams	City's slide down the table was reflected in the attendance, and many more displays like this will reduce the crowd even further. They had some ill-luck, it is true, Wedlock hitting the bar and Nicholson heading against the post but so too did a Pool side who created the best chances.										
13	A	BIRMINGHAM		12	L	0-3	0-2		Ware	Kearns	Jones	**Edwards**	Wedlock	Nicholson	Broad	Bowyer	Butler	Harris	Copestake
		23/11	*20,000*	*1*	12			*Hastings 5, Robertson 20, Smith 60*	*Crossthwaite*	*Ball*	*Fairman*	*Gardner*	*Tinkler*	*Bumphrey*	*Smith A*	*Jones*	*Hall*	*Robertson*	*Hastings*
								Ref: J Howcroft	Over 1,000 City excursionists went to St Andrew's to see their re-arranged attack given a hard time by Birmingham's robust defenders. The Blues forwards, however, created many chances and Smith rounded off their success when he pounced on Ware's fist out to net in fine style.										
14	H	HUDDERSFIELD		13	D	0-0	0-0		Ware	Kearns	Jones	Edwards	Wedlock	Nicholson	Broad	Marrison	Butler	Bowyer	Copestake
		30/11	6,000	*14*	13				*Mutch*	*Blackman*	*Bullock*	*Beaton*	*Fayers*	*Dow*	*Armour*	*Elliott*	*Macauley*	*Howie*	*Jee*
								Ref: H Taylor	City's failure to beat opponents, who had not previously gained a point away from home, was another serious set-back. The goalkeepers stomped up and down between the posts all afternoon in a vain effort to keep warm, as the puerile forwards never seriously troubled them.										
15	A	LEEDS CITY		12	D	1-1	1-1	Brough 22	Ware	Kearns	Banfield	Morgan	Wedlock	Nicholson	Broad	Brough	Butler	Bowyer	Copestake
		7/12	*10,000*	*9*	14			*Robertson 17*	*Scott*	*Law*	*Ferguson*	*Allan*	*Lintott*	*Foley*	*Bainbridge*	*Robertson*	*McLeod*	*Gibson*	*Croot*
								Ref: I Baker	Pure pluck got City a point at Elland Road, where Robertson's brilliant shot hit the bar early in the first half. Ware made a number of fine saves, as City held onto the point earned by Brough's 25-yard angled drive, after Robertson had headed Leeds in front from Croot's corner.										
16	H	GRIMSBY		12	D	2-2	1-0	Bowyer 30, 65	Ware	Kearns	Banfield	Morgan	Wedlock	Nicholson	Gould	Brough	Owers	Bowyer	Copestake
		14/12	6,000	*15*	15			*Mayson 83, Rippon 88*	*Lonsdale*	*Wheelhouse*	*Arrowsmith*	*Andrews*	*Gordon*	*Martin*	*Staniforth*	*Rippon*	*Quinn*	*Mayson*	*Birch*
								Ref: T Kirkham	City, without Broad due to his daughter's death, were shocked by the Mariners' late rally. After Mayson got his foot to a cross by the former City player Staniforth, a 30-yarder from Rippon (no relation to Willis) brought an unlikely point for a Grimsby side that had offered little.										
17	A	BURY		11	W	1-0	1-0	Owers 31	Ware	Kearns	Banfield	Young	Wedlock	Nicholson	Broad	Brough	Owers	Bowyer	Copestake
		21/12	*4,407*	*17*	17				*McDonald*	*Fenner*	*Millington*	*Perry*	*Humphreys*	*Goldie*	*Prior*	*Kay*	*Fitzsimmons*	*Smith*	*Connor*
								Ref: J Pearson	Despite the presence of their new centre-forward from Northwich Victoria, Bury looked a poor side. Even though Bury had most of the play, it was City who took the lead when Owers headed in Broad's cross. It was enough to take the points, but it upset Bury's partisan supporters.										
18	H	FULHAM		10	W	2-1	0-0	Brough 75, Owers 88	Ware	Kearns	Banfield	Young	Wedlock	Nicholson	Broad	Brough	Owers	Bowyer	Copestake
		25/12	10,000	*16*	19			*Kearns 77og*	*Nixon*	*Gray*	*Burns*	*Collins*	*Mavin*	*Marshall*	*Smith*	*Coleman*	*Torrance*	*White*	*Walker*
								Ref: A Briggs	With Wedlock limping on the wing, Ginger Owers headed in City's winner during the dying minutes. A dramatic and happy ending to a keen match that had seen Brough give City the lead with a nice shot, and Fulham quickly equalise when Kearns diverted Mavin's drive past Ware.										
19	H	WOLVES		9	W	3-1	2-0	Brough 37, 40, 58	Ware	Kearns	Banfield	Young	Moss	Nicholson	Broad	Brough	Owers	Bowyer	Harris
		28/12	5,000	*5*	21			*Groves 75*	*Peers*	*Jones*	*Collins*	*Hunt*	*Brookes*	*Bishop*	*Brooks*	*Groves*	*Parsonage*	*Needham*	*Yule*
								Ref: J Sharpe	The hardy band of spectators who braved the incessant rain, which formed large puddles all over the pitch, were rewarded by Brough's two splendid goals before the break. In the second half, when Nicholson's shot rebounded off the bar, Brough was on hand to claim his hat-trick.										
20	A	BRADFORD PA		10	L	1-4	0-2	Brough 70	Ware	Kearns	Banfield	Young	Moss	Marrison	Broad	Brough	Owers	Bowyer	Copestake
		1/1	*10,000*	*11*	21			*Little 20, 38, Smith 47, Howie 65*	*Mason*	*Watson*	*Blackham*	*Halley*	*Dainty*	*Scott*	*Munro*	*Little T*	*Smith*	*Howie*	*Kivlichan*
								Ref: L Bullimer	Despite having their entire half-back line on the injured list, City played better than the score would suggest. Their left-wing pairing was a threat all afternoon in this fast and interesting game but their sole reward was from Bough's close-range shot after Mason conceded a free-kick.										
21	A	LEICESTER FOSSE		12	L	1-3	1-1	Brough 25	Ware	Kearns	Banfield	Young	Moss	Jones	Broad	Brough	Owers	Bowyer	Harris
		4/1	*3,000*	*16*	21			*Osborn 44, Benfield 80, Sparrow 82*	*Mearns*	*Clay*	*Pudan*	*McWhirter*	*Randle*	*Burton*	*Benfield*	*Proctor*	*Sparrow*	*Osborn*	*Harrison*
								Ref: A Adams	With both sides shooting on sight in the drenching rain, Brough headed in from a Harris corner to put City in front. Osborn's oblique drive brought Fosse level almost on the interval after a shot had cannoned off the bar. With time running out, Benfield headed Leicester in front.										

No	Date		Att	Pos	Pt	F-A	H-T	Scorers, Times, and Referees	1	2	3	4	5	6	7	8	9	10	11
22	H	STOCKPORT		9	W	7-2	2-1	Owers 8,44,53,80, Bowyer 70, 88,	Ware	Kearns	Banfield	Young	Moss	Nicholson	Broad	Marrison	Owers	Bowyer	Harris
	18/1		4,000	19	23			Smith 3, Charlton 65 [Broad 75]	McIver	Goodwin	Graham	Chivers	Garratt	Blair	Crossthwaite	Rodgers	Smith	Charlton	O'Brien
								Ref: I Baker	Quite unexpectedly, City found their shooting boots after Smith had headed County into their early lead. Another header brought Owers a quick equaliser from Bowyer's centre, before he put City in front just before the half-time interval with a shot that went in off an upright.										
23	A	PRESTON		10	L	1-5	1-3	Owers 20 [Common 43, 55p]	Ware	Kearns	Banfield	Young	Moss	Nicholson	Broad	Brough	Owers	Bowyer	Harris
	25/1		12,000	1	23			Green 2, Morley 30, Halliwell 60,	Taylor	McFadyen	Rodway	Holdsworth	McCall	Dawson	Morley	Green	Halliwell	Common	Barlow
								Ref: J Pearson (Holdsworth & McCall Benefit)	To those who witnessed this display, the surprise was that City didn't lose more heavily. Preston took control from the off and Barlow made two attempts at goal prior to Green's fired-in opener. Owers brought some respite with his header, but thereafter it was downhill all the way.										
24	H	BURNLEY		11	D	3-3	2-1	Harris 7, Owers 31, Brough 57	Ware	Kearns	Banfield	Young	Moss	Nicholson	Broad	Brough	Owers	Bowyer	Harris
	8/2		11,000 (£291.6.10)	2	24			Freeman 27, 75, Mosscrop 84	Sewell	Gunton	Jones	McLaren	Boyle	Watson	Mosscrop	Lindley	Freeman	Hodgson	Husband
								Ref: G Pardoe (Reuben Marr Benefit)	Whilst the visitors displayed the greater polish, City held the whip hand for the greater part of this game after Harris, with a low angled shot, gave them the early lead. They paid the price of concentrating on defence towards the finish, when Mosscrop headed in Burnley's point-saver.										
25	A	HULL		12	L	1-3	1-1	Jones 20p [Fazackerley 75]	Ware	Kearns	Banfield	Young	Moss	Jones	Broad	Marrison	Owers	Bowyer	Harris
	15/2		7,000	9	24			McQuillan 7p, Lyon 60,	Hendry	Nevins	McQuillan	Wright W	O'Connell	Gordon	McDonald	Fazackerley	Lyon	Boyton	Wright E
								Ref: S Peers	City were far from being a convincing side at Anlaby Road, where they rarely threatened. Jones was frequently beaten by McDonald, who set up two of the Hull goals with his centres. Owers met a masterful pivot in O'Connell, who had chosen not to turn out for Ireland on this day.										
26	H	GLOSSOP		10	D	3-3	2-2	Broad 9, Jones 25p, Allen 83	Ware	Kearns	Banfield	Young	Moss	Jones	Broad	Bowyer	Owers	Allen	Harris
	22/2		4,000	17	25			Stapley 3, Moore 40, 50	Causer	Hampton	Dearnaley	Carney	Bowden	Bamford	Cooper	Stapley H	Moore	Hoare	Law
								Ref: A Shallcross	With his defenders out of sorts, Ware, who had no chance with all three of the close-range goal-getting shots, kept City in the game after the break. Following Allen's late leveller, Ware preserved City's point by diving to his right to save Cooper's penalty after Moss had handled.										
27	A	CLAPTON ORIENT		13	D	0-0	0-0		Ware	Jones	Banfield	Young	Moss	Nicholson	Broad	Brough	Owers	Bowyer	Harris
	1/3		10,000	15	26				Bower	Johnston	Evans	Hind	Liddell	Scott	Parker	Bevan	Dryden	Jonas	Dix
								Ref: S Peers	The rail journey passed all to quickly for those travelling fans who witnessed City's backs-to-the-wall performance at Homerton. Near the interval, Banfield did well to head out Liddell's shot, whilst Orient were fortunate when Owers hustled Evans into an injudicious back pass.										
28	H	LINCOLN		10	W	2-0	0-0	Brough 60, Harris 62	Ware	Kearns	Banfield	Young	Moss	Nicholson	Broad	Brough	Butler	Bowyer	Harris
	8/3		7,750	4	28				Fern	Jackson	Wilson	Barrell	Gardner	Wield	Manning	Miller	Slade	McCubbin	Brindley
								Ref: A Pellowe	The crowd, swelled by the prospect of Wedlock's return after his ankle injury, were dismayed to find that the great man had failed a fitness test. Lincoln, for whom Fern saved Bowyer's penalty, offered little in a game in which the ref was strict in regard to charging infringements.										
29	A	NOTTM FOREST		11	L	1-4	0-1	Brough 88 [Needham 85]	Ware	Kearns	Banfield	Young	Moss	Nicholson	Broad	Brough	Butler	Bowyer	Harris
	15/3		7,000	5	28			Morris 30, 83, Gibson 50,	Hanna	Fisher	Jones	Armstrong	Mercer	Needham	Firth	Reid	Gibson	Morris	Ford
								Ref: J Hornby	Despite having the advantage of the wind, Forest only put on one goal before the break, Morris beating the diving Ware with an 18-yard shot. With the limping Butler put out on the wing for the second half, City were overwhelmed after Gibson headed in to double Forest's advantage.										
30	A	BARNSLEY		12	L	1-7	0-4	Butler 88 [Bartrop 45],	Ware	Kearns	Banfield	Young	Moss	Nicholson	Broad	Brough	Butler	Bowyer	Harris
	21/3		8,000 (£212)	4	28			Moore 25, Lillycrop 40,41,	Cooper	Downs	Bethune	Barson	Bratley	Utley	Bartrop	Travers	Lillycrop	Tuftnell	Moore
								Ref: W Heath [Tuftnell 60, 70, Travers 80]	A severe gruelling for City at Oakwell, where Barnsley didn't get one goal more than they deserved. Surprisingly, City were the better side for the greater part of the first half, and they were only trailing by a single goal until Barnsley quickly added three more shortly before the interval.										
31	A	BLACKPOOL		13	D	1-1	0-0	Jones 87	Ware	Kearns	Banfield	Young	Moss	Nicholson	Broad	Bowyer	Butler	Jones	Harris
	22/3		4,000	19	29			Wilkinson 75	Fiske	Millership	Jones	Thorpe	Connor	Burke	Charles	Reeves	Bainbridge	Wilkinson	Quinn
								Ref: A Adams	The several hundred City fans, not deterred by yesterday's defeat, travelled up to Blackpool on two special trains which left Temple Meads at midnight. They were treated to a fast and exciting game in which a first-time shot by Jones saw City cancel out Wilkinson's close-in drive.										

No	Venue	Opponent / Date	Att	Pos	Pts	Result	H-T	Scorers, Times, Referees	1	2	3	4	5	6	7	8	9	10	11
32	H	BARNSLEY		12	W	3-0	1-0	Jones 45, Bowyer 55, 60	Ware	Kearns	Banfield	Young	Moss	Nicholson	Broad	Bowyer	Butler	Jones	Harris
		24/3	15,000	*4*	31				*Cooper*	*Downs*	*Bethune*	*Cornan*	*Barson*	*Utley*	*Bartrop*	*Travers*	*Lillycrop*	*Tuftnell*	*Moore*
								Ref: G Pardoe	Unlucky when a bouncing ball struck Travers on the elbow just prior to the interval, the Cup holders were further unlucky when Cooper saved the spot-kick at the expense of a corner from which Jones headed City in front. Earlier the play had been held up for repairs to the Barnsley net.										
33	H	BIRMINGHAM		14	L	0-3	0-3		Ware	Kearns	Banfield	Young	Wedlock	Nicholson	Broad	Bowyer	Butler	Jones	Harris
		29/3	6,000	*2*	31			*Reed 20, 35, Robertson 44*	*Crossthwaite*	*Ball*	*Womack*	*Tinkler*	*McClure*	*Bumphrey*	*Gibson*	*Reed*	*Jones*	*Robertson*	*Smith A*
								Ref: J Howcroft	Notwithstanding Wedlock's return, City sustained a humiliating defeat against wonderfully quick and skilful opponents. Reed opened the scoring when he met Smith's centre and then added a second in similar fashion before Robertson's unstoppable shot brought up number three.										
34	A	HUDDERSFIELD		15	L	0-5	0-3		Ware	Kearns	Banfield	Young	Wedlock	Nicholson	Broad	Bowyer	Butler	Jones	Harris
		5/4	*7,000*	*5*	31			*Mann 13, 20, 70, Elliott 18, Jee 55*	*Mutch*	*Blackman*	*Bullock*	*Beaton*	*Fayers*	*Dow*	*Armour*	*Elliott*	*Mann*	*Macauley*	*Jee*
								Ref: H Taylor	Huddersfield were in irresistible form as they chalked up their eighth win to extend their unbeaten run to ten games. 'Tiny' Fayers, even smaller than Wedlock, set up Mann's opener with his free-kick before Elliott notched the second with a magnificent shot from fully 20 yards.										
35	A	FULHAM		15	D	0-0	0-0		Ware	Kearns	Banfield	Young	Wedlock	Nicholson	Broad	Bowyer	Butler	Jones	Harris
		7/4	***2,000***	*10*	32				*Reynolds*	*Coquet*	*Burns*	*Stewart*	*Mavin*	*Marshall*	*Smith*	*Coleman*	*Lee*	*White*	*Walker*
								Ref: A Briggs	Fulham, who had a stiff breeze behind them, did most of the pressing in the first half, but the football generally was poor. After the break play was brighter, but the nearest any side came to a goal was when Reynolds saved brilliantly to keep out fine efforts from both Harris and Butler.										
36	H	LEEDS CITY		13	D	1-1	0-1	Broad 75	Ware	Kearns	Banfield	Young	Wedlock	Nicholson	Broad	Bowyer	Butler	Jones	Harris
		12/4	5,000	*6*	33			*Speirs 42*	*Hogg*	*Copeland*	*Affleck*	*Law*	*Lintott*	*Foley*	*Enright*	*Price*	*McLeod*	*Speirs*	*Croot*
								Ref: I Baker	Wedlock, the City captain, has rarely had such an unprofitable afternoon. Despite a tremendous amount of running about, he seldom got the ball unless it was in the air. Speirs, the most skilful player on the pitch, headed Leeds in front, but Broad fired in City's second-half leveller.										
37	A	GRIMSBY		15	L	0-3	0-2		Ware	Jones	Banfield	Young	Moss	Nicholson	Broad	Edwards	Butler	Bowyer	Harris
		19/4	*4,000*	*7*	33			*Nicholson 1og, Rippon 20, Quinn 75*	*Lonsdale*	*Wheelhouse*	*Arrowsmith*	*Rushby*	*Gordon*	*Martin*	*Staniforth*	*Rippon*	*Quinn*	*Rampton*	*Birch*
								Ref: T Kirkham	Things started badly and ended even worse for Nicholson. In the first minute he sliced the ball into his own net whilst attempting to clear from Birch; then shortly before the finish he was carried off after being kicked in the head. Not a good day for an under-strength City side.										
38	H	BURY		16	L	1-5	0-3	Bowyer 60 *[Peake 36]*	Ware	Kearns	Banfield	Young	Wedlock	Jones	Broad	Edwards	Butler	Bowyer	Harris
		26/4	**4,000**	*11*	33			*Brown 4, Smith 30, 48, 70,*	*McDonald*	*Cameron*	*Millington*	*Humphreys*	*Goldie*	*Bullen*	*Prior*	*Brown*	*Peake*	*Smith*	*Connor*
		Home Ave 8,829	Away 8,232					Ref: J Pearson	After this humiliating defeat it is not encouraging for the fans to find that five of City's six defenders on view have been re-engaged for next season. In conditions that were anything but pleasant for football, City saved their worst display of a very poor campaign right until the last.										

CUP-TIES

FA Cup/Glos Cup			F-A	H-T	Scorers, Times, and Referees	1	2	3	4	5	6	7	8	9	10	11	12 sub used
1 A LIVERPOOL	12	L	0-3	0-2		Ware	Kearns	Banfield	Young	Moss	Nicholson	Broad	Marrison	Owers	Bowyer	Harris	
15/1 *14,000 1:13*					*Goddard 29p, Peake 44, Lacey 89*	*Campbell*	*Pursell*	*Crawford*	*Lowe*	*Peake*	*Ferguson*	*Goddard*	*Metcalf*	*Parkinson*	*Miller*	*Lacey*	
(£357.7.6)					Ref: C Lutwyche	On a pitch hardly any better than it had been when Saturday's game was postponed, Goddard put Liverpool in front with a low shot from the spot after Nicholson was adjudged to have held back Metcalf. The upright then denied Harris before Ware was surprised by Peake's long shot.											
F A BRISTOL ROV	12	L	0-1	0-0		Ware	Kearns	Banfield	Young	Moss	Nicholson	Broad	Bowyer	Butler	Jones	Harris	
GC 25/3 *9,590 SL:14*					*Brogan 65*	*Roney*	*Brown*	*Bennett*	*Harris*	*Walker*	*Morris*	*Peplow*	*Roe*	*Blunt*	*Brogan*	*Palmer*	
(£277)					Ref: L Bullimer	The City had the majority of the play, but lost to a solitary strike from the foot of Brogan, who early on had his shorts badly torn in a tussle with Kearns. Any embarrassment was neatly saved by the referee, who swiftly whipped off his coat and buttoned it round the player's legs.											

FRIENDLIES

			F-A	H-T	Scorers, Times, and Referees	1	2	3	4	5	6	7	8	9	10	11	12 sub used
1 A WYCOMBE		W	10-2	4-1	Br'gh10,50,60,75,Nichol 20,25,70,	Clay	Kearns	Jones	Moss	Wedlock	Nicholson	Butler	Marrison	Nichol	Brough	Copestake	
23/9 *1,000*					*Roberts 5, Pheby 80* [Butler 40],	*Copus*	*Didcock*	*Holland*	*Rolfe*	*Hooper*	*Love*	*Payne*	*Adams*	*Roberts*	*O'Gorman**	*Pheby*	*McDermott*
(£47.10.0)					Ref: H Maisey [Marrison 65, Copestake 85]	In delightfully fine weather, a big crowd at Loakes Park saw City receive an early shock when Roberts opened the scoring with a first-time shot. Fortunately, Brough quickly equalised and thereafter it was bit of a romp as City gave Copus a hot time between the Wycombe sticks.											
2 A EXETER		L	1-2	1-0	Harris 40	Ware	Kearns	Jones	Marr	Edwards	Nicholson	Broad	Brough	Owers	Bowyer	Harris	
1/2					*Whittaker 46, Brooksbank 70*	*Pym*	*Fort*	*Hurst*	*Rigby*	*Lagan*	*Lockett*	*Whittaker*	*Cooper*	*Rutter*	*Brooksbank*	*Ives*	
						Although played under wretched conditions, this clash will surely rank among the best friendlies ever seen on the St James Park ground. City set a rare pace throughout the first half, and they were certainly worth more at the break than only to be leading by a solitary goal by Harris.											

	P	W	D	L	F	A	W	D	L	F	A	Pts
		Home					Away					
1 Preston NE	38	13	5	1	34	12	6	10	3	22	21	53
2 Burnley	38	13	4	2	58	23	8	4	7	30	30	50
3 Birmingham	38	11	6	2	39	18	7	4	8	20	26	46
4 Barnsley	38	15	3	1	46	18	4	4	11	11	29	45
5 Huddersfield	38	13	5	1	49	12	4	4	11	17	28	43
6 Leeds City	38	12	3	4	45	22	3	7	9	25	42	40
7 Grimsby T	38	10	8	1	32	11	5	2	12	19	39	40
8 Lincoln City	38	10	6	3	31	16	5	4	10	19	36	40
9 Fulham	38	13	5	1	47	16	4	0	15	18	39	39
10 Wolves	38	10	6	3	34	16	4	4	11	22	38	38
11 Bury	38	10	6	3	29	14	5	2	12	24	43	38
12 Hull City	38	12	2	5	42	19	3	4	12	18	37	36
13 Bradford PA	38	12	4	3	47	18	2	4	13	13	42	36
14 Clapto'Orient	38	8	6	5	25	20	2	8	9	9	27	34
15 Leicester Fos'	38	12	2	5	34	20	1	5	13	16	45	33
16 BRISTOL C	38	7	9	3	32	25	2	6	11	14	47	33
17 Nottm Forest	38	9	3	7	35	25	3	5	11	23	34	32
18 Glossop	38	11	2	6	34	26	1	6	12	15	42	32
19 Stockport Co	38	8	4	7	32	23	0	6	13	24	55	26
20 Blackpool	38	8	4	7	22	22	1	4	14	17	47	26
	760	217	93	70	747	376	70	93	217	376	747	760

Odds & ends

Double wins: (1) Stockport County.
Double losses: (2) Nottingham Forest, Birmingham.

Won from behind: (1) Stockport County (h).
Lost from in front: (2) Nottingham Forest (h), Leicester Fosse (a).

High spots: Starting the season with a seven match unbeaten run.
Defeating Stockport 7-2 at Ashton Gate on 18 January.
Beating Wycombe Wanderers 10-2 at Loakes Park on 23 September.

Low spots: The 1-3 loss at Glossop that ended City's unbeaten start.
The 1-7 hammering at Barnsley on 21 March.
The injury that prevented Billy Wedlock from playing in England's 4-3 success over Wales at 'Ashton Gate' on 17 March.

Player of the Year: John Kearns.
Ever-presents: (0).
Hat-tricks: (2) Joe Brough, Ebenezer 'Ginger' Owers.
Leading scorer: Overall: Joe Brough (14). League: Ebenezer Owers (13).

Pre-Season Trial Match: 24 Aug Reds 3(1) Blues 0 Ref: F Curtis 6,000 (£71.11s.7d) Harris 20, Owers 60, Bowyer 70
AGM (Ford Memorial Hall, Mill Lane, Bedminster, 26 June 1913):
Loss £1,329.11s.11d. Season Ticket Sales £318.1s.8d.

	Appearances Lge	Cup	Fr	Goals Lge	Cup	Fr	Tot
Allen, Tom	**1**			**1**			**1**
Banfield, Laurie	**25**	2					
Bowyer, Sam	**36**	2	1	**9**			**9**
Broad, Tommy	**37**	2	1	**3**			**3**
Brough, Joe	**14**		2	**10**		4	**14**
Butler, Jack	**15**	1	1	**1**		1	**2**
Clay, Harry	**12**		1				
Copestake, Levi	**8**		1			1	**1**
Edwards, Albert	**4**		1				
Gould, Charlie	**1**						
Harris, Joshua	**32**	2	1	**2**		1	**3**
Jones, Edwin	**25**	1	2	**4**			**4**
Kearns, John	**36**	2	2				
Marr, Reuben	**9**		1	**1**			**1**
Marrison, Tom	**13**	1	1	**1**		1	**2**
Morgan, Jerry	**2**						
Moss, Arthur	**18**	2	1				
Nichol, Billy	**3**		1			3	**3**
Nicholson, 'Jock'	**33**	2	2				
Owers, Ebenezer	**23**	1	1	**13**			**13**
Ware, Tommy	**26**	2	1				
Wedlock, Billy	**23**		1	**1**			**1**
Young, Bob	**22**	2					
23 players used	**418**	**22**	**22**	**46**		**11**	**57**

No	Date	Att	Pos	Pt	F-A	H-T	Scorers, Times, and Referees	1	2	3	4	5	6	7	8	9	10	11
1	H GLOSSOP			W	4-1	3-1	Broad 12, Fuge 40, Harris 42,	**Howling**	Kearns	Banfield	Young	Wedlock	Nicholson	Broad	**Fuge**	**Harrison**	**Tasker**	Harris
	3/9	7,000		2			*Moore 15p* [Cuffe 85og]	*Causer*	*Hampton*	*Cuffe*	*Montgomery*	*Stapley W*	*Carney*	*Toward*	*Clay*	*Stanford*	*Moore*	*Law*
							Ref: E Spiers	Whilst allowance must be made for the fact that Tasker was lamed early on, and that Harris was injured shortly after the interval, City's form was not convincing. Broad's long-shot brought the opening goal before Kearn's trip on Moore allowed Glossop to level from the penalty spot.										
2	H STOCKPORT			W	**5-0**	5-0	Chapple 12, 17, 40, Broad 20,	Howling	Kearns	Banfield	Young	Wedlock	Nicholson	Broad	Fuge	Harrison	**Chapple**	**Burton**
	6/9	12,000		4			[Fuge 44]	*Lunn*	*Goodwin*	*Fagan*	*Tattersall*	*Garratt*	*Bluer*	*Proctor*	*Rodgers*	*Gault*	*Wood*	*O'Brien*
							Ref: J Pearson	City's victory was robbed of some of its merit by the fact that Lunn, in trying to stop Broad from rushing in the third goal, injured his knee and had to go off. Wood took over in goal for the rest of this game, which saw both Wedlock and Rodgers depart following a clash of heads.										
3	A BRADFORD PA		5	L	3-4	0-2	Harrison 53, 80, Burton 65	Howling	Kearns	Banfield	Young	Moss	Nicholson	Broad	Fuge	Harrison	Chapple	Burton
	13/9	*18,000*	*1*	4			*Little 20, 23, Smith 82, 88p*	*Drabble*	*Watson*	*Blackham*	*Thompson*	*Dainty*	*Scott*	*Munro*	*Little*	*Smith*	*Howie*	*Leavey*
							Ref: T Kirkham	City have scarcely taken part in few more extraordinary games than this affair at Park Avenue. Having recovered, against a team playing fast and attacking football, from a two-goal deficit to be in the lead with but ten minutes left, City eventually succumbed to a disputed penalty.										
4	H NOTTS CO		7	D	1-1	0-1	Chapple 50p	Howling	Kearns	Banfield	Young	Moss	Nicholson	Broad	Fuge	Harrison	Chapple	Burton
	20/9	12,000	*11*	5			*Bassett 38*	*Iremonger*	*Machin*	*West*	*Emberton*	*Clamp*	*Craythorne*	*Bassett*	*Flint*	*Williams*	*Richards*	*Haig*
							Ref: J Hall	A Nottingham critic telegraphed into his paper the opinion that the City forwards 'would not have scored in a week, without the aid of a very helpful penalty'. He wasn't far wrong, as City struggled against a side, short of Morley, Waterall and Peart, and with Haig limping early on.										
5	A LEICESTER FOSSE		11	L	0-3	0-1		Howling	Kearns	Banfield	Young	Wedlock	Nicholson	Broad	Fuge	Harrison	Chapple	Burton
	27/9	*16,000*	*1*	5			*Mortimer 2, 47, 50*	*Brebner*	*Clay*	*Currie*	*McWhirter*	*Harrold*	*King*	*Douglas*	*Stoodley*	*Mortimer*	*Benfield*	*Waterall*
							Ref: D Aston	City had a trying afternoon in the oppressive heat at Filbert Street, where they didn't put in a single worthwhile shot until a quarter of an hour from the finish. Mortimer soon got on the way to his hat-trick (completed with shot after an earlier header) when he rushed in Stoodley's cross.										
6	H WOLVES		11	D	0-0	0-0		Howling	Kearns	Banfield	Young	Wedlock	Nicholson	Broad	Chapple	Harrison	Harris	Rose
	4/10	8,000	*6*	6				*Peers*	*Collins*	*Garratly*	*Price*	*Young*	*Bishop*	*Harrison*	*Lockett*	*Hughes*	*Needham*	*Brooks S*
							Ref: T Garner	If City's forwards had played as well as their half-backs, then two points instead of one would have accrued to their account. Still it was a good point to earn, seeing as Nicholson had to take over between the posts for 15 minutes when Howling was carried off early in the second half.										
7	A HULL		7	W	1-0	0-0	Fuge 60	Howling	Kearns	Banfield	Young	Wedlock	Nicholson	Broad	Fuge	Harrison	Chapple	Harris
	11/10	*10,000*	*12*	8				*Hendry*	*Nevins*	*McQullian*	*Edelston*	*O'Connell*	*McIntosh*	*McDonald*	*Stevens*	*Lyon S*	*Wright*	*Lee*
							Ref: L Fletcher	City owed it to their defence that they deprived Hull of their unbeaten record this term as well as ending their long unbeaten home run. A free-kick brought the winner, the ball going to Chapple, whose shot the keeper spilled for Fuge to rush in and kick the ball into the back of the net.										
8	H BARNSLEY		9	D	1-1	1-0	Chapple 5	Howling	Kearns	Banfield	Young	Wedlock	Moss	Broad	**Picken**	Harrison	Chapple	Harris
	18/10	14,000	*6*	9			*Griffin 48*	*Cooper*	*Tindall*	*Bethune*	*Barson*	*Bratley*	*Utley*	*Moore*	*Travers*	*Morton*	*Tuftnell*	*Griffin*
							Ref: A Pellowe	Although City had to share the spoils, they gave easily their best display of the season so far. Chapple put them in front, after taking Harrison's pass on the run, by firing the ball past Cooper. After the break, Wedlock's failure to head away a centre from Moore gave Griffin a clear shot.										
9	A BURY		11	L	1-3	0-2	Harris 75	Howling	Jones E	Banfield	Young	Wedlock	Moss	Broad	Chapple	Harrison	Picken	Harris
	25/10	*9,742*	*1*	9			*Peake 25, 40, 65*	*McDonald*	*Thomson*	*Millington*	*Perry*	*Humphreys*	*Bullen*	*Meadowcroft*	*Peake*	*Wilson*	*Smith W*	*Connor*
							Ref: J Palmer	City didn't get any luck in a fine game at Gigg Lane, where a lofty shot from Harris was their sole reward. The wingers of both sides exhibited grand form and, had all the opportunities they provided been taken advantage off, then the score would have presented a wonderful appearance.										
10	H HUDDERSFIELD		10	W	1-0	0-0	Picken 48	Howling	Kearns	Banfield	Young	Wedlock	Moss	Broad	Chapple	Harrison	Picken	Harris
	1/11	10,000	*16*	11				*Mutch*	*Blackman*	*Bullock*	*Beaton*	*Fayers*	*Dow*	*Armour*	*Smith B*	*Elliott*	*Macauley*	*Jee*
							Ref: C Knight-Coutts	Judging by their form in this match it was difficult to see how Town, who spurned many chances, had beaten Birmingham by seven clear goals the previous week. Although City didn't play as well as in their last home game, Picken's 12-yard cross-drive proved enough to secure victory.										

No Date	Venue	Opponent	Att	Pos	Res	F-A	H-T	Scorers, Times, and Referees	1	2	3	4	5	6	7	8	9	10	11
11	A	LINCOLN		12	L	1-2	1-1	Picken 10	Howling	Kearns	Jones E	**Henry**	Moss	Nicholson	Broad	Chapple	Harrison	Picken	Harris
8/11			*7,000*	17	11			*Kearns 44og, McFarlane 65*	*Fern*	*Meumer*	*Wilson*	*McFadden*	*Gardner*	*McDougall*	*Manning*	*McCubbin*	*McFarlane*	*Barrell*	*Ball*
								Ref: J Hornby	City, without Banfield, Wedlock and Young, and with Jones and Nicholson carrying injuries, deserved a better fate at Sincil Bank. Taking the lead by Picken walking the ball into the net when Fern spilled Harrison's drive, Ball's deflected shot brought the Imps a fortunate equaliser.										
12	H	BLACKPOOL		10	W	1-0	0-0	Harrison 65	Howling	Kearns	**Jones J**	Henry	Moss	Nicholson	Broad	Chapple	Harrison	Picken	Harris
15/11			8,000	*19*	13				*Fiske*	*Rushton*	*Jones*	*Burke*	*Connor*	*Booth*	*Pagnam*	*Charles*	*Bainbridge*	*Buchan*	*Quinn*
								Ref: A Shallcross	The only goal of this poor game owed itself to a sudden dash by Picken, who rounded Connor and beat Rushton before sending in a low drive. Fiske fell in saving and the ball, escaping his grasp, rolled out to Harrison, who had not the least trouble in putting it into the back of the net.										
13	A	NOTTM FOREST		9	D	1-1	1-1	Harrison 13	Howling	Kearns	Young	Moss	Wedlock	Nicholson	Broad	Harrison	**Brown**	Picken	Harris
22/11			*6,000*	*20*	14			*Wedlock 30og*	*Hanna*	*Jones*	*Gibson*	*Armstrong*	*Mercer*	*Needham*	*Firth*	*Bell*	*Allan*	*Derrick*	*Banks*
								Ref: R Eccles	With Harris a limping passenger for two-thirds of the game and Wedlock hobbling on the wing for the last ten minutes, City fought for their point. After Harrison fired in the opener, Forest obtained a fortunate leveller when Bell's long distance effort skimmed in off Wedlock's boot.										
14	H	WLCH ARSENAL		10	D	1-1	0-1	Harrison 75	Howling	Kearns	Banfield	Young	Moss	Nicholson	Broad	Harrison	Brown	Picken	Rose
29/11			15,000	*5*	15			*Hardinge 15*	*Lievesley*	*Shaw*	*Benson*	*Jobey*	*Sands*	*McKinnon*	*Rutherford*	*Flanagan*	*Stonley*	*Hardinge*	*Burrell*
								Ref: T Bryan	City, who had enough chances to have won comfortably, had to be satisfied with a point earned by Harrison's low drive, which caught the keeper by surprise. Weakness amongst the inside-men was the problem as City, after falling behind to Hardinge's long shot, strove to recover.										
15	A	GRIMSBY		11	L	0-1	0-1		Howling	Kearns	Banfield	Young	Harrison	Moss	Broad	**Irving**	Brown	Picken	Rose
6/12			*9,000*	*10*	15			*Rampton 30*	*Spendiff*	*Wheelhouse*	*Arrowsmith*	*Andrews*	*Gordon*	*Martin*	*Quinn*	*Gregson*	*Rippon W*	*Rampton*	*Scott*
								Ref: J Howcroft	So well did Kearns and Banfield perform that Howling was not overworked between the City sticks. Picken, who was the most capable of the forwards, had hard luck with one glorious shot that hit the crossbar, shortly after the unmarked Rampton had headed in the points decider.										
16	H	BIRMINGHAM		12	L	1-2	0-1	Brown 84	Howling	Kearns	Banfield	Young	Wedlock	Moss	Broad	Irving	Brown	Picken	Rose
13/12			10,000	*14*	15			*Gibson 1, Walker 50*	*Crossthwaite*	*Fairman*	*Womack*	*Tinkler*	*McClure*	*Bumphrey*	*Gibson*	*Hall*	*Walker*	*Morgan*	*Smith A*
								Ref: W Heath	Banfield was down injured and Howling appealing in vain for offside as Gibson headed in the opener from Smith's centre. With Banfield a passenger on his return 20 minutes later, City fell further behind when Walker headed in from a free-kick after a silly foul by Kearns on Hall.										
17	A	FULHAM		13	L	1-3	0-1	Chapple 47p	Howling	Kearns	Banfield	Young	Wedlock	Moss	Broad	Brown	Chapple	Picken	Harris
20/12			*10,000*	*6*	15			*Pearce 1, Coleman 46, 85*	*McDonald*	*Charlton*	*Houghton*	*Marshall*	*Russell*	*White*	*Smith*	*Coleman*	*Pearce*	*Taylor*	*Walker*
								Ref: C Hall	Banfield's poor back-pass set up Coleman to make Fulham's victory complete against a City side again exhibiting a lack of thrust and cohesive forward play. Their only success came from the spot, shortly after Coleman's swerver had deceived Howling, when Harris was brought down.										
18	A	CLAPTON ORIENT		14	L	2-5	2-0	Brown 18, 43 *[McFadden 89]*	Howling	Kearns	Jones E	Young	Wedlock	Moss	Broad	Brown	Chapple	Picken	Harris
25/12			*18,000*	*19*	15			*Forrest 63, Dalrymple 68, 83, 85,*	*Clegg*	*Hind*	*Evans*	*Forrest*	*Scott*	*Willis*	*Parker*	*Jonas*	*Dalrymple*	*McFadden*	*Dix*
								Ref: A Shallcross	Brown cleverly converted a Harris centre to open the scoring at Homerton, and then took advantage of a miskick by Evans to put City firmly in charge by the break. Unfortunately, despite controlling the play for lengthy spells, City were unable to withstand Orient's amazing comeback.										
19	H	CLAPTON ORIENT		12	W	3-0	2-0	Brown 10, Chapple 35, 67	Ware	Kearns	Jones E	Nicholson	Wedlock	Moss	Broad	Brown	Chapple	Picken	Harris
26/12			14,000	*9*	17				*Clegg*	*Hind*	*Evans*	*Forrest*	*Scott*	*Willis*	*Parker*	*Dalrymple*	*Jonas*	*McFadden*	*Dix*
			(£466)					Ref: A Shallcross	Trailing to an early opener when Brown nipped the ball home, Orient, with McFadden off for half an hour, fell further behind when an error by Hind allowed Chapple to put away a Harris centre. After the interval Chapple drove the ball in, when a shot from Harris rebounded off the bar.										
20	A	STOCKPORT		13	L	1-5	0-3	Brown 70	Ware	Kearns	Jones E	Nicholson	Wedlock	Moss	Broad	Brown	Chapple	Irving	Harris
27/12			*5,000*	*12*	17			*Rodgers 12, 40, 80, Gault 30, 55*	*Evans*	*Fagan*	*Haughton*	*Mitton*	*Bluer*	*Waterall*	*Proctor*	*Gault*	*Rodgers*	*Wood*	*Ashmole*
								Ref: J Pearson	Despite the advantage of a strong wind in the second half, City were unable to stage a comeback on a pitch that was in a shocking state. Falling behind when Rodgers headed in an early opener from Waterall's free-kick, City no doubt felt the effects of their arduous holiday programme.										
21	H	BRADFORD PA		13	W	2-0	1-0	Chapple 5, Kearns 55	Ware	Kearns	Jones E	Nicholson	Wedlock	Moss	Broad	Brown	Chapple	Picken	Harris
3/1			10,000	*5*	19				*Drabble*	*Watson*	*Blackham*	*Garry*	*Mavin*	*Scott*	*Kivlichan*	*Little*	*Smith*	*McCandless*	*Leavey*
								Ref: T Kirkham	Shortly after Chapple fired the ball home from Broad's judicious pass, City were fortunate not to concede a penalty when Nicholson had his hands up to his face on heading away Smith's capital shot. After the break, Kearns dribbled some 20 yards before firing in goal number two.										

No	Date		Att	Pos	Pt	F-A	H-T	Scorers, Times, and Referees	1	2	3	4	5	6	7	8	9	10	11
22	A	NOTTS CO		14	L	**0-4**	0-1	*[Bassett 84]*	Ware	Kearns	Banfield	Nicholson	Wedlock	Moss	Broad	Brown	**Howarth**	Irving	Harris
	17/1		*10,000*	*1*	19			*Richards 12, 82, Peart 74,*	*Iremonger*	*Morley*	*West*	*Emberton*	*Clamp*	*Allzebrook*	*Bassett*	*Flint*	*Peart*	*Richards*	*Waterall*
								Ref: J Hall	Apart from spells at the start and finish, City had the better of the midfield play, but rarely got close enough to goal to cause Iremonger any real problems. A header by Peart got County moving, and even Howarth, who played for the Army versus the Navy, could make little impression.										
23	H	LEICESTER FOSSE		13	W	1-0	0-0	Broad 75	Ware	Kearns	Banfield	Nicholson	Wedlock	Moss	Broad	Brown	Picken	Irving	Harris
	24/1		7,000	*16*	21				*Bown*	*Pudan*	*Burton*	*Benfield*	*Harrold*	*King*	*Russell*	*Stoodley*	*Mortimer*	*Waterall*	*Douglas*
								Ref: D Asson	It was entirely appropriate that Broad should score the only goal, a swerving shot that beat Bown all the way, as he was the best forward on the frozen pitch. Ware had an easy time between the City sticks, though he was fortunate before the break when the ball rolled against the upright.										
24	A	WOLVES		11	W	2-0	0-0	Howarth 53, Picken 62	Ware	Kearns	Banfield	Nicholson	Wedlock	Moss	Broad	Brown	Howarth	Picken	Harris
	7/2		*5,000*	*10*	23				*Peers*	*Brooks A*	*Bishop*	*Price*	*Groves*	*Crabtree*	*Harrison*	*Howell*	*Francis*	*Needham*	*Brooks S*
								Ref: T Garner	With Wolves feeling the effects of midweek exertions of their FA Cup replay at Sheffield Wednesday, City turned in a capital display to take the points. Howarth opened the scoring with a 20-yard shot on the turn; then Picken took a square pass and easily beat Peers for the second.										
25	H	HULL		11	W	2-1	1-1	Howarth 27, Brown 53	Ware	Kearns	Banfield	Nicholson	Wedlock	Moss	Broad	Brown	Howarth	Picken	Harris
	14/2		10,000	*3*	25			*Stevens 2*	*Hendry*	*McQuillian*	*Morgan*	*Edelston*	*McIntosh*	*Gordon*	*McDonald*	*McCorry*	*Stevens*	*Cameron*	*Lyon J*
								Ref: L Fletcher	Caught napping when Stevens dribbled through to open the scoring with a low shot for his 20th goal of the campaign, City fought back to dominate with a corner count of 18:2. Howarth headed in the equaliser; then after the break Brown touched in the winner from a Harris centre.										
26	A	BARNSLEY		12	L	0-3	0-1		Ware	Kearns	Banfield	Nicholson	Wedlock	Moss	Broad	Brown	Howarth	Picken	Harris
	21/2		*6,162*	*6*	25			*Bartrop 18, Bratley 75, Halliwell 88*	*Cooper*	*Downs*	*Bethune*	*Barson*	*Bratley*	*Wigmore*	*Bartrop*	*Tuftnell*	*Halliwell*	*Moore*	*Griffin*
			(£143.12.3)					Ref: A Pellowe	Having parted with a number of their successful FA Cup side, it wasn't expected that Barnsley would win by such a margin. Facing a stiff breeze, City were pleased to be only one behind at the interval, but couldn't break through in the second half, despite Picken's best endeavours.										
27	H	BURY		12	W	2-0	1-0	Picken 43, 72	Ware	Kearns	Banfield	Nicholson	Wedlock	Moss	Broad	Irving	Howarth	Picken	Harris
	28/2		10,000	*6*	27				*McDonald*	*Millington*	*Allan*	*Goldie*	*Humphreys*	*Bullen*	*Smith J*	*Mercer*	*Wilson*	*Smith W*	*Connor*
								Ref: J Palmer	In spite of the wretched climatic conditions, the spectators had their money's worth as both sides turned on the style, especially in the second half. Picken beat three men before firing in the first-half opener; then doubled the advantage when a shot from Harris rebounded off of Allan.										
28	A	HUDDERSFIELD		11	W	2-1	2-0	Irving 41, 43	Ware	Kearns	Banfield	Nicholson	Wedlock	Moss	Broad	Irving	Howarth	Picken	Harris
	7/3		*5,000*	*16*	29			*Mann 70*	*Davis*	*McLaren*	*Roebuck*	*Beaton*	*Fayers*	*Linley*	*Armour*	*Slade*	*Mann*	*Islip*	*Jee*
								Ref: C Knight-Coutts	After weathering early pressure at Leeds Road, City maintained the form which has brought them twelve points since the turn of the year. Fayers twice struck the crossbar for Town before Irving took advantage of Roebuck's poor clearance to put City in front with a fine shot.										
29	A	GLOSSOP		11	D	1-1	0-1	Picken 48	Ware	Kearns	Banfield	Nicholson	Moss	Irving	Broad	Neesam	Brown	Picken	Harris
	10/3		***1,000***	*19*	30			*Carney 44*	*Causer*	*Hampton*	*Cuffe*	*Montgomery*	*Stapley W*	*Carney*	*Toward*	*Stapley H*	*Doncaster*	*Thompson R*	*Knight*
								Ref: E Spiers	Picken was unlucky with a fine volley that struck the upright early on. Fortunately, against opponents reduced to ten men when Doncaster didn't reappear for the second half, he had better success with his next effort. He drove in a centre from Harris to level Carney's splendid shot.										
30	H	LINCOLN		9	W	4-1	1-0	Harris 44, 55, Picken 57, Brown 80	Ware	Kearns	Banfield	Young	Moss	Nicholson	Broad	Irving	Brown	Picken	Harris
	14/3		**4,000**	*19*	32			*Chesser 70*	*Goldsborough*	*Jackson*	*Wilson*	*Robson*	*Gardner*	*McFadden*	*Manning*	*Barrell*	*Egerton*	*Chesser*	*Brindley*
								Ref: J Hornby	Although much of the football witnessed was rendered farcical by the deplorable state of the waterlogged pitch, City notched up a handsome win. Harris put them in front with a fine shot from an acute angle and then placed Brown's pull-back into an open net to double the advantage.										
31	A	BLACKPOOL		9	W	1-0	1-0	Irving 5	Ware	Kearns	Banfield	Nicholson	Wedlock	Moss	Broad	Brown	Irving	Picken	Harris
	21/3		*4,000*	*14*	34				*Fiske*	*Millership*	*Jones*	*Bainbridge*	*Connor*	*Booth*	*Charles*	*Charlton*	*Lane*	*Buchan*	*Pagnam*
								Ref: A Shallcross	A backs-to-the-wall performance in which City owed victory to their sterling defence after getting off to a magnificent start when Fiske had difficulty in dealing with a free-kick. Irving, filling the centre-forward spot in commendable style, dashed in to drive the ball into the net.										

No	Date	Opponent	Att	Pos	Pts	Res	F-A	H-T	Scorers, Times, and Referees	1	2	3	4	5	6	7	8	9	10	11
32	H	NOTTM FOREST		7		W	1-0	0-0	Wedlock 75	Ware	Kearns	Banfield	Nicholson	Wedlock	Moss	Broad	Brown	Irving	Picken	Harris
	28/3		12,000	*20*	36					*Hanna*	*Fisher*	*Gibson*	*Bell*	*Mercer*	*Needham*	*Firth*	*Derrick*	*Harris*	*Lockton*	*Banks*
									Ref: R Eccles	City didn't play such good football as in most of their recent matches. They won, but it was merely by a solitary strike by Wedlock who placed a shot from 18 yards into the corner of the net. Hardly a satisfactory performance against opponents situated right at the bottom of the table.										
33	A	THE ARSENAL		7		D	1-1	1-1	Brown 5	Ware	Kearns	Banfield	Nicholson	Wedlock	Moss	Broad	Brown	Irving	Picken	Harris
	4/4		***20,000***	*3*	37				*Winship 11*	*Lievesley*	*Shaw*	*Benson*	*Jobey*	*Sands*	*McKinnon*	*Rutherford*	*Flanagan*	*Stonley*	*Lewis*	*Winship*
									Ref: T Bryan	City gave a capital account of themselves at Highbury, where they damaged Arsenal's promotion prospects. After Brown opened the scoring with a left-footed 25-yarder that passed just inside the post, Winship's angled shot over Ware left City having to be content with just a point.										
34	H	LEEDS CITY		6		D	1-1	1-1	Brown 20	Ware	Kearns	Banfield	Nicholson	Wedlock	Moss	Broad	Brown	**Morton**	Picken	Harris
	10/4		**18,250**	*4*	38				*McLeod 15*	*Hogg*	*Blackman*	*Affleck*	*Law*	*Hampson*	*Foley*	*Price*	*Jackson*	*McLeod*	*Speirs*	*Sharpe*
			(£500)						Ref: J Pearson	City received permission from the League authorities in time to play their new centre-forward signing from Barnsley. McLeod followed up to score the opener after Ware had stopped his first shot on the line, but Brown dribbled through to coolly place the equaliser out of Hogg's reach.										
35	H	GRIMSBY		5		W	1-0	1-0	Morton 12	Ware	Kearns	Jones E	Nicholson	Wedlock	Moss	Broad	Brown	Morton	Picken	Harris
	11/4		12,250	*14*	40					*Spendiff*	*Wheelhouse*	*Arrowsmith*	*Andrews*	*Gordon*	*Martin*	*Quinn*	*Rippon T*	*Rampton*	*Gregson*	*Scott*
			(£350)						Ref: J Howcroft	It is likely that Grimsby would have won if ex-City player Willis Rippon, who had to content himself with watching his brother Tom perform, had been fit. As it was, City took the points when Morton's lofty shot from just outside the penalty area appeared to take Spendiff by surprise.										
36	A	LEEDS CITY		7		L	0-1	0-1		Ware	Kearns	Jones E	Nicholson	Wedlock	Moss	Broad	Brown	Morton	Irving	Harris
	13/4		*12,000*	*4*	40				*Turner 25*	*Hogg*	*Blackman*	*Affleck*	*Law*	*Peart*	*Foley*	*Turner*	*Jackson*	*McLeod*	*Price*	*Sharpe*
									Ref: J Pearson	After giving away a penalty not long after the break, Ware redeemed himself by saving Sharpe's kick at the expense of a corner. This, though, wasn't enough to prevent City from losing this exciting game as Turner was able to put the ball away for Leeds following a first-half corner.										
37	A	BIRMINGHAM		8		D	2-2	0-2	Harris 85, Brown 89	Ware	Kearns	Jones E	Nicholson	Wedlock	Moss	Broad	Brown	Morton	Picken	Harris
	18/4		*17,000*	*13*	41				*Smith W 1, Smith A 11*	*Hauser*	*Ball*	*Womack*	*Gardner*	*Hall*	*Barton*	*Ballantyne*	*Smith W*	*Smith A*	*Windridge*	*Eyre*
									Ref: W Heath	At times in this game it seemed likely that City would be beaten by at least four goals, but Brown's capital shot right at the death brought an unlikely share of the points. All credit to City's team of triers against more skilful opponents, for whom Wally Smith headed in the opener.										
38	H	FULHAM		8		L	0-1	0-1		Ware	Kearns	Banfield	Nicholson	Wedlock	Moss	Broad	Brown	Morton	Burton	Harris
	25/4		10,000	*11*	41				*Wood 33*	*Reynolds*	*Charlton*	*Houghton*	*Laws*	*Russell*	*Torrance*	*Smith*	*Wood*	*Lee*	*White*	*Templeton*
	Home	Away							Ref: T Kirkham	Trailing to a headed effort by Wood, City had the chance of salvaging an undeserved point in the second half when a handball in the box gave them a spot-kick. Unfortunately, Morton crashed his kick into the crowd off the top of the crossbar to end the season in disappointing fashion.										
	Ave 10,711	9,942																		

CUP-TIES

FA Cup/Glos Cup			F-A	H-T	Scorers, Times, and Referees	1	2	3	4	5	6	7	8	9	10	11
1 A QP RANGERS	13	D	2-2	1-1	Pullen 6og, Picken 62	Ware	Kearns	Banfield	Young	Wedlock	Moss	Broad	Brown	Chapple	Picken	Harris
10/1	*18,000 SL:6*				*Miller 26, Banfield 84og*	*Nicholls*	*Higgins*	*Pullen*	*Ovens*	*Mitchell*	*Wake*	*Thompson*	*Birch*	*Miller*	*Gregory*	*Fortune*
(£624.17.6)					Ref: R Pook	A tale of two own-goals at Park Royal, where City took the lead when Pullen turned Broad's centre into his own net. Following the exchange of two conventional goals, City were pegged back not long before the call of time when Banfield deflected Birch's shot past his keeper Ware.										
R H QP RANGERS	13	L	0-2	0-0	(aet)	Ware	Kearns	Banfield	Nicholson	Wedlock	Moss	Broad	Brown	Chapple	Picken	Harris
14/1	13,781 *SL:6*				*Birch 113, Gregory 118*	*Nicholls*	*Higgins*	*Pullen*	*Ovens*	*Mitchell*	*Wake*	*Thompson*	*Birch*	*Miller*	*Gregory*	*Fortune*
(£470.2.3)					Ref: R Pook	By the finish City, who missed early chances, were deservedly beaten by the Southern Leaguers. Rangers looked much the fresher side in extra-time when Kearn's poor headed clearance led to Birch firing in the opener. Gregory's cross-shot made the visitors' victory complete.										
F H BRISTOL ROV	7	W	2-0	1-0	Brown 15, Harris 80	Ware	Kearns	Banfield	Nicholson	Wedlock	Moss	Broad	Brown	Irving	Picken	Harris
GC 14/4	8,501 *SL:16*					*Stansfield*	*Harvie*	*Westwood W*	*Nevin*	*Gallagher*	*Westwood J*	*Kay*	*Dixon*	*Roe*	*Murray*	*Griffiths*
(£238.15.4)					Ref: T Kirkham	Given the heavy Easter programme of both clubs, it was somewhat surprising that they managed to put on an interesting display. Brown gave City the lead with a deflected shot, whilst Picken made amends for missing an open goal by giving Harris an opening he just couldn't miss.										

FRIENDLY

			F-A	H-T	Scorers, Times, and Referees	1	2	3	4	5	6	7	8	9	10	11
1 A BRISTOL ROV		W	1-0	0-0	Howarth 83	Ware	Kearns	Banfield	Nicholson	Wedlock	Moss	Broad	Neesam	Howarth	**Irving**	Harris
31/1	*4,000*					*Stansfield*	*Westwood W*	*Bennett*	*Morris*	*Gallagher*	*Roe*	*Kay*	*Dixon*	*Thomson*	*Brogan*	*Griffiths*
					Ref: E Small	The Rovers, missing eight regulars, fielded a side which City could hardly take seriously. The result was a feeble apology of a match, the like of which hasn't been witnessed for a long while. A flying centre from Harris, which Howarth swept up in his stride, settled this dire affair.										

		Home						Away					
		P	W	D	L	F	A	W	D	L	F	A	Pts
1	Notts Co	38	16	2	1	55	13	7	5	7	22	23	53
2	Bradford PA	38	15	1	3	44	20	8	2	9	27	27	49
3	The Arsenal	38	14	3	2	34	10	6	6	7	20	28	49
4	Leeds City	38	15	2	2	54	16	5	5	9	22	30	47
5	Barnsley	38	14	1	4	33	15	5	6	8	18	30	45
6	Clapt' Orient	38	14	5	0	38	11	2	6	11	9	24	43
7	Hull City	38	9	5	5	29	13	7	4	8	24	24	41
8	BRISTOL C	38	12	5	2	32	10	4	4	11	20	40	41
9	Wolves	38	14	1	4	33	16	4	4	11	18	36	41
10	Bury	38	12	6	1	30	14	3	4	12	9	26	40
11	Fulham	38	10	3	6	31	20	6	3	10	15	23	38
12	Stockport Co	38	9	6	4	32	18	4	4	11	23	39	36
13	Huddersfield	38	8	4	7	28	22	5	4	10	19	31	34
14	Birmingham	38	10	4	5	31	18	2	6	11	17	42	34
15	Grimsby T	38	10	4	5	24	15	3	4	12	18	43	34
16	Blackpool	38	6	10	3	24	19	3	4	12	9	25	32
17	Glossop	38	8	3	8	32	24	3	3	13	19	43	28
18	Leicester Fos'	38	7	2	10	29	28	4	2	13	16	33	26
19	Lincoln City	38	8	5	6	23	23	2	1	16	13	43	26
20	Nott'm Forest	38	7	7	5	27	23	0	2	17	10	53	23
		760	218	79	83	663	348	83	79	218	348	663	760

Odds & ends

Double wins: (3) Hull City, Huddersfield Town, Blackpool.
Double losses: (1) Fulham.

Won from behind: (1) Hull City (h).
Lost from in front: (2) Lincoln City (a), Clapton Orient (a).

High spots: The good start with nine goals from the first two games.
Billy Wedlock scoring for England in a 2-0 win over Wales in Cardiff on 16 March, in what proved to be his last international.

Low spots: Losing at 'Park Avenue' on despite leading 3-2 near the end.
Going down to a heavy defeat at 'Homerton' on Christmas Day.
Losing 1-5 on an atrocious pitch at Stockport County on 27 December.
The totally unexpected defeat by Queens Park Rangers in the FA Cup.

Player of the Year: Tommy Broad.
Ever-presents: (1) Tommy Broad.
Hat-tricks: (1) Fred Chapple.
Leading scorer: Overall: Billy Brown (11). League: Billy Brown (10).

Pre-Season Trial Match:
25 Aug Reds 1(0) Blues 1(0) Ref: E Small
2,000 Shortt 75 / *Tasker 60*

AGM (Ford Memorial Hall, Mill Lane, Bedminster, 29 June 1914):
Loss £968.17s.1d. Season Ticket Sales £280.3s.6d.

	Appearances			Goals			
	Lge	**Cup**	**Fr**	**Lge**	**Cup**	**Fr**	**Tot**
Banfield, Laurie	**28**	3	1				
Broad, Tommy	**38**	3	1	**3**			**3**
Brown, Billy	**24**	3		**10**	1		**11**
Burton, Edwin	**5**			**1**			**1**
Chapple, Fred	**16**	2		**9**			**9**
Fuge, Tom	**6**			**3**			**3**
Harris, Joshua	**31**	3	1	**5**	1		**6**
Harrison, Fred	**15**			**5**			**5**
Henry, Tom	**2**						
Howarth, Tommy	**6**		1	**2**		1	**3**
Howling, Ted	**18**						
Irving, Sam	**13**	1	1	**3**			**3**
Jones, Edwin	**9**						
Jones, John	**1**						
Kearns, John	**37**	3	1	**1**			**1**
Morton, James	**5**			**1**			**1**
Moss, Arthur	**33**	3	1				
Neesam, Bert	**1**		1				
Nicholson, 'Jock'	**31**	2	1				
Picken, John	**27**	3		**7**	1		**8**
Rose, Leslie	**4**						
Tasker, Ron	**1**						
Ware, Tommy	**20**	3	1				
Wedlock, Billy	**30**	3	1	**1**			**1**
Young, Bob	**17**	1					
Opponents og				**1**	1		**2**
26 players used	**418**	**33**	**11**	**52**	**4**	**1**	**57**

No	Date		Att	Pos	Pt	F-A	H-T	Scorers, Times, and Referees	1	2	3	4	5	6	7	8	9	10	11
1	H	BLACKPOOL			W	2-1	1-1	Brooksbank 40, 51p	Howling	Kearns	Banfield	Nicholson	Wedlock	Moss	Broad	Brown	**Brooksbank**	Picken	Harris
	2/9		**3,000**		2			*Lane 10*	*Kidd*	*Robson*	*Jones*	*Bainbridge*	*Connor*	*Rooks*	*Charles*	*Turley*	*Lane*	*Yarnall*	*Quinn*
								Ref: J Pearson	Due to the war, only a small crowd saw City fall behind when Lane's first-time shot easily beat Howling. Fortunately, Brooksbank levelled when, with admirable dash, he helped Wedlock's shot into the net, before registering from the spot after Bainbridge brought down Harris.										
2	A	BURY			L	1-2	0-0	Brooksbank 80	Howling	Kearns	Banfield	Nicholson	Wedlock	Moss	Broad	Brown	Brooksbank	Picken	Harris
	5/9		*4,921*		2			*McKnight 60, Parkin 75*	*McDonald*	*Thomson*	*Allan*	*Goldie*	*Perry*	*Bullen*	*Smith*	*Mercer*	*Parkinson*	*McKnight*	*Connor*
								Ref: C Knight-Coutts	Neither side impressed at Gigg Lane and it may be plainly stated that if either expects to make a bid for promotion then the standard will have to improve. Banfield and Kearns, with Howling in goal were the best City players, whilst Brooksbank shaped fairly well as leader of the attack.										
3	H	PRESTON		5	W	4-0	2-0	Harris 15, Brown 23, Morton 72, 88	Howling	Kearns	Banfield	Nicholson	Wedlock	Moss	Broad	Brown	Morton	Picken	Harris
	12/9		4,000	*7*	4				*Hayes*	*Holbem*	*Broadhurst*	*Henderson*	*McCall*	*Holdsworth*	*Broome*	*Macaulay*	*Osborn*	*Toward*	*Morley*
								Ref: R Bussey	Harris's swift shot, which brought the opener, and Brown's hard drive for the second, were deserved reward for City's brilliant combination play. After a 'Bristol's Own' recruitment drive at the interval, Morton's screw-shot put City further ahead, before he walked in the fourth.										
4	A	NOTTM FOREST		3	W	1-0	0-0	Brown 76	Howling	Kearns	Banfield	Nicholson	Wedlock	Moss	Broad	Brown	Morton	Picken	Harris
	19/9		*8,000*	*16*	6				*Iremonger*	*Fisher*	*Gibson*	*Armstrong*	*Mercer*	*Needham*	*Bell*	*Coleman*	*Harris FM*	*Belton*	*Neve*
								Ref: A Pellowe	In fine breezy weather, Wedlock found reserve Bolton a real handful, and just before the break an exciting scrimmage gave the City defence vigorous work. Despite the loss of Banfield with an injury, the wind advantage allowed City to have an equal share of the second-half play.										
5	H	LEICESTER FOSSE		3	W	1-0	1-0	Morton 30	Howling	Jones J	Banfield	Nicholson	Wedlock	Moss	Broad	Brown	Morton	Picken	Harris
	26/9		9,750	*15*	8				*Bown*	*Currie*	*Taylor*	*Thomson*	*Harrold*	*King*	*Douglas*	*Wise*	*Sims Steve*	*Whitfield*	*Anderson*
								Ref: D Aston	An impressive game by reserve John Jones, surprisingly selected instead of his namesake Edwin, in place of the injured Kearns. Whilst the only goal of the game came from Taylor's bungled clearance, it appears that City now have the strength in depth for a realistic promotion bid.										
6	A	BARNSLEY		6	L	1-2	1-2	Picken 29	Howling	Jones J	Banfield	Nicholson	Wedlock	Moss	Broad	Brown	Morton	Picken	Harris
	3/10		*5,000*	*16*	8			*Lyon 25, Tuftnell 40*	*Cooper*	*Downs*	*Bethune*	*Barson*	*Rooney*	*Wigmore*	*Donkin*	*Fletcher*	*Lyon*	*Tuftnell*	*Griffin*
								Ref: G Pardoe	Lyon, after netting an offside goal early on, was more successful later. Picken brought City level, but Tuftnell restored Barnsley's advantage before the interval. There was no more scoring in the second half, although Howling saved a Downs spot-kick not long before the final whistle.										
7	H	GLOSSOP		4	W	3-1	1-0	Broad 44, Cuffe 58og, Chapple 90p	Howling	Jones J	Banfield	Nicholson	Wedlock	Moss	Broad	Brown	Chapple	Picken	Harris
	10/10		10,000	*20*	10			*Sharpe 59*	*Causer*	*Cuffe*	*Dearnaley*	*Carney*	*Stapley W*	*Montgomery*	*Toward*	*Sharpe*	*Hunter*	*Gadsby*	*Knight*
								Ref: H Smith	The City had a huge majority of the play, but couldn't score until close on the interval. Broad took Brown's headed pass and netted with a left-footed drive. On resuming, Cuffe turned a Harris corner into his own net, before Dearnaley's handball brought Chapple his injury-time penalty.										
8	A	WOLVES		3	D	2-2	1-0	Irving 4, Wedlock 75	Howling	Jones J	Banfield	Nicholson	Wedlock	Moss	Broad	Brown	Irving	Picken	Harris
	17/10		*8,000*	*11*	11			*Curtis 46, Brooks 61*	*Peers*	*Garratly*	*Collins*	*Price*	*Groves*	*Bishop*	*Harrison*	*Dunn*	*Curtis*	*Langford*	*Brooks*
								Ref: A Denton	This well-deserved share of the spoils keeps City handily-placed in the promotion race. Following Irving's opener from a Harris centre, City were pegged back by Wolves' fortunate leveller, when Banfield's clearance cannoned against the chest of Curtis and rebounded into the net.										
9	H	FULHAM		4	D	0-0	0-0		Howling	Jones J	Banfield	Nicholson	Wedlock	Moss	Broad	Brown	Irving	Picken	Harris
	24/10		8,000	*10*	12				*Reynolds*	*Charlton*	*Gray*	*Bellamy*	*Russell*	*Torrance*	*Smith*	*Slade*	*Lee*	*White*	*Templeton*
								Ref: T Bryan	City were badly let down by the lack of a capable centre-forward. With the wingers on form, their fine play should have yielded at least a couple of goals, but the nearest City came to netting the leather was a header from Brown, which Gray hooked out of the vacant goalmouth.										
10	A	STOCKPORT		4	D	2-2	0-1	Picken 70, Brown 85	Howling	Jones J	Banfield	Nicholson	Wedlock	Moss	Broad	Brown	Brooksbank	Picken	Harris
	31/10		*5,000*	*15*	13			*Rodgers 27, Gault 50*	*Evans*	*Goodwin*	*Fagan*	*Mitton*	*Bluer*	*Waterall*	*Crossthwaite*	*Gault*	*Rodgers*	*Wood*	*Ashmole*
								Ref: E Spiers	Brown's long-distance left-footed shot crowned City's fine comeback against opponents who have been upsetting the big clubs lately. With Brooksbank replacing Irving, City struggled and it was no surprise when Rodgers netted from a rebound after Ashmole had struck the upright.										

No Date	H/A	Opponent Att			F-A	H-T	Scorers, Times, and Referees	1	2	3	4	5	6	7	8	9	10	11
11	H	HULL	2	W	5-2	3-1	Harris 10, Brooksbank 44, 70, 80,	Howling	Jones J	Banfield	Nicholson	Wedlock	Moss	Broad	Brown	Brooksbank	Picken	Harris
7/11		10,250	13	15			*Stevens 30, 58* [Brown 20]	*Hendry*	*Pattison*	*Betts*	*Edelston*	*Turner*	*Wright*	*Mercer D*	*Cameron*	*Stevens*	*Halligan*	*Morgan*
							Ref: W Heath	Wounded Belgian soldiers were among the crowd who saw Edelston's 80th-minute foul on Harris, which brought City a penalty. Picken had both his initial kick and his effort from the rebound saved, but Brooksbank put the leather into the back of the net to prevent City's blushes.										
12	A	LEEDS CITY	4	D	1-1	1-1	Picken 44	Howling	Jones J	Banfield	Nicholson	Wedlock	Moss	Broad	Brown	Brooksbank	Picken	Harris
14/11		*8,000*	*15*	16			*McLeod 28*	*Hogg*	*Blackman*	*McQuillan*	*Law*	*Hampson*	*Foley*	*Bainbridge*	*Jackson*	*McLeod*	*Speirs*	*Sharpe*
							Ref: J Hornby	City should have won against opponents who, with the loss of the injured McLeod, were down to ten men by the finish. Broad wasted a good chance before McLeod registered from Sharpe's flag-kick. Picken levelled before the break and City started the second half in brilliant style.										
13	H	CLAPTON ORIENT	3	W	3-0	1-0	Brown 17, Brooksbank 47,	Howling	Jones J	Banfield	Nicholson	Wedlock	Moss	Broad	Brown	Brooksbank	Picken	Harris
21/11		7,750	*11*	18			[Picken 83]	*Hugall*	*Johnston*	*Evans*	*King*	*Scott*	*Gibson*	*Parker*	*Forrest*	*Jonas*	*McFadden*	*Dix*
							Ref: D Aston	Watched by a large crowd, close on half of whom were clad in khaki, City improved after an indifferent start. Despite Brooksbank yet again looking unsuited to the centre-forward role, he was in the right place to put the ball into the open goal when Hugall spilled Picken's effort.										
14	A	THE ARSENAL	4	L	0-3	0-1		Howling	Jones J	Banfield	Nicholson	Wedlock	Moss	Broad	Brown	Brooksbank	Picken	Harris
28/11		*7,000*	*3*	18			*Hardinge 16, 63, King 65*	*Lievesley*	*Shaw*	*Benson*	*Grant*	*Buckley*	*McKinnon*	*Rutherford*	*Hardinge*	*King*	*Bradshaw*	*Lewis*
							Ref: A Warner	At the outset, play was very even in the wet, but Howling had to be at his best to save magnificently from King before Hardinge snapped up a splendid centre from Lewis. After the break, Hardinge's shot doubled the advantage before King robbed Wedlock and fired in number three.										
15	H	DERBY	5	L	2-3	2-2	Brown 10, 25	Howling	Jones J	Banfield	Nicholson	Wedlock	Moss	Broad	Brown	Brooksbank	Picken	Harris
5/12		5,000	*1*	18			*Leonard 7, Moore 20, Benfield 85*	*Lawrence*	*Atkin*	*Barbour*	*Walker*	*Eadie*	*Brooks*	*Grimes*	*Benfield*	*Leonard*	*Moore*	*Baker*
							Ref: G Pardoe	Brown headed in City's leveller into the Road End net following Leonard's capital opener. A fierce low drive restored County's advantage before Broad's remarkable run set up Brown to restore parity. Despite being outplayed after the break, Derby escaped with a fortunate win.										
16	A	LINCOLN	5	L	1-3	0-2	Neesam 70	Howling	Jones J	Banfield	Nicholson	Wedlock	Moss	Broad	Brown	Neesam	Picken	Harris
12/12		*5,000*	*16*	18			*Ball 30, Wolstenholme 35, 55*	*Butler*	*Jackson*	*Dunne*	*Wield*	*Gardner*	*Barrell*	*Manning*	*Wolstenh'lme*	*Egerton*	*Chesser*	*Ball*
							Ref: A Warner	Offside decisions caused problems in this game that saw City on the defensive for the most part. The deadlock was broken when Ball banged in the opener from Manning's centre. Wolstenholme claimed a brace from close in, before Neesam's goal made the contest a more even affair.										
17	H	BIRMINGHAM	9	L	2-3	0-3	Harris 65, Nicholson 75	**Blake**	Jones J	Banfield	Nicholson	Wedlock	Moss	Broad	Brown	Neesam	Picken	Harris
19/12		4,000	*4*	18			*Barton 6, Smith A 11, Gibson 39*	*Robb*	*Ball*	*Womack*	*Bumphrey*	*Tinkler*	*Barton*	*Gibson*	*Smith W*	*Smith A*	*Windridge*	*Eyre*
							Ref: J Hornby	Smith's daisy-cutter doubled Brum's advantage after Barton's cross-shot had given them the lead. City looked well out of it when Gibson's fierce drive put on the third but, despite the injured Picken not reappearing after the break, they made spirited recovery with a couple of goals.										
18	A	GRIMSBY	9	W	3-2	2-1	Neesam 17, 28, 49	Howling	Jones J	Banfield	Nicholson	Wedlock	Moss	Broad	Brown	Neesam	Burton	Harris
25/12		***8,000***	*15*	20			*Rippon 40, 80p*	*Summers*	*Wheelhouse*	*Arrowsmith*	*Andrews*	*Kenny*	*Whitchurch*	*Spink*	*Rippon T*	*Rampton*	*Gregson*	*Scott*
							Ref: J Palmer	Neesam's early double set City up for a well-deserved success in front of a good-sized crowd at Blundell Park. After Rippon had put the ball away from a corner, Neesam completed his hat-trick before the Mariner's No 8 registered from the spot to set up a tense and exciting finale.										
19	H	GRIMSBY	5	W	**7-0**	7-0	Harris 16,19, Brown 21, 22,	Howling	Jones J	Banfield	Nicholson	Wedlock	Moss	Broad	Brown	Neesam	Burton	Harris
26/12		11,500	*15*	22			[Neesam 37, 44, Burton 40]	*Summers*	*Wheelhouse*	*Arrowsmith*	*Andrews*	*Kenny*	*Whitchurch*	*Spink*	*Rippon T*	*Rampton*	*Gregson*	*Scott*
							Ref: J Palmer	A strange contest possibly explained by the fact that, despite the sunshine, the Country End goal was a sea of mud. After Harris opened the scoring with a close-range shot, City went on the rampage. The visitors revived after the break and the bar kept out Rampton's brilliant effort.										
20	A	BLACKPOOL	6	L	0-2	0-1		Howling	Jones J	Banfield	Nicholson	Chapple	Moss	Broad	Brown	Neesam	Burton	Harris
1/1		*4,000*	*18*	22			*Quinn 20, Lane 85*	*Kidd*	*Tulloch*	*Robson*	*Bainbridge*	*Wilson*	*Booth*	*Charles*	*Turley*	*Lane*	*Sibbald*	*Quinn*
							Ref: J Pearson	Despite having the gale at their backs at the start, City found themselves troubled by the Seasiders' long passing. Quinn shot in the opener after Neesam, standing almost under the bar, had somehow failed to put away Broad's centre. Lane's free-kick sealed Pool's comfortable victory.										
21	H	BURY	5	W	1-0	1-0	Neesam 25	Howling	Jones J	Banfield	Nicholson	Moss	Chapple	Broad	Brown	Neesam	Irving	Burton
2/1		6,000	*10*	24				*McDonald*	*Greaves*	*Thomson*	*Perry*	*Humphreys*	*Bullen*	*Smith*	*Peake*	*Lythgoe*	*Goldie*	*Duffy*
							Ref: C Knight-Coutts	With Harris joining Wedlock and Picken on the injured list, many feared that Bury would win this game. Fortunately, after Nicholson won the toss and chose to defend the Country End, Neesam earned City a well-deserved success by running through and firing in the game's only goal.										

No	Date			Att	Pos	Pt	F-A	H-T	Scorers, Times, and Referees	1	2	3	4	5	6	7	8	9	10	11
22	23/1	H	NOTTM FOREST	5,000	7 *16*	L 24	1-2	0-1	Burton 58	Howling	Jones J	Banfield	Nicholson	Wedlock	Moss	Broad	Brown	Neesam	Burton	Harris
									Belton 15, Harris 80	*Powell*	*Jones*	*Gibson*	*Armstrong*	*Mercer*	*Needham*	*Derrick*	*Coleman*	*Harris*	*Belton*	*Neve*
									Ref: A Pellowe	City, defending the Country End at the start, monopolised early play, but fell behind when Jackie Belton headed in. Burton put away Broad's centre to level after the break, but Forest amateur Fred Harris ran through from halfway to bring his side their first away success for two years.										
23	6/2	H	BARNSLEY	4,000	6 *5*	W 26	3-1	0-1	Picken 55, 80p, Neesam 70	Howling	Kearns	Banfield	**Hughes**	Moss	Jones E	Broad	Brown	Neesam	Picken	**Batey**
									Moore 10	*Cooper*	*Gittins*	*Bethune*	*Musgrove*	*Rooney*	*Tuftnell*	*Donkin*	*Marshall*	*Moore*	*Lees*	*Griffin*
									Ref: G Pardoe	The visitors were more than a little rough, and thrice they gave away penalties. Fortunately for them, their keeper, John Cooper, was in superb form and twice before the break he denied shots from the spot by Jones, before being eventually beaten by Picken's effort in the second half.										
24	11/2	A	PRESTON	*5,000*	6 *5*	L 26	**1-4**	1-2	Brown 40 *[Howling 75og]*	Howling	Kearns	Banfield	Nicholson	Moss	Chapple	Broad	Brown	Neesam	Picken	Harris
									Osborn 15, Morley 30, Macauley60,	*Jones*	*Broadhurst*	*Holbem*	*Holdsworth*	*McCall*	*Broome*	*Ford*	*Morley*	*Osborn*	*Macauley*	*Dawson*
									Ref: H Smith	On the principle of horses for courses, this defeat at Deepdale wasn't a surprise. Only Broad's pace caused any real concern to a reconstructed North End side giving their best display of the season. Morley brought to their attack the cleverness that had been so lamentably lacking of late.										
25	13/2	A	GLOSSOP	***300***	8 *19*	L 26	1-2	1-0	Harris 40	Howling	Kearns	Banfield	Nicholson	Moss	Irving	Broad	Brown	Neesam	Picken	Harris
									Toward 58, Sharpe 80	*Causer*	*Allen*	*Cuffe*	*Montgomery*	*Stapley W*	*Carney*	*Toward*	*Sharpe*	*Thompson*	*Gadsby*	*Knight*
									Ref: H Smith	Despite losing the injured Nicholson shortly after forcing four successive corners, City took the lead at North Road. However it was often Glossop, fresh from their win at Huddersfield, who looked the better side in the rain and sleet and Toward equalised from Knight's corner.										
26	20/2	H	WOLVES	5,750	10 *11*	L 26	0-1	0-1		Howling	Kearns	Banfield	Hughes	Moss	**Gane**	Broad	Brown	Neesam	Picken	Harris
									Needham 44	*Peers*	*Garratly*	*Collins*	*Price*	*Groves*	*Bishop*	*Harrison*	*Dunn*	*Curtis*	*Needham*	*Brooks S*
									Ref: A Denton	Whilst injuries prevented Wedlock and Nicholson from playing, it was to their forwards that City needed to look for explanation of this defeat. Many chances were spurned and City were forced to concede both points when a clearance by Kearns rebounded off Needham into the net.										
27	27/2	A	FULHAM	*8,000*	10 *13*	W 28	2-1	1-1	Harris 4, Burton 70	Howling	Kearns	Banfield	Nicholson	Wedlock	Moss	Batey	Brown	Picken	Burton	Harris
									Smith 40	*Reynolds*	*Charlton*	*Coquet*	*Maughan*	*Russell*	*Marshall*	*Smith*	*Slade*	*Torrance*	*Taylor*	*Walker*
									Ref: T Bryan	A Harris free-kick, which took a deflection off Charlton, got City off to a good start at Craven Cottage. With the strong wind in their favour, City looked likely to add to their advantage, but Smith levelled for Fulham before the break. Fortunately Burton got City's second-half winner.										
28	6/3	H	STOCKPORT	4,000	10 *7*	L 28	0-2	0-1		Howling	Kearns	Banfield	Nicholson	Wedlock	Moss	Batey	Brown	Picken	Burton	Harris
									Rodgers 25, Crossthwaite 75	*Evans*	*Goodwin*	*Fagan*	*Davies*	*Mitton*	*Bluer*	*Crossthwaite*	*Rodgers*	*Waterall*	*Gault*	*Curtis*
									Ref: E Spiers	City were made to pay for not taking their chances when Rodgers ran through from almost halfway and lobbed the ball over Howling. After the break, Crossthwaite crashed the ball in from a Curtis centre to double the advantage, before Picken skied a spot-kick over the crossbar.										
29	13/3	A	HULL	*5,000*	10 *12*	D 29	1-1	1-1	Neesam 10	Howling	Kearns	Banfield	Nicholson	Wedlock	Moss	Neesam	Brown	Morton	Burton	Batey
									Lee 3	*Hendry*	*Betts*	*Morgan*	*Edelston*	*Deacey*	*Wright*	*Mercer D*	*Cameron*	*Stevens*	*Halligan*	*Lee*
									Ref: W Heath	A recruiting march kept the gate down, but those that chose to attend this game saw Hull take the lead when Mercer set up Lee to obtain the early opener. Fortunately, it didn't take Neesam long to snatch a close-in leveller, but it took much stern defending by City to hold onto a point.										
30	20/3	H	LEEDS CITY	5,000	9 *13*	W 31	1-0	1-0	Neesam 45	Howling	Kearns	Banfield	Nicholson	Wedlock	Moss	Harris	Brown	Neesam	Burton	Batey
										Walker	*Affleck*	*McQuillan*	*Law*	*Hampson*	*Foley*	*Goodwin*	*Jackson*	*McLeod*	*Price*	*Sharpe*
									Ref: J Hornby	Batey was unlucky just before the break when he netted, only to find that play had been called back because George Affleck was lying injured on the ground. Fortunately almost immediately a smart pass from the right allowed Neesam to register almost as the half-time whistle sounded.										
31	25/3	A	LEICESTER FOSSE	*3,000*	7 *19*	W 33	3-1	1-1	Brown 35, 65, Batey 75	Howling	Kearns	Banfield	Nicholson	Wedlock	Moss	Harris	Brown	Neesam	Burton	Batey
									Mills 37	*Bown*	*Currie*	*Taylor*	*Burton*	*Harrold*	*King*	*Douglas*	*Mills*	*Simms Sam*	*Hogg*	*Codd*
									Ref: D Aston	This rearranged game took place before a small afternoon crowd, who witnessed an even first half with Brown's opener being soon countered by a Mills header before the break. City, though, had much the better of matters thereafter, with Brown and Batey's efforts securing the points.										

32	A	CLAPTON ORIENT		9		L	0-2	0-1		Howling	Kearns	Banfield	Young	Wedlock	Nicholson	Harris	Brown	Neesam	Burton	Batey
	27/3		*6,000*	*7*	33				*McFadden 30, Jonas 75*	*Morris*	*Johnston*	*Evans*	*Forrest*	*Steel*	*Scott*	*Parker*	*Dalrymple*	*Jonas*	*McFadden*	*Ridley*
									Ref: D Aston	City won the toss in fine weather at Homerton, where they took up the early initiative without any success. Brown missed an absolute sitter, firing Batey's centre over the top from just two yards, before Richard McFadden gave Orient the lead from Fred Parker's long swinging pass.										
33	H	THE ARSENAL		9		D	1-1	1-1	Burton 23	Howling	Kearns	Banfield	Nicholson	Wedlock	Moss	Broad	Brown	Neesam	Burton	Harris
	3/4		7,000	*5*	34				*Winship 20*	*Lievesley*	*Liddell*	*Shaw*	*Fletcher*	*Buckley*	*Graham*	*Greenaway*	*Flanagan*	*King*	*Blyth*	*Winship*
									Ref: C Illsley	It is probable that more excitement and keenness have attached in the past to meetings with Arsenal than with any other club that City have regularly met with, but not today. Winship's oblique shot, which brought the Gunners their lucky goal, was soon levelled by Burton's drive.										
34	H	HUDDERSFIELD		12		L	0-1	0-0		Howling	Kearns	Banfield	Young	Wedlock	Moss	Broad	Brown	Neesam	Picken	Harris
	5/4		**12,000**	*9*	34				*Mann 65*	*Davis*	*Wood*	*Reid*	*Baker*	*James*	*Linley*	*Richardson*	*Elliott*	*Cook*	*Mann*	*Jee*
									Ref: H Taylor	Town failed to profit from a penalty awarded by the Cup final referee ten minutes after the start, when Mann was brought down by Kearns. Taking the kick himself, the inside man's spot-kick went straight at Howling who easily saved. Wedlock was the only success on the City side.										
35	A	HUDDERSFIELD		12		L	3-5	2-2	Morton 30, 44, 80 *[Richardson 70]*	Howling	Kearns	Banfield	Young	Wedlock	Moss	Broad	Brown	Neesam	Morton	Harris
	6/4		*5,500*	*8*	34				*Shields 5, 10, 75, Jee 60p,*	*Davis*	*Wood*	*Reid*	*Fayers*	*James*	*Watson*	*Richardson*	*Elliott*	*Shields*	*Mann*	*Jee*
									Ref: H Taylor	Shields headed in the early opener in this thriller that was captured on film for the benefit of the local cinema. A mixed afternoon for Jee, who registered from the spot following a foul by Banfield. However, after Richardson found the net with a fine shot, Jee fired another penalty wide.										
36	A	DERBY		12		L	0-1	0-1		Howling	Kearns	Banfield	Young	Wedlock	Nicholson	**Reader**	Brown	Neesam	Morton	Harris
	10/4		*7,000*	*1*	34				*Moore 19*	*Lawrence*	*Atkin*	*Barbour*	*Walker*	*Bagshaw*	*Brooks*	*Grimes*	*Benfield*	*Leonard*	*Moore*	*Baker*
									Ref: G Pardoe	In glorious weather City were unable to get any reward for their fine display. At the outset, Brown finished weakly at the end of a brilliant run, but unfortunately Moore didn't make the same mistake when he raced through in irresistible style to open the scoring with a fine cross-shot.										
37	H	LINCOLN		12		W	2-1	1-0	Harris 40, Broad 85	Howling	Kearns	Banfield	Young	Wedlock	Henry	Broad	Brown	Brooksbank	Morton	Harris
	17/4		4,000	*16*	36				*Dowling 88*	*Butler*	*Jackson*	*Ward*	*Wield*	*Gardner*	*Barrell*	*Manning*	*Dowling*	*Egerton*	*Chesser*	*Ball*
									Ref: J Sharpe	It wasn't until shortly before the interval that Harris made up for some amazing misses by registering with an oblique shot. A mix-up between Joe Butler and Fred Ward allowed Broad to double the advantage, just before Mike Dowling's fine cross-shot brought Lincoln some reward.										
38	A	BIRMINGHAM		13		D	1-1	1-0	Brown 29	Howling	Kearns	Banfield	Young	Wedlock	Nicholson	Broad	Brown	Brooksbank	Burton	Harris
	24/4		***10,000***	*6*	37				*Windridge 60*	*Robb*	*Ball*	*Womack*	*Roulson*	*Barton*	*Bumphrey*	*Gibson*	*Hodges*	*Smith A*	*Windridge*	*Smith W*
		Home	Away						Ref: J Hornby	After Birmingham had won the toss, play was fairly even in the rain before Brown raced past Womack and fired City in front. After the break, City, despite losing the injured Kearns for a short while, had the better of things until Windridge pounced when Howling parried Barton's shot.										
	Ave	6,632	5,933																	

FA Cup						F-A	H-T	Scorers, Times, and Referees	1	2	3	4	5	6	7	8	9	10	11
1	H	CARDIFF		5	W	2-0	0-0	Burton 55, 83	Howling	Jones J	Banfield	Nicholson	Wedlock	Moss	Broad	Brown	Neesam	Burton	Harris
	9/1		14,319 *SL:6*						*Kneeshaw*	*Brittan*	*Layton*	*Harvey*	*Keenor*	*Hardy*	*Beare*	*Goddard*	*Devlin*	*West G*	*Evans*
			(£488.9.0)					Ref: T Bryan	Cardiff's sturdy defence proved a formidable barrier to City's attempts in the first half, but after the break the goals came, despite the visiting right-winger Beare proving a real handful. Kneeshaw's inability to hold Brown's header allowed Burton to run the opener between the posts.										
2	A	EVERTON		8	L	0-4	0-2	*[Wareing 75]*	Howling	Jones J	Banfield	Nicholson	Wedlock	Moss	Broad	Brown	Neesam	Picken	Harris
	30/1		*24,500* *1:4*					*Clennell 15, Kirsopp 30, Parker 55,*	*Fern*	*Thompson*	*Simpson*	*Fleetwood*	*Wareing*	*Makepeace*	*Chedgzoy*	*Kirsopp*	*Parker*	*Clennell*	*Palmer*
			(£776.10.0)					Ref: Mr Conroy	Despite Wedlock's fine form, City couldn't hold Everton at Goodison Park. They had their moments though and Neesam missed a real sitter as well as grazing the bar with a quick shot. Clennell's opener came from close range, whilst Parker's goal-of-the-game was a long-range effort.										

	P	W	D	L	F	A	W	D	L	F	A	Pts
		Home					Away					
1 Derby Co	38	14	3	2	40	11	9	4	6	31	22	53
2 Preston NE	38	14	4	1	41	16	6	6	7	20	26	50
3 Barnsley	38	16	2	1	31	10	6	1	12	20	41	47
4 Wolves	38	12	4	3	47	13	7	3	9	30	39	45
5 The Arsenal	38	15	1	3	52	13	4	4	11	17	28	43
6 Birmingham	38	13	3	3	44	13	4	6	9	18	26	43
7 Hull City	38	12	2	5	36	23	7	3	9	29	31	43
8 Huddersfield	38	12	4	3	36	14	5	4	10	25	29	42
9 Clapt' Orient	38	12	5	2	36	17	4	4	11	14	31	41
10 Blackpool	38	11	3	5	40	22	6	2	11	19	35	39
11 Bury	38	11	5	3	39	19	4	3	12	22	37	38
12 Fulham	38	12	0	7	35	20	3	7	9	18	27	37
13 BRISTOL C	38	11	2	6	38	19	4	5	10	24	37	37
14 Stockport Co	38	12	4	3	33	19	3	3	13	21	41	37
15 Leeds City	38	9	3	7	40	25	5	1	13	25	39	32
16 Lincoln City	38	9	5	5	30	23	2	5	12	17	42	32
17 Grimsby T	38	10	4	5	36	24	1	5	13	12	52	31
18 Nott'm Forest	38	9	7	3	32	24	1	2	16	11	53	29
19 Leicester Fos'	38	6	4	9	31	41	3	1	15	16	48	23
20 Glossop	38	5	5	9	21	33	1	1	17	10	54	18
	760	225	70	85	738	399	85	70	225	399	738	760

Odds & ends

Double wins: (2) Leicester Fosse, Grimsby Town.
Double losses: (1) Huddersfield Town.

Won from behind: (2) Blackpool (h), Barnsley (h).
Lost from in front: (1) Glossop (a).

High spots: Only two defeats in the opening thirteen games.
Winning 3-1 at Leicester Fosse on 25 March.
Knocking Southern League Cardiff City out of the FA Cup.
Billy Wedlock's display in the FA Cup defeat at 'Goodison Park'.

Low spots: The poor display at 'Gigg Lane' on 5 September.
Losing 0-3 at 'Highbury' on 28 November.
The four successive defeats leading up to Christmas.
Failing to score in the second-half on Christmas Day.

Player of the Year: Laurie Banfield.
Ever-presents: (2) Laurie Banfield, Billy Brown.
Hat-tricks: (2) Cliff Brooksbank, Bert Neesam.
Leading scorer: Overall: Billy Brown (13). League: Billy Brown (13).

Pre-Season Trial Match:
22 Aug Reds 1(1) Blues 1(1)
2,000 Picken 40 / *Irving 5*

AGM (Ford Memorial Hall, Mill Lane, Bedminster, 30 June 1915):
Loss £1,417.6s.4d. Season Ticket Sales £79.9s.0d.

	Appearances Lge	Appearances Cup	Goals Lge	Goals Cup	Tot
Banfield, Laurie	**38**	2			
Batey, Tom	**7**		**1**		**1**
Blake, Herbert	**1**				
Broad, Tommy	**31**	2	**2**		**2**
Brooksbank, Cliff	**10**		**7**		**7**
Brown, Billy	**38**	2	**13**		**13**
Burton, Edwin	**13**	1	**4**	2	**6**
Chapple, Fred	**4**		**1**		**1**
Gane, Bert	**1**				
Harris, Joshua	**35**	2	**8**		**8**
Henry, Tom	**1**				
Howling, Ted	**37**	2			
Hughes, Leslie	**2**				
Irving, Sam	**4**		**1**		**1**
Jones, Edwin	**1**				
Jones, John	**18**	2			
Kearns, John	**20**				
Morton, James	**8**		**6**		**6**
Moss, Arthur	**34**	2			
Neesam, Bert	**19**	2	**10**		**10**
Nicholson, 'Jock'	**33**	2	**1**		**1**
Picken, John	**24**	1	**6**		**6**
Reader, Dickie	**1**				
Wedlock, Billy	**32**	2	**1**		**1**
Young, Bob	**6**				
Unknown					
Opponent og			**1**		**1**
25 players used	**418**	**22**	**62**	**2**	**64**

These photographs from *The Illustrated Sporting and Dramatic News* show the action from the Championship decider at St John's Lane on 29 April 1899. City, in dark shirts, lost 3-4 to Southampton